Gower Handbook of Leadership and Management Development

Gower Handbook of Leadership and Management Development

EDITED BY

JEFF GOLD, RICHARD THORPE
AND ALAN MUMFORD

GOWER

Published by
Gower Publishing Limited
Wey Court East
Union Road
Farnham
Surrey
GU9 7PT
England

Gower Publishing Company
Suite 420
101 Cherry Street
Burlington
VT 05401-4405
USA

www.gowerpublishing.com

Jeff Gold, Richard Thorpe and Alan Mumford have asserted their moral rights under the Copyright, Designs and Patents Act, 1988, to be identified as the editors of this work.

British Library Cataloguing in Publication Data
Gower handbook of leadership and management development. -- 5th ed.
   1. Executives--Training of. 2. Executive coaching.
   3. Leadership--Study and teaching.
   I. Handbook of leadership and management development
   II. Gold, Jeffrey. III. Thorpe, Richard. IV. Mumford, Alan.
   658.4'071245-dc22

ISBN: 978-0-566-08858-2 (hbk)
ISBN: 978-0-7546-9213-3 (ebk)

Library of Congress Cataloging-in-Publication Data
Gower handbook of leadership and management development / edited by Jeff Gold, Richard Thorpe, and Alan Mumford.
   p. cm.
Rev. ed. of: Gower handbook of management development / edited by Alan Mumford. 4th ed. c1994.
Includes bibliographical references.
ISBN 978-0-566-08858-2 (hardback) -- ISBN 978-0-7546-9213-3 (ebook) 1. Executives--Training of. 2. Leadership. 3. Management. I. Gold, Jeffrey. II. Thorpe, Richard, 1951- III. Mumford, Alan. IV. Gower handbook of management development. V. Title: Handbook of leadership and management development.
HD38.2.H36 2009
658.4'07124--dc22

2009018773

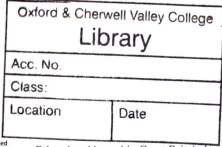

Mixed Sources
Product group from well-managed forests and other controlled sources
www.fsc.org Cert no. SA-COC-1565
© 1996 Forest Stewardship Council
FSC

Printed and bound in Great Britain by
MPG Books Group, UK

Contents

List of Figures

List of Tables

Preface

ALAN MUMFORD

The explicit view about leadership has for many years been that while managers did the boring aspects of defining and achieving results, leaders provided something much more exciting. They were considered to cross frontiers of thinking, engaged in the transformational processes in which their organisations were involved and always out in front. Who was not thrilled to be described as a leader, dusted with an additional bit charisma?

The great change that has occurred in concepts that relate to leadership has been of two kinds. The first has been an acceptance that effective leadership is to a very large extent contextual; time is one of these contexts – what works at one period of time, dealing with one set of circumstances, may not always work in another. A second recognition has been that leadership is not something solely undertaken by one person, someone at the top of organisations, but is in fact invariably exercised by all managers.

Of course one form of development for managers has been to read books by business leaders who are self-proclaimed leaders. In the United States, Lee Iacocca and later Jack Welch gave colourful and direct testimony of what a successful business leader needs to do, whilst in Britain John Harvey Jones was a vivid and effective purveyor of views on leadership both through his books and then later through television. In the political arena the leadership styles of Margaret Thatcher and later of Tony Blair were often dissected and quoted when their policies appeared successful. The transferability of ideas from sport has also been explored, the corporate lecture circuit and after-dinner speaking industry being the most keen, but the parallels here are probably more difficult as sport is different in nature from politics or organisations which have a lot in common with each other. Mike Brearley's views about the captaincy of England were certainly offered as leadership lessons of good in a number of organisations.

Outdoor training has also claimed great success in the delivery and development of leaders. More recently the study of drama and the conductor's role in music or the nature of the role of musicians in a jazz band have been used as metaphors of how the leadership process might work and the role others have in the production of coordinated endeavour. The contrast in leadership styles between Henry V's speeches 'Once more unto the breach', and his later 'A little touch of Harry in the night' is a powerful insight into the need to have different styles of leadership to suit different occasions.

This book shows there are many new ideas on the development of leaders. The best integrate awareness of the contextual requirements for leadership with understanding different ways of developing leaders. Historically, excitement about new ideas has not always been matched by rigour on these two aspects.

Preface to the New Edition

JEFF GOLD AND RICHARD THORPE

When we were asked by Alan Mumford, and Jonathan Norman at Gower, to consider a new edition of Alan's well-known *Handbook of Management Development*, first published in 1973 but last published by Gower in 1994, we knew that we had consider two factors. First, the last edition of the text, even though over 14 years old, was still an important one that retained much influence with its readership. Copies of the book are still to be found on the shelves of many management developers and even quite a few managers and academics. We recognised that there was quite a tradition to be preserved. Secondly, we both believed that for the text to remain credible in the twenty-first century, it would need to demonstrate relevance in what has become a very much extended field which now incorporate a greater emphasis on leadership development. We therefore made it clear that the title and content of the new book had to include leadership whilst retaining its focus on management development. There are many reasons for the incorporation of leadership, and certainly most of these permeate the text you are about to read. One obvious reason is that the market of interest is now generally understood as leadership and management development. Thus, whereas previously, managers and management tended to be conceived of rather narrowly, attention is now focused on a wider range of contexts where both management and leadership have been considered to be vital to performance and success – however defined and measured. This includes private and public sector organisations, including small- and medium-sized organisations as well as those classed as micro-businesses, but also professional and knowledge-based organisations, community and voluntary sector organisations, and increasingly, organisations that operate around the globe. Further, both leaders and managers are meant to concern themselves with or learn about a wide range of issues such as diversity, ethics, corporate social responsibility and the future of their organisations. The events that have been challenging all organisations since the autumn of 2008 seem to have made attention to such issues all the more necessary.

About the Editors

Jeff Gold is Principal Lecturer in Organisation Learning at Leeds Business School, Leeds Metropolitan University and Leadership Fellow at Leeds University where he coordinates the Northern Leadership Academy. He has led a range of seminars and workshops on leadership with a particular emphasis on participation and distribution. He is the co-author of *Management Development, Strategies for Action* (with Alan Mumford), published by the Chartered Institute of Personnel and Development in 2004 and the fourth edition of his textbook *Human Resource Management* (with John Bratton) was published in 2007 with Palgrave Macmillan.

j.gold@leedsmet.ac.uk

Richard Thorpe is Professor of Management Development and Deputy Director of the Keyworth Institute at Leeds University Business School. His interests include performance, remuneration and entrepreneurship, management learning and development and leadership. He has sought to develop these interests at all the institutions in which he has worked. His early industrial experience informed the way his ethos has developed. Common themes are a strong commitment to process methodologies and a focus on action in all its forms; an interest in and commitment to the development of doctoral students and the development of capacity within the sector; a commitment to collaborative working on projects of mutual interest.

rt@lubs.leeds.ac.uk

Alan Mumford has worked in such firms as John Laing and Son, IPC Magazines, International Computers and the Chloride Group. He was also deputy chief training advisor at the Department of Employment. In 1983, he was appointed professor of management development at International Management Centres. He has worked with senior managers and directors and developers in many organisations, including Ford of Europe, Unilever and Unison. He is the co-author of *Management Development, Strategies for Action* (with Jeff Gold), published by the Chartered Institute of Personnel and Development in 2004.

Our Authors

Lisa Anderson is a Lecturer in Management Education at the University of Liverpool Management School. Prior to taking up this appointment, she was Senior Lecturer at the University of Salford where she was primarily involved in CIPD programmes; she has also worked as a manager in the retail sector and in local government. Lisa's research interests centre on social learning, particularly how groups create critical reflection and discursive approaches to the evaluation of management development. She was a member of the Northern Leadership Academy's Think Tank where she focused on the evaluation of leadership development activities.

l.anderson@liverpool.ac.uk

Richard Bolden is a lecturer at the Centre for Leadership Studies at the University of Exeter. His research interests span a wide range of topics, including leadership in higher education, distributed leadership, leadership practice, leadership and management competencies, work-based learning and leadership development for organisational and social change. In addition, Richard teaches and supervises students on a range of programmes, including the Exeter MA in Leadership Studies, MBA and CPD scheme.

Richard.Bolden@exeter.ac.uk

John Burgoyne is Professor of Management Learning in the Department of Management Learning in the Lancaster University Management School and Henley Business School. His primary interest is in management, leadership and organisation development, and the fundamental question of how learning does and can create individual and collective management and leadership capability to enable valuable organisational performance.

john@burgoyne77.freeserve.co.uk

James Collins spent over 20 years in the shipping industry, as a mariner, shipbroker and marine insurance underwriter before taking up academic study and research. Entering the academic world in mid life he undertook his Ph.D. at Cranfield School of Management, where he is a Visiting Fellow at the School's Centre for Executive Learning and Leadership. His principal research interests concern leadership in the public sector and the challenges of leadership in the global context. James now lives and works in Finland where he is an independent consultant

james.collins@cranfield.ac.uk

Murray Dalziel is Professor of Management and Director of the University of Liverpool Management School (ULMS). Murray's current research interests focus on innovation strategies and leadership development. Previously, Murray was Group Managing Director of Hay Group and has worked with large global clients in every continent on their key leadership and organization development issues. He is also actively involved with a number of North American and European venture capital funds on the development of emerging businesses. He received his MA in Sociology from the University of Edinburgh, and has a Ph.D. in Sociology from Harvard University

Murray.Dalziel@liv.ac.uk

Lloyd Davies was the HR Director of Yorkshire Water PLC, a Footsie 100 company. Before retirement, he observed that individuals' greatest personal and professional development usually came from their experiences, rather than from formal programmes. Following retirement he returned to Lancaster University's Department of Management Learning to undertake doctoral research into the various aspects of experiential learning. His book *Informal Learning: A New Model for Making Sense of Experience*, based on his research and published in 2008, explores some of the elements entailed in this process which are usually overlooked but which appear to be critical in personal learning.

jmldavies@lineone.net

Jackie Ford is Professor of Leadership and Organization Studies at Bradford University School of Management. Current research explores leadership as a discursive and performative phenomenon, examining contemporary discourses of leadership and their complex interrelations with gender and identity for managers. She is committed to identifying the human effects of managerial and organisational changes approached from feminist, poststructural and psychoanalytic theoretical perspectives. She has co-authored *Leadership as Identity: Constructions and Deconstructions* (Palgrave Macmillan, 2008); co-edited *Making Public Management Critical* (Routledge, forthcoming 2009) and has published in a range of journals including, *Journal of Management Studies, Leadership, Management Learning, Organization, Sociology.*

J.M.Ford@Bradford.ac.uk

Bob Garvey is Professor of Coaching and Mentoring at Sheffield Hallam University and one of Europe's leading academic practitioners of mentoring and coaching. His Ph.D. (Mentoring in the marketplace: studies of learning at work) investigated mentoring in practice in a range of occupational settings. Formerly a school teacher with experience of primary and secondary schools, Bob has conducted mentoring workshops, designed and established schemes with a wide range of public and private sector organisations. He is co-author of the best selling *The Mentoring Pocket Book* and the schools version *The Pupil Mentoring Pocket Book.* He was a consultant to the videos *Peer Mentoring in Schools, Learning Mentors, New Chances New Horizons* and designer of the video *Mentoring Conversations.* Bob currently coaches and mentors a number of people, including top musicians, art therapists and managers. Bob has published many papers on the practice of coaching and mentoring in a variety of journals.

r.garvey@shu.ac.uk

David Gray is Professor of Management Learning at Surrey University. Work at the University has included the management of a range of programmes, including an MSc in interactive training systems, a postgraduate certificate in the education of adults and the BSc in work-based learning. David has provided consultancy services in a range of areas from executive coaching to e-learning development for organisations, including Toshiba, BP UK Oil, Total Fina, the OECD and the Civil Service. His research interests include leadership, work-related learning (primarily coaching and mentoring), and interactive communications technology in learning (particularly in work-related settings).

d.e.gray@surrey.ac.uk

Bob Hamlin is Professor Emeritus and Chair of Human Resource Development at the University of Wolverhampton. He is active as an independent management and organisation development consultant, both nationally and internationally. His main research interests include managerial and leadership effectiveness, managerial coaching effectiveness and mentoring effectiveness, the results of which have been published widely. Bob is a distinguished Fellow of the Chartered Institute of Personnel and Development, Honorary Treasurer of the University Forum for HRD, and serves on the editorial board of several academic journals, including *Human Resource Development International* and the *International Journal of Evidence-Based Coaching and Mentoring.*

r.g.hamlin@wlv.ac.uk

Jean Hartley is Professor of Organisational Analysis at the Institute of Governance and Public Management at Warwick Business School, University of Warwick. She is an organisational psychologist by background, with research experience in both the public and private sectors. She was the Lead Fellow for the ESRC/EPSRC Advanced Institute of Management (AIM) Public Service Fellows programme. Her research focus is on public leadership (political, managerial, professional and civic) and on innovation and improvement in organisations. She has published four books and a wide range of articles on organisational behaviour and on public management.

Jean.Hartley@wbs.ac.uk

Peter Holt is a leadership development consultant, coach and a member of the Visiting Faculty at Henley Business School. Through Leading People Limited he has designed and applied 360 interventions to build the leadership talent of individuals, teams and organisations. His early career was in the Armed Services. Subsequently he held academic appointments at the Royal Military Academy Sandhurst and The National Police Staff College before taking responsibility for management development in Wiggins Teape – then a global paper manufacturer and merchant. He has written and spoken to conferences about his experience of designing and using 360s.

peter.holt@leadingpeople.co.uk

Paul Iles is Running Stream Professor of HRD at Leeds Business School. He is a chartered psychologist and a Chartered Fellow of the Chartered Institute for Personnel and Development (CIPD). He has published and made presentations on a variety of HRD issues, including leadership and management development, team-building and organisational learning, career development, coaching, mentoring, organisational change and development, international and comparative HRD and recently talent management

p.iles@leedsmet.ac.uk

Kim Turnbull James is Professor of Executive Learning at Cranfield School of Management and Director of the Centre for Executive Learning and Leadership. She is interested in how management learning and leadership development contribute to organisational goals. Kim has worked with a wide range of organisations, including major corporates in the automotive, aerospace, pharmaceutical, insurance and banking industries, as well as public service organisations, such as police, local authorities and the health service. Executive coaching, consulting to teams and leadership development are all part of Kim's portfolio. Kim is a chartered psychologist.

k.james@cranfield.ac.uk

John Lawler is Senior Lecturer Public Sector Management at Bradford University. John trained and practised as a social worker in local authority social work before moving into policy and research and then into academia. He has taught on a wide range of undergraduate and postgraduate programmes and has been involved in management and leadership programmes for organisations in the public and commercial sectors. His research interests are management and leadership development generally, and in public sector organisations specifically; user views of health and social care services; evidence in health and social care; organisational change, and existential thinking in relation to management and leadership. His previous posts include lectureships at Nuffield Institute for Health, University of Leeds and University of Bradford Management Centre.

J.Lawler@Bradford.ac.uk

Becky Malby has a track record in organisational and leadership development in the public sector, in the UK and Europe. She is the Director of the Centre for Innovation in Health Management at Leeds University, a network of 500 leaders; the CIHM work includes organisational development; leadership development and an applied research programme. Becky leads the European Health Management Association Special Interest Group on Management Development. Previously Becky was Director of Complex Systems Associates; Head of Corporate Development at the Nuffield Institute at Leeds University; and a Fellow at the Kings Fund. She has an MA in Public and Social Policy.

R.L.Malby@leeds.ac.uk

Terry McNulty is Professor of Management and Corporate Governance and also Director of Research at the University of Liverpool Management School. His research focuses on processes of management and organisation as they relate to strategic organisation and change, corporate governance and board effectiveness. His work is acknowledged by scholar, practitioner and policy communities. He conducted background research for the Higgs Review into the role and effectiveness of non-executive directors which subsequently informed revisions to the *UK Combined Code of Corporate Governance*. He has presented at expert panels about boards and governance at gatherings organised by the Academy of Management, European Group for Organisational Studies, and European Academy of Management. He has also advised a number of leading organisations, especially in matters related to board of director process and effectiveness.

t.h.mcnulty@liv.ac.uk

Beverly Metcalfe is Senior Lecturer is HRM and Development in the Insititute of Development Policy and Management, University of Manchester. She has worked at Manchester previously and has also worked at Hull University, Staffordshire University, Liverpool Hope and Keele Universities. Beverly is also a Research Fellow in the Centre for Equality and Diversity at Manchester Business School, Research Fellow in the Diversity and Equality in Careers and Employment Research Centre (University of East Anglia) and has held visiting Professor positions at Griffith University and Monash University in Australia. Beverly is currently Chair of the Gender, Diversity and Equality Special Interest Group of EURAM. Her research interests are gender and diversity in the global economy, especially the Middle East; women's leadership development and feminist critiques of management and organization learning and change. She has undertaken consultancy and advisory roles on women's development and empowerment, and HR issues in the Middle East for Bahrain and Islamic Republic of Iran's education ministries.

metcalb@hope.ac.uk

Pero Mićić is the founder and chairman of FutureManagementGroup AG whose mission it is to help top leaders of the world's leading companies to see more of the future markets than their competitors do. Pero is author of six books and he is the developer of the Eltville Model of future management. He is a founding member of the Association of Professional Futurists in the USA, president of the advisory board to the European

Futurists Conference in Lucerne, and president of the conference on international trend and future management in Germany. He gained his Ph.D. in 2007.

pero@micic.com

Alan Murray lectures in Corporate Responsibility at Sheffield University Management School. He is the founding Chair of the British Academy of Management Special Interest Group in CR, and is co-author, with Michael Blowfield, of *Corporate Responsibility: A Critical Introduction* (Oxford University Press, 2008). He was a member of the original United Nations Global Compact Taskforce on Principles of Responsible Management Education (http://unprme.org), and has a continuing role in promoting the principles to schools of business and management in the UK. He sits on a number of policy committees and has visiting positions at a number of UK Universities.

alan.murray@shef.ac.uk

Mike Pedler works with Action Learning, the learning organisation, and leadership development. He is Professor of Action Learning at Henley Business School and co-edits the journal *Action Learning: Research and Practice*.

mikepedler@phonecoop.coop

Kai Peters is Chief Executive of Ashridge Business School. Prior to joining Ashridge, he was Dean, and previously director of MBA programmes, of the Rotterdam School of Management (RSM) of Erasmus University in the Netherlands. Kai serves on supervisory and advisory boards for a number of organisations in the technology and telecommunications sector. He has worked with both IBM in Canada and Volkswagen in Germany in management development. He is interested in strategy and leadership with an emphasis on management development. He holds degrees from York University, Toronto and University of Quebec in Chicoutimi (Canada) and Erasmus University (Netherlands).

Kai.Peters@ashridge.org.uk

Suzanne Pollack is a freelance coach, facilitator and Visiting Executive Fellow of Henley Business School. Her expertise lies in helping senior executives, and top teams, to reach their full potential through coaching and learning programmes/interventions. Suzanne adopts a pragmatic approach, drawing on a blend of NLP (an enabler of swift and effective personal change), best business practice, her own senior leadership experience and proven psychological techniques, to enable executives to move forward. She is skilled in using instruments such as the Myers–Briggs type indicator, Firo-B, 360s and emotional intelligence questionnaires.

David A. Preece is Professor of Technology Management and Organisation Studies, Head of the Centre for Leadership and Organizational Change, and DBA Programme Leader in the Business School, University of Teesside, Cleveland, UK. He has previously worked at the universities of Leeds, Bradford, Coventry and Portsmouth. His main research interests are in the areas of organisational and technological change and leadership development. He has published a number of refereed journal articles and book chapters, and is editor/author of six books, including *Technological Change and Organizational Action* (Routledge, 2003) with J. Laurila and *Technology, Organizations and Innovation*, four volumes (Routledge, 2000) with I. McLoughlin and P. Dawson. He is editor of the Routledge Research Monograph Series Work, Technology and Organizations. d.preece@tees.ac.uk

Phil Radcliff specialises in supporting senior teams and individual managers in the management of change. Phil's international career involved working in the engineering, food and drink industries, predominantly in organisation development roles, culminating in the management of a series of mergers in the formation of Diageo and a period of time as the HR director of United Distillers and Vintners. Following this, Phil established a network of specialist consultants to support major businesses and the voluntary sector. He focuses on the coaching of senior management and facilitation of top teams managing organisational change. He is a Visiting Faculty member at Henley Business School.

phil.radcliff@changeconnections.co.uk

Michael Reynolds is Emeritus Professor of Management Learning at Lancaster University Management School and has been director of full-time and part-time postgraduate programmes in the department of Management Learning and Leadership. His research interests are in illuminating differences between tutor intentions and students' experiences in experiential learning designs, and in the application of critical perspectives to management learning design. He was co-editor with John Burgoyne of *Management Learning: Integrating Perspectives in Theory and Practice* (1997) and with Russ Vince of *Organising Reflection* (2004) and the *Handbook of Experiential Learning and Management Education* (2007).

m.reynolds@lancaster.ac.uk

Simon Robinson is Running Stream Professor of Applied and Professional Ethics at Leeds Metropolitan University. He has a degree in Philosophy at Edinburgh University and he began his career in psychiatric social work, before training in Oxford for the Anglican priesthood. This took him to curacies and hospital chaplaincy in the Durham diocese, before moving back to Edinburgh and higher education as chaplain to Heriot-Watt University and postgraduate work at New College, Edinburgh, on Christian social ethics. He has a concern to locate ethical reflection in practice and everyday decision-making. Simon has published extensively on business ethics, bioethics, the ethics and spirituality of healthcare and values and care in higher education.

s.robinson@leedsmet.ac.uk

Eugene Sadler-Smith is Professor of Management Development and Organizational Behaviour in the School of Management, University of Surrey. Dr. Sadler-Smith's research interests are centred currently on the role of intuitive judgement in management decision-making, management development and leadership. His research has been published in journals such as the *Academy of Management Executive, Academy of Management Learning and Education* and *Organisation Studies*. He is author of *Learning and Development for Managers* (Blackwell, 2006), *Learning in Organisations* (with Peter J. Smith, Routledge, 2006), *Inside Intuition* (Routledge, 2008) and *The Intuitive Mind: Profit from the Power of your Sixth Sense* (to be published by John Wiley and Sons in 2009).

e.sadler-smith@surrey.ac.uk

Erella Shefy is Founder of Humanager Organizational consulting, life and business coaching. She has over 18 years expertise working with managers and leads coaching development programmes in organisations and in Humanager private coaching school. Her interests are centred currently on the role of using mind-bypass tools (MBT) in developing intuition in management coaching and leadership development. Her research has been published in journals such as the *Academy of Management Executive*, *Academy of Management Learning and Education*, *Journal of Management Development*, *Human Relations*. Erella Shefy has a Masters in Management from Tel Aviv University and a Master of Arts in Holistic Health and Arts from Lesley University.

Tim Spackman is Head of Organisational Development at HML, a wholly-owned subsidiary of Skipton Building Society. He has worked in human resource management for over 15 years. Having obtained a BA Hons degree in business studies, he joined Barclays, where he spent 9 years working in a variety of roles in people management and development before joining HML. A firm believer in lifelong learning and a qualified coach, he has six postgraduate qualifications, including an MA in strategic human resource management. He is a Fellow of the CIPD and is passionate about coaching, employee engagement, leadership and organisational development.

Tim.Spackman@hml.co.uk

Jim Stewart is Director of the DBA Programme and Professor of HRD at Ashcroft International Business School. He has held previous professorial and academic appointments at Leeds, Nottingham and Wolverhampton Business Schools. As an active researcher Jim has undertaken projects funded by the UK Government, the European Union, ESRC and LSC among others. He is the author and co-author/editor of 12 books and numerous articles, most of which draw on these research projects. Jim is Chair of the University Forum for HRD and holds three national roles with the CIPD, including Chief Examiner for Learning and Development.

j.d.stewart@leedsmet.ac.uk

Paul Tosey joined Surrey University in 1991, where he is a Senior Lecturer in Management. Previous experience includes management and internal consultancy in local government, freelance coaching and consulting, and lecturing at the University of Edinburgh. He became a Higher Education Academy National Teaching Fellow in 2007, and has trained to Master Practitioner level in NLP (1992). He has published widely on transformative learning, on Gregory Bateson's work, and on NLP. In 2008 he chaired the world's First International NLP Research Conference. *NLP: A Critical Appreciation*, co-authored with Dr Jane Mathison, is being published by Palgrave Macmillan in 2009.

P.Tosey@surrey.ac.uk

Kiran Trehan is Director of the MA in Human Resource Development and consulting at Lancaster University and visiting professor at Birmingham City University, where she undertakes research, teaching and consultancy with a variety of organisations in the area of management learning and leadership development. Prior to this Kiran was head of department and professor of management learning/HRD at Birmingham City University. Her current research includes critical thinking in Management learning and leadership development, emotions in learning, critical reflection and action learning in practice with particular reference to management/leadership development. She is Joint Editor of *Action Learning: Research and Practice*.

k.trehan@lancaster.ac.uk

Alison Trimble has worked in the voluntary and community sector for over 20 years and was a founding member of the Bromley by Bow Centre team. Allison was CEO of the Centre and in particular was responsible for developing the Bromley By Bow model of community participation and approach to partnership working. Allison now works as an associate of various leadership and organisational development groups, including the Kings Fund and The Centre for Innovation and Healthcare Management. Allison has worked with a range of social regeneration partnerships across the public, private and community sectors, as well as her advisory role on community regeneration issues, including as a neighbourhood renewal adviser with the Department of Communities and Local Government.

Russ Vince is Professor of Leadership and Change in the School of Management and the School for Health, the University of Bath. His research interests are in organisational learning, leadership and the management of change. His books include: *The Handbook of Experiential Learning and Management Education* (Oxford University Press, 2007), *Rethinking Strategic Learning* (Routledge, 2004); *Organizing Reflection* (Ashgate, 2004); *Group Relations, Management and Organization* (Oxford University Press, 1999) and *Managing Change* (Policy Press, 1996). Russ is Editor-in-Chief of the international academic journal *Management Learning*.

rv212@management.bath.ac.uk

PART 1

Leadership and Management Development in the Twenty-first Century

CHAPTER 1

Leadership and Management Development: The Current State

RICHARD THORPE AND JEFF GOLD

Introduction

'Leadership' has always been a popular term, and has appeared in an ever-increasing number of books, all offering insight into how managers and very often those carrying the title of leader can develop themselves and their organisations in the context of rapid change and globalisation. There has also been a growth in leadership centres – often called 'academies' – that purport to improve the leadership skills of particular groups of professionals.[1] Those involved in developing managers have long been puzzled by leadership being so prominent at the expense of management, and there has been a great deal of speculation as to why this should be so.

One explanation we offer is that management literature has always drawn a distinction between management and leadership, acknowledging a difference between aspects of an organisation that might be said to be in steady state or routine, and aspects that might be depicted as in flux, unprogrammed, complex, and ambiguous and so on, for which where there are no 'correct' answers and management decisions require judgement. Herbert Simon's[2] studies on decision making in the 1950s and Bennis's[3] research on leadership in the 1980/90s exemplify this point. Leadership might be seen as activity that is visionary, creative, inspirational, energising and transformational, whereas management might be seen as dealing with the day-to-day routine, much more transactional and so requiring good operational skills. In one sense then, the growth and interest in leadership might simply reflect the changing nature of managerial work.

However, commentators also detect some degree of inflation in the use of the word 'leadership' compared to 'management'. When management is defined in relation to administration, for example, it is the word 'management' that conveys the sense of strategy and creative endeavour, with 'administration' seen as embodying notions of efficiency and routine. When leadership is defined in relation to management, however,

---

1   For example, the National College for School Leadership at http://www.ncsl.org.uk/ seeks to provide support for 'current and future school leaders so that they can have a positive impact within and beyond their schools'.

2   Simon, H. A. (1957) *Administrative Behaviour*, 2nd edn, New York: Macmillan.

3   Bennis, W. and Nanus, B. (1985) *Leaders*, New York: Harper Row.

it is leadership that is then cast as the creative function, with management seen as relating more to day-to-day work. It is perhaps interesting to point out that the MBA degree, the only general master's qualification in management that is truly international, and still relatively popular, is actually a Master of Business Administration, although leadership will undoubtedly be a prominent aspect of its content.

A related issue that might account for the increased interest in leadership detected by management development professionals is that real long-term changes in the economy and society may be affecting the nature of the task of managing. This argument suggests that management was, in a past industrial age, primarily associated with those who manage the factors of production on behalf of owners or shareholders. Leadership, in contrast, has a longer pedigree and is the term traditionally used in the management of professionals.[4] With the increase in knowledge in the new economy, and a commensurate increase in professional employment, the term 'leadership' has become dominant when discussing the way powerful, self-directing and knowledgeable workers might be 'managed'. As with all professional workers, these individuals often have complex if not independent relationships with the organisations in which they work. First, they belong to a distinct community of practice, often a professional society, whilst at the same time often reporting to a range of individuals in the organisations in which they work. Second, their tenure in a job can be a brief one, working on projects, or within teams that disband and reform to focus on new activities.

There have also been other forces at work which provide a strong impetus for promoting leadership as a missing ingredient in the search for improvement and modernisation, especially in the public sector. In the UK, the Council for Excellence in Management and Leadership (CEML)[5] was set up in 2000 to provide a strategy for management and leadership development and made particular reference to the need for more leaders to enable an improvement in UK's economic performance. The Cabinet's Performance and Innovation Unit, very much driven by a modernisation agenda in the public sector, tried with little success,[6] to draw lessons about leadership from private and public sectors on the qualities required for effective leadership and the impact of development programmes on organisational outcomes.

More recently, there has been growing interest in the importance of diversity as an issue for inclusion in leadership and management programmes, as well as attention to ethical and more socially responsible behaviour by leaders and managers.

We feel it is important to raise these issues at the beginning of a book focused on developing managers and leaders, so that readers are clear that leadership hasn't suddenly made the need for management and administration redundant within organisations. Nor is leadership a substitute for many of the activities and roles that managers and administrators need to discharge. Rather, it is a different aspect of the role that is for many embodied in the same person, and an aspect that may well have been missing from the way we have developed our managers in the past. As society changes, professionals'

---

4   A useful reminder provided to us by our friend and colleague, John Burgoyne in Thorpe, R., Gold, J., Anderson, L., Burgoyne, J. G., Wilkinson, D. and Malby, B. (2008) *Towards 'Leaderful' Communities in the North of England*, Cork: Oak Tree Press.

5   The Council's final report, *Managers and Leaders, Raising Our Game*, was published in 2002.

6   See PIU (2001) *Strengthening Leadership in the Public Sector: A Research Study by the PIU*, London: The Cabinet Office.

work increases and we expect more from our public services, the need to address the development of leadership does so as well.

Not withstanding this increasing interest in leadership as a phenomenon, there is still a dearth of literature that clarifies just what leadership is and how leaders can be developed. A systematic review of the leadership literature[7] revealed it to be not particularly robust, with few convincing empirical studies and a sense that little progress has been made since Stogdill[8] first suggested the absence of any clear personality traits that reliably predict leadership potential. Of interest to us is the observation by Pfeiffer[9] who pointed out the fact that the performance of a business is often outside the control of single individuals – yet the search for the individual as leader and hero continues. In this chapter, we hope to indicate the distributed, collective nature of leadership and help readers to identify how both individual working within collectives might be more appropriately seen as the unit of account and what this means for leadership learning and development.

In addition to these comments on leadership, more broadly it seems that it remains an act of faith than an investment in management development will be linked to measures of success, whether at the level of organisations or the nation as whole. It is very much part of conventional wisdom that management development is a good thing.[10] However, there is now growing research to suggest that there is a link between management development and organisation performance, although this link is very much connected to the priority and support given to it by those in senior positions – the leaders.[11] Thus leadership development is very much connected to management development, and this theme will be evident in this chapter and throughout the book.

So What is Leadership and Does it Differ from Management?

A number of years ago, when the dean of a British business school visited North America, he asked an Indian chief, to whom he was introduced, why it was he who became the leader of the tribe. His response was that when he was hunting for buffalo on the great plain and the track forked left and right, if he rode right and his braves followed him, he was reaffirmed as the leader; but if he rode right and his braves rode to the left, then he was no longer the leader. The inference is here that for leaders to be leaders, they have to have followers; how leaders create confidence in others to follow is one of the subjects of this chapter.

Charles Handy, when presenting BBC Radio 4's *Thought for Today* some years ago, suggested leaders had three qualities – 'the trinity' – which connect to the Indian chief's theme:

7   Thorpe, R., Lawler, J. and Gold, J. (2007) *Leadership – a systematic review*, SELIG working paper series: http://lubswww. leeds.ac.uk/selig.

8   Stogdill, R. M. (1974) *Handbook of Leadership*, New York: The Free Press.

9   See Pfeiffer, J. (1977) The ambiguity of leadership, *Academy of Management Review*, 2: 104–112.

10   The Leitch Review of skills (2006) *Prosperity for All in the Global Economy – World Class Skills*, London: HM Treasury, linked an improvement in management skills to the improvement in business performance.

11   See Mabey, C. and Ramirez, M. (2005) Does management development improve organizational productivity? A six-country analysis of European firms, *International Journal of Human Resource Management*, 16(7): 1067–1082.

1. *Do they understand?* Understanding means that leaders can both read the external drivers that will affect the organisation's success and understand internal drivers, such as the organisation's capabilities, the views and values held by the stakeholders involved in the enterprise, and the possibilities for change.
2. *Do they have a vision?* Vision means that leaders see a bigger picture: what some writers[12] have called the 'helicopter factor'. They can see not only this bigger picture but also how it can be translated into operational actions.
3. *Can they inspire others?* Inspiration means that leaders can release the energy within their subordinates and connect with them to obtain their willing if not wholehearted support.

So, in a general sense, leadership demands a sense of purpose, and an ability to influence others, interpret situations, negotiate and debate their views, often in the face of opposition. If this image is one that seems to set a standard for leaders, we perhaps need to explore how far those who are appointed to the role of leader or manager match this standard by observing how they behave and the roles they perform.

A Retrospective Look at the Roles Managers and Leaders Perform

What is clear to leadership and management developers is the way in which the early idea of what management[13] is and what managers do is still deeply embedded in the management psyche today. The early studies, undertaken at the beginning of the last century,[14] imply that management is at its core a rational scientific process that can be behaviourally studied, systematically trained for and performance-measured. These early writings suggest a number of functions that managers perform:

- Planning: managers determine the direction of the organisation by establishing objectives, and designing and implementing strategies.
- Organising: managers determine the specific activities and resources required to implement the business plan, as well as making decisions about how work should be allocated and coordinated.
- Directing: managers communicate to others their responsibilities in achieving the plan, as well as providing an organisational environment in which employees are motivated and able to improve their performance.
- Controlling: managers guide, monitor and adjust work activities to ensure that performance remains in line with the organisation's expectations.

---

12   Handy, C. (1982) *Understanding Organisations*, 2nd edn, Harmondsworth: Penguin Books.

13   Most research at first tended to focus on management with leadership implicitly seen as part of the work.

14   For the classical texts, see, for example, Fayol, H. (1916) *General and Industrial Administration*, translated from the French by C. Storrs (1949) London: Sir Isaac Pitman; Taylor, F. W. (1947) *Scientific Management*, New York: Harper and Row; Brech, E. F. L. (1965) *Organisation: The Framework of Management*, 2nd edn, London: Longman.

This very much remains the orthodoxy for both managers and leaders and forms the basis of many programmes, frameworks, books and articles. However, what have we learnt about what managers and leaders actually do?

From various studies,[15] we have learnt that when we imagine a manager or leader sitting quietly behind a desk making decisions and thinking of the future. The observation studies conducted reveal managers and leaders at all levels within an organisation to be working at a frenetic pace, often on a variety of tasks simultaneously, and often being reactive to events – a far cry from the image of a proactive individual. From these studies, a number of themes can be distilled that helpfully illuminate a number of aspects of management and leadership work:

1. *Elements:* we have already discussed the fact that managers and leaders are seen to undertake both specialist and generalist work, but more important is the fact that they often carry out very similar tasks in completely different ways and, in so doing, achieve similar results. This is, of course, most perplexing for those brought up within the behavioural school, where jobs are thought to be reducible observing what managers and leaders actually do couldn't offer a more different picture from their functional components, and where training programmes are developed to improve the performance of individuals carrying out these functions. What is not open to debate, though, is that a number of roles can be identified that all leaders especially appear to perform, regardless of company size or sector. One of these is to act as figurehead for the organisation, division or group. Leaders also represent the organisation to outside bodies, visitors and new recruits, and perform important liaison roles, connecting to those outside the organisation. They also allocate scarce resources and sort out disruptions in work, often by negotiating with people when these arise.

2. *Distribution of time:* a second feature of a manager and leader's work is the amount of time spent planning ahead and thinking about the future. Not only did these activities rarely get observed but those that did were of short duration and, as a consequence, agendas were often used to identify what needed to be done. Agendas link closely to notions of their use of recipes or 'agendas' that have been thought to help managers save time. As with single-loop learning,[16] these kinds of shortcuts save managers and leaders time in analysing problems or enacting strategy.

3. *Ways of interaction:* one striking feature of the studies into the ways managers and leaders behave is the amount of time they spend in communication of various forms. Even though electronic media now reduce the degree of face-to-face contact, the latter is still seen as important. Lateral communication – where managers talk to other managers of the same rank or status – appears to occupy a large part of their time, and of course there are those endless rounds of meetings. What can't be so easily observed is time taken to stand back and reflect on strategic issues important for the future.

---

15   For insights into what managers and leaders do, see Mintzberg, H. (1975) The manager's job, folklore and fact, *Harvard Business Review,* July–Aug: 49–61; Kotter, J. P. (1990) What leaders really do?, *Harvard Business Review,* May–June: 103–111; Watson, T. (2000) *In Search of Management,* London: Routledge.

16   Single-loop learning is a concept used by Argyris to describe learning from past activities that saves managers reassessing each problem afresh. Double-loop learning occurs when the manager realises important aspects of the problem have changed and new solutions are required. See Argyris, C. (2006) *Reasons and Rationalizations: The Limits of Organisational Knowledge,* Oxford: Oxford University Press.

Another interesting feature of communication (and one we will pick up on later) is its informality – in humour and references to matters seemingly unconnected to work. This highlights the importance placed on individuals' interpersonal skills and what academics have begun to call 'human capital': a quality managers and leaders need to have, to benefit from others. 'Social capital', meanwhile, refers to the quality of the relations managers and leaders develop. It is through social capital and a manager and leader's networks that a great deal of information is gained.[17] This links to the importance of understanding how managers and leaders gain their knowledge. Knowledge has so often been viewed as simply data that can be transferred, as opposed to information that might be gained through informal contact and involvement with peers, in what academics refer to as 'communities of practice'.[18]

4. *The political nature of management practice:* what has been understated for many years is the political and symbolic nature of managerial and leadership work. Dalton,[19] as long ago as 1959, showed the way in which power struggles and information alliances affected the way managers operated. Also recognised has been the way managers and leaders have not always followed organisations' goals but instead pursued personal agendas. The political nature of work can be the way individuals manipulate incentive bonus schemes to reward themselves in the short term, whether or not it produces problems for the organisation in the long term. An illustration of this might be the recent problems that have occurred within the financial services industries.

5. *The symbolic dimension:* this is another theme of activity that, although recognised, has been undervalued by both managers, leaders and academics alike. Yet it is a particularly important feature of the way leaders operate,[20] especially in how they create change and set agendas for certain kinds of activity. Managers and leaders can't influence individuals to change their behaviours directly but achieve this through one or more *mediating means.* The weapons the manager or leader has in their armoury to achieve this include the use of compelling rhetoric, which might work to persuade individuals or groups of the importance of one thing or another. Another might be the way in which the physical settings and infrastructures are designed. Stories told within the organisation also play their part. Stories with often dramatic narratives of past events are used to suggest to employees the benefits of particular practices or activities, and serve to signal the way the organisation was successful in the past.[21] Rituals – also an important aspect of organisational life – serve to signal the success of individuals in the organisation, such as being promoted or achieving some kind of success or another. Successful leaders use these kinds of symbols and rituals to send important messages to employees about what is valued within the organisation.

---

17   For an understanding of the way human and social capital is generated see Thorpe, R., Jones, O., Macpherson, A. and Holt, R. (2008) The evolution of business knowledge in SMEs, in Scarborough, H. (ed.) *The Evolution of Business Knowledge*, Oxford: Oxford University Press; or Jones, O., Macpherson, A., Thorpe, R. and Graham, A. (2007) The evolution of business knowledge in SMEs: conceptualising strategic space, *Journal of Strategic Change*, 16(6): 281–294.

18   A term usually attributed to Etienne Wenger, go to http://www.ewenger.com/theory/index.htm.

19   Dalton, M. (1959) *Men Who Manage: Fusion of Feeling and Theory in Administration*. New York: Wiley.

20   See Pfeffer, J. and Sutton, R. (2006) *Hard Facts, Dangerous Half-Truths, and Total Nonsense Profiting from Evidence-Based Management*, Boston, MA: Harvard Business School Press.

21   See Weick, K. (1995) *Sensemaking in Organizations*, San Francisco, CA: Sage.

The issues raised above indicate the importance of understanding aspects of the nature of a manager and leader's work. We are not suggesting that managers and leaders don't plan and think about the future, but rather that their day-to-day activity is, necessarily, a far cry from what many expect, yet the roles they perform are often quite similar. It is from the relatively informal everyday processes that most managers and leaders derive much of their learning, and a recognition of this forms part of the trend towards relatively informal learning and development provision that includes mentoring, coaching, including executive coaching and 360-degree feedback as well as management development methods such as action learning.[22] Of course, the very informality of such learning poses difficulties for those concerned with proving the value of provision, an issue that will be considered later in the book.

One way of considering the distinction between leadership and management is to view them as processes that require two very different systems of action. Kotter[23] argues that both are important for success, and that far from being mystical, mysterious processes, management and leadership aren't so much linked to particular personality traits or individual displays of 'charisma', but rather to distinctive systems of action that rub alongside the everyday functions of management, shown in Table 1.1. The real danger (especially in the small organisation) is over-management at the expense of leadership. Drawing on Kotter's ideas, Chell[24] illustrates how good organisational management might deal with the issues of complexity, through the process of planning, organising, controlling and solving problems, whilst those responsible for the organisation's leadership help to create direction and vision, through communication, motivation and the inspiration they instil in subordinates.

Table 1.1   Leadership and management as systems of action

Management	Leadership
Planning; setting targets Identifying steps to goal achievement and allocating resources to achieve them	Envisioning; setting direction Creating a vision for the future along with strategies for its achievement
Organising – creating a structure Identifying jobs and staffing requirements, communicating the plan and delegating responsibility to those job holders for carrying them out	Aligning people Communicating the vision and marshalling support; getting people to believe the management and empowering them with a clear sense of direction, strength and unity
Controlling and problem solving Installing control systems to direct deviations from the plan, the purpose being to complete routine jobs successfully	Motivating and inspiring Energising people through need, fulfilment and involvement in the process, including supporting employees' efforts, and recognising and rewarding their success. Coordination occurs through strong networks of informal relationships

Source: Kotter (1990) adapted from Chell (2001).

22   See other chapters in this book and Hirsh, W. and Carter, A. (2002) *New Directions in Management Development, Report 387*, Brighton: Institute for Employment Studies.

23   Kotter, J. P. (1990) op. cit.

24   Chell, E. (2001) *Entrepreneurship: Globalisation, Innovation and Development*, Part 3, Chapter 9, Leadership and management, are they different?, pp. 188–190. London: Thomson.

Readers will notice that the headings in the management column follow closely the classical view of the functions managers perform, as discussed earlier, whereas the headings that describe the leaders' qualities and roles include a number of those identified from the observation studies, including the informational roles and a number of generic competences put forward by Richard Boyatzis.[25]

Good leadership is a lot about the ability to cope with change and, in this context, a distinction has been drawn between two types of leadership – transactional and transformational approaches – which will be discussed in the following section.

Linking Theory to the Observation of Roles

When managers and developers look to academics for theories that might help them understand how they may be developed, they are faced with a bewildering array of competing approaches.[26] There appears to have been no cumulative building of theory in respect to leadership with all the studies that have been done, offering only a partial perspective on leadership. This is not to suggest that each in its own way is not useful; so long as managers and leaders don't look for a single correct explanation, the theories do help to shed some light on leadership or management as an activity. Rather like eating the elephant, it is possible only by tackling one small bit at a time. So at this stage in the chapter, we will outline some of the most influential theories produced by academics over the last 50 years. We conclude this section with the notion of distributed leadership: an idea whose time we believe has come[27] and one that we are currently exploring more widely.

Trait theory. From this perspective, leadership or management is seen as embedded in individuals. Debates continue as to whether particular traits are born or bred. The approach involved identifying the traits (psychological and physiological) of successful leaders, often in war situations, and highlighting those qualities that appeared to correlate with their success as leaders. So leaders, for example, were thought to have to be very small or very tall to have integrity and good social skills. The problem, of course, came in considering just how desired personality traits might be developed and how the observations could be adapted to different contexts or cultures.

Functional views. This approach views leadership[28] very much as a job. Leaders need to attend to various important aspects of most work. So, for example, the task in hand needs to be achieved, the needs of individuals are to be taken care of, and how individuals work together as a group or team must be managed, to gain the optimum from the resources available. Used extensively by the British Army even today, the approach suggests that by striking the correct balance between the needs of the task, the teams and the individual, optimum performance can be managed regardless of the styles the leader adopts, which in any event might depend on the nature of the tasks undertaken.

---

25   See Boyatzis, R. E. (1982) *The Competent Manager: A Model for Effective Performance*, New York: John Wiley and Sons, and Chapter 12 of this book.

26   Thorpe, R., Lawler, J. and Gold, J. (2007) *Leadership – A Systematic Review*, SELIG working paper series, http://lubswww.leeds.ac.uk/selig.

27   A comment adapted from Gronn, P. (2000) Distributed properties: a new architecture for leadership, *Educational, Management and Administration*, 28(3): 317–338.

28   Adair, J. (1983) *Effective Leadership*, Aldershot: Gower.

Style approaches. In this perspective on leadership, paramount to success was the leader's influence, as opposed to accepting that subordinates should always have an influence on work decisions. The research studies often depict a continuum of styles where at one end the leader tells or sells to subordinates what *the leader* thinks are the important priorities, whilst at the other end the leader abdicates responsibility to subordinates. On balance, the research suggested that leaders would be most effective when adopting a consultative style that balanced the views of subordinates with their own views. However, in the majority of research studies, the margin of error was really quite large and there was little definitive proof that one style was in fact much more successful than other, even though, for many, the quality of working life might have been improved. In later years, this stream of research on style was extended to incorporate a contingency component that stressed the importance of striking an appropriate balance between a concern to achieve tasks and a concern for those individuals undertaking them, dependent on the organisational context and circumstances at the time. Even today managers remain familiar with 'Blake and Mouton's managerial grid'.[29]

Contingency theories. Contingency theories were very much in vogue in the 1960s and 1970s, and the study of leadership was no exception. This approach to leadership, advocated by writers such as Vroom and Yetton,[30] further developed the contingency approach and brought into play even more variables that would predict the best choice of leadership style. The variables considered included the personality of the leader, the nature and urgency of the task to be completed, the dynamics of the context, and the personality of those subordinates being led.[31] Later, writers went further, suggesting that leadership styles might also need to change depending on the maturity of the group or team, with early engagement potentially requiring more autocratic styles, but familiarity and experience of working together allowing a more participatory style. This approach is one that many schoolteachers will readily recognise as they seek to stamp their authority on a new class but relax as patterns of work become more established.[32]

The use of power. Often absent from the more traditional explorations of styles, research on power is nevertheless important. From a traditional or classical point of view, leaders will enjoy power and authority from the formal role they occupy within the organisation. Here, their authority comes from their position in the organisational hierarchy; however, this is not always so, and even in terms of the contributions individuals make within teams, writers such as Belbin[33] illustrate how power can also be exerted on decisions and performance through an individual's expertise.

Expertise can also have a reputational dimension and might therefore emanate from past performance. This links closely with the symbolic aspects of leadership discussed above, where the leader performance is seen as a consequence of past performance in the job. Another source of power can emanate from the respect and admiration that an

---

29   Blake, R. R. and Moulton, J. S. (1964) *The Managerial Grid*, Houston, TX: Gulf.

30   Vroom, V. H. and Yetton, P. W. (1973) *Leadership and Decision Making*, Pittsburgh, PA: University of Pittsburgh Press.

31   For an early account of a contingency view of leadership see Fieldler, F. E. (1964) A contingency model of leadership effectiveness. In Berkovitz, L. (ed.) *Advances of Experimental Social Psychology*, New York: Academic Press.

32   Conger, J. (2004) Developing leadership capability: what's inside the black box?, *Academy of Management Executives*, 18(3): 136–39.

33   Belbin, R. M. (1981) *Management Teams: Why they Succeed or Fail*, Oxford: Butterworth Heinmann.

individual commands, due to their charisma. Recent work by Bryman[34] highlights the importance of this quality, but readers need look no further than the phenomenal success of Barack Obama in winning the hearts and minds of many hitherto disenfranchised Americans through his charismatic personality.

Power, of course, can also play a significant part in the political activity of individuals. Picking up some threads from earlier, we can mention that researchers examined the way in which successful leaders can influence others through giving access to individuals who want to get their points across. The power that comes from gate-keeping and occasionally opening the gate is considerable and often involves reciprocity. Here favours are often offered in the expectation of their being returned some time in the future. Such a process sets up new obligations on individuals and a network of exchange relationships.[35]

TRANSACTIONAL OR TRANSFORMATIONAL?

These ideas emerged in the 1980s, principally as a response to dissatisfaction of prevailing views of leadership or management styles and a concern that leaders were too bogged down in detail to provide the inspiration needed in challenging times.[36] As part of a 'new paradigm', transactional approaches to leadership are usually based on a clearly understood bargain being struck between leaders and subordinates who are clear about the rewards they can expect to receive for certain actions or behaviours taking place. Leaders, therefore, promise rewards for effort, with an underlying assumption that individuals will work for self-interest[37] to gain the rewards offered. By contrast, transformational approaches to leadership relates closely to organisational change. It involves leaders presenting visions of new possibilities and individuals rising to the challenge. Through enacting the vision, individuals can both improve and fulfil themselves.[38] By inspiring people through this transformational style, leaders create new possibilities for their subordinates that move them beyond the basic self-interest that is the bedrock of transactional approaches. There is of course a danger that transformational leadership can overspill into a more coercive and totalitarian ethos that others dare not challenge. In the twenty-first century, the behaviour of leaders such as Enron, who were consistently seen as transformative, nevertheless have served to prompt a more considered and ethical treatment of how to engage hearts and minds.[39]

This 'rediscovery' of the idea of leaders as inspirational, visionary and charismatic had and still does have much attraction for developers and a range of instruments have been

---

34   Bryman, A. (1992) *Charisma and Leadership in Organisations*, London: Sage.

35   Boissevain, J. (1974) *Friends of Friends*, Oxford: Blackwell.

36   For an overview on transactional and transformational approaches to leadership see Bennis, W. (1984) Where have all the leaders gone? In Rosenbank, W. E. and Taylor, R. L. (eds) *Contemporary Issues in Leadership*, Boulder, CO: West View Press.

37   For an account of the effect reward bargain see Bowey, A. M. (ed.) (1982) *Handbook of Wages and Salary Systems*, Aldershot: Gower.

38   The person who first coined the term transformational leadership was Burns. Burns, J. M. (1978) *Leadership*, New York: Harper Row.

39   Ethics and corporate social responsibility are growing elements of leadership and management development programmes. See Simon Western's (2008) *Leadership, A Critical Text* (London: Sage) for a more considered critique of coercion and totalisation in leadership practice.

offered to assist.[40] There is a link to the phenomenon of emotional intelligence.[41] However, there has also been something of a reaction against the promotion of transformation, perhaps at the expense of transactional approaches. For example, the effort–reward bargain may well be much more sophisticated than simply a monetary one. Reward can be far more than pay and bonuses; it can extend to other rewards such as flexible working, personal development and even a guaranteed car-parking space in a busy city. On the other side of the equation, effort is often seen as far more than physical or mental application; with the growth of the knowledge economy, often of greater importance are things such as the flexibility and reliability of staff, their commitment, and possibly their ability to be creative and innovative. In some ways, transactional leadership, with its basis in the striking of a bargain, could be seen as having a strong moral base. Leaders set out what they require from subordinates and subordinates know what they will get by adopting certain behaviours.

Dialogical. Both transformational and transactional approaches link closely to something we will discuss later: *authorship*.[42] This is where a leader and/or manager creates a landscape of possibilities for individuals whilst at the same time it remains clear just what everyone's obligations and responsibilities are if they are to make the new landscape a reality. The leader is not so much a hero, but just as much a listener and sometimes a servant.[43] In order to operate within a context requiring transformation and to be successful in getting others to buy into what needs to be done, leaders need to be reflective enough to be aware of the language they use and the way they structure what they want to say to others in their daily transactions. The subject of linguistic philosophy, as it is known, is not new;[44] it relates to how conversations can be shaped in order to create shared meaning and understanding.[45] Critical is the sensitivity that leaders need to have towards the audience with which they engage. This includes using language that will connect with whomsoever they are communicating, and this sense of being grounded in the local, yet understanding the global, is an important skill of the leader. In the 1960s, a colleague of ours worked as an assistant to Anthony Wedgwood-Benn, who was then the Energy Minister. One of the most striking things he remembers was the way Tony Benn, as he is now known, could moderate the way he spoke to very different audiences. So, for example, his manner of speaking to a group of senior business leaders was quite different from his manner of speaking to a group of trade unionists in a works canteen. In the former situation he would sit at a boardroom table, while in the latter he might well stand on a table in a suit, shirtsleeves and no tie as he spoke.

---

40   Probably the most well known of these is the Multifactor Leadership Questionnaire (MLQ) – go to http://www.mindgarden.com/products/mlq.htm.

41   See Goleman D., Boyatzis, R. and McKee, A. (2004) *Primal Leadership: Learning to Lead with Emotional Intelligence*, Boston, MA: Harvard Business School Press.

42   Authorship is a term coined by John Shotter in his book *Conversational Realities*: Shotter, J. (1993) *Conversational Realities: Constructing Life Through Language (Inquiries in Social Construction Series)*, London: Sage.

43   See Robert Greenleaf's idea of servant leadership at http://www.greenleaf.org/ and Joseph L. Badaracco's (2002) notion of the quiet leader in *Leading Quietly: An Unorthodox Guide to Doing the Right Thing*, Boston, MA: Harvard Business School Press.

44   Austin, J. L. (1959) *Sense and Sensibility*, Oxford: Oxford University Press.

45   Holman, D. and Thorpe, R. (2003) *Management and Language*, London: Sage.

Leadership and distribution. There is an emerging body of knowledge relating to what is referred to as distributed leadership and this concept does not fit easily with most of the research which tends to focus on what individual leaders should learn to do to improve their performance. What an insight into distributed leadership provides is an understanding of how leaders at all organisational levels are able to use influence and how influence might be seen within organisations as part of work practice and the deployment of talent. Leadership is distributed through the work of people working together for the good *or otherwise* of an organisation. We qualify this statement because there is no certainty that people will align their efforts for a common good. This of course poses quite a difficulty for those appointed into leadership roles because, we mentioned earlier, leaders cannot directly influence others but instead need to use a range of mediating means. Distributed leadership is in many ways the antithesis of hero leadership, where a single individual is reified as the saviour of the firm. Hero leadership dominates so much of the leadership literature, particularly the academic literature from North America, where the highly individualistic culture serves to reinforce the view that individuals matter more than collectives.[46] Such views, though, do not sit comfortably in the British and European traditions. Academic research by writers such as Peter Gronn[47] and Jim Spillane[48] has illustrated how adopting a distributed view, and embracing and developing the talents of people throughout the organisational hierarchy and even outside the organisation, can have substantial positive effects on leadership performance. James and others[49] show how distributed leadership has been embraced in the teaching profession, requiring the collaboration of the many as opposed to the few and where leaders are beginning to be seen more as *lead learners*. Significantly there is now growing evidence of the value of an understanding of this perspective on leadership and organisations that experience positive outcomes.[50]

For those involved in developing leaders and managers, the emerging evidence on distributed leadership does rather set the cat amongst the pigeons because it blurs a long recognised distinction between the leaders as agents appointed to a role and leadership as process of influence and interdependencies. As Richard Barker once asked, 'How can we train leaders if we do not know what leadership is?'[51] However, what the concept of distributed leadership is able to do is enable developers to find a new range of development opportunities that focus on a variety of interdependencies where, influence and interests can be aligned. Figure 1.1 suggests some of these possibilities with solo leaders and collective leadership seen at opposite ends of a continuum that serve to clarify for developers exactly what units might lend themselves for attention.

---

46   Hofstede, G. (1991) Motivation, leadership and organisation: do American theories apply abroad?, *Organisational Dynamics*, 9(1): 42–63.

47   Gronn, P. (2000) Distributed properties: a new architecture for leadership, *Educational, Management and Administration*, 28(3): 317–338.

48   Spillane, J. (2006) *Distributed Leadership*, San Francisco, CA: Wiley.

49   For a contemporary account of distributed leadership in a school setting see James, K. T., Mann, J. and Creasy, J. (2007) Leaders as lead learners: a case example of facilitating collaborative leadership learning for school learners, *Management Learning*, 38(1): 79–94.

50   Although such evidence is still mainly confined to education. See Harris, A. (2008) Distributed leadership according to the evidence, *Journal of Educational Administration*, 46(2): 172–188.

51   See Barker, R. (1997) How can we train leaders if we do not know what leadership is? *Human Relations*, 50(4): 343–362.

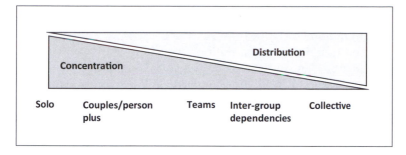

Figure 1.1   A continuum of leadership development possibilities

It is undoubtedly the case that most development is focused towards the solo end of the continuum, an investment in what David Day[52] sees as human capital which enhances the capability of certain individuals. Movement toward the collective end of the continuum affords greater weight to relationships, networks, collaboration and cooperation or what Day sees as social capital.

The above overview of the academic research needs, in our view, to be seen as contributing to explaining just what we observe when we examine what leaders and managers do, as described earlier in the chapter. Unfortunately, rather than being seen as partial perspectives, the different models are seen as competing alternatives that vie against each other for prominence. However, we believe they are actually pieces of a jigsaw that need to come together for us to gain a better picture of how leadership and management operate and how they might be developed.

Developing Leaders and Managers

Our consideration of what managers and leaders do, and some of the key ideas and theories drawn from research, suggests that those involved the business of learning and development do have quite a lot to learn themselves in order to cope with the many challenges presented by our analysis.

One source of help, at least in terms of how to think about the choices, is provided by David Holman, a valued colleague of ours, who rather neatly sets out some ways of thinking about management and, we would argue, leadership development.[53] Holman suggests four conceptually different approaches:

1. Academic liberalism – the pursuit of objective knowledge as principles and theories to be applied rationally and relatively scientifically. Managers and leaders have the image of a 'scientist', applying ideas and principles gained from experts.
2. Experiential liberalism – rather than theories, experience is the source of learning which provides ideas and insights which can be used in practice. A crucial is skill is to become a 'reflective practitioner' to make learning from experience a deliberate

52   See Day, D. (2001) Leadership development: a review in context, *The Leadership Quarterly*, 11: 581–613.

53   See Holman, D. (2000) Contemporary models of management education in the UK, *Management Learning*, 31(2): 197–217.

process, perhaps with others in a joint process or by taking responsibility for self learning and development.

3. Experiential vocationalism – organisations are where managers and leaders practice so what is needed is relevant knowledge and skills, as required. The image is that of a 'competent manager', as defined by an agreed a model of competences.

4. Experiential/critical – where 'emancipation' is sought by managers and leaders and others. While there is a body of knowledge drawn from critical theory, the image for managers and leader is of a 'critically reflective or reflexive practitioner' who seeks to work with others to deal ambiguous, paradoxical and intractable problems in a complex world.

All of these approaches to some extent inform what is offered as leadership and management development, and the chapters in this book certainly reflect aspects of the conceptual models.

MANAGERS AND LEADERS AS SCIENTISTS

We live in knowledge-rich world, so it is not surprising that there is a high expectation that managers and leaders will be able to analyse issues and apply theories and principles. Learning about leadership and management and the issues that need to be faced strategically is a significant part of any management and leadership development intervention, whether offered in-house or by external providers.[54] It is also often the unique selling point of programmes such as the MBA degree, learning through exposure to those 'experts' who know through formal instruction seminars, case studies and perhaps increasingly e-media and in-house access to databases.

Competent Managers and Leaders

We began our characterisation of past approaches to the development of leadership and management by suggesting their links to behaviourist approaches to development. The view here is that good leadership and management can be studied and desired behaviour subsequently developed through an appropriately designed instructional process. Over the decades, developers have sometimes seen this process in highly structured ways, such as in profiles of competences that need development. Often such approaches have been achieved through scientific processes such as the functional analysis of jobs. These assume close relationships between behaviour and performance. On the other hand, others[55] have built a great deal of flexibility into both the definition of the competence and the approach that might be used for its development. Whatever the approach, there is usually an instructional process through which the desired outcomes are obtained. Knowledge is seen in the form of a category, principle or definition that, if the process of development is followed properly, can be improved and measured. Although not often undertaken over the longer term, leadership performance is measured against these predefined objectives, which are often the stuff of annual appraisals.

---

54   See Storey, J. (2004) *Leadership in Organisations*, London: Routledge.

55   Boyatizis, R. (1982) *The Competent Manager: A Theory of Effective Performance*, New York: John Wiley and Sons.

Although this approach is seen to benefit those involved with leadership and management development, it raises a number of issues. One issue, highlighted earlier in the chapter, relates to how different leaders and managers can achieve similar results in very different ways. If this is indeed the case, then knowing which approach is the correct one to adopt becomes extremely difficult. Add to this the uncertainty of the unknown, and complications become greater still. A pure behaviourist philosophy also assumes that the leader will adopt a passive role in their own development, whereas we have also shown the way managers and leaders often behave proactively and in ways that may be at odds with the immediate goals of the organisation.

Behavioural statements, when produced, also say little about the moral or ethical basis of leadership decisions: aspects of the role we have identified as important. In the management education literature, concerns have recently been expressed, particularly in respect to the MBA degree, that managers may not be taught enough about subjects such as corporate social responsibility, and their understanding may not be sufficiently embedded in a close knowledge of practice and so not be properly grounded in events, practices and experiences.[56, 57] This we see as extremely important, particularly where distributed leadership is concerned, as it is from the understanding of the practitioner's approach to the general that true understanding emanates.

MANAGERS AND LEADERS AS REFLECTIVE PRACTITIONERS

Recognising the limitations of the models above, many management and leadership developers have grasped the importance of situating and grounding development in the context of day-to-day reality. This has led to programmes that are both problem- and learner-centred. Starting from this position, a number of approaches to management and leadership development have emerged, including action learning, coaching and mentoring, where managers and leaders are helped to reflect on their day-to-day activities as well as the sense they make of their work for themselves. These are related to their current knowledge and understanding, as well as to their current practice needs. From this perspective, a view has developed that sees organisational development as inextricably linked to an individual's personal development and where learning takes place through reflection and as a consequence of problems and opportunities that the individual faces at work. Many also recognised that learning often occurs naturally, particularly as a consequence of significant work-related events,[58] whether these are problems or opportunities. From this perspective, it follows that learning and development can be significantly enhanced if the learning can be structured and captured, and if the issues the manager or leader faces can be reflected upon.

The process might be further enhanced if managers are encouraged to work through what a number of researchers[59, 60] have referred to as the learning cycle. This cycle includes

56   Khuana, R. (2007) *From Higher Aims to Hired Hands: The Social Transformation of American Business Schools and the Unfilled Promise of Management as a Profession*, Princeton, NJ: Princeton University Press.

57   Starkey, K. and Tiratsoo, N. (2007) *The Business School and the Bottom Line*, Cambridge: Cambridge University Press.

58   Davies, J. and Easterby Smith, M. P. V. (1983) Learning and developing from managerial work experiences, *Journal of Management Studies*, 21(2): 169–182.

59   Kolb, D. A. (1984) *Experiential Learning*, Englewood Cliffs, NJ: Prentice Hall.

60   Honey, P. and Mumford, A. (2000) *The Learning Style Helpers Guide*, Maidenhead: Peter Honey Publications Ltd.

undertaking an activity, and reflecting on its outcome and result, how the learning from the activity might be captured and conceptualised, and the implications all this might have for learning and for future actions. This kind of development philosophy makes full use of an individual's experience and places the person firmly at the centre of the development process. It is also self-directed and action-oriented.

However, the approach is not without problems, as pointed out by academics such as Holman and others:[61] the approach predominantly focuses on individuals and, whilst not ignoring social relationships, does not explicitly take into account the interaction between individuals within the organisation. In addition, individuals are often seen as divorced from their social, cultural and historical context; and, in the way the learning cycle is characterised, the various components – for example, thinking and action – are portrayed as separate parts of a circular process. Although learning cycles have for many years been seen as the underpinning rationale for the management development vehicle of action learning, the latter can often, through careful discussion and facilitation, overcome these challenges. This is particularly so where individuals learn together in the context of their own organisation, and where conceptual knowledge and information are fed into the process to help managers make sense of complexity and, when they need to, find ways of viewing their organisations and themselves afresh. Programmes and 'tools' that promote reflection are important to the development of managers and leaders and they can often help managers see situations and their role differently. This focus on the development of managers closely links for the CEO the development of strategy with learning and change.[62, 63]

MANAGERS AND LEADERS AS CRITICALLY REFLECTIVE OR REFLEXIVE PRACTITIONERS

Models that emphasise knowledge, the right way of behaving or finding practical responses to problems through the development of reflective practices, can only ever offer partial success, because managers and leaders are frequently having to find responses to problems which, as Einstein was quoted as suggesting 'cannot be solved at the same level of thinking we were at when we created them'. Instead, managers and leaders need, according to Chia and Morgan,[64] to embrace 'the management of life in all its complexions'. So instead of simply embracing knowledge and skills that reinforce conventional wisdom and reflection that leaves assumptions unchallenged, managers and leaders need to consider their 'ignorance', and challenge the abstractions which often become confused for truth and embedded in taken-for-granted ways of behaving and thinking. The challenge to this state of affairs is to encourage more critical approaches as part of the development process, but an inevitable tension is created by action-oriented,

---

61   Holman, D. and Pavilia, K. and Thorpe, R. (1996) Rethinking Kolb's theory of experimental learning: the contribution to social constructionist and activity theory, *Management Learning*, 25(4): 489–504.

62   Gold, J., Holman, D. and Thorpe, R. (2002) The role of argument analysis and story telling in facilitating critical thinking, *Management Learning*, 33(3): 338–371.

63   Gold, J., Thorpe, R. and Holt, R. (2007) Writing, reading and reason, management and the three r's of management learning. In Hill, R. and Stewart, J. (eds) *Management Development: Perspectives from Research and Practice*, London: Routledge.

64   See Chia, R. and Morgan, S. (1996) Educating the philosopher-manager: de-signing the times, *Management Learning*, 27(1): 37–64.

fast-paced development events which provide little time for critical challenge to the assumptions of managers and leaders that might change their thinking and by so doing find solutions for longer term problems.

A FINAL IMAGE: MANAGERS AND LEADERS AS PRACTICAL AUTHORS

We end this chapter with one of our own preferred images which serves to inform our own development activities – this is an image which carries elements of all the models outlined above. The image is one of a manager or leader as a practical author and is taken from the writing of John Shotter.[65] Shotter suggests that one of the key skills of a successful leader or manager is an ability to analyse and read situations so as to be able to find the subtext behind situations or actions observed. Managers and leaders must evaluate problems or situations critically and arrive at preliminary judgements. Whilst this competence would undoubtedly give some managers and leaders an advantage over others, reading situations is not the only thing that leaders need to be able to do. In addition to simply reading situations from different perspectives, managers and leaders need also to generate order out of situations that have become for others perhaps chaotic, confusing or contradictory. Taking this argument further, we see attempting to restore order and clarity in situations of ambiguity and, by so doing, establishing new and more stable flows of activity, as an important task.

If conversations are central to communication, and the processes of learning and leadership are central to change, then what becomes important are the ways in which conversations can lead to the promotion of learning and purposeful action by others and how these people can be developed within organisations.

In most organisational contexts (particularly where professional or technical staff are concerned), it is often the case that the person in charge – the leader – knows little more about the job role and its content than those they are managing.[66] Even when the employees are not professional leaders, the person in charge perhaps needs to be aware that staff often make use of tacit and informal knowledge to make sense of their work and that, by its nature, this kind of knowledge is often well hidden from view. Nevertheless, as researchers have identified, it remains an essential ingredient in maintaining an efficient work process. Given this, one implication (as we have already seen) is that greater knowledge does not necessarily translate into greater authority; the implication for leadership is that the activity needs to be seen less about imparting 'superior knowledge or vision' to those who know, and more about facilitating or acting as a catalyst to groups of individuals, all of whom have a common purpose and who, given the opportunity, might well be capable of painting in the details themselves. To achieve this, they need to tune into conversations and argue persuasively in order to create alignment; this is part of the process of learning about distributed leadership.

From this perspective, leaders and managers serve to help others to make sense of situations and to develop connections within and between a whole range of perspectives

---

65   See Shotter, J. (1993) *Conversational Realities: Constructing Life Through Language,* Inquiries in Social Construction Series, London: Sage.

66   Barnley, S. (1996) Technicians in the workplace: ethnographic evidence for bringing work into organisation studies, *Administrative Science Quarterly,* 41: 404–441.

and tasks. This in turn supports the task of promoting understanding and action, and in developing ways in which this can be more effectively achieved.

These images of leaders and managers do provide differing views for learning and developing. The images of managing and leading as scientific or standardised by the definition of competences both imply development as a more formal process which can be deliberately planned and specified in advance. By contrast, images of leaders and managers as reflective practitioners or critically reflective/reflexive both imply a more involved and engaged view of development which has to be recognised, often retrospectively, but takes account of the moral and ethical work of managers and leaders, the often complex and difficult decisions to be made and the informal nature of how learning occurs. We therefore can suggest a dimension of deliberate and more emergent options of leadership and management development, shown as Figure 1.2, with our fifth image, managers and leaders as practical authors, oscillating between the two poles of the spectrum.

Conclusion

As this chapter suggests, there are a variety of reasons why an investment in the development of managers and leaders might be viewed as a necessity, including dealing with the many challenges facing our economies, dealing with rapid change, embracing the global agenda, improving public services, promoting diversity and embracing more ethically and socially responsible behaviour within our practice at all levels. Although there has been scant evidence to prove that leaders are directly responsible for a better-performing organisation, nevertheless there has of late been a revival of interest in leadership development, a feature of which has been the bifurcation between leadership and management which in some ways might have been somewhat overstated, particularly in the light of recent evidence that suggests the importance of local leaders who must also manage.[67]

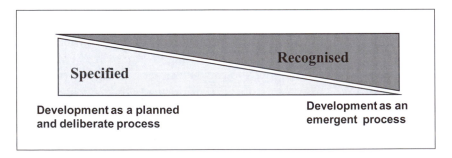

Figure 1.2   A dimension of deliberate emergent options of leadership and management development

67   See Alimo-Metcalfe, B. and Alban-Metcalfe, J. (2005) Leadership: time for a new direction, *Leadership*, 1(1): 51–71.

In this chapter then, we have presented some of the key ideas from research, theory and practice that raise issues for the choices that need to be made when learning and development is considered. We have identified a variety of perspectives and shown the importance of leaders and managers embracing a more holistic approach to development. The scientific/behaviourist approaches take developers some way along the road, but we show how over-specification of behaviour can lead to only partial solutions and also be problematic. We also show the importance of leaders and managers being well grounded in the context of their organisation and work. Real knowledge, we believe, is embedded in practice and the ability to understand this practice through reflection and where necessary, a critique of assumptions made that hinder effective action is an important quality.

We have also argued that good leadership is not simply the ability to read situations; it also requires leaders to understand fully the organisations in which they work. Only by doing this will they be able to explain to others what needs to happen when perhaps for many all that is seen are vague contestable positions not readily understood without the benefit of the clarity of explanation provided by the leader. For us, the essence of leading is giving a sense of shared significance that offers direction and a sense of purpose to others who already share feelings, however vague, and then having the commitment to continue to work hard to argue for it persuasively for the sense they make of the direction the organisation should travel.

Our view remains that those charged with development continue to offer a rather narrow focus when developing individual leaders and managers. However, as we indicate, it is our view that it has now become an imperative that individuals learn about the distribution of influence in and between organisations. We argue strongly that leadership and management development activities need to address both distributed forms and the way in which leaders and managers need to develop a greater awareness and vision for the future, make judgements and act creatively. This aspect we refer to as 'making history'. Retrospective sense-making takes individuals only so far in a rapidly changing world: what is also required is imagination, judgement and vision.

2 National and International Developments in Leadership and Management Development

KAI PETERS

Introduction

Two distinct fault lines can be traced across the landscape of international management development literature over the past 20 years. The first was unleashed by Geert Hofstede's oft-cited work[1] from the early 1980s looking at cultural similarities and differences between international managers at IBM. The second literature stream is anchored around a post-colonial perceived inappropriateness of a Western, specifically American, economic world view. Both often generate 'how-to' guides which provide checklists of what to do where.

In parallel, there is a much more sophisticated literature which looks at management development through a conceptual lens. What is missing, however, is a general overview of the strands of the international literature, and more critically, a synthesis of the international literature with conceptual management development frameworks. This chapter, therefore, sets out to fill this gap. By thus anchoring the international components of the management development challenges within a more holistic overall model, the chapter seeks to provide an approach which both advances the academic conceptualisation of international management development but, importantly, also provides practitioners with a useful approach to management development design which transcends the excessively narrow approaches too often found in individual international management development articles.

1   Hofstede, G. (1980a) *Culture's Consequences*, London: Sage; (1980b) Motivation, leadership and organisation: do American theories apply abroad? *Organisational Dynamics,* Summer: 42–63; (1993) Cultural constraints in management theories, *Academy of Management Executive,* 7(1): 81–94.

Background Literature

A 1988 article by Clement[2] surveyed the literature on management development between 1981 and 1988 and found that most significant was 'a trend towards management development in the international realm' both in terms of international assignments and of the development of international managers in their domestic markets. Much of this literature was influenced by the pioneering work on intercultural differences conducted by Geert Hofstede who, between 1967 and 1973, had developed an extensive database of survey responses which looked at cultural values among IBM employees across the world. This work was popularised through the 1980 appearance of the book *Culture's consequences, international differences in work-related values*, in which value continua were described in terms of individualism, power-distance, masculinity, and uncertainty avoidance. Subsequently, when an Asian data set was added, a further dimension, long-term orientation, was added.

Since then, Hofstede has applied his work not only in his original field of social psychology but invariably also in management development, as have many others. Given that Hofstede himself has data sets for 56 countries and that the questionnaire is available for others to use in their own research, it is not surprising that in a world with close to 200 countries, the literature is extensive. As an indication, Richards[3] looked at Brunei and noted low individualism, strong uncertainty avoidance and high power distance. In discussing the implications for management development, Richards notes that open discussions around organisational goals and challenges were undermined by strong organisational hierarchies which did not allow for Western-style agenda-setting and problem-solving. Kirkbride and Tang[4] look at the Nanyang Chinese societies of South East Asia (Indonesia, Hong Kong, Macao, Malaysia, Philippines, Singapore, Taiwan and Thailand) where, based largely on Hofstede, they note the Confucian characteristics of strong family values and the related long-term orientation. Jones[5] looks towards Africa. Basing his study on managers and their subordinates in Malawi, he concludes that transplanted Western concepts around discussion-based problem solving are unsuccessful and offers Hofstede-based advice on how to design management development initiatives. Jones, together with Blunt,[6] revisits Africa in an article contrasting African and Asian management development – again drawing attention to the different cultural values at play and how they are different from those values prevalent in Western societies. McFarlin, Coster and Mogale-Pretorius[7] focus on South Africa. Mbigi and Maree[8] survey Africa

---

2   Clement, R. W. (1988) Management development in the 1980s: a field in transition, *Journal of Management Development*, 7(1): 45–55.

3   Richards, D. (1991) Flying against the wind? Culture and management development in South East Asia, *Journal of Management Development*, 10(6): 7–21.

4   Kirkbride, P. S. and Tang, S. F. Y. (1992) Management development in the Nanyang Chinese Societies of south-east Asia, *Journal of Management Development*, 11(2): 32–41.

5   Jones, M. (1986) Management development: an African focus, *Management Education and Development*, 17(3): 202–216.

6   Blunt, P. and Jones, M. L. (1997) Exploring the limits of Western leadership theory in East Asia and Africa, *Personnel Review*, 26(1/2): 6–23.

7   McFarlin, D. B., Coster, E. A. and Mogale-Pretorius, C. (1999) South African management development in the 21st century, *Journal of Management Development*, 18(1): 63–78.

8   Mbigi, L. and Maree, J. (1995) *Ubuntu: The Spirit of African Transformation Management*, Randburg: Knowledge Resources.

generally. Bollinger[9] performs the same service for Russia, this time from the perspective of a French management development consultant, noting that Russia and France have similar values. Littrell and Valentin[10] compare and contrast Romania, Germany and the UK. Branine[11] looks at China. Liu and MacKinnon[12] compare Europe and China.

Suffice it to say that the literature is extensive and the conceivable permutations and combinations endless. In some cases, advice is based purely on a Hofstede-derived perspective. In the majority of cases, Hofstede forms part of a discussion anchored around aspects of culture and how that should guide a management development initiative.

The second strand of literature vigorously notes the inappropriateness of a Western-derived management paradigm and the related distrust of Western management development approaches without reference to Hofstede. Many begin with a historical overview deemed to have been overlooked or misunderstood internationally. Kiggundu[13] writes that 'the problem is that most scholars write of Africa as if there was no organised African political economy before the colonial era' and then proceeds to list examples of historical good governance ranging the great empires of Ghana to the construction of the pyramids. The article concludes with a checklist of 'practical guidelines for management development professionals for Sub-Saharan Africa'. Neal and Finlay's[14] article title is enough to provide an indication of its orientation – American hegemony and business education in the Arab world – with, in this case, a focus on business school students in Lebanon.

Templar, Beaty and Hofmeyr[15] write more dispassionately about the challenges of management development in South Africa, again anchoring management development within the historical and socio-economic context of the South African environment. Cases for specificities historically embedded in society are made in many further articles focusing on any number of countries and regions. Manning and Poljeva[16] outline the post-Soviet situation and the challenges of management development in the Baltic States in the twenty-first century. Avery, Donnenberg, Gick and Hilb[17] look to the German-speaking countries and Mitku and Wallace[18] seek to prepare East African managers for the twenty-first century. Very recently, a literature has been emerging focusing specifically on

9   Bollinger, D. (1994) The four cornerstones and three pillars in the 'House of Russia' management system, *Journal of Management Development*, 13(2): 49–54.

10   Littrell, R. F. and Valentin, L. N. (2005) Preferred leadership behaviours: exploratory results from Romania, Germany, and the UK, *Journal of Management Development*, 24(5): 421–442.

11   Branine, M. (2005) Cross-cultural training of managers: an evaluation of a MD programme for Chinese managers, *Journal of Management Development*, 24(5): 459–472.

12   Liu, J. and Mackinnon, A. (2002) Comparative management practices and training: China and Europe, *Journal of Management Development*, 21(2): 188–132.

13   Kiggundu, M. N. (1991) The challenges of management development in Sub-Saharan Africa, *Journal of Management Development*, 10(6): 32–47.

14   Neal, M. and Finlay, J. L. (2008) American Hegemony and business education in the Arab World, *Journal of Management Education*, 32(1): 38–83.

15   Templar, A., Beatty, D. and Hofmeyr, K. (1992) The challenge of management development in South Africa: so little time and so much to do, *Journal of Management Development*, 11(2): 32–41.

16   Manning, P. A. and Poljeva, T. (1999) The challenge of MD in the Baltic States in the 21st century, *Journal of Management Development*, 18(1): 32–45.

17   Avery, G., Donnenberg, O., Gick, W. and Hilb, M. (1999) Challenges for management development in the German-speaking nations for the 21st century, *Journal of Management Development*, 18(1): 18–31.

18   Mitku, A. and Wallace, J. B. (1999) Preparing East African managers for the 21st century, *Journal of Management Development*, 18(1): 46–62.

the challenges generated through the nationalisation initiatives in a number of locations. Rees, Mamman and Bin Braik[19] can be cited as an example by way of their article 'Emiratization as a strategic HRM change initiative: case evidence from a UAE petroleum company'. No doubt a survey article will soon appear comparing and contrasting such initiatives in countries like Saudi Arabia, South Africa and the United Arab Emirates as there are many similarities.

Making sense of this labyrinth of national values, traits and characteristics is indeed a challenge. Littrell[20] had obviously hoped that some clustering was possible. Instead, Littrell's study looking into leadership behaviour in Hong Kong, Singapore and Taiwan among Chinese speakers, found that very little was transferable to mainland China. This research result was confirmed anecdotally from the personal experience of the author. Intuitively, one could expect that were the study to be conducted again today, thereby taking China's development into account, there would be more similarities.

Safavi[21] tries at the very least to describe the potential categories to which one could allocate the various national typologies. The author differentiates between a *polycentric orientation* which 'has claimed that development needs of managers are different in just about every country and thus require individually designed programmes for each nation and, at times, for diverse ethnic groups within a nation'. The second option is a *regiocentric orientation* that assumes 'that management development needs within a geographic region are sufficiently similar for application of a unified approach'. The final perspective is described as an *ethnocentric orientation* which is 'focused on similarities between the development needs across national boundaries' which 'has faith in the universality of management functions, and global applications of the North American management development model'. The author suggests that countries like South Africa and Vietnam are polycentric while a number of areas like the German-speaking countries, the Baltics, East Africa and Australia/New Zealand can be bundled in regional groupings.

Limitations of the Literature

Two distinct challenges arise within the international management development literature as described above. The first is simply the challenge of the broad range and mix of nationalities on offer. Litrell and Valentin's[22] article on Romania, Germany and the UK, for example, presents rather a random selection of countries to focus on. Jones's[23] article on Malawi, similarly, may genuinely provide guidance when in Malawi, but Malawi is actually quite small. Are the lessons learned useful in neighbouring Tanzania or Mozambique? Furthermore, there is a huge potential bias which is not acknowledged in the cultural differences literature on management development which concerns the origin of the author and in practical management development terms of the provider of

19   Rees, C. J., Mamman, A. and Bin Braik, A. (2007) Emiratization as a strategic HRM change initiative: case study evidence from a UAE petroleum company, *International Journal of Human Resource Management*, 18(2): 33–53.

20   Littrell, R. F. (2002) Desirable leadership behaviours of multi-cultural managers in China, *Journal of Management Development*, 24(5): 421–442.

21   Safavi, F. (1999) The evolving world of management development: salute to the 21st century, *Journal of Management Development*, 18(1): 5–17.

22   Littrell, R. F. and Valentin, L. N (2005) op. cit.

23   Jones, M. (1986) op. cit.

training. There is no intention of belabouring this point here, although this issue figures prominently in the anthropology literature and is seen as a genuine concern.

The second major limitation of the articles which have been reviewed above is that there is not tremendous clarity on what types of management development initiatives were studied and how they relate to each other. Branine[24] describes a seemingly straight 'chalk and talk' United Nations Development Programme, thus a short, open attendance programme, aimed at explaining capitalism to managers from Chinese state-owned enterprises, evidently in the late 1990s or in the early 2000s. Jones's[25] study also focuses on a short open programme in Malawi. Bollinger[26] covers the establishment of training centres for entrepreneurs in Almaty, Kazakhstan in 1992. If one wants, one can also search for other articles which look at the challenges presented specifically by international MBA programme participants, for example, Peters.[27] Kirkbride and Tang's[28] study is much broader and describes a whole range of activities covering formal courses, self-development, coaching, job rotation as well as action learning and more esoteric transactional analysis in Hong Kong and beyond.

From a management development perspective, there are simply worlds of difference between individual coaching, straightforward content transmission open courses, and an entrepreneurship training centre in 1992 Kazakhstan. These differences manifest themselves in the design, delivery and reception and the intervention: in who will say what where; in whether the intervention is designed to help the individual or the organisation; and in who delivers what, whether they are an academic, a trainer or a coach. All of these factors call into question many of the assertions which are made in the previously cited articles about how people are, what they like, and about what is a cultural taboo which must be avoided in the classroom and what is a prize winner .

MANAGEMENT DEVELOPMENT WITHOUT THE 'INTERNATIONAL'

These same differences between types of interventions also, of course, apply to national courses, in national contexts, provided by national providers in whatever one considers to be a 'national market'.

Thus, to begin to put some order into the interesting but occasionally frustrating literature around international management development, it is worth taking a step back and looking at some definitions of leadership and management development more generally. Wexley and Baldwin[29] differentiate between management education – cognitive, MBA-type courses; management training – time management and delegation skills for example; and on-the-job experience like action learning, job placements and mentoring. Paauwe and Williams[30] introduce a special journal issue of the *Journal of Management*

---

24   Branine, M. (2005) op. cit.

25   Jones, M. (1986) op. cit.

26   Bollinger, D. (1994) op. cit.

27   Peters, B. K. G. (2001) Recruitment and selection of lecturers for international classrooms. In Farkas-Teekens, H. (ed.) *Teaching and Learning in the International Classroom*, Den Haag: Nuffic Press.

28   Kirkbride, P. S. and Tang, S. F. Y. (1992) op. cit.

29   Wexley, K. N. and Baldwin, T. T. (1986) Management development, *Journal of Management*, 12(2): 277–294.

30   Paauwe, J. and Williams, A. R. T. (eds) (2001) Of management development from a Dutch perspective, *Journal of Management Development*, 20(2): 90–105.

Development by also citing Baldwin, this time with Patgett[31] about the differentiation between education as knowledge acquisition; training for a specific task; and management development as 'the complex process by which individuals learn to perform effectively in managerial roles'.

They posit that each of these goals has a different delivery mechanism and place special emphasis on the fact that the transition from classroom-based to real life learning requires four elements. First, the issue(s) must be seen to be important. Second, some analysis must be involved. Third, creativity must be called on and fourth, importantly, practical application is necessary. Thus, it is only through active participation that effective management performance can be developed.

In the same issue, Jansen, van der Velde and Mul[32] outline a typology of management development from a different perspective, looking not from management development cognition, but from organisational style and structure. In looking at nearly 100 organisations spread across the private, public and not for profit sectors in the Netherlands, they classify organisations by their level of development. Some organisations are classified as administrative organisations likely to provide life-long employment, others as organisations in technological and innovative environments in which human capital is valued and required. Another group is classified as up-or-out companies where management progression and management development are directly linked and strictly planned. Finally, a group of organisations is classified as being 'turbulent'.

To try and make sense of these differences, the authors created a small table (Table 2.1) to illustrate how these different types of organisations balanced the personal development and organisational development components of management development.

Table 2.1   How these different types of organisations balanced the personal development and organisational development components of management development

High personal development (strong emphasis on PD within organisation)	*Leading* MD aimed at developing the skills of leaders so that they can help the rest of the organisation get through the turbulence	*Partner* MD in which human capital and social capital is jointly developed in order that intelligent individuals can create something greater through cooperation than from individual initiative
Low personal development (no attention paid to PD by organisation)	*Administrative* MD aimed primarily to keep stability	*Derived* MD with strict planning and a close link to the strategy of the organisation rather than to the development of the individual
	Low organisational development (no attention)	High organisational development (strong emphasis)

Adapted from Jansen, van der Velde and Mul.[33]

31   Baldwin, T. T. and Patgett, M. Y. (1994) Management development: a review and commentary. In Cooper, C. L. and Robertson I. T. (eds) *Key Reviews in Management Psychology*, New York: Wiley.

32   Jansen, P., van der Velde, M. and Mul, W. (2001) A typology of management development, *Journal of Management Development*, 20(2): 106–120.

33   Jansen, P., van der Velde, M. and Mul, W. (2001) ibid.

It is not only across organisations, however, that these types of differentiation come into view, but within organisations as well. There are clearly different levels and calibres of individuals within a company – the high potential managers of the future are different from the pool of technical specialists who are again different from the pool of competent and capable, but not high-flying middle managers.

Lubitsch et al.[34] and Blass and April[35] set out to explore this territory within the organisational context. Their report expands the perspective considerably by viewing management development not in isolation but within an overall talent management framework. The framework is a continuum ranging from recruitment and selection, through retention, reward and development because all of these areas are critical for an organisation's ability to benefit from the skill of their people, right through to exit. While this may sound simple enough, 'talent management is a controversial territory and even the first step of defining what is meant by talent can force organisations into some difficult internal debates'.

Within the talent management literature, there are not only debates on the size of the talent pool which range from all of those who are above average, thus the top 50 per cent, through to the idea of a high-performing elite of 3–5 per cent of the organisation.[36] Furthermore, there are debates about how to identify talent. Should it be based on past performance, future potential or on a combination of the two? The logical extension of this thought process is that somewhere between 50 and 95 per cent of the organisation is not to be considered as 'talent' by these definitions. As one can imagine, this may not be universally acknowledged by those individuals in the organisation who have been classified as not having talent.

Peters,[37] without suggesting ratios, suggests a model which addresses both the challenge of the 'talent' and 'non-talent' pools within an organisation. In the model, basic business competence forms the groundwork. As such, this basic business understanding should be widely diffused within the organisation among all staff. At the next level, there is a need for an understanding of the context in which the organisation operates and how that influences the present and potential future strategy. The author suggests that this is a point at which 'talent' should be more extensively involved. At a third level, an ability to influence people must be developed. Implementing a strategy involves working with others so that goals are shared across the organisation rather than simply being understood theoretically by senior management. This is not a simple task. Lastly, strong reflective skills are required for those in or reaching an organisation's highest level. These reflective skills promote a well-rounded view of the needs of the individual manager with an ability to understand others and by extension reflect well on the overall direction and culture of the organisation.

Such a typology sees leadership development as having a closed level where there are information transfer goals aimed at creating alignment with an organisation's way of doing things. Thereafter, there are open learning goals which seek to create the future

---

34   Lubitsh, G., Devine, M., Orbea, A. and Glanfield, P. (2007) *Talent Management – A Strategic Imperative*, Berkhamsted: Ashridge Consulting Report.

35   Blass, E. and April, K. (2008) Developing talent for tomorrow, *Develop*, 1: 48–58.

36   See Berger, D. R. and Berger, L. A. (eds) (2004) *The Talent Management Handbook*, New York: McGraw-Hill.

37   Peters, B. K. G. (2006) The four stages of management education, *Biz Ed*, May/June: 36–40.

for the organisation. Everyone should understand the closed learning goal while 'talent' must be given free reign in the second realm.

Much of the material concerning closed learning goals can be delivered through a traditional classroom or e-learning setting, whether in open programmes attended by delegates from a variety of organisations or from a group specific to an organisation, increasingly delivered internally through a corporate university or otherwise in conjunction with a business school or increasingly, through the larger consultancies who have increased their presence within the educational arena. Thereafter, however, the individual and organisational development goals tend to involve a broad range of activities ranging from seminars and action learning groups through to mentoring, consulting and coaching and job placements both nationally and internationally. These different interventions will then also be delivered by different people with faculty, consultants, behavioural coaches and psychometricians all playing their part.

INNOVATION IN MANAGEMENT DEVELOPMENT

In the past few years, research has tended to focus on the modes of delivery for the more open learning goals required for senior management levels. There is an extensive literature on appreciative inquiry, action learning and applied, hands-on activity and a lesser focus on traditional, passive, classroom information transfer. The former is something interesting and innovative while the latter is seen to be a commodity.

Voller and Honore,[38] as an example, conducted a study into innovation in international executive education on behalf of Unicon, the International University Consortium for Executive Education. The authors confirm the trend to the commoditization of knowledge and the delivery of the knowledge deemed useful by a specific organisation to that organisation's internal mechanisms. Competency frameworks combine generic management skills and abilities with organisation-specific approaches. These frameworks then lead to curriculum design which can be centrally planned and broadly rolled out, often in a combination of face-to-face and electronic delivery.

What is interesting in this realm is that while electronic delivery of generic content cannot be described as something new or particularly interesting, the sophistication of electronic delivery platforms continues to develop. Electronic learning management systems which incorporate audio and video clearly improve asynchronous learning.

In the middle ground, combinations of proprietary information and proprietary platforms are being linked with consumer-led social networking platforms like wikis, chat and blogs to create asynchronous/synchronous hybrids. By combining structured content with user input, learning is becoming increasingly active. Additionally, an increasing use of publicly available material is being added to the learning environments. Thus, even within the domain of generic or organisation-generic content, environments are being created which add to the learning in a cost-effective manner.

If one fast-forwards these developments and thinks creatively, one will most certainly end in a virtual world of learning. At present, most of leadership and management development initiatives in virtual worlds are at the experimental stage with meeting simulations and classroom simulations, primarily in Second Life. Once virtual worlds

---

38   Voller, S. and Honore, S. (2008) *Innovation in Executive Education: A Case-based Study of Practice in International Business Schools*. Berkhamsted: Ashridge and Unicon Report.

are no longer constrained by the need to install extensive software on local computers, but can instead be accessed freely without the need to download, the second wave of development will begin. This is dependent on Internet bandwidth sufficiency which will surely be available within the next few years.

More prosaically, Voller and Honore[39] signal a change in the approach to time taking place within leadership and management development initiatives which go beyond the transfer of knowledge to focus on strategy formulation and implementation. On the one hand, specific interventions continue to shorten. Whereas events lasting multiple weeks were not uncommon in the past, face-to-face activities have gravitated to two- or three-day sessions spread over time and supported electronically. That said, the view of what constitutes development has lengthened to a talent management based view of continuous development spanning many years.

In terms of pedagogy, the trend to an emphasis on experience rather than classroom learning has been noted earlier. There is nevertheless very much that remains unknown around the role of experience in learning. McCall[40] discusses how different experiences can provide different learning opportunities. These, in turn, are taken up differently by participants who have had different previous experiences to build on and who may well also react differently to different experiential activities. Additionally, experience does not automatically provide learning or at least not learning which is deemed valuable by the individual and the organisation. To increase the likelihood that learning is effective, forethought must be given to the nature of the assignment and senior management sponsorship must be secured. Even then, the action learning intervention tends not to stand on its own, but may well require facilitation, debriefing or coaching in order to generate something worthwhile.

In parallel to the increased domination of action learning is an ongoing trend Voller and Honore describe as active learning. This domain includes business simulations, games, improvisation, outdoor learning and a whole host of increasingly esoteric learning metaphors ranging from African drumming through to horse-whispering and community engagement. The goal is generally to create a time-compressed simulation of getting something done collectively. This provides the facilitator with the opportunity to facilitate a discussion about leadership and group interaction around a completed assignment. Additionally, the experience is not the same as a normal workday – something that can be used to overcome normal organisational patterns. At their best, these interventions bring participants to see things from another perspective and inspire change. Alternatively it is also possible that they tend to simply be a bit of fun. This can also be fine when an active learning activity is used to refresh participants through a change of scenery. There is, however, also a potential downside. At their worst, these activities can be seen as pointless or more worryingly as offensive if issues of hierarchy, gender, diversity and good behaviour are not taken into consideration up front.

Not surprisingly, initiatives which aim to go beyond the learning of the individual to incorporate organisational learning require significant cooperation between providers of leadership and management development services and the organisations which use them. Interventions are increasingly co-designed and co-delivered with senior organisational managers providing internal perspectives. Furthermore, external providers often

39   Voller, S. and Honore, S. (2008) ibid.

40   McCall, M. W. (1988) Developing executives through work experiences, *Human Resource Planning*, 2(1): 1–12.

transcend the expected training and development to the participants by also training internal trainers in consulting skills, coaching skills or organisational development design in the process.

From 20 respondents to the study interviewed by Voller and Honore[41] from around the world, six in-depth case studies were conducted among business schools in South Africa, Australia, the US, the UK and Norway concerning innovative customised programmes developed for clients. In order to genuinely apply recent leadership and management development thinking, it became clear that the client organisations needed to have a culture which allowed for experimentation and acknowledged that deep learning required the active engagement and taking of responsibility among participants. This strongly suggests that not all organisations are willing or able to engage in such projects.

When the characteristics of the projects brought forward by the overall pool of 20 schools were mapped in terms of the interventions' purpose and delivery methodology, similarities emerged. Overall, projects were initiated which sought to develop holistic, global leaders who were in it for the long term and who focused strongly on the needs of the organisation. To accomplish these goals, programmes were experiential and discussion based and aimed to promote reflection through the extensive use of storytelling and action learning. All programmes were firmly grounded in the realities and culture of the host organisation rather than based on external case studies or generic management knowledge. Given that managers prefer short, intensive management development initiatives, projects relied extensively on intense, high-energy interventions coupled with an ongoing use of technology to promote longer term learning and continued learning once often multiple-session interventions had come to an end.

Of the six specific projects investigated further, two were technology-based. The first used technology to encourage executive experience-sharing and the second to facilitate culture mapping and online narrative capture. Two cases discussed the up-front use of theoretical leadership and development frameworks which incorporated the extensive self-responsibility of the learner for learning. The last two focused on experiential learning. The first programme, involving the use of historical narratives *in situ*, by, for example, bringing Norwegian managers to London to learn about leadership by using Queen Elizabeth I as an anchor. The second intervention simulated real management challenges by forcing participants to take charge in a programme that looked completely disorganised and fraught with disasters which were changed depending on how programme participants reacted to this particular style of experiential learning.

REFLECTIVE LEADERSHIP DEVELOPMENT – A CAVEAT

The examples sited above were selected to highlight the possibilities available to encourage in-depth reflection about leadership. While participant feedback was generally positive, the interventions also generated a small but significant volume of criticism from the subset of participants who simply did not feel that simulation and reflection worked for them. In some cases participants stated that they did not feel that unstructured learning was right and they preferred something 'more organised'. In other cases, participants simply are not interested in reflecting on how their own behaviour impacts on others and on the environment. This is a genuine challenge to overcome when the problem

---

41   Voller, S. and Honore, S. (2008) op. cit.

is indeed that the manager's own behaviour hinders the cooperation and coordination required in organisational life. Highlighted here is the point at which learning blends into the psychology of the individual and content is replaced by a need to overcome individual denial.

To tackle these challenges, both the provider and client for leadership and management development initiatives need to cooperate in tackling these issues. This problem arises sporadically in a number of situations, for example when managers senior to the management development team within the organisation prove to be a problem and the organisation is not willing to act upon the challenge. More generally, this type of an issue arises in environments in which performance rewards for the individual are based more on the results of that individual rather than of the organisation overall, even when that leads to overall suboptimisation. Examples here often come from finance and from professional service firms.

TOWARDS A HOLISTIC FRAMEWORK

Up to this point, this chapter has provided an in-depth look at the international management development literature and a short snapshot view of the directions in which management development has been progressing today. In drawing these various strands together, an overall framework can be developed which can guide thinking about the design and delivery of management and leadership development, whether that be national or international in nature (Table 2.2).

At the highest level, leadership and management development is anchored within an overarching purpose of generating the highest possible outcomes from the people working for an organisation. To this end, one seeks to recruit the best possible staff available at that time and place.

From that point forward, one seeks to develop people so that they can perform to the best of their ability within the context of the present and future challenges faced by the organisation, something which is easier said than done. Immediately, two major challenges must be faced by designers of leadership and management development interventions. First, for the broad range of people within the organisation, what are the actual requirements in terms of knowledge, skills and self-development which are required by individuals and groups of individuals? Second, how does one define the present and future context in which the organisation will be required to act successfully? Thereafter,

Table 2.2   A holistic talent framework

Talent management	Recruit/develop/reward or remove
Purpose	Competencies of knowledge, skills and self-development/world view
Context	External to company (international or technology development) as well as internal to company (industry, stage of development)
Methodology	Formal or informal (ranging from courses and coaching to mentors and models)

the biggest challenge of all arises: how does one draw these two interlinking challenges together?

Storey, for instance, notes wrily that 'management development really ought to be closely tied to corporate planning'.[42] It is easy to arrive at a complete atomisation if one thinks logically in these terms. A young engineer in a multinational company who works in a new acquisition in a Kazakh oilfield has completely different leadership and management development needs from a board member who is based in London, whose background is in accounting and who is originally from the Philippines.

The challenge, however, is in thinking in practical terms. There are clearly some common goals which apply across an organisation which are function and geography independent. These goals must be commonly shared and must permeate all management development initiatives. Thereafter, there are knowledge competencies and skills which are shared by groups of people within the organisation. These can also be mapped out with a reasonable level of detail and can generally be divided into specific technological requirements for a variety of roles and more general functional business skills. By mapping competencies against groups of people within the organisation, one arrives at a basis framework of purpose. In general, the framework is simpler for the broader rank and file than for those identified as talent.

This framework must then be reflected against the realities of the organisation, taking into consideration a whole host of issues ranging from the characteristics of a particular industry through to the stage of development of the specific company. These issues, from the author's experience, tend to influence leadership and management development significantly and are as, if not more, important than national cultural traits and characteristics. Young technology companies around the world look remarkably similar, sharing a fast-paced engineering world view. State-owned, or recently state-owned infrastructure organisations around the world also look remarkably similar with long histories, extensive bureaucracies and a tendency to move slowly. As an example, an Indian IT company is more influenced by the fact that it is an IT company than by the fact that it is Indian. Within that company, Indian software developers will have more in common with other, international software developers based in California or Cambridge than they will with their Indian colleagues in the marketing department.

None of this is to deny that national traits and characteristics are not an important consideration. It is simply to state that national specificities must be considered within a much broader framework rather than as ends in themselves. National characteristics do not lead the design process for management development but simply form a part of the consideration of management development.

This focused approach also applies to the specific methodologies of delivery, where world views and learning styles have a tremendous influence on what can and should be done. Some people like courses, others do not. Some like coaching, others do not. Here again, the challenge of not atomising arises. Decisions must be made about which approaches provide the best management development outcomes that are actually deliverable to smaller or larger groups, in different geographies, over time.

The reality, unfortunately, is that tremendous atomisation is rampant in many organisations. Over time, decentralisation processes have led to national and operating

---

42   Storey, J. (1989) Management development: a literature review and implications for future research, Part 1: conceptualisations and practices, *Personnel Review,* 18(6): 3–19.

company autonomy. This is exacerbated by years of merger and acquisition activity. In all too many cases a hodge-podge of leadership and management development activities has arisen involving thousands of different courses provided by hundreds of different organisations in many different languages – all with different design principles employing different methodologies – which are then tracked by complicated software products, simple card files or not at all. Not only is this tremendously costly as the wheel is constantly reinvented, but it is also a major hindrance for mobility, as no one is quite sure about who is where and what they have done. It also means that there is little chance to develop an organisation-specific culture of shared goals and values.

There is also another genuine danger in thinking in terms of specific nationalities. Even in cases where there is a relative homogeneity within the national part of an international organisation, or within a large purely national organisation, ever-increasing globalisation means that managers do come into contact with international colleagues or business partners. Designing for a specific national group, in a way which specifically suits the need of that group, can actually be counterproductive.

Leadership and management development initiatives can purposely be designed to challenge acceptable cultural approaches so that managers can experience the different perspectives they are likely to encounter when they interact with other cultures. This is not cultural imperialism, but purposeful design. When done well, such purposeful dissonance can create extremely powerful learning experiences which draw out new insight among participants. Such approaches naturally require careful consideration as it is quite possible to lose the goodwill of participants because the leap from the accepted to the challenging is done too quickly for a particular culture. By gradually introducing a more participative, reflective learning style and by signposting the reasons why one is doing this, participants acknowledge and accept something different.

One must acknowledge limits, though. There is a continuum between the untried and unknown and the uncomfortable and unacceptable. Encouraging participation is one thing; criticising the company or the boss is another. Mixing genders in the classroom in the Middle East is possible even if uncomfortable. Mixing genders in experiential outdoor learning exercises during which there is a need for physical contact is much beyond what is possible.

Case Study

A multinational non-governmental organisation (NGO)

The client, a multinational development bank with headquarters in the US and field operations throughout the world, sought to develop a set of common values to ensure corporate social responsibility was pursued in the investment process, while at the same time ensuring that the diversity required in field operations was acknowledged and respected. Following extensive interviews with staff from the head office and from the field operations, a design was developed which created a common experience for a trial group of 20 individuals split evenly between the two groups and thus involving participants from countries as diverse as India, Pakistan, Senegal, South Africa, Cameroon, Mexico, Macedonia and Hungary. Additionally, four regional action learning groups, two in the US and one each in Central Europe and Africa, supported regional needs. Both the common and regional experiences were conducted in English. Finally, individual coaching for participants was provided in English or where possible, in the participant's mother tongue, allowing them to best express their personal circumstances. Faculty involved in the project reflect participant diversity as much as possible so that there is not a 'them and us' situation. The programme sought to combine the overall, the regional and the individual perspectives in both abstract and practical terms. Participants noted that they learned extensively about the politics at play in their own organisation, how to navigate through the politics and how to get things done. They did so through dialogue rather than on the basis of faculty member expertise, which allowed expert voices from within the organisation to be facilitated by tutors specialising in organisational development and consulting.

Case Study

A European electronics company

A major European player in the medical devices and electronics sector sought to create a programme which challenged high-potential managers to explore new product and market opportunities. The programme was designed to understand both major metropolitan markets with launch sessions, depending on the cohort, in Singapore/Shanghai; Amsterdam/London or New York. Subsequent field-based studies took place outside the participants' comfort zones and included sessions involving local communities in India which brought together villagers and NGOs for sessions to brainstorm new product ideas. Finally, participants presented business plans to senior management. Little of the programme is straight teaching. Instead, an experiential design was chosen which emphasised going out to meet people, understand countries and discuss experiences. Finally, a real challenge, the creation of a business plan presented to participants' bosses ensured that the programme was indeed taken seriously and met business needs. The overall design was clearly communicated to participants who were also briefed on the cultural issues at play in the field sessions. These sessions have subsequently also been conducted in Iran, Central Africa and in the United Arab Emirates.

Blunt and Jones[43] assert that culture should lead management. While they make a strong case which states that not taking local conditions into account leads to failure, there is also another view which needs to be set alongside this assertion. In some cases, certain cultural attributes and historical legacies can be dysfunctional when they lead to conflict and corruption. More importantly, from the perspective of leadership and management development, is the fact that in order for people to be able to interact successfully within complex global organisations, management sometimes simply has

---

43   Blunt, P. and Jones, M. L. (1997) op. cit.

to lead culture by ideally creating a new culture which is a hybrid of the positive aspects of a variety of cultures rather than the subsuming of other cultures by one particular dominant world view. Kirkbride and Tang,[44] in writing about course design, point to Nancy Adler's call for culturally synergistic approaches which build upon common values while transgressing the fewest possible norms whereby the faculty member actively seeks dialogue and insight and learns from successes and failures. This same view of cultural synergy has been termed 'crossvergence' within the field of anthropology. Ward et al.[45] and Ralston et al.[46] propose that when two cultures meet, a blend of economic and cultural values takes place creating a more balanced perspective between global and local perspectives. More recently, Mendelek-Theimann, April and Blass[47] apply a crossvergence perspective to management development and thus overcome the foreign versus local debate.

The Development of Management Developers

The challenge for management developers, especially for those without extensive international experience is, of course, in knowing what is or is not an uncomfortable or unacceptable approach in a particular culture. Even worse is the situation in which problems arise because of the age, gender or ethnicity of the tutor in question. Both the latter and the former dilemmas actually arise from the same source: a lack of preparation beforehand. Whether an intervention is being designed for a national or a non-domestic audience, good preparation is the key. This preparation takes two primary forms. The first involves an in-depth needs analysis of not only the direct client, often a management development professional, but also dialogue with a pool of potential participants of the intervention. Here, if there are issues of cultural differences, they can take place in small groups and can be smoothed over in a give-and-take discussion among people who understand that they are at the design and not delivery stage of a project. One can politely conclude that there is a gender mismatch, or that a confrontational challenge will not work with a particular group. This is certainly much safer than if these issues are only discovered once the intervention has gone live with participants who were not involved in the design stage. Once an intervention has gone off the rails in a real setting, recovery is very difficult.

The second form of preparation involves sensitizing individual tutors to issues in general. Experience has shown that a mentoring and development programme for tutors is invaluable. For tutors within a management development organisation, whether it be a business school or a consultancy, a combination of internal training, combined with external training, ideally in an international setting not involving one's own colleagues, is invaluable. In the first instance, there are courses in which trainers come together. Even better are settings in which trainers, thus suppliers, come together with purchasers of

44   Kirkbride, P. S. and Tang, S. F. Y. (1992) op. cit.

45   Ward, S., Pearson, C., Entrekin, L. and Winzar, H. (1999) The fit between cultural values and countries: is there evidence of globalization, nationalism or crossvergence? *International Journal of Management*, 16(4): 466–473.

46   Ralston, D. A., Gustafson, D. J., Cheung, F. M. and Terpstra, R. H. (1993) Differences in managerial values: a study of U.S., Hong Kong and PRC managers, *Journal of International Business Studies*, 24(2): 249–275.

47   Mendelek-Theimann, N., April, K. and Blass, E. (2006) Context tension: cultural influences on leadership and management practice, reflections, *The Society for Organizational Learning Journal*, 7(4): 38–51.

management development and can openly air their viewpoints. In a number of situations, training trainers has been an overt part of the intervention where clients understand that some of the tutors are there as observers 'under development' and that, in some cases, some of the clients' own management development staff are also there in an 'under development' role. In such cases, both sides benefit tremendously.

Conclusion

None of these steps are easy. Defining the right competencies of knowledge, skills and reflective practice for different levels of managers within an organisation is a challenge. Clearly articulating the influence of a particular industry or stage of development is difficult as is defining the next stage of development which an organisation requires if it is to succeed in the future. Invariably, some parts of the organisation are younger, or have been acquired, therefore making design more difficult. Clearly defining the influence of external factors like technology development is a challenge. Over what time frame? And what technology should be considered, given that predicting the future of technology is an inexact science at best? Mapping the likely effectiveness of different educational and developmental approaches, whether they are more traditional classroom experiences or more behaviourally anchored experiential and reflective initiatives, is a challenge. Thinking through existent cultural norms and values, from the more innocuous through to complete taboos, for every country and culture in the world is simply impossible. Then, when one must consider myriad people from multiple cultures all lumped together in one multinational organisation, it is even more impossible.

Leaving these small details aside, one must nevertheless try. In a world in which technologies and management systems are instantly diffused and easily replicable, people and organisational cultures are the differentiating factor. Not only the organisational literature but also the strategic management literature recognises this. People, in the resource-based view of the strategy literature, are the valuable, rare, inimitable and non-substitutable assets held by an organisation. Collectively, they form a culture which is influenced by a range of historical and contextual realities.

From wherever one starts, it is possible to develop individuals and organisations through a range of interventions. This chapter has sought to illustrate that in looking at international leadership and management development, the literature on national and international culture makes a contribution to understanding one set of influential components. The literature concerning leadership and management development provides another. When these literatures are combined and considered within a framework, and when design is thoroughly thought through rather than simplistic and linear, significant results can be achieved within all organisations.

3

Crafting a Leadership and Management Development Strategy I

JOHN BURGOYNE

Despite the fact that Keith Grint claims that leadership is an 'essentially contested concept',[1] I want to start with a clear claim about what leadership is.

Leadership is the point of origin of meaning, structure and activity, the core of agency, and works in, on and through organised systems (and is the origin of this organisation) on the boundary between order and chaos/complexity.

This way of thinking helps define the difference between leadership and management. Leadership works on the chaos/complexity side of the boundary and management works on the order side. Both are needed and need to work closely together, often through the same person or team.

It follows from this that if leadership development creates leadership, and leadership creates organisation and order in the face of complexity and chaos, then leadership development is itself the true source of leadership.

It may be that leadership development, as often carried out as a human resource management (HRM) practice, is a takeover bid for leadership by that function, and I am sure it often is. However, it is more often the case that in leading successful organisations senior leadership spends a very high proportion of its time on leadership development, developing the people that they work through and who work for them, and who may be their successors. *Fortune* magazine lists the world's best lead organisations, according to a panel of expert judges, and supports this point. Their top three in 2007 were General Electric, Proctor and Gamble and Nokia.

The role of HRM is better thought of as setting up the systems and facilitating the processes through which leaders and leadership functions conduct leadership development.

If a case needs to be made for the order/chaos complexity view of leadership and management, then I would point out that the idea has an enduring presence in management and organisation theory, appearing in different forms with different authors over the years.

---

1   Grint, K. (2004) *What is Leadership? From Hydra to Hybrid*, Working Paper, Said Business School and Templeton College: Oxford University.

Herb Simon makes the distinction between 'programmed' and 'unprogrammed' decisions, the former gravitating to technical specialism's, the latter to management.[2] Burns and Stalker used the distinction between 'mechanistic' and 'organic' forms of organisation, or ways of understanding them.[3] Within the tradition of action learning the distinction is made between 'p', programmed knowledge, and 'q', questioning knowledge.[4] The idea is clearly used within complexity theory itself.[5] Finally, for now, the idea is used within leadership theory in the form of the distinction between 'transactional' and 'transformational' leadership.[6]

The distinction between leadership as dealing with the chaos/complexity side, and management as dealing with the order side, has been subject to semantic slippage over time. The distinction I am now making used to be made in the contrast between administration and management, the management term occupying the space we now label with leadership, and administration labelling what we now refer to as management.

To summarise, I am arguing that leadership is dealing with the boundary between order and chaos/complexity, from the chaos/complexity side – management is the other way round. Both are concerned with finding and implementing viable new activities, and disposing of old ones as they become non-viable.

So much, for now, for leadership. What about leadership development? The oldest debate, almost certainly, about leadership development is whether leaders are 'born' or 'made'. This is the leadership application of the foundational question in psychology of which behaviours are innate or learnt nature or nurture. The questions can be endlessly debated, but I think the most useful conclusion comes from evolutionary psychology.[7, 8] This comes down to the proposition that the will to lead is largely innate, but the ability to do it well is largely learnt. In terms of corporate practice this corresponds to the American Airlines slogan: 'recruit for attitude, train for skill'. Here we have the familiar 'make' or 'buy', recruit or train choice.

Organisations can, of course, select for learnt ability, and some pursue this as a strategy: others train for their industry, and develop their networks in this way, like many of the big consultancy firms and General Electric. However, if the evolutionary psychology view is right, they cannot train for attitude.

It is clear from this that the two strands of a strategy for leadership development are acquisition and development. There is a third, which is utilisation. Many organisations may have leadership capability that they do not make full use of.

The normal elements of the utilisation strand of a leadership development strategy are performance management, career development and 'hard' organisation development – the restructuring of organisations to pursue new strategies, creating new leadership roles to be filled.[9]

2   Simon, H. A. (1957) *Administrative Behaviour*, 2nd edn. New York: Macmillan.

3   Burns, T. and Stalker, G. M. (1961) *The Management of Innovation*. London: Tavistock.

4   Revans, R. W. (1998) *The ABC of Action Learning*. London: Lemos and Crane.

5   Stacey, R. D. (1992) *Managing Chaos: Dynamic Business Strategies in an Unpredictable World*. London: Kogan Page.

6   Bass, B. M., Avolio, B. J. and Atwater, L. (1996) The transformational and transactional leadership of men and women, *International Review of Applied Psychology*, 45: 5–34.

7   Nicholson, N. (1997) Evolutionary psychology: toward a new view of human nature and organizational society. *Human Relations*, 50(9): 1053–1078.

8   Nicholson, N. (1998) How hardwired is human behaviour? *Harvard Business Review*, 76: 134–147.

9   Burgoyne, J. G. (2008) Competency frameworks: love 'em or lose 'em? *Talent Management Review*, 2(2): 7.

To summarise this, leadership development in the widest sense involves the acquisition, development and utilisation of leadership capability or the potential for it, and in the narrower sense it is the middle 'strand' of this 'bundle'. Either way, the intended meaning of the bundle metaphor is that the strength of the whole is greater than the sum of its parts. In other words, organisations need to do all three in a balanced and integrated way.

There is some evidence for this.[10, 11] Figure 3.1 shows the correlation between the degree of integration of career development and management development, in a sample of about 50 private sector organisations, and their return on capital. Having a high level rather than a low level of integration gives about a 15 per cent improvement.

One useful way of thinking about the integration of leadership development and career management for leaders is offered by Charan and colleagues,[12] in the form of their idea of managing the leadership pipeline in organisations. This is based on their case study work with the highly successful General Electric Company. Their approach is shown in Figure 3.2.

The idea here is that there are seven phases or stages in a leader's career – obviously not everyone follows all of them. They are managing oneself, managing a team, managing a group of managers managing teams, managing a function, managing a business unit, managing a group of business units and playing a part in the overall management of a large enterprise like General Electric. The key points at which people need developmental help is the transitions, or passages as they call them, between these stages. This is because the change is too great for it to occur by natural learning from experience.

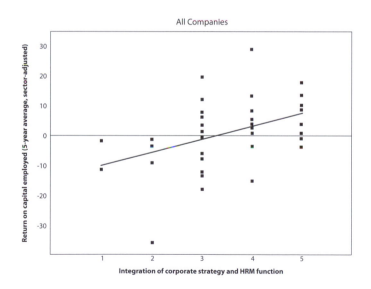

Figure 3.1   Developing leaders for contemporary organisations

10   Fox, S. and McLeay, S. (1992) An approach to researching managerial labour markets: HRM, corporate strategy and financial performance in UK manufacturing. *International Journal of Human Resource Management,* 3(3): 523–554.

11   Fox, S., McLeay, S., Tanton, M., Burgoyne, J. and Easterby-Smith, M. (1990) *Managerial Labour Markets: Human Resources Management and Corporate Performance,* Lancaster: Lancaster University for the ESRC Project.

12   Charan, R., Drotter, S. and Noel, J. (2001) *The Leadership Pipeline: How to Build the Leadership Powered Company,* San Francisco, CA: Jossey Bass.

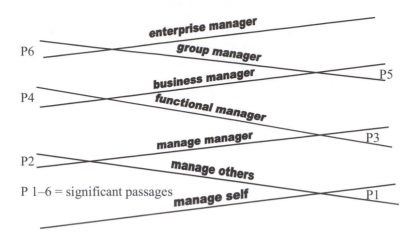

Figure 3.2   Critical career passages in large organisations

The model may apply differently in different organisations, and may often have fewer phases or stages, but the underlying idea may be a useful one.

To summarise, Table 3.1 sets out the elements of the bundle.

Table 3.1   The leadership development bundle

Acquisition	1. Recruitment and selection of people: (a) directly into leadership roles; (b) into other roles but with potential for career progression into leadership. 2. Acquisitions of organisations and teams, including mergers and acquisitions as discussed above, with leadership capability as part of the equation.
Development	3. Job/work placements with leadership capability development as one of the purposes. 4. Education, training and development of individuals, including: (a) the 'context-sensitive' methods of coaching, mentoring and action learning (b) more formal education – training and development programmes. 5. 'Soft' organisation development initiatives including: (a) culture change initiatives (b) team building (c) 'hearts and minds' collective mission/values creating initiatives.
Utilisation	6. Performance management systems. 7. Career management and development systems. 8. Reward systems. 9. 'Hard' organisation development – organisation structuring and restructuring, organisation design and its implementation, the change management involved in redesign and restructuring.

The General Electric example also provides an example of the use of performance management and rewards systems in an integrated way to support the utilisation of leadership capability. Managers are measured rigorously on performance, and the bottom 10 per cent eliminated if they do not improve.

But what is involved in setting up leadership development systems for organisations? Our study for a consortium of organisations known as Careers Research Forum[13] suggested there are five *strategic,* two *pivotal* and four *operational* choices to be made.

The *pivotal* questions link the *strategic* and the *operational* because they are the fundamental 'mindset' questions that both shape and are shaped by the strategic view and set the fundamental parameters for operational decisions.

We suggested that the eleven questions are an essential framework for any organisation wishing to audit, review or plan its leadership development activity. To have 'fit for purpose' leadership development an organisation needs to have answers to all of these questions that hang together.

The eleven fundamental questions are below. They are each followed by brief comments on how we found they are usually dealt with.

STRATEGIC

1 What is the 'business case' for leadership development?

What is the organisation seeking to achieve through the investment it makes in leadership development?

Answers to this were usually in the form of a short-term and long-term case. The short term was about implementing a current strategy, the long term about ensuring, as far as possible, the long-term viability of the organisation, which includes the ongoing capability to continually revise the strategy.

2 How does leadership development link to organisational strategy?

What is the relationship between leadership development and the formation and implementation of organisational strategy?

This was and is possibly the most interesting question of all. As stated in the introduction, leadership has a chicken-and-egg relationship with strategy, which is what makes it different from any other form of development in organisations, the logic for which can start with the strategy and analyse how any other role or job helps implement it, and the skills involved. Leadership involves the skills in implementing the current strategy but also those involved in developing the next one – corresponding to the short- and long-term case referred to above.

---

13   Burgoyne, J. G., Boydell, T. and Pedler, M. (2005) *Leadership Development: Current Practices, Future Perspectives*: 65. London: Corporate Research Forum.

3 How has organisational leadership development changed over time, and what will happen in the future?

How has the organisation changed over time and within that the role of leadership and leadership development? What further trends are anticipated for the future?

We found in our case studies that no organisation forming or re-forming leadership development starts with a green field site. There is always a history and tradition of leadership and, implicitly or explicitly, informally or formally, leadership development.

4 Who is responsible for leadership development?

Who takes prime responsibility for leadership development and how is their job/role located?

From our case research we found three main dimensions of choice on this one. The first is whether the person or people concerned are relatively new to the organisation or have a long history with it, and a deep understanding of its past and its traditions. The second was where they were organisationally located and the third was whether they were a leadership development/HR professional or an experienced leader/senior manager stepping out of line responsibility to take charge of leadership development.

On the first of these there is probably a largely positive self-correcting process at work. Organisations that have an unexpected crisis – implying the failure of previous leadership and the leadership development behind that – are more likely to look for a new approach and a 'fresh broom' to introduce it, a newcomer able to see things with fresh eyes. Organisations with an ongoing history of success are more likely to use the time-served insider who has a feel for the dynamics of the continuing success. There are dangers either way – throwing babies out with bathwater with the 'new broom' or failing to see new kinds of upcoming challenge with the traditional approach, or indeed the fear of changing anything through lack of certainty about what is maintaining success.

On the second choice, in the great majority of cases leadership development seems to be located in HR, but in a small number of cases they were in a separate organisation development unit reporting directly to the board or equivalent. The numbers are really too small to tell, but there may be a trend towards the latter. What is important is that there are open lines of communication and influence between leaders and managers at all levels, and across the processes described in the 'bundle' above.

On the last point, the professional form of leadership seems to be in the majority, though not necessarily by a long way. What is important is the credibility of the person or people in the role(s) and this may be the deciding factor. It is the case, however, that there is some professional knowledge or skill to be had, and this is important. Line managers taking on the job should at least read this book and particularly this chapter!

5 Are leadership development practices stable or changing?

Are corporate leadership development practices well established and stable, or under development or revision?

This is very much the issue just discussed in terms of the self-correcting process of ongoing success seeking to replicate itself, and failure looking for a new direction. However, leadership development is a longer-term process, though often short cut by using recruitment rather than development in turnaround situations. None the less, making best use of existing talent and using the momentum of previous leadership development is a serious challenge in turbulent times.

It is worth noting that crises are the times when senior managers/leaders do take back the reigns of leadership development from HR and specialists.

PIVOTAL

6 Where is 'leadership' in this organisation?

To whom is leadership development investment applied? Where is the leadership development investment located?

Figure 3.3 shows the diagram developed to explain the choices we found in addressing the question of 'Where is the leadership capability that matters?' and hence 'Where do we focus our leadership investment?'

The two dimensions are 'leadership by the few' vs. 'leadership by the many', and leadership as something done by individuals vs. leadership as something done by teams or larger collective groups – leaders vs. leadership if you like (so far in this chapter the terms have been used rather interchangeably). This latter distinction is, on one sense of the terms, the distinction between human capital and social capital – the latter being a property of the collective as, for example, residential communities where people look out for each other and their property – the kind of thing that Neighbourhood Watch schemes try to inculcate. The distinction is applied to leadership by Day.[14]

In terms of leadership development, education training and development can be seen as targeting human capital, while organisation development targets social capital.

Leadership by the few	HERO	TOP TEAM
Leadership by the many	EMPOWERED EMPLOYEES	CULTURE, TRADITIONS, PROCEDURES
	Leadership as the total of individuals' capability	Leadership as proper of the collective

Figure 3.3   Where is the leadership capability that matters?

14   Day, D. D. (2001) Leadership development: a review in context, *Leadership Quarterly*, 11(4): 581–613.

Heroic leadership is the top individuals that are often celebrated and held up as examples, the captains of the ship to whom the success or failure of the voyages are attributed.

Top teams attribute the same kind of achievement to the quality of boards and the like, and subscribe to the view that this should be the target of development.[15] Along similar lines, Garratt supports the view as an organisational metaphor that 'the fish rots from the head' – the head being the board or equivalent.[16, 17]

Leadership by the many attributes importance to large numbers of leaders near the coalface of an organisation's work. In the Health Service a programme called 'Leadership at the Point of Care' targeted 25,000 people who were first live leaders at ward level or equivalent targets in this population. One of the sayings in Tesco, allegedly, is that 'One of the most important forms of leadership is that immediately behind the people who serve our customers' – the same idea.

Leadership as embedded in culture, traditions and procedures is perhaps difficult to think about. However, many long-term successful organisations remain so, despite the comings and goings of individuals at all levels. It is tempting, in these situations, to think that ongoing leadership may be more embedded in culture and so on. In long-standing organisations (better thought of as institutions) like ancient universities (Oxford and Cambridge) and the Roman Catholic Church, it looks as though figurehead leaders – vice-chancellors and popes–are thrown up, often by a collegiate process, to represent the culture, rather than come in from somewhere else, heroic-leader style, to define or redefine it.

In the great majority of organisations in our study most of the leadership development budget was spent on the top heroic managers and the up-and-coming managers likely to succeed them. There was some senior management teambuilding and some 'hybrid' programmes that aimed at social capital as well as human capital by, for example, working on shared organisation problems in action-learning mode.

There were exceptions, like retail organisations working on leadership near the customer interface, or Barnardo's where leadership in the high street charity shops was identified as a critical point in the business model, facing the particular challenge of leading largely volunteer groups.

In terms of Figure 3.3, my belief is that it is not a question of choosing one or other of the four corners of the diagram and going for that, but thinking about how to address them all, and getting them to hang together. According to the situation some of the corners may dominate, or even lead the others, but it is important that they hang together.

7 How is 'leadership' defined in this organisation?

What does leadership mean? How it is understood?

---

15   Kakabadse, A., Jackson, S. and Fandale, E. (2002) *Meeting the Development Needs of Top Teams and Boards*, London: CRF.

16   Garratt, R. (1987) *The Learning Organisation*, London: Fontana/Collins.

17   Garratt, R. (1990) *Creating a Learning Organisation*, London: Director Books.

While I may be clear, as in my opening paragraphs, about what leadership is, or more precisely what it does, in general terms, how it does it seems much more varied and contested and closer to the Grint view.[18]

What seems to be important is that each organisation has a uniting and integrating leadership concept – and in many ways this has to be unique to give the organisation its unique character and distinctive advantage in a way that both builds on its past and takes it into the future.

However, I think there are some broad patterns. In large parts of the private sector, with the shift to knowledge work and the knowledge economy, the emphasis is on *people* leadership, since this is what it takes to align individual effort with corporate purpose.

In public sector leadership *public* leadership has become important – this is, developing and meeting the expectations of the public that they serve.

Many organisations these days still rely on professional work – education, health, law, accountancy, the big consultancy firms – and here *professional* leadership matters, meaning leadership of professional activities rather than a professional style of leadership. Very few universities or business schools are led by people who do not have at least a reasonable past performance in research and teaching. Professional leadership is about advancing the craft of the profession and developing newcomers into it.

Almost all organisations I know have leadership competency frameworks by this or another name. Both academics and practitioners have a love–hate relationship with them.[19] While the way they are arrived at may not satisfy the academic, and the way they are used (or not used, or solely served by tick boxing) may not satisfy the practitioner, it seems to me that the benefit comes from the dialogue that creates them, rather than their use, though the dialogue on how to use them across the spectrum of recruitment, development, performance and career management may well be part of what holds the 'bundle' together.

I have come to the conclusion that there are three kinds of competencies that are important.

First there is a foundational, and largely generic, set of basic competencies that are the building blocks for all the rest, the reading, writing and arithmetic of management and leadership if you like, which are necessary but not sufficient for effective management and leadership. These are probably best captured in the Council for Excellence in Management and Leadership review.[20] While these competencies are unlikely to give an organisation a competitive advantage, they are unlikely to be able to have it without them. If they are absent they are probably the best investment for leadership development, and they often are, particularly in situations where professionally and technically skilled people like doctors or engineers move into management and leadership.

Secondly there are the organisation-specific competencies, which are about knowing the basic facts and technologies of the organisation and its sector, and skills relevant to its current strategy and business model.

---

18   Grint, K. (2004) *What is Leadership? From Hydra to Hybrid*, Working Paper, Said Business School and Templeton College: Oxford University.

19   Burgoyne, J. G. (2008) Competency frameworks: love 'em or lose 'em? *Talent Management Review*, 2(2): 7.

20   Perren, L. and Burgoyne, J. G. (2002) *The Management and Leadership Nexus: Dynamic Sharing of Practice and Principle*, p. 13. London: Council for Excellence in Management and Leadership.

Thirdly there are the competencies to do with strategy formation and implementation, which may again be largely generic. These are to do with seeing the big picture, the total systems that an organisation and its business model are part of. It has been suggested that a high level of education of any kind will do the trick here – it is the higher level mental abilities of critical thinking that allow people to see more possibilities in situations and be prepared to make bold moves, rather than pursue incremental change.[21]

OPERATIONAL

The operational choices that we found were (8) deciding on the balance of recruitment and retention, and how to implement this, (9) working out how to align development to career, performance and reward management – making the bundle work, in other words, (10) the difficult one of deciding the best development methods, and finally, (10) the question of how to evaluate leadership development initiatives.

On (8) recruitment, we found, is largely favoured either in pursuing rapid expansion or finding a new direction after a crisis, but we also found those concerned with leadership development much preoccupied with mergers and acquisitions.

In the planning-for-takeover situation, the question of whether another firm is strong in terms of management and leadership, and thus may be an asset to be advantageously acquired, or weak, and hence one to which value can be added, is there, whether or not it is the main consideration in the decision. In a post merger/acquisition situation there are two populations to be integrated, and two sets of bundle systems to be integrated.

On the integration of career and leadership development specifically, and the elements in the bundle generally, my previous research, originating in evaluation work for British Rail,[22] has produced a six-step ladder model which describes six progressively better steps to integrated leadership development (see Figure 3.4).

This is the horizontal dimension of Figure 3.1, which shows the real bottom line pay-off for being higher on this ladder. I have described and made the case for the ladder in various publications.[23, 24]

The ladder is about the degree of integration and coordination with leadership development tactics, career development tactics (like succession planning or running an internal leadership jobs market) and the implementation and formation of organisational strategy.

At the first level there is no deliberate leadership development or career management. It is left to chance, natural processes or last-minute ad hoc arrangements in the case of the career side.

At the second level there is one or the other or both, but they are not connected to each other or anything else. They are often introduced in response to a crisis – a lack of skills, for example, financial skills for engineers – and then carry on out of habit and with their own routine momentum.

---

21   Bosworth, D. (2006) Management skills, strategy and performance. In S. Porter and M. Campbell (eds) *Skills and Economic Performance*, pp. 225–236. London: Caspian.

22   Burgoyne, J. G. (1985) Management development policy: the British Rail case. In C. Clegg *et al.* (eds) *Case Studies in Organisational Behaviour*, pp. 150–156. London: Wiley.

23   Burgoyne, J. G. (1988) Management development for the individual and the organisation, *Personnel Management*, June: 40–44.

24   Burgoyne, J. G. (1999) *Develop Yourself, Your Career and Your Organisation*. London: Lemos and Crane.

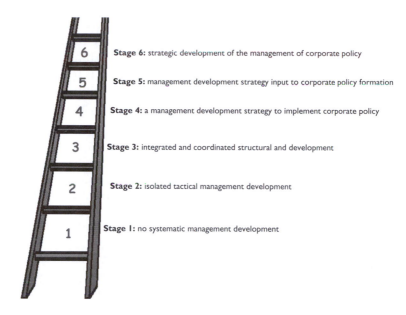

Stage 6: strategic development of the management of corporate policy

Stage 5: management development strategy input to corporate policy formation

Stage 4: a management development strategy to implement corporate policy

Stage 3: integrated and coordinated structural and development

Stage 2: isolated tactical management development

Stage 1: no systematic management development

Figure 3.4   The integration of leadership and career development

At the third level they are connected to each other, but nothing else. When people are considered for a development programme the question of whether this is for current or future role-performance is asked, for example. From the other side, if someone were considered for a succession list, then the question of whether a development programme for them would be useful would be asked.

The difficulty with the third level is that there tends to be an assumption, for career planning purposes, that the organisational chart is a stable map across which career journeys can be planned, and that the capabilities that have worked for leaders and managers in the past will serve similarly in the future. However, we know that both of these assumptions are changing. Most organisations are being frequently if not continuously restructured, and their leaders face new challenges requiring new skills.

Organisations reaching the fourth level address this problem, and this is the level of strategy implementation. At this level all that is known about new strategies being implemented is fed into the career and leadership development planning process: the extent to which the future is uncertain, and there is usually a large element of this, is allowed for by the development of the capabilities of coping with learning and change themselves, and maintaining flexible talent pools rather than detailed succession plans.

The fifth level moves beyond strategy implementation to strategy improvement. Here leadership development events are used to review and improve strategies as well as planning to implement them, and career development discussions can generate new ideas for the future that lead to new roles.[25]

---

25   Burgoyne, J. G. and Germain, C. (1984) Self development and career planning: an exercise in mutual benefit, *Personnel Management*, April: 21–23.

The sixth level, which I often call the icing on the cake, is where effort is put into the development of the most senior leadership team in terms of both their strategy and their ability to form and implement it.

The individual can use the ladder idea to try to manage their own development and career progression too, and as a basis for negotiating these with their employer(s). As a first step they can try to ensure that they get some development, and some planning of any future career moves. As a second step that these two link, so that they support each other – development opens up career opportunities, and makes them more likely to happen. As a third step they can try to see that their development and career planning fits in with any new strategic organisational directions. At the next levels they can try to see if their ideas can contribute to the formation of new strategy directions, and at the last stage they can see if they can be formally involved in this process.

The fifth level and above represents the breakthrough to becoming a learning organisation.[26, 27, 28, 29, 30, 31] Note that Senge takes a similar line of argument to me – leadership is about taking charge of the development process.[32]

Most organisations, in my experience, are at levels 2–4, so there is considerable scope for improvement here. Various diagnostics and further resources for this approach are available.[33]

Returning to the British Rail case, which was the starting point of the 'ladder' model, the long-term outcome is interesting. As the reader is likely to know, British Rail was split up and is no more. I met my client for the British Rail evaluation some years later, and said, semi-jokingly, that the long-term evaluation was not very good from the organisational point of view. He said: 'What you do not know, John, is that many of the people who went through those management development programmes have gone on to become multi-millionaires through using their business knowledge from the programme, and their insider information, to cherry-pick the best management buy-outs'. The moral of the story supports the ladder model: capability development ran ahead of career development, with the result that the individuals concerned created their own rewarding career options.

The choice of teaching/learning methods does not beg any simple answers. This is probably because what works is highly variable, with context, what is to be learnt, the prior experience, learning styles and cultural settings of the learners. Having said this there is a strong preponderance towards experiential methods, and particularly the ones that are context-sensitive in themselves: coaching, mentoring and action learning.[34] Being steered by short-term evaluation is probably the best approach.

26   Dixon, N. (1994) *The Organizational Learning Cycle*. Maidenhead: McGraw-Hill.

27   Garratt, R. (1987) *The Learning Organisation*. London: Fontana/Collins.

28   Garratt, R. (1990) *Creating a Learning Organisation*. London: Director Books.

29   Pedler, M., Burgoyne, J. G. and Boydell, T. (1996) *The Learning Company*, 2nd edn. Maidenhead: McGraw-Hill.

30   Senge, P. (1990) *The Fifth Discipline, The Art and Practice of the Learning Organisation*, New York: Doubleday.

31   Senge, P., Kleiner, A., Roberts, C., Ross, R. B. and Smith, B. J. (1994) *The Fifth Discipline Fieldbook. Strategies and Tools for Building a Learning Organisation*, New York: Currency Doubleday.

32   Senge, P. (1990) The leader's new work: building learning organizations. *Sloan Management Review,* 32(1): 7–23.

33   Burgoyne, J. G. (1999) *Develop Yourself, Your Career and Your Organisation*. London: Lemos and Crane.

34   Horne, M. and Stedman Jones, D. (2001) *Leadership: the challenge for all?* London: Institute of Management. HMSO.

Lastly to evaluation, which may seem logical enough, but by one argument it should be first.[35, 36] The argument is that planning a leadership development initiative should start by drawing on lessons of past evaluations in terms of what has worked in the organisation and context specifically and as shown by research in general.

In practice, evaluation tends to be an add-on afterthought, and while many see the logic of building in evaluation from the beginning, fewer do it, though it is seen as best practice to try to do so. The Pawson argument lifts best practice to another level.

Leadership development is a special case as far as evaluation goes, for reasons already explained. Development for all other roles can be evaluated in terms of whether this enhances the delivery of strategy, but this does not work for leadership development because leadership, in part at least, is about forming strategy.

Evaluation of leadership development has to be to some extent open-ended, because it is about bringing useful forms or order from the other side of the boundary with complexity and chaos. It is the problem of evaluating the success of a journey into unknown territory.

The model proposed by Easterby-Smith[37] for the four functions of evaluation works for all forms of development except leadership (see Figure 3.6).

However, for the evaluation of leadership development, a modification proposed by Anne Murphy (work in progress) is needed (see Figure 3.7).

Having said that, the success of leadership development should be manifest in the success of the organisation and, again, it is the job of leadership to define and achieve success in a way that is sustainable for the organisation (unless it is a temporary organisation, the aim of which is to deal with a problem and put itself out of business – a possible if rare situation).

The problem is not so much how to measure success, as how to know whether it can be attributed to leadership development. This is the problem faced by the American

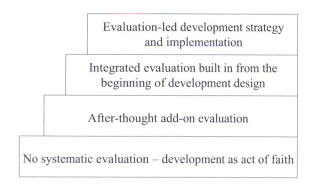

Figure 3.5   Levels of best practice in evaluation

35   Pawson, R. D. (2002a) *Evidence-based Policy: I. In Search of a Method*. London: ESRC UK Centre for Evidence Based Policy and Practice: Queen Mary College University of London.

36   Pawson, R. D. (2002b) Evidence-based policy: in search of a method. *Evaluation*, 8(2): 157–181.

37   Easterby-Smith, M. P. V. (1981) *The Evaluation of Management Education, Training and Development*. Aldershot: Gower.

Purpose of:	PROCESS	OUTCOME
SUMMATIVE	CONTROLLING Is it going according to plan?	PROVING Is it achieving what was intended?
FORMATIVE	IMPROVING Is a there a better way of doing what we are trying to do?	LEARNING Can we re-visualise what we are trying to do?

Figure 3.6   The purposes of evaluation

Purpose of	PROCESS	OUTCOME
SUMMATIVE	CONTROLLING Is it going according to plan?	PROVING Is it achieving what was intended?
FORMATIVE	IMPROVING Is there a better way of doing what we are trying to do?	LEARNING Can we re-visualise what we are trying to do?
TRANSFORMATIVE	GENERATING Is what we are doing causing a fundamental re-think of why we are doing this is the first place?	INNOVATING Are we doing something other than we imagined which also satisfies external/social stakeholders?

Figure 3.7   The purposes of evaluation extended to include transformation

evaluation guru Jack Phillips.[38] His solution is to trust the judgement of those closest to the process – presumably the leaders themselves.

By way of summary, Figure 3.8 shows the strategic, pivotal and operational choices that are involved in leadership development, which have been discussed above.

The best advice I can give on forming and implementing a corporate leadership development strategy is to work backwards and forward and across these eleven questions making sure that the answers are consistent with each other, using the pivotal questions as the cornerstones for this.

Conclusion

It has been argued that leadership can be defined in a general way, as dealing with the chaos/order boundary from the chaos side. Beyond that, it creates its own definition in

---

38   Phillips, J. (1994) *ROI: the Search for Best Practice*, American Society for Training and Development.

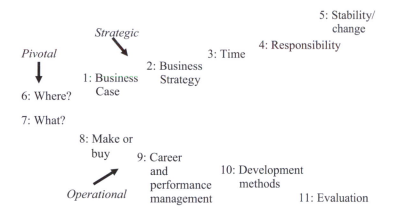

Figure 3.8   Essential choices in forming a leadership development strategy

specific contexts. It is a bootstrap operation. Leadership development works in tandem, from an organisational point of view, with the acquisition of leadership capability or the potential for it, and the utilisation of leadership capability. All three are needed in a coordinated way. The bundle of these activities is held together by evaluation, which takes the form of the challenge of evaluating a journey into the unknown, rather than over already mapped territory.

4 *Crafting a Leadership and Management Development Strategy II*

TIM SPACKMAN

Introduction

Based in Skipton, North Yorkshire, HML is the UK's leading third-party mortgage administration company, with over 40 clients and £50 billion worth of assets under management. It is home to 2,000 employees at four sites.

This is the story of HML's journey over the last five years. It is a story that will hopefully stimulate ideas, thoughts and questions, but it is our story. And although there will undoubtedly be many similarities with others, there are likely to be just as many differences. For the idea of 'best fit' rather than 'best practice' is of paramount importance to any such journey. It is true there is much to be learned from different organisations and an external view is essential for the practitioner, yet I believe the key is to 'adapt, not adopt'[1] examples of good practice in a way that is right for your business, its strategy, culture and environment.

My previous experience undoubtedly shaped my approach in many ways at my present organisation. However, had I adopted the kind of practices deployed by a large high street bank as soon as I joined HML, my ideas would have not fitted with the culture or the maturity[2] of the organisation. Going from a global multinational customer-focused organisation to a small, ambitious, rapidly growing client-focused company was a personal transition for me, yet never losing sight of 'best fit' has enabled us to craft a leadership and management development strategy that is right for our business.

HML has grown exponentially over the past five years, as shown in the graph in Figure 4.1. This story will incorporate examples of both long-term strategic aims and shorter-term objectives over a five-year period. The challenge of delivering both the proactive and the reactive in a fast-moving environment is a key one for practitioners.[3]

1   Ulrich D. and Smallwood N. (2003) *Why the Bottom Line Isn't!: How to Build Value Through People and Organisation.* Hoboken, NJ: John Wiley & Sons.

2   Mumford, A. and Gold, J. (2004) *Management Development, Strategies for Action.* London: CIPD.

3   Mayo, A. (2004) *Creating a Learning and Development Strategy.* London: CIPD.

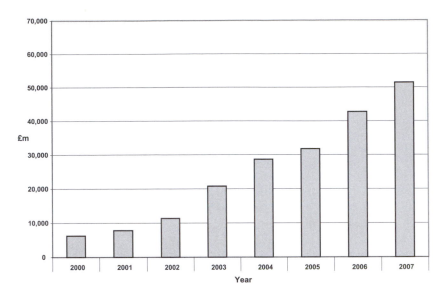

Figure 4.1   HML growth

This chapter is intended to tell a story for two reasons. First, storytelling is a highly effective methodology for leadership development, the skilful use of which has the potential to effect culture change. Secondly, I believe it is important for those of us leading this type of development activity to role-model, live and breathe the approaches we advocate.

A note about language. In HML, leadership development means leadership *and* management development. The development of leadership capability, style and behaviour will only be successful for us if combined with an ability for operations-management excellence and the requisite technical skills and knowledge that enable us to demonstrate expertise in our chosen market.

Strategy and Culture

In our experience, leadership, strategy and culture are so entwined that any discussion of leadership development must also involve discussion of strategy and culture. The importance of culture cannot be underestimated. Over the recent period of growth, HML's culture has, like any culture, been in a state of flux influenced by a melting pot of variables such as growth, leadership style, our parent company and geographical expansion.

As might be expected, some of the supportive, paternalistic aspects of its parent, Skipton Building Society, remain part of the culture. In addition, HML's growth has been achieved through commitment, entrepreneurialism and strong relationships – within the organisation and with its clients and communities in the fairly diverse areas of Londonderry, Glasgow, Yorkshire and Lancashire. In recent times challenging market conditions and the need for developing operational excellence have resulted in an increased focus on performance, coaching, quality and continuous improvement.

The model[4] in Figure 4.2 explains the key links between mission/strategy, leadership and culture.

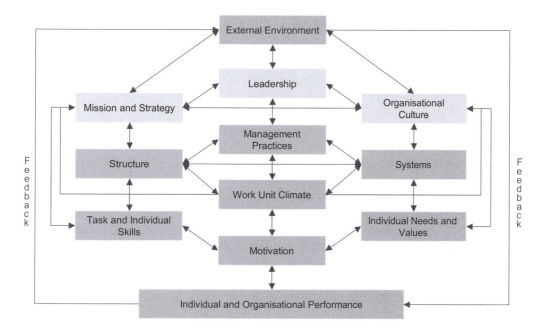

Figure 4.2   The Burke–Litwin model

This model suggests leadership influences the ongoing creation of strategy and culture. Desired strategic and cultural direction clearly need to influence leadership development strategy, yet leadership development itself can also influence and create organisational strategy and culture in a systemic way. The model is used both explicitly and implicitly to articulate why and how leadership needs to change in order to deliver organisational strategy and create an organisational culture that enables change to happen rather than hinders it. Questions such as 'What do we need our leaders to excel at?', 'What kind of leadership does our strategy require over the next three to five years?' and 'What kind of leadership will drive the culture we desire to deliver our strategy?' are key for us in identifying a leadership and management development strategy. Like all models, it has its limitations, yet it does help us view subjects such as leadership systemically, highlighting how our relationship with our external environment (especially clients and regulatory influences) impacts on our leadership behaviours and our culture.

Our aim in leadership development is to craft our approach with this model in mind. In 2008 our managing director successfully challenged 15 talented people from all levels of the organisation to play an active role in defining business strategy. This stretching task had to be completed in just one month, involving primary and secondary research and analysis. Interviews and the classic strengths, weaknesses, opportunities, threats (SWOT)

---

4   Burke, W. W. and Litwin, G. H. (1992) A causal model of organisational performance and change, *Journal of Management,* 18(3): 523–545.

and political, economic, social, technological and environmental (PESTLE) methodologies were used. It needed to result in credible strategic options for our business, which would be presented to the 40 most senior leaders and subsequently our parent company. The team achieved their goal and the business outcome was an approved three-year strategy informed by bright ideas, rigorous research and intelligent thinking and debate. The long-term *learning* outcomes for the team, which included all levels within the organisational structure, included business knowledge, teamworking, strategic knowledge, research skills, working under pressure, presentational and influencing skills.

Strategy

HML's three-year strategy with high-level goals is complemented by an annual corporate plan with organisational and divisional objectives. Corporate goals and objectives are set in line with the balanced scorecard approach[5] under the headings Effectiveness, Commercial, Profit and Engagement. In order to ensure strategic alignment to these goals,[6] HML's leadership development programme has been designed along the same lines, with modules and learning objectives against each of the four areas to provide a balanced approach to leadership development. Yet this programme also features prominently within the overall strategy as one of the 'key strategic inputs' – it is of key strategic importance in attaining our three-year goals.

In order to craft a leadership development strategy, we need to 'make sense' of the business strategy that captures the overall direction and thrust of the business. This is the planned element of leadership development whereby our team develop policies and practices which allow us to enable the strategy to be delivered.

Just as strategy itself must be flexible, given the unpredictable nature of the world around us, so must leadership development. The impact of the external environment on the organisations of today cannot be underestimated. Some of our most recent business challenges illustrate how a leadership development strategy must be as flexible and responsive to changes driven by external factors as it is in responding to internal business needs. A selection of our business challenges is listed below, together with the corresponding leadership challenge.

Table 4.1   Integrated leadership development

Business challenges	Internal leadership challenge
2008 'Credit Crunch' and meltdown of sub prime mortgage industry	Agility and adaptability to change; culture change
Development of online technology; changing customer demands; exploiting new opportunities; speed to market of new products	Delivery focus; can-do attitude; tolerance of ambiguity; marketing; commercial awareness; entrepreneurialism; leading change across teams

---

5   Kaplan, R. S. and Norton, D. P. (1992) The balanced scorecard – measures that drive performance, *Harvard Business Review*, January–February: 71–79.

6   Holbeche, L. (1998) *High Flyers and Succession Planning in Changing Organisations*. Horsham: Roffey Park Institute.

Table 4.1 *Concluded*

Business challenges	Internal leadership challenge
Development of new products	Systemic thinking; external and future focus; commercial awareness
Legal and regulatory demands	Quality assurance; risk and compliance awareness
Increasing focus on customers in arrears and arrears management	Credit management leadership, behavioural learning and development
Pressure from clients to reduce prices and improve service	Financial awareness; operational excellence; relationship management
Operations management excellence and quality – focus on being the best	Lean-thinking tools and techniques; facilitation of ideas; performance coaching; change leadership; continuous improvement; feedback skills
Developing relationships with new and existing clients	Commercial awareness; relationship building; emotional intelligence
Improving employee engagement and reducing employee turnover	Inspirational leadership; authentic leadership; developing trust; coaching; communication
Focus on being proactive and project delivery	Articulating vision, strategy and desired culture; project management; change management; stakeholder management

In addition to a focus on and within our business strategy, our leadership development strategy seeks to adopt a cultural, learning and business focus.

CULTURE FOCUS

- Developing what leaders pay attention to, measure and control.
- Highlighting leaders' reactions to critical events in relation to our values.
- The stories leaders tell; the words and phrases they use.
- Strong emphasis on values-led strategy.

LEARNING FOCUS

- Need to learn faster than the speed of change.
- Everyone has responsibility for their learning.
- People learn in differing ways and at different speeds.
- Leadership and management development as a key strategic lever.
- Every manager expected to coach and develop their people.

BUSINESS FOCUS

- Centrally driven consistency for organisational needs (leadership, talent, induction, education and regulation).
- Expert local business partners and change agents enable business to achieve objectives and lead change.

- Internal consultancy approach identifies real needs and flexible, tailored solutions.

In order to continue our business growth, HML as a business needs to learn faster than the speed of change, embedding learning, coaching and performance-improvement into all aspects of HML life, creating a true learning organisation where every challenge, every project and every day brings an opportunity for learning and therefore improving how we perform.

Everyone has a responsibility for learning. Every manager is expected to coach and develop their people in order to deliver performance improvement and every individual is expected to take ownership for their own performance and development.

Our people and development team aim to act as strategic business partners and change agents to enable the business to achieve its objectives. Our aim is to adopt a more strategic, challenging, value-adding approach to enhancing business performance and enabling organisational change. We aim to be role models in adopting the values and behaviours that will make HML successful and seek to challenge those who do not.

Acting as internal consultants, professional expertise is available for advice and guidance on all performance issues. The ultimate goal will always be to improve performance – of individuals, teams, departments and the organisation as a whole.

People learn in so many different ways. HML do not adopt a menu-driven, 'sheep-dip', course-based approach to learning. Informal learning is increasingly promoted and facilitated, using methodologies such as mentoring, coaching, volunteering and action learning. This brings benefits of greater relevance, ability to apply learning and further developing a learning culture.

CULTURE

The work on the cultural web,[7] developed by Gerry Johnson and Kevan Scholes in 1992, provides an approach for looking at and changing and organisation's culture. It defines six elements that help to make up a culture (Figure 4.3). More recently living systems approaches to change by the likes of Margaret Wheatley have been influential for us in understanding culture and also recognising challenges around culture change in complex, adaptive systems that cannot be controlled in a mechanistic manner.

Towards the end of 2007, we began a process of culture inquiry through sessions with around 150 people from all hierarchical levels and business areas, where we asked 'What kind of organisation do you want to work for?' Using a values sort exercise[8] we identified that our existing culture, whilst strong in the areas of striving for client satisfaction, friendliness, commitment and corporate social responsibility, needed to change to enable our emerging strategy around continuous improvement, operational excellence, new products and services and agility.

The key transformational factors of strategy, culture and leadership, led by a new managing director, were identified as a way to drive a real change in the business in a time of economic turmoil. Our culture of reacting to growth demands, client focus and strong personal relationships had served us well in times of growth. Our strategy now

---

7   Johnson, G. and Scholes, K. (1993) *Exploring Corporate Strategy*, 3rd edn. Englewood Cliffs, NJ: Prentice-Hall.

8   Cook, S., Macaulay, S. and Coldicott, H. (2004) *Change Management Excellence: Using the Four Intelligences for Successful Organizational Change*. London: Kogan Page.

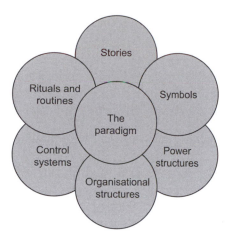

Figure 4.3   The cultural web

requires a shift towards more balance between internal and external focus, continuous improvement of processes, performance management and both client and customer focus.

The senior leaders of the organisation were brought together for sessions on strategy, culture, leadership, engagement and continuous improvement. The impact leaders and leadership have on culture was explored as a senior leadership team, with an emphasis on them developing understanding of their impact on culture through storytelling, reactions to critical incidents and role modelling.

There are many ways of identifying and embedding organisational values to develop a culture to enable a business strategy and our approach was to task senior leaders with identifying the values that they would need to live and breathe in order for the strategy to land. This was conducted through a challenging, unstructured cross-functional session, where the group were expected to self-organise and come up with the appropriate values for our strategy and culture. Previous to this, the group had listened to a presentation detailing research on some of the positive and less-than-positive characteristics of our existing culture, as described by people at all levels of the organisation, most of which they recognised. They had also conducted a gap analysis themselves on our capabilities in many areas. So the need for change had been recognised and the counterproductive elements of our culture identified. People respond more readily to change when they themselves have been part of the diagnosis of the need to change.

The leaders were also asked to engage in metaphor and storytelling by telling some positive stories of when they had seen new values demonstrated. Whilst recognising that this could only be one small step on a difficult journey of culture change, it did have the effect, in terms of leadership development, of engendering a spirit of collaboration and real buy-in to the cultural changes needed within the business. The leaders were asked to physically sign the flip chart they had drafted to present the values, showing their commitment to living them.

Culture change is notoriously difficult to achieve and our approach aims to develop our culture through meaningful conversations. Our next step was to further define our values by asking a wide range of leaders to consider what the organisational values actually mean, why they are important, some 'positive' stories of when they had seen them being lived, some 'negative' stories of when they had not been lived and the inherent paradox within the values – the dangers associated with overplaying the value or misinterpreting the intended meaning of it. These thoughts were summarised and distributed around the group, resulting in greater clarity and shared understanding of the values. This group has subsequently co-created the values further with their teams in their respective contexts, identifying the behaviours they as a group need to stop, start and continue in order to embody the values.

Any culture change programme takes years to take effect and we are realistic about the challenges ahead. Our intention is to constantly reinforce the values, encouraging dialogue, storytelling and especially feedback to embed them. We are also making values and our desired culture a core element of the new leadership development programme – for example, using the values for contracting in action learning sets and activities in the residential event such as asking delegates to work on a task which they choose that has a stated purpose – 'To shape the culture of HML' – which results in commitment to actions individually and as a cross-functional group in the workplace.

People and Structure

In order to craft and deliver a leadership development strategy, build and maintain credibility with the business, all members of my team are expected to invest time and energy in their continuing professional development. Our facilitators develop learning contracts with each other when working together and are expected to adopt high levels of support and challenge as a team – we think it is key that we, to paraphrase Ghandi, 'are the change we wish to see in the world' as we seek to develop a learning culture.

Benchmarking with other organisations helps maintain an objective, progressive approach. With five Chartered Fellows of the Chartered Institute of Personnel and Development (CIPD) in the department and four people qualified to Masters level, the commitment to our own development is clear.

As HML grew, its learning and development team grew with it. The demands of high numbers of new starters meant induction training was a high priority to get right. It also meant rapid career progression for a number of aspiring managers. In a not untypical tale, many of these customer-facing employees found themselves promoted on the basis of their technical expertise rather than their people-management competencies, posing a challenge for leadership and management development.

A central management development team was set up to provide training, coaching and support for these managers, with the initial focus on first-line managers. This served the organisation well for three years as a high priority on core organisational needs such as recruitment and selection, coaching, performance management and handling discipline, and capability meant a large volume of workshops, e-learning and one-to-one internal consultancy was required.

With further growth came new sites in Lancashire and London Derry. The need to take the learning to the learner became ever more apparent and we soon devolved the delivery of these core modules to each local site, retaining ownership and accountability for a consistent overall framework centrally.

With greater organisational maturity came more sophistication of people processes, and the human resources and learning and development teams were restructured in a manner designed to ensure a horizontally integrated provision of service.

Now, service delivery has responsibility for all aspects of day-to-day delivery of recruitment, induction, management development and support; business partnering for internal consultancy and organisational development for strategic people objectives around employee engagement, talent management, leadership development and organisational performance.

Our current structure brings talent management and leadership development closely together. Policy development also sits within organisational development, knowing as we do that policy becomes 'dead on the page' as soon as it is written[9] – the intention being that policy development and formulation includes implementation into our leadership and management development framework.

The team structure is helpful to us in developing our leadership development strategy, but how people work together across boundaries is what is most important (Figure 4.4).

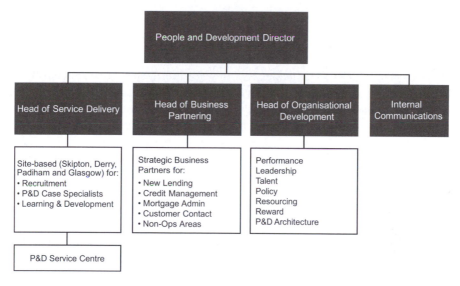

Figure 4.4   People and development

The Leadership Development Journey at HML

The evolution of our leadership development strategy is ongoing. It is important to recognise that the pace with which any development strategy evolves is a function of both the rate of change within and outside the business and the maturity of the organisation.

Our leadership development strategy has been informed by the thrust of a successful, growing business. There are 'design' features of our strategy, such as the frameworks and development programmes we have put in place in order to deliver business strategy;

9   Shotter, J. (2000) Constructing 'resourceful or mutually enabling' communities: putting a new (dialogical) practice into our practices. Paper delivered at the Meaning of Learning Project Conference, Denver, October 25–28.

and 'emergent' features,[10] which have been shaped by events and feedback from key stakeholders with rapidly changing business needs. For example, an initial 'bottom-up' focus on first-line managers and their development led to feedback from this population which suggested some needs in the middle management population, who were providing inconsistent levels of support and challenge for their direct reports.

Recent developments in leadership theory and practice have emphasised the increasing role of values, communication and interpersonal relationships, and the central importance of responding to, and shaping, continuous change for all those in leadership roles. Our approach has been to focus on these areas. Perhaps unsurprisingly given the pace of change, 'learning to learn' is also seen as an increasingly important meta-skill for managers.[11] This key skill is very much at the forefront of our leadership and management development strategy.

Figure 4.5 shows the changing nature of Leadership Development within HML over the past five years, a time in which employee numbers more than doubled. Over a number of years, change has taken the form of growth and expansion, resulting in new people-managers and the setting up of new sites, new teams and processes. The ability to respond to the needs of expansion has become a core competence of the company and leading change a required competence for leaders.

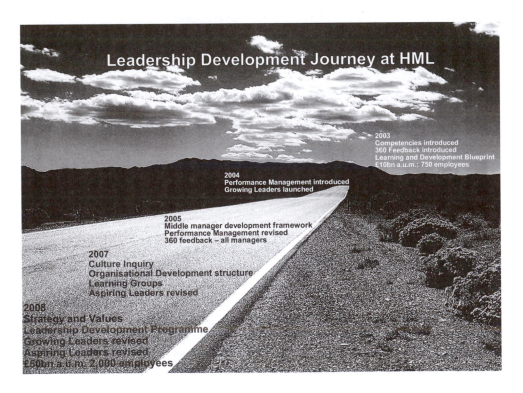

Figure 4.5   The leadership development journey at HML

---

10   Mintzberg, H. (1994) *The Rise and Fall of Strategic Planning: Reconceiving Roles For Planning, Plans, Planners*. New York: The Free Press.

11   Winterton J., Parker M., Dodd M., McCracken M. and Henderson I. (2000) *Future Skills Needs of Managers*. London: DfEE Research Report RR182.

The milestones along the journey will be different for different organisations yet the constantly shifting nature of organisational life will be similar. As with any leader, no leadership development framework or programme has ever 'arrived' – the constantly changing nature of organisational systems requires a similarly fluid, adaptable approach to developing leaders and leadership within the organisation.

In 2003, HML was about to take off. A combination of attracting new, larger clients and the growth in the mortgage industry meant exciting times ahead. Perhaps unsurprisingly, HML's people strategy and processes were relatively underdeveloped, with an old-fashioned appraisal system, a legacy of promotion based on technical expertise and dependent trainer-led approaches to learning and development.

A learning philosophy was outlined in a strategy document called the 'Learning and Development Blueprint', with aspirations to the idea of Senge's learning organisation. Senior leaders were invited to leading-edge sessions on distributed leadership and action learning partly as development and partly as a way of creating some engagement and alliance amongst the senior leadership population to help support a shift towards a learning culture.

A platform for learning needed to be built. Following the introduction of a competency framework, an exercise in 360-degree feedback was conducted for the whole of the management population. Inexperienced team leaders, many of whom had taken the opportunity provided by a growing business to seal promotion, were shown to be struggling in the key people management competencies of the time – developing and empowering, clarity for performance and motivating and inspiring.

There were clear benefits to us in identifying real needs for a large population. Analysis of the results of this exercise on a global basis looking at norm groups for team leaders and department managers highlighted key development areas for the different levels of management as a whole. It also enabled us to repeat the exercise two years later as a method of evaluation, when the results showed a 10 per cent improvement in competency scores across the board.

In 2004 the team leader 'Growing Leaders' programme was designed and implemented for the first time. Performance management was introduced to provide the bedrock necessary for facilitating learning conversations and improving performance. It proved to be an important element of the business achieving the training and competence requirements of mortgage regulation the following year – another example of the external environment impacting leadership within the organisation systemically.

In 2005, a Masters dissertation conducted on 'middle manager development' within HML highlighted the challenging role of the middle manager within HML in a time when there was dramatic growth. At this time, around 65 per cent of the organisation had less than 12 months' service and a young inexperienced management population (the vast majority of managers aged between 25 and 44 years old), wrestled with HML's growing pains.

Research showed HML's managers to be inexperienced, but well-qualified; demonstrating an appetite for learning that may have been frustrated by the perceived lack of time available; they typically performed well in managing client relationships, which they found relatively easy, and not so well in communicating, motivating and developing those around them in order to lead the business through change – skills which they recognised were absolutely crucial to HML.

A since-abandoned 'Middle Manager Development Framework' was implemented, which had a strong emphasis on informal and self-directed learning. This proved to be a learning experience. Although in itself the framework was robust, reflection since suggests that it was too early for the business to embrace such an approach, with more structure required, and uptake from the target group was low. More recently, however, elements are working successfully in the leadership development programme – suggesting it was the right idea at the wrong time.

At this point, a decision was taken to not conduct 360-degree feedback again over the whole management population; a decision based on the need to shift our culture to one where individuals direct their own learning. The expectation now was that 360 was there as and when they needed it as a tool to support their development. Pleasingly, many did continue to undergo the 360 process on a regular basis. However, it was noticeable that of those who did not, many had not scored well previously. The introduction of a new leadership development programme now means that, as part of the programme, leaders are expected to undertake 360 at the beginning and end of the process – still not a blanket exercise, but perhaps a good balance enabling identification of the whole spectrum of leadership capability at that level.

There was an increased emphasis on leadership in 2006, having focused primarily on management development needs for two years. The 'Leadership Ideals' provided a behavioural framework for all formal leaders to aspire to. Talent management was introduced and the Aspiring Leaders programme provided support for many soon-to-be team leaders in a still rapidly growing business. Further development opportunities were made available through an increasing focus on corporate social responsibility initiatives, especially volunteering and cross-sector programmes developing leadership beyond authority.

In 2007, HML underwent further significant change. This time, however, the focus was internal as the organisation restructured to become aligned with the core internal processes associated with mortgage administration. The effect of this change was greater than that which had gone before and a series of informal 'learning groups' were introduced in order to support middle managers. The approach taken was one of action learning sets; the groups were self-organising and were facilitated by the group members themselves. The vision for the groups was to provide an environment where a group of peers could discuss their experiences of leading change and the challenges they were facing, with a view to reflecting on their leadership practice, planning and reviewing action.

The success of these groups was mixed. Some individuals found great value in having the ability to make sense of change and to develop a wider understanding of the business through a cross-section of managers. Other groups were a success for a while, but petered out. Others barely got off the ground. The reasons for these groups not working this time were around managerial time pressures, a lack of facilitation skills, a lack of clarity around their focus within the overall framework and perhaps inadequate sponsorship and visibility.

Perhaps another good idea too soon. Despite these problems, our conviction that action learning was a valuable methodology for us in developing leadership and a learning culture was undiminished. The problems associated with the learning groups were not due to the methodology and could be mitigated with facilitation and strategic positioning. The learning we gained from this experience stood us in good stead when designing the Leadership Development Programme in 2008.

Leadership Ideals

Leadership is guided by HML's leadership ideals, a set of desired leadership behaviours arranged into three areas (Figure 4.6).

1. *Leading self.* Here the focus is on self-awareness, self-development and leadership style.
2. *Leading people.* The focus here is on the leadership of the individual's immediate team.
3. *Leading the business.* A more systemic view; the emphasis here is on leading change, bringing the organisation's vision and strategy to life and working as one team across the business.

These behaviours were developed through semi-structured interviews with 32 of the most senior leaders within the organisation. Stories of great leadership and poor leadership were elicited and the behaviours suggested by them were captured. A view as to the strategic challenges of the organisation and the type of leadership behaviour required for the next three to five years was also sought. The behaviours are assessed as part of the performance management process and are also used in recruitment and selection, for competency-based interviews.

There are different ways in which an organisation can choose to assess leadership performance, and the value placed on leadership as part of overall performance assessment will vary from organisation to organisation. Some, whilst critical of competencies in

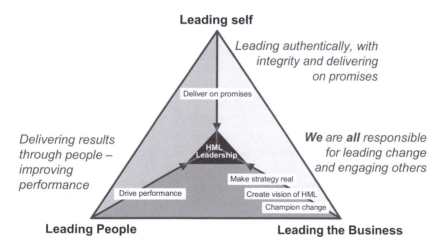

Figure 4.6   Leadership ideals

general, argue a preference for organisation-specific models,[12] although there is a limited shelf life of such models when the business changes[13] – something we have experienced in our rapidly changing organisation where we have made five changes to our competency framework in as many years.

In seeking to assess leadership using these ideals in performance management, we are faced with a number of choices. Do we make demonstrating effective leadership behaviour a prerequisite for meeting expectations? (The 'gateway' or 'hurdle' model.) Do we assess leadership behaviour as a separate entity to objectives? (The 'what and the how' or '50/50' model.) Or do we attempt to measure leadership as a single objective amongst other objectives? ('Integrated model'.) All of these options have advantages and disadvantages and unfortunately leave a lingering feeling of dissatisfaction. Yet despite measurement being troublesome, our belief is that it has to be better to at least try to assess leadership behaviour and performance. What gets measured *does* seem to get done and including an assessment in the process appears to drive the behaviours of observation, feedback and recognition of the impact an individual's leadership style is having on their team and their results – in other words, it benefits leadership development.

Our current approach is to measure leadership behaviours using the 'gateway' model, although in line with our approach to talent identification, we are considering moving towards the '50/50' approach at the time of writing. There is also an employee engagement objective in all senior leaders' performance plans, based around scores in the annual employee opinion survey.

Leadership Development Principles

Key to all of our development programmes a core set of principles, which guide the design of our interventions and act as a way of conveying our underlying philosophy. They are important from a learning and a cultural perspective, with a focus on sustainable self-directed learning. There is a challenge for us as developers here in terms of recognising the importance of informal learning, so the principles stress action-based learning. In our experience, there has been a necessity to facilitate an education process around this in that many people still carry with them traditional pedagogical notions of learning. The principles are:

- Individuals learn at their own pace and in differing ways.
- Individuals focus their development best by owning their learning.
- Individuals learn more quickly through real actions.
- Individuals learn in context to their environment.
- Individuals cannot develop leadership without developing followership.
- Individuals' learning takes them somewhere unique.
- Individuals' learning creates 'thinking performers'.

Setting these principles out explicitly often drives a conversation around what is learning and the individual's role in making it happen. They are informed by theories

---

12   Mumford, A. and Gold, J. (2004) *Management Development Strategies for Action*, 4th edn. London: CIPD.

13   Holbeche L. (1998) *High Flyers and Succession Planning in Changing Organisations*. Horsham: Roffey Park Institute.

of self-directed learning.[14] We present this explicitly to our learners but perhaps more importantly, we adopt it implicitly in much of what we do. Hence, encouraging self-direction and taking responsibility for learning through the setting of goals and plans, and providing an environment for reflection on action through, for example, action learning sets and manager one-to-ones. We also spent a great deal of time on helping leaders understand their 'real selves' through diagnostics and feedback.

The principles are illustrated in our 360-degree feedback process, where the individual will kick-start the process by identifying whom they will get feedback from. The feedback, once completed, will be collated into a report which is fed back face-to-face by an objective internal coach who has not been involved in the process. The individual will then sit down with their line manager and summarise the feedback, gaining support and challenge on their proposed development plan as a result. This way the individual getting feedback takes ownership for the process from start to finish.

We aim to build flexibility into our programmes so that leaders can take their learning in different directions according to their own agendas. There is tension here – the need to work to organisational outcomes as well as individual agendas is a difficult balancing act. It is essential to pursue, however, given the nature of learning and the motivation that needs to be there for it to occur.

Leadership Development Framework

At HML we seek to adopt all three types of learning[15] in our approach to leadership development:

- Type 1 – informal, incidental;
- Type 2 – integrated, opportunistic; and
- Type 3 – formal, planned.

We seek to encourage our managers to see every day as a learning opportunity, where a meeting, project or phone call can be rich in learning given a 'learning mindset' where the individual reflects on or gets feedback on their performance. Informal learning plays a major part in our philosophy, with individuals given the tools to make the most of everyday learning through structured reflection, internal coaching and ongoing development plans.

Increasingly in recent times, we have sought to leverage the value from managers using real planned experiences as a vehicle for their ongoing development. Examples of this are many and include manager one-to-ones, project 'lessons learned' sessions, using a facilitator to review group process as a cross-functional group working on a project together and facilitated off-site team development sessions. Planned activity such as reflecting on a recent one-to-one coaching session with a view to setting a development goal prior to a coaching workshop shows how the informal can meet the formal in an integrated way.

---

14   Goleman, D., Boyatzis, R. and McKee, A. (2006) *The New Leaders*. London: Little, Brown.

15   Mumford, A., Gold J. (2004) *Management Development Strategies For Action*, 4th edn. London: CIPD.

After some years' development, HML now has formal Type 3 learning programmes for virtually all levels of manager – together, these form our Leadership Development Framework. Yet even in planned programmes, we signpost and encourage informal learning, in line with our principles. Our Type 3 programmes are largely run internally, but we have some key strategic external partners who run and co-run some elements. They have been chosen because of their expertise in the field, for example, we use a company for training on lean production tools and techniques. We also have a long-term relationship with Sheppard Moscow who have co-designed and co-facilitate our residential experiential event, due to their strong track record in this area. This brings added credibility and strong design and facilitation skills to the event.

We have sought to provide an integrated framework, where our stakeholders can see the key formal interventions and transitions in the journey of a leader within HML. In even a medium-sized organisation, a progressive approach to leadership development will lead to a high number of interventions, both formal and informal, over time and it is important that development looks and feels consistent and familiar to leaders progressing in their career.

Formal interventions revolve around three levels of leadership development programme according to different needs of leaders within the organisation's structure, combined with talent management which spans the whole population. It is important to note that this framework is continually refined, improved and adapted to business needs, learner and stakeholder feedback. In the last five years our programmes have been reviewed and adapted three times (Figure 4.7).

Table 4.2 outlines the purpose and broad outcomes of programmes and interventions aimed at different levels of manager within HML.

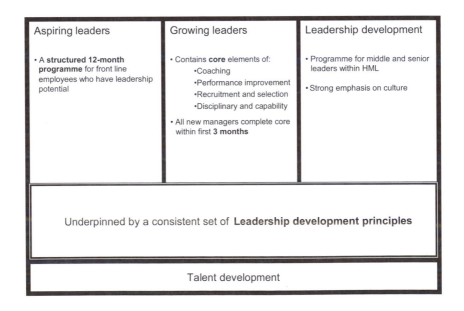

Figure 4.7   Integrated leadership developments

Table 4.2   The purposes and outcomes aimed at different levels of manager within HML

Level	Purpose	Broad outcomes
Aspiring	Supporting fundamental behavioural development needs in those identified as having both potential and aspiration for a people management role	Leadership expectations Intrapersonal and interpersonal skills Performance management Team working Leading self (assertiveness, self-development, self-reflection)
Team leader (first line management)	Familiarisation for new managers. Developing awareness and skills for leadership at HML at team level, focusing on first 12 months	Management development (performance reviews, disciplinary/capability, interviewing skills, legal framework, managing attendance) Intrapersonal and interpersonal skills Coaching and feedback skills Supporting the client Customer focus Continuous improvement Leading change Mortgage knowledge
Middle/senior manager	Develop managers' awareness of broader business and their own leadership brand	Financial awareness Operational excellence (including lean sigma) Commercial awareness and entrepreneurialism Coaching and feedback skills Leading change Leading the business (creating vision) Neurolinguistic programming Employee engagement
Board	Further develop awareness of broader business and their own leadership brand	Strategic thinking External focus Intrapersonal and interpersonal skills Benchmarking leading thinking Coaching skills Leading the business (creating vision) Employee engagement

These outcomes should be cumulative, so a team leader would be expected to have the skills/knowledge/attitude outcomes that result from the Aspiring leader programme. The outcomes are also not intended as a 'sheep dip' list. As stated in the principles, a leader's development journey is unique and these outcomes would look different from one leader to the next.

You will see the significance of intrapersonal and interpersonal skills, featuring as they do in all four levels. This area of 'leading oneself' is key for us, and a number of different approaches are used to help our leaders develop their self-awareness and awareness of their impact on others, including sharing their personal leadership journey, psychometrics such as the Occupational Personality Questionnaire (OPQ), Myers–Briggs Type Indicator (MBTI), Fundamental Interpersonal Relations Orientation – Behaviour (FIRO-B) and Wave, learning styles inventory and providing opportunities for motivational and developmental feedback.

Programme Overviews

The programme overviews for the different levels of leader can be seen in Table 4.3.

Table 4.3   Programme overviews

Level	Programme	Methodologies	Length	Admission
Aspiring	Aspiring leaders	Orientation workshop Learning contract meetings Skills workshops Project-based event, often community activity supported by group coaching	12 months	In line with talent identification. Limited annual intake, selected by business
Team leader	Growing leaders	Familiarisation process – online support and one-to-one with internal coach Directed on-the-job activity and reflection Skills and knowledge blended learning on core areas Online support	12 months Further development under talent development if appropriate	All new team leaders
Team leaders/ managers	Refresher	Online support and workshops on key areas of leadership for those who last completed training 4+ years ago or who have not attended core elements Online support	Stand alone units can be delivered as needed.	All team leaders and managers
Manager/ senior manager	Leadership development programme	Orientation Learning contract Action learning sets Modules in finance, lean, commercial and coaching – led by senior managers and business experts Identification of new product/service as output Transformational residential learning event after 7 months Celebration of success Accreditation All events facilitated but led and dictated by delegates and groups	12 months Further development under talent development if appropriate	All managers at this level

Table 4.3   *Concluded*

Level	Programme	Methodologies	Length	Admission
Board	Bespoke	Methodology and principles same as manager programme, forming a discrete group	Ongoing	All board
Team leader and above	Talent development	Orientation Career goal-setting Business project Mentoring Calendar of events	12 months	All high potentials and rising stars

There is also a three-month familiarisation period for all leaders, regardless of level, where they are able to access orientation learning materials (for example, people processes, client knowledge) at entry point to a role, as well as annual refresher sessions for key organisational needs such as objective-setting, attendance management and performance reviews.

Aspiring Leaders

Aspiring leaders is our development framework for those individuals who are generally employed in entry-level roles, for example customer service advisors, who have career aspirations to move into a people-management role.

In a period of extreme growth and career opportunity, there was a clear organisational need to develop our aspiring leaders in a way that would support them to 'hit the ground running' when they took on their first people-management role. The programme originally offered formal learning around core aspects of a team leader's role such as coaching and performance management. Aspiring leaders would attend modules in these areas alongside existing team leaders, providing insight for them into real experiences in leading a team. They and their line managers would also be encouraged to find ways in which they could gain on-the-job preparation through deputising, running team meetings and shadowing their manager. In effect, aspiring leaders were being given access to the training and learning a new team leader would typically get within their first six months in the role.

Having run for around 18 months, feedback from some stakeholders suggested that there were some issues hindering the success of the programme. A cross-site review was held including key operational stakeholders at all levels of the organisation, including some aspiring leaders. Despite some positive feedback, three main issues emerged.

First, people were being nominated for the aspiring leaders programme who were not suitable for people-management and sometimes not even willing! In some cases, their line manager took an 'easy option' in providing access to a formal programme focused on people-management, rather than conducting an in-depth development discussion with the individual exploring career aspirations and technical and specialist development routes. Secondly, some aspiring leaders were accessing the formal learning with little or no opportunity to the crucial on-the-job informal learning opportunities such as standing in for their team leader in one-to-ones, interviewing and team meetings. Finally, there was some feedback from the learners themselves around the lack of prestige associated with entry onto the programme – at that time line manager nomination was all that was required.

These issues were addressed by tightening up the selection process so that sign-off was made at a senior management team meeting once a year; by conducting three-way-learning, contracting meetings between the individual, their line manager and a development specialist; and by developing a more generic 'springboard' programme for people with both technical and people-management career aspirations.

Aspiring leaders has since gone on to prove a highly successful programme in preparing people for the challenges of their first people-management role. It is now more structured and relevant to needs of individuals and the business. Almost without exception, successful candidates for the team leader role are now people who have participated in the programme.

Growing Leaders

Growing leaders is HML's long-standing team-leader development brand. Although the programme has changed a number of times, its core components have remained in place: specifically, learning modules in performance management, recruitment and selection, discipline and capability and coaching.

With any core programme such as this, ongoing feedback from a wide range of stakeholders and sources can be very helpful in ensuring relevance to business needs. The content of Growing leaders is currently being revised again to align it with the Leadership development programme, business strategy and feedback sought by both HR business partners and through focus groups of team leaders. The design progress will be communicated via an online 'Growing leaders live' intranet page in order to gather further collaborative ongoing feedback. Feedback received in a cross-functional 'workout' session on recruitment and selection also led to the introduction of annual 'refresher' sessions – we have found this kind of opportunistic approach to gathering feedback in addition to more structured approaches works well for us.

The revised programme will include 13 modules geared towards supporting a new team leader in their role, including feedback, managing relationships, leading change, coaching, team dynamics, commercial awareness, leadership brand and influence and persuasion. Some of the anticipated changes will be in the methodologies adopted, with each module comprising on-the-job activities (for example, a coaching session), an online or workshop element and action planning, supported by action learning. Working on the basis that the first 90 days within a leadership role are essential, a familiarisation module is being developed to guide all new leaders through this period, with an emphasis on performance management and the four elements of our balanced scorecard.

Leadership Development Programme

This is a new programme designed to address the organisational and individual learning needs of HML's middle and senior management population. Built around both 'hard' and 'soft' elements – HML's leadership ideals and its strategy around our balanced scorecard elements of effectiveness, client, profit and engagement, it is a key strategic programme with a high level of executive sponsorship and a roll-out period of around two years.

Figure 4.8 identifies the drivers and enablers of the programme, including a mix of internal and external factors.

Strategic drivers are identified through discussion with board members and in strategic plans. Other drivers reflect the need to look outside the organisation at the external environment, including feedback from clients, good practice in other organisations, and the use of external consultants.

Our leadership ideals represent what we need our leaders to pay attention to. The employee opinion survey provides a rich source of information for identifying global leadership development needs. The climate a leader creates has a direct correlation to the results and employee engagement. Equally, Investors in People remains a useful diagnostic tool for identifying strengths and weaknesses in our current approach to leadership and for us it has highlighted inconsistencies in certain areas in relation to the application of people management policies and practices.

Leadership learning groups were action learning sets set up to support managers during a period of change and internal reorganisation. Their introduction proved to be of value to many managers and ultimately led to this methodology becoming a core part of the Leadership development programme.

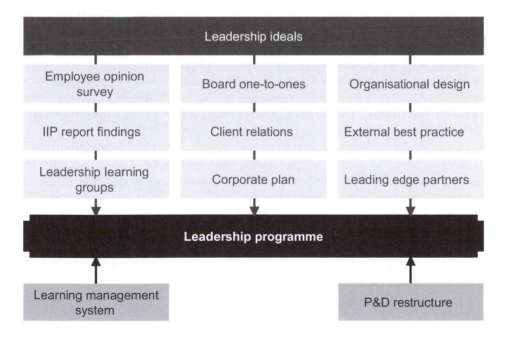

Figure 4.8   Drivers and enablers

Enablers for the programme include the introduction of an online learning management system to enable a more blended approach and the restructure of the people and development department, creating an organisational development function with the remit of driving forward strategic people change programmes.

Figure 4.9 shows some key strategic drivers from the corporate plan, together with how they have been translated into leadership development priorities.

The overall aims of the Leadership Development Programme are:

- Develop leadership capability.
- Develop agility, engagement, productivity and client/customer focus.
- Create leaders who can teach, coach and learn.
- Drive culture change.
- Develop individuals' self-awareness and adaptability of own leadership style.

In order to drive culture change, our new organisational values are woven into the fabric of the programme. Hence, contracting within action learning sets is against the four values and the whole of the three-day residential event, designed in partnership with an external provider, is structured around conversations and storytelling in relation to culture and values.

Key to this programme is our principle that a leader's journey will take them somewhere unique. We are striving to achieve the difficult balancing act of providing a framework where many different paths can be taken according to the learner's needs, aspirations and motivation, whilst focusing on developing people in key strategic organisational needs. Developing self-awareness is integral to the programme and leaders are encouraged to reflect on and share their 'leadership brand' – the style, experiences, values and beliefs they bring to their role as leader, with a view to adopting an authentic approach to leading their people.

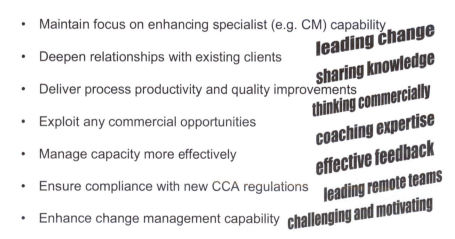

Figure 4.9   Strategic drivers and implications for leadership development

It is too early to evaluate the success of this programme, although evaluation has been built into the design of every stage of the 12-month journey, including the identification of tangible business revenue and cost savings in all action plans, 360-degree feedback, portfolios of learning and application, the delivery of commercial ideas and regular management information assessing progress against learning outcomes. As part of the accreditation of the programme, participants are expected to take part in a group exercise designed to review the programme itself with a view to continually improving the content, methodology and facilitation. The structure of the programme is detailed in Figure 4.10.

The intention is to gradually decrease the level of support and dependency on the facilitators over the length of the programme, aiming to create self-directed learners who will continue with their ongoing development beyond the programme timetable. Hence, topic-led learning around profit, client, effectiveness and engagement are at the front end of the programme and replaced by self-directed modules towards the end.

We see one of the most important aspects of the programme being the way that it is run for the business by the business. Facilitators from people and development hold the framework together with action learning, coaching and facilitation, but the programme is opened by the managing director, the profit module is delivered by the heads of financial accounts and procurement and the client module is facilitated by the commercial director and the business development director. The idea of 'leaders as teachers and coaches' is at the forefront of our thinking.

The programme combines many different blended methodologies, and seeks to enable individuals to deliver their current and future business objectives as well as the overall business strategy. The use of monthly action learning sets which link the different elements together is key, with task planning and task review discussions to draw out learning from on-the-job activity.

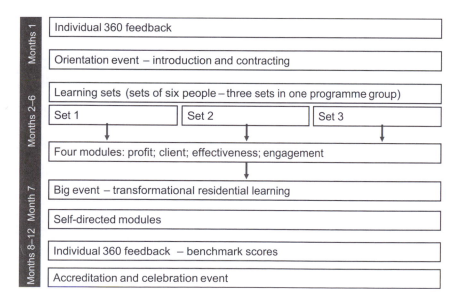

Figure 4.10 Leader development programme

Coaching plays a key role in the programme and learners are expected to develop their coaching practice throughout. A coaching module places an emphasis on practice and coaching supervision is provided through the action learning sets. Facilitators also hold supervision meetings amongst themselves. The organisation is gradually developing a small number of professionally qualified coaches who can provide expert internal coaching and with senior level external coaching in the mix there are signs that a coaching culture is beginning to emerge.

Talent Management

For HML, talent management spans all hierarchical levels of the organisation and all levels of ability, and is inextricably linked with leadership development. Where leadership development focuses on strategic organisational needs, role transitions and the whole management population, talent development focuses additional development on those people assessed as having potential to take on roles of greater responsibility and complexity.

One of the first things we did to introduce talent management was research good practice, including reading, attendance at conferences, networking and visits to other businesses. We found many organisations doing the same and it continues to be an area where people in different organisations are eager to learn from each other and share ideas – an interesting trend given the much-quoted perception of a 'war for talent'.

HML introduced its talent management process in 2005. Its introduction in the first year took the form of a strategic business project managed using PRINCE2 project management methodology. Like leadership development, this is a journey not a destination and at times the project environment posed some challenges for us. Unlike projects, there was not a beginning, middle and end and the benefits of talent management are by their nature long term, so inevitably it was difficult to identify short-term benefits. Nevertheless, there were benefits from adopting a project management approach at first – deliverables were clearly defined, the scope was set and agreed at a senior level, visibility and sponsorship were high from the start and the tracking of costs was clear.

Our approach combines the full cycle of talent attraction, identification, development, retention, risk mitigation and succession planning. As this chapter relates primarily to leadership development, there follows an overview of our current 'talent journey' – a development programme for high potentials which combines offline coaching, business projects, mentoring and masterclasses aligned to our leadership development principles to develop leaders of the future (Figure 4.11).

Our journey with talent has had some successes and some learning along the way and we have been open with key stakeholders in expecting this, including sharing mistakes when they have been made – a necessity in an area where there needs to be commitment for the long haul.

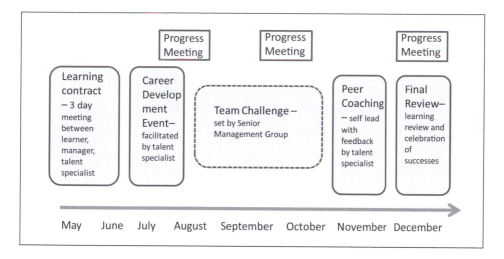

Figure 4.11 The HML potential development journey

Conclusion

Learning needs to stay ahead of the pace of change for it to be a key strategic lever for the organisation, and this chapter has sought to convey how HML have developed learning for leaders in a period of dramatic, fast-paced change. The need for agility in leadership development is as pronounced as it is for organisations in general and applies equally whether the organisation is growing, contracting or consolidating. The ever-changing external environment will always drive a need to adapt in order to prosper and leaders and leadership are at the forefront of this challenge.

We have chosen to embrace the relationship between strategy, culture, leadership, structure and the environment in our approach. Our specific interventions will not necessarily work for all organisations, but holding a systemic view of the organisation should do. The real value in adopting this mindset lies in the questions it prompts the leadership development practitioner to ask of the organisation.

Our leadership development strategy, guided by leadership behaviours and development principles, seeks to combine formal and informal learning to raise leadership capability. It aims to develop individual and organisational leadership within the context of our mission, strategy and culture. Our intention is to continuously improve programmes, encourage a learning culture and adopt flexible frameworks.

The journey continues…

5

Developing the Board Through Corporate Governance Reform and Board Evaluation

TERRY MCNULTY

Introduction

Corporate governance is about the direction and control of corporations. A substantial research literature has developed over the last two decades, along with considerable regulatory activity directed at developing mechanisms of corporate governance including more effective boards of directors. This chapter is about the effectiveness of boards.[1] Using theory and empirical research it seeks to further conceptualize board effectiveness in order to identify issues that are important to the practice of board evaluation and development. This interest is set against a context of corporate governance reform which is pursing processes of board review and evaluation as a principle of good corporate governance.[2] This is an important development, not least because processes of organizational and managerial review and development are often thought to stop before they reach the executive echelons and doors of the boardroom. If this is true there are signs that the situation will not persist, as one of the principles of the *UK combined code of corporate governance* is that boards of companies listed on the UK Stock Exchange should undertake and report an annual evaluation of board performance.

The main purpose of this chapter lies with the practical challenge of board review and evaluation. In particular it is interested in considering further issues that may be central to the substantive content of a board evaluation. Working from theoretical debate and empirical research about board effectiveness, the chapter offers a model to guide the focus of a board evaluation. Underlying the model is the argument that research, debate and regulation tends to focus on issues of board structure and composition, particularly non-executive independence, as proxies for improving board effectiveness. However, the

---

1   It is claimed that board effectiveness is 'among the most important areas of management research'. Forbes, D. P. and Milliken. F. J. (1999) Cognition and corporate governance: understanding boards of directors as strategic decision-making groups, *Academy of Management Review,* 24: 489–505.

2   See the *UK Combined Code on Corporate Governance* issued by the Financial Reporting Council (2006).

practical development of boards as effective entities for corporate direction and control requires more attention to board processes and outcomes. By drawing on empirical research on boards and directors, a theoretical model of board effectiveness[3] is adapted to extend beyond matters of board structure and composition to identify key issues of board task performance and process that should be addressed in any evaluation of board effectiveness.

Following this introduction the remainder of the chapter is organized as follows. The first part of the chapter introduces the concept of corporate governance. The next section discusses developments in research and our understanding of board effectiveness. A theoretical model of board effectiveness is explained along with complementary empirical evidence from research about boards and directors. Following a discussion of corporate governance reform, the second half of the chapter turns to developing a conceptual framework to guide board evaluation. The framework emphasizes issues to do with board outcomes and processes. Specifically, it is argued that to develop board effectiveness it is important that board evaluation addresses the performance of tasks associated with the service, control and resourcing roles of the board. However, task performance will be shaped and mediated by the internal working of boards, hence, board evaluation must also focus on the following aspects of board process: strategic decision processes; the board agenda; the conduct of the board meeting; special board events; relations and dialogue outside of the board meeting; chair and chief executive relationship.

Boards of Directors as a Mechanism of Corporate Governance: the Research Literature

Agency theory continues to have a profound influence on corporate governance research, reform and practice. Agency theory assumes that corporations can be governed through two broad sets of controls: an external mechanism, the market for corporate control, and internal mechanisms, primary among them the board of directors. Agency theory as applied to boards regards decision-making responsibility as delegated by shareholders to executives within an organization but potential agency costs are then reduced by boards of directors exercising decision control, which involves monitoring executives through independent non-executive directors or outside directors, as they are variously called in the UK and US respectively.

Corporate governance reform directed at boards and incumbent, independent non-executive directors chimes with the assumptions of agency theory in that board effectiveness is assumed to be a function of board independence from management and the 'control' role of the independent non-executive director is emphasized. This is explained as a reaction to recent governance failures and scandals whereby non-executive directors have been the target of both blame and reform. By way of blame non-executives on boards are thought to have contributed to governance problems through behaviour that suggested passivity, capture or collusion on their part. By way of a solution to such problems of board involvement, distance and independence from executives, changes to the *UK Combined Code on Corporate Governance* have pursued a separation of the

---

3   See Forbes, D.P. and Milliken, F. J. (1999) Cognition and corporate governance: understanding boards of directors as strategic decision-making groups, *Academy of Management Review*, 24: 489–505.

roles of chairman and chief executive, a progressive increase in the prescribed number of 'independent' non-executives on boards, and an insistence that independent non-executive directors should dominate sub-committees of the board for audit, remuneration and audit to reduce conflict of interest.[4] Undoubtedly some recent governance scandals such as that experience by the ENRON corporation bear out the assumptions and fears of agency costs associated with agency theory. However, doubts exist as to the efficacy of agency theory and its associated prescriptions. Reviews of the literature[5] show few findings to link structural characteristics of boards (some of which are used as proxies for board independence), to board outcomes and firm performance. The implication is that there is more to the relationship, by way of intervening 'variables' or processes (as will be discussed below) between the board and firm-level outcomes. Others challenge a monitoring and oversight approach to governance from a shareholder-value perspective.[6] Alternative theories for developing our understanding of boards as mechanisms of corporate governance and performance are being advanced, notably stewardship theory[7] and resource dependency theory.[8] Calls have been made for methodologies that involve studying the operation of the board itself, the lived experience of directors and the potential effects on board performance of the quality and dynamic of board relationships.[9] This chapter proceeds to discuss writing and research which supports this call.

Researching and Understanding Board Effectiveness

Specifically, this chapter engages with the challenge of better understanding the 'inner workings of boards'.[10] Problems of access to boards and directors are well recognized, but some research studies do shed light on the metaphorical 'black box' of the boardroom by examining perceptions of roles and tasks and analysing dynamics of board power and influence.[11]

In contrast to the agency model of the board as a control mechanism, studies suggest that boards can have a broader, more inclusive role, with non-executive directors

---

4   See the *UK Combined Code on Corporate Governance* issued by the Financial Reporting Council (2006).

5   Hermalin, B. E. and Weisbach, M. S. (2003) Boards of directors as an endogenously determined institution: a survey of the economic literature, *Economic Policy Review – Federal Reserve Bank of New York*, 9(1): 7–26.

6   Daily, C., Dalton, D. R. and Cannella, A. A. Jr (2003) Corporate governance: decades of dialogue and data, *Academy of Management Review*, 28(3): 371–383.

7   See Davis, J. H., Schoorman, F. D. and Donaldson, L. (1997) Towards a stewardship theory of management, *Academy of Management Review*, 22: 20–47.

8   See Pfeffer, J. (1972) Size and composition of corporate boards of directors: the organization and its environment, *Administrative Science Quarterly*, 17: 218–228. Also Pfeffer, J. and Salancik, G. (1978) *The External Control of Organisations: A Resource-Dependence Perspective*, New York: Harper and Row.

9   See Pettigrew, A. M. (1992) On studying managerial elites, *Strategic Management Journal*, 13: 163–182.

10   A focus emphasized as important by both Pettigrew (1992) op. cit. and Hermalin, B. E. and Weisbach, M. S. (2003) Boards of directors as an endogenously determined institution: a survey of the economic literature, *Economic Policy Review – Federal Reserve Bank of New York*, 9(1): 7–26.

11   See studies by Mace, M. L. (1971) *Directors: Myth and reality*, Boston, MA: Harvard University Graduate School of Business Administration; Lorsch, J. W. and MacIver, E. (1989) *Pawns or Potentates: The Reality of Americas' Corporate Boards*, Boston, MA: Harvard University Graduate School of Business Administration; Pettigrew, A. M. and McNulty, T. (1995) Power and influence in and around the boardroom, *Human Relations*, 48: 845–873.

involved in giving advice and enhancing strategy discussions.[12] A study of UK boards found non-executives to be involved in reviewing and refining the strategic decisions of their organizations, and concluded that evidence for the divergence between the interests of shareholders and managers was scant, with managers wanting to be seen as good professionals running the company.[13] Research presents an understanding of 'corporate directing' as activity that involves strategizing, governing and leading. These studies also show that even in the absence of overt interventions, the expectation of non-executive scrutiny has an important disciplinary effect on executives, raising the standard of proposals that come before the board.[14] The development of closer social ties between the CEO and the board has also been argued to provide strong benefits, including the enhancement of mutual trust, allowing space for advice-seeking on the part of the executives, a reduction in defensive and political behaviour within the board, and the opportunity for enhanced learning.[15]

Research has distinguished between minimalist and maximalist boards.[16] Minimalist board cultures are those in which a set of conditions severely limit the involvement and influence of the board and its incumbent non-executive directors on the affairs of the firm. By contrast, a maximalist culture is one where the board and non-executives actively contribute to dialogue within the board and build their organizational awareness and influence through contacts with executive directors, managers and other non-executives beyond the boardroom. Differences, it is argued, stem from a range of factors, including board size and composition, the attitudes of a powerful chairman or chief executive, the nature of the board process, and the will and skill of the non-executive directors to exert influence. Subsequently, a development of the study[17] identifies three levels of board involvement in respect of strategy, described as taking strategic decisions', 'shaping strategic decisions' and 'shaping the content, context and conduct of strategy'. In a similar vein,[18] other studies have highlighted how non-executives' review of strategic initiatives is a central feature of their contribution and that their presence in the minds of the executive helped to 'raise the bar' in terms of the quality of strategic proposals and the effectiveness of decision making. Also the relationship between chairmen and chief executives has been characterized into two broad types – competitive and complementary – each, of course, with very different consequences for board effectiveness.[19]

These studies of boards and directors suggest that the work and functioning of boards are empirically variable, and that the involvement and influence of boards within the host firm will be mediated not only by external conditions and the structural features of

---

12   Lorsch, J. W. and E. MacIver (1989). *Pawns or Potentates: The Reality of Americas's Corporate Boards*, Boston, MA: Harvard University Graduate School of Business Administration; Demb, A. and Neubauer, F. F. (1992) *The Corporate Board*, New York: Oxford University Press.

13   Hill, S. (1995) The social organisation of boards of directors, *British Journal of Sociology*, 46: 245–278.

14   McNulty, T. and Pettigrew, A. M. (1999) Strategists on the board, *Organization Studies*, 20: 47–74.

15   Westphal, J. D. (1998) Board games: how CEOs adapt to increases in structural board independence from management, *Administrative Science Quarterly*, 43(3): 511–537.

16   Pettigrew, A. M. and McNulty, T. (1995) Power and influence in and around the boardroom, *Human Relations*, 48: 845–873.

17   McNulty, T. and Pettigrew, A. M. (1999) Strategists on the board, *Organization Studies*, 20: 47–74.

18   Stiles, P. (2001) The impact of boards on strategy: an empirical examination, *Journal of Management Studies*, 38(5): 27–50.

19   Roberts, J and Stiles, P. (1999) The relationship between chairmen and chief executives: competitive or complementary roles?, *Long Range Planning*, 32(1): 36–48.

boards, but also by board processes and the motivation and skill of individual directors acting as members of a functioning group.[20] Contrary to agency theory assumptions, this work also suggests that non-executives place a high premium on the closeness and openness of their relationships with executives.

A Model of Board Effectiveness

Complementing such empirical research about board and director behaviour are attempts to theoretically model board dynamics. One particularly useful model is described below.[21] In the model, boards are viewed as strategic decision-making groups. Drawing on existing knowledge of group dynamics per se it is possible to analyse what boards need to do to discharge their tasks and responsibilities more effectively. Developmentally the implication is that we need to look beyond matters of group composition to highlight the importance of board processes to board outcomes. In short, the argument is that the effectiveness of boards depends on social–psychological processes, related to group participation and interaction, the exchange of information and critical discussion. Key elements of the model are rehearsed below as a necessary conceptual precursor to discussion later in the chapter about the practical developmental challenge of board evaluation. The definition of an effective group guiding the model is of a group that achieves task performance and sustains cohesiveness.

Task performance and cohesiveness are two group 'outcome' constructs identified in the model to help us conceptualize and reach judgements of group effectiveness. Applied to boards, the implication is that boards perform tasks related to 'service', 'control' and 'resourcing' roles. The board's control task refers to its legal duty to monitor management on behalf of the firm's shareholders and to carry out this duty with sufficient loyalty and care. Decisions relating to hiring, compensation and replacement of the firm's most senior managers and approval of major initiatives proposed by management relate to the 'control' role of the board. The board's 'service' task refers to its potential to provide advice and counsel to the CEO and other top managers and to participate actively in the formulation of strategy. It is evidenced by analysing activities that involve the board and incumbent directors imparting their expertise and insight during major corporate decisions, events and processes such as acquisitions and restructuring.

Board cohesiveness draws attention to the affective dimension of board membership and reflects the ability of the board to sustain positive group working over time. At issue here are matters to do with member attraction to the board, satisfaction or dissatisfaction with the board, levels of commitment to the board; motivation to remain as a member of the board, and thoughts and actions re resignation and re-election. The relationship between board task performance and cohesiveness is theorized as curvilinear. Task performance by boards requires 'extensive communication and deliberation' raising the need for positive interpersonal relations, engagement and trust between board members. Curvilinearity, however, recognizes that within decision-making entities such

---

20   Pettigrew, A. M. and McNulty, T. (1998) Sources and uses of power in and around the boardroom, *European Journal of Work and Organisational Psychology*, 7 (2): 197–214.

21   Forbes, D. P. and Milliken, F. J. (1999) Cognition and corporate governance: understanding boards of directors as strategic decision-making groups, *Academy of Management Review*, 24: 489–505.

as boards, high level(s) of cohesiveness can be dysfunctional and result in a reduction in independent critical thinking and an absence of cognitive conflict (discussed below). Using the Janus' concept of 'group-think', it is argued that that the most effective boards will be characterized by high levels of interpersonal attraction (cohesiveness) and task oriented disagreement (cognitive conflict). Cognitive conflict can help to prevent the emergence of group think in cohesive groups by fostering an environment characterized by a task-oriented focus yet tolerance of multiple viewpoints and opinions. The point is powerful as it is apparent how processes of cognitive conflict may be an antidote to the passivity, capture and collusion on boards discussed earlier.

Here a connection is made between board processes and board outcomes. The corporate board is viewed as a particular form of group that is highly susceptible to 'process-losses'. Boards are characterized as having a size that may be relatively large and a membership that may involve elite individuals, working on a part-time basis, with a primary responsibility and affiliation 'outside' the corporation. Furthermore, boards are recognized to engage in episodic decision-making involving the processing complex strategic issues, wherein they are expected to monitor and influence – but not implement strategy. Hence the 'output' of the board is said to be entirely cognitive in nature. These characteristics make boards prone to 'process losses', defined as interaction difficulties that prevent groups from achieving full potential. Consequently, for effectiveness, boards are heavily dependent on social-psychological processes, particularly those pertaining to group participation and interaction, the exchange of information, and critical discussion. To accompany the 'outcome' constructs of task performance and cohesiveness, the model contains the three 'process' constructs of 'efforts norms', 'cognitive conflict' and the board's 'use of knowledge and skills'.

Effort norms is a group level construct that refers to a group's shared beliefs regarding the level of effort each individual is expected to put to a task. It relates to individual's motivation and task-performance behaviour. In practice, effort norms may be revealed by the time that the board devotes to tasks as well as matters of attendance, attentiveness, engagement, participation, analysis and scrutiny. Cognitive conflict refers to task-oriented differences in judgement among group members – for instance, differences of views and opinions in relation to the group task. Cognitive conflict is concerned with the presence of issue-related disagreement among members and is likely to arise in groups, like boards, that are interdependent and face complex decision-making tasks. The issue for board effectiveness is leveraging differences of perspective for positive purposes and avoiding conflict becoming negative and dysfunctional.

From a positive perspective, cognitive conflict involves the use of 'critical and investigative interaction processes' that can enhance the board's performance of its control role. It can serve to remind management of the power and role of the board and the importance of shareholder interests in the formulation of strategy within and beyond the boardroom. On a negative note, cognitive conflict can arouse negative emotions that diminish interpersonal attraction amongst members, lowering satisfaction with the group and desire to remain with the group. People, including those on the board, can react to high levels of cognitive conflict by reducing their commitment.

The use of knowledge and skills refers to the board's ability to tap knowledge and skills available to it and then apply them to its tasks. Boards require a high degree of specialized knowledge and skill to function effectively, both in terms of functional knowledge as well as firm-specific knowledge and skills. As a construct in the model, 'use of knowledge and skills' is the behavioural dimension of social integration, which refers to a group's ability to cooperate, build upon each other's contributions, learn and develop creative and synergistic endeavour.

Empirical research about board effectiveness lends support to the model and in particular the focus on interpersonal processes. Recent research amongst UK directors[22] concluded that actual board effectiveness does depend upon the behavioural dynamics of a board, and how the web of interpersonal and group relationships between executive and non-executives is developed in a particular company context. In the context of the UK unitary board (a scenario where non-executives and executives are members of a single board) an effective non-executive both support executives in their leadership of the business and monitor and control their conduct. Both aspects of the role can only be achieved through strong and rigorous processes of accountability within the board which is in turn achieved through a wide range of non-executive behaviours – challenging, questioning, probing, discussing, testing, informing, debating and exploring – that draw upon non-executive knowledge and experience in support of executive performance. Through such conduct, non-executives are constantly seeking to establish and maintain their own confidence in the conduct of the company: that is the performance and behaviour of the executive in respect of, for example, the development of strategy; the adequacy of financial reporting and risk assessment; the appropriateness of remuneration and the appointment and replacement of key personnel.

This finding is an outcome of research commissioned[23] for a review of corporate governance which informed in a revised code of corporate governance.[24] From a developmental perspective one of the most interesting aspects of the review and subsequent revisions to the *UK Combined Code on Corporate Governance* is the attention to relationships on the boards. Furthermore, one particular recommendation – that boards of directors undertake annual appraisal – is now a principle of good corporate governance. With reference to theoretical developments and empirical research discussed above, the remainder of the paper discusses this 'principle of UK corporate governance' and the practical challenges of board evaluation and development.

Developing Board Effectiveness through Corporate Governance Reform and Board Evaluation

Corporate governance reform is part of the contemporary context of publicly listed corporations and boards of directors. The Cadbury Report[25] in particular focused attention on boards of directors as institutions of corporate control and leadership. In essence, Cadbury probed deeply the structure and systems of corporate governance in UK firms as exercised by boards of directors. Subsequently, further developments such as

---

22   Roberts, J., McNulty, T. and Stiles, P. (2005) Beyond agency conceptions of the work of the non-executive director: creating accountability in the boardroom, *British Journal of Management*, 16(special issue): S5–S26.

23   Higgs, D. (2003) *Review of the Role and Effectiveness of Non-Executive Directors*, London: Department of Trade and Industry, HMSO.

24   Financial Reporting Council (2006) UK *Combined Code on Corporate Governance*, London: Financial Reporting Council.

25   Cadbury, A. (1992) *The Financial Aspects of Corporate Governance, Report of the Committee on the Financial Aspects of Corporate Governance*, London: Gee and Co.

the Hampel Report[26] contributed to the creation of the UK Combined Code on Corporate Governance. The most recent development of the Code resulted from the Higgs Review, an independent review of the role and effectiveness of non-executives led by Derek Higgs, at the behest of the UK government[27]. While other countries, such as the USA responded to recent governance scandals and shocks by introducing legislation[28] and new listing rules – the UK's response was to conduct a review to explore what, if anything, could be done to strengthen to the Combined Code on Corporate Governance in relation to the role and effectiveness of non-executive directors.

The Higgs Review reveals a process-oriented view of board effectiveness and an innovative focus on developing board relationships and behaviours[29]. Revisions to the UK Code on Corporate Governance have sought to maximize the potential for the development of positive dynamics on boards as evidenced by: provisions to do with evaluating the balance of skills, knowledge and experience on the board, in advance of making new appointments; encouraging clarity about the nature of likely time commitments; and recommendations about induction and professional development directed at ensuring that non-executives are and remain sufficiently knowledgeable about the company on whose board they serve. A symbol of the development ethos reaching the higher echelons and the realm of the boardroom is the principle of board evaluation now embodied in the UK Combined Code on Corporate Governance as follows:

The Board should undertake a formal a rigorous annual evaluation of its own performance and that of its committees and individual directors.

Furthermore, the board should state in the annual report how performance evaluation of the board, its committees and its individual directors has been conducted. The non-executive directors, led by the senior independent director, should be responsible for performance of the chairman, taking into account views of executive directors.[30]

Attention to the practical challenge of board evaluation and appraisal is growing as evidenced by recent literature about the pressures and reasons for board evaluations in the contemporary corporate context,[31] the politics of board evaluation and appraisal,[32] and suggested frameworks for evaluating boards of directors.[33]

For the purpose of developing the practice of board evaluation noteworthy points made in this literature are those which suggest that board evaluations can help prevent

---

26   Hampel, R. (1998) *Committee on Corporate Governance: Final Report*, London: Gee and Co.

27   Higgs, D. (2003) *Review of the Role and Effectiveness of Non-Executive Directors*, London: Department of Trade and Industry, HMSO.

28   Sarbanes–Oxley Act (2002) US Congress website, at H.R.3763.ENR.

29   Roberts, J., McNulty, T. and Stiles, P. (2005) Beyond agency conceptions of the work of the non-executive director: creating accountability in the boardroom, *British Journal of Management*, 16(special issue): S5–S26.

30   Financial Reporting Council (2006) UK *Combined Code on Corporate Governance*, p. 10, London: Financial Reporting Council.

31   Minchelli, A., Gabrielsson, J. and Huse, M. (2007) Board evaluations: making a fit between the purpose and the system, *Corporate Governance: an International Review*, 15(4): 609–622.

32   Ingley, C. and Van der Walt, N. (2002) Board dynamics and the politics of appraisal, *Corporate Governance: An International Review*, 10(3): 163–174.

33   Kiel, G. C. and Nicholson, G. J. (2005) Evaluating boards and directors, *Corporate Governance: An International Review*, 13(5): 613–631.

governance failures of which there can be four types: strategic failure; control failure; ethical failure and interpersonal relationship failure.[34] Also that, pragmatically, board evaluation processes must recognize the unique 'board architectures' and 'environmental factors' such as company life-cycle, corporate structures, board cultures and embedded processes.[35] Finally the approach to board evaluation must suit the circumstances of the board and organization. In this respect four systems of board evaluation are proposed using a distinction between board evaluation systems that, on one axis, are either internally or externally focused and, on the other axis, are conducted either by internal or external parties to the board.[36] Judged against this advice it seems that the principle of evaluation in the UK Combined Code resonates with 'board to board' and 'board to market' evaluations systems. In other words, UK corporate boards are being asked to undertake (self) evaluation of internal board processes and performance, albeit with the aim of raising and sustaining confidence of external constituents, notably investors, in the board as a transparent and effective mechanism of corporate control and performance.

Notwithstanding these important points made in the literature about ensuring the process of board evaluation is sensitive to particular circumstances and contingencies of the board and host company, it is difficult to move away from the view that the core of the developmental challenge for any corporation undertaking board evaluation is to examine the quality of the board as a collective body or functioning team. This requires attention to relational and behavioural dynamics in and around the boardroom. For these reasons, the theoretical model described earlier[37] and published empirical research amongst UK boards and directors can guide the focus of board evaluation. To develop this point, Figure 5.1 offers a model of board effectiveness as an indicative guide to develop and conduct a board evaluation that engages with key board processes and outcomes.

Utilizing, yet adapting, the earlier model,[38] Figure 5.1 has three elements: board characteristics, board process and board outcomes. The main focus of attention in academic literature and even policy debate is on board characteristics, for example, the UK Combined Code offers a lot of prescription about the structure and composition of boards. For these reasons the emphasis here is on board outcomes and processes.

Evaluating Board Outcomes

As observed above, different intellectual traditions and research on boards have produced a three-role categorization to capture the most significant duties and functions of boards

34   Kiel, G. C. and Nicholson, G. J. (2005) Evaluating boards and directors, *Corporate Governance: An International Review,* 13(5): 613–631.

35   Long, T. (2006) This year's model: influences on board and director evaluation, *Corporate Governance: An International Review,* 14(6): 547–557.

36   Minchelli, A., Gabrielsson, J. and Huse, M. (2007) Board evaluations: making a fit between the purpose and the system, *Corporate Governance: An International Review,* 15(4): 609–622.

37   Forbes, D. P. and Milliken, F. J. (1999) Cognition and corporate governance: understanding boards of directors as strategic decision-making groups, *Academy of Management Review,* 24: 489–505.

38   Forbes, D. P. and Milliken, F. J. (1999) Cognition and corporate governance: understanding boards of directors as strategic decision-making groups, *Academy of Management Review,* 24: 489–505.

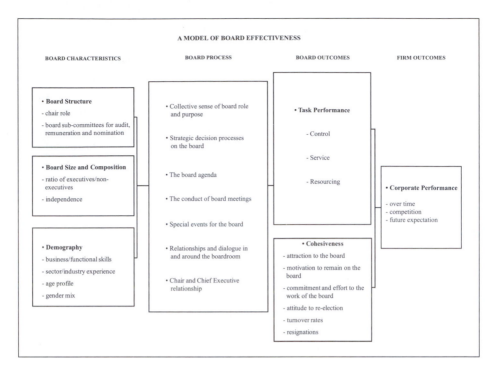

Figure 5.1   A model of board effectiveness

and directors. The roles are labelled as 'service', 'control' and 'resource-dependence'.[39] The control role flows from agency theory and related conceptions of the role of the board as monitor of the executive. The service role involves advising the CEO and top managers on administrative and other managerial issues as well as more actively initiating and formulating strategy. The resource dependence role refers to boards' ability to provide resources – financial, material and symbolic – that are critical to firms, drawing on relationships and networks established with the firm's external environment. However, for the practice of evaluation it is necessary to go beyond a conceptual and abstract view of roles to identify and probe how boards act with respect to particular tasks, decisions and issues that they face as a collectives. To this end, Table 5.1[40] identifies tasks associated with the three-way categorization of service, control and resourcing roles of the board. The tasks were initially identified by research based on interviews with directors.[41] The tasks and issues listed in Table 5.1 are meant to be indicative, not exhaustive, of many of the key tasks and issues addressed at board level. More tasks were identified that relate to the strategy role of the board as compared to the control and resource dependence role. For the practice of board review the list could serve to guide reflection, analysis and development of board task performance across a range of board- and company-related

39   Johnson, J. L., Daily, C. M. and Ellstrand, A. E. (1996) Boards of directors: a review and research agenda, *Journal of Management*, 22: 409–438.

40   McNulty, T., Pettigrew, A., Morris, C. and Jobome, G. (2008) The Role, Power and Influence of Chairmen on the Boards of UK listed Companies. Working paper.

41   McNulty, T. and Pettigrew, A. M. (1996) The contribution, power and influence of part-time board members, *Corporate Governance: An International Review*, 4(2): 160–179.

matters that may impact on overall firm performance. In this way the evaluation can develop a multi-dimensional review of outcomes of the board.

Table 5.1   Roles and tasks of the board

Service (strategy)	Control (monitoring)	Resource dependence (relationships)
Structure of the company's business activities	Remuneration of full-time executive board members	Relations with institutional shareholders
Response to a takeover bid	Replacement of executive board members (other than the CEO)	Relations with government
Management succession planning within the company	Appointment of executives to the main board	Relations with non-institutional shareholders
How the company develops strategy	Policy-making in board subcommittees, e.g. audit, remuneration and nomination	Relations with industry regulator
Entry into new markets	Selection of non-executive directors	Annual general meeting of shareholders
Decisions about joint ventures	Replacement of the chief executive	Social responsibility issues within the company
Decisions about merging businesses	Creation of board subcommittees, e.g. audit, remuneration and nomination	
Management culture within the company	The process and conduct of the board meeting	
Exit from markets	Appointment of the chief executive	
Marketing behaviour of the company		
Decisions about disposing of business operations		
Use of information technology		
Management structure within the company		
Decisions about acquiring other companies		
Issues of dividends		
Raising finance		
Ethical conduct of the company		
Appointment of senior executives to the company		
Financial planning and control in the company		

Cohesiveness is another key outcome variable and can be developed using a range of subjective and objective indicators. Subjective perceptions of board member satisfaction, desire to stay as a member of the board and attitude to re-election may be sought. Objectively, data about board members turnover, directors not choosing to stand for re-election, resignations from the board could also be used to shed light on cohesiveness.

It was observed earlier how a key argument is that how board 'outcomes' will be impacted upon by board processes. In other words, the effectiveness of the board as a working group is dependent on avoiding 'process losses' or interaction difficulties that prevent boards from achieving full potential. The model presented earlier pointed to three process constructs: effort norms, cognitive conflict and the use of knowledge and skills as important. Drawing on research findings the suggestion here is that for a board evaluation it is desirable to develop these processes via attention to processes that board members experience and may be able to articulate, for instance: strategic decision processes; the board agenda; the conduct of the board meeting; special board events; relations and dialogue outside of the board meeting; chair and chief executive relationship. Each of these points is discussed below.

Developing Board Processes

DEVELOPING STRATEGIC DECISION PROCESSES

The argument here is that board evaluation should examine board involvement in strategy and ensure that the board is not an inauthentic ritual of collective decision-taking. In effect, the board should not be a passive entity but duly involved in key processes of strategic choice, change and control. Such involvement cannot be assumed. Research has identified there to be a significant gap between prescription that boards should be active in strategy and empirical evidence that boards are indeed active in strategy.[42] Empirical studies closer to boardroom behaviour also provide a mixed set of findings about the involvement of the board and part-time board members in strategy. Early work is sceptical about board involvement in strategy, concluding that boards are not involved in strategy formation.[43]

More recent research has conceptualized board involvement in strategy at three levels: 'taking strategic decisions', 'shaping strategic decisions' and 'shaping the content, context and conduct of strategy'[44]. Each level of the three levels of involvement in strategy conveys different sets of behaviours, which in turn are a function of power relations between full-time executive board members and non-executive directors. For instance, 'taking strategic decisions' is the level of minimal involvement in strategy. At this level, non-executive directors are largely reactive to executives. This is a minimalistic role and would not reflect well in an evaluation of board task performance. The other

---

42   McNulty, T. and Pettigrew, A. M. (1999) Strategists on the board, *Organization Studies*, 20: 47–74.

43   Mace, M. L. (1971) *Directors: Myth and Reality*, Boston, MA: Harvard University Graduate School of Business Administration; Lorsch, J. W. and MacIver, E. (1989) *Pawns or Potentates: The Reality of Americas' Corporate Boards*, Boston, MA: Harvard University Graduate School of Business Administration.

44   McNulty, T. and Pettigrew, A. M. (1999) Strategists on the board, *Organization Studies*, 20: 47–74.

two levels of involvement afford non-executive directors a greater impact on strategy and corporate affairs. This greater involvement is underpinned by a more balanced power relation between non-executive and executive directors. 'Shaping strategic decisions', draws attention to antecedents of decision-taking processes in the boardroom to uncover important processes and behaviours outside of the boardroom which shape the making of strategic decisions. 'Shaping the content, content and conduct of strategy' conceptualizes non-executive influences of strategic decision processes in the context of wider behavioural and process issues.

Employed in the context of board evaluation the use of this model of board involvement in strategy supports attention to signs of a minimalistic role for boards, as implied by 'taking strategic decisions'. If present the practical implication is that the board would not be exercising due influence on decision processes and outcomes that may prove fateful for form performance. At the other end of the involvement spectrum, a board evaluation should also seek to establish whether there is excessive involvement and influence of the board in strategy as vicious dynamics and relationships can ensue on boards where executives perceive non-executives as inappropriate in terms of role performance and contribution.[45]

DEVELOPING THE BOARD AGENDA

If strategy involvement can guard against the perils of a passive board, the board agenda is an important mechanism for alleviating the threat of capture of the board by the executive. As leader of the board the chair has a key role in ensuring that the agenda enables the board to exercise effort, to be engaged, to contribute opinions and make the best use of the knowledge and skills at its disposal. Board agendas differ between firms. On some boards, the agenda is populated by procedural items such as reports of the business performance, reports of board subcommittees, reports of budget planning exercises, publication of company results and dividend policy. The items on the agenda encourage only review of past performance rather than discussion about critical strategy-related issues facing the firm in the future. This kind of board agenda restricts board members' opportunity to influence strategy and the future direction of the company. In effect, non-executive directors are not being consulted by executives about strategy and that responsibility for strategy is perceived to lie with the executives away from the boardroom.

By contrast, a board agenda can be an important mechanism for drawing the board and the non-executives into the strategy process. The agenda is constructed in ways that board members have a genuine opportunity to support or challenge executives as they deliberate taking bold and risky decisions. 'Real issues' are brought to the board for early discussion rather than confirmation. It is not perceived as a sign of weakness on the part of the executive for issues to be brought to the board for resolution. Further, issues are placed on the agenda early enough for non-executive directors to influence the resolution of issues. The board agenda is planned carefully to ensure that an issue which may require a decision by the board in the future is raised at the board, and the board is given time to prepare a view and construct a decision. Indeed, the agenda may allow an issue to

---

45   Roberts, J., McNulty, T. and Stiles, P. (2005) Beyond agency conceptions of the work of the non-executive director: creating accountability in the boardroom, *British Journal of Management,* 16(special issue): S5–S26.

proceed through several iterations over time, enabling a more continuous dialogue about strategy at board level, in which there is greater opportunity for non-executives to use their knowledge and skills to shape the thinking of executives and vice versa.

DEVELOPING THE CONDUCT OF BOARD MEETINGS

The agenda is a necessary but insufficient condition for board effectiveness. It is necessary that space on the board agenda be accompanied by actual processes of information sharing, challenge and open debate amongst all board members. Without these accompanying processes the time of the agenda may lead only to ritualistic and superficial consideration of strategy rather than genuine debate. Board involvement in strategy is greatest in those firms where the board meeting is conducted in ways that ensure that executives bring information to the board for non-executives as a precursor to debate. This point resonates with creating due cognitive conflict and using knowledge and skills.

Presentations by executives to the board are valuable mechanisms for sharing information, and bridging gaps between executives and non-executive knowledge and understanding of situations and issues. Presentations about firms' profitability, levers of profitability, business trends and market share are valuable for increasing part-time board members' understanding of important issues facing firms. Presentations open up the board process to the acquisition of information and debate. Presentations alone are not sufficient for involving the board and non-executive directors in strategy. Presentations need to be a precursor to deeper understanding and debate across the whole board rather than an end in themselves. It is important that within the board process executives spend time listening to the board as well as reporting to the board. The time spent at board meetings between presentation by executive and debate is an important indicator of board behaviour in this respect. Furthermore, it is important that presentation and debate involve the whole board and, for instance, are not solely channelled through an over-dominant chief executive. Boards do vary in the extent to which there is open debate during which executive directors, other than the chief executive, are allowed to speak their minds as directors of the company and members of the board. Where 'shades of opinion' amongst the executive are allowed to be revealed, non-executives have a wider flow of information and perspective against which they can probe and question strategy.

USING SPECIAL EVENTS TO DEVELOP THE BOARD

Special events such as strategy 'away days' involving the whole board in strategy can provide all board members with a more informal setting to contribute. Once again, process is important as these events appear to work best for boards, when they are deliberately planned to be more informal and relaxed than a regular board meeting and when the purpose of the event is for executives to share their thinking with the board as a whole as opposed to justifying or convincing non-executives about a particular course of action.

DEVELOPING RELATIONS AND DIALOGUE OUTSIDE OF THE BOARD MEETING

Construction of the board agenda and the conduct of the board meeting must be seen in the context of the behaviour of board members between board meetings. Opportunities for non-executive board members to contribute are considerably increased in those firms where there is an informal dialogue between executives and non-executives between board meetings. Informal dialogue between executives and non-executives is another mechanism for informing the board about company affairs and drawing them into the strategy process. The number of times executives, including the chief executives, ask non-executives for a view about a strategic issue, outside board meetings, is one indicator of executives' willingness to use and involve the board. Informal dialogue between executive directors and non-executive directors is a sign that executives feel that board members are sufficiently important to make sharing information with them desirable. It opens up relationships exposing each party to new information and perspectives. It allows people to develop personal relationships, and they gain access to new information, which place them in a better position to make judgements in the boardroom. Informal dialogue is also a way of the non-executive exerting influence without undermining executives in front of the whole board. Some of the most decisive action by boards is predicated on the basis of this informal contact between non-executive directors outside of the boardroom.[46]

DEVELOPING THE CHAIR/CHIEF EXECUTIVE RELATIONSHIP

The above point raises the issue of the quality of relationships between board members. Empirical research reveals that a complementary relationship between the chairman and chief executive is a necessary condition of an effective board.[47] Such a relationship not only contributes directly to the performance of the chief executive through providing informed counsel and advice, but also gives the chairman the knowledge and understanding of the company that then allows him or her to create the conditions under which the non-executives can be effective. It is argued that the chairman's work in managing the board, in building non-executive knowledge through induction, strategy events and various off-board meetings, in structuring the board agenda and ensuring the quality and timeliness of board papers, and in chairing the meetings themselves is 'pivotal' in creating the conditions for non-executives to be effective.

Conclusion

The last decade and more has seen numerous governance failures often with severe implications that extend throughout and beyond the corporation. Effective boards are important to the fabric of corporate life and societal in general. Nevertheless boards have largely been invisible. Research, regulation and activism are now rendering boards more

---

46   McNulty, T. and Pettigrew, A. M. (1999) Strategists on the board, *Organization Studies*, 20: 47–74.

47   Roberts, J. (2002) Building the complementary board: the work of the plc chairman, *Long Range Planning*, 35: 493–520; Roberts, J and Stiles, P. (1999) The relationship between chairmen and chief executives: competitive or complementary roles?, *Long Range Planning*, 32(1): 36–48.

visible and subject to scrutiny. Board evaluation is part of that process. What this chapter has sought to do is argue that board evaluation should attend to board processes and outcomes. Specifically the challenge is to analyse and develop the complex behavioural and relational dynamics involved in the highest processes of strategic choice, change and control. In this way, board evaluation can be a genuine stimulus and opportunity for board effectiveness and good governance though the development of internal working arrangements. If boards take us the challenge then board evaluation can be a meaningful and highly developmental aspect of corporate governance rather than a superficial, intrusive and costly reporting exercise.

6 *Strategies for Leadership and Executive Development*

MURRAY M. DALZIEL

Introduction

This chapter focuses particularly on the preparation of executives to lead today's organisations. There are some real differences for crafting a strategy for this level of any organisation. The fundamental premise of this chapter is that there are significant differences in crafting an executive development strategy because the work of executives is vitally different from the work of managers.

Executive development is a relatively new concept in management learning. While management education and learning have a fairly rich history, the idea that executives need development is fairly recent. The idea that this could be core to strategy is even more recent. This is not to say that previously individual executives did not foster learning. However, there was a common assumption that some stimulating lectures from leading business school thinkers and maybe the odd book or two on a management topic was all that was necessary.

The drivers for this change offer some basic propositions for crafting an executive development strategy. One of the seminal turning points was the publication in 1982 of Peters and Waterman's *In Search of Excellence*[1] which climbed rapidly to the top of all publication lists. The propositions have long been overtaken and the fundamental premise questioned because most of the companies mentioned in the book either do not survive to this day or lost their mantle of excellence.[2] Some companies which became the 'heroes' later, such as General Electric, were not on their list. However, it is worth understanding the context in which *In Search of Excellence* came to prominence. The USA had just suffered one of the worst recessions since the Second World War, almost bringing to a close a period of steady and significant growth. There was widespread admiration mixed with concern about the dominance of the Japanese, and in this climate there was a

---

1   See Peters, P. and Waterman, R. (1982) *In Search of Excellence*. New York: Harper and Row.

2   Colville, I. D., Waterman, R. H. and Weick, K. E. (1999) Organizing and the search for excellence: making sense of the times in theory and practice, *Organization*, 6(1): 129–148.

lot of searching for new answers.[3] Peters and Waterman provided a stimulus, grounded in nationalism, to the view that there were solutions. US executives, in particular, widened their vistas. They came to see that there are multiple models available and trust that they were in control, could make choices and lead their companies towards different directions.[4]

These and the other historical contexts give some propositions and a starting road-map for crafting executive development strategy.

Proposition 1: Executive development becomes salient when actors believe that there are a number of choices they can make about their environment and that there are models they can choose to drive their future.

The search for models took new significance with the rise of Jack Welch at General Electric (GE).[5] As one of the largest US multinationals GE had a rich history for promoting management development, but Jack Welch took this to another dimension. Early in his tenure as CEO he hired academics from University of Michigan – Noel Tichy and Steve Kerr – not just to lead a single programme but to develop interventions and actually run the overall management and executive development programme. Executive development became integrated as a practice in the business like any other practice and a key to driving overall strategy development.[6]

Proposition 2: Executive development can operate as part of the overall management process and not separate from it.

The GE experience gave legitimacy to the concept of strategic executive development. Today 'leadership development' or 'talent management' in general are among the most prominent themes companies cite as important to their future.[7] A key driver is fundamental change in demographics. The rate at which executives will retire in advanced industrial countries far outstrips the supply of managers to succeed them.[8] One clear consequence of this is that managers will rise to executive roles at a much younger age than in previous decades. This not only gives strategic executive development extra weight in corporate life, but it also places new demands on executive development.

---

3   The President's Commission on Industrial Competitiveness (1987) *Human Resources and Competitiveness. Report of the Committee on Human Resources*, Research Report Series RR-87–27. Washington, DC: US Government Office.

4   For a sobering counterbalance to this see McKendrick, D. G., Doner, R. and Haggard, S. (2000) *From Silicon Valley to Singapore: Location and Competitive Advantage in the Hard Disk Drive Industry*. Stanford, CA: Stanford University Press.

5   Tichy, N. (1993) *Control Your Destiny or Someone Else Will*. New York: Doubleday.

6   Tichy, N., Charan, R. and Welch, J. (1989) Speed, simplicity, self confidence, *Harvard Business Review*, September–October: 112–120.

7   Guthridge, M., Komm, A. and Lawson, E. (2008) Making talent a strategic priority. *The McKinsey Quarterly*, http://www.haygroup.com/ww/Best_Companies/Index.aspx?id=156, has a number of references to senior management's focus on this topic.

8   'The baby boomer generation is about to retire en masse. Some 75 million workers in the US will retire in the next 5 to 10 years and with them 50 per cent of the CEOs of major organizations. The available talent to replace them will need to be picked from the next generation of just 45 million.' Hay Group (2007) *The War For Leaders: How to Prepare for Battle*, p. 4. Philadelphia, PA: Hay Group.

Proposition 3: Executive development includes accelerating managers to take up more senior and demanding posts earlier in their careers.

Organisations have changed fundamentally in the last 25 years. Large organisations previously had the luxury of letting executives emerge by going through a number of progressively more senior roles – sometimes over 20 in the course of a career. However, as organisations become flatter the availability of roles to test managerial skills lessens. Therefore, developing executives needs to be a more deliberative activity and future executives need to be actively involved in making choices about how they will develop.

Executive Development is Different from Management Development because Executive Work is Different

What is the executive audience? The definition of the 'executive population' is quite diverse. In a large multinational organisation people considered executives can be up to three layers of management below the chief executive. In smaller organisations the executive population is the chief executive and perhaps one or two others. Whatever the definition, there needs to be a clear view of the challenges facing executives in order to build development programmes. This differentiation between executive and managerial work is not well documented, particularly what defines when managers become executives. These factors make executive work different:[9]

- The time horizon for decision-making is significantly longer than in managerial work.
- The impact of their decisions is broader (for example, affecting a whole division, country unit or key function).
- The context is more complex – changes are more discontinuous and solutions less obvious or well known.

These factors imply that fundamentally executive work is different from managerial work. While the boundary between managerial work and executive work is indistinct there are some key areas that illustrate just how that work is different. The largest differences are around the scope of influence of an executive versus a manager. The further away from front-line delivery, the more executives depend on others to actually execute work. Take a sales role. The sales person can influence by their own actions whether they make the sale or not. Their front-line manager can have an influence on results through, for example, changing calling rates, the size of territories or the types of clients that the salesperson calls on, but they themselves cannot make the sale. Of course, that front-line manager might have been a great salesperson and so stands-in from time to time to help the salesperson, but there will be limits on the time they have available to do this. The sales managers' own managers are even further away from results. They may make decisions that affect how sales are to be made. For example, they may initiate policies

9   Jacques, E. and Clement, S. D. (1991) *Executive Leadership*. Arlington, VA: Cason-Hall and Co.
Jacques, E. (1997) *Requisite Organization: Total System for Effective Managerial Organization and Managerial Leadership for the 21st Century,* London: Gower; Garonzick, R., Nethersell, G. and Spreier, S. (2006) Navigating through the new leadership landscape, *Leader to Leader,* 39: 30–39 .

that directly help or hinder the sales person by changing terms that the salesperson can offer the customer. They can affect the motivation and effectiveness of the salesperson by determining how many salespeople should be allocated across territories. But again, they cannot make the sale. Likewise with the managers of these managers of sales managers, who we have to assume depending on the size of the company, are in the group we would commonly call executives. They can affect sales by developing key policy areas: they could, for example, change the mix of products, or change the organisation so that sales people cover different portfolios of products. These executives will all assume that these actions will affect sales, but they do not make the sale.

Looking at this range of actions we can clearly see that the time to affect decisions greatly increases as one goes up an organisational hierarchy. A salesperson can change their sales approach and they will immediately get feedback about whether this works or not. The sales manager will get a fairly short-term reaction if they change sales territories around or make good or poor hiring decisions. The policies that their managers set out may take different lengths of time to take effect. Changing terms of sales may have an immediate effect. However, recalling that these types of policies are applied across potentially quite different segments (for example, across different regions) the results may not be as predictable. If we look at four territories: the results in territories A and B go up after the policy is implemented and go down in territories C and D. In the former case, many executives congratulate themselves that they have made the right decision and in the latter bemoan how it did not work, but in many cases we find that in territory A the sales went up irrespective of policy.

Perhaps the demand conditions are stronger there or the sales person is extraordinarily good. Likewise, in the cases that do not work further investigation will show that perhaps the new policy prevented an even more precipitous decline, or in one case this happened and in the other the results became worse because that particularly sales person was de-motivated.

These differences need to be taken into account when crafting executive development programmes. Certainly, any strategic executive development programme needs to address:

- Will participants be able to balance and assess their impact across several time horizons clearly?
- Will the participants make decisions, assess their broad impact and then bring on board whole units, a range of functions or several layers in an organisation?
- Will participants be able to deal with situations and make decisions in ambiguous situations or when the parameters and consequences are not predictable?

Competencies, Context plus Processes and Practices are the Key Ingredients of Executive Development

Executive development, like development at other levels in the organisation, needs to provide mechanisms for developing the skills and competencies to perform in the role. However, given these considerations, the more senior an executive the more important the *context* in which they operate.[10] Executives set business agendas. The content of these agendas and the judgements that they need to make are not necessarily foreseeable but the texture and domain of the situations they encounter are often very similar. For example, at some point a general manager in a consumer goods company will need to resolve some dilemmas around marketing spend, size and deployment of their sales forces, and research and development investment. There are a key set of skills and practices that will enable the executive to weigh the alternatives logically and make judgements about information they are receiving from others. However, timely and definitive judgment comes from having been in some of these contexts before.

Therefore, executive development needs to ensure that executives not only have skills and knowledge but also that they have been in the right contexts to make judgements. Consider an executive who has to manage a far-flung international organisation where the sources of growth are far from their own domestic marketplace. Would it be reasonable to assume that an executive with little experience outside their domestic market will be able to assess the subtleties and biases in overseas marketplaces?

The majority of larger organisations with international operations accept the desirability of developing executives to run global operations by having some international exposure. However, there are other more tricky dilemmas in exposing potential executives to the contexts they have to operate in. Consider a common situation in some global pharmaceutical companies. The functions where the brightest often sit and where they get a chance to shine early in their careers are research and development, if they are scientists, and marketing and product development if they have an advanced business degree. Progressing through these functions early in careers is dependent on technical excellence. High-potential managers will obtain exposure to management but the types of people they manage more often come from the same background and have similar profiles to the manager. Sometimes, the first time that they encounter people from diverse backgrounds with varied motivations is when they become a general manager. This becomes a steep learning curve on how to manage people when they, themselves, cannot personally make a technical contribution that will make a difference. Perhaps exposure to sales management earlier in their career, where they would have had to manage people with different profiles, would provide a better context for some aspects of the general manager role.

There is also a warning about use of context in managerial learning. Some executives stop thinking or assessing situations, preferring to rely on 'rules of thumb' which they learned from successful application over time. This works well in terms of time efficiency: no executive can afford to deal with every new scenario from scratch. However, relying too much on rules of thumb prevents executives from seeing that a new situation is occurring which may need a new approach.[11] Rules of thumb become barriers to creative solutions.

What are the *processes* and *practices* that executives need to learn? There will always be a few key processes embedded in organisations and there will be variations by sector. Practices are the substance of executive life. Figure 6.1 describes a possible schema.

---

10   For example, Mayo, T. and Nohiria, N. (2005) Zeitgeist leadership, *Harvard Business Review*, 83(10): 45–60; Snowden, D. J. and Boone, M. E. (2007) A leader's framework for decision making, *Harvard Business Review*, 85(11): 68–76.

11   For example, Drummond, H. (2001) *The Art of Decision Making: Mirrors of Imagination, Masks of Science*. Chichester: Wiley.

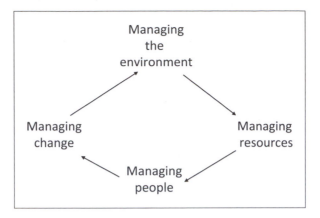

Figure 6.1 Executive leadership

There are few organisations who would claim that strategic planning was irrelevant, that budget planning was beside the point, that appraising people was inappropriate or that performance management was inconsequential. These would be among the practices that executives need to learn. There may well be fashions around practices. Twenty years ago there would have been eyebrows raised if someone suggested that executives needed to learn 'quality processes', but for those organisations that have adopted total quality or 'six sigma' programmes, their executives need to learn and apply this theory.

Many of these practices are so fundamental for organisations that they need to be embedded and learned at different levels in the organisation. Again there are some stepwise differences between managers and executives. In most organisations executives would be expected to play the lead role in a particular process or practice and therefore have the accountability for bringing the pieces together. As leaders there would be a high expectation that they innovate around these processes: indeed innovation itself may be one of the key processes executives would be expected to drive.[12]

In terms of practices and processes, the key difference between executives and managers is that executives must integrate a number of practices and change them if necessary. Imagine a manufacturer who sells key pieces of equipment to customers and then provides materials on an ongoing basis. Conventionally value will be created by how many new customers the company attracts to install new machinery plus the power of customer service to keep providing the materials for these machines. Executives in different companies with the same model will lead and integrate a number of sales processes. Client relationship management would be the key practice. However, the company may over time develop other practices that it feels gives them competitive edge – for example, they may own the machinery themselves and lease back to the customer. Imagine that there is a serious tightening of credit. If the company is leasing then the cost of servicing these leases may be too high and pricing practices will need to be altered. If the company is selling the machinery then its customers may not be able to raise capital or payment terms may need to be altered. What if it were to loan their clients the

---

12   There are good examples in Leavy, B. (2005) A leaders guide to creating an innovation culture, *Strategy and Leadership*, 33(4): 38–45.

machinery, using their own balance sheet to finance and perhaps securing commitments for their materials at slightly higher costs? This strategic choice makes a significant change to sales and client relationship practices. The role of the executive is to learn how to deal with and integrate these types of scenarios. Ultimately, the decision has an effect across a number of practices which the executive must manage.

A key process that might be distinctive for executives is *learning as a process*. Earlier in careers the disposition to keep learning is often cited as a key competency that predicts success throughout careers.[13] Later in careers it is not so much the capacity for learning as executives carving out time for real critical reflection.[14] This is counterintuitive to some executives, who see executive life as one in which they are required to take action and be continuously on top of what's going on around them – but this is precisely why executives need reflective and critical thinking. They are required to position their institution in the wider environment. They need an antidote to quick, intuitive, rule of thumb decision-making. They need reflection because although the practices may be predictable the situations and changes to environment may be quite different. Lack of critical thinking and reflective skills dooms them to potentially miss cues about issues or opportunities for their organisation[15].

ARE COMPETENCY MODELS USEFUL?

Almost any major organisation makes use of a competency model. There is a whole industry almost entirely devoted to the development of competency models.[16] Some commentators assert that there is a concise and well-known set of competencies that should underlie any managerial and executive development.[17] However, there is sufficient

---

13   Lomardo, M. and Eichenger, R. W. (2000) High potentials as high learners, *Human Resource Management*, 39(4): 321–329 and Eichenger, R. W. and Lombardo, M. (2004) Learning agility as a prime indicator of potential, *Human Resource Planning*, 27(4): 12–15.

14   Antonacopoulou, E. (2007). Reflexive critique in the business curriculum. In Wankel, C. and DeFillippi, R. *University and Corporate Innovations in Life Long Learning*. Connecticut: Information Age Publishing; Antonacoulou, E. (2001) The paradoxical nature of the relationship between training and learning, *Journal of Management*, 38: 307–350.

15   These are some methods of developing critical reflective skills in executives. Chris Argyris has proposed a number of methods over the years which involve executives developing real cases or analysing some living cases and looking at the types of assumptions that underlie their thinking. For example, see Argyris, C. (2000) *Flawed Advice and the Management Trap*, Oxford: Oxford University Press; Argyris, C. (1996) Actionable knowledge: intent versus actuality, *Journal of Applied Behavioral Science*, 32(4): 390–406; Argyris, C. (1991) Teaching smart people how to learn, *Harvard Business Review*, 69: 99–109. Using behavioural event interviews with this in mind in individual executive assessment exercises can also be helpful (see Spencer, L. and Spencer, S. (1993) *Competencies at Work: Models of Superior Performance*, New York: John Wiley, especially Chapter 11). The participant discusses critical incidents and describes at some length what they were doing, saying, feeling and thinking. The interviewer tries to collect the data with the minimal interpretation of events by the participant. Then this data can be 'coded' for key competencies or other attributes (Boyatzis, R., 1998, *Transforming Qualitative Information*, Thousand Oaks, CA: Sage) then presented back to the participant. Another exercise is the personal application assignment (PAA) in which the participant journals an event that is very salient to them and then reflects to what degree all the elements of experiential learning are contained in this reflection (Kolb 2000, *Facilitators' Guide to Learning*, Boston, MA: Hay Group.

16   There is a very good history of the development of competency models by Boyatzis in the preface to Spencer, S. M., Raja, T., Narayan, S. A., Mohan, S. and Lahiri, G (2007). *The Indian CEO: A Portrait of Excellence*. Mumbai: Sage.

17   For example, see Ulrich, D. and Smallwood, N. (2007) *Leadership Brand: Developing Customer-Focused Leaders to Drive Performance Amd Build Lasting Value* (New York: Perseus Distribution Services), which has some good descriptions of systemic executive development beyond this premise on competencies.

academic evidence that competencies can be quite different depending on situations, so the predictors of success are not always so obvious.[18]

To use an existing competency model in strategic executive development the key question must be why the model was developed in the first place. Some models are developed specifically to provide a common language to discuss promotions or succession planning. In that case, the organisation needs to ensure that the language is reflective of the level of executive work. Will the behaviours describe give a clear map as to what would be expected of an executive?

Some competency models are not designed with any level in mind: organisations wish competency models to reflect behaviours and even values that drive the organisation's culture. In these cases, executive development programmes use competency models to ensure that executives understand and meet the aspirations of the organisation but they are not be necessarily predictive of success in the organisation.

WHAT TYPES OF COMPETENCIES SHOULD DRIVE EXECUTIVE DEVELOPMENT?

Competencies, context and practices work together. Competencies predict whether an executive can deal with processes and practices in any domain. Context enables an executive to learn how competencies may be applied and gives a backdrop to set judgements or speed up decision-making. Competencies give the executive the capability to develop and take forward solutions and context offers some alternative views about which practices could work.

Based on the view that there are differences in the nature of executive work there are three key questions that need to be addressed when looking at executives:[19]

*   How do they form agendas and make decisions?
*   How do they take others with them?
*   Do they have the resilience to sustain their own and other's performance?

Executives Set the Agenda

At the heart of any executive work is the practice of setting strategy. Strategy is about finding a distinctive position in a market and ensuring that the company organises itself around that position to obtain a competitive advantage that they believe they can maintain for some time in the future.[20] If executive development is to support strategy it needs to nurture mindsets that can distinctively focus and position organisations and

18   Spencer, L., and Spencer, S. (1993) *Competence at Work* (New York: Wiley), provides a good review of earlier literature; McClelland, D. (1998) Identifying competencies with behavioural event interviews, *Psychological Science,* 9(5): 331–339 is an interesting study demonstrating that it is not the number of competencies a person possess that necessarily makes the difference but rather having the right combination for a particular situation.

19   Dalziel, M. (2003) Competencies: the first building block of talent management, in Berger, L. A. and Berger, D. *The Talent Management Handbook,* pp. 53–63, New York: McGraw-Hill; and Dalziel, M. (2003) Determining every employee's potential for growth, in Berger, L. A. and Berger, D. *The Talent Management Handbook,* pp. 129–138, New York: McGraw-Hill discuss these areas in greater detail.

20   Porter, M. (1998) *Competitive Strategy Techniques for Analyzing Industries and Competitors.* London: Free Press, is classic reference work.

ensure skills to develop and bring together the activities that bring about the strategy. Executive development is a key part of successful execution of strategy.

But strategy is a dynamic process. In fact, it is positively dangerous for a firm to maintain a totally inflexible position, so a strategy has to be enduring but is often a 'work in motion'.[21] Executive development should provide frameworks for making strategy dynamic, and for executive development to be strategic, it really needs to help executives define distinctive and enduring positions while offering models that help executives dynamically change strategy and evaluate new or emerging positions. Strategy provides the focus for executive development but executive development should enable strategy development to be dynamic. Consider a profitable media name at the end of 2007. Assume that the firm has in place executives with the skills to take the firm forward but the firm sees that they could be an attractive target for private equity investors. This particular route might even provide better value to shareholders. The firm conducts an exercise with its board and senior executives where they pretend that they are not a publically traded company but owned by private equity. They envision what that world is like and they propose the actions they would take in this context. This then leads to a challenging discussion with the board about the desirability of following these actions whether or not they are publically traded or owned privately. As a result the strategy is modified. This is an example of a strategic executive development activity. The executives learn new concepts and evaluate actions for the future critically.

A well-defined strategy provides focus. One way to test focus is to look at value chains.[22] Does executive development lead to building strength in those parts of the value chain that build competitive advantage? A pharmaceutical company, for example, might decide that all senior executives irrespective of functional background need to gain real exposure either in drug development or in sales and marketing. A large multi-service bank might decide that all executives should be exposed to risk management at some point in their career.

Changes in strategy and changes in priorities in the value chain often go hand in hand. Consider the industrial manufacturer highlighted earlier who decides on the option to capture customers in a new economic climate by leasing rather than selling the equipment. One approach for executive development is to focus on enhancing financial analysis skills throughout the sales function. An alternative would be to enhance the finance function as a whole not only to perform financial analysis but also to spot opportunities in existing or potential customers' financial situation.

What competencies help executives to make this happen? There are two sources: an achievement drive and cognitive ability. Achievement drive is a major source for managers and executives in developing agendas. The drive focuses on being motivated to develop goals, make improvements, set and exceed standards of excellence.[23] At the executive

---

21   Cf. Mintzberg, H. and Waters, J. A. (1985) Of strategies, deliberative and emergent, *Strategy Management Journal*, 6(3): 257–272.

22   A very useful workbook and guide is Kaplinksky, P. and Morris, M. (2001) *A Handbook for Value Chain Research*. Brighton: Institute of Development Studies, University of Sussex.

23   The classic reference is McClelland, D. C. (1953) *The Achievement Motive*, New York: Appleton-Century-Crofts. Surveying the competency literature there is no doubt about the requirement for these types of competencies in managers and executives: McClelland D. C. (1965) Achievement motivation can be developed, *Harvard Business Review*, 43(6): 6–18. However, strength in this area to the exclusion of development in other areas can cause problems. See Spreier, S., Fontaine, M. and Malloy, R. (2006) Leadership run amok: the destructive potential of overachievers, *Harvard Business Review*, 84(6): 78–82.

level achievement drive has to be played out on a larger platform. The drive must focus on more than improvements in operations. Therefore, goal-setting is wider and more strategic. The focus turns to larger scale enterprise development which is much more about capturing larger opportunities than day-to-day improvements and more focused on breakthroughs than incremental change.[24]

Likewise, for cognitive ability the expression of these capabilities has to be at a higher level. Executives with these abilities combine two fundamental attributes: analytical thinking and conceptual thinking. Although the higher-order abilities in either one might come into play in different executive situations it would be a deficit for an executive to have one set of skills and not the other. Higher levels of analytical thinking involve being able to make logical and complex arguments with different textures of argument. This could involve imagining several potential consequences of a decision or a chain of connections ('if this happens then this which implies this and that leads to ...'). Clearly in complex planning situations this level of competence is helpful. On the other hand, analytical thinking does not necessarily imply creative or breakthrough thinking. Higher ends of conceptual thinking involve turning a concept on its head or developing a new concept from scratch. The ability to develop concepts is useful both for breaking through and encouraging creativity and as a skill to develop clear communications. One way this is often observed in executives is in their use of metaphors. Thinking with metaphors can be a way of breaking through a problem ('I realised that this situation was like ...') or of communicating a complex idea to others so that they remember it.

Executives Take Others with Them

Undoubtedly, a key aspect of managerial or executive life lies in persuading or convincing others about a course of action. What makes the executive requirements at this level different from managers is the scope of influence. Executives' sphere of influence reaches down through a much larger organisation or across a wider number of units. Of course, by their very nature being an executive carries some authority. Nevertheless, authority in itself is not sufficient to convince or persuade across multiple levels. This is one of the great shocks for managers who come from quite specialised backgrounds where there technical knowledge has often been a large factor in their success to date. When they face wider audiences of people with different levels of experience and from different backgrounds their previous skills of persuasion seem to evaporate!

There are a number of ways in which executives express higher levels of influence to take others with them. One approach involves being quite sensitive to the overall 'political' environment in an organisation or even across a set of organisations, and being skilled in developing influence strategies as a result.[25] In some executives these strategies can be quite complex and involve using multiple approaches or even other people as the key influencers.

---

24   This is not to suggest that executives should not be concerned about day-to-day improvement or incremental change. However, the absence of the higher order elements of achievement is a detriment to executive performance.

25   For example, French, J. and Raven, B. (1959) The bases of social power. In D. Cartright, *Studies in Social Power*, pp. 150–167. Ann Arbor, MI: University of Michigan Press and Tjosvold, D., Andrews, I. R. and Struthers, J. (1992) Leadership influence: goal interdependence and power, *Journal of Social Psychology*, 132(1): 39–50.

Experienced executives are also sensitive to the 'authority' that goes with office and use occasions or specific events to make a point. A modification of the well-known 'elevator speech' exercise helps executives to think like this:

> *You step into an elevator and just as it takes off a manager who sits about three levels away from you in the organisation steps in. You vaguely remember him or her. Get a message across before you step off in six floors.*[26]

What is common about these types of influence is that executives recognise that with so many people they may have to win over they cannot depend solely on their own presence to be influential. They have to find ways to be economical with their time and to cover a lot of people without being present all the time.

One area that is somewhat controversial for executives in taking others with them is in how they use teams. There is a lot of anecdotal evidence that being able to lead a team is a fine executive competence. There is less evidence that executives actually use it as frequently as some suggest. For an executive, 'team leadership' is an example of a higher level of influence competency only if it involves being able to use a team to develop, mobilise and implement an agenda. This is because at this level the executive is using the team as an extension of their leadership. Team leadership at this level is much more than running meetings or keeping others involved. At its heart it involves being able to create the interdependencies that an organisation might need to create and execute a strategy.[27]

Executives are Resilient

In considering moving managers into executive ranks a number of organisations look at the personal characteristics of executives to predict who can adapt to the larger environment described previously. There are two complimentary approaches to this. One is to identify whether the executive has a high degree of emotional or social competency.[28] Like the previous two areas, there is an assumption that these sets of competencies are not uniquely executive level competencies but found throughout the organisation.

---

26   The author has had many different responses from this exercise. A number of executives find it difficult. One executive even tried to get off at an earlier floor without saying anything. He claimed that he was showing his commitment to people by getting off at the human resources department floor! After some practice he decided that the manager was an account executive and he asked about what was happening in a key account. We discussed whether the message about his interest in account strategies was more impactful than a statement he had made about this in the company newsletter.

27   Wageman, R., Nunes, D., Burruss, J. and Hackman, D. (2008) *Senior Leadership Teams: What it Takes to Make them Great* (Cambridge, MA: Harvard Business Press) not only contains a good review of why some top teams succeed and others don't but offers very practical approaches to developing executive teams. There is a good body of academic evidence that executive teams can be a critical element for achievement of strategy but are by no means necessary; for example, see Iaquinto, A. (1997) Top management team agreeement about the strategic decision process: a test of some of its determinants and consequences, *Strategy Management Journal*, 18(1): 63–75 and Hambricht, D. (1995) Fragmentation and other problems CEOs have with their teams. *California Management Review*, 37(3): 110–127.

28   This is a well-documented area. Goleman, D. (2006) *Social Intelligence: The New Science of Human Relations* (New York: Bantam Books) provides good descriptors. Goleman, D. (2000) Leadership gets results, *Harvard Business Review*, 78(2): 78–90 shows impact on organisational results. Goleman, D., Boyatzis, R. and McKee, A. (2002) *Primal Leadership: Realizing the Power of Emotional Intelligence* (Cambridge, MA: Harvard Business Press) and Boyatzis, R., McKee, A. and Johnson, F. (2008) *Becoming a Resonant Leader* (Cambridge, MA: Harvard Business School Press) describe examples and approaches to developing these.

There are two views about what differentiates at this level. One view would be a tremendous amount of self-confidence with clear ability to resiliently deal with setbacks, conflicts and stress.[29] Another view would see that the absence of a set of competencies or a mismatch will predict issues and therefore raise red flags in any promotion decision.[30] In this view many of these factors should be identified early in a person's career.

Implementation Steps

Competency models are pervasive in larger organisations and there are numerous popular writings about the characteristics of leaders, but are these sufficient to define executive development? One strand of thought suggests that competencies need to be identified earlier in people's careers and that other areas can be taught or learned thereafter. This reasoning assumes that competencies are well-defined concepts that are either present or not in a person. The richer view of competencies sees them as developing over time, existing with varying degrees of complexity. Competencies are also attributes in which the issue is less a question of whether some people possess them and more one of whether they actually use them with any frequency.

This is critical in thinking through what competency development at an executive level might be. Consider the influencing scenarios mentioned above. Most executives have some skills in persuasion or they would not have progressed that far in an organisation. However, some executives have never developed this attribute beyond their own ability to conduct face-to-face conversations where they try to persuade with facts. This is often not enough to convince larger parts of an organisation where they will rarely have the opportunity to be present. What's necessary here is to develop the kernel of competency that they do have and enable them to apply this in the larger context.

WHAT ABOUT PERFORMANCE?

Is performance really the best indicator of executive development? There are some who believe that the programmatic development of executives is not worth the expense and that performance is a better predictor of future potential. There is no doubt that without performance in a particular role it is hard organisationally to see how a person could advance. An exception is when there is something about a role that makes it particularly difficult to perform and there is a lot of other evidence about the person's performance elsewhere (for example, someone who has had a very good history of obtaining results as an operations manager who cannot settle into a service or advisory role in headquarters). Given the differences in roles between managers and executives, described above, how can success in a managerial role predict success in executive roles? Likewise, success in some executive roles does not necessarily predict success in another role where the context is quite different.

---

29   Reivich, K. and Shatte, A. (2002) *The Resilience Factor: 7 Keys to Finding Your Inner Strength and Overcoming Life's Hurdles* (New York: Random House) provides detailed studies plus approaches to developing resilience in managers.

30   Lombardo, M., Ruderman, M. N. and McCauley, C. D. (1988) Explanations of success and derailment in upper-level management positions. *Journal of Business and Psychology*, 2(3): 199–216; Leslie, J. B. and Van Velsor, E. (1996) *A Look at Derailment Today: North America and Europe*. Greensboro, NC: Center for Creative Leadership.

CAN COMPETENCIES BE LEARNED AND DEVELOPED?

There is a definite view by some that competencies should be used for selection: processes and practices can be taught and context learned through experience. In this view competencies are very difficult to develop, but Richard Boyatzis and his colleagues provide a good deal of evidence that with the right conditions and structure competencies can be developed.[31] Boyatzis' model is presented in modified form in Figure 6.2. The model starts with a sharp focus on individual exploration, looking at who or what the person would ideally want to be along with where they see themselves at present. This discovery leads to realisation of strengths and potential gaps which leads to constructing a learning agenda.

Adapted from Boyatzis[32]

Boyatzis proposes two processes which enable that agenda to come to fruition. First, there is a process of re-creation. Learning takes root when participants experiment with new behaviours, thoughts and even feelings that relate back to the learning agenda (building on strengths and eliminating significant gaps). Practice then embeds these new behaviours, thoughts and feelings. Boyatzis and his colleagues view this as a physical act – neural pathways are being recreated.

Second, all these processes work better if participants are supported by people whom they trust and can relate to throughout this process. Therefore, in building programmes to develop competencies facilitators need to focus on providing an environment where people can discover what they really want and concentrate on building relationships within a group or between participants and others that will support learning and change.

EXPLORATION	REALISATION	AGENDA BUILDING	RECREATION
'Ideal self': Who do I want to be?	My strengths	Learning agenda	Experiment to discover new behaviours thoughts etc.
'Real self' => Who am I?	Gaps between My 'ideal' and 'real' self	Build on strengths reduce gaps	=> Practice to embed

'Resonant relationships: to support process'

Figure 6.2 Boyatzis' theory of self-directed learning

31   Boyatzis, R. (2001) Developing emotional intelligence. In C. Cherniss and D. Goleman, *The Emotionally Intelligent Workplace*, pp. 234–253 (San Francisco, CA: Jossey-Bass); Boyatzis, R. (2006) Intentional change theory: from a complexity perspective, *Journal of Management Development*, 607–623; Boyatzis, R. E., Leonard, D., Rhee, K. and Wheeler, J. (1996) Competencies can be developed but not in the way we think, *Capability*, 2(2): 25–41; Boyatzis, R. E., Stubbs, E. C. and Taylor, S. N. (2002) Learning cognitive and emotional intelligence competencies through graduate management education, *Academy of Management Journal on Learning and Education*, 1(2): 150–162.

32   Boyatzis (2001) op. cit.

SOME USEFUL EXERCISES THAT INTEGRATE CONTEXT, PRACTICES AND COMPETENCIES

The concepts of 'experimentation' and 'practice' lead some organisations to focus solely on classroom settings for development. Thinking more broadly it is possible to develop settings that enable experimentation and practice not only around competencies but also integrating context, practices and competencies into organisational life.

Since setting strategic agendas and integrating practices are critical in executive life, exposing potential executives to business planning exercises from the bottom up helps to accelerates development. A consumer electronics firm saw potential confusion in a number of product lines because of interlocking technologies. They set up task forces of younger managers to develop and propose solutions.

If company policy allows it, placing high-potential executives onto the board of small or start-up companies enables them to see how business agendas can be crafted in a different setting, but one where they can more quickly grasp the overall context. Being on the board of such a company also tests their ability to take others with them in quite different settings. Likewise, exposure to social enterprises offers a way to change the context in which potential executives operate.[33]

International exposure, as mentioned previously, is essential for executives who are going to run global operations. Other methods for widening how potential executives look at context include putting them in situations where they may see solutions that they had not thought of previously. A major consumer products company had some of their potential executives change places with a Formula 1 organisation. Both learned different contexts about how innovation and continual improvement happen in different settings.

HOW DO YOU BUILD THIS INTO PROGRAMMES YOU CAN COMMUNICATE?

Boyatzis' model and the exercises above do demonstrate a tension in crafting executive development programmes – do you focus on individual or organisation development or both? This needs to be considered as a strategic design decision and should be accompanied by having a clear view of who is actually driving learning – the participants themselves or expert facilitators?

This consideration of strategy leads to choices along two fundamental dimensions – see Figure 6.3.

One dimension is whether the focus is around organisation change and therefore is about developing collective skills or whether the focus is on changing and developing individuals – for example to develop them to take roles in the future or to improve their skills now. The second dimension is the basis of the intervention. Is it participant-led so that participants construct their own learning and direction or is it led by experts who transmit learning to the participants? These need not be discrete choices. Organisations can build programmes at points along these dimensions, but the choices produce quite different approaches – see Figure 6.4.

In the upper right quadrant are interventions in which the focus is on individuals. They construct their own personal learning and development. This quadrant is most

---

33   http://www.mercnetwork.org/ is an example of a resource for this type of assignment.

consistent with the Boyatzis model but it could include other interventions which many organisations use to stimulate development in executives. An example would be job assignments or rotations shaped around individual development needs. How this works in practice depends on whether this executive sees the situation as a learning experience – an experience to realise learning and practice or experiment with new approaches. Some organisations employ executive coaches to help executives reflect and then shape their actions in this situation.

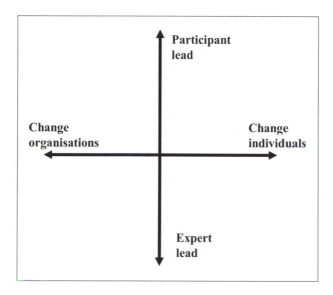

Figure 6.3   Crafting the nature of executive development interventions

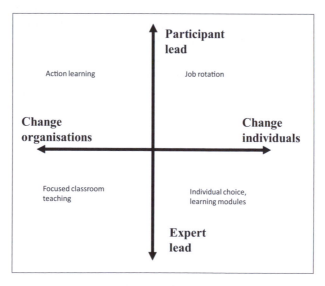

Figure 6.4   Examples of executive development interventions

The bottom right-hand quadrant contains interventions in which the focus is more on transmitting learning but still focused around individual skills. A typical intervention would involve an exploration of an individual's strengths and weaknesses often with a particular focus – short-term or long-term – and then prioritise reducing any gaps. In this setting participants seek out experts to reduce the gap. Organisations typically deal with this by sending and individual or group into a classroom or some other type of training to address these issues.

Interventions in the bottom left-hand quadrant focus on addressing a collective issue such as an organisational change, and do so by imparting know-how or skills which are for the group as a whole. For example, a professional services firm has traditionally sold to clients from distinct expertise-related practices. The firm changes its strategy and decides that it needs a 'key account' strategy. This would have a single senior partner as the coordinating point for all sales and relationships with major clients. In order to implement this strategy, the firm's board decides that there needs to be training around strategic selling and key account skills and employs a firm to lead this training to support the strategic change.

The top left-hand quadrant describes interventions which, like the one above, involve a focus on a collective issue like strategic or organisational change. These interventions enable participants to explore in multiple ways what they have to learn in order to make the change happen. Action learning is a key example here.[34] Action learning is organised around a problem which needs to be solved by a group. The group can call on the resources they need to learn how to solve the issue. They can also break up the task so that individuals contribute and so have to either learn from others or explore issues on their own. Likewise teams or subgroups of the overall programme can do the same together.

Organisations often adopt particular methods, more from the point of view of which practice they or their people are most comfortable with rather than more strategic consideration. None the less, a company could use a mix of these strategies. For example, a company intent on organisational change can decide that they will use an action learning approach but there may some threshold knowledge that all team members need before they can become executives so individuals are sent to particular programmes or courses to reduce some skill gaps. Likewise, a company could decide that job placement was the most appropriate method but that there were some key organisational development issues (for example, adapting to global markets) where they need to improve skills and so they develop programmes for groups of executives that address these issues.

Each quadrant has pluses and minuses in their exclusive use. Individually focused discovery methods such as job placement have the advantage of happening in real time and are almost guaranteed to be relevant to the organisation's overall purpose, but they do depend on the participant being willing to engage in learning. Their effectiveness is also dependent on time. If the person is too long in the assignment the extra-ordinary learning experience diminishes.[35] On the other hand, if the person has too little time in the assignment there is a real question as to whether they have really had time to embed

34   There is a big literature: see Revans, R. (1982) *The Origins and Growth of Action Learning*, Bromley: Chartwell-Bratt; Garvin, D. (2000) *Learning in Action*, Boston, MA: Harvard Business School Press; Kuhn, J. and Marsick, V. (2005) Action learning for strategic innovation in mature organizations, *Action Learning: Research and Practice*, 2(1): 27–48.

35   We assume all job assignments require some learning.

new practices. Doubts can be avoided by setting the learning objectives from the start and deciding how success in the assignment will be measured. Looking for hard business outcomes as part of learning is problematic, because the nature of executive work means results may not be known for a number of years.

Individual classroom learning has the advantage of concrete learning objectives, which can be measured. Likewise, focus on gaps can be made measurable so that there are possibilities for developing cost-effective solutions. On the other hand, classroom programmes and particularly those that are focused on individual learning, suffer from a common criticism that participants find it hard to apply when they return to the workplace. They miss the dimensions of experimentation and practice outlined in the Boyatzis model. Classroom interventions need to be carefully designed with clear objectives and are usually used in conjunction with other interventions.

Classroom learning focused on collective learning, like individual classroom learning, can have well-defined learning outcomes. Like any classroom effort the learning objectives must be matched with an appropriate mix and variety of teaching methods in order to be effective. Since these types of interventions are by definition 'collective' the success depends heavily on the skills of the facilitator to create group learning and traverse the corporate, group and individual issues which emerge.

Action learning has the advantage of being run in real time on problems that are relevant to the business and organisational change. For executives this can be particularly powerful. Often the topics will be issues that executives need to grapple with anyway. The method of addressing them can look much more natural than straightforward classroom learning. Reflect on a global pharmaceutical company that takes its most senior executives on an action learning exploration in India. They are guided by an outside facilitator but they embark on a series of explorations ranging from meeting in health care with physicians, policy makers and patients. They also meet up with a number of other executives and explore both indigenous development of industry and the impact of international companies in Indian expansion. It is doubtful they would have invested four days to do this in a seminar format in the classroom. Of course, they might have done the meetings with health care stakeholders anyway but that would normally have been delegated to executives with key responsibilities in that area. In this intervention, everyone learns the issues. They may see some applications they had not thought of in their own territory. This also takes seriously one of the most important tenets of adult education – namely, that the participants carry much of the knowledge in themselves. The role of an educational intervention is to help make that knowledge more explicit, or more importantly and particularly for this level of participant, to help them integrate what they know in potentially new and more creative arrangements.

A key issue in action learning over time as a development method is that the organisation runs out of problems to be solved. The method positively disintegrates if the problems are seen as irrelevant. There needs to be a recognition, though, that just defining the learning objectives can oscillate in different directions. The domains can be clear but the overall objectives will be determined by the groups. This has the advantage of giving the participants a lot of ownership over their learning. However, individual learning objectives may get swamped by the groups and there needs to be a degree of skill in facilitating the groups to ensure that they really do have concrete learning objectives within the scope of the overall collective programme.

The issue of balancing individual and company needs is critical to effectiveness. As the Boyatzis proposition cited above states, if individuals do not tie the intervention to their personal aspirations it will be less effective. On the other hand, if a company's strategic position needs urgent attention some executives will be reluctant to pass up the opportunity to address this in strategic executive development. A potential intervention that enables these to come together is 'open systems technology'.[36] Participants are placed in a setting early in the intervention in which they can explore themes and learning in an open way. These themes could be a combination of personal and company. As a result they form networks with people with similar learning motivations and develop programmes which could essentially use methods from any of the four quadrants of intervention.

Conclusion

Executive work is significantly different from managerial work and executive development needs to take that into account. A well-crafted leadership and executive development strategy will focus on helping participants understand current and future contexts, the practices that executives need to use and particularly how these are integrated and how to deploy competencies to build agendas, take others with them and maintain resilience. Integrating these practices themselves into the heart of company processes ensures that they will have some degree of permanence and contribute to the organisation's performance.

---

36   Owen, H. (1997) *Expanding Our Now: The Story of Open Space Technology.* San Francisco, CA: Berrett-Koehler Publishers.

7 Leadership, Management and Organisational Development

RICHARD BOLDEN

Introduction

In this chapter I suggest that leadership, management and organisational development are all parts of the same process – namely enhancing the capacity of organisations and the people within them to better achieve their purpose. As such, they are closely tied to strategic mission and all the systems that support it, as the *Center for Creative Leadership Handbook for Leadership Development* concludes:

> To be fully effective, a development system must be integrated with the organization's other processes: management planning, performance management, job selection, reward and recognition systems, and even mistake systems. The confluence of these processes determines the relative effectiveness of any one development activity.[1]

Despite the interdependence of these systems, however, they are often treated in relative isolation – as a series of discrete initiatives outsourced to different parts of the organisation: human resources (HR), finance, information and communications technology (ICT), and so on. – and consequently it is not surprising that many fail to deliver on their promise. Furthermore, leadership and management development (LMD) activities are often commissioned with little consideration of the underlying theories and assumptions on which they are based. Without an informed appreciation of the logic on which such initiatives are founded, however, and the proposed mechanism(s) by which they may lead to improved capacity and, in turn, enhanced performance it is unlikely that the desired outcomes will be achieved – to use the analogy 'you reap what you sow'!

I begin this chapter by reviewing recent trends in LMD, before outlining the conceptual underpinnings of the most common approaches and exploring the relationship of LMD to other organisational development activities. The chapter concludes with a framework that can be used when considering which approach(es) to utilise, along with a number of recommendations on choosing a provider.

---

1   McCauley, C., Moxley, R. and VanVelsor, E. (1998) *The Center for Creative Leadership Handbook of Leadership Development*, San Francisco, CA: Jossey-Bass, pp. 228–229.

Current Trends in Leadership and Management Development

Management and executive education is big business, with an estimated US$50 billion spent per year on leadership development alone.[2] In a 2003 survey the *Financial Times* found leading European companies to be spending on average £3,336 per participant per year on executive education; 42 per cent of respondents had a corporate university (with a further 12 per cent looking to establish one over the next couple of years); and of the topics offered leadership, followed by general management, were the most popular.[3]

Within higher education (HE) provision, there are now 117 members of the Association of Business Schools in the UK (up from just two in the whole country in the mid 1960s) and in the years between 1996–97 and 2006–07 the number of students of business and administrative studies rose by 40 per cent (from 222,321 to 310,255) with the greatest rate of change for postgraduate students (up by 66 per cent), especially those on business and management programmes such as the MBA.[4]

Such trends are typical of the expanding global market for LMD – driven, in part, by the desire of educational providers to enter into what is seen to be a lucrative market, and fuelled by political and corporate assertions about the value of effective leadership and the need to address a leadership and management 'skills gap'. From an employer perspective the primary triggers for investing in LMD are considered to be the rapidly changing nature of the external environment, closely followed by business needs and HR strategy, and students are increasingly regarding leadership and management-related programmes as enhancing their employability and career prospects.

Despite an explosion in the provision of and demand for LMD, however, the link to improved performance remains inconclusive. Empirical research has remained unable to produce consistent evidence of either the relationship or the mechanisms by which it might occur. There are many reasons why this might be, including variations in the quality of provision, variable levels of integration with organisational processes, personal and contextual differences in the most appropriate forms of development and even the possibility that such relationships are tenuous or non-existent. Whatever the cause, however, organisations are well advised to consider when and how to invest in LMD – after all, whilst it may be concluded that:

> *there is strong statistical evidence that management development leads to superior performance across companies of all sizes, sectors and national location ... an impressive 16 percent of variance is explained by three factors: the extent to which HR is integrated with business strategy, the degree to which the firm takes a thoughtful, long-term approach to developing managerial capability and the belief by line managers that their employer is taking management development seriously.*[5]

In effect, factors outside the classroom.

---

2   Raelin, J. (2004) Don't bother putting leadership into people, *Academy of Management Executive*, 18: 131–135.

3   Financial Times (2003) Companies still value training, *Financial Times*, 8 September, Special Report on Business Education.

4   Higher Education Statistics Agency (2008) *Student Tables by Subject of Study 1996/7 and 2006/7*, available at http://www.hesa.ac.uk, accessed 9 June 2008.

5   Mabey, C. and Ramirez, M. (2004) *Developing Managers: A European Perspective*. London: Chartered Management Institute.

Increasing dissatisfaction with traditional approaches to LMD, along with an expanded marketplace, changing business challenges and advances in leadership theory, development and practice have led to a diversification in the range of programmes and initiatives on offer. In particular there has been increasing demand for postgraduate and short course or executive education within university provision; greater modularisation, flexibility and work-based learning from all providers; and more informal and personalised development such as mentoring, coaching, 360° feedback, project assignments, action learning sets and team facilitation (see Table 7.1).

Table 7.1   Changing trends in leadership development[6]

Key trends	From	To
Type of provision	• Prescribed course • Standardised • Theoretical/academic	• Intervention/development programme • Customised • Applied/based on real-life challenges
Time frame	• One-off • Discrete start and end points	• Continual • An ongoing development 'journey'
Format	• Didactic: lectures and presentations • Abstract/conceptual	• Participatory: interactive activities and group work • Experiential/reflective
Location	• Classroom-based • Offsite	• Blended (variety of methods) • Work-based as well as offsite
Focus	• Development of individuals • Generic	• Development of individuals and groups • Vocational/for a specific purpose
Role of provider	• Supplier • Expert	• Partner, collaborator and coach • Co-designer/facilitator
Nature of support	• Limited • Primarily concerned with accreditation • Theoretical/academic	• Extensive – relationship management • Primarily concerned with client experience • Coaching/mentoring

Such trends pose major practical and developmental challenges to providers of LMD. First, alongside the modularisation of formal programmes into 'bite-sized chunks' there is increasing pressure to provide holistic programmes applicable to leaders and managers at all levels of the organisation. Secondly, the increase in personalised learning and customisation of programmes poses serious resourcing challenges through the increased time required for developing and supporting provision and the high level of practical expertise required by staff. And thirdly, with the shift away from traditional career structures and employment arrangements managers are increasingly expected to determine and address their own development needs rather than being directed to

6   Adapted from West, M. and Jackson, D. (2002) Developing school leaders: a comparative study of school preparation programmes. Paper presented at the AERA Annual Conference, New Orleans.

provision via their employer (hence increasing the need for promotion and legitimisation of development activities).[7]

Given the difficulty in implementing the changes highlighted above it is perhaps not surprising, therefore, that most HE provision remains in a traditional face-to-face, classroom mode and that where approaches such as e-learning are utilised this tends to be to support rather than replace traditional education (e.g. via a 'blended' approach). Furthermore, whilst employers clearly place great value on work-based learning, much of this remains ad hoc rather than via formalised job rotation, placements, exchanges and assignments.

Whilst much leadership development remains focussed on the acquisition of knowledge and skills, however, it is proposed that one of the main benefits for practising managers is the opportunity for reflection. For managers in fast-paced and demanding jobs, leadership development can offer a protected space in which they can take time to slow down and reflect on past, current and future events – a period of calm in which they can regroup and re-energise for the challenges ahead – although, as John Storey argues, there may well be insufficient time allocated to this.

> There is a fundamental dilemma that haunts many leadership development events. Because leadership is perceived as fundamentally about 'doing' rather than 'knowing', there is an inherent bias towards activity-focussed and indeed briskly paced encounters ... In consequence, there is little time for reflection or strategic thinking. These characteristics of leadership development events are self-evidently in tension with the kind of clear thinking supposedly required of top leaders.[8]

The key to successful leadership development, it would appear, is achieving an appropriate balance between knowledge-exchange, action and reflection, and alignment between the needs and wants of the individual and those of the organisation. From an extensive review of the literature Burgoyne, Hirsh and Williams conclude:

> the evidence on how management and leadership works is that it works in different ways in different situations. The practical implication of this is that to get the benefit of management and leadership development requires the design of appropriate approaches for specific situations rather than the adoption of a universal model of best practice.[9]

– a case of not so much *what you do* but *how you do it*.

For example, 360° feedback, although increasingly in vogue, like many approaches is found to be most effective when integrated within a comprehensive development programme and is significantly affected by the following three factors:

1. a work context supportive of skills development;

7   Hirsh, W. and Carter, A. (2002) *New Directions in Management Development, IES Report 387*, Brighton: Institute for Employment Studies.

8   Storey, J. (2004) Changing theories of leadership and leadership development. In J. Storey (ed.) *Leadership in Organizations: Current Issues and Key Trends*, p. 27. London: Routledge.

9   Burgoyne, J., Hirsh, W. and Williams, S. (2004) *The Development of Management and Leadership Capability and its Contribution to Performance: The Evidence, the Prospects and the Research Need*, p. 49. London: Department for Education and Skills, Research Report 560.

2. the belief of the participant that people can improve their skills; and
3. a belief that they themselves are capable of improving and developing.[10]

Indeed, factors contributing positively towards individual development performance across all approaches include

1. opportunities for receiving and discussing individual feedback;
2. the quality of management processes preceding, supporting and reinforcing development activities;
3. the extent to which they are tailored to personal requirements; and
4. the extent to which they draw on and develop personal experience.[11]

Thus, the choice of development approach is not a simple one. For maximum effect, we need to consider carefully what it is that we seek to develop and how best this can be achieved. If, for example, we wish to develop a culture of shared, considerate and reflective leadership within our organisation is it wise just to send individual 'leaders' on action-packed or highly prescriptive leadership training courses? Robert Chia[12] recounts a Japanese management development programme for high-potential leaders that adopts a rather different approach – they were taken to a retreat in the mountains and encouraged to learn the art of tea pouring and observing the movement of carp. Such a programme, it is argued, sought to develop a sensitivity, self-discipline and capacity for pattern recognition that could not be achieved through more mainstream approaches. A clearly espoused theory of change that leads to desirable forms of behaviour, linked to ongoing monitoring and evaluation of impact(s), is increasingly deemed a crucial factor influencing the success of an LMD intervention.

It is also worth noting that the LMD process serves many purposes beyond simply developing talent. Executive education can be an effective retention strategy that helps maintain the motivation, enthusiasm and commitment of participants; it can serve as a reward; and can also help in team-building and engendering a sense of shared purpose. On the flipside, singling out certain individuals over others for involvement in LMD can lead to unintended consequences such as disappointment, alienation and resistance – little can be more demotivating than having a colleague or superior go off on all-expenses-paid trip only to try to change everything and tell you how to do your job better upon their return!

Theoretical Perspectives on LMD

The trends and challenges outlined above point towards a number of competing pressures and purposes for LMD. There are, of course, the practical concerns of creating more effective managers and leaders, enhancing the competitiveness of organisations and

---

10   Maurer, T. J., Barbeite, F. G. and Mitchell, D. R. (2002) Predictors of attitudes toward a 360-degree feedback system and involvement in post-feedback management development activity, *Journal of Occupational and Organizational Psychology*, 75: 87–108.

11   Burgoyne *et al.* (2004) op. cit.

12   Chia, R. (1996) Teaching paradigm shifting in management education: university business schools and entrepreneurial imagination, *Journal of Management Studies*, 33(4): 409–428.

providing programmes that people will pay for, but associated with these are a number of rather diverse philosophical perspectives on the role of management and leadership within organisations and how best to develop them.

David Holman[13] has identified four contrasting models of management education, each founded upon differing philosophical beliefs about the nature of knowledge, learning, and the role of managers (see Table 7.2). In outlining these perspectives he argues that 'academic liberalism' and 'experiential vocationalism' are somewhat wanting as approaches to the development of practicing managers – the former due to its overreliance on theory and the latter for its overreliance on action – proposing instead that 'experiential liberalism' and 'experiential/critical' approaches are most likely to create managers capable of meeting the future needs of organisations and society. Their experiential methods go a long way to promoting learning and development because of the way in which they build upon how managers naturally learn at work and their ability to address the complexities of actual management practice. They are also likely, however, to produce managers who are more questioning of traditional authority and prepared to challenge organisational vision, values and practices. Clearly the perspective chosen will have major impacts on the kinds of management and leadership capacity developed within organisations yet, despite this, remarkably few LMD initiatives explicitly articulate what constitutes an effective manager or leader, or the educational processes associated with their development.[14]

Table 7.2   Models of management education

Approach	Main assumptions	Main aims	Teaching methods
Academic liberalism	Management education is concerned with the pursuit of objective knowledge about management that can be applied in a relatively scientific and rational manner	To create the management scientist, capable of analysis and the application of theoretical principles	Primary teaching methods include lectures, seminars, case studies and experimentation
Experiential liberalism	Shares many of the same assumptions as academic liberalism but argues for a more applied approach, grounded in managerial experience rather than theory	To create the reflective practitioner equipped with appropriate practical skills and knowledge and the ability to adapt to and learn from the situation	Primary teaching methods would include group work, action learning and self-development

13   Holman, D. (2000) Contemporary models of management education in the UK, *Management Learning*, 31(2): 197–217.

14   Clarke, M., Butcher, D. and Bailey, C. (2004) Strategically aligned leadership development. In J. Storey (ed.) *Leadership in Organizations: Current Issues and Key Trends*, pp. 271–292. London: Routledge.

Table 7.2   *Concluded*

Experiential vocationalism	Arises from economic and organisational concerns to argue that the main role of management education is to provide managers with the relevant skills and knowledge required by organisations	To create the competent manager equipped with the necessary interpersonal and technical competencies required by organisations	Primary teaching methods would include competence based approaches such as the National Occupational Standards in Management and Leadership
Experiential/critical	Seeks to 'emancipate managers *and* other employees in the organisation from oppression and alienation' (Holman, 2000: 208). It has much in common with experiential liberalism although it demands a more critical level of reflection that enables people to become reflexive about their own knowledge and actions and to formulate practical, non-instrumental and emancipative forms of action	To create the critical practitioner able to challenge and develop new modes of action	Primary teaching methods would include approaches incorporating critical action learning and critical reflection

Adapted from Holman.[15]

Another area of confusion in this field is the similarity and difference between 'leadership' and 'management' development. In the discussion so far the terms have been used largely interchangeably because there is a significant degree of overlap, but what exactly *is* leadership (as opposed to management) development and how can individuals and organisations get the most out of it?

Day[16] argues that leadership development is distinct from management development in the extent to which it involves preparing people for roles and situations beyond their current experience. Whilst management development equips managers with the knowledge, skills and abilities to enhance performance on known tasks through the application of proven solutions, leadership development seeks to build capacity to deal with unforeseen challenges. He goes on to make a further distinction between leader and leadership development, whereby *leader development* is about developing individuals in leadership roles, whilst *leadership development* is concerned with the development of the collective leadership capacity of the organisation.

---

15   Holman, D. (2000) op. cit.

16   Day, D. (2000) Leadership development: a review in context, *Leadership Quarterly,* 11(4): 581–613, p. 582.

In this way, each person is considered a leader, and leadership is conceptualised as an effect rather than a cause. Leadership is therefore an emergent property of effective systems design. Leadership development from this perspective consists of using social (that is, relational) systems to help build commitments among members of a community of practice.[17]

Hence 'leader development' can be considered primarily as an investment in the *human capital* of selected individuals, whereas 'leadership development' is an investment in *social capital* via the nurturing of interpersonal networks, cooperation and collaboration within and between people and organisations. Both are important, although traditionally development programmes have focused almost exclusively on the former.

Whilst Day's distinction is helpful in drawing attention to the wider social dynamics of leadership, the boundary between leader, manager and, in fact, personal development remains blurred – participants on development programmes are usually managers and during their studies may well build and extend social networks for themselves and their organisations. There is a risk, therefore, that leadership development could be viewed as *any* understanding that develops individual(s) and that *all* development activities could be regarded as equally effective. Campbell, Dardis and Campbell[18] argue that the field of leadership development is currently dominated by individualistic approaches that seek to enhance the intrapersonal attributes, interpersonal qualities, cognitive abilities, communication skills and task-specific skills of individual participants. At the *intrapersonal* level they argue, however, that 'there is little reason to label this *leadership* development, except in the broad sense that the developing individuals hold leadership positions'.[19] The *interpersonal* level fits more closely with the notion of leadership development as a social influence process, whilst the additional three categories (cognitive, communication and task-specific skills) are a range of personal capabilities that help enhance an individual's interpersonal influence. In each case a challenge remains as to how to differentiate the types of skills required by 'leaders' as opposed to 'managers' and/or 'followers' and the response remains largely dependent on one's theoretical and philosophical views on the nature of leadership. Campbell and colleagues own view is that the primary aim of leadership development is to enhance interpersonal influence *over and above* that which stems directly from a person's positional authority or legitimate power, and that the development of core influencing skills (including values that can serve as a 'moral compass', problem-defining and problem-solving skills, task facilitation skills, and communication and motivational skills) should be the main focus.

In our own experience of developing leaders at the Centre for Leadership Studies in Exeter we take the view that it is important to develop all of these skills with a contextual appreciation of the cultural and organisational environment. When considering leadership, rather than management, development the primary emphasis is on enabling people to think beyond the apparent restrictions of their current role and to develop the critical capabilities to move between operational and strategic modes as required – to balance an attention for detail with an understanding of the bigger picture. 'All in all, leadership

---

17 Ibid., p. 583.

18 Campbell, D., Dardis, G. and Campbell, K. (2003) Enhancing incremental influence: a focused approach to leadership development, *Journal of Leadership and Organizational Studies*, 10(1): 29–44.

19 Ibid., p. 31.

development within management education should develop the 'character', integrity, skills and discursive intelligence necessary for the responsible exercise of power'.[20]

To this extent, leadership development may well incorporate elements of more typical management and self-development programmes (including time management, planning, delegation and self-awareness) but with the objective of creating a reflexive space in which the leader/manager can reflect critically upon their current practice and experience. There is no reason to consider, therefore, that leadership development should only be offered to senior managers and, indeed, there would be good reason to encourage this kind of development opportunity throughout the organisation to enhance collective as well as individual capacity. The nature of the required intervention, however, is likely to vary according to the job role, experience and personal abilities/attributes of participants.

Choosing an LMD Approach

With the array of development initiatives on offer, the differing theoretical perspectives that inform them, and the wide range of providers in the marketplace, the practical issue of deciding which to select can be overwhelming. From extensive experience of working with management and leadership development over many years and in different contexts Jonathan Gosling and Henry Mintzberg propose seven basic tenets upon which management (including leadership) education should be built:[21]

1. Management education should be restricted to practising managers, selected on the basis of performance.
2. Management education and practice should be concurrent and integrated.
3. Management education should leverage work and life experience.
4. The key to learning is thoughtful reflection.
5. Management development should result in organisation development.
6. Management education must be an interactive process.
7. Every aspect of the education must facilitate learning.

The implications of these tenets are manifold both for those purchasing and participating in management and leadership development as well as those providing it. Of particular significance is the emphasis on the interplay between practice and reflection, individual and organisational development, and the provider and participant. Gosling and Mintzberg argue 'there is a certain quality of conversation that takes place in a well-managed classroom that is almost unique, where the fruits of experience, theory and reflection are brought together into a new understanding and commitment'.[22]

This approach argues for increased dialogue and partnership between companies and LMD providers that enhances the depth of conversation about the nature of management and organisation. Leadership development, particularly the opportunity to step back

---

20   Gosling, J. (2004) Leadership development in management education, *Business Leadership Review*, 1(1): 5, available at http://www.mbaworld.com/ blrissues/article1.htm.

21   Gosling, J. and Mintzberg, H. (2004) The education of practicing managers, *Sloan Management Review*, 45(4): 19–22.

22   Ibid., p. 22.

and reflect upon practice, should be built into all aspects of organisational functioning. Development doesn't just occur in the classroom – there are opportunities to learn from just about everything and, indeed as many large organisations now recognise through their application of the 70–20–10 principle,[23] a richness and diversity of learning is pivotal to developing balanced, reflective, yet decisive leadership as and when required

So, on this basis what can we do to ensure that we get the most out of leadership development? From a review of the literature Yukl[24] proposes that conditions for successful leadership training include:

- clear learning objectives;
- clear, meaningful content;
- appropriate sequencing of content;
- appropriate mix of training methods;
- opportunity for active practice;
- relevant, timely feedback;
- high trainee self-confidence; and
- appropriate follow-up activities.

Thus, as indicated earlier, a well-considered approach that clearly articulates how particular interventions will impact upon management and leadership capacity and, in turn, influence individual and organisational performance is most likely to yield effective results. The content and style of the preferred intervention, however, will vary according to the context as the following nine points for reflection will clarify.

1. *Critically evaluate current conceptions of the nature of leadership and learning within your organisation*. As discussed earlier you tend to reap what you sow – if development and reward systems favour individual recognition over collective action then they are unlikely to result in a culture that encourages collaboration and shared leadership.

2. *Think carefully about the development needs of both individuals and the organisation*: 'needs analysis provides the crucial information to ensure that professional learning is appropriate, valid and relevant'.[25] Consider ways in which the impact of development can be evaluated from a range of perspectives; how benefits can be optimised both for individuals and the organisations they serve; and how development needs may change over time.

3. On the basis of these considerations, *explore a range of development options from a number of providers*. Enter into a discussion with providers to see how programmes could be tailored to your requirements; how they could maximise the benefits of experiential and reflective learning; and how the learning can be transferred and sustained within the workplace. Approaches that integrate a variety of learning methods are particularly effective, especially when combined with opportunities for receiving and discussing individual feedback.

---

23   The Center for Creative Leadership's 70–20–10 model of leadership development – 70 per cent on-the-job learning, 20 per cent interpersonal feedback and 10 per cent formal training courses – is now used as a framework for development in organisations including Mars, Lilley, Thompson Reuters and ITT.

24   Yukl, G. (2006) *Leadership in Organizations*, 6th edn. Upper Saddle River, NJ: Pearson Prentice Hall.

25   West-Burnham, J. (1998) 'Identifying and diagnosing needs'. In J. West-Burnham and F. O'Sullivan (eds) *Leadership and Professional Development in Schools*, p. 99. London: Financial Times/Prentice Hall.

4. *Ensure that learning and development are recognised as essential and valued activities within your organisation* and that everyone is encouraged and supported in their learning. The quality of management processes preceding and following development activities are a key predictor of impact and instrumental in ensuring that newly learned competencies are put into practice.

5. *Review other organisational systems and processes (especially HR) and how these interface with and support LMD.* Research evidence indicates that the manner in which HR practices are implemented is a greater predictor of success than which practices are adopted. A sophisticated approach that enables one to 'go the extra mile' is most likely to be effective: 'those organisations with the Big Idea that were value-led and managed were much more likely to sustain their organisational performance over the long-term'.[26]

6. *Identify and reduce personal barriers to learning and the exercise of leadership.* There are a range of psychological barriers to effective leadership, including low self-esteem, lack of self-confidence, fear of failure or disapproval, cognitive 'constriction' and adverse consequences of stress. To overcome these, a range of techniques including desensitisation, reinforcement, psychological re-enactment, social skills development and group dynamics may be used.[27]

7. *Consider the role and impact of organisational culture and context.* What is the nature of the task? How experienced and able are employees? And what are appropriate ways of conceiving of performance? In many sectors, focusing on economic outcomes alone is wholly inappropriate. What drives people to work in health care, education or the military is quite different one from another, and from more commercially oriented sectors. To engage, motivate and inspire people, goals and objectives must be couched in culturally appropriate values and language.

8. *Take an appreciative rather than deficit approach to development.* Build upon strengths that already exist and find ways of working with or around weaknesses. The key to effective leader development is not filling in gaps in competency, but nurturing a unique and genuine approach to leadership.[28] Consider too the importance of continuity in the change process – there may be a time and place for dramatic transformation, but in the majority of cases a more subtle and considered approach that builds upon existing individual, group and organisational capabilities is what is required.

9. Finally, *take the long-term view to leadership and organisational development.* In creating genuine and sustainable leadership within organisations there is no quick fix (despite what some providers may promise!). A series of initiatives following the latest management fads is more likely to engender a climate of cynicism than engagement. 'Leadership' too, has suffered at the hands of faddism, with each guru stating their 7, 8, 9 or 10 principles more vociferously than the last. It pays to be selective and critical in what you sign up to and to consider how development activities fit within the longer-term life and career span of organisations and individuals.

---

26   Purcell, J., Kinnie, N., Hutchinson, S., Rayton, B. and Swart, J. (2003) *Understanding the People and Performance Link: Unlocking the Black Box.* London: CIPD – cited in Burgoyne *et al.* (2004) p. 37.

27   Gill, R. (2006) *Theory and Practice of Leadership.* London: Sage Publications.

28   Buckingham, M. (2005) What great managers do. *Harvard Business Review,* 83(3): 70–79.

An Integrated Approach to Leadership, Management and Organisational Development

So far in this chapter I have focused specifically on the development of individual managers and leaders as well as the development of the more relational and collective aspects of leadership. What is evident, however, from this review is the dynamic interplay between each of these factors and the wider organisational context. It is clear, for example, that developing individual leaders in isolation is unlikely to be sufficient to improve leadership across the entire organisation. Furthermore, building networks and relationships may prove unproductive if the individuals within them do not have the necessary knowledge, skills or competence to exert influence, or find themselves faced with inflexible and unsupportive organisational structures.

Many authors now recognise the interdependent nature of organisational systems and processes and the key role played by people in leadership roles. Purcell *et al.*, for example, in their analysis of HR practices recognise the central role of first line managers (FLMs) in moderating employee experience:

> *It is clear that the crucial link is between the employee experiences of people management, the formation or modification of attitudes towards the employing organisation and the job, and the inducement these provide to engage in certain types of discretionary behaviour, It is not, however, simply the quality of HR practices per se which causes this chain reaction, but crucially the way in which FLMs apply these practices. Employees' experience of these is inexorably linked with their relationship with their FLM who is seen as the agent of the organisation and the deliverer of the people management practices.[29]*

Hence the paradox is that LMD (and other forms of organisational development) are more likely to be successful where leadership and management is already effective than where it is problematic. The question, therefore, for those people involved in such activities is how to create a virtuous cycle whereby individual, team and organisational practices and performance become mutually reinforcing. Whether or not LMD and other organisational processes are aligned, they each transmit powerful messages about what the organisation values and rewards, and where messages are consistent they are far more likely to drive desired behaviours.

The final part of this chapter presents an integrated framework for leadership and organisational development developed from an extensive review of leadership theory and practice.[30] It does not claim to be comprehensive, but rather to serve as a map of the terrain, identifying some key milestones and landmarks that should be of value to those exploring this area. The model, shown in Figure 7.1, is not to be regarded as static but in a continual state of flux, whereby each element informs and influences the others. It incorporates three levels (individual, group/team and organisation) and series of five steps (direction setting, structures and processes, leadership development, learning transfer, evaluation and review). For each step a series of key factors are highlighted, along

---

29   Purcell, J., Kinnie, N., Swart, J., Rayton, B. and Hutchinson, S. (2008) *People Management and Performance*. London: Routledge.

30   Bolden, R. (ed.) (2006) *Leadership Development in Context*. Exeter: Leadership South West Research Report, Centre for Leadership Studies, Exeter. Available at http://www.centres.ex.ac.uk/cls/research/publish.php.

with some key questions to consider. The entire model is embedded within a broader context which should be considered when determining appropriate forms of action. In presenting this model, the intent is that it be used as a structure for facilitating discussion and reflection rather than as a prescriptive framework for deciding on a leadership development approach.

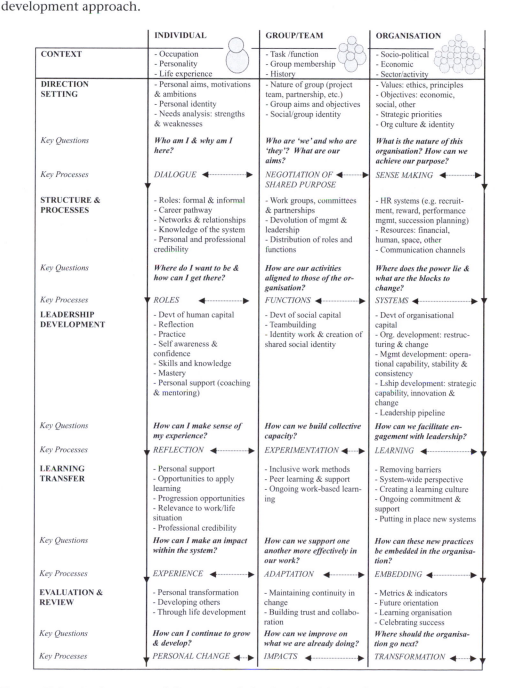

	INDIVIDUAL	GROUP/TEAM	ORGANISATION
CONTEXT	- Occupation - Personality - Life experience	- Task /function - Group membership - History	- Socio-political - Economic - Sector/activity
DIRECTION SETTING	- Personal aims, motivations & ambitions - Personal identity - Needs analysis: strengths & weaknesses	- Nature of group (project team, partnership, etc.) - Group aims and objectives - Social/group identity	- Values: ethics, principles - Objectives: economic, social, other - Strategic priorities - Org culture & identity
Key Questions	*Who am I & why am I here?*	*Who are 'we' and who are 'they'? What are our aims?*	*What is the nature of this organisation? How can we achieve our purpose?*
Key Processes	*DIALOGUE* ◄·········►	*NEGOTIATION OF SHARED PURPOSE* ◄·········►	*SENSE MAKING* ◄·········►
STRUCTURE & PROCESSES	- Roles: formal & informal - Career pathway - Networks & relationships - Knowledge of the system - Personal and professional credibility	- Work groups, committees & partnerships - Devolution of mgmt & leadership - Distribution of roles and functions	- HR systems (e.g. recruitment, reward, performance mgmt, succession planning) - Resources: financial, human, space, other - Communication channels
Key Questions	*Where do I want to be & how can I get there?*	*How are our activities aligned to those of the organisation?*	*Where does the power lie & what are the blocks to change?*
Key Processes	*ROLES* ◄·········►	*FUNCTIONS* ◄·········►	*SYSTEMS* ◄·········►
LEADERSHIP DEVELOPMENT	- Devt of human capital - Reflection - Practice - Self awareness & confidence - Skills and knowledge - Mastery - Personal support (coaching & mentoring)	- Devt of social capital - Teambuilding - Identity work & creation of shared social identity	- Devt of organisational capital - Org. development: restructuring & change - Mgmt development: operational capability, stability & consistency - Lship development: strategic capability, innovation & change - Leadership pipeline
Key Questions	*How can I make sense of my experience?*	*How can we build collective capacity?*	*How can we facilitate engagement with leadership?*
Key Processes	*REFLECTION* ◄·········►	*EXPERIMENTATION* ◄·········►	*LEARNING* ◄·········►
LEARNING TRANSFER	- Personal support - Opportunities to apply learning - Progression opportunities - Relevance to work/life situation - Professional credibility	- Inclusive work methods - Peer learning & support - Ongoing work-based learning	- Removing barriers - System-wide perspective - Creating a learning culture - Ongoing commitment & support - Putting in place new systems
Key Questions	*How can I make an impact within the system?*	*How can we support one another more effectively in our work?*	*How can these new practices be embedded in the organisation?*
Key Processes	*EXPERIENCE* ◄·········►	*ADAPTATION* ◄·········►	*EMBEDDING* ◄·········►
EVALUATION & REVIEW	- Personal transformation - Developing others - Through life development	- Maintaining continuity in change - Building trust and collaboration	- Metrics & indicators - Future orientation - Learning organisation - Celebrating success
Key Questions	*How can I continue to grow & develop?*	*How can we improve on what we are already doing?*	*Where should the organisation go next?*
Key Processes	*PERSONAL CHANGE* ◄·········►	*IMPACTS* ◄·········►	*TRANSFORMATION* ◄·········►

Figure 7.1   An integrated framework for leadership and organisational development

1. The first step of the model is labelled *direction setting* and is underpinned by the processes of dialogue, understanding and creating shared purpose. At an individual level this involves identifying motivations, ambitions, identity, personal strengths and weaknesses. It is summed up by questions such as 'Who am I?' and 'Why am I here?' These can be deeply philosophical questions and may remain with the individual throughout the leadership development process if not their whole life. At a group and organisational level it involves identifying a common and connecting set of values, objectives, shared identity and strategic priorities. It is about how groups and organisations determine who/what they are and what they seek to achieve. Such expressions may be captured in ethics or value statements, organisational mission, business plans and group norms, and define the ultimate purpose, and hence desirable form, of leadership within the group/organisation.

2. The second step involves *examining structures and processes* and incorporates a review of systems, roles and functions. At an individual level this means focusing on formal and informal roles (both within and outside the organisation), career progression and development opportunities, networks and relationships (again within and beyond the organisation), and an in-depth and practical understanding of how the system works – such a perspective should help reveal any barriers, conflicts and sources of support for taking on/developing a leadership role. At a group level it involves considering the distribution of expertise and issues relating to the social dynamics of the work group and how various tasks are distributed. At the organisational level it involves reviewing how HR practices, resource allocation, communication processes, management and leadership approach and partnership working influences the distribution of power and any resistance to change within the system.

3. The third step, *leadership development*, corresponds to the actual process of enhancing the leadership capacity of individuals, groups and the wider organisation. For individuals this involves offering opportunities for learning, reflection and experimentation that builds on and extends prior experience. Whilst an element of this may be about straight skills and knowledge acquisition, it must also go deeper so as to engage with the bigger questions and issues raised in steps one and two. At the group level it involves building and strengthening relationships, trust and commitment. At the organisational level this requires the integration of organisational development, management development and leadership development. It may occur at a number of levels, through multiple channels, be associated with organisational change, and involve longer-term planning for staff development and succession. Ultimately the question here is 'How can we facilitate an active engagement with leadership?'

4. The fourth step is about *learning transfer*. Without application to, and implementation in, the work and life context of individuals and organisations leadership development will fail to bear fruit. Thus individual leaders will require ongoing support, opportunities to apply their learning, and the ability to be recognised as credible in front of their peers and colleagues. They need to take stock of their situation and discover how they can influence the system from their position within it. Groups may find that where several members have engaged in the same development process a greater momentum for change may be sustained through opportunities for peer learning, discussion, joint projects and a shared vocabulary about leadership. For organisations, the transfer involves embedding the learning within organisational systems and processes, eliminating barriers, developing a sense of community and

the establishment of new systems and processes where required. Fundamentally, to be effective leadership development requires long-term top-level support and investment and an ongoing commitment to supporting and developing participants.

5. Finally, the leadership development process requires evaluation and review. Without personal transformation, sharing the learning with others and a commitment to life-long learning individuals will not maximise on the value of their development. Likewise, at the group and organisational levels there should be attempts to identify success, future needs and requirements and meaningful measures and indicators of impact and performance. Given the mediated and time-dependent nature of many of these impacts the measures will need to be qualitative as well as quantitative, which together can be used to create a compelling story or account of why and how the development initiative gave rise to such outcomes and how this might change in the future.

Each of these steps is interconnected such that they influence the others, affect the overall context and help define future directions and priorities. Undoubtedly, proposing an integrated approach such as this is far easier said than done but the message is simple: without taking a holistic, system-wide perspective on LMD the potential benefits will be severely limited. LMD needs to be considered as a key strategic concern, endorsed and supported from the very top of the organisation, with implications for everyone, at all levels.

Conclusion

In this chapter I have attempted to outline the manner in which leadership, management and organisational learning and development are connected and how through considering them as parts of the same process we may be able to enhance the integration and consistency of approaches, thereby improving the likelihood that investments will be worthwhile.

It has also been argued that there has been a massive expansion of LMD supply and demand over recent years, with an increasing tendency towards customised, flexible and experiential initiatives. Despite this trend, however, the realities of LMD are subject to a number of pressures and tensions that mean that individuals and organisations may not always invest in the most effective forms of provision and that providers may find it difficult to deliver precisely what is required. Indeed, evidence of a causal link between LMD and organisational performance remains elusive: however, it would appear that where initiatives are well thought through and aligned with strategic processes and priorities they are far more likely to produce positive and enduring results.

In thinking through how organisations determine an appropriate approach to LMD, they would be well advised to consider the theoretical and philosophical assumptions upon which different forms of provision are based, and to articulate a clear rationale as to how LMD may lead to enhanced individual, group and/or organisational capability and subsequently impact upon performance. To assist readers in deciding upon an LMD provider a number of points of guidance are provided.

The chapter concludes with an integrated framework for leadership development that highlights some of the key issues and questions that organisations, groups and individuals are advised to consider when attempting to line up organisational, leadership and management development.

A large amount of material has been covered and it is possible that this chapter will have raised more questions than it has answered. The exploration of such questions however, I would argue, is the most fundamental part of the enquiry. Developing leaders, managers and organisations is ultimately a process that emerges through collective dialogue. It is the shared meanings, understandings, identities and purpose that hold organisations together. There is no Holy Grail or quick fix but through working together as critical and reflective practitioners we may find new, more efficient, inclusive and sustainable ways of growing, structuring and running our organisations.

Further Reading

For further elaboration on the arguments in this chapter please see the following:

Bolden, R. (ed.) (2006) *Leadership Development in Context*. Exeter: LSW Research Report, Centre for Leadership Studies, University of Exeter. Available at http://www.centres.ex.ac.uk/cls/research/publish.php.

Bolden, R. (ed.) (2005) *What is Leadership Development: Purpose and Practice*. Exeter: LSW Research Report, Centre for Leadership Studies, University of Exeter. Available at http://www.centres.ex.ac.uk/cls/research/publish.php.

Burgoyne, J., Hirsh, W. and Williams, S. (2004) *The Development of Management and Leadership Capability and its Contribution to Performance: The Evidence, the Prospects and the Research Need*. DfES Research Report 560. London: Department for Education and Skills. Available at http://www.dfes.gov.uk/research/data/uploadfiles/RR560.pdf.

Day, D. (2001) Leadership development: a review in context, *Leadership Quarterly,* 11(4): 581–613.

The following websites also have useful material relevant to LMD:

Business Leadership Review http://www.mbaworld.com/blr
Centre for Leadership Studies http://www.exeter.ac.uk/leadership
Northern Leadership Academy http://www.northernleadershipacademy.co.uk
National College for School Leadership http://www.ncsl.org.uk

CHAPTER 8

Leadership and Management Development in Small and Medium-Sized Enterprises: SME Worlds

JEFF GOLD AND RICHARD THORPE

Introduction

In most economies, small and medium-sized enterprises (SMEs) play a major role both in job creation and as the source of regeneration and innovation. SMEs are the acorns from which future oak trees might grow and, as a consequence, understanding how they develop is of considerable importance. Yet, until fairly recently, business schools had considered the study of SMEs to be a Cinderella activity. In a programme of work[1] for the Council for Excellence in Management and Leadership (CEML) in 2002, very few examples were found of business schools that offered programmes specifically designed for SMEs or indeed for entrepreneurs: a trend that has in recent years reversed. Today, no self-respecting business school would be without its chair of entrepreneurship.

Of course, small businesses are often synonymous with their owners, meaning that it is through the development of the owner that the business as a whole is developed. However, it is often the case that the managers of small businesses are those least enthusiastic about development. Often they are short of time and focused on the here and now, so they don't see the relevance of development. This observation is consistent throughout many studies including the Bolton Report as long ago as 1971. A turning point perhaps arrived with the CEML work mentioned above, which, through its wide-ranging remit, was able to offer a more considered understanding of SMEs and how they operated. One of the study's key findings was that overlapping agendas had existed for years between the various government departments charged with small business support, each offering management and leadership services for SMEs that often created a 'jumble of funding drivers'. One consequence was that all too often, too much emphasis was placed on the

---

1   See Perren, L., Davis, M. and Kroessin, R. (2002) *Mapping of UK SME Management and Leadership and Development Provision*. London: Council for Excellence in Management and Leadership.

size of the intervention (for example, learning and development programmes) rather than on identifying those businesses with the potential to develop, and on considering the most appropriate mechanisms to help them do so.

Having each worked in the field for 30 years now, we have many anecdotal examples of how various support initiatives have been offered to exactly the same clients, delivered through very different means. Despite these overlapping agendas, there does appear to be more coherence now in the way SME leadership and management development is approached, and this chapter outlines one of these interventions.

The government, for its part, now has an action plan to offer a more 'joined-up' service so that initiatives that seek to 'stimulate demand' do meet the needs of the SMEs and are delivered in a much more informal way. For example, programmes have been delivered locally that provide 'tailored support and funding for managing directors' of SMEs. As opposed to simply offering packaged solutions, these kinds of programmes enable managers to identify their development needs. This new emphasis on understanding and stimulating the demand for development was one of the features highlighted in the Leitch Review[2] – although there was little elaboration on how this might be achieved! Another related aspect is the amount of funding now available for management and leadership training, rising steadily year on year and clearly indicating the importance now placed on securing high-quality management and leadership within the SME sector. Unlike in times past, this funding does appear to be targeted on 'personal' as opposed to 'business' development: an emphasis that further reinforces the link between managers and their firms.

We begin this chapter by considering some of the context in which leadership and management learning takes place in SMEs. Particular attention is given to the notion of the 'world' of the SME. We see this as important to understanding how demand might be stimulated at either a business or a personal level. We also consider the importance of how performance is measured, which we consider vital in raising managers' horizons to the potential that might exist within the business. It is so often the way managers perceive their businesses, emanating from their past experience and knowledge, that limits their view (or in other words their worlds) that, we believe, need to be challenged for development to take place. We conclude the chapter by considering how provision might become more focused on processes that add value to the business, how knowledge might be embedded and absorbed through networks, and how different associations with communities of practice can often be key to a development process.

Management and Leadership Learning in SMEs

As we have indicated elsewhere in the book, there is no general agreement about the nature of leaders, even if some of the roles they perform have over the years become clearer. This fact has prompted Peter Senge[3] to suggest that in this day and age 'there's not a snowball's chance in hell of redefining leadership'.

---

2   See Leitch, S. (2006) *Prosperity for All in the Global Economy – World Class Skills. The Final Report of the Leitch Review of Skills*. London: HMSO/HM Treasury.

3   Senge, P. (1999) The gurus speak (panel discussion): complexity and organizations, *Emergence*, 1(1): 73–91.

In Chapter 1, we discussed the difference between leadership and management, suggesting the split is not particularly helpful. We recognise that both are important in the context of SMEs. When it comes to understanding SMEs, one problem is that they are often referenced against practice in larger organisations,[4] which is not always helpful. What we do know, however, is that crucial to running an SME is a combination of day-to-day activity and overall responsibility for the ownership, governance and direction of the business, and that many of the building blocks important in leadership have a shared foundation with those identified in the literature on entrepreneurship. So it matters little whether we call it 'management' or 'leadership' development; what is important is how the learning relates to how managers experience and undertake their work.

There are clearly managers who want to grow their businesses in markets that are able to grow but who soon become stuck, overwhelmed by the day-to-day issues faced; these wish to develop into oak trees. However, we also know that there are others with little interest in growth (although they still might need support); these are businesses that we might characterise as healthy bonsais that wish not to grow, but simply to retain their independence and survive. It is generally agreed that most managers of SMEs lack the time to stand back and reflect – yet this is exactly what they need to do in order to take stock and develop. This often means that most learning in SMEs takes place at work, outside formal educational settings such as universities and colleges. This is borne out by relatively few managers' registering to undertake formal programmes of development, preferring instead to learn more actively by working through problems, and talking to customers, staff and other SME managers they meet during the course of their day. It is unlikely that these activities are counted as SME learning activities, as the learning tends to occur naturally and simply becomes part of work. There is nothing new in recognising this kind of 'informal learning', and Allan Gibb and his team at Durham University[5] championed a variety of learner-centred, problem-centred approaches over many years.

There is now growing recognition that informality in learning and development is important for SME management and leadership development. Government bodies talk about the 'three-legged gazelle': all that this type of firm needs to take a leap forward is to gain the knowledge that will enable it to take that leap forward. At a national level, the government's *Action plan for small business* seeks to provide a more 'joined-up' service, with initiatives that stimulate demand that work through brokers who serve an important role in diagnosing needs and thereby provide an appropriate matching of activity. This use of brokers is now seen as increasingly important in the connecting of SMEs that would normally avoid contact with the agencies that administer funding; we will highlight the role of such brokers later in this chapter.

The Importance of Performance Measurement

How SME managers learn from informal events will of course vary, and this is now recognised as a key factor affecting the growth of a business. There is also growing

---

4   The work of Fuller-Love, N. (2006) Management development in small firms, *International Journal of Management Reviews*, 8(3): 175–190 is very useful here.

5   See for example, Gibb, A. A. (1997) Small firms' training and competitiveness: building upon the small business as a learning organisation, *International Small Business Journal*, 15(3): 13–29.

evidence that SME managers, rather than 'struggle to grow', in fact 'struggle to survive'. We can point to a whole a range of factors that affect the disposition of managers to learn and develop: some are external, such as the structure of the industry and the market competition, and education and past training also play their part. As for internal factors, we know that many SMEs have inherited problems, for example from family ownership or from sets of values, which will impact on learning.

One crucial factor, which has been subject to considerable research, is individuals' approach to the way they view performance.[6] For example, we know that SME managers find it difficult to participate in projects owing to a lack of time and that, even when a performance model is employed, its implementation is often only partial. Of course, many of these models are also those designed for use in larger organisations. Perhaps most importantly, the performance measurements used are often narrowly focused, concentrating unduly on financial and operational aspects rather than attempting to deal with more qualitative aspects that are important for survival and development, and often with little attempt at integration. Finally, performance measurement is unplanned, simply responding to problems. As a result, the measures used are often backward-looking and support control as opposed to innovation and change.

What we also know is that performance, in the mind of an owner–manager, is an idiosyncratic concept that can be properly understood only with a thorough understanding of the desires, aspirations and ambitions of the manager. Many SME managers use measures that are partial and short-term, reflecting the pressures they face from day to day. Often the very idea of thinking about the business strategically is anathema, and the limitations of the performance measures used by SMEs serve to play a key role in how managers think about their businesses. This appears to be the case in respect to development, and recent research has shown a significant association between an SME manager's approach to strategic planning and the firm's business performance.[7] Our point is that those who engage in a 'strategic' approach to performance management are likely to be more profitable, with a greater capacity to grow, innovate and develop new products.

In an attempt to represent SME performance and develop discussion in this area, we use the framework displayed in Figure 8.1, which shows a range of measures on two dimensions. In this way, we can depict different stages in considering performance, and the progression that needs to take place for SME managers to adopt a more strategic approach to performance management. The horizontal axis represents a range of approaches to performance evaluation – from goal-based approaches that measure specific, relatively tangible, simple, short-term, and visible aspects of business performance, to those (on the right) that offer more systemic approaches taking into account many more variables within a business and the interaction between these variables. The vertical axis shows the planning horizon often associated with the use of a measure. A short-term horizon might be associated with daily or weekly output measures such as hours worked as a percentage of turnover, whereas long-term measures are often financially based and invariably include some qualitative dimensions that need to be assessed over a much longer period

---

6   See in particular Garengo, P., Biazzo, S. and Bititci, U. S. (2005) Performance measurement systems in SMEs: a review for a research agenda, *International Journal of Management Reviews*, 7(1) 25–47.

7   See Perry, S. C. (2001) The relationship between written business plans and the failure of small business in the US, *Journal of Small Business Management*, 39(3):201–209 and Roper, S. (1997) Strategic initiatives and small business performance: an exploratory analysis of Irish companies, *Entrepreneurship and Regional Development*, 9: 353–364.

(at least a quarter, and sometimes several years). The diagonal line in the diagram shows the direction of travel that we consider the manager might need to take if they are to raise their horizons and think more about the future. Those at the bottom left might be associated with recording changes in inputs and outputs that might affect the day-to-day operations of the business in a given period of time. These measures are the kind that give managers information on key survival indicators but don't take account of the wider context in which the business operates, including changes that the environment might bring.

The group in the centre of the diagram represents efficiency measures that assess the steady state. Efficiency is a notion that helps managers make comparisons internally as well as externally; in assessing the potential for improvement, many firms use the technique of benchmarking to gauge their relative performance levels.

At the top right of the diagram are the more strategic measures, which capture those capabilities that a firm needs in order to protect and develop activities that will enable it to continue to be successful. These kinds of measures often take into consideration a much wider range of factors, as well as considering how measures might be devised to account for important linkages within and outside the organisation. The dynamic in a small firm so often tends to rest in the short term (those in the bottom-left corner of the diagram); yet, to grow and develop, the measures that increasingly need to be used are those towards the top right. As quantitative data can't measure all aspects of a business, there will undoubtedly be a need to take account of a range of qualitative aspects, for example flexibility of response. The issue here is that many of these qualitative aspects of performance are far more difficult to measure than the quantitative ones, yet their assessment may be vital to monitoring the success of the business.

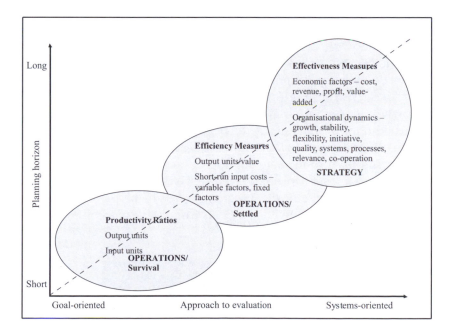

Figure 8.1   Hierarchy of productivity measures

Adapted from: Bowey, A. M. and Thorpe, R. (1986) *Payment Systems and Productivity*, London: MacMillan.

Considerations such as these are important to those who seek to bring learning and development to SME managers. They form part of the SME 'world' we speak about, as well as playing a key role in what a manager will accept as useful, and indicate the extent to which the learning can be 'stretched forward' to offer the manager scenarios of how the business might develop in the future.

The Demand for Management and Leadership Development in SMEs

So far we have argued that most SME managers learn informally, but we have also recognised the need for flexibility of provision if development opportunities are to meet managers' needs. Figure 8.2 presents a number of possibilities along a dimension that ranges from highly informal to highly formal approaches to learning.

We show five possible approaches to learning, ranging from one extreme of highly informal, depicted as 1, to another extreme of highly formal, depicted as 5. However, between these poles is a raft of possible practices, depicted as 2, 3 and 4. Factors that determine the preferred approach to learning include the following:

- Place: *Where learning takes place* can range from purely on-site to more formal settings, such as the classroom or off-site training suites, with many permutations. For example, managers might be prepared to move away from their workplace, but wish still to remain on-site. This would explain position 2 on the dimension.
- Problem: This factor considers *the speed with which a problem must be solved* and the extent to which tools are available to do so, as opposed to applying abstract ideas that could then be used in solving a range of problems, both then and in the future. Again, there are permutations – for example, learning might be theoretical (involving abstract ideas) but with some indication of when the theory might be inapplicable: this would indicate position 3 on the diagram.
- Sociality: In *the social setting of learning, who will be involved* in the discussions can range from those who are immediately present as part of the problem-solving process to experts who may not be familiar to the manager. Those who are prepared to learn from others both inside and outside the organisation would be at position 3.
- Impact: This considers *how quickly any changes through the learning would become apparent*, ranging from immediate application, as required, to an extended period during which the impact can be deferred or given time to work. Thus, models or frameworks learned from an MBA programme might be used later in a manager's career; this would be an example of position 5 on our dimension.

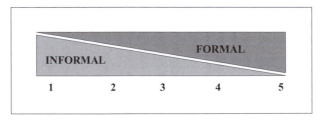

Figure 8.2   Dimensions of learning in SMEs

By applying these factors, embodied in the diagram above, we noticed that the demand for development proved mainly informal, using coaches, mentors and advisors. These people work with managers at work on a one-to-one basis, on issues seen as of immediate use to managers. This represents mainly a position 2 on our dimension. Our observations reinforce research evidence that emphasises the 'soft' nature of relation-building approaches within SME advising. It is clear to us that most SME managers prefer relatively informal learning, even when making use of outsiders such as mentors and coaches.

Providing Management and Leadership Development in SMEs

One of the features from the findings of the CEML was the plethora of provision in SME management and leadership development that was seen as bureaucratic and disconnected from the needs of SMEs. Our view is that the funding targets drive the growth and diversity of provision, resulting in there being a poor take-up of the schemes, even when these achieve a relatively high profile.[8]

As we have indicated, the disposition of SME managers towards performance measurement and growth, and a desire to stay small and survive, is also manifest in their response to the provision of management and leadership skills. Thus, where survival and the constraint of current operations are the priority, managers are preoccupied with meeting short-term goals and use measurement processes accordingly. As a consequence, management and leadership development needs to reflect these concerns for managers who wish to take a step towards growth, and to help them stretch themselves and plan more for the longer term (which will require a more strategic focus). We suggest these two possibilities can be presented as dimensions along a continuum of provision of management and leadership development, shown in Figure 8.3.

The kinds of factors that will determine a development provider's approach to considering management and leadership development include the following:

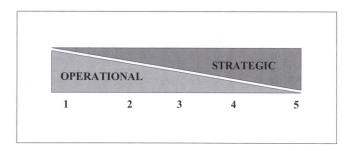

Figure 8.3   Possible provision of management and leadership development

---

8   See the work of Matlay, H. (2004) Contemporary training initiatives in Britain: a small business perspective, *Journal of Small Business and Enterprise Development,* (11)4: 504–513.

- Time frame: This relates to *the length of time needed for the provision to impact on the manager and organisation.* At position 1, an immediate impact is expected but at position 5, the impact might be over many years.
- Horizon: This considers *how provision might broaden the scope of thinking of managers.* The range here is from the short term and satisfaction with status quo to the longer term and thinking 'outside the box'. This notion of stretch is crucial for managers as it considers the extent to which their understandings can be changed.
- Measurement: Any provision implies *how performance might be measured.* This could range from the immediate performance of a task, through the setting of performance targets, to more systemic approaches to measurement.
- Ownership: This factor considers *the process of aspects contained in any provision and how this might occur.* Ownership ranges from the person themselves (at position 1), through the involvement of others (at position 2), to the use of outside experts (at position 5).
- Cost: Participating in any learning activity does entail some cost, in terms of time, commitment, money, or a combination of these.

Figures 8.2 and 8.3 illustrate the variations in SME learning and so the possibilities for provision. They can be combined to create a framework that allows us to match SME managers' requirements with provision. This framework is shown in Figure 8.4.

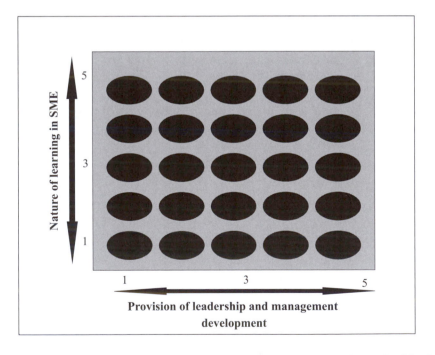

Figure 8.4   Learning requirements of SME managers (L) against the kinds of programmes on offer (P)

Using this framework, we suggest 25 possible combinations of learning and provision, or (following the CEML) 25 SME 'worlds'. We accept that this is an oversimplification, since all SMEs are unique, with their own contexts, histories and cultures. However, in a general way, we are seeking to add complication to learning and provision. Each combination of learning (L) and provision (P) represents a possible position based on particular judgements. We believe that the value of the framework lies in helping us understand SME 'worlds' in terms of the learning preferences of SME managers, and their desires and expectations for provision.

L1P1 indicates highly informal learning and highly operational provision. This is a position of normal working and learning for most SMEs, where survival might be the main mode of operation. It might also be the starting point for what we could call 'pure' entrepreneurism, with a movement along the floor of the framework to L1P5. Crucially, this movement occurs without external business support, where learning is continuous as the managers stretch the business and themselves. Such managers are prepared to 'boldly go' forward, and are committed to developing themselves and their businesses.

A contrast can be drawn with managers at other points on the framework. For example, a manager at L4P2 might be prepared to go on training courses away from work and might be more accepting of theories that could eventually be applied at work. At P2, managers have moved beyond a reactive focus and basic measures, so they will consider small improvements and incremental changes to improve efficiency. Other positions show different dispositions toward learning and what is on offer. However, as we know, many SME managers become stuck at L1P1 and do need help in making a move, if they desire to do so.

Engaging with the 'Hard-to-Reach'

We know that while many SME managers do not undertake more formal management and leadership development, business size is not necessarily the main determinant of this:[9] they might still undertake development if they see value in it and if it serves their interests. Many SME managers find the value hard to see, partly because their interest lies in surviving and in managing problems on a day-to-day basis. Learning is centred on coping with problems, so they tend not to see value in connecting with others, even if the programmes of development are fully funded and of no cost to the business. Such managers we refer to as the 'hard-to-reach' or the 'tough nuts to crack'.[10] Engaging with such managers is not easy, first because there are very many such SMEs. Second, lack of awareness about offers of learning and development is not one of the difficulties, and mailshots and publicity campaigns have not proven effective. However, we also know that many such managers have a desire for growth but are 'stuck and struggling'. They also tend have a sceptical view of any attempt at interference from the outside.

Nevertheless, there is evidence that with the right approach and set of skills, even 'hard-to-reach' managers can be attracted into development. The work of a small number

---

9   See Thomson, A., Storey, J., Mabey, C., Gray, C., Farmer, E. and Thomson, R. (1997) *A Portrait of Management Development*. London: Institute of Management/Open University.

10   See for example, Devins, D. and Gold, J. (2000) Cracking the tough nuts: mentoring and coaching the managers of small firms, *Career Development International*, 5(4/5): 250–255.

of intermediaries or brokers, whom we have referred to as 'door-knockers',[11] is becoming recognised. Through the efforts of these brokers, SME managers can express what they need. Engagement with managers is the crucial starting point in helping SMEs grow and develop, even after many years of survival being the priority. Our own research has shown that these door-knockers have a way of working that involves physically presenting themselves to SME managers with offers of learning and development. We found such engagement to be a strategic and tactical process, with a clear plan of engagement using information from agencies such as Business Link on hard-to-reach SMEs and on the funding offered. A target for engagement could be set, taking into account the payment that the SME would receive if evidence was provided that managers had set an action plan for development, including considering the needs and desires of managers, the provision required and how its impact could be measured.

When it comes to engagement, particularly striking was the effort of the brokers to make conversation based on the interests and concerns of managers. It was also evident that such conversations could seldom be predicted, and that a considerable repertoire of conversational skills is needed to start and sustain the relationship with managers. Often, it was necessary to engage initially with those who 'protected' managers from 'outsiders', such as receptionists and secretaries. In one case, for example, a receptionist 'in a good mood' was attracted into a conversation using a joke, which then led to a conversation about a funded programme of management development. Eventually, success was achieved but it still needed four more phone calls to make progress. Even if SME managers agreed to meet with a broker, it was often the case that suspicion and previous experience of funded programmes had to be tackled. Perceptions of heavy paperwork and the time involved to begin participation were frequently encountered as preconceptions.

A key skill seems to be to use the indicators available to begin a conversation, which may not immediately be about the business. For example, in one case, football and golf photos on the wall and an interest in cars were used to establish common ground in 'plain English'. This process established the social credentials of the broker, removed potential threat and allowed agreement to a second visit to focus specifically on management and leadership needs.

Between the first and second visits, the issues for discussion can be clarified. Some managers already know exactly what needs to be done and the help required, but others need more time and more discussion. Crucially, the paperwork required to access funds, usually via the public purse, does need to be completed, for reasons of accountability, but this can be minimised and simplified by the broker. The development of trust between the broker and the manager prevents the latter's past experiences with agencies becoming a barrier to progress. Once the manager's needs are expressed and approved, it is quite possible that others can become involved in the relationship. We found that the door-knockers were able to facilitate the connection to particular providers, who would join the conversation to ensure that a close understanding of the SME was generated.

What is important about these processes is that they point the way to how SME managers, even those that are seen as the hard-to-reach, can be engaged with to consider learning and development needs. The value of the work of intermediaries – the door-knockers – is that, through persistent efforts to put themselves physically in front of

---

11   See Gold, J. and Thorpe, R. (2008) *Mapping of UK SME Management and Leadership Development Provision* 'Training, it's a load of crap': the story of the hairdresser and his suit, *Human Resource Development International*, 13(3): 385–389.

managers, they can then create a conversation that results in a plan for learning. Such skills seem entirely conversational, and the grant alone is not enough to attract managers. Once the plan is made, appropriate provision can then be found and, if this is suitable, managers can explore new possibilities, having solved existing problems. In the next section, we explore how managers might move from one world to another and beyond. We will provide an example of this movement through the story of one manager, the owner of a hairdressing business in Huddersfield, who stopped struggling for the first time in 19 years and started a path of growth that continues.

Moving Worlds: the Role of Coaching and Mentoring

Coaching and mentoring are both processes of helping that are proving to be effective approaches to SME learning and development. Both allow managers to work on issues that are meaningful in a local context, and both give prominence to building relationships and stimulating demand for learning within these. Although more expensive than other approaches, coaching and mentoring are particularly important in helping survival-oriented managers make progress. Informal learning is used and, if this is correctly pitched and timed, SME managers can be moved to consider new possibilities that they have previously found inconceivable. In terms of the framework shown in Figure 8.4, L1P1 might be the typical position of a hard-to-reach SME manager. To achieve movement from this position, those engaging and helping must understand the current capabilities and how these are used in work. In each case, culture and history are bound to play a role, and feature as part of an SME manager's story. This all adds to gaining a greater knowledge of the SME world we referred to earlier. Anyone involved in helping a manager in this sector will need to understand the peculiarities of their world, so the helper can judge what degree of stretch can be built into provision. Figure 8.5 represents such a consideration.

In World 1, the current capabilities are shown as the inner oval. If access is granted, a coach or mentor can work with these capabilities and then attempt to move into the area between the inner oval and the outer boundary. The edge of the world represents the limit of acceptable movement, at that moment. However, through achievement, it might become possible to stretch the manager beyond the boundary of World 1 towards

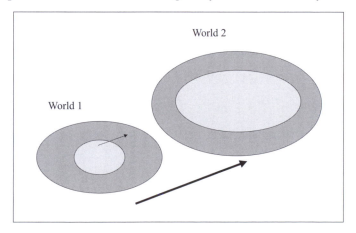

Figure 8.5   Stretching SME managers and leaders

World 2. Crucially, coaches and mentors need to understand how this movement can occur, based on how new capabilities can be developed.[12] In the case that follows, the relevance of this can be clearly seen.

The story concerns Mark Riley, who is a well-known hairdresser in Huddersfield;[13] for many years, his views about learning and development were typical of those of many SME managers. More concerned about survival than growth, he had a poor record in responding to training initiatives, even being antagonistic and highly sceptical about their benefits. Mark had been 'stuck and struggling' in running his business, and this had been the pattern for 19 years, even though he felt he was sitting on a goldmine waiting to be exploited.

It was through a door-knocker, Kent Mayall of Inspire to Independence,[14] that Mark became aware of how he could exploit his goldmine. The work took place within a national programme of management and leadership development for SMEs, which provided £1,000 for learning and development for each manager, following a needs assessment leading to a personal development plan. Crucial to this process was the way Kent was able to engage with Mark to ensure he was aware of the programme. But this awareness was not achieved without a struggle. First, it took five telephone calls before Mark agreed to meet Kent, and then it took a further four meetings before Mark's scepticism subsided and he agreed to meet Brian Wadsworth,[15] a specialist mentor of SME managers, over breakfast in a café.

Importantly, through this series of meetings, Mark's needs and desires became more evident and he ended up no longer stuck and struggling, but now a 'man with a plan for change', which he agreed to implement with Brian.[16] Working with Brian, Mark soon identified major inefficiencies in current operations that were causing cash-flow problems; indeed, the business was a 'mess'. One change needed was the introduction of a supervisory infrastructure that would allow Mark more time to focus on operational and financial performance. He could also take time away from cutting hair to meet with Brian to think strategically and talk business. Part of this involved articulating Mark's special vision of the 'Mark Riley Experience', based on a 'journey of well-being for customers' and growth of the business to over 10 salons across Yorkshire by 2010.

This vision would need trained staff who could enact the values that went with the vision. So it was not enough that trainees went college to get their NVQ in Hairdressing; it was also important that they understood and worked with Mark's notion of the journey of well-being for customers. Here, Mark's doubts reflected concerns more widely expressed about the United Kingdom's National Vocational Qualifications framework, which does not carry the support of all employers.[17] One way for Mark to ensure that trainees met his requirements was to do more training in-house, rather than at college. With Brian's

---

12   This analysis has been developed from the work of the Russian psychologist, Lev Vygotsky. See Vygotsky, L. S. (1978) *Mind And Society: The Development Of Higher Mental Proces*. Cambridge, MA: Harvard University Press.

13   You can contact Mark Riley at mark@mark-riley.co.uk.

14   You can contact Kent Mayall at kent.mayall@i2i-ltd.co.uk.

15   You can contact Brian Wadsworth at brian@isds2.co.uk.

16   For an evaluation of this programme, see Learning and Skills Council (2006) *Impact Evaluation of the National Phase of the Leadership and Management Development Programme*. London: Learning and Skills Council.

17   See Raggatt, P. and Williams, S. (1999) *Government, Markets and Vocational Qualifications: An Anatomy of Policy*. London: Falmer.

help, a partnership deal was struck with Brighouse College to allow Mark to establish an academy for 20 trainees, with a forecast to expand to 50 as the business grows.

The significance of this story rests on its demonstration of how hard-to-reach SME managers, many of whom have long-frustrated aspirations for growth and development, require persistent efforts to secure engagement that leads to a process of development. It is only through these efforts that the 'world' of the manager can be understood and assessed. Like many SME managers, Mark did not lack awareness of support, but his experience of such offerings failed to attract him. And yet, for nearly 20 years, Mark had suspected that his business was a goldmine, waiting for exploitation. Furthermore, this opportunity was possible not through being in the classic high-growth sector but through the vision and aspiration of the manager. Mark was a three-legged gazelle, requiring support for take-off.

We can see that coaching and mentoring can work in tune with a manager's capabilities, while providing the necessary stretch into uncharted waters. This requires a process of conversation that creates the space for more strategic considerations and a movement from one 'world' to another.[18] One of the most important results of this movement is that while Mark initially received £1,000 to pay for his work with Brian, within three months he was willing to pay for his development because he could measure the impact from the support he received. Indeed, this was a feature of greater awareness of performance measurement.

Crucially, business development was the rationale for Mark's management and leadership development, and subsequently for the training initiatives for his staff.[19] Like many employers, Mark was not impressed with formal qualifications but, as a passionate believer in his industry, he wanted to 'give something back' and to construct a vision or plan for his business that provided the backdrop against which skills development could be referenced.

What Else Works?

Clearly then, coaching and mentoring offer significant potential in working with the specific interests of SME managers and leaders, helping them find solutions to immediate problems they face and then stretching them towards new possibilities and ways of working. We are also aware that many managers are prepared to discuss problems and issues with other managers.[20] We know there are many local networks, forums and business clubs that provide an ideal environment for this to happen. Although managers may not regard the activity as learning, there are many possibilities for changes in behaviour, partly because of the informality. One example in which we are involved is the Yorkshire Leadership Group. This is a programme of facilitated peer-group development, with participants from a wide range of non-competing organisations. Each group has no more than 15 members and meets every 2 months. Members can also arrange one-to-one

---

18   This is a crucial finding from the Evolution of Business Knowledge Project: see Thorpe, R., Holt, R., Macpherson, A. and Pittaway, L. (2007) *Studying the Evolution of Knowledge within Small and Medium-Sized Firms*, London: Economic and Social Research Council/Engineering and Physical Sciences Research Council.

19   This slightly reverses the idea of skills-led business development.

20   See Zhang, J. and Hamilton, E. (2006) Enterpreneurial learning through peer networks: a process model. Paper presented at the British Academy of Management Conference, Belfast, September.

business coaching, mentoring, advisory or non-executive director services to supplement the group meetings.[21]

Action learning programmes also serve to create similar conditions. In action learning, there is informality and challenge between peers, but learning has a more central place in the process. For example, recent evidence from the evaluation of a regional action learning programme for over 150 SME managers suggested significant benefits: the chance to reflect on and question key issues within a context of challenge and support led the managers to take considerable action to overcome the constraints they faced. It also became apparent that the move to more formality, and the chance to escape operational concerns, was for many a key feature in becoming more strategic and more capable as leaders.[22] Action learning has also been shown to be successful in programmes supported by the Sector Skills Councils in addressing leadership development for micro and SME owner–managers. The Action Learning for Leaders programme ran from 2004 to 2006, with three groups of SME owner-managers from across the UK meeting in Glasgow, Nottingham and Guildford. The results, which were rigorously evaluated, showed the process of action learning and on-the-job coaching to be very successful. Comments from participants included the following:

I have benefited greatly from this programme and have been able to bring the benefits directly back to my business.

The programme has really helped me to gain the confidence and achieve changes.

This programme has probably saved my company from potential oblivion on my retirement.

One interesting development in action learning for SME managers has been occurring in Sheffield, where a programme starts as peer-to-peer learning but, after nine months of participation, offers members the option of beginning their own action learning set. This creates the potential to multiply the number of participants over time, hence the programme's name: Six-Squared. As reported, 'the model is designed to be a sustainable "self-help" approach, which is entrepreneur-led and that does not depend on external agencies or government funding'.[23]

A further possibility is carefully to combine coaching and mentoring with action learning, and to introduce further inputs such as lectures, masterclasses and seminars that seek to further open the managers' horizons and desire for growth, and to make use of genuine 'strategic space'. For example, the pilots of the LEAD programme at Lancaster University (between November 2005 and March 2006) incorporated coaching, mentoring and peer learning, as well as strategic workshops led by experts. The evaluation revealed the importance of the 'soft aspects' of formal provision, including acknowledging the need for affirmation and growth in confidence, principally achieved by building relationships and supported by reflective and peer learning. The concept of strategic space was a key finding

---

21   For more details, go to http://www.yorkshireleadership.co.uk/.

22   See Clarke, J., Thorpe, R., Anderson, L. and Gold, J. (2006) It's all action, it's all learning: action learning in SMEs, *Journal of European Industrial Training*, 30(6): 441–455.

23   Taken from the interim evaluation of the Six-Squared Learning Sets for Entrepreneurs and Small Business Owners, Sheffield University, December 2007.

of research that suggested SME managers and leaders need space to think strategically so that new ideas can be considered and absorbed into normal work.[24]

Taking this evidence together, we discern a pattern of possible provision that appears to meet the needs and aspirations of SME managers and leaders, providing that sufficient attention is given to the process of engagement. This approach is important as many SME managers in the UK and elsewhere remain detached from the provision, often because too little attention has been paid to their interests and needs, or because there has been a failure to communicate with them appropriately. As a consequence, the importance of door-knockers to access those SMEs traditionally categorised as hard-to-reach is essential. If access is then gained, the likely path to development will connect them to someone who can provide help for their immediate needs, usually through coaching and mentoring. From this point on, however, other kinds of provision become possible but will always depend on the desires and preferences of the individual SME manager. Our view is of a ladder of possible intervention and provision, as shown in Figure 8.6.

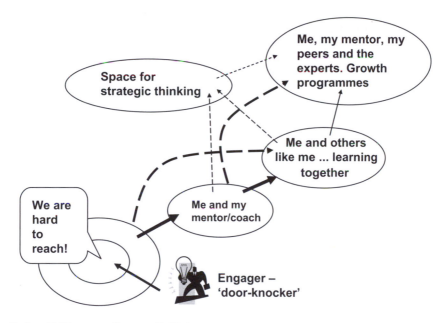

Figure 8.6   SME growth possibilities

Conclusion

To conclude this chapter, we offer principles of good practice for those interested in SME leadership and management development, based on the evidence we have examined as

24   See Thorpe, R., Jones, O., Macpherson, A. and Holt, R. (2008) The evolution of business knowledge in smaller firms. In H. Scarbrough (ed.) *The Evolution of Business Knowledge*, Oxford: Oxford University Press. This is a chapter that develops the importance of social and human capital and develops the notion of strategic space in the development of small firms. The project was funded within the ESRC The Evolution of Business Knowledge Programme: RES-334-25-0015.

part of our work with the Northern Leadership Academy.[25] We make no claim that these principles represent a definitive statement of what must be done, but they have emerged from evidence and so can be used to guide policy-makers and practitioners. We recognise that as more evidence accumulates, the principles will need to be adapted.

1. *Engage with the identity and interests of the manager.* For managers in SMEs, learning becomes meaningful when it is strongly related to their concerns, problems and desires. It is important to explore their situation and how this has come about. Every manager will have a story of who they are, how they came to be where they are, and, possibly, what they are trying to achieve. They personally value the organisations they manage and lead, both emotionally and financially. There may also be a long history behind their position and this needs to be appreciated. Abstract concepts are unhelpful if they do not form part of the sense-making activities that help managers and relate to the image of themselves as leaders. They are also often very sceptical (if not cynical) about outside help, and sensitive to exposing potential 'weakness'. It is therefore also fundamental to gain confidence, and to build mutual respect and trust, as well as to establish perspective and relativity.

2. *Understand the context and build on it.* The experience of the SME manager both shapes and is shaped by the context of the organisation, so it is important to understand this before any activity can be provided. The 'best practice' approaches of leadership development in larger organisations start from the wrong premise for many SME managers, whose desire to be self-employed greatly shapes their disposition to learning. SME managers must establish 'balance' between strategic and operational performance, as well as between management and leadership. However, running through their experiences of running their business, themes of loneliness and isolation are common. They want to understand whether the ways they run their businesses are appropriate, and this opens the possibility of exploring new ideas, so long as there is connection to the realities they face.

3. *Respond to the time-frame as appropriate.* It is important to understand a manager's thinking about time frames. The reality is that most SMEs have extremely short planning horizons, and order books that barely last more than one or two months at a time. Indeed, SMEs that operate at survival levels work with a time frame that can best be summarised as 'here and now'. Thus, strategy development and long-term business growth are, more often than not, relegated to the background or do not feature at all in the 'thinking' of SMEs. For such managers, attempts to move too quickly beyond immediate concerns are likely to be rejected. However, recent research has shown there is a significant association between an SME's approach to strategic planning and its business performance: those who engage in a strategic approach to their organisations, working with time frames of between one and five years, are likely to be more profitable and to have a greater capacity to grow, innovate and develop new products.

4. *Determine the measurement and what is valued.* How SMEs measure their performance is strongly connected to the managers' response to what they learn. The measures that

---

25   The Northern Leadership Academy was founded in 2006 with the aim of developing entrepreneurial growth in the North of England through increasing leadership talent. For more details, go to http://www.northernleadershipacademy. co.uk/.

managers use can constrain and limit learning, especially as research suggests that most SMEs find it difficult to participate in performance-measurement projects due to lack of time for anything other than operational activities. Further performance measurement is narrowly focused, usually on financial and operational aspects, with little awareness of integration or systemic consideration. Even where a performance model is employed, the implementation tends to be partial or incorrect – a consequence perhaps of most models being more suited to larger organisations. Measurement is not planned but is responsive to, and emerges from, solving problems, with the consequence that any measures that do emerge are past-oriented and developed to support control.

5. *Stimulate entrepreneurship and stretch.* SME managers are generally concerned with present interests, seeking to repair or improve current ways of working. It is important to assess existing capacity and capabilities, and to explore the potential for making an advance. Each manager will attach a meaning to such an advance, which simultaneously provides the potential and the limit for development. Attempting to move the manager too far beyond this point will be seen as inappropriate or unrealistic. However, over time, and through the development of relationships with others, it may become possible for the manager to gain command of new capabilities, setting a new and higher limit for the potential and development.

6. *Develop communities of practice.* Learning by managers in SMEs most often occurs naturally by completing work and solving problems as part of an everyday process. Such learning is the by-product of a work process rather than its focus, and is shared with everyone involved in the process. The accumulation of such learning over time, and the meanings attached to what is done, become accepted by everyone connected to the organisation. SME managers also like to learn with and from others who have similar concerns and face similar issues. Managers need learning to connect to action, and being able to consider the possibilities with others who can understand the realities they face is more likely to lead to success. The social and interdependent dimension of learning is therefore crucial. Through conversations during which managers share information, seek help and generally give meaning to their work, collective knowledge is created that enables, sustains and constrains – but also advances – its practice.

7. *Enhance belief, confidence and awareness.* Any attempt to provide support for SME management and leadership development requires a space to attract managers into a conversation. Development interventions must recognise the need for appropriate language and learning contexts (often the managers' own or other businesses), and for a pedagogy that is premised on exchanges of experiences and ideas. There is the need to help managers identify how interventions relate to their business, and how these help develop both the business and the managers themselves, from which they can aspire to an appropriate identity. A key characteristic of this approach is the extent to which managers are able to set the agenda, and influence the direction and speed of conversations, according to their interests, gaining confidence as they do so. Similarly, there is a need to reinforce the identity-development process by focusing on areas of competence and skill development.

9 *Leadership and Diversity Development*

BEVERLY DAWN METCALFE

Injustice anywhere is a threat to justice everywhere. We are caught in an inescapable network of mutuality, tied in a single garment of destiny. Whatever affects one directly, affects all directly.
Letter from Birmingham Jail, 16 April 1963, Martin Luther King

We are caught in an inescapable network of mutuality, tied in a single garment of destiny. All life is interrelated.
Nobel Peace Prize Lecture, Norway, 11 December 1964, Martin Luther King

Introduction

The increasingly diverse workforce demographics, coupled with a growing global economy, are beginning to force organizations to rethink models of business success and how they will ensure organizational development for effectively aligning business strategies with current and future demographic and market realities.

The impetus to address issues of inequity in employment has elicited concern about how leaders and managers will respond to increasing diversity. Workforce mobility is growing as migration increases across the globe. Electronic communication affords opportunities to build and develop diverse work teams from many different ethnic and gender backgrounds, but also in respect of other difference dimensions such as culture and religion. The quotations from Martin Luther King at the beginning of this chapter remind us that all human activity is interrelated and the valuing of difference is a social justice concern for managers, organizations and communities alike. In short, management development practioners are under increasing pressure to demonstrate an understanding of diversity issues and facilitate commitment to inclusive values and behaviours.

The chapter examines how managers respond to diversity so defined, how they work for and with diversity. The first sections of the chapter examine briefly the changing nature of global workforce demographics and what is meant by diversity, and highlights how understanding of the concept has moved on from organizational policies associated with equal opportunities. The reader is introduced to a number of well-known approaches to diversity management which although evolved in the USA reflect how organizations and managers are only now beginning to grapple with the complexities of difference and diversity, and how to capitalize on these dynamic capabilities in organizations. In order to highlight the diversity competencies at the individual and organizational level, that is, an understanding of diversity demographics, the politics and emotions of inclusion and difference, and how diversity can positively contribute to organizational performance, the benefits of diversity are briefly outlined. The remaining sections of the chapter examine how managers and leaders can develop a deeper understanding of diversity and difference in organization contexts, and reflect on their own perspectives of doing diversity management. In addition to encouraging critical reflection of management practice several case analyses provide examples of how organization and management development interventions have sustained commitment to diversity.

Global Demographics

The changing global workforce demographics have demonstrated that future organizations and managements will be markedly different. In the Western economies the current white majority is ageing. This is shown by the number of same-sex relationships; an increasing number of British and Americans citizens identifying themselves as multiracial, as well as the recognition that people's work identity is shaped by a number of intersecting difference dimensions. In the US Latinos now surpass the number of African Americans as the largest minority segment. African, Hispanic and Asian American women are moving into the labour force in greater numbers, as the country's population becomes more diverse. In the USA for example, the workforce is projected to consist increasingly of workers that were once considered minorities. The Asian American workforce is set to rise 42 per cent to 7.5 million by 2010; Hispanic women's employment is set to increase to approximately 8.5 million in 2010; African women, currently comprising 8.5 million workers, currently the highest female population are expected to increase in numbers by 22 per cent by 2010.[1]

The dramatic demographic shift was highlighted by Lorbiecki and Jack,[2] who reported that in the future the USA working population: 'would be African Americans, Hispanics, Native Americans, women and other "minority" groups ... the relegation of white males to minority group status caused organizations in the USA to consider who their future managers might be'.

Other countries in the developed world have also reported similar accounts of dramatic demographic change.[3] According to the Australian Human and Equality Rights Council, 40 per cent of Australians are either themselves migrants or children of migrants and almost one-sixth speak a language other than English at home.

The UK's diversity landscape is also evolving due to migration shifts from Eastern European and Asian countries such as India, and the increasing number of working Muslims. In addition, the number of women entering the labour force and pursuing

---

1   Giscombe, K. (2005) 'Best practices of women of colour in corporate America', in Burke, R. and Matis, M. (eds) *Supporting Women's Career Advancement*, Cheltenham: Edward Elgar.

2   Lorbeicki, A. and Jack, G. (2000) 'Critical turns in the evolution of diversity management', *British Journal of Management*, 11(3): 17–31.

3   See cataylyst.org. Various reports include: *Advancing Asian Women in the Workplace* (2004); *Advancing Latinos in the Workplace* (2004); *Moving Women of Colour up the Ladder* (2002).

professional careers in leadership and management development has risen markedly over the last 20 years.[4]

While business is demonstrating efforts to increase the representation of traditionally minority groups in the workforce, these efforts are not as effective as they could be. A key concern across all Western economies is not so much in recruitment efforts, but in efforts to retain, develop and advance minority groups.

What is Diversity?

Singh nicely summarizes diversity as 'representing the mosaic of pattern of equality through difference'.[5]

Diversity refers to including and managing people in the workforce who have traditionally been marginalized because of their race, gender, ethnicity, sexual orientation and/or disability. There has also been discussion about the impact of diversity on the bottom line as well as the economic and legal consequences for failing to recruit, professionally develop and promote women and ethnic minorities. There are also broader societal concerns relating to how governments maintain social cohesion in communities if some groups are excluded or marginalized. Recently the focus has been on diversity as a strategic device that impacts both organizational performance and environmental positioning within an increasingly global market. While theories of organization management and change have focused on the benefits of a diverse workforce, very little has been written about the processes by which organizations and managers can develop diversity knowledge and competencies, and pursue diversity strategies to aid organizational improvement. Nor have many studies shown how diversity is understood and how diversity impacts organizational structures and culture across time.

The use of the word diversity is increasing in public and private discourse, although organizations and managements differ in what exactly the term means. For instance, it has become perceived as yet another management fashion, while others view it as a means of making a real difference in developing socially conscious organizations, and contributing to the performance of key business functions. All the definitions of diversity share some common elements and the Chartered Institute of Personnel and Development (CIPD) definition includes these:

> *Diversity is the concept that people should be valued as individuals for reasons related to business interests, as well as for moral and social reasons. It recognizes that people from different backgrounds can bring fresh ideas and perceptions which can make the way work is done more efficient and products and services better.*[6]

CIPD argue that people make the difference at work. A diverse workforce includes many types of diversity. All workforces are diverse whether by role and function, length of

---

4   Metcalfe, B. D. (2006) 'Gender and communication in international business', in Barrett, M. and Davidson, M. *Gender and Communication Issues at Work*, pp. 95–108. Aldershot: Ashgate.

5   Singh, V. (2002) *Managing Diversity for Strategic Advantage*. London: Council for Excellence in Management and Leadership.

6   CIPD (2006) *Managing Diversity: People Make the Difference at Work But Everyone is Different*. Aldershot: Ashgate. Available at http://www.cipd.co.uk.

service, and personal characteristics (age, gender, and ethnicity, background and so forth) (see Table 9.1). Different forms of diversity create different challenges and opportunities. Without appropriate management development in diversity principles, the benefits of a diverse organizational culture may not be realized. Management development has a responsibility to encourage creative thinking about diverse workforce characteristics, and their potential. However, all managers need support and guidance to develop relationships, and better ways of managing diversity in organizations and dealing with culture change.

Table 9.1   Categorizing diversity

Social category diversity	Demographic differences such as age, race, gender, sexuality, disability, class, religion
Informational diversity	Organizational differences such as education, tenure and function
Value diversity	Psychological differences in personality and attitudes

It is important to note that diversity concepts have also been influenced by international economists, in particular Martha Nussbaum's work on the development of human capabilities, rights and freedoms. This has strongly influenced the diversity philosophies of international agencies and resonates with diversity scholarship in management and organization. The United Nations organizations for example have begun to mainstream diversity in the HR and development programmes worldwide. They argue:

Diversity takes many forms. It is usually thought of in terms of obvious attributes – age differences, race, gender, physical ability, sexual orientation, religion and language. Diversity in terms of background, professional experiences, skills and specialisation, values and culture, as well as social class is also a prevailing pattern.[7]

The development of an understanding of diversity then extends to diversities and difference that comprise the make up of organizations, communities and societies.

Understanding Equal Opportunity and Diversity Management

The recognition that the 'difference' of specific social groups, such as women, and ethnic minorities was something to appreciate and 'be managed', have their roots in the equal opportunities systems in the UK, and affirmative action programmes in the USA. Equal opportunity and affirmative approaches relied on moral-based arguments and the enforcement of legal measures to aid equality advancement. Another key focus was in developing management skills and intervention programmes that helped assimilate the marginal group into the dominant organization culture. There is now recognition that these approaches failed to address the intersecting quality of individual differences, and

---

7   See the United Nations Website, http://www.un.org, and Nussbaum, M. (2002) 'Women and equality: the capabilities approach', *International Labour Review*, 138(3): 227–245.

the implications this had for organization and management development. Consequently, a core argument proposed is that diversity or diversity management represents a discourse that is distinct from previous equal opportunities initiatives. Table 9.2 summarizes the equal opportunity and management diversity approaches.

Table 9.2 Summary of the equal opportunity and management diversity approaches

Equal opportunities (EO) – the old paradigm	Managing diversity (MD) – the new paradigm
Externally driven	Internally driven
Rests on moral and legal arguments	Rests on business case
Perceives EO as a cost	Perceives MD as an investment
Operational	Strategic
Concerned with progress	Concerned with outcomes
Rational organization model	Internalized by managers and employees
Externally imposed on managers	Systematic understanding
	Appreciation of organizational culture
Difference perceived as other/problematical	Difference perceived as asset/richness
Deficit model	Model of plenty
Ethnocentric, heterosexist	Celebrates difference
Assimilation advocated	Mainstream adaptation advocated
Discrimination focus	Development focus
Harassment seen as individual issue	Harassment seen as organizational climate issue
Group focused	Individual focused
Group initiatives	Individual initiatives
Family-friendly policies	Individual development
	Employee friendly policies/cafeteria benefits
Supported by a narrow positivist base	Supported by a wider pluralistic knowledge base

Sources: Wilson and Iles (1999) and Girton and Greene (2000).[8]

Recent research by Morrison *et al.*[9] found that diversity was conceptualized and understood in many ways. A common strand was that diversity was understood as involving many differences that comprise an individual identity. This is a departure from

---

8   See Girton, G. and Greene, A. (2003) *Dynamics of Managing Diversity*, London: Butterworth Heinmann; see also Wilson, E. and Iles, P. (1999) 'Managing diversity: an employment and delivery challenge', International Journal of Public Sector Management, 12(2): 27–48.

9   Morrison, M., Lumby, J., Maringe, F., Phopal, K. and Dyke, M. (2007) *Diversity Identity and Leadership, Centre for Excellence in Leadership*, Lancaster: CEL, Lancaster University; see also Lumby, J. and Coleman, M. (2007) *Leadership and Diversity*. London: Sage.

equal opportunity initiatives which focused on the special needs of specific social groups. A second theme that emerged from their work was that individual differences incorporated not just race and gender identities, but background characteristics including experience, expertise and personality. However, the study found there were master identities or groups that people did strongly adhere to.

The implication of this research is that the harnessing of difference offers many challenges for organization and management training specialists. Leadership and management development approaches for the twenty-first century must be grounded in values and norms that are more relevant in the post-industrial era of rapid change and globalization. Deetz *et al.*[10] argue that important social movements and changes in the nature of products and work processes have created a crisis in contemporary organization. They cite such changes as the rise of professionalized knowledge workers, internationally mobile workforces, geographically dispersed facilities and decentralized and unstable markets that have led to the difficulty of management coordination and control. These economic and social challenges signal a move toward more fluid and ambiguous leadership communications, in which identities are not fixed, but are continuously reformed and negotiated. Increasingly, it is argued that successful organizational development needs to move away from the myth of the 'triumphant individual', leading alone, and begin focusing on new approaches, such as creative collaboration, teamwork, network and coalition building and maintenance within and among communities and organizations.

These new approaches to what have been called learning leadership[11] point to the need for norms and values such as concern for the common good, diversity and pluralism in structures and participation, client orientation and consensus-oriented policy making. This involves a critical interpretive view of leadership which shifts the focus away from structural-functionalist, management-oriented news, toward the process of leadership that develops through meaningful interaction, and how it can facilitate social change and emancipation. Approaches to leadership diversity development, then, engender learning diversity management as 'practice'. The forgoing clearly suggests that the leaders and management developers of tomorrow will need a solid understanding of diversity principles. Diversity management is a systemic and planned programme or procedure that is designed to improve interaction amongst diverse people, especially of different ethnicities, sexes or cultures, and make this diversity a source of creativity, complimentarity and organizational effectiveness.[12] In the following section I examine different models of diversity management that have evolved.

Approaches to Diversity Management

Over the years, several models have been developed to help organizations and leaders understand and manage the complexity of the diverse workforce. Cox developed a model of different organization approaches to managing diversity, detailed in Table 9.3.

10   Deetz, S. A., Tracy, S. and Simpson, J. L. (2000) *Leading Organizations Through Transitions: Communication and Cultural Change.* Thousand Oaks, CA: Sage.

11   Antonacopoulou, E. P. and Bento, R. F. (2005) 'Methods of learning leadership: taught and experiential', in Storey, J. *Leadership in Organizations: Current Issues and Key Trends.* London: Routledge.

12   Stockdale, M. S. and Cosby, F. J. (2004) *The Psychology and Management of Workplace Diversity.* Malden, MA: Blackwell Publishers. See also Western, S. (2008) *Leadership: A Critical Text.* London: Sage.

Table 9.3   Cox's diverse organization structures model

Type	Characteristics
Monolithic	The traditional dominant form of organization in the USA. These organizations did not manage diversity and HR function was underdeveloped. Instead, through assimilation, minority members were expected to adapt to organization norms which had been shaped predominantly by white heterosexual males.
Pluralistic	The pluralistic organizations first emerged in the late 1960s and represents the dominant model in the USA today. They engage in diversity management. They recruit and hire minority employees, monitor their reward systems for fairness and offer diversity training.
Multicultural	The new multicultural organization is the model for the future. Pluralism is dominant and organization members do not differ in their identification with the organization as a function of their demographics. Furthermore, prejudice, discrimination and intergroup conflict are minimal. A key characteristic between the pluralistic and multicultural organization is that minority employees are not only valued as contributing to the organization, but are also formally and informally integrated.

Cox's model was further modified and identified key components necessary for eliminating discriminatory practices in HR systems. These included:

- Equal training provision for women.
- Corporate-wide education programmes on diversity.
- Development of cultural value systems that incorporate diversity and inclusiveness.[13]

The model, however, offered little detail for management development practioners who were concerned with trying to engender diversity principles in management processes and systems. Specifically it failed to address the complexities of learning about difference, how differences materialized, and how this could be capitalized upon in organizations.[14] Ely and Thomas advanced understandings of diversity management principles by proposing three different perspectives, or philosophies, which underpin diversity management training.[15] The third approach, the *integration and learning* perspective, outlines how difference needs to be fully internalized and valued as central to an organization's management value system.

---

13   Cox, T. (2001) *Creating the Multicultural Organization: A Strategy for Capturing the Power of Diversity.* Michigan, University of Michigan.

14   Reynolds, M. and Trehan, K. (2003) 'Learning from difference', *Management Learning,* 34(2): 163–180.

15   Ely, R. J. and Thomas, D. A. (2001) 'Cultural diversity at work: the moderating effects of work group perspectives on diversity', *Administrative Science Quarterly,* 46(2): 229–273.

ELY AND THOMAS'S MODEL OF DIVERSITY MANAGEMENT

Ely and Thomas argued that an organization's diversity perspective, which refers to organizational members' normative beliefs and expectations about cultural diversity and its role in their organizations, is a key moderator of the relationship between diversity and work outcomes. An organization's diversity perspective stands for the values that drive its diversity management practices. Ely and Thomas developed three models of diversity management: discrimination and fairness, access and legitimacy, and integration and learning. The authors refined their arguments in a qualitative study of workgroups from three US firms. They found that workforce diversity had the most positive effects on workgroup functioning when the workgroup stood for an integration and learning perspective. These dynamics were shaped by group functioning including the quality of intergroup relations, feelings of being valued and respected and the positivity of employees' racial identity at work.

On the basis of their theory-generating study, Ely and Thomas offered a refined description of the three diversity perspectives.

1. *The discrimination-and-fairness perspective* focuses on ensuring equal and fair treatment and avoiding discriminatory employment practices. Diversity is not explicitly related to an organization's work, and the predominant diversity management strategy is one of ignoring or playing down differences (demographics are ignored because they are assumed not to affect performance or organization culture). Ironically the focus on fairness inevitably leads to concerns about unfairness, resulting in strained relationships among minority groups. These relationships are characterized by defensive claims of innocence. White employees become apprehensive about their racial identity, and employees of colour feel powerless. The discrimination and fairness perspective reduces the opportunities for learning from each other.
2. *The access and legitimacy perspective* is characterized by using diversity as a means of gaining 'access to legitimacy with a diverse market'.* The resulting staffing patterns (for example, more minority employees in certain roles/grade versus more white employees in certain roles/grades) produce perceptions of differential status: the higher percentage of white employees in a business unit, the higher its status. Minority employees question their value for the organization and feel uncertain about the value of their racial or difference identity at work. The access and legitimacy perspective, like the discrimination and fairness perspective, prevents ethnically different employees learning from each other.
3. *The integration and learning perspective* of diversity management assumes that the 'insights, skills and experiences employees have developed as members of various cultural identity groups are potentially valuable resources'.† These resources can influence organizational thinking on a variety of strategically important dimensions, such as market and product choices. Different cultural experiences are associated with different patterns of problem solution strategies and insights for optimizing organizational development. Organizational members openly discuss the impact of their race, gender and ethnic based experiences and value viewpoints of ethnically different employees as an opportunity for learning and development.

---

* Ely, R. J. and Thomas, D. A. (2001) 'Cultural diversity at work: the moderating effects of work group perspectives on diversity', *Administrative Science Quarterly*, 46(2): 229–273, p. 265.
† Ely, R. J. and Thomas, D. A. (2001) 'Cultural diversity at work: the moderating effects of work group perspectives on diversity', *Administrative Science Quarterly*, 46(2): 229–273, p. 240.

The Business Benefits of Diversity

Recognizing the importance of leading for diversity is essential for long-term business development. Yet it is unlikely to succeed unless an effective strategy is developed for inclusion through a commitment to diversity at all levels in the workforce, especially at the senior management levels. Organizations will not devise diversity strategies unless they can expect an increased profit and metrics that substantiate the necessity to expand the emphasis on diversity.

A joint survey by The Society for HRM and *Fortune* magazine was conducted to ascertain the benefits of diversity management strategies. The survey was mailed to 839 HR professionals at Fortune 1000 companies and to the organizations on *Fortune*'s list of the 100 best companies to work for. Respondents were asked to indicate how diversity initiatives have affected 20 different issues relating to the bottom line. The most evident measurable benefits are competitive advantage, superior business performance, employee commitment and loyalty, strengthened relationships with multinational communities and attracting the best candidates. Table 9.4 gives the survey results.

Table 9.4   Survey showing the positive effects of embracing diversity[*]

Initiative	% responding, n = 87
Improves corporate culture	79
Improves recruitment of new employees	77
Improves client relations	52
Higher retention of employees	41
Decreased complaints and litigation	41
Enables the organization to move into emerging markets	37
Positively affects profitability indirectly	32
Increases productivity	32
Positively affects profitability	28
Maximizes brand identity	23
Has not impacted bottom line	7
Increased complaints and litigation	1
Negatively affects profitability	0
Lower retention of employees	0
Impedes organization from moving into emerging markets	0
Deteriorates client relations	0
Deteriorates corporate culture	0
Hinders recruitment of new employees	0
Negatively affects profitability indirectly	0
Decreases profitability	0
Detracts from brand identity	0
Other	0

Note: Percentages will not equal 100 per cent as multiple responses were allowed.
Source: Adapted from SHRM/*Fortune* survey (2001).
[*]   McCusiton, V. E. and Wooldridge, B. R. (2004) 'Leading the diverse workforce: Profit, prospects and progress', *Leadership and Organization Development Journal*, 25(1-2): 73–89

The survey showed the positive effects of embracing diversity also included improving corporate culture, helping recruit new employees, improving relationships with clients, higher retention of employees, and decreasing complaints.

ORGANIZATION PERFORMANCE

Generally the survey argued that a commitment to organization diversity improved business performance. Diversity in gender, race and age on senior management teams is correlated with superior business performance in worker productivity, market share and shareholder value. Generally, top leaders in organizations believe that diverse teams will outperform teams that are not diverse.

TALENT MANAGEMENT

Promoting diversity is more likely to attract recruits from a wider pool including multi-ethnic students, affiliations under multicultural organization and active campaigns on jobsites aimed at diverse candidates. IBM have specifically embraced diversity as a key business principle. They argue that: 'Creativity flows when diverse minds meet, when people with a broad range of experiences work together to find a solution. This is why we value our employees for their individuality, their uniqueness and their difference.' This was recently demonstrated when IBM won the 2008 Stonewall Award for being the UK's top employer for the gay and lesbian workforce.

EMPLOYEE LOYALTY

A further reason to invest in diversity is that it will foster greater employee commitment and loyalty. Organizations with good track records of diversity initiatives and equality opportunities will find it easier to recruit and retain talented women and ethnic minorities who prefer to work where they can receive support for training and achieve promotion. If new minority hires see little evidence of role models in senior positions they will conclude they have to move elsewhere for advancement. Strong CEO and senior management support for diversity initiatives, along with special and minority support groups, mentoring programmes and work–life policies build employee job satisfaction and commitment to a company's business goals.

IMPROVED CLIENT RELATIONS

The greatest loss to a company when diversity is not a priority is loss of potential business in the form of new customers in growth markets, customers who are proving increasingly loyal to companies that understand their culture and their needs.

The case study below from IBM reveals how leading diversity from the top can significantly impact the organization's cultural diversity and commitment to inclusion of all differences.

Case Study

Diversity improved the bottom line at IBM

Like many companies IBM took big strides to eliminate discrimination by attempting to ignore cultural, racial and other differences in its vast worldwide workforce. That ended when Lou Gerstner became CEO. Gerstner initiated a diversity work task force initiative that would 'uncover and understand differences among the groups and find ways to appeal to a broader set of employees and customers. Since then the number of female executives in the company has grown by 370 per cent, ethnic minority executives have jumped 233 per cent, and the number of self-identified gay, lesbian, bisexual and transgender executives gained 733 per cent.' David Thomas of HBS reported that IBM, by deliberately seeing ways to reach a broader range of customers, improved bottom line results.*

* Thomas, D. (2004) IBM finds profit in diversity, Harvard Business School Working Knowledge: hbswk.hbs. edu/item/4389.

Organizations, Diversity and Leadership

The chapter so far has reviewed the nature of diversity and approaches to diversity management. How though as managers and leaders can we develop the skills necessary to be able to nurture a commitment to diversity in everyday working relationships and practices? The key driver in business is to ensure that a more heterogeneous workforce would function as productively as a more homogeneous one. As already argued, a diverse workforce will bring a wider range of perspectives to bear, improving decision making. This perhaps underplays the complexity of managing for inclusion and in embedding commitment to difference and diversity as an organizational value, as part of broader organizational development changes. DiTomaso and Hooijborg argue that greater diversity in populations and the workforce interconnects with changes in organizations and organizational practice (see the box overleaf).

- Increasing permeability of organization boundaries.
- Increasing interconnections among organizations (networks, alliances, partnerships).
- Increasing educational and technological specialization.
- Increasing interdependence in work among all employees.
- Increasing customization of products and services.
- Externalization of risk, through subcontracting, licensing.

The learning leader then needs to be reflective in considering their own individual differences and values, engender commitment to the appreciation of difference, as well as ensure that these are effectively managed in context of evolving organization systems changes and relations. DiTomaso and Hooijberg state that this requires more than just offering greater support and commitment to a diverse culture: 'Leadership in a (diversity) context means to "do" diversity in the origination, interpolation and use of structures

... it means to remake (or reengineer) the relationships of people in various categories to resources, power and opportunity.'

This amounts to a number of layers of change and includes encouraging attitudinal change, rearranging or reforming power structures in organization and human relationships, as well as decision-making processes. This would not necessarily focus on rectifying the differences of particular groups, but rather to reconfigure organizations as democracies which therefore offer the power to shape choice and action. The aim would not be to have more women and ethnic minorities in top positions, but by having systems and structures in place which promote equity.

This approach relies on arguments that certain approaches to organizational and leadership development, such as feminist and antiracist critiques 'prefer' or 'privilege' specific difference. This would include for example recruitment processes which advocate quota systems for certain social groups. Sinclair argues a generic approach to diversity management is more beneficial premised on a number of grounds detailed in the box below.

---

1. Diversity approaches are inclusive. They encompass all the characteristics that might result in disadvantage to an individual or group.
2. As diversity group approaches are inclusive, they encompass the tensions between the interests of different groups.
3. Diversity aligns with the practice of leaders and managers who do not relate to women, ethnic minorities but work with people, each of whom have multiple identities.
4. As diversity approaches are inclusive they are perceived as less threatening, spark less resistance and are more successful in supporting organizational change.[*]

---

[*] Sinclair, A. (2007) 'Teaching leadership critically to MBAs', *Management Learning*, 38(40): 461–475; and Sinclair, A. (2002) 'Teaching managers about masculinities: are you kidding?', *Management Learning*, 31(1): 89–104. See also Simpson, R. (2006) 'Feminising the MBA', *Academy of Management Learning and Education*, 5(2): 182–194.

Sinclair further argues that diversity fosters a commitment to all diverse characteristics including those that are not visible, which may be met with discrimination. Significantly, it is the intersecting and multilayered composition of difference and diversity that needs to be acknowledged by leaders and organizations alike. Leaders and managers thus need to be aware of broad organization diversity principles and how they interrelate if they are to develop their own capacities for doing diversity.

Developing Diverse Leaders and Managers

The forgoing arguments have highlighted that diversity is complex and requires organizations to rethink their business models. Significantly diversity, while adopting an integrative and learning approach to valuing difference, can aid organizational benefits. A new generation of leaders will require different skill sets and competencies to manage the diverse workforce. They will require sensitivity, listening, learning, coaching and networking with each other and to cultivate new leaders. A key focus will be the development of cross-cultural leaders resulting in a generation of multicultural professionals.

A focus on personalized or 'learning leadership' will enable individual leaders to manage the complexity and fluidity of diverse work cultures.[16] Learning leadership as practice as previously highlighted, presents a fluid image beyond attributes and tasks, behaviours and situations. This requires that leaders develop an awareness and alertness to one's own and another's diversity learning needs, being able to be flexible and open so as to challenge one's own existing framework. This will involve learning to value difference and embrace change on a number of intersecting levels, which is detailed in the box below.

First, to instil confidence not just in themselves but also to build employees' confidence in each other.

To redistribute power and difference beyond a numbers game.

To attend to the politics of differences as well as the organization's requirements.

To move beyond notions of sameness and difference, and appropriate multiple and interconnecting different positions.*

*   Lumby, J. Coleman, M. (2007) *Leadership and Diversity*. London: Sage.

A way of starting this development process at the individual level is to consider our own assumptions and values about how we manage and interact in the workplace. To become an effective manager of diverse work teams mangers need to 'get comfortable with being uncomfortable'. The following questions can act as a self guide by which managers can assess whether their behaviours encourage inclusion.

EXAMINING DIVERSE OPINIONS, ASSUMPTIONS, BEHAVIOURS[17]

1. How inclusive are you about socializing with those from different backgrounds?
2. What priority do you give to providing institutional support to staff members who are from backgrounds different from yours?
3. Do expectations of women of colour and ethnic minorities vary from other staff?
4. Do you ever use stereotypical assumptions about different groups?
5. How do you assess competence?

---

16   Storey, J. (2004) *Leadership in Organizations: Current Issues and Key Trends*. London: Routledge.

17   Giscombe, K. (2004) 'Best practices for women of colour in corporate America', in Burke, R. J. and Mattis, M. C. *Supporting Women's Career Advancement*, Cheltenham: Edward Elgar.

6. Do you assume competence when a staff member has a similar cultural knowledge, speech and behavioural style as you?
7. Do you judge marginal groups in management such as women, women of colour and ethnic minorities as exceptions?
8. How comfortable are you acknowledging superior expertise in someone from their outsider group?

FEMINIZING THE MBA AND CREATING DIVERSE MANAGEMENT CURRICULA

The forgoing has argued for the development of diversity awareness for managers to be able to harness the benefits of difference. However, while the MBA and similar postgraduate courses are increasingly seen as a requisite for senior posts for many women as a way of breaking the glass ceiling, as well as other marginal groups, its offerings in UK business schools rarely reflect this multicultural component. Despite the continued popularity of the MBA, doubts exist concerning the value of the course for managers and organizations.[18] Critics argue that the MBA relies too much on analytical skills to the neglect of softer skills seen as increasingly important for managers. The importance of interpersonal skills development includes associated changes such as the flattening of hierarchies, a greater reliance on teamwork and an enhanced customer/client focus, all of which draw on the ability to manage diverse relationships inside and outside the organization. Early work by Mintzberg, for example, exploring the significance of interpersonal skills in management activities found that leadership development processes (including motivating, inspiring and nurturing individuals, as well as building teams) infuse all managerial work and that 40 per cent of managers' time is devoted to communication and a sharing of information through talking, and in particular listening. While these skills are regarded as important they remain a neglected component of management education.

Management education has an important role to play in the creation of managerial identity and in acquiring the skills of an appropriate selfhood, one that is aware and sensitive to the diverse needs and experiences of employees. Significantly, it is argued that predominately MBA's reassert the values of stereotypical masculinist behaviours and attitudes.[19] In sum, management education may be reinforcing and maintaining a masculine way of organizing and seeing the world, and underplaying different cultural perspectives.

To counter this male bias in management education Simpson has argued that MBA curriculum's be remodelled to include 'feminine aspects'. The feminization of the MBA would assist in developing more critical perspectives of gender, race and other differences. While feminization is often taken to mean the spread of feminine qualities and attributes culturally associated with women, and while some work has attempted to define this nature to include interdependence, cooperation, imagination, creativity and the priority of feelings; feminization incorporates more critical understandings of the intersecting and multiple difference in organizations. At a more foundational level, feminization

---

18   Simpson, R. (2006) 'Feminising the MBA', *Academy of Management Learning and Education,* 5(2): 182–194; and Grey, C. (2004) 'Reinventing business schools: the contribution of critical management education', *Academy of Management Learning and Education,* 3: 178–187.

19   DiTomaso, H. and Hooijberg, R. (1996) 'Diversity and the demands of leadership', *The Leadership Quarterly,* 7(2): 163–187.

encourages critical reflection of the values of the management as a body of knowledge and as a political and moral practice.

The forgoing discussion has raised issues of how diversity management can be conceptualized and how it may influence individual perspectives of doing diversity. In the following the focus is on how organizations can develop diversity management approaches that foster inclusion, and value difference.

Creating Inclusive Work Environments

In assessments of diversity policy strategies undertaken by the CIPD, and Catalysts assessment of Fortune 5000 companies it was found that all the companies had started the process of developing managerial accountability for diversity, and most had undertaken development programmes to target disadvantaged groups. However, it was noted that in both the USA and UK there was divergence between the companies' stated diversity policies and the perception by employees of the effectiveness of their companies diversity policies. An issue with creating polices or managerial practices that address inequities is guaranteeing the implementation by all levels in the organizations.

Successful management developments efforts include:[20]

- Assessment of work environments and careers.
- Support from senior leadership.
- Clearly developed business case.
- Effective communication strategy.
- Workforce development strategies that emphasize talent development.
- Diversity strategy design.

ASSESSMENT OF WORK ENVIRONMENTS AND CAREERS

A first step in work environment assessment is to benchmark the progress of marginalized groups, which can involve both internal and external measurements. External research uncovers practices of industry peers or companies with highly regarded best practices. Internal research should provide metrics on recruitment, retention and advancement of minority groups and identify best practices in areas of the company which may not be well known. Creating benchmarks or standards against which the company compares itself is key to evaluating the ongoing progress and effectiveness of diversity initiatives. Specific practices to benchmark include performance appraisal, succession planning, access to training and mentors and access to flexible work arrangements. In addition to quantitative measures, qualitative measures can assist benchmarking efforts. Qualitative research gleaned through focus groups and interviews provides an understanding of how different employee groups perceive the corporate culture and work environment. Qualitative measures of diversity performance should include perceptions by different demographic groups of the work environment in general, access to developmental

20   Giscombe, K. (2004) 'Best practices for women of colour in corporate America', in Burke, R. J. and Mattis, M. C. *Supporting Women's Career Advancement*, Cheltenham: Edward Elgar.

opportunities, support from supervisors, feedback on performance, reward systems and perceptions for career development opportunities.

SUPPORT FROM SENIOR LEADERSHIP

Long-term goals require long-term commitment of top leadership in addition to the commitment of financial and staff resources. Therefore it is critical that a company's succession planning should provide for strong and consistent leadership in this area so that there is continuity despite changes in organizational leadership. In addition to senior management involvement companies often designate influential senior executives to champion the initiative. Alliances between employee networks, including women's networks for example, are another means to create an inclusive, problem solving and comprehensive approach to evaluating diversity initiatives.

CLEARLY DEVELOPED BUSINESS CASE

The benefits of embracing diversity as part of the corporate culture and value systems were highlighted previously. It is important however that an organization's inclusion strategy builds on and contributes to overall business goals. Companies that have integrated their diversity and business goals and strategies are more likely to be successful in gaining ownership for diversity initiatives among managers. Developing a clear business case also provides for continuity of initiatives in the face of competing priorities and changing organizational needs. Below is a case example of a clearly articulated business case for developing Asian employees.

Case Study

The Asian Value Proposition in IBM

In 2000 the IBM Asian Task Force defined the Asian Value Proposition which outlined why IBM should care about the attraction, retention and development of Asian employees at IBM. Teams of IBM Asian executives met with 41 members of IBM's worldwide management council. Through these meetings the strong business case for investing in efforts targeting Asians was made and IBM leaders learned of the importance of developing a specific initiative to meet the needs of their growing diverse population.

COMMUNICATION, DIVERSITY AND LEADERSHIP

The entire workforce in an organization needs to understand the business case and the programmes and policies of a diversity strategy. Managers play a key role as gatekeepers of formal and informal information and of the use of corporate initiatives. The case study of Hewlett Packard (HP) shows how communication strategies were harnessed to instill a deeper understanding of diversity dynamics in personal and work relations.

WORKFORCE STRATEGIES THAT EMPHASIZE TALENT DEVELOPMENT

Workforce strategies typically capitalize on talents and assist in developing diverse leadership competencies through an integrated strategic HR approach including recruitment, remuneration systems and diversity and education training. Thus diversity principles should be core to effective people management and development. Diversity programmes should ensure that they address differences among subgroups. Diversity interventions include the following:

- *Employee networks.* Support networks are an important development for marginal groups given lack of access to informal networks, as well as mentors and role models. Support networks provide critical tasks such as advising management of issues facing network members, organizing network events for members and assisting with mentoring programmes
- *Mentoring.* Networks support marginalized groups but cannot be seen as a substitute for formal access to senior executives. Research has shown that mentoring systems have assisted women and ethnic minorities to attain senior executive roles.

The following case studies outline how HP created opportunities for communicating and valuing difference, how KPMG succeeded in nurturing women's talent and how HSBC have devised global approaches to talent development of minorities through a range of management training initiatives and HR support systems.

Case Study

HP communicating the value of diversity and difference

HP developed a programme called Addressing Diversity Issues.* The company did not feel that it had an understanding of the experiences and positions of its top women and minority talent. As HP became more dominant in consumer markets, its customer base continued to diversify and there was greater and greater need to reflect these changes. The diversity focus was central to leadership development and review processes which evaluated how diversity issues were communicated and represented. They found that diversity was more complex that envisaged. They revealed that multiple group identities (race, gender, culture, sexual orientation) that all people bring to organizational life mean that each person embodies several and often competing social realities. For some these perspectives are contradictory, while for others they are mutually reinforcing. For example with white men, both their racial and gender identity place them in socially privileged groups that classically have power over white women and people of colour. In contrast, white women and black men belong to both dominant and subordinate identity groups, while women of colour in the USA are typically on the bottom in terms of race and gender. By opening up questions the cultural values, beliefs, and norms within an organization, and having employees respond to them from their race, gender and organizational group perspectives, communication about the impact and experiences of diversity challenged the links between who has power, influence and access to organization rewards, and the race/gender stratification in the organization structure. As the leadership and various groups at HP interacted and developed new understandings about group and minority experiences, the organizational discourses, the ways in which knowledge (sources of meaning) and power (structures, relations and processes) started to shift.

*   Fumler, R., Gibbs, P. A. and Goldsmith, M. (1999) 'The new HP way: merging strategy with diversity: leadership development and decentralization', *Strategy and Leadership,* October–December: 21–29.

Case Study

KPMG talent management*

In 2008 KPMG in the UK launched Reach, a two-day development programme for women aspiring to senior manager positions and beyond. The programme addresses a number of issues which women and men perceived as potential barriers to the career progression of women in the firm. These include leadership skills, career visioning and management, effective networking and direct access to role models and mentors. The objectives of Reach are: to help strengthen the pipeline of women to more senior grades; to support the retention and career progression of talented women at KPMG, and to send a clear message to women who perceive barriers to their career progression that the firm is committed to enabling women as well as men to achieve their full potential.

It is too early to quantify the impact of Reach on the career progression of participants but it is clear that individual women benefit enormously from the programme. Here is how one participant recently described the experience:

Beforehand, whilst I thought it was worth a go, I was somewhat sceptical about the value of a women-only programme. Having been on the course last week, I can honestly say that this was the most inspirational and truly useful course I have ever attended. I already feel so much more empowered and in control, and I am following through on actions and learning.

Reach is one of a number of activities in Retaining Talented Women, a programme which was established in 2006 with the sponsorship of the CEO to address the drop-off in the representation of women at middle manager grade. Since 2006 the percentage of women in middle-manager grade has increased by 5 per cent to 44 per cent.

*   Sealy, R. and Sing, V.(2008) *Female FTSE Index and Report 2008,* Cranfield: Cranfield University.

Case Study

HSBC – Global Diversity Approaches

HSBC aims to provide a fully inclusive working environment that gives all employees the opportunity to reach their full potential. We endeavour to create a working environment that lets them balance their personal and professional lives. In the Asia Pacific region this has meant changing working practices within cultures where women have traditionally stayed in the background. We have established regional and local diversity committees that aim to enable women of different ages, ethnic background and cultures to progress their careers and achieve their full potential based on meritocracy. HSBC has effectively established a family-friendly working environment. Successfully enabling women to balance work and home helps HSBC to recruit and retain women and enables them to pursue full careers. For example, in Hong Kong where we have a large workforce, the Wayfoong Nursery School was established by HSBC in the early 1990s to provide day care facilities for children of more than 130 employees. The school is open longer than other nurseries and during term breaks so that our employees do not have to worry about taking care of their children during the school holidays. Child care facilities are also available in several other Asia Pacific countries where HSBC operates. Family-friendly policies must extend beyond this type of facility and into the actual workplace itself. We also have flexible work arrangements, leave options and free counselling for those who feel they need some assistance, all designed to enable working mothers to thrive in their careers while raising a family.

HSBC also encourages employee networks to provide informal coaching and mentoring, which facilitates career and personal development outside of the formal corporate hierarchy. Mentoring programmes by professionals and senior management have been introduced to share experiences and best practices on successful career management with all staff, enabling the most capable talent to succeed regardless of gender.

All these initiatives could not succeed without the wholehearted support of HSBC senior management. This has helped a large number of women attain senior positions within the bank. In Hong Kong, women make up more than 58 per cent of our workforce, and women also hold 49 per cent of our senior management positions. HSBC was named the Best Company for Women by the American Chamber of Commerce in Hong Kong and the South China Morning Post in 2007, based on the high number of women in senior management in Asia and our commitment to supporting our people in every aspect of their lives.

In other areas of Asia Pacific, women hold senior management posts at the highest levels. The CEOs of our India, Malaysia and Turkey operations are women.

DIVERSITY DESIGN

The nurturing of commitment to diversity is often incorporated as part of a broad scale culture change initiative. The case of the Diversity Change Design Strategy at Eastern Bank[21] in the USA (see Figure 9.1) described by Zane is significant because it maps the process of learning about *and* with diversity over a three-year period. Also significant is that the champion for the programme was the chief executive and that he encouraged the development of minority employee groups to create the diversity change processes and agendas. It can be seen in the diagram that as time progresses more employee groups were formed, illustrating how the organization terrain of learning about diversity was unfolding. In the initial stages, for example, part-time employees and gay and lesbian employees felt that their voice had not been heard, whereas in year three they had contributed a distinct voice. In Phase 1 the CEO defined and communicated the banks' diversity vision. Simply, this referred to the 'valuing of people', which embraced management communication and behaviours that represented 'respect, courtesy and caring'. Senior leaders were fired, and an Equality Action Committee was formed comprising different employee groups. This group helped formulate key organizational values which focused on people, performance,

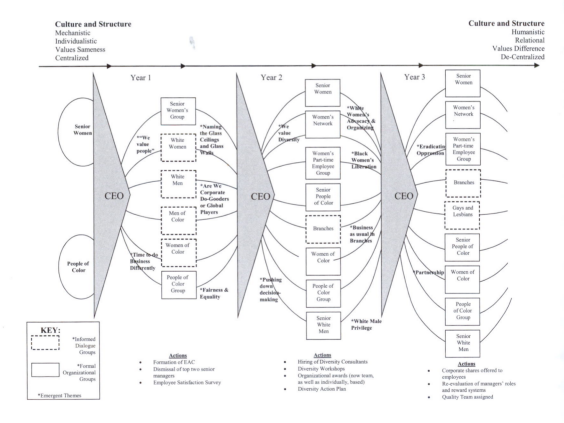

Figure 9.1   The Diversity Design Change Strategy at Eastern Bank

21   Zane, N. C. (2002) 'The glass ceiling is the floor my boss works on: leadership challenges in managing diversity', *The Journal of Applied Behavioural Science*, 38(3): 334–354.

teamwork, diversity, commitment and integrity. During this phase the organization encountered the complexity of difference identities and began to appreciate that perhaps not all voices had been included. In Phase 2 the focus on valuing people was changed to 'valuing diversity' in an attempt to create an inclusive language. A diversity action plan was initiated which introduced diversity awareness workshops for all employees, as well as diversity management development programmes. The skills focus for managers and leaders was on relationship-building competencies such as counselling and mentoring as a specific way of demonstrating support to diversity. This was a particularly challenging time for the organization as it brought to the surface feelings about supposed meritocracy in organization design and promotion. For white women the lack of merit was reflected primarily in promotional practices. For people of colour, while they also experienced promotional discrimination, they were more concerned about basic issues such as who was being hired in the first place. White men, on the other hand, felt that discussions of race and gender were preferring specific identities. Over time however, through ongoing connections via diversity consultants, employees began learning about difference, and constructing new ways to understand connections between themselves, other groups and the organization as a whole. Of key importance is that through this diversity journey the CEO came to learn about the power relationships that specific employee groups held, and came to appreciate that. In Phase 3 the shifts in dialogues between employee groups was reflected in the identification of sections of the workforce establishing their own groups, the gay and lesbian group and part-time worker group, signalling that culture was beginning to change and be more inclusive. At this stage the phrase 'partnership' had become embedded as part of everyday organizational discourse, representing reciprocal forms of mutual respect and engagement.[22]

Global Challenges for Developing Diverse Leadership and Knowledge

While diversity approaches advocate the valuing of differences, and pose models of organizational change and development that are inclusive, much of the aforementioned debate on diversity management and in developing diversity awareness is rooted in the Western management paradigm. Global diversity strategies assume that a generic label cannot shade or shadow difference. However, diversity discourses and meanings are socially constituted, highly variable and subject to ongoing change and development. That is, difference and diversity agendas change according to sociopolitical and geographic context. For example in both Middle East and Asia the concepts of diversity management are not commonly understood in respect of HR programmes or leadership development initiatives. In many Arabian countries for example equality measures that focus on one difference category, sex, would be recognized and encouraged. Indeed, women's leadership development and political advancement development is cornerstone to the United Nations Empowerment Goals. Yet issues of valuing the rights of homosexual workers, or understanding different needs of ethnic and national identities such as Israelis would not be countenanced at the organization policy level, or in institutional frameworks in

---

22   It is important to note that this diversity initiative was highly successful. Zane reports that it did not grapple with the complexities of class.

Arabian societies. A similar picture is prevalent in China and Russia. HR and leadership development programmes that favour one group over another, for example, women or ethnic minorities, would not be politically accepted.

While unquestionably this chapter has argued for embracing a broader approach to managing equality through valuing difference, the naming of difference, and targeting 'differences in specific groups' is a tactic that is still advocated by senior leaders and policy development advisors. The recent Cranfield FTSE[23] study which tracks the reasons for obstacles facing women in attaining executive and board leadership positions, as well suggest organization and government strategies to foster women's advancement on boards, has for the first time in 20 years advocated a radical approach to improving the number of women leaders. They suggest a more prescriptive approach that requires adherence to regulatory frameworks, something which many professional institutions and employer organizations have resisted. The rationale for this was that voluntarism has not yielded many changes to boardroom composition over the last twenty years. They recommend that:

1. All directors in the private sector be advertised (as occurs in the public sector).
2. Longer lists for director appointments reflect an aspirational target of female targets.
3. Search consultants be more proactive in building relationships with potential non-executive directors.
4. Companies set gender targets and report on progress in annual teleports, including settling and monitoring of key performance indicators at each level of the organizational pipeline.

The above recommendations spark a potential return to equal opportunity versus diversity management debates, with suggestions for tighter measurement and evaluation of organizational progress in supporting difference and inclusion.

Conclusion

In this chapter we have highlighted common attributes to diversity management, the benefits of diversity management to corporate success, and provided case examples of leading companies who have integrated diversity traits in their competency frameworks. Above all diversity management requires that leaders themselves engender commitment towards inclusiveness. This requires that leaders be self-reflexive, through feedback processes that include the learners themselves, providers and facilitators and other stakeholders. Underpinning the arguments presented is the importance of management and leadership development programmes in challenging dominant curriculums that ignore difference and diversity, by feminizing and integrating notions of how is diversity formed and reformed in everyday organizational relations. At the strategic development level it was highlighted that diversity interventions needed to be integrated with HR policy, and that the valuing of diversity and difference is most likely to influence management behaviours and styles when it is embedded in the cultural values of organization. The chapter concluded by introducing global cultural challenges relevant to all management

---

23   Sealy, R. and Sing, V. (2008) *Female FTSE Index and Report 2008*. Cranfield: Cranfield University.

educators and leaders. As the quotations from Martin Luther King at the beginning of this chapter stress, diversity is a much contested concept and is undergoing constant reformation and change. Yet diversity and difference are woven together in an inescapable network of mutuality. Leaders who learn to value these dynamic capabilities can play a key role in enhancing organization performance, as well as work towards the goals of social justice and inclusion of all.

10 *Leadership Ethics*

SIMON ROBINSON

This chapter begins with a case study around ethical decision-making and leadership. It will show the importance of developing ethical awareness as a leader and how the very nature and purpose of leadership involves developing and handling moral values and identity. I will then look at how the study of leadership ethics has been developing, with an introduction to ethical theory. This provides a general basis for the applied ethics of leadership but does not say anything particular about leadership ethics as distinct from professional ethics. Focusing on the purpose of leadership I will move into a discussion of good leadership, and into a consideration of the key issues, including leadership and power, leadership and trust, integrity and virtues of the leader. As part of this I will critically examine theories of leadership which are associated with ethics, in particular, transformational leadership. I will argue that these are useful but not sufficient and that ethical leadership is best focused in the concepts and practice of responsibility and integrity.

Horror in the Antarctic

Following the success of a computer game based upon a scenario set in the Antarctic a computer software development company was commissioned by a major media company to develop a second game.

This time the client requested two developments: increased shock value, and the inclusion of the explicit death of young children. An added incentive to do this would be that if the computer company agreed to this there would be rapid release of monies still outstanding from the first game.

John, the manager of the computer games company, employed 90 people and they depended on regular commissions to survive. However, the manager was very uneasy about the commission, and initially felt that he ought to turn it down. He decided to share his feelings with the staff, who were also very unsure what to do. They felt there might be wider issues about how such games affect players and about how their firm might be perceived. However, they decided that the next step was to get back to the media company and to clarify the position, to begin to understand why they wanted such a commission. The result was that the manager wrote to his client's legal department and asked if they would confirm in writing that the company wished him to develop a second game and that it was their intention that this should involve increased horror and the explicit death of children. No such confirmation was received, the new game was developed without the initial additions, and the money owed for the first game was rapidly released.

At the centre of this true story was a leader. He was not trained to be a leader, having risen to that position through his IT expertise and a strong sense of enterprise. A key part of his job as leader was to keep his company functioning, so that his employees could maintain their families and lifestyles, and could practise their profession. In other words, as a leader he had a responsibility to his workers and colleagues. Just what that responsibility meant began to be questioned when he was faced by this lucrative contract offer, introducing a wider responsibility. Initially John was not sure how to articulate that responsibility. Did he and his company have a responsibility to the people who might use such a game? Did they have a responsibility to society at large? Might such a game contribute towards the desensitisation of young people and thus of society as a whole? He knew that the empirical evidence about such games was inconclusive, and yet could not help imagining a slippery slope with himself at the top. Leadership in all this involved working through a response to this issue. It was more than just getting a job done.

By implication, it also involved working through what the value base of his company was. The question that he put to his colleagues was 'Where do *we* stand?' This would seem to indicate that a leader has responsibility for at least enabling the group that they lead to establish its ethical meaning, and thus to establish an ethical community of practice. This means the development of a company that can articulate its purpose, its underlying values, and can develop over time a way of embodying those values. Beneath all of that were also beliefs about purpose, identity, how the corporation related to society, how computer games related to society, and so on. To make matters worse for the leader, none of this had actually been worked out beforehand. Yes, they had something of a mission statement, with some general values, but that statement did not actually tell them what they should do, or how he should lead.

This last point took him into a new related area of concern. Just how should he lead the firm in responding to the issue? Had it been a larger group he might have decided to look to leadership from some other source. He might, for instance, have turned to the chair of the board. After all, the board represents the natural authority of that group, the owners. It could be argued that they should take the leadership role, and that part of his task as executive leader was to recognise his limitations and hand over to them. As it was, he jointly owned the firm. Was he then going to lead from the front, to affirm his identity as a leader of integrity and charisma, and to stand out against any suggestion that such a game should be produced? As a man with three young children, he was sorely tempted. With equal determination, he might have thought rather about the future of his firm and those who depended on him, and quickly signed the contract, noting en passant that any responsibility for the final product and consequences of its sale would lie with the commissioning firm. Perhaps the responsibility would be with the law, who would impose an age limit on the game. Instead, he chose to share the decision-making, and thus the responsibility, with his colleagues. He saw them as colleagues, and not as followers, because he felt that if a decision was to be made about their future they should share in the responsibility for it. He also felt that he had limited skill in this area and wanted to hear how they might contribute to making sense of the whole thing.

Once he began to share the issue with them, greater clarity began to emerge. The groups questioned the data that they were given. How far would the firm budge on this? What did it mean to show the explicit death of children? Perhaps this was gratuitous horror, or perhaps the end of children could be shown in a moral context that did not involve the player in their death and was seen to be the result of unacceptable behaviour. Most of the staff were uneasy and many had strong moral feelings against the initial proposal. The majority also wanted more time to see how those moral intuitions would play out in dialogue around their plans and practice. One thing all were agreed on was need to asses the effect of any option on the reputation of the firm, and thus on their survival.

In the event, the leader represented the view of his colleagues, and began a dialogue with the commissioning firm. There are two interesting things about that dialogue. First, he was really asking the commissioning company what they meant. As Minnow[1] notes in her reflection on the prisoner abuses in Iraq and other areas, this is a powerful question. Most of the orders that led to such abuses were not direct or explicit. Minnow argues for the importance of clarifying orders. The clarification question invites the person or groups to reflect on and take responsibility for the words they have used.

Secondly, by recording the question in a letter, John was placing the dialogue firmly into the public domain, and thus ensuring transparency and accountability. The commissioning firm would now need to be aware that their shareholders, colleagues and potential clients might be listening, and would need to work out their accountability. This is precisely why a firm with a strong family market chose not to pursue the initial commission. Plato, in the *Republic*, raises this issue in the story of the ring of Gyges.[2] The ring that Gyges finds makes him invisible. If you are invisible do you then have to be good? In one sense, John was reminding the large media firm that no one is invisible and therefore everyone is accountable.

This case and its brief analysis introduces the idea of ethical leadership.

First, it may be noted that leadership is not confined to management. The leader in this case was a manager, but other players might have taken leadership roles and the computer games staff shared the leadership.

Second, the case shows that it is very difficult to see ethics as the unthinking application of principles or codes. John had to work through ethical deliberation that was both rational and affective. Getting the decision right really mattered to him, reminding us of Charles Taylor's argument that any significant decision involves 'strong valuations'[3] that are constitutive of the person's identity. This could only be worked out in the light of the issues and the people involved in the situation. In turn, this required taking responsibility for articulating and testing moral meaning.

---

1   Minnow, M. (2006) What the rule of law should mean in civics education: from the 'Following Orders' defence to the classroom. *Journal of Moral Education*, 35(2): 137–162.

2   Plato (1974) *Republic*. London: Penguin.

3   Taylor, C. (1989) *Sources of the Self*. Cambridge: Cambridge University Press.

Third, the case shows that ethics, in the sense of discerning right and wrong, and embodying underlying values are essential to leadership. Ciulla[4] argues that ethics is at the heart of leadership. At no point in this case was the manager able to avoid questions of value and of how the underlying values might relate to practice. It could be argued that the shared concern about the reputation and survival of the firm was not so much ethics as pragmatism.

However, the distinction between ethics and pragmatism can be strained. There are perfectly good pragmatic motives for being good, not least the survival of the group and anyone dependent on the group.

Given the importance of ethics in leadership it is not surprising that the study of ethics in leadership should be gathering pace. Ciulla,[5] however, notes that in the general literature of leadership there is little evidence of a focus on ethics other than reference to the importance of integrity. She goes on to suggest much of the writing on leadership pays little attention to ethical theory. Rost,[6] for example, argues that ethical theory has little relevance to leadership studies. Ciulla argues that without such theory it is difficult to determine what is meant by ethics. Hence, it is to theory that we now turn.

Ethical Theory

One might not expect the term ethics to be understood in the same way by everybody. However, postmodernism suggests that any convincing overview of ethics has gone. The effort of sustaining some overarching prescriptive framework about what is good is now too great.[7] The immense differences in cultures and religions across the globe lead to a plurality of ethical views, all of which, so the argument goes, we have to respect. In effect, this accepts ethical relativism. Some theorists argue that ethics can only be worked out 'locally' in the light of tradition, the responsibility of persons or groups to the local community and environment. Others argue that in any case we have every right to follow what we feel is morally acceptable, unless it is harming another.

In attempting to make sense of moral meaning, philosophy has offered several different theories of ethics, the first of which argues for the possibility of shared ethical meaning.

DEONTOLOGICAL THEORY

This theory argues that ethical meaning is found in absolute or general principles, such as the Ten Commandments, applicable to all situations. This approach is summed up in Natural Law thinking which argues that there is shared and self-evident ethical meaning based in an analysis of underlying values and purpose. The ethical principle that says it is wrong to kill, for instance, is based in the self-evident or natural value of the sacredness of life.

---

4   Ciulla, J. ed. (2004) *Ethics the Heart of Leadership*. Westport, CT: Praeger.

5   Ciulla (2004) p. 4.

6   Rost, J. (1991) *Leadership in the Twenty-First Century*. New York: Praeger.

7   Connor, S. (1989) *The Post Modern Culture*. Oxford: Blackwell.

Critics, however, argue that it is difficult to see how principles alone can act as the foundation to ethics. Few, if any, principles are absolute and thus apply to all situations. There are exceptions to the principle against killing, for instance, from self-defence to the context of war. In any case, Finch and Mason[8] suggest in their research on families that few people actually use principles in ethical deliberations. Instead, they argue that ethics, and thus ethical identity, is developed through the active negotiation of responsibility in the situation. As Fletcher[9] also noted there is also the danger of simply applying ethical principles without any thought about the situation, and thus losing individual responsibility or agency.

Despite this, principles and any ethical rules are an important element in ethics, for several reasons:

- Principles, such as it is wrong to kill another person, remain generally true. The exceptions have to be justified.
- Principles can sum up the accumulated wisdom of the group or society. Whilst this must not be accepted uncritically, there is little point in reinventing insights into what is right or wrong.
- It is important to have general moral injunctions, exemplified in the Declaration of Human Rights, to test out any 'local' views of ethics in terms of overarching justice and values. Nussbaum[10] argues that this guards against attempts to justify exploitative behaviour, such as child labour, on economic or cultural grounds. Kung[11] goes further, to argue that shared views of justice and responsibility are necessary to respond to the global environmental crises. At the very least, this suggests that ethics has to involve a continual dialogue between general principles and the particular situation.
- Beauchamp and Childress[12] suggest ethical principles also have a broad function in guiding practical response. They suggest principles for professional practice in general, which could happily apply to leadership. These involve:

  - Respect for the autonomy of the client.
  - Justice, a concern for fairness in dealing with stakeholders.
  - Beneficence, always aiming to maximise the good in any situation.
  - Non-maleficence, aiming to avoid harm.

Again, such functional principles are guidelines to how we behave, and have to be worked through in the situation. Hence, many of these principles were involved in the case above. John was concerned with fairness and justice for his colleagues and the other stakeholders in terms of the effects of any decisions, and to respect their autonomy in working through the decision. He was also deeply concerned about any harm to children. Another functional principle, that of precaution, caused him not to take decisions too

8   Finch, J. and Mason, J. (1993) *Negotiating Family Responsibilities*. London: Routledge.

9   Fletcher, J. (1966) *Situation Ethics*. London: SCM.

10   Nussbaum, M. (1999) Human functioning and social justice: in defence of Aristotelian essentialism. In Koggel, C. (ed.) *Moral Issues in a Global Perspective*, pp. 124–126. Peterborough, Ontario: Broadview.

11   Kung, H. (1991) *Global Responsibility*. London: SCM.

12   Beauchamp, T. and Childress, J. (1989) *Principles of Biomedical Ethics*. Oxford: Oxford University Press.

early in the light of limited grasp of all the possible consequences, hence the letter to the commissioning firm.

UTILITARIANISM

Faced by some of the problems of principles in ethics, philosophers such as Mill[13] have argued for a more pragmatic foundation to ethical thinking, summed up in the theory of utilitarianism. This suggests that moral meaning is discovered though calculating how any action might maximise the good for the most people. A classic, if crude, illustration of this is the case of the potholers, or cavers, who invite the most rotund of their number to go through the final exit first, only for him to get firmly stuck. Meantime, subterranean waters are rising, rapidly threatening the life of the 25 cavers behind their fellow. A simple calculus tells you that the fate of the 25 people outweighs that of the one and that therefore it ethically right, indeed necessary, to use means that might endanger his life in order to save the others. Hard luck on the imaginary overweight caver.

Of course, it makes sense to calculate the benefits and risks involved in any option, and John was roughly doing this. The trouble is that in real life it starts to become very difficult. How do you weigh the good to 90 colleagues, of a contract that will keep them and their families, against the good of not helping to develop a game that might adversely affect many more vulnerable people?

The weaknesses of this approach become obvious. First, utilitarianism does not make clear what the good is that should be maximised. Faced by competing views of what is good it cannot provide criteria for choice. Second, it does not provide good reasons for why the good of the majority should be taken over that of the minority. There may be fundamental issues of justice that overturn this. Children who are forced into labour, for example, may be in a minority, but their plight is unjust nonetheless. Third, and related, using this approach as the only foundation to ethics runs the danger of ends justifying any means, such as torture in the context of the so-called 'war against terror'.

Finally, it is often very difficult to know what the consequences of any action might be. It would be easy to assume that not to take the contract would have adverse effects on the business, or for that matter to assume that games that include the gratuitous death of children might lead to the desensitisation of some people. Both are in fact speculative. There simply is not clear evidence one way or the other. Hence, many utilitarians would invoke the precautionary principle – it is best not to do something, in case these certain negative consequences might ensue. A related approach is the slippery slope argument, to the effect that if a particular action is taken then this might result in a breakdown of standards, ushering further negative consequences. A good example of this was in the opposition to the unsuccessful Assisted Dying Bill of 2007.[14] It was argued that if this were passed that it would allow a slippery slope at the bottom of which would be death on demand, and the casting-off of the elderly who have become a nuisance. However, as Lee[15] notes, the slippery slope argument is a fallacy, based on neither empirical nor logical evidence. John and his colleagues were careful to steer clear of such arguments.

---

13   Mill, J. S. (1960) *Utilitarianism*. London: Dent and Son.

14   http://www.publications.parliament.uk/pa/ld200304/ldbills/017/2004017.htm.

15   Lee, S. (2003) *Uneasy Ethics*. London: Pimlico.

Utilitarian ethics then is more of a calculus than a theory. Hence, Beauchamp and Childress[16] use cost–benefit and risk–benefit analysis, but only in the light of the four guiding principles.

OTHER THEORIES

Several other approaches to ethical theory have emerged in the last century, each trying to develop a view of ethics that is richer, more complex, and focused in practical reflection:

Virtue ethics

Building on the ethics of Aristotle this argues that ethics is not so much about determining what is right or wrong, but rather about building a good character. The character is informed and sustained by the stories of the community, which embodies the virtues. The virtues are learned through practice focused in a community or practice,[17] and good character will lead to good ethical decisions. The virtues, such as courage, justice and temperance are 'of the mean', that is, between extremes. Courage, for instance, lies between cowardice and foolhardiness. At the heart of this approach is practical wisdom or phronesis, the capacity to identify the core purpose of a person or project and embody that in practice. This was seen by Aristotle as an intellectual virtue. John, in effect, was trying to enable all the different participants to reflect on their different views of purpose. In particular, his letter was inviting the commissioning firm to contrast their vision and purpose with their practice in this case.

Feminist ethics

Feminist writers contrast justice with care.[18] Justice, they argue, is solution-driven and based upon power. This approach to ethics has dominated Western history. In contrast, care as the foundation of ethics is concerned not simply to solve ethical dilemmas, but rather to understand the nature of any dilemma and to include all who are involved in working it through. This is an ethics that looks to develop trust and is dependent upon key attributes such as empathy.

Post-Holocaust ethics

Writers such as Bauman[19] reflect on the experience of the Holocaust. At the heart of the Holocaust was denial that certain groups any human characteristics or rights. Hence, responsibility for the other, in these cases, was denied. This denial was exacerbated by management techniques such as the division of labour, which further distanced any sense of responsibility. Bauman argues that any ethics has to begin with the inclusive awareness and appreciation of the other, and, hence, responsibility for the other. That, of course,

---

16   Beauchamp, T. and Childress, J. (1989) *Principles of Biomedical Ethics*. Oxford: Oxford University Press.

17   McIntyre, A. (1981) *After Virtue*. London: Duckworth.

18   Koehn, D. (1998) *Rethinking Feminist Ethics*. London: Routledge.

19   Bauman, Z. (1993) *Postmodern Ethics*. Oxford: Blackwell.

is an impossibility. You cannot take responsibility for all others. Hence, Levinas[20] argues that responsibility is not simply individualistic but rather shared and therefore essentially social. The rest of ethics then is how that responsibility is worked out together.

Discourse ethics

Habermas[21] suggests that ethical meaning emerges from dialogue, enabling reflection on values and the discovery of shared norms. Getting the process right for such discourse is thus of the highest importance, and Habermas suggests basic conditions for this. Benhabib[22] goes further, noting that whilst the discourse may reveal shared moral meaning, the conditions of discourse themselves already embody moral meaning, not least respect. Such discourse, in turn, requires attributes such as empathy.[23]

Global ethics

Building on the sense of connectedness stressed by the feminist ethics, global ethics stresses our responsibility for the environment and human kind globally. In one sense, this is also a natural progression from post-Holocaust ethics, stressing responsibility for all on a global scale, and a concern for structural global response to issues that dwarf the all too often individualistic focus of ethics.[24]

These approaches overlap. All have some reference to:

- Character, involving virtues or qualities.
- Awareness of and openness to the other.
- Process focused on reflectivity and dialogue that embodies core values.
- A starting point of taking and sharing responsibility for the other.

ETHICAL DECISION-MAKING FRAMEWORK

Any ethical decision-making would have to take into account all of these factors, pointing to a process of ethical decision making that is not value-free, but that rather embodies such ethical insights.

The important elements of such a framework, noted in Robinson *et al.*[25] include:

- Data-gathering. Often this requires all stakeholders to ensure a balanced perspective.
- Value reflection. This will uncover the different values underlying the situation and the views of the stakeholders. This may involve dealing with value conflicts, as well as searching for an agreed value or principle base.

20   Levinas, E. (1998) *Entre Nous: On thinking-of-the-Other.* New York: Columbia University Press.

21   Habermas, J. (1992) *Moral Consciousness and Communicative Action.* London: Polity Press.

22   Benhabib, S. (1992) *Situating the Self.* London: Polity.

23   Benhabib (1992) p. 52.

24   Kung, H. (1991) *Global Responsibility.* London: SCM.

25   Robinson, S, Dixon, R., Preece, C. and Moodley, C. (2007) *Engineering, Business and Professional Ethics.* London: Butterworth-Heinemann.

- Responsibility analysis. This looks to analyse the resources and responsibilities of all involved and how they might be shared through negotiation.[26]
- Planning in the light of resources and constraints, and analysing options in terms of the core values.
- Implementation. This demands creative partnership.

Of course, the deadlines of work mean that embodiment of values cannot be 'perfect', and the fitting of values to practice will be a matter of ongoing reflection and monitoring of professional practice. Nonetheless, the use of a framework that is understood and accepted by colleagues can enable rapid critical reflection for the immediate situation. This embodies and reinforces a view of ethics that is dialogic, participative, collaborative and transformative.

Elements of most of this ethical framework are used by John in the case as he enabled clear data-gathering about the intentions and motivations of the commissioning firm, and the beginnings of reflection on values and responsibility, worked with his colleagues around responsibility, and waited a response from the commissioning firm before moving to next steps.

The Ethical Identity of Leadership

Ethical theory then, despite Rost's suggestion, does provide a useful framework for working through the ethics of leadership in practice. However, it can be just the same framework for any professional or applied ethics. The question may be asked, what is distinctive about *leadership* ethics? In what sense does ethics lie at the heart of this activity, as Ciulla[27] suggests? The question would not be lost on Aristotle, who argued that ethics and ethical identity are developed through reflection on the purpose or telos of the person or group.

Ciulla suggests that the one reason why this ethical identity has not been explored more is because of the stress on positivist approaches to leadership. This focuses on a scientific approach, trying to understand what it involves and from that how leaders might be trained. Calas and Smircich[28] argue that this tends to focus on fine detail, leading to a fragmentation of leadership practice. This aspires to value neutrality and takes the focus away from any sense of overarching purpose that gives meaning and identity.

Another reason why ethical identity in leadership is not easily pinned down is the problem of definition. Rost,[29] for instance, claims that there are over 221 different definitions of leadership. There is much debate about whether these are descriptions, definitions or paradigms, and whether the differences are substantive or simply arise from different contexts.

However, it is possible to reflect on core purposes of leadership and from this to focus on the responsibilities of leadership. This will involve examining issues such as power and leadership, and the moral context of leadership.

---

26   Finch, J. and Mason, J. (1993) *Negotiating Family Responsibilities*. London: Routledge.

27   Ciulla (2004) p. 4.

28   Calas, M. and Smircich, L. (1988) Reading leadership as a form of cultural analysis. In Hunt, G., Baliga, B., Daschler, H. and Schriesheim, A. *Emerging Leadership Vistas*, pp. 222–226. Lanham, MD: Lexington Books.

29   Rost, J. (1991) *Leadership in the Twenty-First Century*. New York: Praeger.

LEADERSHIP AND POWER

All leadership involves making use of power in enabling meaningful practice to happen. How that power is exercised then becomes a matter for value judgement. Is leadership a function of expertise or greater knowledge, with the leader taking the group in the right direction? If so, who determines what the right direction is? What is the basis of the leader's authority?

Some argue that charismatic leaders are essential in enabling groups to work through necessary change. Others see leadership as a function of the group, and look to involve different stakeholders, much like John. Others argue for the importance of formal democratic process, with leadership enabling a consensus.[30] This involves developing a form of contractual leadership, embodying core transactional values, such as fairness or responsibility.

Greenleaf[31] goes further to see the leader as essentially not involving the overt use of power at all. Servant leadership, as he calls it, involves putting the needs of those who are being led first. He focuses on higher needs, resulting in mature and holistic development, involving autonomy, freedom, wisdom and increased focus on service. The core characteristics of the leader, then, include listening, empathy, healing, awareness, conceptualisation, foresight and the building of community. In turn, such leadership looks to make a difference within the institution or project and beyond the group in terms of affecting those in society with the least resources.

THE MORAL CONTEXT OF LEADERSHIP

Such views place leadership firmly in a moral context, including a moral purpose in leadership itself and the pursuit of moral purpose in the group or project.

In the context of business, Friedman[32] and Sternberg[33] argue against this approach. They stress competence over care and service, and argue that the ethical basis of leadership is the contract between leader and owner. The shareholders own the company and the primary legal and ethical purpose is to increase the profits, whilst staying within the law. The idea of making a difference to members of group and beyond is secondary to that core contract. Of course, this will involve respecting laws to do with respect, tolerance and diversity, but the responsibility for developing and maintaining such practice is with politics and the development of social policy. Such an argument is often characterised as trying to avoid ethical concern with leadership. In fact, it is based in teleological argument (telos = purpose) about the proper focus of ethics in leadership, and Friedman's argument is that leader's ethical job is to enable the group or project to stay focused on its proper purpose.

Friedman's argument has been critiqued on several grounds, including:

---

30   Rost (1991).

31   Greenleaf, R. (1977) *The Servant as Leader: A Journey into the Nature of Legitimate Power and Greatness*. New York: Paulist Press.

32   Friedman, M. (1983) The social responsibility of business is to increase its profits. In Donaldson, T. and Werhane, P. (eds) *Ethical Issues in Business*, pp. 239–243. New York: Prentice Hall.

33   Sternberg, E. (2000) *Just Business*. Oxford: Oxford University Press.

- There is not a priori reason why purpose should be restricted to one. It possible to both be concerned for the well-being of the groups as well as for the owner. Moreover, any 'proper purpose' needs to be worked out in context, and cannot be simply determined beforehand and applied.
- It could be argued that concern for the well-being of the staff will lead to a more motivated workforce and therefore increased productivity.[34]
- Behind the Friedman/Sternberg argument is a concern for the freedom of the manager/ leader. Stakeholder theory suggests that any project involves a plurality of groups or person with a concern for, or affected by, it. This points to an underlying view of humanity as interdependent. At the very least, this demands that a leader should be aware of these relationships and respond to them in taking the group forward.
- The Friedman argument has a deterministic view of shareholders, that they must have the single purpose of raising money. However, this ignores the autonomy and responsibility of shareholders and thus their potential in developing a leadership role in determining what the ethos and purpose of the groups might be.

Burns[35] aims to take the moral base of the leader beyond this. He argues for a view of the leader as essentially moral, excluding figures such as Hitler from the very definition of leadership. Burns agrees with Rost that the purpose of the leader is by definition transformative, but argues that this involves more than simply finding a consensus. This process of transformation can be painful and conflictual. He acknowledges that Rost's view on leadership developing a consensus for change is value-based, but argues that these values are transactional rather than transformational. Transactional, or modal, values are about the means of any process, and include responsibility, fairness, honesty and promise-keeping. Transformational leadership, however, focuses on the ends. Burns suggests that there are key moral ends that transcend the purpose of any particular group. These include justice, freedom and equality. The task of the leader is to lead the project and its members into these uplands of moral maturity, through stages akin to Kohlberg's stages of moral development.[36] These move from the early stages where values are developed through peer pressure to the mature stages where the members of a group or project can both belong to the group and also have autonomy of rational decision-making. The effect of all this is to enable group members to develop into responsible leaders, becoming fully moral agents.

Burn's position is potentially creative but problematic. Keeley[37] argues that it assumes that collective ends are more legitimate or morally powerful than individual ends. Keeley notes research by Birnbaum[38] into leadership in higher education that questions the three myths that underlie the Burns view. The first myth is that leaders have to create a vision that will transcend the interests of the individual. Birnbaum found that in fact successful leaders reflect the many interests and values of the different stakeholders. Effective listening in this was seen to be more important than communicating a vision. The second myth

---

34   Robinson *et al.* (2007).

35   Burns, J. (1978) *Leadership*. New York: Harper and Row.

36   Kohlberg, L. (1984) *Essays on Moral Development*, vol. 2. San Francisco, CA: Harper Row.

37   Keeley, M. (2004) The trouble with transformational leadership: towards a federalist ethic for organizations. In Ciulla, J. (ed.) *Ethics the Heart of Leadership*, pp. 149–176. Westport, CT: Praeger.

38   Birnbaum, R. (1992) *How Academic Leadership Works*. San Francisco, CA: Jossey-Bass.

was that university heads should be transformational leaders. The research suggested that change was in any case a given in the life of the academic community and that the most effective way of handling this was through reflection on the values already held by the members of that community, using these as the basis for working together. Finally, Birnabum noted that charisma was not essential in this leadership. On the contrary, charisma can easily subvert the lower levels of management through diminishing their responsibility and authority in relation to the leader.

A further problem for the Burns position is his choice of transformational values. The values of equality, justice and the like are in effect general moral principles. They certainly transcend the concern of any group. However, their very generality means that it is difficult to work through what they actually mean in practice. The term equality, for instance, can have over a hundred logically distinct meanings.[39] Hence, meaning has to be worked out in context and this is difficult to do in any group or project without the people involved being engaged in dialogue around these values and how they can be embodied in their community of practice, including any transactions. This further suggests that the rigid distinction between transactional and transformational values is an unhelpful dichotomy. Transaction and transformation are intimately connected. Transactional values involve the development of broad contracts where expectations are shared. These are precisely a way both of generating trust[40] and embodying the so-called transformational values. The contract relationship can embody freedom, creativity, equality and trust.

In both the Burns and Greenleaf models there is a strong sense that they know what is good for the group or workforce and have to bring them up to the required level of altruism. This seriously questions what they mean by autonomy. The stress on altruism (especially in Greenleaf) is also problematic. Much feminist ethics has argued that stress on service runs the danger of devaluing self-concern, and that it is important to balance the two.[41]

GOOD LEADERSHIP

Ciulla[42] also argues against Burns' exclusively moral definition of leadership. It is not clear that moral leaders alone can be defined as leaders. The issue, as Ciulla puts it, is what makes a good leader, not what makes a leader. Hitler clearly had claims to being a leader. The very word *fuehrer* means leader. Hitler aspired to an ethical vision, one that included a belief system and well-developed value system, and sought to enable his followers to take responsibility for all of that.[43] The point is that he was a morally bad leader. At one level, this can be seen in terms of the characteristics of cult leadership – the term cult often refers to a closed religious movement.[44]

The characteristics of such a leader include:

---

39   Rae, D. (1981) *Equalities*. Cambridge, MA: Harvard University Press.

40   Robinson, S. (2001) *Agape, Moral Meaning and Pastoral Counselling*. Cardiff: Aureus.

41   Robinson *et al.* (2007).

42   Ciulla (2004) 8ff.

43   Burleigh, M. (2000) *The Third Reich: A New History*. London: McMillan.

44   Barker, E. (1989) *New Religious Movements*. London: Stationery Office Books.

- Control of the truth. The leader is the source of truth, and others have to accept it. There is no space for critical reflection.
- A strong affective content. What binds the cult member to the leader is fulfilment of non-reflective emotional need.
- Those outside the group are seen as enemies to the group, hence a threat. In extreme cases this involves failure to accept their full humanity.
- Emphasis upon the members proving their loyalty through making sacrifices for the group.

Sims and Brinkmann[45] argue such a leadership broadly characterised the Enron disaster. Geoff Skilling, the CEO, for instance, became the source of all information, internally and externally, about the company. This set up a culture in which no practice was questioned, including suspect accounting practices. This spread outside Enron, even to their accountancy firm of Arthur Andersen.

Some might argue that this is not unethical leadership per se, not least because members of such groups choose to belong to them, the groups satisfy their need for belonging, and for the most part no harm is done. However, the example of Enron shows that significant harm that can be done to the group and to individuals through this kind of leadership. Arthur Andersen collapsed, the leaders of several connected firms suffered legal terms, and the Enron staff lost their jobs and pensions. Such leadership also encouraged a restricted and conditioned the view of community. You only belong to the group if you fit in with their view. Its view of freedom and autonomy is also narrow, not least because it limits any learning, through discouraging discussion and critique at any level. Because of all this, it discourages members of the group from taking responsibility for their thoughts and actions.

From this it could be argued that a core purpose of leadership is to enable the development of responsibility at all levels.

Responsibility

Schweiker[46] suggests three modes of responsibility, the first two of which originate in Aristotle's thinking:

- *Imputability.* Actions can be attributed to a person. Hence, the person can be seen to have been responsible for those actions and the decisions that led to them.
- *Accountability.* The person is responsible or answerable *to* someone.
- *Liability.* The person is responsible *for* something or someone.

45   Sims, R. R. and Brinkmann, J. (2003) Enron ethics (or culture matters more than codes). *Journal of Business Ethics*, 45(3): 243–256.

46   Schweiker, W. (1995) *Responsibility and Christian Ethics*. Cambridge: Cambridge University Press.

Imputability

There are strong and weak views of imputability. The weak views[47] simply refer to the causal connection between the person and any action. This shows that the action can be attributed to the person. Such a view does not help in determining just how much the person is actually involved in and therefore fully responsible for the action. A stronger view suggests that responsibility involves a rational decision-making process that enables the person to fully own the action that arises from the decision. Taylor[48] argues that this decision-making constitutes a strong valuation that connects action to deep decision-making, and is what constitutes the moral identity of the person. In order to be fully responsible the person would have to be aware of their social context, the significant relationships, and the mutual effect of those relationships and so on. John clearly tried to develop a strong sense of responsibility.

Accountability

The second mode of responsibility is accountability. This is based on contract relationships. The contract sets up a series of mutual expectations. At one level, these are about discernible targets that form the basis of any job, and without which the competence of the person cannot be assessed. At another level, there will be broader moral expectations of how one should behave in any contract. This would include the importance of openness and transparency in relationships and other such behaviours that provide the basis for trust.

In John's case, there was a strong sense of accountability to his colleagues through a contract that was sustained through dialogue.

Liability

Liability (as distinguished from legal liability) goes beyond accountability, into the idea of caring for others, of sense of wider liability for certain projects or people. Each profession has to work these out in context, without an explicit contract. Working that out demands an awareness of the limitations of the organisation, avoiding taking too much responsibility, and a capacity to work together with others and to negotiate and share responsibility. This was the stage that John was entering into with the commissioning firm. It is in this mode that different areas of responsibility begin to emerge: personal, professional, corporate, civic, environmental and global.

Leadership and Responsibility

The purpose of the leader in all of this is to enable responsibility to be taken in each of these different 'modes'. In terms of immutability this is about empowering the members

---

47   McKenny, G. (2005) Responsibility. In Meilander, G. and Werpehowski, W. (eds) *The Oxford Handbook of Theological Ethics*, pp. 237–253. Oxford: Oxford University Press.

48   Taylor (1989).

of an organisation to take responsibility for their values and practice. At one level, this has to involve empowering group members to critique their own and the group's myths – the big stories that give value and identity to the group. In the case of Enron, all the staff accepted without question the presentation of the corporation as benign and caring, driven forward by the next ambitious big idea. No one asked how this related to actual practice, and there were no objective means of reporting on this.

The leader is also about enabling accountability at all levels. Again, the Enron case is instructive. There was a reluctance to be critical or to be accountable in the firm. This was no doubt partly because of fear of what befall anyone who raised problems. Which is why developing a culture of critical openness becomes so important.[49] Regardless of motive, the work of Milgram,[50] Bauman[51] and Zimbardo[52] suggests that a majority of people tend to try to avoid accountability. The Milgram experiments, for instance, used participants who thought they were involved in an experiment about the relationship between pain and learning. Behind a screen was a subject (actually an actor) attached to 'electrodes' and the participant was in charge of the administering shock to the subject whenever he got the answers wrong. The participant was invited by a person in authority to increase the shocks on a regular basis. Over 60 per cent took the shock to what was clearly marked as levels of high danger. They were more or less content to deny their responsibility in the face of authority. Bauman develops this view and notes that the practice of the division of labour further reinforces such a dynamic. Once you decide not to accept responsibility this affects how you perceive reality. In the Milgram case the participant can see the effects that they are having on the person but simply does not ascribe any moral significance to them. Assessing moral significance becomes a matter for the person in authority. In the Enron case, one Arthur Andersen director sent an email advising colleagues they should avoid any 'smoking gun' in any report or communication. A week later he clarified this by saying that a 'smoking gun' meant any evidence of guilt.[53] These communications involved over a dozen colleagues and not one questioned the meaning or probity of these statements. They simply did not see it as morally significant. From this and many other cases, one can see the pragmatic moral argument that organisations that do not attend to the development of a culture of responsibility run the danger of another Enron disaster, one that was not unique. In all this, individual responsibility and corporate responsibility are intimately connected.

The other point about leadership that attends to a culture of responsibility is that it could be argued that this leads to more effective leadership in practice.[54] It leads to more effective data-gathering, better-motivated staff, and more efficient and effective practice.

The focus on responsibility and the empowering of all stakeholders and groups members to develop responsibility at all these levels is different from both Rost's and Burns' positions. First, it is not simply about achieving consensus. It is about enabling

49   Borrie, G. and Dehn, G. (2002) Whistle-blowing: the new perspective. In Megone, C. and Robinson, S. *Case Histories in Business Ethics*, pp. 96–105. London: Routledge.

50   Milgram, S. (1971) *The Individual in a Social World*. Reading, MA: Addison and Wesley.

51   Bauman, Z. (1989) *Modernity and the Holocaust*. London: Polity.

52   Zimbardo, P. (2007) *The Lucifer Effect*. London: Rider.

53   I am indebted to Andrew Weissmann, one of the federal prosecutors of Enron, for this data, shared in an unpublished paper in the Conference of the Centre for Applied and Professional Ethics, Kingston University, 2 July 2008.

54   Tyler, T. (2005) Fairness as effectiveness: how leaders lead. In Ciulla, J. Price, T. and Murphy, S. (2005) *The Quest for Moral Leaders*, pp. 113–130. Cheltenham: Edward Elgar.

reflective and responsible practice, such that the groups as a whole and the members can own and work through purpose and practice at all levels. The responsibility model may in fact question or challenge consensus. It was, after all, consensus that was at one point apparently shared in Enron. Second, leadership in this is not about enabling transformation as such, but more about empowering the group to take responsibility for their own change. The idea that leadership should be transformational smacks of a leader-centred agenda imposed on the led.

The Virtues of the Leader

It is a short step from the idea of responsibility to focusing on the virtues of the leader. Most of the emphasis on writings in this area has been on the virtues that would inspire trust in the leader. This has included all the core virtues of courage, patience, wisdom and justice, all of which enable better decision- making and better relationship-building. Others even include virtues such as serenity.[55] Perhaps the most important candidate for this has been the virtue of integrity,[56] alongside technical excellence/competence in the chosen field of the leader. This chimes with the stress in Burns on authentic as well as transformative leadership.

INTEGRITY

It makes sense to argue that trust depends upon integrity rather than image both at a corporate as well as a personal level. Solomon[57] suggests that integrity is not one but several virtues and Robinson and Dixon[58] bring together some of these elements:

- *Integration* of the different parts of the person: emotional, psychological and intellectual. This leads to holistic or integral thinking, and an awareness of the self alongside awareness and appreciation of external data.
- *Consistency* of character and operation between: value and practice; past, present and future; and in different situations and contexts. The behaviours will not necessarily be the same in each situation, but will be consistent with the ethical identity of the person.
- *Transparency*. This is perhaps the most powerful ethical tool, in that it assumes an openness such that all are or will be held to account. It provides a very basic ethical test, 'Would you be happy if what you had done or intend to do was reported in the newspapers tomorrow?' Such a test demands the development of honesty.

---

55   Harle, T. (2005) Serenity, courage and wisdom: changing competencies for leadership. *Business Ethics: A European Review*, 4(4): 348–356.

56   Solomon, R. (1992) *Ethics and Excellence*. Oxford: Oxford University Press.

57   Solomon, R. (1992) *Ethics and Excellence*. Oxford: Oxford University Press. Solomon, R. (2005) Emotional leadership, emotional integrity. In Ciulla, J., Price, T. and Murphy, S. (2005) *The Quest for Moral Leaders*, pp. 28–44. Cheltenham: Edward Elgar. See also Worden, S. (2003) The role of integrity as a mediator in strategic leadership: a recipe for reputational capital. *Journal of Business Ethics*, 46(1): 31–49.

58   Robinson, S. and Dixon, R. (1997) The professional engineer: virtues and learning. *Science and Engineering Ethics*, 3(3): 339–348.

- Taking *responsibility* for values and practice. Without accepting responsibility for ethical values and for response neither the individual nor the profession can develop a genuine moral identity or agency.
- Integrity as essentially a *learning concept*. Absolute integrity is impossible to attain. Hence, an important virtue is humility, the acceptance of limitations, of weakness as well as strengths.[59] Equally important therefore is the capacity to reflect, to evaluate practice, to be able to cope with criticism and to alter practice appropriately. This capacity to learn means that integrity should not be seen as simply maintaining values and ethical practice come what may, but as involving the reflective process, such that values can be tested in the light of practice and either appropriately maintained or developed. This is very close to Aristotle's intellectual virtue of phronesis, the capacity for rational deliberation that enables the wise to reflect on their conception of the good and to connect this to practice.

Brown[60] develops this further in the light of corporate integrity. He argues that corporate integrity involves consistency, awareness, inclusion and purpose. The purpose of the organisation has to be worked through and awareness involves five dimensions: cultural, interpersonal, organisational, social and natural. In other words the leader has to enable patterns of conversation between the significant internal relationships and the relationships of the group to the social and physical environment

This involves handling plurality of responsibilities from civic to professional, and the starting point of shared responsibility, seeing all parties as global citizens, provides the basis from which integrity can be worked through.

The recent report of the Institute of Chartered Accountants in England and Wales[61]sees integrity as being at the heart of how the profession relates and reports. One of the core drivers, they argue, is leadership. Leadership partly involves modelling integrity, but is much more than charisma. Leadership needs to enable 'the strategy, policies, information, and culture to sustain a reputation for integrity'.[62] Brown sees this as creating the conditions for corporate and personal integrity, that will be evidenced in a community of practice. The signs of that integrity at one level will involve values such as openness, respect, respectful challenge, reflexivity, awareness of the others and so on.[63]

Learning Ethical Leadership

In the light of a stress on responsibility, it becomes clear that ethics in leadership is itself a learning experience. There is no question of simply applying principles to a situation without thinking. Any of the general principles can only be understood as they are worked out in practice and in dialogue with the different stakeholders. This means that every situation will have new elements and learning points in relation to ethics.

---

59   Robinson and Dixon (1997) p. 341.

60   Brown, M. (2005) *Corporate Integrity*. Cambridge: Cambridge University Press.

61   ICAEW (2007) *Reporting with Integrity*. London: Institute of Chartered Accountants in England and Wales.

62   ICAEW (2007) p. 36.

63   Brown (2005) p. 215.

At the core of this the role of leadership is about enabling such learning. This can be summed up as a dynamic process:

- *Articulation of principles and values*. For most groups these are summed up as value or mission statements. However, such statements soon lack any real meaning if there is no opportunity to reflect on them and critically test them. Only through such critical reflection can the members of the group begin to take responsibility for them, as distinct from simply parroting them. This means providing space for real dialogue. This might be an annual reflection as part of any staff development exercise. This is a vital part of enabling ethical learning, precisely because it begins to test integrity and moves away from image. The Enron case was a good example of the way in which image, including an 'ethical image', became more important than integrity. Ethics thus became instrumental rather than real. de Woot[64] argues that instrumentality in business is about the bottom line of always keeping up the share values. The Enron case, however, shows that even shared values are dependent upon genuine trust, and that once trust based in integrity is lost the effect on shares can be devastating. This was especially poignant for the employees of Enron. Fuelled by an 'ethical' stress on sharing profits most of the employees had significant shareholdings that formed the basis of their pension planning. Trust in Enron was based around the idea of non-critical acceptance of the leadership. Hence, part of ethical learning is that the leadership should open itself to critique and question. The mature handling of such critique can then model the development of corporate integrity.
- *Transparency around action and data*. This is partly a narrative transparency. The group needs to know the story of what the organisation is doing, and how that affects the organisation and those outside. This is a further stage in developing ethical identity. A leader should not expect this to represent 'perfect ethics'. On the contrary, the point about ethical learning is that one should reflect on the challenge to practice and note the inevitable 'ethical failures'. One example of this is the *Report to Society* from the Anglo American Corporation (2005). This tells many different stories about how the firm relates to wider society, but also includes reference to legal challenges. I am not suggesting this is a perfect example, and once again such a narrative needs to be open to critique from members of the organisation. The effect of both of these is to invite members of the organisation to take responsibility for values and practice. The case of Enron once again showed how it was not open to such learning. The leaders were rather concerned how to avoid opening narrative out for critical dialogue, and thus to avoid learning.
- *Ethical decision-making*. The reflective overviews of the two elements above have also to be embodied in actual decision-making. This involves careful consideration of how any decision impacts on and relates to ethical values and practice. Such decisions do not have to be open to all, but do need to take account of the ethical thinking that has been open to all.
- *Handling ethical crises*. The three parts above are designed to put ethical reflection into the every day management of the institution and of decisions within the institution. The argument here is that it is best to have such considerations attended to in the

---

64   de Woot, P. (2005) *Should Prometheus be Bound*. Basingstoke: Palgrave.

project process itself.[65] However, even careful attention this will not prevent all ethical crises. Hence, any process of transparency needs to have a culture and means of whistleblowing. The whole point of such a culture is to enable members to safely question what seems to be unacceptable behaviour.[66] Whistleblowing is really focused on what is often just one person taking responsibility for ethical challenge. Sharon Watkins was famously the whistleblower in the Enron case, but by that time it was too late for Enron and Arthur Andersen. There had been others who were aware of the problems but who could not see how to raise the issue and keep their jobs. Hence, the need for a culture that accepts the need to examine all critiques, and see this as critical to effective as well as ethical leadership and management.

- *Negotiating responsibility.* The negotiation of responsibility involves identifying the different stakeholders, noting their purpose, view of responsibility, identity and resources, and then negotiating how any shared responsibility might be effected. Increasingly, large organisations of very different kinds, such as NGOs and corporations, see the importance of working together to effect ethical identity and response.[67] This is a creative approach to ethics which less about harm reduction and more about maximisation of good. Hence, it stresses liability and how this can be worked through. The Enron case focused only on accountability, and with that an attempt to deny responsibility. Hence, even at the end, the management looked to blame particular individuals, in particular Andy Fastow.
- *Planned response.* Ethics is as much created as it is applied. Working with different stakeholders for an ethical response leads the organisation into ethical possibilities that would not have been possible had there not been shared planning. This in turn provides the narrative that can be opened to critique from inside and outside the organisation.

Such a process enables ethical learning at a personal and corporate level, and a corporate and community level. It is an ethics that is based in relationships in practice, not simply about abstract concepts. How it is worked through in corporation will differ. The practicalities are not necessarily onerous. Adequate reports, good communication, and the achievement of safe space for dialogue simply demand efficient management, including annual reflections. All this demands of the leader the capacity to develop reflective dialogue, and to handle in that dialogue what may be perceived as criticism. For some leaders this will involve a reinterpretation of the meaning of strength, to include the capacity for handling critique respectfully. The point of ethical leadership then is to enable this culture of responsibility and learning.

---

65   See Armstrong, J., Robinson, S. and Dixon, R. (2002) *The Decision Makers: Ethics in Engineering.* London: Thomas Telford.

66   See Borrie, G, and Dehn, G. (2002) Whistleblowing: the new perspective. In Megone, C. and Robinson, S. (eds) *Case Histories in Business Ethics*, pp. 96–105. London: Routledge.

67   See Robinson, S. (2008) Can the marketplace be ethical? In Wetherly, P. and Otter, D. *The Business Environment*, pp. 187–211. Oxford: Oxford University Press.

Globally Responsible Leadership

Integrity, holistic thinking and responsibility come together in the concept of globally responsible leadership. This term was developed through the Globally Responsible Leadership Initiative (GRLI), an offshoot of the UN Global Compact.[68]

The GRLI argue in their *Call to Engagement*, that the global challenges take the issue of responsibility and leadership up to a new level.[69] It explicitly combines the need for leaders to maintain inclusivity and the broadest awareness of the social and physical environment within which we operate, with the need to be alert to diversity of value and the need for dialogue around change. The first assumes that as individuals and as groups we are prone to move away from such awareness. Hence, leadership requires the development of structures and ethos, a moral climate that will empower the development of such reflection.[70] Holistic thinking also demands enabling reflection on context, and underlying beliefs and values.[71] The second area focuses on the skills of listening and dialogue, such that difference is effectively engaged. All this sets up a central and mutual dialogue, between the universal and the particular ethical voices, focused in responsible practice and shared response.

The *Call to Engagement* therefore looks to develop new paradigms of leadership based in dialogue and partnership, requiring 'introspection, courage, humility, openness to learning, deep thought and careful planning, as well as a conviction to face and engage while being willing to acknowledge both intended and unintended consequences of ... decision and actions'.[72]

The implication of this is the need to develop learning models both in work and academia to a more whole person learning approach,[73] with ethics itself seen as a learning experience.

This brings us back to the original case. For John and his firm the ethical challenge occasioned by the commission, was, above all, a learning experience. As a leader John enabled the organisation to learn what it stood for and how to defend that position rationally, so that responsibility was developed at all levels; a challenging engagement with the commissioning firm that did not demand a breakdown in relationship; the further development of integrity at all levels, enabling the capacity to handle ethical diversity.

---

68   http://www. globallyresponsibleleaders.net.

69   Available at http://www. globallyresponsibleleaders.net and http://www.efmd.org/component/efmd/?cmsid= 041207trlv.

70   See Groejan, M. Resick, C., Dickson, M. and Smith, D. (2004) Leaders, values and organizational climate: examining leadership strategies for establishing and organizational climate regarding ethics. *Journal of Business Ethics*, 55: 223–241.

71   Hamilton, F. and Bean, C. (2005) The importance of context, beliefs and values in leadership development. *Business Ethics: A European Review*, 14(4): 336–347.

72   GRLI (2005) *Call to Engagement*, p. 18. New York: UN Global Compact.

73   Taylor, B. (2007) *Whole Person Learning*. Wetherby: Oasis Press.

Conclusion

This chapter has:

- Focused on ethical issues faced in leadership.
- Surveyed ethical theory.
- Outlined an ethical decision-making process.
- Examined different approaches to the ethical understanding of the purpose of leadership.
- Developed the ethical ideas of responsibility and integrity, viewing them as core to leadership. It argues that the role of leadership is not to transform so much as to enable responsibility to be owned by the group or organisation and the members of that group, embodying core values of freedom, community and equality.

At the heart of much of this view of leadership is practice-centred dialogue that itself enables the development of responsibility.

First, mutual dialogue enables the development of agency. It demands articulation of value and practice, which clarifies both what we think and do. Articulation, the development of narrative, becomes essential for reflection and learning. It will enable the person or corporation to see just how values and practice relate, leading often to surprise, and clarification of practice and its meaning and value.

Second, dialogue demands the development of commitment to the self and the other. It is not possible to develop dialogue without giving space and time for it to develop, and this in turn demands a non-judgemental attitude. Commitment to the self and others is also essential if the potential critique of values and practice is to emerge from articulation and reflection.

Third, dialogue enables listening, and with that, empathy, appreciation and responsiveness. We learn about the other as well as ourselves only if we are open to both.

Fourth, dialogue enables the development of a more realistic and truthful assessment of the data in any situation. There are many examples in corporate responsibility of NGOs and business arriving at a very different view of the data, that could have been avoided through more effective dialogue.

Fifth, dialogue itself sets up a continued accountability with those involved. This is partly because it sets up a contract, formal or informal, that establishes expectations and which is continually being tested by the dialogue.

Sixth, dialogue enables the development of shared liability, not simply the recognition of shared interests. This leads to the negotiation of responsibility.

Seventh, dialogue not only enables challenge, it extends the imagination and develops creativity. It shows what is possible, especially where responsibility is shared, and so increases the capacity to respond.

Eighth, in doing all of this it enables real partnerships and everyone involved to engage personal as well as group responsibility.

Ninth, dialogue enables core underling values of freedom (through agency), community (through shared responsibility) and equality. Equality may not chime easily with some views of leadership. However, it is possible to see equality in terms of equality of respect and mutuality. Dialogue enables mutuality, without this having to be symmetrical. Hence, Tawney[74] can argue for equality and respect for leadership.

Finally, such dialogue enables the handling of core ethical tensions, between justice for all and care for the particular (respect), and between shared values and different values that emerge from plurality, in any organisation and beyond.

---

74   Tawney, R. H. (1930) *Equality*. London: Allen and Unwin.

11 *Evidence-based Leadership and Management Development*

BOB HAMLIN

Introduction

The purpose of this chapter is fourfold. First, to explain what is understood and meant by 'evidence-based leadership and management development' (EBLMD) secondly to argue the case that most if not all LMD practitioners should increasingly adopt an evidence-based approach to their professional practice, thirdly to outline various obstacles and dilemmas they will have to contend with in becoming evidence-based; and fourth to illustrate with practical examples how some of these difficulties might be overcome.

The arguments to be presented are based on two assumptions.[1] First, that management development (MD) and leadership development (MD) are major components of the modern day conceptualization of human resource development (HRD), which places as much emphasis on organization development (OD) as on people development. Secondly, the activities of 'leading' and 'leadership' are constituent parts of the everyday task of most if not all managers within organizational hierarchies. This second assumption rests on the fact that, although many traditional management and leadership theorists argue the concepts 'manager' and 'management' are different from 'leader' and 'leadership', most practitioners, plus many scholars, actually see little distinction and use the terms interchangeably. Indeed, leading and leadership appear to be part of the everyday grass roots activities and behaviours of most managers who, consequently, can be thought of as 'managerial leaders'. Similarly, most business and organizational leaders appear to engage in managing as well as leading, which means they are also 'managerial leaders'.

---

1   Evidence supporting these two assumptions can be found in Hamlin, R. G. (2007a) Towards evidence-based management development. In Rosemary Hill and Jim Stewart (eds) *Management Development: Perspectives from research and practice*, pp. 95–119. Abingdon: Routledge.

What is Meant and Understood by Evidence-based Leadership and Management Development?

In addressing and discussing what is meant and understood by evidence-based leadership and management development (EBLMD), a first requirement is to present readers with my understanding of leadership and management development (LMD). This is not made easy by the fact that, as with HRD, the process of defining LMD by academics, researchers and practitioners is proving to be problematic, with no single definition having as yet emerged. There are many conceptualizations of MD and LD. These vary widely in focus and emphasis, as revealed and discussed by Mumford and Gold[2] and Gill[3] respectively. Consequently, I have considered it appropriate to offer my own definition of LMD:

> *LMD, being a component part of HRD, encompasses planned activities and processes designed to enhance organizational, group, and individual learning, and to develop human potential, in order to maximize managerial, leadership and organizational effectiveness, and to help bring about effective and beneficial change within and even beyond the boundaries of organizations.*

Adapted from the definition of HRD offered by Hamlin.[4]

Historical Roots of Evidence-based Practice

Regarding the various conceptualizations of evidence-based practice emergent in the fields of management and HRD/LMD, all have been strongly influenced by the concepts of evidence-based medicine and evidence-based healthcare, which are now firmly established and institutionalized in health service organizations worldwide. Although originating in the UK during the 1970s, the term 'evidence-based medicine' was first coined in 1992 by the McMaster Medical School, Ontario, Canada. In the UK, it was defined by Sackett *et al.*[5] *as the conscientious explicit and judicious use of current best evidence in making decisions about the care of individual patients*. The term *judicious use* means balancing the risks and benefits of alternative sources of evidence, including research evidence, clinical expertise, beliefs and values of therapists and patients, clinical assessment of the patient, and the patient's preferences. Although evidence is perceived as encompassing a wide range of information sources, the term 'best evidence' primarily refers to scientific evidence derived from good research, albeit of varying scientific strength. In medicine and healthcare such research falls into two categories. The first increases understanding by concentrating on the development of the knowledge base from which new ideas can be created for evaluation using the second category of research. The second category enables an assessment of the [medical] interventions, which is primarily concerned with the evaluation of ideas in practice. In the broader field of healthcare, evidence-based practice is perceived to be about integrating

---

2   Mumford, A. and Gold, J. (2004) *Management Development: Strategies for Action*. London: CIPD.

3   Gill, R. (2006) *Theory and Practice of Leadership*. London: Sage.

4   Hamlin, R.G. (2002a) Towards evidence-based HRD practice. In Jim McGoldrick, Jim Stewart and Sandra Watson (eds) *Understanding Human Resource Development: Research-based Approach*, pp. 93–121. Abingdon: Routledge.

5   Sackett, D. L., Rosenberg, W. N. G., Gray, J. A. M., Haynes, R. B. and Richardson, W. S. (1996) Evidence-based medicine: what it is and what it isn't, *British Medical Journal*, 312: 71–72.

individual expertise with the best available external evidence from systematic research. In nursing, critical thinking and research utilization competencies, and the ability to use research as a process, are also perceived as inherent to evidence-based practice.

CALLS FOR EVIDENCE-BASED MANAGEMENT

The broader definitions of evidence-based practice in healthcare and nursing strike a chord with various calls for evidence-based management (EBM). For example, Rosemary Stewart[6] argues that although evidence-based medicine can draw on more clear-cut scientific research than that available in the field of management, it is still desirable to practise evidence-based management. For her, it is an attitude of mind that thinks in terms of evidence for decisions and about the nature of the evidence, asks questions such as 'What is happening?', 'How is it happening?', 'Why?', and 'What are the consequences?', that is aware of the potential limitations of the different answers, and is interested in research to try to find the answers, or at least to reduce the ignorance. She goes on to suggest that managers need to build a questioning approach into their everyday management practice, and encourage the creation of a research culture. More recently, Stewart[7] has defined EBM as *the conscientious, explicit and judicious use of current best evidence in making decisions.* She also argues that a broad view must be taken of what is meant by current best evidence. Similarly, Axelsson[8] argues that evidence-based approaches can and should be applied to healthcare management. He conceptualizes EBM as meaning that managers should examine the scientific basis for their practice by learning to search and critically appraise empirical evidence from management research as a basis for decisions. This means they should be asking questions such as 'What do we know empirically about different aspects of organization and management?', 'What is the scientific state of this knowledge?', 'What is the effectiveness and efficiency of different models of management?', and 'What is the experience of these models from different organizations?' In the USA, evidence-based health-services management is conceptualized as management applying the idea of evidence-based decision making to business processes, including both operational and strategic decisions in health services organizations. Kovner and Rundall[9] succinctly define this as *the systematic application of the best available evidence to the evaluation of managerial strategies for improving the performance of health services organizations.* They suggest the best available evidence explicitly incorporates the results not only of rigorous formal research, but also of studies conducted with smaller samples and weaker designs than would otherwise be desirable, including systematic surveys and experiential judgement.

Regarding evidence-based management in general (EBM), Pfeffer and Sutton[10] suggest it proceeds from the premise that using better, deeper logic, and employing facts to the

---

6   Stewart, R. (1998). More art than science?, *Health Service Journal*, 26: 28–29.

7   See page 23 in Stewart, R. (2002) *Evidence-based Management: A Practical Guide for Health Professionals.* Oxford: Radcliffe Medical Press.

8   Axelsson, R. (1998) Towards an evidence-based healthcare management, *International Journal of Health Planning and Management*, 13(4): 307–317.

9   See page 6 in Kovner, A. R. and Rundall, T. G. (2005) Evidence-based management reconsidered, *Frontiers of Health Services Management*, 22(3): 3–22.

10   See page 219 in Pfeffer, J. and Sutton, R. I. (2006) *Hard Facts, Dangerous Half-Truths and Total Nonsense: Profiting from Evidence-based Management.* Boston, MA: Harvard Business School Press. See also http://www.evidence-basedmanagement. com.

extent possible, permits leaders to do their jobs better, and is *a way of thinking about what they and the company know and what they don't know, what is working and what is not, and what to try next.* Their conceptualization is based on the belief that facing the 'hard facts' about what works and what doesn't, understanding the 'dangerous half-truths' that constitute so much conventional wisdom about management, and rejecting the 'total nonsense' that too often passes for sound advice, will help organizations perform better. Drawing upon the developments of evidence-based practice in health services management and psychology, Rousseau,[11] sixtieth President of the Academy of Management, claims EBM *derives principles from research and translates them into practices that solve organizational problems,* and that it *links how managers make decisions to the continually expanding research base on cause–effect principles underlying human behavior and organizational actions.* Consequently, the features that characterize EBM include managers learning about cause–effect connections in professional [management] practice; isolating the variations that measurably affect desired outcomes; creating a culture of evidence-based decision making and research participation; using information-sharing communities to reduce overuse, underuse, and misuse of specific practices; building decision supports to promote practices the evidence validates, along with techniques and artefacts that make the decision easier to execute and perform (e.g. checklists, protocols), and having individual, organizational, and institutional factors promote access to knowledge and its use. Rousseau also argues that an 'evidence' orientation in management shows that decision quality is a direct function of the available facts, thus creating a demand for reliable and valid information when making managerial and organizational decisions. However, she makes a useful distinction between what she calls 'Big E evidence' and 'little e evidence'. Big E evidence refers to generalizable knowledge regarding cause–effect connections (for example, specific goals promote higher attainment than general or vague goals) derived from scientific methods. Little e evidence is local or organization-specific as exemplified by root cause analysis, and other fact-based approaches to organizational decision-making and total quality management.

CALLS FOR EVIDENCE-BASED HRD INCLUDING LMD

For well over a decade there have been various calls in the UK for research-informed HRD, and more recently for evidence-based HRD.[12] In the USA, Holton[13] has called for a national movement to embed evidence-based practices throughout the HRD business, and suggests the definition used in the US mental health sector – *evidence-based practices are interventions for which there is consistent scientific evidence showing that they improve client outcomes* – could be introduced into the HRD lexicon. I have been advocating and providing examples of evidence-based HRD ever since 1998, and first offered my own working definition in 2000.[14] A slightly modified version of this definition is equally applicable for the practice of LMD, as follows:

---

11   See page 256 in Rousseau, D. M. (2006) Is there such a thing as 'evidence-based management?', *Academy of Management Review,* 31(2): 256–269.

12   See Hamlin, R. G. (2002a) op. cit. and Hamlin, R. G. (2007a) op. cit.

13   Holton, E. F. (2004) Implementing evidence-based practices: time for a national movement. *Human Resource Development Review,* 3(3): 187–188.

14   Hamlin, R. G. and Ash, K. (2000) Towards evidence-based organisational change and development. Paper presented at NHS-P Research Into Practice Conference, Birmingham, UK, January.

EBLMD is the 'conscientious, explicit and judicious use of current best evidence in making decisions about the development of managers, leaders, teams, and organizations, and integrating individual LMD practitioner expertise with the best available evidence derived from systematic research'.

Adapted from the definition of evidence-based HRD offered by Hamlin.[15]

I have suggested 'best evidence' within the context of HRD (including LMD) can be comprised of the systematic feedback of opinions and preferences of client (or colleague) managers/leaders and organizations; good critically reflective evaluation data; a combination of relevant, good-quality empirical research of all kinds including both 'pure' and 'applied' research; the consensus of recognized professional experts in the field of management, leadership and HRD (including LMD); and any affirmed professional experience that substantiates practice. EBLMD means that trainers and developers not only use the results of good research to inform their practice, and, as required, engage in action research as part of the process of LMD interventions, but also they use established principles of cause–effect and relevant conceptual frameworks or theoretical models to evaluate and reflect upon their practice critically. This requires practitioners to possess the academic skills of critical thinking and critical reflection. Such competencies enable them to select and scrutinize relevant little e or Big E evidence, critically evaluate its soundness and strength, and determine whether it has been derived from good or poor management-related fact-finding investigation, research or science. This means asking such questions as 'Why are we doing this and in this way? What is the empirical evidence that supports this LMD? What theory or principle has worked well in practice, but also what has not and why? What lessons should be learned for future practice? What research is now called for, not only to help identify what needs to be done next to improve practice, but also to help advance the field of general knowledge?' Additionally, I suggest practitioners need to be open to questioning long established, taken-for-granted, dominant beliefs about management and leadership. This may mean utilizing, within their own LMD practice, the results of organization and management studies based on critical management perspectives, in order to challenge the predominant traditional bureaucratic management paradigm.[16]

Four Compelling Reasons Why LMD Practitioners should become Evidence-based

Despite the above calls, and the increasing rhetoric in both the management and HRD literatures supporting the concept of research-informed and evidence-based practice, there is as yet little evidence of EBLMD becoming a reality. There are few 'real-life' practical examples illustrating how practicing managers, leaders and LMD practitioners use empirical evidence derived from good research, whether of the Big E or little e kind,

---

15   See Hamlin, R. G. and Ash, K. (2000) op. cit. and Hamlin, R. G. (2002a) op. cit. p. 97.

16   For a good insight into 'critical management' thinking see Alvesson, M. and Willmott, H. (2003) *Studying Management Critically*, London: Sage; Grey, C. and Willmott, H. (2005) *Critical Management Studies: A Reader*, Oxford: Oxford University Press; Learmonth, M. and Harding, N. (2006) Evidence-based management: the very idea, *Public Administration*, 84(2): 245–266.

in order to inform, shape and evaluate their practice. However, I believe there are four compelling reasons why it is important and timely for most LMD practitioners, as well as other HRD professionals, to move increasingly towards becoming evidence-based.

1 THE IMPACT OF EBM WITHIN ORGANIZATIONS WHERE THE EVIDENCE-BASED MOVEMENT IS ALREADY WELL ESTABLISHED

A significant hurdle confronting LMD practitioners working in medicine and health service organizations worldwide is the fact that the evidence-based movement has become firmly established and institutionalized. Furthermore, it has spread to many other public sector fields including, for example, social care, education, criminal justice and policing. This means that practising managers and leaders such as clinical directors, directors of nursing, and middle and first line managers of doctors, nurses, therapists, as well as their professional equivalents in other evidence-based public sector organizations are likely to resist LMD initiatives and interventions if they are not based on relevant 'best evidence'. Responding to the many calls for EBM, it is likely most managers and leaders in these organizations will increasingly wish to incorporate evidence-based approaches into their personal everyday management and leadership. Already, the rise of evidence-based clinical practice has caused people to start questioning how clinician managers, other healthcare managers, and policy makers make decisions, and what role evidence plays in the process. As Stephen M. Shortell, dean and Blue Cross of California Distinguished Professor of Health Policy and Management at the School of Health, University of California-Berkeley contends, there needs to be a 'marriage' between evidence-based medicine and EBM to achieve sustainable improvement in the delivery, quality, cost and outcomes of care. He also contends that an effective partnership between academics and practitioners is needed in order to ensure that relevant practice-grounded research is correctly translated for, and used by practising healthcare managers in their day-to-day activities.[17] A development of this kind will likely result in much questioning of how HRD and LMD practitioners operating in the healthcare sector make their decisions, and of the role that evidence plays in the training and development of healthcare managers and leaders. Those practitioners who fail to use best evidence to inform and shape the content and process of their management and leadership development programmes could find themselves severely challenged by course delegates who happen to be role models and strong advocates of evidence-based medicine, evidence-based healthcare and EBM.

2 THE FAILURE OF SO MANY ORGANIZATIONAL CHANGE AND DEVELOPMENT (OCD) PROGRAMMES

Over the past decade or so, both large and small organizations, whether in the private, public or voluntary and not-for-profit sectors, have been and continue to be subjected to enormous competitive and environmental forces of change. These have led to major transformations in organizational structures and contexts in which management and their staff have to operate and succeed. Such organizational changes continue to increase in frequency, pace, and complexity. The major challenge facing managers is how to

---

17   See Grazier, K.L. (2004) Interview with Stephen M. Shortell, Ph.D., FACHE, University of California-Berkeley, *Journal of Healthcare Management*, 49(2): 73–79.

help people through the transitions of organizational change, and help them cope in working environments that are in a state of constant flux. However, many managers and managements fail to rise to that challenge. Whether concerned with downsizing, delayering, cost reduction, total quality management (TQM), business process re-engineering (BPR), culture modification, or IT-related interventions, 60–80 per cent of OCD programmes in the UK, Europe and the USA fail, or are not wholly successful in achieving their objectives. For example, in the USA, Schaffer and Thompson[18] found from their survey of electronics companies that of the 229 companies implementing some form of TQM programmes, 63 per cent failed to yield improvements in quality, and only 10 per cent were deemed successful. With regard to BPR programmes, Hammer and Champney[19] revealed a failure rate in the region of 50–70 per cent. In the UK, Wilkinson, Allen and Snape[20] found that although over two-thirds of the top 500 companies in Britain had introduced TQM programmes, only 8 per cent of managers in these companies believed they had been successful. Furthermore, of the UK companies that Nelson and Coxhead[21] had surveyed, only 10 per cent achieved major breakthroughs from introducing and applying BPR principles, and they estimated that over 50 per cent of BPR change initiatives failed to achieve the results intended.[22] Similarly, as Pfeffer and Sutton[23] tell us, study after study shows most mergers – some estimates are 70 per cent or more – fail to deliver their intended benefits, and destroy economic value in the process. Additionally, many OCD programmes are poorly or even badly handled, and consequently fail badly with unintended human and business consequences. For example, people whom the organization wishes to keep become disaffected and leave, and the survivors of change feel guilty for still being in a job. The remaining workforce loses confidence in management, becomes fearful, suspicious, cynical and demoralized and possibly less loyal. Such failure to manage the people-dimension risks disruption, political infighting, bad feelings, high stress levels, employee alienation and possible psychological withdrawal from the organization, all of which impact negatively on business performance. Over the past ten years the effects of organizational change within most UK organizations have been and continue to be largely negative, as revealed by Worrall and Cooper.[24] Based on their '2007 Quality of Working Life' study, they report that as a result of organizational change 71 per cent of managers felt that morale had declined, 64 per cent felt their job security had declined, 60 per cent felt less motivated, 57 per cent felt less loyal to their organization and 50 per cent reported a decline in their well-being. This begs the question: why is there

18   Schaffer, R. and Thompson, H. (1992) Successful change programs begin with results, *Harvard Business Review*, 70(1): 80–89.

19   Hammer, M. and Champney, J. (1996) *Re-Engineering the Corporation: A Manifesto for Business Revolution*. London: Nicholas Brealey.

20   Wilkinson, A., Allen, S. and Snape, E. (1993) *Quality and the Manager: Institute of Management Report*. London: Institute of Management.

21   Nelson, T. and Coxhead, H. (1997) Increasing probability of re-engineering/culture change success through effective internal communication, *Strategic Change Journal*, 6(1): 29–48.

22   For other examples of the failure rate of different kinds of OCD programmes, see Hamlin, R. G. (2001) A review and synthesis of context and practice. In Bob Hamlin, Jane Keep and Ken Ash (eds) *Organizational Change and Development: A Reflective Guide for Managers, Trainers and Developers*, pp. 13–38. Harlow: FT Prentice Hall.

23   Pfeffer, J. and Sutton, R. I. (2006) op. cit.

24   See Worrall, L. and Cooper, C. (1997–2001) *The Quality of Working Life: Surveys of Managers' Changing Experiences*, London: Institute of Management; and Worrall, L. and Cooper, C. (2007) *The Quality of Working Life 2007: Managers's Health, Motivation and Productivity*, London: Chartered Management Institute.

so much failure and so many unintended consequences in bringing about organizational change and transformation? In endeavouring to answer this same question several years ago, I highlighted six root causes of OCD failure[25] of which five were attributed to managers, and one to trainers and developers:

- Failing 1: Managers not knowing the fundamental principles of change management.
- Failing 2: Managers succumbing to the temptations of the quick fix and simple solution.
- Failing 3: Managers not fully appreciating the significance of the leadership and cultural aspects of change.
- Failing 4: Managers not appreciating sufficiently the significance of the people issues.
- Failing 5: Managers not knowing the critical contribution that the human-resource development function can make to the management of change.
- Failing 6: Trainers and developers lacking credibility in the eyes of line managers.

All of the five OCD 'failings' of managers can be attributed to a lack of knowledge and understanding of theory and practice relating to the effective management of organizational and cultural change, or a lack of confidence in their change agency capabilities, or a lack of clarity as to what specifically needs to be changed. All can be interpreted as a failure of managers to use best evidence to inform and learn how to bring about strategic change effectively and beneficially. Historically, many management and leadership development programmes do not attempt to address, or fail adequately to address, these types of failings. Furthermore, as will be demonstrated later, the traditional bureaucratic, reactive and authoritarian management culture prevailing in the majority of organizations has not been conducive for LMD/HRD practitioners to operate strategically as internal or external change agents. These have precluded the development of appropriate LMD initiatives, and other types of HRD, that could help managers to overcome their failings and blind spots concerning the effective management of change. As I have argued elsewhere,[26] a vicious circle seems to be in play where the five OCD failings of managers contribute to the credibility problems of LMD and HRD practitioners. This in turn leads to an absence of appropriate LMD/HRD effort incorporated into OCD programmes, which then fail to question the appropriateness of the LMD programmes offered to leaders and managers. Consequently, such programmes fail to address and overcome the five particular OCD failings of managers. To break this vicious circle, and create in its place a virtuous circle that leads to more effective management of strategic change, LMD and HRD practitioners need to acquire strong change-agency capabilities and competencies themselves. Without such expertise and experience they will be ill-equipped to train and develop managers as effective change agents. But this means they need to adopt a research-informed and evidence-based approach that draws upon all the available best evidence relating to the effective management of organizational change and development.

---

25   These six root causes of OCD failure are fully articulated in Hamlin, R. G. (2001) op. cit.

26   Hamlin, R. G. (2001) op. cit.

Another associated reason for LMD practitioners to engage seriously with EBLMD is the likely progressive spread of EBM into the private sector, which has already begun in specific industries such as software engineering and manufacturing.[27] I suggest this trend will gain momentum as managers and business leaders increasingly buy into the message that EBM can lead to superior business performance and sustained competitive advantage, as claimed by Pfeffer and Sutton[28] in their book *Hard Facts, Dangerous Half-Truths and Total Nonsense: Profiting from Evidence-based Management.* They attribute the high failure rate of corporate mergers and acquisitions to poor business decisions which, more often than not, are based on hope or fear, or on what others seem to be doing, and on what senior leaders have done and believe has worked in the past, or on their dearly held ideologies – in short, on lots of things other than the facts. In other words, the fads, half-truths and self-laudatory accounts of business leaders, and the formulaic prescriptions of business consultants as proffered in populist management books sold at most airports around the globe. Guest[29] suggested almost two decades ago that the success of writers of such books is much based on their capacity to present a coherent, positive and optimistic philosophy about management, even though the claims they make are generally highly susceptible to critical scrutiny, and their supporting empirical evidence is either hinted at rather than clearly presented, or extremely weak or negligible. As a counter to this, Pfeffer and Sutton[30] advocate that for business leaders and managers to make better decisions to produce superior results and sustainable business success, they need to adopt a mindset with two critical complements:

> *First, willingness to put aside belief and conventional wisdom-the dangerous half-truths that many embrace – and instead hear and act on the facts; second, an unrelenting commitment to gather the facts and information necessary to make more informed and intelligent decisions, and keep pace with new evidence and use the new facts to update practices.*

I suggest this mindset is of equal relevance and timely importance for LMD practitioners.

3 THE FAILURE OF MUCH LEADERSHIP/MANAGEMENT EDUCATION, TRAINING AND DEVELOPMENT AS DELIVERED IN BUSINESS SCHOOLS AND PROVIDED BY LMD PRACTITIONERS

Unfortunately, there is a paucity of empirical research demonstrating the relationship between investment in LMD programmes and organizational/managerial performance and transformation. Regrettably, very little is known about the processes of management or leadership training that contribute to the improvement of managerial and organizational

---

27   See for example, Dyba, T., Kitchenham, B. A. and Jorgensen, M. (2005) Evidence-based software engineering for practitioners, *Software, IEEE,* 22(1): 58–65; and Sloan, D. M. and Boyles, R. A. (2003) *Profit Signals – How Evidence-based Decisions Power Six Sigma Breakthroughs,* Seattle, WA: Evidence-Based Decisions.

28   Pfeffer, J. and Sutton, R. I. (2006) op. cit.

29   Guest, D. (1992) Right enough to be dangerously wrong: an analysis of the *In Search of Excellence* phenomenon. In G. Salaman and C. Mabey (eds) *Human Resource Strategies,* pp. 5–19. London: Sage.

30   See Pfeffer, J. and Sutton, R. I. (2006) op. cit. p. 14.

effectiveness. As Fiedler[31] notes, there has been hardly any meaningful, rigorous research carried out in this area of management research. Although some LMD programmes are effective, many tend to fail. For example, a large scale meta-analysis of US-based studies of LMD programmes from 1982 to 2001, carried out by Collins and Holton,[32] revealed a wide variation in their overall effectiveness. Some were tremendously effective but others failed miserably. However, the factors contributing to this wide variation in programme effectiveness could not be determined, because there was a general lack of any empirical assessment and critical evaluation data provided in the compared studies. Nevertheless, an investigation in the UK of why, despite massive investment, most leadership development initiatives in public and private sector organizations were regarded as failures, revealed three formidable barriers.[33] First, top managers regarded leadership development for themselves was unnecessary, though they believed that the managers below them needed it. Second, when managers returned from their leadership training, they became much more aware of the poor quality of the leadership exhibited by their senior managers, which increased their frustrations. The third barrier was the fact that those managers and leaders newly returned from development activities were rejected or ignored by their somewhat defensive and/or reactionary bosses, and this resulted in disenchantment, greater cynicism and lower morale.

That so many LMD programmes appear to have little effect in terms of managers applying their newly acquired knowledge and skills back in the workplace to beneficially impact the organization, and the fact that many organizational leaders and managers perceive LMD of little or no relevance to them, should not be a surprise. As various writers contend,[34] much of what is taught and delivered in business schools and on LMD programmes is not perceived to be part of the manager's real world, or of practical relevance. That this should be the case is also reflected by the fact that HRD (including LMD) does not register on the radar screen of many if not most organizational leaders and managers: but when it does, it is at best only a fourth order consideration[35] that has little impact.

Despite the strong rhetoric in the management literature that emphasizes the importance of leadership styles based on *empowerment* and *trust*, Worrall and Cooper's study[36] showed that managers below director level were far more likely to feel that the prevailing management and leadership styles in their organizations were *bureaucratic*, *reactive* and *authoritarian*, all of which appeared to have a negative impact on motivation, health and productivity levels. Furthermore, their research also showed that these negative impacting styles were most associated with declining businesses, while *accessible* and *empowering* managerial styles were most associated with growing businesses. In sharp

31   Fiedler, F.E. 1996) Research on leadership selection and training: one view of the future, *Administrative Science Quarterly*, 41: 241–250.

32   Collins, D.B. and Holton, E.F. (2004) The effectiveness of managerial leadership development programs: a meta-analysis of studies from 1982 to 2001, *Human Resource Development Quarterly*, 15(2): 217–248.

33   Alimo Metcalf, B. and Alban Mecalfe, R.J. (2003) Stamp of greatness, *Health Service Journal*, 113(5861): 28–32.

34   See for example, Bones, C. (2007) What's wrong with business education, *MBA and Business Education Guide*, *Management Today*, October: 70–71; Mintzberg, H. (2004) *Managers Not MBAs: A Hard Look at the Soft Practice of Managing and Management Development*, San Francisco, CA: Berrett Koehler; Mumford A. (1997) *Management Development: Strategies for Action*. London: Institute of Personnel and Development.

35   Gold, J., Rogers, H. and Smith, V. (2003) What is the future for the human resource development professional? A UK perspective, *Human Resource Development International*, 6(4): 437–456.

36   Worrall, L. and Cooper, C. (2007) op. cit.

contrast, only a small percentage of directors thought that the leadership styles prevailing in their organizations (including their own styles) were bureaucratic, reactive and authoritarian. This was very widely at variance with the perceptions of managers below them. It would seem from the Worrall and Cooper findings that the traditional 'bureaucratic management paradigm' of command, control and coercion still predominates in the UK, and that far too few organizations are led by senior executives who embrace the 'new management paradigm' of inclusion, participation and empowerment. Yet for decades, this latter paradigm has been taught in business schools on most MBAs, and advocated through much formal and informal leadership/management training and development conducted by LMD consultants, either on open courses or as part of 'bespoke' in-house programmes.

I suggest one reason for the poor uptake of *accessible* and *empowering* management/leadership styles that are known to be associated with superior performance, and the persistent use of styles known to be largely ineffective, is because HRD and LMD practitioners, as well as academic teachers and professors in business schools, are insufficiently evidence-based to convince managers as to the causal link between certain types of management practice, and the delivery of superior performance and long-term sustainable success.

4 THE WEAKNESSES OF COMPETENCY-BASED LMD SYSTEMS

According to the 2007 Learning and Development Survey[37] conducted for the Chartered Institute of Personnel and Development (CIPD), the use of competencies seems to have become a common feature of a modern organization. Of the sample of organizations surveyed, 60 per cent had a competency framework in place, and a further 19 per cent intended to introduce one. Of those organizations with competence-based systems, 50 per cent appeared to be using a single competency framework covering both managerial and non-managerial employees across the organization. This data suggests the arguments promulgated by the competency movement in the UK have been compelling, effective and largely accepted by top management. However, there have been many criticisms of competency-based management and competency-based LMD systems. Most organizations introduce competencies and competency frameworks for the purpose of improving managerial performance and managing progression more effectively, but in many cases the benefits of a competency-based system either don't materialize, or they don't match up to expectations. As Whiddett and Hollyforde[38] claim, many managers find it hard to use competencies and competency frameworks to help achieve their own goals and the goals of the organization. Typically, the framework is either too general, in that it contains statements that do not provide enough guidance as to the specific types of managerial behaviour expected, or it contains too many competencies with little indication given as to those that are critical for success, or is too detailed which means processes become too cumbersome and too time consuming. This often leads to

---

37   To see the full survey results go to http://www.cipd.co.uk/subjects/perfmangmt/competnces/comptfrmwk.htm and follow instructions.

38   See Whiddett, S. and Hollyforde, S. (2007) *Competencies Toolkit*. London: Chartered Institute of Personnel and Development, and also their article in the July 2007 issue of *People Management*.

a lack of credibility and then disengagement on the part of hard-pressed managers and individuals.

Such weaknesses in the creation and design of competencies and competency frameworks result not only from poor LMD practice, but also from insufficient insight and understanding of the particular effective and ineffective managerial and leadership behaviours that contribute to good or bad management, as perceived and judged by managers and employees within organizations.

Other critics of competency-based LMD argue that competencies are usually out of date and ineffective because they are derived from managerial behaviours captured in the past. They also claim competency frameworks cannot be kept up to date because of the fast-changing world. I suggest the weaknesses reflected by the many criticisms levelled at competency frameworks, many of which are well justified, have been significant factors contributing to the failure of many LMD initiatives and programmes. However, as I suggested previously in (3), an evidence-based approach to the identification and creation of competencies and competency frameworks using better little e evidence, or preferably Big E Evidence, could overcome many of the current weaknesses of competency-based LMD systems. Examples of UK public, private and third sector organizations that have either created new, or validated and revised existing context-specific management competency frameworks, derived from the findings of good organizational-based research, have been reported recently in various management and HRD related academic journals.[39] I fully recognize that investing in academically rigorous, applied, empirical research is costly in time and money for most organizations, whether large or small. No doubt cost is a key factor that deters many organizations from doing so. Interestingly, the cost factor might explain why there has been a growing interest in 'generic management competencies' that can be applied in any context, as recently reported in the management literature.[40] Despite ongoing debates about whether this is possible, recent multiple cross-case analyses of findings from replica case studies of managerial and leadership effectiveness are beginning to demonstrate empirically the existence of generic management behavioural competencies that are generalized and transferable to many different organizational contexts in the UK.[41]

Difficulties and Dilemmas

In my view, most LMD practitioners and managers can readily become evidence-based should they so wish. This can be achieved by being committed to fact-based decision making and using hard facts and best evidence comprised of little e evidence. However, there are several significant difficulties and dilemmas confronting those attempting to become evidence-based using best evidence comprised of Big E Evidence. I focus here on the three which I suggest can impede the most.

---

39   Details of the organizational-based empirical case studies I have in mind at this juncture will be found in the section of this chapter entitled 'Guidelines on practice and implementation'.

40   See for example, Mumford, A. and Gold, J. (2004) op. cit.

41   These are the same case studies as referred to in footnote 39. Also see Hamlin, B. (2009) *Universalistic Models of Managerial and Leadership Effectiveness: A Cumulative and Multiple Cross-case Empirical Study of Effective and Ineffective Managerial Behaviour.* Saarbrücken: VDM Verlag Dr. Müller.

Lack of a Sound and Sufficient Body of General Knowledge Derived from Empirical Research

Despite the volumes of published management and managerial behaviour research, few studies have produced empirical results that can be generalized beyond particular organizational settings. Similarly, the research designs adopted by most researchers of leadership/leader behaviours have limited the possibility of comparing – or made it difficult if not impossible to compare – the findings from one study to another. Consequently, the amount of generalizable knowledge regarding the cause–effect connections between particular aspects of management practice that could be translated and transferred across organizations, sectors and cultures, is sparse. Indeed, many writers question the generalizability of management and leadership research carried out from one country to another. Nevertheless, other expert commentators believe in the existence of universal or near-universal effective-leader behaviours, leadership styles and functions, generic managerial competencies and in the idea of universalistic models of managerial competency. However, although logic suggesting the universality of management and leadership is compelling, it has yet to be demonstrated empirically. Consequently, in the absence of relevant empirically derived general knowledge, most LMD programmes remain founded upon anecdotal and opinion-based prescriptions.[42]

Lack of Relevance and Utility of most Management Research

Chris Bones, Principal of Henley Management College, argues that most academic institutions involved in management and business education today are becoming ever less relevant to the organizations and individuals they purport to help.[43] His opinion accords with the claims of many other expert commentators who have criticized management science for being overly theoretical and abstract, and for not being sufficiently concerned with the problems and challenges facing the acting manager. There is ample evidence to suggest that management research has had, and continues to have, a low level of 'face validity' among practitioners, and has had little impact in management practice. As Adler et al.[44] claim, management research continues to be too divorced from the world of management practice, with few research initiatives actively seeking to bridge the much talked about 'research–practice' gap. These concerns resonate with debates in the USA about the lack of relevance and utility of most management research, and about its lack of impact on management practice because little attention has been given to the 'soft stuff' of managing.

Yet similar research–practice gaps do not exist in other professional fields such as medicine, dentistry, pharmacy, law and engineering. Much of the research carried out in universities relating to these particular professions is done in collaboration with organizations and professional bodies, and is perceived by practitioners as having direct

---

42   For evidence supporting the arguments made in this paragraph, see for example Hamlin, R. G. (2002b) In support of evidence-based management and research-informed HRD through professional partnerships: an empirical and comparative study, *Human Resource Development International*, 5(4): 467–491.

43   Bones, C. (2007) op. cit.

44   Adler, N., Rami Shani, A. B. and Styhre, A. (2004) *Collaborative Research in Organizations: Foundations for Learning, Change, and Theoretical Development*. London: Sage.

relevance and utility for informing and shaping professional practice. For example, as Starkey and Tempest[45] observe, 'medical and pharmacy school staff are more involved in the practical application of knowledge to patient care than business school staff are committed to improving the practice of management'. Instead, business school staff tend to be 'more committed to the generation of knowledge about management (the *what*), rather than knowledge that generates better management practice (the *why so*, and *how best* to)'. Similarly, Murray[46] argues that although managers want research that is enmeshed with action, this is resisted by academics. Murray's view is echoed by Bones,[47] who claims the drive to gain academic respectability for business and management studies has driven business school academics into building academic careers at the expense of sharing insights into developing better practice in the workplace. Unfortunately, this, he argues, has led to the pursuit of the arcane just to achieve academic publication.

Various other related debates regarding management research have led to a distinction being made between Mode 1 knowledge production, which is purely academic and monodisciplinary using predominantly the 'scientific method', and Mode 2 knowledge production which is multidisciplinary, and aims at solving complex and relevant field problems using pluralistic methodologies. The challenge confronting management researchers is how to deal with the seemingly opposing ends of Mode 1 rigour and Mode 2 relevance. Vermeulen[48] argues research should be done that synthesizes rigour and relevance by asking research questions that matter to practice, but in a way that does not sacrifice rigour in searching for the answers. Brannick and Coughlan[49] offer two ways forward: 'collaboration between academics and practitioners', and 'forms of research which integrate action and knowledge creation'. These suggestions coincide with the ideas of van Aken.[50] He argues a possible product of Mode 2 research is *general knowledge* that can be used in contexts other than those in which it has been produced. van Aken likens this to inquiry in the *design sciences* such as medicine and engineering, where the aim of most research is to develop knowledge that the professionals of the discipline in question can use to design solutions for their field problems. Such design science approaches to management research offer the prospect of bodies of Big E Evidence being created in order to support the concept of EBM and EBLMD. However, this means much stronger connections need to be forged between academe and industry. Additionally, far more applied research should be carried out by business school academics in collaboration with practitioners, aimed at addressing questions of direct relevance to the world of practice.

45   See pages 25–26 in Starkey, K. and Tempest, S. (2004) Researching our way to economic decline. In Niclas Adler, A. B. Rami Shani and Alexander Styhre (eds) *Collaborative Research in Organizations: Foundations for Learning, Change, and Theoretical Development*, pp. 23–36. London: Sage.

46   Murray, J. (2006) Management research: who to talk with, what to say, *Irish Journal of Management*, 26(1): 8–21.

47   Bones, C. (2007) op. cit.

48   Vermeulen, F. (2005) On rigor and relevance: fostering dialectic progress in management research, *Journal, Academy of Management*, 48(6): 978–982.

49   Brannick, T. and Coughlan, D. (2006) To know and to do: academics' and practitioners' approaches to management research, *Irish Journal of Management*, 26(2): 1–22.

50   van Aken, J. (2005) Management research as a design science: articulating the research products of Mode 2 knowledge production in management, *British Journal of Management*, 16: 19–36.

The Failings of Business Schools in Educating and Developing Managers and LMD Practitioners to become Evidence-based

As previously mentioned, for managers and LMD practitioners to become evidence-based they need, in addition to being convinced about the merits of EBM and EBLMD approaches to practice, the academic insights and abilities to differentiate good from poor research, and to recognize strong from weak evidence. This requires them to possess the critical skills to evaluate effectively the validity, credibility and trustworthiness of the claims that research makes, or the potential organizational damage that the quick-fix and simple prescriptive solutions proffered in the populist management literature can bring about. In other words, they need to become *critically-reflective research-informed practitioners,* which is a first-step requirement for becoming an *evidence-based* expert professional manager, trainer or developer. Such expertise ought to be acquired by all students of MBA programmes, and of other management and LMD related postgraduate masters degrees.

Unfortunately, many business schools fail badly in this regard, as bemoaned by various writers. For example, Starkey, Hatcheul and Tempest[51] claim business schools have conspicuously failed to generate critical thought and enquiry about business and management, whilst Rousseau[52] expresses great disappointment that the findings of management research do not appear to transfer into the workplace. Rouseau observes that managers, including those with MBAs, continue to rely largely on personal experience to the exclusion of more systematic knowledge, or alternatively follow bad advice from business books or consultants based on weak evidence. The most important reason she gives is that professors, and other academics, do not adequately educate their students to know or to use scientific evidence. She suggests that research evidence is not a central focus of study for undergraduate and postgraduate management students, including executives on MBA programmes. Instead, popular concepts from non research-oriented magazines, such as the *Harvard Business Review,* take precedence. Furthermore, she asserts that management education in the US is itself often not evidence-based. In place of evidence, behavioural courses tend to focus on general skills, such as team building and conflict management, and on current case examples which perpetuate the research–practice gap. This is not helped by many management educators being adjunct professors who base their teaching on classical management theory and their own practical experience, rather than on the latest scientific knowledge which often they do not possess because many full-time educators fail to share it with them. Additionally, Rousseau claims tenured professors in many business schools tend also to teach what they learned in graduate school, rather than what current research supports. This means that few managers and potential managers graduating with MBAs leave with a clear idea of how to update their knowledge as new evidence emerges. This is not helped by there being few role-models of competent evidence-based managers within organizations whom they can emulate.

The situation is somewhat less bleak in Europe and the UK. This is because the curriculum of MBAs and management related MA/MSc degrees offered by universities, business schools and other higher education institutions, contains a significant research

51   Starkey, K., Hatcheul, A. and Tempest, S. (2004) Rethinking the business school. *Journal of Management Studies,* 41(8): 1521–1531.

52   Rousseau, D. M. (2006) op. cit.

focus. This is in the form of a research project at the final stage of each Masters programme, which culminates in the production of an academic dissertation or thesis. However, the majority of MBA projects tend to be organization-specific case studies that are poorly grounded in theory, and are often disengaged from, or totally unconnected to the literature review provided by the student. Furthermore, the research tends to be methodologically weak, and conducted with only a limited amount of academic rigour and robustness. Unfortunately, too many MBA projects seem to address irrelevant problems, whilst others seem little more than management consultancy-type investigations. Although the findings from most MBA research can be of practical use within the specific settings of the respective case study organizations, they are likely at best to fall within the little e category of evidence. Few MBA research designs reach out for any degree of relative generalization aimed at producing empirical results that might be classed as Big E Evidence. Furthermore, I suspect far too many UK managers studying for an MBA see it primarily as a means to enhance their status and career, rather than as a learning and developmental experience to improve their current work performance. I suspect also that after their MBA studies, most managers tend not to engage actively with research ever again, but instead succumb to the quick-fix prescriptions and simple-solution answers to the dilemmas of managing and leading which they read about in the populist management literature. To counteract this undesirable situation, academic management researchers need to undertake more applied research that has high theoretical and methodological rigour, as well as high practitioner relevance and utility. Furthermore, they need to ensure this type of pragmatic research is shared, and used far more extensively as essential underpinning for their teaching on MBA programmes. By so doing, they will more likely convince their students as to the value of research, and instil in them a desire to become competent as critically reflective, research-informed, and ultimately evidence-based leaders and managers.

Guidelines on Practice and Implementation

An essential requirement to resolve the difficulties and dilemmas outlined above would be the closing of the research–practice gap in management and HRD. Rousseau suggests there is a lot that can be done by business school academics. These include, for example:

1. managing student expectations with regard to the role of behavioural course work in students' present and/or future jobs, and in their broader careers;
2. providing models of evidence-based practice and evidence-based managers;
3. promoting the active use and assessment of evidence; and
4. building collaborations among managers, researchers and educators.

Much could also be done by LMD practitioners who, in my opinion, could and should take a lead by proactively adopting a research-informed and evidence-based approach to their own LMD and management practice. By so doing, they would then become role models to the managers and leaders for whom they provide LMD training and development, and to those managerial leaders they help and support in their role as internal or external expert change agents/OCD consultants. As already mentioned, in the field of management and LMD there are few examples of evidence-based practice, or role models of competent evidence-based managers and LMD practitioners. However, there has been some growth in the number of large-scale international collaboration studies in management, notable examples being the Globe leadership research of House, Javidan, Hawges and Dorfman,[53] and the multi-nation charismatic leadership study of Carl and Javidan[54] respectively. Furthermore, Adler, Rami Shani and Styhre[55] claim collaboration and partnering between academics in universities and practitioners in industry is on the increase, both in Europe and the United States. The various contributors to their edited book *Collaborative Research in Organizations: Foundations for Learning, Change, and Theoretical Development*, offer not only various perspectives on the purposes, processes, mechanisms and added value to management practice of collaborative research based on the experiences and perceptions of both academics and practitioners, but also eight 'alternative roadmaps' that can be followed. These are well illustrated by a collection of practical examples of successful academy–industry partnership experiences drawn from several European countries and the USA. A comparative overview of the respective research approaches or orientation of these distinctly different alternative roadmaps is provided by Shani, David and Willson.[56] These approaches include action research, action science, appreciative inquiry, clinical field research, developmental action inquiry, intervention research and table-tennis research. Hatcheul's[57] model of intervention research is based on a negotiated partnership arrangement set up between academic researchers and collaborating host organizations. Such research becomes focused on addressing historically and contextually grounded problems in the respective organizational settings. The prime aim of the researcher or researchers is to locate these problems within a more theoretically grounded context, and to conduct the research with academic rigour. In so doing, a research capability is developed within organizations as a direct result of the structured engagement with academic researchers.

Another type of collaborative inquiry that helps bridge the research–practice gap is HRD professional partnership research of the kind defined by Jacobs[58] in the USA, and strongly advocated by me in the UK. In this type of partnership-research, universities and organizations engage in a collaborative partnership within which individual scholars and HRD (LMD) practitioners jointly conduct a programme of pragmatic research focused on issues of concern to management. However, they do so with their own mutually exclusive yet complimentary goals. Maintaining the integrity of both sets of goals for the common good is considered important. Thus, there is a dual goal to improve the organization through the application of academically rigorous but timely applied research, whilst at the same time advancing the HRD (LMD) field of general knowledge.

53   House, R., Javidan, M., Hawges, P. and Dorfman, P. (2002) Understanding cultures and the implicit leadership theories across the globe: an introduction to project GLOBE, *Journal of World Business*, 37: 3–10.

54   Carl, D.E. and Javidan, M. (2001) Universality of charismatic leadership: a multi-nation study, Academy of Management Conference, Washington, DC, August, Best Paper.

55   Adler, N., Rami Shani, A. B. and Styhre, A. (2004) op. cit.

56   Shani, Rami A. B., David, A. and Willson, C. (2004) Collaborative research: alternative roadmaps. In Niclas Adler, A. B. Rami Shani and Alexander Styhre (eds) *Collaborative Research in Organizations: Foundations for Learning, Change, and Theoretical Development*, pp. 83–100. London: Sage.

57   Hatcheul, A. (2001) Two pillars of the new management research, *British Journal of Management*, 12(Special Issue): S33–S39.

58   Jacobs, R. L. (1997) HRD professional partnerships for integrating HRD research and practice. In R. Swanson and E. F. Holton III (eds) *Human Resource Development Research Handbook: Linking Research and Practice*, pp. 47–61. San Francisco, CA: Berrett-Koehler.

I have been involved as the principal academic partner in several near-replica HRD professional partnership research studies carried out in both public, private and third/charity sector organizations in the UK, as I will discuss later. But first, I wish to draw attention to a wide range of practical illustrations of evidence-based HRD/LMD reported in *Organizational Change and Development; A reflective guide for managers, trainers and developers* by Hamlin, Keep and Ash.[59] In this edited book there are 18 reflective case histories of OCD change agency. These were contributed by various research-informed senior executives and HRD/LMD practitioners drawn from private, public, and not-for-profit organizations in the UK, Ireland and the Netherlands. Each contributor was asked to critically reflect upon a particular OCD programme with which they had been personally involved as a change agent. In doing this they described the contextual background of the organizational setting and situation that needed to be changed, plus the triggers and drivers of the planned OCD programme; the theoretical perspectives and principles used to inform and shape the approach adopted for making sense of the organization through organizational analysis and diagnosis; an outline of the key decisions made in formulating the adopted OCD strategy and what happened in practice; and finally, an evaluation of the OCD programme plus the valuable lessons learned resulting from their critical reflection. These case history examples cover such change management issues as transformational/cultural change, quality improvement, OD processes and interventions and various training and development initiatives. All are examples of critically reflective, research-informed practice, and some are examples of EBM.

For information and interest, the reflective case history contributed by Margaret Reidy[60] is a clear example of the evidence-based HRD and management. It relates to the OCD efforts of Dick Shepherd, the then Executive Head of HM Customs and Excise (Anglia Region), and his research officer/internal OD consultant (Margaret Reidy) to bring about effectively and beneficially strategic organizational and cultural change within the organization. In summary, they used empirical evidence resulting from (1) an extensive and comprehensive 'longitudinal ethnographic study of cultural change' carried out by Margaret Reidy as part of a doctoral study, and (2) a related empirical study of managerial effectiveness that Dick Shepherd had commissioned from me. The latter research was conducted jointly with Margaret Reidy within an HRD professional partnership arrangement, using critical incident and factor analytic techniques as the primary research methods. The aim of this partnership research was to identify the criteria of managerial/leadership effectiveness and behavioural competencies associated with effective and least effective/ineffective management within the changing organizational context of 'Anglia'. The findings were then used to develop a range of OD/HRD intervention tools in order to reveal and help bring about the desired and necessary changes in the management culture. The power and efficacy of these research-informed tools rested on the fact that they had been derived from internal research that had strong academic credentials, and were expressed in the organization's own language, which struck a chord with 'Anglia' people. Consequently, the research findings were readily perceived as being directly

---

59   See pages 13–38 in Bob Hamlin, Jane Keep and Ken Ash (eds) (2001) op. cit.

60   Reidy, M. (2001) Managing organizational and cultural change in the Anglia executive unit of HM Customs and Excise. In Bob Hamlin, Jane Keep and Ken Ash (eds) (2001) op. cit.

relevant and usable in the organization. Further details of this professional partnership research can be found in Hamlin[61] and several of the journal articles he cites.

Building upon the 'Anglia' research, and using this as a template, six near-replica professional partnership research studies have been carried out in the UK since 2001. The results of these have been presented at numerous AHRD/UFHRD[62] international research conferences held in Europe and the USA, and reported in various management and/or HRD related international academic journals. The collaborating organizations included an acute NHS Trust hospital (see Hamlin[63]), a specialist NHS Trust hospital (see Hamlin and Cooper[64]); a local government social care department (see Hamlin and Serventi[65]); a professional communications services company (see Hamlin and Bassi[66]), a telecommunications-related Group plc,[67] and a third sector/charity organization[68] respectively. The practitioner partners in all but one of these studies used the research to inform and shape various HRD and LMD initiatives and interventions, such as:

1. validating an existing leadership and management competency framework;
2. creating a behavioural competency framework where none existed before;
3. developing an OD intervention tool that could be held up as a mirror to the organization so as to secure top management buy-in to the need to change the predominant traditional bureaucratic management style;
4. helping embed and nurture a desired redefined management culture by identifying with a high degree of clarity and precision those positive (effective) managerial behaviours that need to be valued, nurtured and rewarded, and those negative (least effective and ineffective) managerial behaviours that need to be minimized or eliminated; and
5. reviewing and revising an organization's existing management and leadership development programme, or introducing a new one.

The empirical findings from the above replica and near replica studies, together with an earlier study by Hamlin[69] used as a template for the 'Anglia' research, have been cumulatively subjected to multiple cross-case analysis. These analyses have revealed high

---

61   Hamlin, R. G. (2007a) op. cit.; Hamlin, B. (2009) op. cit.

62   AHRD is the US based Academy of Human Resource Development (http://www.ahrd.org), and UFHRD is the UK-based University Forum for Human Resource Development (http://www.ufhrd.org).

63   Hamlin, R. G. (2002b) op. cit.

64   Hamlin, R. G. and Cooper, D. (2007) Developing effective managers and leaders within health and social care contexts; an evidence-based approach. In Sally Sambrook and Jim Stewart (eds) *Human Resource Development in the Public Sector: The Case of Health and Social Care*, pp. 187–212. Abingdon: Routledge.

65   Hamlin, R.G. and Serventi, S. (2008) Towards generic behavioural criteria of managerial effectiveness: an empirical and comparative case study of UK local government, *Journal of European Industrial Training*, 32(4): 285–302.

66   Hamlin, R.G. and Bassi, N. (2008) Behavioural indicators of manager and managerial leader effectiveness: an example of Mode 2 knowledge production in management to support evidence-based practice, *Journal of Management Practice*, 3(2): 115–130.

67   Hamlin, R. G. and Sawyer, J. (2007) Developing effective leadership behaviours: the value of evidence-based management, *Business Leadership Review*, 4(4): 1–16.

68   Hamlin, R. G., Sawyer, J. and Sage, L. (2009) Behavioral indicators of managerial and leadership effectiveness: a case study example of HRD professional partnership research from the UK Third Sector. Paper presented at the 2009 Academy of Human Resource Development International Research Conference in the Americas, Washington, DC, USA, February.

69   Hamlin, R. G. (1988) The criteria of managerial effectiveness within secondary schools, *Collected Original Resources in Education*, 12(1). Published MPhil thesis.

degrees of relative generalization across all of the cases. The identified commonalities and universals have led to the development of a progressively refined model or framework of generic behavioural criteria of managerial and leadership effectiveness which is presented in Table 11.1.

Table 11.1   Framework of emergent generic behavioural criteria of managerial and leadership effectiveness

	Positive generic behavioural criteria		Negative generic behavioural criteria
1	Effective planning and organization, and proactive execution and control	1	Shows lack of care and concern for staff
2	Active supportive management and managerial leadership	2	Inappropriate autocratic and non-consultative management style
3	Delegation and empowerment	3	Unfair, inconsiderate, self and self-serving behaviour
4	Care and concern for staff and other people	4	Undermining and/or intimidating behaviour
5	Fights for the interests of their staff	5	Weak/slack management and tolerance of poor performance from others
6	Actively addresses the learning and development needs of staff	6	Ignoring and avoidance behaviour
7	Open, personal and trusting management approach	7	Abdication
8	Involves and includes staff in planning, decision making and problem solving	8	Depriving and withholding behaviour
9	Communicates and consults well with staff and keeps them informed	9	Closed mind and negative approach

It is hoped this generic framework,[70] which can already be identified as a well-defined body of *instrumental knowledge*, will lead to the creation of a well-defined body of *general knowledge* about the type of managerial behaviours associated with effective and ineffective leading and managing. Even in its present stage of refinement, the framework could be used as best evidence in support of EBM and EBLMD.

A comprehensive bibliography of other empirical research and scholarship, of general relevance to LMD professionals, can be found in the *Evidence-based Coaching Handbook:*

---

70   The earliest version of the generic framework, including the behavioural constructs underpinning the 11 constituent behavioural criteria, was reported in Hamlin, R. G. (2004) In support of universalistic models of managerial and leadership effectiveness, *Human Resource Development Quarterly,* 15(2): 189–215. This framework was derived from public sector-related empirical data only. Full details of the subsequent public and private sector-related version, now comprising 18 behavioural criteria, can be found in Hamlin (2007b) Generic behavioural criteria of manager and managerial leader effectiveness: generating HRD related 'general knowledge' through Mode 2 research. Paper presented at the UFHRD Eighth International Conference on HRD research and Practice Across Europe, Oxford, England, UK, June, and in Hamlin, B. (2009) op. cit. A recent multiple cross-case analysis by Hamlin and Hatton has led to the development of a public, private and third/charity sector-related version of the generic framework, details of which are not yet in the public domain.

Putting Best Practices to Work for your Clients by Stober and Grant.[71] Additionally, Nutley, Walter and Davies[72] provide potentially useful insights into the type of strategies that can be adopted for promoting the use of research in practice. These are based on what can be learned from three areas of social science literature, namely those relating to individual and organizational learning, knowledge management and the diffusion of innovations. The learning perspective encourages practitioners to think carefully about the processes of knowledge acquisition within individuals and across groups and organizations. It also encourages dialogue, critical reflection and local experimentation, and emphasizes the potential importance of local collaborations between researchers and practitioners; particularly research collaborations that focus on the practitioners' needs and those that are sustained over time. Such interactive approaches to research use in practice, combined with local experimentation and analysis, are likely to lead to learning which changes fundamental assumptions about organizations, and, with the support of LMD practitioners, helps managers bring about effective organizational change and transformation.

The knowledge management perspective focuses the attention of practitioners on the ways in which knowledge is created, captured and shared within organizations. A key insight for LMD practitioners from this perspective is the view that knowledge cannot be separated from action, and that research findings only make sense when situated in practitioner actions. The knowledge management literature also emphasizes the importance of developing an organizational culture that both values knowledge (resulting from good research) and recognizes the importance of knowledge sharing within organizations. The 'diffusion of innovations' perspective focuses the attention of practitioners on the spread of ideas, technologies and practices among individuals and organizations, and also on the adoption of knowledge across populations. This includes the spread of research ideas and research-based technologies and practices. Consequently, a key insight for LMD practitioners committed to promoting EBLMD and EBM, is to use the diffusion of innovations literature to understand the organizational reconfigurations that might support better research use within organizations, plus the establishment of evidence-based approaches to practice.

Value Added

In light of the foregoing, I suggest to readers that there are compelling reasons why leaders, managers and LMD practitioners should increasingly become evidence-based in their professional practice. From a management perspective, EBM offers the prospect of added value for business leaders, managerial leaders and managers in terms of:

1. better business decisions based on systematically gathered hard facts, rather than on anecdotal and opinion-based fads, half-truths and inappropriate ideology;
2. more effective implementation of business and management decisions;

71   Stober, D. R. and Grant, A. M. (2006) *Evidence-based Coaching Handbook: Putting Best Practices to Work for your Clients.* Hoboken, NJ: Wiley. Also go to http://www.brookes.ac.uk/schools/education/ijebcm/home.htlm.

72   Nutley, S. M., Walter, I. and Davies, H. T. O. (2007) *Using Evidence: How Research can Inform Public Services.* Bristol: The Policy Press.

3. better leadership and management as a result of improved managerial competence; and
4. real managerial and organizational learning derived from valid information and evidence, as well as from a systematic understanding of the principles governing organizations and human behaviour.

From an LMD perspective, the added value to be derived from EBLMD includes, for example:

1. better focus and direction of the LMD effort in line with the strategic thrust of the organization, which results from a more systematic and rigorous diagnosis and analysis of the organizational and individual development needs;
2. greater relevance and utility of the content and process of LMD programmes as a result of them having been informed and shaped by best evidence;
3. enhanced learning through the application of research methods, including action research, as part of the learning and behaviour change processes of LMD;
4. more effective and beneficial individual, group and organizational outcomes from OCD change agency interventions and initiatives;
5. enhanced transfer of LMD learning to the workplace through a better understanding of the identified enabling/inhibiting factors, and better diagnosis of the transfer climate issues; and
6. better evaluation and demonstration of the impact of LMD on organizational, group, and individual performance.

Conclusion

Mumford and Gold[73] offer a 'model of management development activities and learning' which outlines three types (methods) of LMD:

1. Type 1 Informal managerial – incidental and accidental processes.
2. Type 2 Integrated managerial – opportunistic processes.
3. Type 3 Formal management development – planned processes.

In my view, an evidence-based approach to practice has relevance and utility for all three LMD methods, and should be encouraged, developed and role modelled by LMD practitioners. At an *informal* level, there is nothing to stop individual managers and organizational leaders voluntarily 'using better, deeper logic, and employing facts to the extent possible' in all of their managerial activities, as advocated by Pfeffer and Sutton.[74] At the *integrated* level, there is nothing to stop organizational leaders, managers, and LMD practitioners becoming critically reflective and research-informed practitioners, using at least bodies of 'little e evidence' as discussed by Rousseau.[75] At the *formal* level, I suggest that for LMD practitioners to maximize their contribution to improved organizational

---

73   See pages 116–124 in Mumford, A. and Gold, J. (2004) op. cit.

74   Pfeffer, J. and Sutton, R.I. (2006) op. cit.

75   Rousseau, D.M. (2006) op. cit.

effectiveness and performance, and to the achievement of long-term sustainable organizational success, they will need increasingly to become fully evidence-based in their practice. The future of LMD, as Mumford and Gold[76] suggest, will be determined by the 'significant and identifiable trends and drivers for change which will affect what managers (and leaders) must learn and how learning will be delivered'. The key trends they identify include globalization, technology and science, new knowledge, deregulation/regulation, and socio-economic factors. Anticipating, analysing and responding appropriately and effectively to these external drivers of change calls for a high order of change agency capability on the part of managers, trainers and developers, as discussed several years ago by Hamlin and Davies.[77] As these authors claim, a key to success as a change agent is *organizational understanding*. Making sense of an organization is of crucial importance, because structure, function and their relationship to the core activity of the organization (the culture) need to be analysed in depth before effective strategies for change can be devised, including specific LMD strategies. Most consultants, change gurus and academics influencing OCD practice tend to agree that the analysis of the organization must take place as the important first step. Understanding gained from the analysis acts as a sound basis for the development and implementation of appropriate OCD and LMD strategies for change. This calls for a strong evidence-orientation in management and LMD, using the findings of instigated local or organization-specific research (little e evidence) and/or, as appropriate, existing relevant and utilizable generalizable knowledge derived from academic management research/science (Big E evidence).

I am hopeful that the hard facts and logic of the arguments presented in this chapter have demonstrated beyond doubt that critically reflective and evidence-based approaches to management and LMD practice, particularly when informed by best evidence resulting from collaborative professional partnership research, can lead to considerable value added benefits both for managers, trainers and developers, and for the organizations they serve. However, I recognize there is a paradox in the views that I have expressed. Although the proposition of evidence-based approaches to LMD practice may appear sound to most if not all readers, for some it may appear logically unacceptable, bearing in mind the current lack of a sound and sufficient empirical base. Unless and until many more LMD practitioners and managers engage in collaborative activities that will close the research–practice gap in management and HRD, there is a risk that EBLMD will remain more rhetoric than reality.

In conclusion, I strongly urge all LMD professionals who wish to maximize individually and collectively their contribution to organizational effectiveness, the development of high-performing organizations, and the achievement of sustainable business success, to give serious consideration to the concept of evidence-based leadership and management development.

---

76   See page 240 in Mumford, A. and Gold, J. (2004) op. cit.

77   Hamlin, R. G. and Davies, G. (2001) Managers, trainers and developers as change agents. In Bob Hamlin, Jane Keep and Ken Ash (eds) *Organizational Change and Development: A Reflective Guide for Managers, Trainers and Developers*, pp. 39–60. Harlow: FT Prentice Hall.

Acknowledgement

I wish to acknowledge the help given by Dr Alf Hatton, Helen Wilcock and Geoff Westwood who acted as my critical readers for this chapter.

12 *Measuring and Assessing Managers and Leaders for Development*

JEFF GOLD AND PAUL ILES

Introduction

Can we honestly say that we know how to measure and assess leaders and managers? If we consider for a moment the underlying assumptions of any measuring and assessing process, first it is possible to say with some certainty that we know what makes for good/better/effective leadership and management. Secondly, such knowledge can be expressed in terms that are accepted and understood in measureable terms. Thirdly, measurement and assessment against whatever terms are used, are accepted by leaders and managers and can result in a willingness to engage in some form of development. A moment's reflection on each of these would suggest that there are bound to be different views of how honest an answer to our first question can be. Nevertheless, there does seem to be quite a lot of faith invested in the measuring and assessing process. Organisations very much need to know how to express their requirements for the performance of leaders and managers, highlighting deficiencies or gaps that can be met through learning and development activities. Further, because we are dealing with the behaviour of particular people in particular work positions, there is support from psychology to explain why people behave in the way they do, although there are inevitably different perspectives. What we hope to do in this chapter is at least provide some way through to what is important; that leaders and managers find some way of understanding how they can learn and develop to be better at what they do.

Is There a Model?

There has, of course, been a long search for a model of management and/or leadership performance which can be expressed in terms of knowledge, skills, attitudes, abilities, behaviours and results. The search continues but along the way, terms such as 'effective' or 'excellent' are applied to management performance and to leaders especially, such terms as 'high-performing' and 'transformational'. Science purports to have a role here or at least some degree of rigour in developing anything approaching a model but there are bound to be disagreements and what may be seen as 'excellent' at one time may soon become obsolete. One assumes that leaders of the various financial institutions that have failed in recent years were selected and developed on the basis of some definition of leadership and management.

There are some key issues to consider with reference to models and the implication of best, excellent, competent or otherwise.

1. Is there one model which can be applied to all managers and leaders, in all contexts? or
2. Are there different models appropriate to different situations and places?
3. Do models, however specified, take sufficient account of the dynamic aspects of leading and managing?

There continues to be an interest in providing generalised or generic models of management and leadership which can be applied in all contexts of practice. As we will see below, such models are often expressed as competences but any generalised statements or typology of skills or abilities would answer the first question above. One example might be Perren and Burgoyne's[1] framework of management and leadership abilities shown as Figure 12.1. The framework was developed from various texts and other frameworks, seeking to find some common basis of 'excellence in management and leadership'. This resulted in the identification of 83 abilities – enough for a lifetime of development. A quick Google search will reveal a variety of other models of excellence (or otherwise) for managers and leaders. Some would argue that generic ideas are especially important for identifying and developing leaders. For example, there has for many years been an interest in cognitive abilities or IQ as part of a model of leadership and since the late 1990s, emotional intelligence or EI has been added to the list.[2]

While the words of generic models may be considered attractive, it is their meaning in context of work which is more important to managers and leaders. Organisation-specific models may look similar to generic models but they purport to reflect the meaning and understanding of what is important in particular situations and this is the basis of the investment by many organisations in their own competency models, which we consider later in the chapter.

Both generic and organisation-specific models are highly favoured in organisations, especially among those who seek enough clarity about management and leadership to 'pin it down' as objective, so to speak. The large availability of measurement tools, many claiming validity and reliability, bear testament to the need to be seen to act on the basis of research and rigour. However, there is a contrasting view which questions the starting point of such models. This view considers both managing and leading as processes which occur between people in a time, place, culture, and so on. Dynamic activities are inherently unpredictable and less controllable by one person. Recent studies of management and leadership work give more prominence to the ongoing processes of managing and leading relationships and this is bound to complicate measurement and assessment.[3]

---

1   See Perren, L. and Burgoyne, J. (2002) *Management and Leadership Abilities: An Analysis of Texts, Testimony and Practice*, London: Council for Excellence in Management and Leadership.

2   See Dulewicz, V. and Higgs, M. (2005) Assessing leadership styles and organisational context, *Journal of Managerial Psychology*, 20(2): 105–123 and Goleman, D. (1998) *Working With Emotional Intelligence*, New York: Bantam.

3   See Tony Watson (2001) The emergent manager and processes of management pre-learning, *Management Learning*, 33(2): 221–235 and Lawler, J. (2005) The essence of leadership? Existentialism and leadership, *Leadership*, 1(2): 215–231.

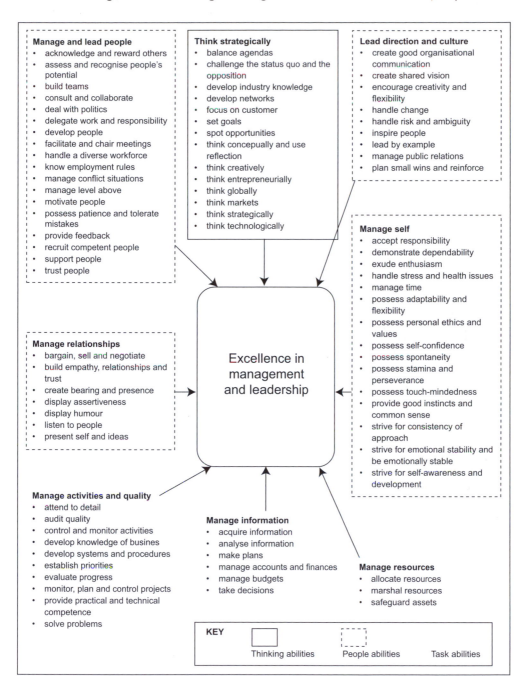

Figure 12.1 A framework of 83 management and leadership abilities

Source: Perren and Burgoyne (2002).

Psychological Foundations of Measuring and Assessing Leaders and Managers

Most occupational psychologists are interested in the consistent patterns of differences displayed by individuals, especially those falling into the categories of personality (differences in temperament or disposition) and cognitive ability (capacity to process information). Such differences are usually assessed by psychometric tests, which include, for example:

- General and specific ability tests, for example, manual dexterity tests for semi-skilled workers; technology tests; tests of general abilities for administrative and clerical staff; tests of aptitude for customer contact; verbal and numerical critical reasoning tests for managers.
- Tests of occupational preferences.
- Tests of personality.

A well-established framework for understanding and assessing differences in cognitive ability is given in Figure 12.2. At the most general level there is general intelligence or general mental ability. People who do well on one kind of cognitive test such as verbal ability also tend to do well on others, such as numerical ability. However, some people do relatively well at verbal rather than numerical ability, or vice versa, so at another level there are more specific cognitive abilities – a two-factor theory of intelligence (others argue for even more specific abilities or 'multiple intelligences': we shall look at one kind, emotional intelligence, in more detail).

However, most researchers now accept that behaviour is not just a function of the person, but also of the situation (even the biggest extraverts are likely to be quiet at a church service, for example). So behaviour at work is not just a function of personality, but also the product of situational demands.

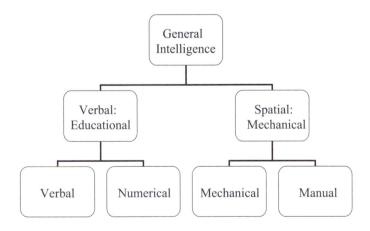

Figure 12.2 Vernon's model of cognitive ability[4]

---

4   See Vernon, P. E. (1950) *The Structure of Human Abilities*. London: Methuen.

The hypothesised link between personality trait, job competence, and job performance is shown in Figure 12.3.

Figure 12.3 refers to the popular 'Big Five' model of personality or the five-factor model. Research on it indicates that there are some important relationships between personality factors and job performance which personality tests will attempt to measure. For example, some research suggests that Extroversion and Agreeableness are positive predictors of transformational leadership.[5] However, there are some doubts about the use of tests for assessing managers and leaders, whose work is bound to be complex and beyond the narrow measurement of a psychological profile.[6] This also applies to the assessment of intelligence where it is argued that intelligent behaviour is strongly linked to setting, task, location and other people involved.

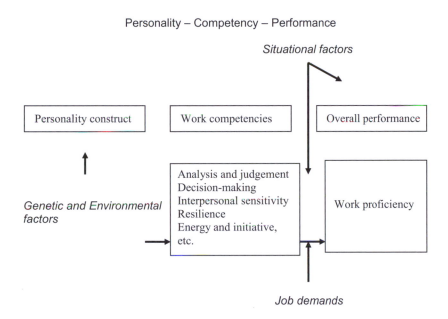

Figure 12.3 refers to the popular 'Big Five' model of personality or the five-factor

Figure 12.3 Links between personality, competence and performance[7]

There has been growing interest however in assessing emotional intelligence (EI), especially among leaders. Salovey and Mayer[8] argued that people vary in their capacity to process emotional information and relate this to wider cognitions, defining EI as 'the ability to perceive accurately, appraise, and express emotion; the ability to understand emotion and emotional knowledge; and the ability to regulate emotions to promote

5   See Judge, T. and Bono, J. (2000) Five-factor model of personality and transformational leadership, *Journal of Applied Psychology*, 85(5): 751–765.

6   See Robertson, I. T., Baron, H., Gibbons, P., Maciver, R. and Nyfield, G. (2000) Conscientiousness and managerial performance, *Journal of Occupational and Organizational Psychology*, 73(2): 171–180.

7   See Cooper, D., Robertson, I. T. and Tinline, G. (2003) *Recruitment and Selection: A Framework for Success*, London: Thomson.

8   Salovey, P. and Mayer, J. D. (1990) Emotional intelligence, *Imagination, Cognition and Personality*, 9: 185–211.

emotional and intellectual growth'. Goleman[9] took this further by associating ability in this area, called 'emotional intelligence' or EI, with leadership and business success; successful people are more able to perceive, understand, and regulate their emotions than unsuccessful people low in EI. They can monitor their own feelings, as well as others', discriminate amongst them, and use the information to guide their thinking and action. Consequently they can manage both themselves and others more effectively. Cognitive processes are clearly influenced by emotional factors, and these affect success in all areas of life; often the 'competencies' used in assessment centres are social or emotional in nature – achievement drive, initiative, proactivity, influence, and so on. EI is seen as providing the bedrock for these 'emotional competencies'.

Interest in EI has resulted in an assessment instrument, the Emotional Competence Inventory,[10] which is meant to be filled in not just by the focal individual but by their peers, subordinates, superiors and customers (a form of 360-degree feedback). It covers the following areas:

- *Self-awareness*: self-confidence and accuracy of emotional self-assessments; recognition of emotions, knowing strengths and weaknesses, being open to feedback and having assurance and presence
- *Self-management*: self-control, self-regulation, adaptability, initiative, optimism, achievement; being able to manage one's own emotions, stay composed, focussed and poised, having integrity, being trustworthy, ethical and principled, being conscientious, taking responsibility and meeting promises and commitments, being flexible and being open to, and comfortable with, new ideas and information; having achievement drive, commitment, initiative and persistence.
- *Social awareness:* empathy, organisational awareness, a sense of service; sensing others' feelings and perspectives, anticipating and meeting others' needs; offering feedback, coaching and mentoring; respecting people in an unbiased way; and understanding power relations and networks
- *Relationship management*: social skills, inspiration, influence, developing others, fostering teamwork and managing conflict; being persuasive, clear in communication, listening, aiming for mutual understanding, leading by example, initiating and championing change; negotiating disagreements, building bonds and networks, sharing information and resources in a collaborative way and creating synergies between people.

EI is seen as particularly important in *leadership*. The higher up the organisation, the more difference EI is seen to make to performance, and leaders who 'derail' often show deficiencies in emotional competencies like interpersonal relationships, teamwork and dealing with change. One illustration of this is from research using the Leadership Dimensions Questionnaire (LDQ) as developed by Dulewicz and Higgs.[11] This contains measures of context, as well as 15 leadership dimensions:

---

9   Goleman, D. (1996) *Emotional Intelligence*. London: Bloomsbury.

10   Sala, F. (2002) *Emotional Competence Inventory: Technical Manual*. Philadelphia, PA: McClelland Center For Research, HayGroup.

11   Dulewicz, V. and Higgs, M. (2005) Assessing leadership styles and organisational context, *Journal of Managerial Psychology*, 20(2): 105–123.

- the *intellectual* dimensions of critical analysis and judgement, vision and imagination, and strategic perspective;
- the *managerial* dimensions of resource management, engaging communication, empowering, developing and achieving;
- the *emotional* dimensions of self-awareness, emotional resilience, intuitiveness, interpersonal sensitivity, influence, motivation and conscientiousness, as assessed by the EIQ.

They report that all dimensions reached conventionally acceptable levels of reliability and that all 11 dimensions were significantly related to the current job performance of British naval officers, as assessed by appraisal. A further study of managers showed that personality factors did not moderate the relationship between leadership competencies and leadership style and performance, challenging the importance of personality in earlier models of leadership. The overall conclusion is that EI plays an important and increasingly critical role in leadership, and that it can be assessed through conventional psychometric instruments.

Competences[12]

Competences for managers and leaders are the usual route to clarification of what is requirement and objectivity in the process of measuring and assessing for development. This is confirmed by some evidence over the last 30 years of use. Such evidence suggests that competences allow the identification of needs, the design of programmes and the facilitation of feedback.[13] It has also been shown competences can result in managers taking more responsibility for developing others because this is an aspect of the framework in use. The recent attention to emotional intelligence, expressed as competences for leaders, seems to confirm the adaptability of competence frameworks to emerging research on leadership behaviour.[14] The work Richard Boyatzis[15] (and others) is a common thread here because it was his work in the early 1980s which raised awareness of the link between a person's characteristics or abilities and effective performance in terms of results that are achieved. For Boyatzis, characteristics or abilities were difficult to assess directly but were shown in behaviours which could be seen, and his work resulted in 5 clusters of behaviour and 19 competences. It is worth showing the basic Boyatzis framework in Figure 12.4 because of its significance: most frameworks have similar terms.

---

12   There has been a confusion around the term competences for quite a long time. Some texts use the spelling competencies to refer to behaviour approaches to specification reserving the term competence for standards and results specification. Over time the single term competences tends to be used for both approaches but it is always necessary to check which approach is referred to.

13   See Strebler, M., Robinson, D. and Heron, P. (1997) *Getting the Best Out of Your Competences*, Brighton: Institute of Manpower Studies.

14   Goleman, D., Boyzatis, R. and McKee, A. (2003) *The New Leaders: Transforming the Art of Leadership into the Science of Results*, New York: Time Warner Paperbacks.

15   See Boyatzis, R. (1982) *The Competent Manager: A Model for Effective Performance*, New York: John Wiley. It is worth stating that the origin of competences probably started with the work of McLelland in the 1960s and then the McBer consultancy in the 1970s.

Each competence is specified by a description and some way of measuring and assessing behaviour. Boyatzis was careful to ensure that factors such as the requirements of the job and the environment of the job, including the roles of others, should also be part of the consideration of effective performance. This does stretch competences toward the dynamic action version of models, although most competence frameworks are aimed at individuals. From the mid 1980s many organisations in the US and UK began to develop their own frameworks to take account of particular business needs and strategies. According to writers such as Holbeche,[16] competence frameworks could link management behaviour directly to organisation objectives and align various HR activities. Based on research completed within an organisation, competences allow for clarity in how effectiveness is explained and consistency in assessment. The language is meaningful to managers and others in the business. Further, during the rapid structural changes in the 1990s such frameworks could also be extended to others in the organisation, so competences could be expressed at all levels of the organisation – from shop floor to the executive suite (see Chapter 11). In particular, during the late 1990s and into the 2000s, with leadership high on the agenda in both public and private organisations and even the third sector of voluntary and community organisations (see Chapter 25), leadership competence frameworks began to be used. Figure 12.5 shows, for example, the Leadership Qualities Framework used in the National Health Service.

Most of the frameworks chime with the attraction of the transformational view of leadership and the agenda of modernity sought in the public sector, although as we suggest below, evidence during the 2000s was already shifting in a different direction.

Goal and Action Cluster
- Efficiency orientation
- Proactivity
- Diagnostic use of concepts
- Concern with impact

Leadership Cluster
- Self-confidence
- Use of oral presentations
- Logical thought
- Conceptualisation

Human Resource Cluster
- Use of socialised power
- Positive regard
- Managing group process
- Accurate self-assessment

Directing Subordinates Cluster
- Developing others
- Use of unilateral power
- Spontaneity

Focus on others Cluster
- Self-control
- Perceptual objectivity
- Stamina and responsibility
- Concern with close relationships

Figure 12.4 Boyatzis' competency clusters

Source: Boyatzis (1982).

---

16   Holbeche, L. (1999) *Aligning Human Resources and Business Strategy*, Oxford: Butterworth-Heinnemann.

In the UK, as well as the various generic and organisation-specific frameworks of competences specifying behaviours for managers and leaders, there has also been an approach to specification that gives more attention to results against a standard. This approach puts management competences in the same mould as the National Vocational Qualifications (NVQ) framework which has been developed since the late 1980s. The so-called Management Standards provide an inventory of management requirements which are said to be 'widely acceptable', reflecting best practice. Responsibility for the standard is held by the Management Standards Centre of the Chartered Management Institute, so there is a clear link to the aspiration of professionalism in management. The latest version of the standards extends the coverage to leadership and following the basic formula of a NVQ, begins with a key purpose: 'The Key Purpose of Management and Leadership is to ... Provide direction, gain commitment, facilitate change and achieve results through the efficient, creative and responsible deployment of people and other resources.'

The standards are expressed through six functional areas, shown as Figure 12.6.

Figure 12.5 The NHS Leadership Qualities Framework

Figure 12.6 Functional areas of management and leadership standards

Each functional area is further specified as units and then elements of competence with performance criteria for assessment. There has tended to be a criticism that the standards approach became to difficult to work with; from 1997 there were 77 units. However, the most recent revision reduced the number of units to 47. In addition, the current framework includes behaviours that underpin performance, a move closer to generic and organisation-specific models covered earlier.

It is claimed that the standards, presented as National Occupational Standards, provide a benchmark of best practice. A brief glimpse at the website reinforces the view of total coverage with best practice guides for business planning, organisation development, performance management, succession planning and so on. Another publication refers to 'One hundred uses of the management and leadership standards'.[17]

Competences seem to have endured as a claimed objective view of what leaders and managers need to learn to do their work well. This has occurred in spite of continuous efforts to highlight difficulties. These range from suspicions about the conflict of use, for pay and development for example, to critiques of competences based on their dominating effects, a critique inspired by the work of French philosopher, Michel Foucault.[18] One persistent criticism relates to our earlier point about the need for models that capture the dynamics of activity. In 1989, John Burgoyne[19] doubted that competences could account for the 'holistic nature of management' and this has to include the flux, movement, ambiguity and uncertainty which are not especially prone to a technical interpretation implied by competences. This becomes even more pronounced perhaps when applied to leadership. Bolden and Gosling[20] provide a wide coverage of criticisms of leadership competencies, highlighting the neglect of relational aspects of leadership and its distribution which arise due to the focus on individuals – 'a simple representation of a highly complex and changing landscape'. The language of measurement that competence frameworks provide may be too impoverished, too mean and too limp to capture the movement of managing and leading.

Performance Management Systems and Feedback

A performance management system (PMS) is now considered something of a panacea for an organisation's credibility that it is business-oriented, able to set and measure the achievement of targets and is basically under control.[21] The CIPD, for example, found that over 87 per cent of organisations in a survey of 500 operated a PMS with most using appraisals for review, objective-setting and developments.[22] About a third of organisations

---

17   Go to http://www.management-standards.org.uk/. Other institutes also work with NVQs – go to the Institute of Leadership and Management at http://www.i-l-m.com/. The Institute of Directors offers qualifications too at http://www.iod.com.

18   A useful summary of criticisms can be found Chapter 4 of Mumford, A. and Gold, J. (2004) *Management Development, Strategies for Action*, London: CIPD.

19   See Burgoyne, J. (1989) Creating the managerial portfolio: building on competency approaches to management development, *Management Education and Development*, 20: 56–61.

20   Bolden, R. and Gosling, J. (2006) Leadership competencies: time to change the tune? *Leadership*, 2(2): 147–163.

21   See Stebler, M. and Bevan, S. (2001) *Performance Review, Balancing Objectives and Content*, Brighton: Institute of Employment Studies.

22   Go to http://www.cipd.co.uk/subjects/perfmangmt/general/perfman.htm, a CIPD resource that provides good information on PMS.

seem to also use appraisals for pay-related decisions, something that many years of research suggests is a sure way of confusing the purpose of appraisal. We will consider this issue in more detail below. A PMS is considered a way of ensuring that organisation objectives are communicated and met by alignment with each person's needs. The ideal situation is that there is a common understanding of goals, shared expectations of each person's contribution, skills and abilities to respond to expectations and commitment to organisation aims.[23]

As a process, PMS does rely on a flow of information about performance and behaviour using tools such as psychometric assessment and competences. However, and this is the crux, any information about performance and behaviour requires interpretation and requires some form of judgement about a person. Such judgements can lead to decisions about contribution, value, worth as well as potential for development. Both are forms of feedback and suddenly we are into a rather tricky area because many years of research suggest that no one really likes to give feedback nor get it. The possibilities, from the receiver's point of view, are summarised in Figure 12.7.

There seem to be two possibilities. First, if there is agreement with feedback being provided, this could result in improved performance, perhaps through the identification of development needs. Alternatively, a defensive posture in response to negative feedback could result in a failure to agree with development needs and also deterioration in performance. Research on the relationship between feedback and performance[24] has found that in one-third of cases, feedback has a negative effect on performance. Feedback can help a person focus on what needs to be done or learned and this can result in improved performance, but the danger lies in how people view themselves. Managers and leaders might be particularly prone to defensive postures. One finding on the impact of feedback on managers found that there were 13 criticisms during an appraisal interview for managers.[25] No surprise about defensive behaviour if this is continued over time. One of

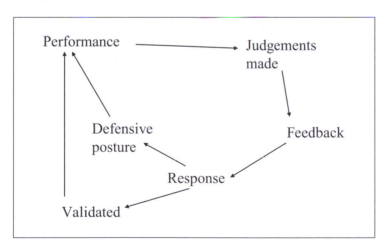

Figure 12.7 Responses to feedback

---

23   See Holbeche op. cit.

24   See DeNisi, A. S. and Kluger, A. N. (2000) Feedback effectiveness: can 360-degree feedback be improved? *Academy of Management Executive,* 14(1): 129–139.

25   This was the classic finding reported in Meyer, H. H., Kay, E. and French, J. R. P. (1965) Split roles in performance appraisal, *Harvard Business Review,* January/February: 123–129.

crucial considerations here is that most managers and leaders are likely to rate themselves usually quite well or above average, so any feedback which is less favourable is bound to lead to defensiveness, eventually. Of course, it is one of the aims of feedback to encourage self-awareness and allow managers and leaders to consider strengths and weaknesses so that development needs for improvement can be identified. Being subjected to increasing amounts of feedback, both formally through PMS processes but also informally through daily interactions, is bound to impact on a manager's or leader's sense of self and the value of who they are, what they can do and what they are achieving – their very identity as a manager or leader.

Many managers and leaders are very much more proactive about feedback. These 'feedback-seekers'[26] have a willingness to develop new skills and master new situations, referred to as 'learning-goal orientation'. By contrast, some managers and leaders may be more concerned with showing and proving that their competences are adequate by avoiding negative judgements; this is referred to as performance-goal orientation and research suggests this drives out feedback-seeking and learning. The research also suggests that contextual factors such as culture and leadership influences the overall stance towards goal orientation.

Development Centres

A development centre (DC) consists of multiple participants undertaking multiple activities, performance in which is assessed by multiple observers. The observers use their observations to assess participant strengths and development needs against a profile of behaviours or competencies identified as critical to the job/role performance of participants through a series of critical incidents with jobholders. DCs, of course, do have a strong similarity with assessment centres which can create a degree of confusion over purposes – assessment or development. Indeed, in some organisations, the purposes are combined and this is partly to do with the use of centres for recruitment, promotion, assessment of high potential as well identifying development needs. Crucially, the participants need to be aware of the purpose because, as Woodruffe[27] argues, 'Assessment centres masquerading as development centres are wolves in sheep's clothing.' How the results are used will affect how centres are viewed by participants.

The first stage in a DC is to identify the criteria against which performance is to be assessed – that is, the 'dimensions' of behaviour or behavioural framework (for example, communication skills, and so on). This could be done by a job analysis, for example, repertory grid or critical incidents analysis of post holders.

The second stage is to identify the activities holders engage in, which form the exercises they take part in. A sequence of daily activities, so one exercise leads into the other in the course of a typical day (for example, I read documents, do a report, do a presentation on my views, take part in a strategy/management meeting on what to do about an issue) is one way of structuring the process.

---

26   See Van De Walle, D., Ganesan, S., Challagalla, G. N. and Brown, S. P. (2000) An integrated model of feedback-seeking behaviour: disposition, context and cognition, *Journal of Applied Psychology*, 85(6): 96–103.

27   Woodruffe, C. (2000) *Development and Assessment Centres: Identifying and Developing Competence*, London: CIPD Publishing.

The third stage involves devising a matrix of dimensions against exercises, indicating which dimensions are to be assessed against which exercises. (Not all dimensions will be in each activity.)

The fourth stage involves training the assessors in the use of the matrix, how to use the scoring system, and how to give feedback.

The fifth stage involves running the centre, ensuring each person is assessed by at least two assessors in the course of a day.

The sixth stage involves the assessors meeting to agree an assessment for each participant, and giving feedback on performance to mutually identify training needs, as well as also identifying OD needs that seem to run across the cohort and might apply generally (for example, strengths in verbal presentation, not in data analysis).

Figure 12.8 shows the stages involved in designing and running a development centre.

The difference is the focus of the centre, and what the centre results are used for; in the case of assessment centres, to make pass/fail or 'red/green light' decisions, for example, whether to select a person for a job or training course, or promote a person; in the case of a development centre, what development options/opportunities to recommend. In both, behaviour is observed, detailed performance feedback is provided, and dimensions observed are keyed to competences. However, in a development centre, the output is used to inform a personal development plan and enable development activities to be more focused and targeted than in most training and development initiatives. Figure 12.8 shows how development/assessment centres can be placed on a continuum, from 'development' to 'assessment'. Many organisations run 'hybrid' centres mixing assessment and development: feedback following assessment in the case of 'identification of potential' centres; diagnostic centres profiling strengths and weaknesses; cultural change programmes. Centres may be classified into different 'generations'.[28]

Figure 12.8 Stages of development centre design

28   Goodge, P. (1995) Design options and outcomes: progress in development center research, *Journal of Management Development,* 14(8): 55–59.

The development centre can use a series of scenarios drawing on the critical incidents technique used by, for example, Sheaff and West[29] in their research into the ethical environment of NHS board members. Some of the scenarios used in the Sheaff and West study are outlined in Table 12.1.

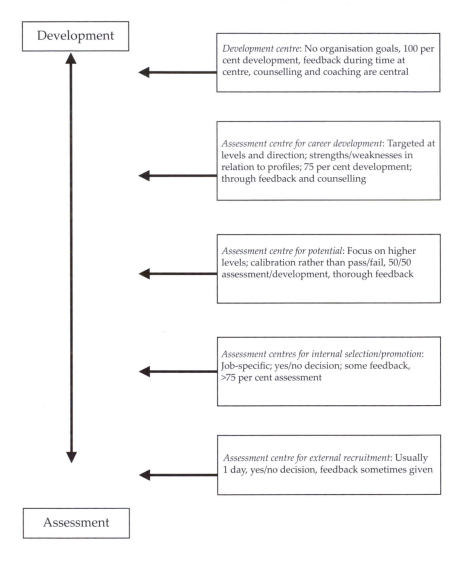

Figure 12.9 The assessment centre continuum[30]

29   Sheaff, R. and West, M. (1997) Marketisation, managers and moral strain: chairmen, directors and public service ethos in the National Health Service, *Public Administration,* 75(2): 189–206.

30   Adapted from Vloeberghs, D., de Rijke, T. R. and Strokappe, A. J. (2000) The development of a competence centre as a self-management instrument, *Career Development International,* 5(3): 155–170.

Table 12.1 Scenarios from Sheaff and West's NHS study

Scenario 1	Turn a blind eye to infractions of rules or standing orders when these are in the NHS organisation's interest
Scenario 2	Invite NHS staff to do work for oneself out of hours
Scenario 3	Use NHS hospitality budgets to reward deserving members of staff in kind
Scenario 4	Mention major gains of new business but not major losses of existing business in the annual report
Scenario 5	Mention details of competitor's bids in discussions with potential suppliers

Measuring and Assessing: Appraisal

As indicated by the CIPD research, appraisal of some form is the most widely used method of measuring and assessing. Indeed, symbolically, appraisal represents the most visible indicator that an organisation is trying to measure, monitor and control the activity of managers and leaders, although for more senior staff there may be difficulty in finding someone to make it happen. Such is the ubiquity of appraisal that it can become the pathway for a variety of purposes, including information for succession and resource planning, clarity of roles, identifying potential, deciding about remuneration and so on. We need to add identifying development requirements, even though this purpose may become submerged by the other purposes. Appraisal in the word of one writer is a 'panacea'.[31] With so many purposes attached to appraisal, it is likely that conflicts will feed through into delivery. This does explain why appraisal has a long and troubled history, especially where managers are required to make judgements about other managers' performance. Research showed in the 1950s that managers do not like 'playing God' and even more recently, appraisal was viewed by many as a 'tick-box' exercise.[32]

We really do need to learn some key lessons if appraisal is to have any value on leadership and management development, and a good starting point is the research completed in the 1960s at GEC in the US.[33] The study took place among 92 managers appraised by their superiors. Each manager was appraised twice over two weeks, the first to consider performance and salary, the second to consider improvement. Reactions were obtained by observation, questionnaires and interviews. As we mentioned earlier, one finding was the level of critical comments and defensive posture by managers in response, mainly caused by 90 out of 92 managers rating themselves as average or above. The key lessons from this study were:

- Criticism often has a negative impact.
- Praise has little effect.
- Performance improvement needs specific goals.

---

31   Taylor, S. (1998) *Employee Resourcing*, London: CIPD.

32   See Ferlie, E. and McGivern, G. (2007) Playing tick-box games: interrelating defences in professional appraisal, *Human Relations*, 60(9): 1361–1385.

33   See Meyer, H. H., Kay, E. and French, J. R. P. (1965) Split roles in performance appraisal, *Harvard Business Review*, January/February: 123–129.

- Participation in setting goals is vital.
- There needs to be a clear separation between appraisal for development purposes and remuneration discussions.
- Coaching on a regular basis can improve the appraisal process.

Making appraisal more developmental is certainly espoused by many organisations although it is likely that the word *appraisal* remains a source of ambiguity. Research suggests that the conflict on purposes remains with power and politics having an impact. All managers and leaders do need to be prepared on how to use feedback more purposefully and tie it to action. Further, organisations need to see appraisal as genuine space for reflection between managers and leaders for consideration of the factors that affect performance and how that performance is judged. Appraisal needs to become a relationship-building vehicle that can have culture enhancing qualities. Again, research shows that with persistent efforts, appraisal can be valued[34] as a way to set objectives and develop personal development plans. Regular reviews, rather than one-off yearly appraisals, also seem to be a requirement since this brings the two parties into more contact. Perhaps there is a key point here since most appraisal images are based on outdated notions of organisations as machines with bureaucratic controls a necessity. As Henry Mintzberg[35] once argued, the form of structure called 'machine bureaucracy is not just a way to organize, it is the way to organize' reflected in statements like 'getting organized' and 'being rational'. With so many organisations now concerned with the production and delivery of customised services, based on the work of professional and knowledge-based expertise, managers and leaders often are not able to observe or even understand the performance process of others and in turn, this makes their own assessment and measurement more problematic. This would suggest that self-assessment and measurement and feedback from a variety of others would be more useful.

Measuring and Assessing: Self and Others

The various tools now available for measurement and assessment imply a degree of distance from those measured and assessed which is necessary to ensure objectivity, reliability and even validity. However, managers and leaders are bound to have an opinion of how they are performing so self-appraisal is inevitable but often dismissed as one-sided, subjective and a distortion. This may be the case, but judgements about self can provide the foundation for learning and development which is more acceptable to managers and leaders. Based on research by Campbell and Lee,[36] we suggest that self appraisal is based on four stages:

1. Managers and leaders have their own beliefs and views about what they need to do to meet goals.

---

34   See Redman, T., Snape, E., Thompson, D. and Ka-Ching Yan, F. (2000) Performance appraisal in an NHS hospital, *Human Resource Management Journal*, 10(1): 48–62.

35   See Mintzberg, H. (1989) *Mintzberg on Management*, New York: Collier.

36   Campbell, D. J. and Lee, C. (1988) Self-appraisal in performance evaluation: development versus evaluation, *Academy of Management Review*, 13(2): 302–314.

2. Such beliefs and views inform managers and leaders in how they meet goals.
3. Judgements are made on whether their behaviour meets the desired results.
4. Such judgements are used to either reinforce or change beliefs and views about their work and what needs to be done.

Of course, the judgements made are likely to be biased because they based on the views of managers and leaders about their own performance and this is likely to differ from judgements made by others. Campbell and Lee identified three such differences:

1. Information – disagreements about work to be done, how it is done and the judgement of results.
2. Cognition – simplifying complex behaviour involved in managing and leading resulting in different perceptions of what happened.
3. Affective – defensive posture when judgments are made which distort interpretations.

None of this is surprising, but helping managers and leaders measure and assess their own behaviour and performance is probably the most crucial step in moving towards a more developmental purpose for measurement and assessment. Given the differing stances towards development and varying degrees of openness to feedback, any process to encourage self-appraisal needs to based on the interests and concerns of managers and leaders. It will also probably involve reflection or even critical reflection (see Chapter 18). For example, we worked with one CEO to help him consider development needs based on a self-appraisal of performance, but we started with what was important to him based on the problems he currently faced. We asked him to write about the problem as a story and this reflective process immediately puts some distance between what he is thinking and what he sees on paper. It does allow a consideration for seeing things differently but the words written are still his. We allowed the leader to collect two more written reports on problems faced and his feelings about them. We used a process of considering beliefs about performance which is based on a model of arguments presented by the philosopher, Stephen Toulmin.[37] This is a step towards revealing assumptions but it allows the leader to retain some degree of control over what is revealed and judgements about performance. If there is a discrepancy revealed, the leader can decide what to change and so learning becomes possible. We can take this process further, by allowing the leader to accumulate a written record of issues faced, chart the finding to reveal patterns of behaviour over time and then work out possible development needs. The chart completed for the CEO is shown as Figure 12.10.

The chart contains important judgements about the CEO's performance in his own terms. For example, there is a critique of his behaviour as someone who 'wants to be in total control' and the pattern of emotion that emerged across the range of different events. We can also see how his identification of Actions were oriented toward changing how he related to his team; he wants to 'understand my team' and 'find a mechanism to have a debate'. Following the charting process, the CEO made significant progress with all his issues, particularly in managing relationships with his bank and working with his team.

---

37   See Gold, J., Holman, D and Thorpe, R. (2002) The role of argument analysis and story telling in facilitating critical thinking, *Management Learning*, 33(3): 371–38.

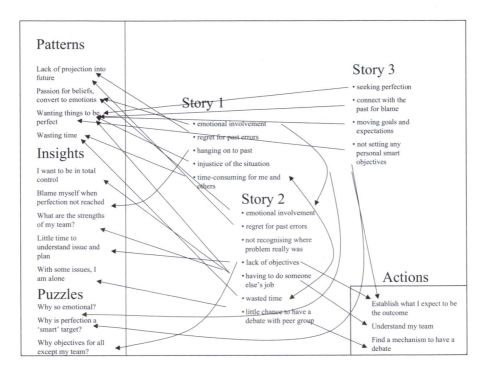

Figure 12.10   Revealing patterns of behaviour

This process of self-appraisal uses the opportunity to generate feedback to self. It carries face validity but it is still based on views of one person, so it remains subjective and partial. Here we would like to suggest that no leader or manager, can 'lift themselves up by their own hair';[38] they need to consider the views of others and this can occur through multi-source feedback processes which be found in other chapters in this book. This includes 360-degree feedback (Chapter 19), coaching (Chapter 20), mentoring (Chapter 23) and action learning (Chapter 22). All these process can augment self-appraisal and can allow learning and development, although the influence of culture and the way feedback is provided along perceptions about the need to change are very influential in how acceptable multi-source feedback will be considered by managers and leaders.[39]

Conclusion

We began this chapter by asking the simple question of whether we can honestly say that we know how to measure and assess leaders and managers. Six thousand words later, we are not sure an answer has been found – not an honest answer and certainly not a simple one. Nevertheless, there does seem to be a whole range of options available, including

---

38   A phrase we have developed from our reading of the works of the Russian writer and philosopher, Mikhail Mikhailovich Bakhtin.

39   See Smither, J. W., London, M. and Reilly, R. R. (2005) Does performance improve following multisource feedback? A theoretical model, meta-analysis, and review of empirical findings, *Personnel Psychology*, 58(1): 33–66.

a variety of tools and instruments that have scientific rigour as a mark of quality. The trouble is that there is a large space between their use and their acceptance by managers and leaders as accurate indicators of gaps in performance and requirements for learning and development. There is no escape from the fact that measurement and assessment of managers and leaders requires judgements to be made about performance and this is bound to create difficulties relating to who makes the judgements and how, and whether these are accepted by managers and leaders so that learning and development ensues. It would seem that over half a century of effort to create the tools of measurement and assessment has not changed what is a fundamentally human process of interpretation. Thus, as research has tended to suggest, the tools and models employed may well provide a logic and a language for measuring and assessing but the very process of judgement unleashes a range of possible responses. One obvious tension is the variety of purposes that information derived from measurement and assessment can be used for. Learning and development can easily be denigrated when combined with purposes such as pay or promotion. Another comes from years of research which make it clear that, like other human beings, managers and leaders do have a view of who they are and how they perform, and this tends to be at least on a par with others, so any criticism sooner or later will lead to defensive responses.

Organisations are under significant pressure to demonstrate to stakeholders that they are being led and managed rationally and correctly. The performance of managers and leaders needs to be shown to be in line with organisation objectives and learning and development should serve as a means to bring this about. Given the difficulties we have raised in this chapter, it becomes clear that relationships, context and culture and not a little bit of politics all play a part. As we have suggested above, probably the most crucial step is encouraging managers and leaders to measure and assess their own performance and work out their own needs for learning and development, even if this means a subjective distortion of information. Nevertheless, such an interpretation is more likely to be seen as valid and can then supplemented by the views of others through processes such as mentoring, coaching and multi-source feedback. We do take the view that how such processes work with the assessments of managers and leaders themselves provides the foundation for a culture of learning and development.

13 *Talent Management and Career Development*

PAUL ILES AND DAVID PREECE

Introduction

In recent years, talent management (TM) has become a common phrase, but it did not appear on the HR scene until the late 1990s, when McKinsey and Company first coined the term in their report, later book, *The War for Talent*,[1] which exposed this issue as a strategic business challenge and a critical driver of corporate performance. The main impact on the organization was said to be in the identification, development and redeployment of talented staff. Subsequently, the proposition that the success of organizations is at least partly dependent upon a group of 'super performers' has proved influential, especially with top managers. Narratives around TM now often refer to 'fulfilling human potential' and 'transforming organizations' as well as 'fighting a war for talent'.

In a recent CIPD study, over 90 per cent of the respondents agreed that TM activities can positively affect an organization's bottom line, and over half of the respondents had already undertaken TM activities.[2] In an IOMA (Institute of Management and Administration) survey nearly three-quarters of the respondents said TM was at the top of their HR 'critical issues'.[3] According to an IDC study,[4] TM is anticipated to be the next core competency in HR domain expertise. Thus, it can be argued that TM approaches to HRM are emerging as the most favoured means of managing people in the organization, and TM is an emerging critical competency for the HR function.

An extensive number of books, articles, and surveys on TM have been published, and consulting firms have been attracted by the market potential of TM. More organizations are coming to see talent as a, if not the, major source of competitive advantage and scarcest resource in the knowledge-based global marketplace. The management of 'high-potential' individuals who are seen as critical to the company's success and survival has therefore come to be seen as a key role for the corporate HR function, especially in the international firm.[5] As the knowledge economy continues to develop, the value

1   See Michaels, E, Handfield-Jones, H. and Beth, A. (2001) *The War for Talent.* McKinsey and Company, Inc. Boston, MA: Harvard Business School Press.

2   See Clarke, R. and Winkler, V. (2006) *Reflections on Talent Management.* London: CIPD.

3   See Sandler, S. (2006) Critical issues in HR drive 2006 priorities: # 1 is talent management, *HR Focus,* 83(1): 1–3.

4   IDC (2005) *HR BPO (Business Process Outsourcing) Vendor Analysis: The Evolving Landscape.* London: IDC.

5   Scullion, H. and Starkey, K. (2000) In search of the changing role of the corporate human resource function in the international firm, *International Journal of Human Resource Management,* 11(6): 1061–1081.

of outstanding talent will continue to be recognized.[6] Proponents of TM argue that it challenges:

- Tayloristic approaches to organization–employee relationships, as it champions the need to develop skills and talents.
- Emphases on systems and structures; talent is something that cannot be contained in one compartment or box (such as within the HRM function), and requires the development of a TM 'mindset'.
- Egalitarian models of HRM, as it presents a differentiated/segmented view of the workforce, where some 'talents' are more highly valued than others. Talent is a relational term: the talented exist in relation to the 'untalented' or the 'less talented'.

Because of organizational investment in TM, there is much practitioner-focused literature and activity, but the concept of TM has not to date attracted a corresponding amount of critical scrutiny, and there is relatively little empirical work on the effectiveness of TM strategies and the issues arising from them.[7] Questions include:

- What is talent? How is the term socially constructed in a range of contexts, and why do these constructions differ?
- How does being placed on a fast-track, talent list, or talent pool influence employee identity?
- What theoretical perspectives can be applied to TM, and how can its theoretical basis be developed?
- How and why do TM strategies differ across organizations, cultures and sectors?

There are many opportunities for further theoretical development and empirical study; indeed, one can question whether TM is fundamentally different from HRM. In essence, there are two divergent views. On the one hand, some believe that TM is simply a repackaging: 'new wine in old bottles'.[8] Guest has claimed that:

Organizations espouse a lot of notions about TM and give it a lot of emphasis, but in practical terms it doesn't have a very different meaning to what most organizations have always done ... TM is an idea that has been around for a long time. It's been re-labelled, and that enables wise organizations to review what they are doing.[9]

Interestingly, many current ideas in TM, now often presented as novel and best practice, such as assessing potential, 360-degree feedback, assessment centres, and coaching, come

---

6   See Martin, G. (2008) Talent management and the older worker, Scottish government public policy seminars on Talent Management and the Older Workforce, March 2008; Orr, K. and Swailes S. (2008) EURAM conference Liverpool 2009, Track proposal: talent management: critical perspectives.

7   Iles, P. A. (2007) Employee resourcing and talent management, in Storey, J. (ed.) *Human Resource Management: A Critical Text*, 3rd edn, pp. 97–114. London: Thomson Learning.

8   Adamsky, H. (2003) Talent management: something productive this way comes, available at http://www.ere.net/articles/db/76E79D059FEB4637A7F0FBD4439490C6.asp, retrieved in February 2008.

9   Warren, C. (2006) Curtain call, *People Management*, 12(6): 24–29.

from the 1950s era of large stable bureaucracies and sophisticated succession planning as part of more general 'manpower planning'.[10]

Others assert that TM incorporates new content and is not a management fashion: 'TM is a lot more than yet another HR process; the talent mindset is not just another HR fad.'[11]

A search for journal articles with the key words 'talent management' in the Emerald and British Business Premier databases between 1985 and 2006 showed a dramatic increase in the numbers of articles during this period.[12] In Emerald, the number rose from 0 in 1990 to 109 in 2000 to 275 in 2006; in British Business Premier, from 0 in 1985 to 230 in 2000 to 760 in 2006. This shows trends resembling other 'management fashions'[13] and the cyclic influences of managerial innovations.

Talent management is a term that can be seen as another management fad which has gained currency through fashion rather than through relevance and value – rather like previous terms and management techniques such as total quality management (TQM), business process re-engineering (BPR) or just in time (JIT) which have been subject to academic and professional criticism.[14]

This interest in TM follows earlier work on careers, the breakdown of lifetime employment and the move towards more market-driven employment relationships. Interest in TM emerged in the USA to explain how employers were managing careers and developing talent in the context of moves towards a more open labour market, with lateral hiring and lay-offs. Most US companies have not been managing talent at all; those that have – older, large 'academy' companies with a long legacy of human resource and succession planning – have been acting as if they still had lifetime employment models, but in practice are losing most of their employees to competitors. US employers have either done little or nothing, making no attempt to anticipate needs and making no plans to address them; or have used old complex legacy systems of forecasting and succession planning.

The basic challenge in both career management and TM is to identify demand, and then manage supply to just meet demand, a challenge shared with other business disciplines. If TM is defined as 'the process through which employees anticipate and meet their needs for human capital',[15] then it is closely related to both career management and supply chain management. Common failures in both TM and career management then include mismatches between supply and demand, such as having too many employees ('inventory') leading to lay-offs and restructuring and high turnover due to perceptions of lack of career opportunities on the one hand; or on the other hand too few, leading to shortages. Both undershooting or overshooting carry costs, and failures in managing this balance have led employers to lurch from surpluses to shortages, as in the IT industry. Organizations need to reduce talent bottlenecks, speed processing time,

---

10   Cappelli, P. (2008) *Talent on Demand: Managing Talent in an Age of Uncertainty*. Boston, MA: Harvard Business Press.

11   A comment from *Identifying and Managing your Assets: Talent Management* by Rhea Duttagupta of PricewaterhouseCoopers. Available at http://www.buildingipvalue.com/05_SF/374_378.htm.

12   See Iles, P. A., Chuai, X. and Preece, D. (2008) Is talent management just another management fashion or fad? Paper submitted to EURAM conference, Liverpool, UK, May 2009.

13   Abrahamson, E. (1996) Management fashion, *Academy of Management Review*, 21(1): 254–285.

14   See Jim Stewart's *Developing skills Through Talent Management*, available from http://www.ukces.org.uk/pdf/SSDA per cent20Catalyst per cent206 per cent20talent per cent20management per cent20.pdf, accessed 17 December 2008.

15   Cappelli P (2008) op. cit. p. 1.

improve forecasts of need, manage flow rates, waiting times, and queueing problems, and avoid mismatches, as well as ensure returns on investments in development. Issues for employers include the leaking of talent pipelines (more sieves than pipes due to neglect of retention and engagement issues – career development is a significant retention practice here), and accounting pressures to show returns on investment in development practices. Decentralized TM programmes may make the problem worse, as managers hoard or hide talent. Employee and employer interests may be balanced by using an internal market; internal job boards are one example.

Most companies now fill vacancies from outside, having started to do this in earnest in the 1980s when they began to abandon the old 'employment security with internal development' model. The failure of these was not that they did not 'work' in developing talent, but were too expensive to maintain, failing to manage the unpredictability of the demand for talent. Complicated planning techniques are both expensive and inappropriate to an era where business is very unpredictable (given changes of strategy, restructuring, regulatory regimes, business models, mergers, acquisitions, alliances, etc.) and their models are highly inaccurate. Talent pipelines in old 'academy' companies have continued to turn out talent, producing an excess; whereas consequent reactive external hiring then led companies into retention problems, causing many to reduce investment in development as their long-term and therefore expensively developed talent 'walked', often to competitors. 'Just in time' hiring has also failed, leading to renewed concerns with talent shortages and renewed interest in TM and especially talent development. In part this has also been driven by strategic interest in the internal resources of the firm and in knowledge management.

Both the bureaucratic planning model and the free agency model of individual career planning are rooted in transient historical and economic circumstances; there needs to be a balance between outside hiring and internal development and between organizational and employee interests, with shared responsibility in career development, as seems to be emerging in the UK at least.[16]

What is Driving this Interest in TM?

Technological change, changing business models, the 'knowledge economy' and globalization of markets have increased the demand for highly skilled people. Meanwhile, workforce ageing and an inadequate supply of young talent have created a supply gap in many labour markets. The creation, development and retention of a 'talented' workforce, which is more mobile and informed than ever before, has increasingly come to be the focus of HRM strategies and attention.

Due to *demographic shifts*, organizations across the globe have faced a major and potentially long-term struggle to fill job vacancies with appropriately skilled employees. Associated with these demographic shifts, the nature of the *psychological contract* has changed. Talent shortages have meant that the labour market has swung back towards the job-hunter's advantage (though it may swing back again in any recession). *Globalization*

---

16   See Iles, P. A. (1997) Sustainable career development: a resource-based view, *Career Development International,* 2(7): 347–353 and Thomson, A., Mabey, C., Storey, J., Iles, P. A. and Gray, C. (2000) *Changing Patterns Of Management Development.* London: Routledge.

has meant that professional and managerial people can more readily obtain employment information (and IT helps here, too) and take up global job opportunities. Thus, such workers find it easier to choose employers based on considerations such as career development, compensation and work–life balance. However, this driver of interest in TM may become less important as the recession bites and labour markets become tighter.

Technological change and *networking* have had a significant impact upon organizations and the nature and conduct of work, including the HR function, and this has made the boundaries between organizations much more permeable.[17] An initial impetus for TM came into being in the late 1980s when client/server technology, optical character recognition software and equal employment opportunity reporting made job applicant tracking possible and necessary for most large corporations. It then took off in the mid 1990s with the advent of the Internet, web browsers and database technology, and went mainstream in the late 1990s with the explosion of online job boards, e-recruiting companies and corporate employment websites.[18] Today, talented individuals are no longer limited to marketing their skills within one country or region, but can market themselves to organizations across the world.

In conclusion:

> *The universal shift from 'industrial age' managerial thinking and practices to a necessarily very different 'information society' leadership mindset has seen the management of knowledge and talent evolve as critical competences, at all levels, within businesses.*[19]

In view of these shifts in many aspects of social and economic life, it is not surprising that many observers predict that the competition for talent will intensify globally, and therefore debates over how talent is recruited, retained, developed and managed will gain more attention.

What is Talent?

'TM requires HR professionals and their clients to understand how they define talent, who they regard as "the talented" and what their typical background might be'.[20] Many organizations prefer to formulate their own meaning of talent rather than accept a universal or prescribed definition. Thus, they tend to have different talent targets. Microsoft UK focuses its attention on its 'A list', the top 10 per cent of performers, regardless of role and level, whilst Six Continents targets executives below board level and high-potential individuals, as the two cadres are likely to provide their leaders of tomorrow.[21]

Whilst talent can be categorized as valuable, rare and hard to imitate, the specific prescriptions regarding talented employees are unclear, and there is no universal definition of great talent. The definitions-in-use of talent will depend on an organisation's business

---

17   See Martin, G. (2005) *Technology and People Management: The Opportunity and the Challenge*. London: CIPD.

18   See Schweyer, A. (2004) *Talent Management Systems: Best Practices in Technology Solutions for Recruitment, Retention and Workforce Planning*. New York: John Wiley and Sons.

19   See Williams, M. (2000) *The War for Talent: Getting the Best from the Best*, p. 108. London: CIPD.

20   CIPD (2007) *Talent: Strategy, Management, Measurement*. London: CIPD.

21   See *Identifying and Managing your Assets: Talent Management* by Rhea Duttagupta of PricewaterhouseCoopers. Available at http://www.buildingipvalue.com/05_SF/374_378.htm.

strategy, the type of firm, the overall competitive environment and so on. Therefore, it is often argued that definitions of talent should be tailored to individual organizations, and each company should be encouraged to 'understand the specific talent profile that is right for it'.[22] An in-depth assessment of the key elements of organization culture and job structure, followed by a matching with candidates who have specific backgrounds, work experiences, and personal qualities, therefore becomes crucial in the process of talent identification

Notwithstanding the range of conceptualizations of talent, most if not all of them fall into one of the following four perspectives:

1. *Exclusive people*. 'Key' people with high performance and/or potential (irrespective of position)
2. *Exclusive position*. The right people in key positions (position-related)
3. *Inclusive people* Everyone in the organization is seen as actually or potentially talented (given opportunity and direction)
4. *Inclusive social capital*: importance of networks, trust, relationships and teams.

Let us now discuss each in turn.

EXCLUSIVE PERSPECTIVE PEOPLE

This perspective adopts a rather narrow understanding of talent: individuals who have the capability to make a significant difference to the performance of the company. For example, 'critical talent' refers to groups and individuals who drive a disproportionate share of an organization's business performance and generate greater-than-average value for customers and shareholders. One exclusive definition of talent is:

> *A code for the most effective leaders and managers at all levels who can help a company fulfil its aspirations and drive its performance, managerial talent is some combination of a sharp strategic mind, leadership ability, emotional maturity, communications skills, the ability to attract and inspire other talented people, entrepreneurial instincts, functional skills, and the ability to deliver results.*[23]

For example, in the capital markets and investment banking sector, one form of demarcation is between those employees who are seen as direct revenue generators – the front office, and those that support them – the middle and back offices. Key challenges in managing the former are managing 'stars' and the development of 'player managers'. Front office personnel are often highly visible, well paid and sought after by competitors.

The CIPD survey[24] sees talent as 'those individuals who can make a difference to organizational performance, either through their immediate contribution or in the longer term by demonstrating the highest levels of potential (p. xi)'.

---

22   Michaels, E, Handfield-Jones, H. and Beth, A. (2001) op. cit. p. xii.

23   Ibid., p. xiii.

24   CIPD (2007) *Talent: Strategy, Management, Measurement*. London: CIPD.

Others[25] talk about 'superkeepers':

Superkeepers are a very small group of individuals, who have demonstrated superior accomplishments, have inspired others to attain superior accomplishments, and who embody the core competencies and values of the organisation; their loss or absence severely retards organisation growth because of their disproportionately powerful impact on current and future organisation performance.

Such views see talented individuals as those who enhance the companies' competitive advantage, driving companies forward through their outstanding competence and ability; not everyone in the organization can be considered a talent, as talented employees are fundamentally different from others in terms of their current and past performance as well as their future potential and competence. Some argue that 20 per cent of the workforce can contribute 80 per cent of the value, according to the Pareto principle.[26]

Future potential, as well as past and current performance, is often emphasized; performance is often measured against specific objectives and performance reviews that describe current and past behaviour, and may or may not be an indicator of potential. Potential, on the other hand, is about looking forward and predicting what an employee may be capable of in the future. It is more difficult to determine because it requires inferring future contribution based on current data. A focus of TM here, then, is to align existing *performance* appraisal processes with *potential* identification processes.[27] Others are more critical of potential-based programmes like fast-track and high-potential programmes, based on assessing long-term potential; these raise equity and expectation issues. Instead, assessment should be based on performance in, for example, try-outs and low-cost job/project opportunities, as well as on self-selection.

This *exclusive people* TM perspective, then, implies or asserts that talent is neither title nor position-related. This perspective is based upon differentiation or *segmentation,* that is, the division of the workforce into parts that are to be treated differently. TM is seen as impractical without segmentation, for then managers would treat all employees as equally valuable, regardless of performance, competence, potential, or other characteristics that distinguish one employee from another. Therefore, it is both fair and essential to invest scarce resources on the most promising talent, although this should not be at the expense or neglect of all the other employees.[28] In this sense, segmentation is a practical version of labour economics, as can be illustrated in the following two examples: (i) the segmentation of 'A' (the top 10–20 per cent), 'B' (the middle 70 per cent), and 'C' (the lowest 10–20 per cent) employees in GE, and (ii) segmentation into 'superkeepers' (those who greatly exceed organizational expectations), 'keepers' (those who exceed expectations), 'solid citizens' (those who meet expectations) and 'misfits' (those who fail to meet expectations).[29] One can also detect some affinity with aspects of the marketing literature: instead of defining market segments in terms of customers, and tailoring specific 'value propositions' to

25   Such as Larson, P. and Richburg, M. (2004) Leadership coaching, in Berger, L. and Berger, D. (eds) *The Talent Management Handbook*, p. 5. New York: McGraw-Hill.

26   Branham, L. (2005) Planning to become an employer of choice, *Journal of Organizational Excellence*, 24(3): 57–69.

27   Mucha, R. T. (2004) The art and science of talent management, *Organizational Development Journal*, 22(4).

28   Ledford, G. and Kochanski, J. (2004) Allocating training and development resources based on contribution, in Berger, L. and Berger, D. (eds) *The Talent Management Handbook*, pp. 218–219. New York: McGraw-Hill.

29   Mucha, R. T. (2004) op. cit.

those segments, it divides the actual/potential workforce into segments, and then offers employees/potential employees different 'value propositions'. This view is even more evident in the next approach to be considered, the *exclusive perspective positions*.

EXCLUSIVE PERSPECTIVE POSITIONS

A particularly influential perspective on TM sees the talent defining process is closely allied with the identification of 'key positions' in the organization.[30] The starting point is to identify strategically critical jobs ('A positions'); the claim is that just as effective business and marketing strategy requires differentiating a firm's products and services in ways that create value for customers, an effective HR strategy also requires workforce differentiation. Only the 'right' staff ('A players') occupying those positions can be considered as talents, and they should get a disproportionate amount of financial and managerial investment. Focusing on A players alone, the exclusive people perspective may not lead to high-performance if such players are not in strategically important positions. These are not necessarily revealed by hierarchical title or level of difficulty in filling positions, but are both strategically important and exhibit wide variations in work quality (customer service in some firms, heads of clinical trials in others). Whilst failing to attend to B positions, such as pilots in airlines, may have great risks, investing in them to the same extent as A positions does not offer the same return. People in A positions are then guaranteed maximum opportunities for their development. A perfect match of A players and A positions is expected to lead to 'A' performance. A positions carry great autonomy, reward is performance-based, and they create value by enhancing revenue or reducing costs. Consequences of mistaken hires carry significant expense, and their careers need to be managed centrally. Given the limited financial and managerial resources available in most organizations to attract, select, develop and retain top performers, companies simply cannot afford to have A players in all positions; thus, a portfolio approach is recommended, which involves placing the best A employees in strategic positions, good B performers in support positions, and eliminating non-performing jobs and C employees that do not add value, or outsourcing such positions. Following the identification of A, B and C positions, the right people who do the right things in those positions are respectively considered as A, B, C players.

This talent-defining perspective shares something in common with the first one by emphasizing 'workforce differentiation' and argues that A, B and C players should get disproportionate attention and investment.

INCLUSIVE PERSPECTIVE PEOPLE

In contrast to the above two exclusive approaches, which target the elite few, the third perspective on TM adopts a more inclusive approach, taking the position that everyone in the organization has talent; everyone has a role to play and contribution to make to the success of the business, hence everyone should be viewed as potentially at least source of competitive advantage. This approach to TM is comparatively rare in practice,[31]

30   Huselid, M. A., Beatty, R. W. and Becker, B. E. (2005) A players or A positions? The strategic logic of workforce management, *Harvard Business Review*, 83(12): 110–17.

31   Clarke, R. and Winkler, V. (2006) op. cit.

but is advocated by some commentators; 'an inclusive talent management strategy is a competitive necessity'.[32] Similarly, others claim:

> The talent is inherent in each person … HR' s most basic challenge is to help one particular person increase his or her performance; to be successful in the future we must restore our focus on the unique talents of each individual employee, and on the right way to transform these talents into lasting performance.[33]

TM should take a broader, more inclusive, approach by recognizing that everyone has the capability and potential to display talent, therefore everyone should have opportunities to be considered and developed, and in effect go through the same talent identification process.[34] Employees may have the abilities, but they may not be given the *opportunity* to display and use them in the workplace; thus it is essential that opportunities are provided for everyone to learn, grow, and strive to fulfil their potential.

SOCIAL CAPITAL PERSPECTIVE

This approach[35] sees the other TM perspectives as too dependent on an individualistic focus, one that views talent in '*human* capital' terms. It differentiates 'leader development' (individually focused development programmes aimed at enhancing the human capital of leaders) from 'leadership development' (collectively focused programmes aimed at enhancing *social* capital through, for example, developing bonds, bridges, trust and networks). In a similar vein, extant TM perspectives can be argued to overemphasize individual talents (attributes of individuals) and downplay the influence of roles, teams, organization structuring, networks, culture and leadership in giving talent direction and opportunity.

An example from the banking sector illustrates the value of taking a more collective, social capital approach. UBS set up a Leadership Institute in 2002, and its Global Leadership Experience is targeted at senior management, with an Accelerated Leadership Experience aimed at high-potentials. The point of departure here is that each business unit has a TM team and line managers are seen as key 'owners of talent'; a 'line manager engagement programme' has been introduced, and is seen as having an important role to play in the identification and nurturing of talent.[36]

A second case study illustration of the purchase which can be obtained from taking a social capital perspective on TM comes from research[37] which focused on tracking high-flying CEOs, researchers, software developers, and professionals in investment banking, advertising, public relations, management consulting and the law. It found that when a company hired a 'star', the star's performance plunged, there was a sharp decline in the

---

32   Warren, C. (2006) op. cit. p. 9.

33   Buckingham, M. and Vosburgh, R. (2001) op. cit. p. 17.

34   See Stainton, A. (2005) Talent management: latest buzzword or refocusing existing processes?, *Competency and Emotional Intelligence,* 12(4): 39–43.

35   Iles, P. A. and Preece, D. A. (2006) Developing leaders or developing leadership? The Academy of Chief Executives' programmes in the north-east of England, *Leadership,* 2(2): 317–340.

36   Iles, P. A. (2007) op. cit.

37   See Groysberg, B., Nanda, A. and Nohria, N. (2004) The risky business of hiring stars, *Harvard Business Review,* 82(5): 93–100.

functioning of the group the person worked with, and the company's market value fell. What is more, stars did not stay with the organizations for long. Thus, companies were not gaining competitive advantage by hiring stars from outside. They recommended that organizations focus on growing talent and retaining the stars they create, as company-specific factors impact on any star's success (these factors were: resources and capabilities, systems and processes, leadership, internal networks, training and membership of teams).

The above suggests that the attainment of competitive advantage through people is mediated by the complex organizational structures, processes, and so on, within which people work, and thus draws attention to the need to manage talent in particular – and always changing – social and organizational contexts: social capital comes to the forefront, as does talent *management*.

What is Talent Management?

Just as with talent per se, a review of the literature on TM reveals a lack of agreement regarding the definition and scope of TM. Clearly, there isn't a single consistent or concise definition of TM. TM can be defined as:

> *A conscious, deliberate approach undertaken to attract, develop and retain people with the aptitude and abilities to meet current and future organisational needs. TM involves individual and organisational development in response to a changing and complex operating environment. It includes the creation and maintenance of a supportive, people oriented organisation culture.*[38]

For others

> *TM is the strategic management of the flow of talent through an organisation. Its purpose is to assure that supply of talent is available to align the right people with the right jobs at the right time based on strategic business objectives.*[39]

TM can encompass all the usual HR processes and practices:

> *It commonly refers to the sourcing (finding talent), screening (sorting of qualified and unqualified applicants), selection ... on-boarding (offer generation/acceptance ... payroll, facilities, etc.), retention ... development ... deployment ... and renewal of the workforce with analysis and planning as the adhesive, overarching ingredient. In other words, talent management is what occurs at the nexus of the hiring, development and workforce management processes and can be described alternatively as talent optimization.*[40]

---

38   Stockley, D. (2005) Talent management concept – definition and explanation, available at http://derekstockley.com.au/newsletters-05/020-talent-management.html, retrieved in October 2007.

39   See Duttagupta, R. (2005) *Identifying and Managing your Assets: Talent Management*, p. 2. London: PricewaterhouseCoopers.

40   Schweyer, A. (2004) op. cit. p. 18.

For the CIPD, 'TM is the systematic attraction, identification, development, engagement, retention and deployment of those individuals with high potential and who are of particular value to an organisation.'[41]

This study of nine UK private and public sector organizations across a range of sectors found that:

- What is seen as talent and how it is developed is highly varied.
- There is no one definition of TM.
- Talented individuals are often associated with leadership behaviours, creativity, expertise and initiative.
- The main drivers of TM are changes in the external labour market, increased competition and skills shortages, recruitment and retention difficulties and succession planning.
- There was little evidence of employers adopting a formal TM strategy.
- Top-level support for TM was necessary.
- HR played a main role in TM.
- TM programmes varied in terms of who they were aimed at and how.
- There were issues relating to the demotivation of individuals not selected for TM, especially if this meant they had fewer resources and opportunities for progression.
- There was often a lack of integration with other HR programmes.
- A blend of formal and informal learning interventions was necessary.
- Coaching and mentoring were important.
- Challenges remained for deploying talent in the organization.
- The evaluation of TM, given its future focus, was difficult.
- TM is a dynamic process that needs continuous review in the light of changing business priorities.

Within this variety of conceptualizations of TM, it seems to us that two main strands can be identified: (1) TM as a collection of integrated HR practices, targeted at a differentiated workforce and (2) TM as talent continuity/succession planning.

TM as a Collection of Integrated HR Practices Targeted at a Differentiated Workforce

This perspective defines TM as a collection of typical HR practices and activities covering the various HR functions, such as recruitment, development, deployment and retention of talented individuals. In this sense, the components of a TM system have been widely discussed without producing much new thinking. The different models of TM put forward by different authors are, in essence, quite similar to each other (as in the definitions above). From these models a more generalized version of TM activities can be developed: attracting, retaining, developing and deploying/transitioning talent. CIPD[42] echoes this view by suggesting that TM is joined-up thinking, combining the different elements of

41   CIPD (2007b) *Talent: Strategy, Management, Measurement*. London: CIPD.

42   CIPD (2007) *Talent: Strategy, Management, Measurement*. London: CIPD.

human resourcing in a structured approach, with its key processes supportive of each other.

ATTRACTING TALENT

In attracting new employees to the organization, two main activities are normally involved: (1) employment branding and employee attraction, and (2) recruitment and selection.

1. Employment branding forms a key part of many talent strategies, starting from the corporate culture and involving systematic efforts to strengthen the corporate image in order to help attract potential talent. According to Sullivan,[43] employment branding is the process of developing an image of being a 'great place to work' in the minds of the targeted candidate pool. When developing employment branding, organizations try to make their talent requirements clear in order to promote an appropriate match between a potential applicant, the organization culture and the role(s).
2. Recruitment and selection: talented individuals are then recruited on the basis of careful and systematic screening and selection methods.

RETAINING TALENT

Given the time and expense involved in nurturing and rewarding talents, retention should form a key element of TM. Without the right organizational mix of values, attitudes, terms and benefits, talented individuals are likely to leave. Thus, emotional attachment and engagement should be included in any retention strategy.

DEVELOPING TALENT

Developing talent involves processes such as development and training, coaching and mentoring and performance management, including career development.

DEPLOYING AND TRANSITIONING TALENT

TM also involves transitioning talents out of the company. The benefits of a successful implementation of talent transition can be significant, including 'exit management' and the elimination of C players.[44]

To summarize, TM as a collection of integrated HR practices targeted at a differentiated workforce involves highlighting and supporting a set of carefully selected employees (referred to as talented individuals or A players) seen as critically valuable to the success of the organization. The central challenges are thus to attract, recruit, develop and retain such individuals. TM here is an umbrella phrase including employee recruitment, retention, performance management, skills and competency management, succession planning,

---

43   Cited in Levoy, B. (2007) *222 Secrets of Hiring, Managing and Retaining Great Employees in Healthcare Practices*, p. 20. London: Jones and Bartlett Publishers.

44   See Huselid, M. A., Beatty, R. W. and Becker, B. E. (2005) op. cit.

redeployment, learning management, training, career development, developing internal career centres and identifying internal career paths.

However, defining TM in terms of the functions of traditional HR seems to add little new to our understanding of how to manage talent. Managing talent through recruiting, developing and deploying talent may require the addition of new skills to an HR practitioner's skill-set, but does not fundamentally change traditional HRM principles and practices. Thus, if organizations are often unclear about what they mean by talent, and concentrate on specialist areas within HR, such as branding, TM as such will be superfluous, and the terms TM and HRM may be used interchangeably. TM could then in effect become a new label for HRM for many managers,[45] satisfying demands to re-brand HR practices to keep them seemingly new and fresh, but not advancing the practice of the strategic and effective management of talent.

TALENT CONTINUITY AND SUCCESSION PLANNING

The second perspective on TM focuses primarily on talent continuity, with links to the well-established concept of succession planning. TM here is a set of practices put in place in an attempt to ensure a smooth continuity of talented employees into roles throughout the organization.[46] TM initiatives designed to create talent pools that feed particular job classifications, and which focus on the individual skills, competencies and behaviours that make those jobs and employees successful in the future. This encompasses much of the work done in traditional succession and workforce planning, and therefore quite close to what is usually known as 'succession planning' (SP) or 'human resource planning'.[47]

SP initially arose in family businesses, whereby the management of the business could be passed down from generation to generation. When the corporate world became interested, it focused concerns on the CEO position. Over time, corporations began to realize that the ongoing stability of their entire senior management teams was just as important as ensuring a plan for the CEO role. More recently, SP has developed yet again, as organizations have sought to attract people to be part of an organization's future plans. Through *talent relationship management*, an organized ongoing relationship with potential new recruits, they enhance the chances of having a wide choice of those who may make a significant contribution to the organization in the future.

SP can be defined as:

> *The attempt to plan for the right number and quality of managers and key-skilled employees to cover retirements, death, serious illness or promotion, and any new positions which may be created in future organisation plans.*[48]

45 Barlow, L. (2006) Talent development: the new imperative? *Development and Learning in Organizations*, 20(3): 6–9.

46 See Kesler, G. C. (2002) Why the leadership bench never gets deeper: ten insights about executive talent development, *Human Resource Planning*, 25(1): 32–44 and Pascal, C. (2004) Foreword, in Schweyer, A. (ed.) *Talent Management Systems: Best Practices in Technology Solutions for Recruitment, Retention and Workforce Planning*. New York: Wiley.

47 Jackson, S. E. and Schuler, R. S. (1990) Human resource planning: challenges for industrial/organizational psychologists, *American Psychologist*, 45(2): 223–239 and Rothwell, W. J. (1994) *Effective Succession Planning: Ensuring Leadership Continuity and Building Talent from Within*. New York: AMACOM.

48 Sambrook, S. (2005) Exploring succession planning in small, growing firms, *Journal of Small Business and Enterprise Development*, 12(4): 41.

SP can be seen in terms of identifying successors for key posts and then planning career moves and/or development activities for these potential successors; processes need to be designed around purpose, population, principles, processes and players, with senior manager engagement and HR championing. The highest-potential employees are then offered accelerated development and career paths. Of course, the downside is that non-selected employees may feel that they are less valued and have less access to development opportunities.

In reality, however, few companies would appear to have such programmes. One SP leadership development programme in a large US healthcare conglomerate aimed to achieve a more precise matching of executive talent to business needs and build an executive team of high-performing leaders with enterprise-wide experience. Mentoring played a key role, and the strengths of the programme were reported to include the matching of participants, training of mentors and mentees, programme structure and integrity, ongoing evaluation and feedback, identification of leadership potential and teambuilding. Problems included the limited involvement of mentee's line managers and an inadequate selection process for participants.[49]

Others are more critical of SP or attempts to equate SP with TM, arguing instead for a 'talent on demand framework' based on managing risk (not overestimating the places to be filled) and using talent pools that span functions to develop broad competencies and create a balance of employer/employee interests. Risks include vacancy (vacant critical leadership positions), readiness (under-developed successors), transition (poor assimilation) and portfolio (poor deployment against business goals). SP is often associated with the old, complex legacy systems of forecasting and succession planning from the 1950s; these can be both inaccurate and expensive, and no plans may really be better than poor plans as mistakes (for example, talent excess) are very costly, and employees' expectations may be built up, leading to retention problems if disappointed.

Others are more positive about the value of SP for TM; 'leadership pipelines' can:[50]

- focus on development.
- identify crucial 'lynchpin roles'.
- create transparent succession management systems.
- regularly measure progress.
- ensure flexibility.

Organizations can become 'talent factories' so as to ensure a free-flowing pipeline of high-potential employees, becoming more aware that future development opportunities have often been sacrificed by the elimination of many positions formerly exposing high-potentials to a range of problems.[51] Such attention to talent development requires the attention of the board to ensure both functionality (rigorous talent processes supporting strategic and cultural objectives) and vitality (managers' emotional commitment, engagement and accountability).

---

49   Boverie, P. (2008) *A Succession Planning Leadership Mentoring Program: Working Report on the Evaluation and Success of Mentoring for Executive Development.* Presented to the 9th International Conference on Human Resource Development.

50   See Ready, D. A. and Conger, J. A. (2007) Make your company a talent factory, *Harvard Business Review,* 85(6): 68–77.

51   Ready, D. A. and Conger, J. A. (2007) Make your company a talent factory, *Harvard Business Review,* 85(6): 68–77.

Senior managers and executives appear to be increasingly concerned about the ageing population and how it will impact on their workforce profile, thus making the identification of talent and the development of future leaders a priority. Policy developments in the Scottish Parliament relating to human capital issues and the talent management of an older workforce are in part focused on labour-supply shortages in key public services and the retention of the talents of older workers.[52]

It can thus be seen that SP has gone beyond the reactive replacement of exiting employees to the proactive facilitation of the deployment of an organization's talent as needed, now and in the future. Much SP has become a forward-looking process, and one of its primary assumptions is that the future will be different from the present. At the same time, SP has also become the proactive management of the organization's entire talent pool – it is no longer sufficient or appropriate to focus on a small pool of talented employees exclusively from the upper ranks.[53]

Therefore, enlightened organizations may be more willing and ready to integrate SP into their strategic business planning processes and corporate policies. One example is Procter and Gamble (PandG), which can search global databases of talent profiles to identify candidates for international joint ventures and other initiatives in merging markets and is developing a global talent supply-chain process, coordinated globally whist executed locally by local managers. This often involves hiring local talent; high-potential prospects and stretch assignments, such as country-manager in a small country like Taiwan, are also identified globally and managed at the executive level. The company uses formal training and external executive education programmes, but most development takes place on the job, with peers, coaches and mentors and job assignments, projects and taskforces. People and positions, as well as diversity, are tracked in a technology-based TM system, especially middle and upper management, at the country, category and regional level. A global talent review process monitors the TM capacity of every business, function and country, including the effectiveness of recruitment and promotion. PandG engages employees in their own career development, plotting moves that will build 'career development currency' into moves to 'destination jobs', so that job assignments are seen through a career development lens.[54]

SP is also growing in importance in the public sector, as illustrated in the following case study of TM and SP in Derby City Council.

---

52   See McGoldrick, J., Kelley, L., Feeley, L., Clark, G., Appleton, L., Martin, G. and Bushfield, S. (2008) *HRD, Human Capital and Talent Management of an Older Workforce: Evidence-based Policy Development in the Scottish Government Symposium*. Presented to 9th International Conference on Human Resource Development Research and Practice across Europe, 21–23 May 2008 IESEG Lille France; see also http://www.esrcsocietytoday.ac.uk.

53   Carey, D. and Odgen, D. (2004) CEO succession planning: ensuring leadership at the top, in L. A. Berger and D. R. Berger *The Talent Management Handbook*, pp. 243–252. New York: McGraw-Hill.

54   See Ready, D. A. and Conger, J. A. (2007) op. cit.

Case Study

Succession Planning and Talent Management in Derby City Council

Derby City Council (DCC) has been a unitary authority since 1997 and employs some 12,000 people; it is the largest single employer in the city providing all local government services which include education, social services, highways and transportation, arts and cultural events, refuse collection and recycling, and parks. There is an age imbalance: 42.5 per cent of the workforce is over 45, with the average age of senior managers being 50 and 28 per cent of the workforce will reach retirement age within the next 15 years, including the CEO. A Workforce Development Plan for 2007–2010 has been developed, with TM and SP as key themes.

Developing leadership skills has been identified as a key challenge for the organization, resulting in a Leadership Charter and Leading Manager programme designed and delivered jointly with the local University. The Council has introduced a coaching programme for senior managers to address leadership needs at first and second tier levels. Promotion to Head of Service, reporting to Assistant Directors, has historically been a significant jump, with little training in place for this group (in contrast to supervisors and middle managers).

The main rationale for growing talent at DCC is succession planning to develop an Assistant Director succession pool, and stems from the identified need to develop managerial skills and experience within the organization. This has much to do with the age profile of senior staff and the demographics of the wider labour market, which is seen as likely to reduce the numbers of talented individuals attracted to local government in the longer term. Due to a long-established policy of recruiting through external as well as internal advertising to promote equal access to Council job opportunities, there has hitherto not been a tradition of internal SP. The Chief Executive identified that the Council requires 'more managers with generic management skills as opposed to more technically competent people. It has been the problem of local government that people tend to get promoted through their professional and technical competence and that is not always what we are looking for.'

A talent pool of over 70 employees has been identified through the completion of a Leading Managers programme. Whilst these are keen to take on new challenges, for most of them the reality has been a continuation in their current job role. A benefit of the initiative, though, has been emerging awareness of the senior management team that these employees need to be better deployed for the benefit of the organization and the individuals themselves.

The importance of an integrated approach to the Council's Achievement and Development process as the central hub of its performance management initiative, and the value of coaching as a core managerial skill to support TM, are increasingly recognized and have formed part of the new HR strategy for the authority. This is reflected in a change in approach away from simply attending courses to a greater emphasis on self-development, coaching and mentoring, using secondments, project working and shadowing as the means of developing the work force. A Succession Planning Board has been set up, chaired by an Assistant Director, to oversee the establishment of a succession planning programme in 2008 and accelerate the development of high-potential managers, reducing the costs of external recruitment and the lead-in time in taking up a new role.

A major issue for DCC is that (in common with much public sector employment) it has a commitment to open access to all jobs through external advertising. On the one hand, giving special opportunities to a managerial talent pool challenges long-established principles and practices on equal opportunities and diversity. On the other, it is recognized that the talent pool has to be utilized, otherwise it will be detrimental to employee retention and motivation. It is also acknowledged that there needs to be a proactive approach to developing existing internal capability to address the current lack of women on the senior management team and the underrepresentation of minority ethnic groups in managerial roles. An Equality Impact Assessment was conducted for the Succession Pool, and targets set to increase diversity at HoS level. Selection of participants was the responsibility of individual departments, with an emphasis on self-nomination through appraisal. Self-assessment against leadership principles to assess readiness, with comments by the line manager and director, are used for selection and consideration of access to the Leading Manager programme. Applicants remain in the pool for three years or until they have been promoted, with annual appraisals. Pool participants agree a schedule of responsibilities, including study programmes (possibilities include modules, mentoring, 360-degree feedback, work shadowing, project work/ secondments, and a Developing Future Leaders course), and application of learning to the workplace and the development of a Personal Development Plan.

Budgetary constraints have been a key concern, and some respondents felt that the Leading Manager programme used up limited central resources when general supervisory capability was a central concern for organizational performance. It was also recognized that the role of the immediate line manager was pivotal in spotting and nurturing talent, but that this could be a mixed experience for a variety of reasons – for example project work might develop the individual and provide wider benefits for the organization, but the focus on service delivery meant that for operational management this could mean a loss of a key resource.

*   See Dexter, B. P. (2008) *Developing Future Council Leaders: A Case Study of Succession Planning at Derby City Council*. Presented to the 9th International Conference on Human Resource Development Research and Practice across Europe, 21–23 May 2008 IESEG, Lille, France and Dexter, B. P., Franco, G. and Chamberlin, J. E. (2006) Educators as change agents: how far can we go? *The International Journal of Knowledge, Culture and Change Management*, 6(1): 168–174.

Conclusion

This chapter has explored the increasing importance of talent management or TM to HRM theory and practice, especially since the 'war for talent' came to be identified as an important issue for organizations since the late 1990s. Interest in TM has been driven by the development of a global market in talent, especially professional and managerial talent, as economies become more knowledge-driven, and by cultural and demographic changes such as ageing societies and lower organizational commitment and loyalty, as well as by technological changes allowing for greater applicant tracking and employee profiling.

Talent management also shows the increasing importance of economic and marketing theories of labour market segmentation and employee branding on HRM, as many conceptions of TM challenge egalitarian models of HRM by differentiating the workforce into 'talented' (for example, those employees/applicants showing high performance and/or high potential) and 'less talented', though organizations differ over how exclusive their definitions of the talent pool are. Some organizations seek to also differentiate roles and positions (for example, A, B and C positions) and seek to match differentiated talent to such positions. TM is often linked to career development, career planning and succession planning, and the matching of talent supply (talent pipelines) with talent demand, though it is problematic how much either can be accurately predicted in times of change, instability and uncertainty. In addition, an overly individualistic human capital model of TM may neglect social context, social capital, teamwork and networks, as well as the contribution of organizational structures and processes such as leadership, structure and culture to high performance.

TM can be seen in terms of both integration (the holistic understanding of attraction, retention, deployment and development policies) and differentiation (their application to different workforce segments), as well as in terms of continuity (ensuring a smooth flow and supply of talents) This is shown in the case study of Derby City Council, which also shows its links with career development and how TM is gaining in importance in public services as well as in the corporate sector.

14 *How Leaders and Managers Learn*

JEFF GOLD, RICHARD THORPE AND ALAN MUMFORD

Introduction

As a way of introducing some of the key themes concerning how leaders and managers learn, we are going to present the results of a recent, and totally unscientific, experiment with over 40 leaders and managers who were our audience at an event organised by a management professional association. We asked them to identify some aspect of their work which was current and seen to be problematic. This was not a difficult question to answer and more a case of identifying which among many could be surfaced for this particular experiment. In accordance with research on the lives of leaders and managers,[1] we know that the realities leaders and managers face are far removed from the smooth world of Gantt charts and neat plans. Instead, there is always a plethora of difficult, complex and uncertain issues that, to a greater or lesser extent, must be dealt with. Of course, learning how to deal with such issues is what leaders and managers are there for and why they command a remuneration premium for their efforts. Further, leaders and managers can learn some important ideas and theories from a variety of sources, but principally from the management and business schools. Indeed, in our sample, there were several who could make claims about their learning in such contexts via the possession of MBAs and professional qualifications such as CIPD and CIM. So we would expect some evidence of this learning to be part of practice. We asked the audience to consider how they were dealing with the issue they had identified from the point of view of ideas and theories being used in practice and set up a scale as shown in Figure 14.1.

There are five choices available, ranging from the use of pure theory to what feels right and reasonable according to the situation. In between these extremes, managers and leaders could choose models or other conceptual devices like typologies of styles[2] or perhaps more localised versions or theories as rules of thumb. At point 4 on the scale are stories, recalled from other occasions or events or new constructions, but used to work out what to do or to explain a point to others in particular events.[3] We were not surprised

---

1   The research of Kotter, J. (1982) *The General Managers*, New York: Free Press; Mintzberg, H. (1975) The manager's job: folklore and fact, *Harvard Business Review*, July/August: 49–61 and Watson, T. J. (1994) *In Search of Management*, London: Routledge, are three sources among several we could invoke.

2   Any typology of leadership style would fit here because they are still very popular on training programmes.

3   This scale has been developed from our reading the work of the philosopher Stephen Toulmin in his book *Return to Reason*, Cambridge, MA: Harvard University Press, 2001.

to find that nearly all our audience chose points 4 and 5 on the scale. That is, in terms of their behaviour, there was little evidence of having learned the very many models and theories relating to management and leadership. Now, we do need to make a slight adjustment here, because in discussion with the audience, many pointed to the value of theory and the need for guidance from theory on what to do. Some even claimed to have enjoyed their time on courses or getting their qualifications; it just seemed that in using what they learnt, there was little opportunity. This apparent contradiction has been the source of much concern in the business schools and some of the commentators on management and leadership[4] but, crucially for this chapter, what does it suggest about how managers and leaders learn? This is an important question, because managers and leaders are vital to organisation success and social well-being. We want those who occupy such roles to learn to be effective in the whole range of situations they are responsible for. Further vast amounts of resources are invested in the learning endeavour, so it matters if learning does or does not happen.

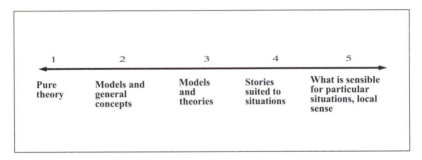

Figure 14.1 A scale of dealing with management and leadership issues

Because it matters, explanations of how managers and leaders learn have been a hot topic for many years. There are conferences, journals, many books and even whole academic departments devoted to the issue. There are inevitably many theories devoted learning generally,[5] and we should remember that it is not just managers and leaders who learn or should learn; there is now a very clear requirement for lifelong learning for everyone in our society. Nevertheless, we believe that managers and leaders do warrant some specific consideration because of their importance, although we must recognise that the origins of the various ideas on learning are seldom directed at managers and leaders per se.

---

4   Simon Caulkin's column in the *Observer* regularly expresses doubts about formal management and leadership education, but even academic writers such as Bennis and O'Toole (2005) How business schools lost their way, *Harvard Business Review*, May, 96–104 have declared that 'business schools are on the wrong track' (p. 96). They particularly cite the failure of MBA programmes to provide managers with useful skills, for not preparing them adequately for leadership roles and for not imbuing them with appropriate norms of ethical behaviour.

5   Go to http://www.learning-theories.com/ for a useful coverage of various learning theories.

Learning and Effectiveness

It should be clear from the example above that the managers and leaders in our audience were live evidence of contradictions when learning is considered. Most had attended events when learning was going on in terms of some delivery of a process relating to something to be learned – perhaps a theory or the latest thinking about some area of leadership work or a new skill or a challenge to current attitudes. They knew they had been part of a process of learning and were even perhaps attracted by the possibility of learning about new ideas and theories. After all, there is an expectation that managers and leaders need to be rational, objective, neutral and dispassionate in how they go about their work and the learning of theories and skills is a way to do this.[6] However, on this occasion at least, there did not seem to be any evidence that the process of learning had resulted in a change in behaviour which could be demonstrated. We do not know enough about each person's circumstances to know whether there had been a change in behaviour but this had not been sustained. Essentially, we are suggesting that learning is both a process – we become involved in acquiring new skills, knowledge or ways of relating to others – and an outcome – a change in behaviour which is sustained or built on over time. Managers and leaders need to show evidence of both for learning to have occurred.

There has to be a further qualification to this dual definition which is that whatever leaders and managers learn, they are in a context. That is, all managers and leaders learn somewhere and usually with somebody, whether trainers, tutors, other managers and leaders or anyone else. Nobody can be nowhere when they learn. This obvious fact has become increasingly important in leadership and management learning and highlights both a social context, in terms of the role of others, and also a more physical or structural context which might include how work is set out or defined. Both can enable or inhibit learning, especially in terms of application of new ideas or practices. A further layer of context lies in the background, an unnoticed 'hurly-burly',[7] this can include not just the immediate context, with an infusion of values and norms that make a culture, but also the effect of past formations of these factors, the history. Some learning theories explicitly attempt to consider culture and history, and how such factors can help or hinder learning.

Before we begin to consider particular theories and their use in leadership and management development, we want to explore some meanings of effectiveness. Clearly, when the audience we featured in our experiment were asked to consider how they were dealing with a particular issue of their choosing, it would have been effective if learning had enabled them to deal with the situation against some criteria (of satisfaction or excellence). So, effectiveness in leadership and management development needs to consider three factors:

1. What a leader or manager needs to achieve to get something done against some criteria.
2. A development process that is focused on what needs to be done against the criteria.

---

6   Some would say the learning of theories justifies or legitimises the work of managers and leaders.

7   Both ideas of the background and hurly-burly are drawn from the works of the philosopher Ludwig Wittgenstein. Go to http://www.iep.utm.edu/w/wittgens.htm for more about Wittgenstein.

3. A process of learning that brings these together and ensures impact and sustainability.

It is important for all of these factors to be considered for effective leadership and management development and this becomes clear when only two factors are present without the third. Thus if only 1 and 2 are present but there is no process of learning employed, it is most unlikely that there will be impact and sustainability. If 2 and 3 are present but there is no consideration of what a leader or manager needs in the context of their work, this is bound to affect motivation to participate. The importance of combining all three factors is summarised in the well-known effectiveness triangle by Alan Mumford, shown in Figure 14.2.

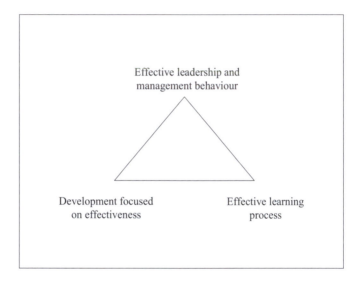

Figure 14.2 A triangle of effectiveness[8]

It is not always clear just how managers and leaders have learned what they require to complete their work. We did not press the audience we had, but it would be a fair assumption that many would not have been able to specify where they learnt what they actually did in the situation identified. While there may have been some connection with a past training event or a module on their qualification programme, in all likelihood most of the learning would have come from less formal or what Michael Eraut[9] calls 'non-formal learning'. Further it is quite possible that managers and leaders might not be consciously aware that they were learning, in which case the learning is implicit. This highlights something that has been long recognised in leader and manager learning; that learning is probably occurring every day, in a variety of working contexts or otherwise,

---

8   See Mumford, A. and Gold, J. (2004) *Management Development, Strategies for Action*, p. 89, London: Chartered Institute for Personnel and Development.

9   See Eraut, M. (2000) Non-formal learning, implicit learning and tacit knowledge in professional work. In F. Coffield (ed.), *The Necessity of Informal Learning*, Bristol: Policy Press.

and that that this 'natural learning'[10] is achieved in the course of normal dealing with people and situations, attending meetings, tackling problems and so on. In the particular circumstances, if the right results or responses are achieved, the learning might be considered effective although others might disagree. Further, because it is natural without an intent to learn, it is not usually recognised *as* learning, and managers and leaders might not even be able to talk about it because they are not consciously aware of what was learned and how it has changed what they do.[11] Implicit learning is closely associated with the development of what is often called 'know-how' – a knowing what to do according to the requirements of a situation. It is highly personal and allows managers and leaders to deal with new or unexpected events, not usually covered in the textbooks or theories they may have studied. This kind of knowledge is tacit and as Polanyi,[12] one of first writers in this area, once wrote 'this knowledge cannot be put into words'. Ever since, there have been arguments and debates relating to how tacit knowledge might be put into words, and this has created a degree of ambiguity around the meaning of tacit knowledge. Stephen Gourlay[13] is a key researcher in this area and has sought to remove some of this ambiguity by suggesting that that tacit knowledge should only be used when there is evidence of behaviour but the 'actors could not give an account'. This does mean that there are times when know-how can be presented to others. For example, managers and leaders often present what they know as pictures or diagrams rather than words.

Because managers and leaders use 'know-how' and 'know-what' to deal with regular situations, they can usually recognise when errors are occurring or problems are arising, so they can respond to bring things back to normal, as required. This kind of learning is routine and based on embedded assumptions which, if they work, do not need challenging. Chris Argyris[14] uses the term single-loop learning to describe this kind of response and works with the analogy of a thermostat to explain the idea. So, if the temperature drops from that which is desired – say 68 degrees – the thermostat comes on. Once the desired temperature is restored, the heating is switched off, no questions asked. However, if the thermostat did ask the question, 'Why am I set at 68 degrees?', it would be questioning the routine and assumptions behind it and this is referred to as double-loop learning. Argyris makes the point that professionals, and this includes managers and leaders, are very good at single-loop learning as a consequence of the discipline of their training and education and their exposure to many real-world problems. However, they are less able to do double-loop learning. Indeed, success at single-loop learning is based on assumptions which have brought success in the past. So when certain practices and ways of behaving do not quite work any more, when managers and leaders find difficulties where the usual responses do not work as intended, there is a need to challenge and be critical of what is happening and of the assumptions which underpin particular ways of behaving. However, rather than engage in second-loop learning, managers and leaders might prefer to find ways of avoiding challenge and criticism, adopting what Argyris calls defensive

---

10   See Stuart, R. (1984) Towards re-establishing naturalism in management training and development, *Industrial and Commercial Training*, July–August: 19–21.

11   See the work of Reber, A. S. (1993) *Implicit Learning and Tacit Knowledge: An Essay on the Cognitive Unconscious*, Oxford: Oxford University Press.

12   See Polanyi, M. (1967) *The Tacit Dimension*, Garden City, NY: Doubleday.

13   Gourlay, S. (2006) Towards conceptual clarity for 'tacit knowledge': a review of empirical studies, *Knowledge Management Research and Practice*, 4(1): 60–69.

14   See Argyris, C. (1991) Teaching smart people how to learn, *Reflections*, 4(2); 4–15.

routines. As other writers in this handbook will explore, asking managers and leaders to reflect on experiences is now a common approach to make learning deliberate. Further, such reflection might become more critical if assumptions are revealed and patterns of behaviour are challenged to enable new possibilities to be found.[15] This is all part of a frequent call for leaders and managers, but especially leaders to engage in deep learning, so that underlying values are exposed and challenged and new meanings are constructed. This is seen as part of a promotion of creativity and the development of transformational leadership skills.[16]

Some Theories and Models of Learning for Leaders and Managers

While informal or non-formal learning can be considered the most usual kind of learning for leaders and managers, this does not explain how the learning is occurring or what theory is relevant. Theories of learning are important, as we have suggested, and this is particulary the case when more formal events for leadership and management development are provided. We are talking here about degrees of formality. For example, there are clear occasions when learning is the explicit purpose of participating in events including accredited programmes such as MBAs and off-site training courses. On other occasions, the purpose might be to combine learning and work on difficult issues in an action learning set or to take responsibility for learning in a self-directed learning process. It is even possible to give more attention to using work incidents, surprises or challenging moments to recognise what has been learned and how this might be used. All these possibilities can be informed by learning theories. It is our intention here to outline some of the more well-known theories of learning, currently used in leadership and management development. There is a need to make one simple point before we do this and that is, for most of the twentieth century theories of learning we formulated on the basis of their explanation of how children learned, and this was often based on the behaviour of experiments with animals. We would not for a moment claim that these were not valuable; however, at least from the 1960s, there was recognition that adults needed to be considered differently and managers and leaders are clearly adults. The main element of adultness we need to mention is that unlike children and animals, managers and leaders are people who have already accumulated experiences and we need to recognise this. There are many adult learning theorists that provide guidance on this but one we might mention straight away is Malcolm Knowles,[17] who even suggested using the term 'andragogy' to indicate adult learning in contrast to 'pedagogy' as a reference to the teaching of young people. The key ideas for adult learning are that adult learners do have experience which could be a resource for learning, adults learn to do things not just for the sake of learning and adults are ready to learn when they see the need for it.

---

15   See Gold, J., Holman, D. and Thorpe, R. (2002) The role of argument analysis and story-telling in facilitating critical thinking, *Management Learning*, 33(3); 371–388.

16   See Nailon, D., Delahaye, B. and Brownlee, J. (2007) Learning and leading: how beliefs about learning can be used to promote effective leadership, *Development And Learning In Organizations*, 21(4): 6–9.

17   See Knowles, M. (1973) *Adult Learner – A Neglected Species*, Houston, TX: Gulf Publishing Co. Read more about Knowles at http://www.infed.org/thinkers/et-knowl.htm

BEHAVIOURISM

Having mentioned the adult learning movement, we begin by returning to the theoretical developments in the first half of the twentieth century which produced the key ideas and theories referred to as behaviourism. Of course, the influence continues. The main ideas are, and this has to be a simplification, that learners are essentially passive and that any change in their behaviour requires some kind of stimulation from the outside: this produces a response from the learners which, if correct, is reinforced through feedback. It is also assumed that thoughts and feelings are less relevant because they cannot be observed; what is important is behaviour change. Sophistication of this basic view includes the specification of what change is desired before the stimulus occurs, and measurement of outcomes achieved, so that learning can be said to have happened. Behavioural psychologists such as Skinner, Pavlov (and dog) and Hull and Thorndike[18] did seem to assume a machine-like response of people to particular kinds of stimuli which is reinforced by reward. If the right result is not achieved, reinforcement can be negative to move people towards the right direction. Practice can make perfect if the measurements indicate this.

Without stretching a point too far, behaviourism as a learning theory has a resonance with the machine-like quality of industrial organisations and bureaucracies. We are certainly not the first to comment on this but when we consider the learning of skills, behaviourist ideas inform the specifying of jobs as parts which are clearly delineated in terms of skills. People can be trained against the specification of parts, until they get it right. There is a semblance of this in some management and leadership development. For example, there are typologies of skills with definitions of behaviour required and criteria for judgement. In the UK one such typology is the National Occupational Standards for Management and Leadership,[19] a competence framework composed of specified functional areas, broken down into units each of which is specified in terms of outcomes that are measured and behaviour that produces the outcomes. Such frameworks can have much use in management and leadership learning. One benefit, for example, is to set objectives for learning. For example, one of the standards is concerned with achieving results and UNIT F1 is specified as 'Manage a project'[20] which is further specified in terms of:

- 12 outcomes of effective performance such as (1.) Discuss and agree the key objectives and scope of the proposed project and the available resources with the project sponsor(s) and any key stakeholders.
- 9 behaviours which underpin performance, such as (4.) You create a sense of common purpose.

---

18   Of course there are many others – visit http://www.learningandteaching.info/learning/behaviour.htm for more.

19   Visit http://www.management-standards.org for more details.

20   Other units for achieving results are:

F2 Manage programme of complimentary projects	F8 Work with others to improve customer service
F3 Manage business processes	F9 Build your organisation's understanding
F4 Develop and review a framework for marketing	of its market and customers
F5 Resolve customer service problems	F10 Develop a customer-focused organisation
F6 Monitor and solve customer service problems	F11 Manage the achievement of customer satisfaction
F7 Support customer service improvements	F12 Improve organisational performance

- 20 areas of general understanding and knowledge such as (1.) The fundamental characteristics of projects as opposed to routine management functions/activities.

There is also a requirement for industry-specific knowledge and context-specific knowledge.

Assessment against the requirements of the standards results in an identification of gaps and allows objectives to be clearly set. The assumption here is that managers and leaders become motivated by this process. There is concern perhaps that the objectives set belong to the framework-owner rather than the managers and leaders. This might apply to all assessment processes that use an external standard against which to measure managers and leaders for training purposes. We are not suggesting that all programmes that specify objectives or outcomes to be achieved are informed by behaviourist assumptions, but there is certainly a neat linear way of presenting management and leadership development which ties objectives to measurement in terms of behaviour and the valuing of changes which can be using in evaluation. If only life were so simple.

One aspect of behaviourist thinking in learning, perhaps even more so for managers and leaders, is the importance of reinforcement as feedback. This would require the chance to practise new skills so that good performance can be recognised, via feedback or adjustments made for less good performance. As we saw earlier, managers and leaders don't always get the chance to apply their learning at work and this may be due to context factors as well as the ability of the manager. One way of reinforcing learning and supplying feedback is through the growing use of coaches and mentors. However, corrective feedback can easily be interpreted as criticism and research has for many years shown that managers and leaders will only accept so much negative feedback. On the other hand, it does seem that some managers become 'feedback-seekers'[21] which does affect performance improvement. However, there are many variations in the response to feedback, which does suggest some variations in how managers and leaders consider feedback. This leads us to the next set of theories, based on learners as people as thinkers and processors of information.

COGNITIVISM

Cognitivism was and is very much a challenge to the dominance of behaviourism by exploring that aspect of learning that behaviourists prefer to leave out – the way we process information through thinking, and with thinking, how memory plays a part along with other aspects of brain functioning. If the machine seemed to be at work with behaviourists, cognitivists might be said to see learning like information processing in a computer where inputs are registered through the senses, then processed in some way prior storage in memory or rejected, to be recalled as required to deal with particular situations such as decision-making. Learning is a process of acquiring new information that connects to what is already stored but makes it something different which can then inform action taken. With so much information available, and we are living in the so-called information or knowledge society, there is considerable interest in how this is all organised so that overload can be avoided. Here cognitivists make use of the idea of

---

21   See VandeWalle, D. and Cummings, L. L. (1997) An empirical test of goal orientation as a predictor of feedback-seeking behaviour, *Journal of Applied Psychology*, 82: 390–400.

schema[22] as a way of explaining how information is organised as knowledge into patterns which can be called upon as required. Schemas can play role in choosing what is selected for attention in our perception. In this way, managers and leaders might be helped to build their cognitive schema so as to organise what they already know into meaningful patterns which can lead to new insights and produce creative and useful responses to difficult and challenging situations.

Of course, there is also a danger that in the process of selecting, managers and leaders can choose not to attend to certain features of the environment. Managers and leaders can become attached to particular ways of thinking and understanding and this will produce what they are interested and believe in, how they feel and what they are motivated to do or not do. Therefore, it is argued, managers and leaders need to understand *how* they understand and be challenged to test their assumptions. For example, MBA programmes will use problematic case studies to encourage managers and leaders to follow key steps in a systematic manner to challenge existing ways of thinking and explore new possibilities. If successful, and the judgement of success would be provided by an 'expert', this could be called learning through the refinement of patterns of thinking. A command of models and theories might be considered a way of proving such refinement.

Because this is all occurring in the brain, the internal mental state, there are inevitable difficulties in gaining access to what is going on. However, such is the interest in cognition that psychologists have developed a wide range of tests to enable managers and leaders to understand how they process information. For example, there are tests for cognitive styles which measure the different ways managers and leaders build preferences for organising and processing information from experiences. One of the most well-known tests which has shown reliability over time is the Cognitive Styles Index, developed by John Hayes and Chris Allinson[23] to be used specifically in organisational settings. The test provides results which show preferences on a bipolar dimension between two ways of processing, labelled 'analytic' and 'intuitive', shown as Figure 14.3.

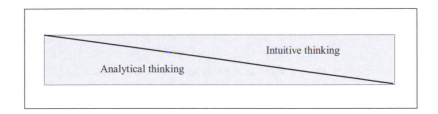

Intuitive thinking

Analytical thinking

Figure 14.3 A dimension of preferences for organising and processing information

The basics of this dimension are drawn from studies of the different functions of the hemispheres of the brain[24] where analytic and rational information processing is linked

22   Read more about schema and the cognitivist approach to learning in Sadler-Smith, E. (2006) *Learning and Development for Managers*, Oxford: Blackwell Publishing, especially p. 109.

23   See Christopher W. Allinson and John Hayes (1996) The cognitive style index: a measure of intuition–analysis for organizational research, *Journal of Management Studies*, 33(1): 119–135.

24   Check the work of Roger Sperry at http://nobelprize.org/educational_games/medicine/split-brain/background.html and http://www.rogersperry.info/.

with the left brain and more intuitive and less rational processing is associated with the right brain. A preference for analytic thinking in managers and leaders would result in more structured decision-making based on systematic investigation. There is a preference for step-by-step approaches, models and formulas that provide a solution. By contrast, an intuitive preference would result in more open approaches to decision-making, taking more factors into account in working on problems, and would be prepared from more creative possibilities. The variations in preferences are said to have an impact in how managers and leaders behave, how they solve problems, how they relate to others and, of course, how they learn.

Other measures of how the brain processes information included Herrmann's 'whole brain' model and the Herrmann Brain Dominance Instrument (HBDI),[25] the Myer–Briggs Type Indicator and the Kirton Adaption–Innovation Inventory.[26]

Although not intentional, it could be argued that various measures of cognitive style and information processing could lead to a degree of simplication and even polarization around one style, at the expense of another – a bit like a see-saw, you can't be analytic and intuitive at the same time.[27] Others argue that there is interaction and interdependence between the different styles. So, as a consideration, you might consider analysis and intuition as not so much contrasting opposites but as two dimensions ranging from high to low on each, which can be combined to product four broad categorisations such as high intuition and low analytic or high intuition and high analytic.[28] In the latter case, managers and leaders would be able to show versatility in processing information, being able to show openness and consider a range of factors while also being structured and systematic.

EXPERIENTIAL AND SOCIAL LEARNING

While behaviourism is mainly considered with stimulation from the outside and the evidence of response, and cognitivism concerned with the human processing of information, other theories of significant use in management and leadership development are concerned with the interdependence and interaction between learners and their environment, be it physical or social or even self-produced by a lively imagination. These all provide experiences, and the crucial element is whether they become a source of learning in both the process and outcome sense. This is the concern of those who support management and leadership development as a process of 'learning from experience', wherever and whenever possible.

The focus on experience in learning has roots in the work of John Dewey[29] and Carl Rogers,[30] but probably the most well-known model is that of David Kolb and his version of the learning cycle, shown as Figure 14.4.

---

25   Read more at http://www.hbdi.com/WholeBrainProductsAndServices/thehbdi.cfm.

26   See http://www.kaicentre.com/.

27   Our thanks to Eugene Sadler-Smith for this image. See Chapter 21, Intuitive intelligence, in this Handbook.

28   See Hodgkinson, G. P. and Clarke, I. (2007) Exploring the cognitive significance of organizational strategizing: a dual-process framework and research agenda, *Human Relations*, 60: 243–255.

29   More details on Dewey at http://dewey.pragmatism.org/.

30   More details on Rogers at http://www.carlrogers.info/aboutCarlRogers.html.

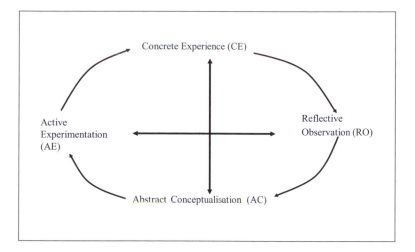

Figure 14.4 Kolb's learning cycle[31]

The cycle provides an explanation of how learning both might and should occur. The cross arrows indicate two tensions and contradictions which need to be reconciled for learning to occur, first between experience and forming new concepts, and secondly between reflection and action. This occurs through what Kolb calls transformation. Thus the sensing and grasping of experience is transformed through reflection and this allows the emergence of ideas which can then be tried out through action. Kolb's theory of experiential learning focuses on individual needs and goals concerning the types of experience sought and utilised. However, it is likely that managers and leaders develop preferences for the different stages of learning in the cycle and this will be determined by patterns of assumptions, attitudes and aptitudes. Managers and leaders who are introduced to the learning cycle can assess their preferences by use of Learning Styles Inventory (LSI).

Kolb's cycle has provided inspiration for the work of Peter Honey and Alan Mumford.[32] Accepting the basic ideas of a cycle and preferences and styles, Honey and Mumford's version of the theory gives more attention to planning action and assessment of particular learning styles at each stage of the learning cycle. They formulated their own version of a Learning Styles Questionnaire (LSQ) which, they claim, managers and leaders can make use of both when they are on development programmes and when they work. Thus, managers and leaders can come to understand their preferred learning style and less preferred styles, as shown in Table 14.1.

---

31   See Kolb, D. A. (1984) *Experiential Learning: Experience as the Source of Learning and Development*, Englewood Cliffs, NJ: Prentice-Hall.

32   See Honey, P. and Mumford, A. (1992) *The Manual of Learning Styles*, Maidenhead: Peter Honey.

Table 14.1 A dimension of cognitive processing

> *Activists* Learn best from relatively short here-and-now tasks. These may be managerial activities on the job or on courses: such things as business games and competitive team-work exercises. They learn less well from situations involving a passive role such as listening to lectures or reading.
>
> *Reflectors* Learn best from activities where they are able to stand back, listen and observe. They like collecting information and being given the opportunity to think about it. They learn less well when they are rushed into things without the opportunity to plan.
>
> *Theorists* Learn best when they can review things in terms of a system, a concept, a model or a theory. They are interested in and absorb ideas even where they may be distant from current reality. They learn less well from activities presented without this kind of explicit or implicit design.
>
> *Pragmatists* Learn best when there is an obvious link between the subject matter and the problem or opportunity on the job. They like being exposed to techniques or processes which can be applied in their immediate circumstances. They learn less well from learning events which seem distant from their own reality. 'Does it apply in my situation?'

This typology of learning styles[33] has been used to design management and leadership development events and the learning cycles used to help participants understand and gain benefit from experiences by including attention to each stage of the cycle. The LSQ results can also indicate if there is preponderance of particular styles within a group. For example, it is not unusual to find among managers a preponderance of Activists and Pragmatists and few Reflectors, and the revelation of this can have use for how managers work together. The LSQ results are meant to indicate rather than prescribe and they should certainly not be used for decisions about selection and promotion.[34] However, we do know of many managers and leaders that have found the LSQ results helpful and the learning cycle useable. There are two features worth highlighting. First, as identified by Kolb, the stages of the learning cycle are analogous to the skills of managing problems and Alan Mumford also saw a connection between learning and dealing with the reality of management work.[35] Kolb suggested that problem management is a primary skill for managers, starting with finding problems by analysing the situation, analysing and understanding the causes, deciding on appropriate solutions and then working with others to plan actions and implement. Each of these steps is connected to the learning cycle. Thus a low preference for concrete experience might show itself in giving little time to finding and defining problems. Or perhaps, a strong preference for active experimentation would result in a preference for implementing, maybe without proper analysis of causes and developing new solutions. Connecting learning preferences to dealing with work problems can provide managers and leaders with a good understanding of how to make

---

33 While the LSI and LSQ are probably the most well-known learning styles tools, there are many more, details of which can be found at http://www.support4learning.org.uk/education/learning_styles.cfm.

34 It is worth recording that despite the continuing popularity in the use of learning styles, this has not been without criticism. In a wide-ranging report on 13 learning and cognitive styles instruments, including LSI and LSQ, it was found that none had been validated independently, their use was 'questionable' and the research on the instruments lacked coherence. See Coffield, F., Moseley, D., Hall, E. and Ecclestone, K. (2004) *Learning Styles in Post-16 Learning: A Systematic and Critical Review*, London: Learning and Skills Council.

35 See Mumford, A. (1997) *How to Choose the Right Development Method*, Maidenhead: Peter Honey.

changes to the way they are working. A second features is the attention given to reflection in the learning cycle, and in our experience, a preference or style many managers and leaders avoid, partly caused by the frantic pace of work or drive to take action. Reflection by writing about experiences or reviewing them with others is a highly valued skill and one considered more deeply in another chapter in this handbook. However, we do see it as a process that provides managers with a chance to consider their view of a situation or problem or simply to take advantage of learning from experience. Reflection can lead to new opportunities for action.

How managers and leaders form learning preferences may well be an issue that arises in reflection. This can also be explored more carefully in an examination of personal meanings, feelings and emotion. For example, neurolinguistic programming (NLP) examines representations of the world and how thoughts are ordered through language which in turn lead to responses to situations (see Chapter 17 this volume). Similarly, patterns of personal meanings can be considered by completing a repertory grid, based on George Kelly's Personal Construct theory.[36]

Another theory that provides a link between cognitive and behavioural theories of learning and interaction with environment is Bandura's Social Learning theory.[37] He suggested an ongoing process of 'reciprocal determinism' between the behaviour of a person, their psychological processes and the environment. In particular, he argued that much learning involved modelling what others did by observing their behaviour and attitudes. If a manager, for example, observes another completing a team briefing, modelling will occur if the manager can see enough value in doing so and the model is recognised as someone with similar attributes. The behaviour observed is then retained by images or words so that it can be reproduced when appropriate: this can include mentally rehearsing the behaviour.[38] One interesting aspect of this process is how a leader might feel about their ability to perform certain actions and how setbacks might be coped with. This is Bandura's idea of self-efficacy and is concerned with the conviction a person has about their ability to carry out behaviour to produce a particular outcome. Self-efficacy depends on the situation, so if a manager does not believe they can chair a team meeting, this would indicate low self-efficacy and even if a training course had been completed, the manager might avoid using the skill learnt because of the lack of belief. If forced to chair the meeting, the resulting poor performance will reinforce the lack of belief and will not lead to efforts to try to improve this; indeed, the manager would try their best to not chair meetings. In contrast, where there is high self-efficacy, a manager would keep trying to improve if performance was below requirements.[39] These ideas on self-efficacy are particularly useful in exploring how intentions from leadership and management development events can be implemented back at work. Managers and leaders need to be prepared for what they will do, how to recognise success and, very importantly, how to deal with setbacks. Managers and leaders can be encouraged and persuaded to keep trying

---

36   Try http://www.enquirewithin.co.nz/theoryof.htm for more details on Kelly's theory and the use of repertory grids.

37   See Bandura, A. (1977) *Social Learning Theory*, New York: General Learning Press.

38   This theory should also remind managers, leaders and developers that their behaviour is potentially modelled by others.

39   Read more about self-efficacy in Robertson, I. T. and Shadri, G. (1993) Managerial self-efficacy and managerial performance, *British Journal of Management*, 4: 37–45.

but experience of success is the most powerful source of completing learning and raising self-efficacy.

SOCIOCULTURAL LEARNING

While experiential learning and Bandura's social learning explicitly recognise interaction with an environment, there is still much more of a focus on individuals in terms of styles or preferences or convictions about completing behaviour. Sociocultural ideas on learning devote much more attention to how environment explicitly affects learners, both in an enabling sense and in terms of possible constraints. Such ideas are mainly drawn from the work of a Russian psychologist who was writing and working in the Soviet era. There is also a connection to Marxist theory, which we will not explore here. However, we do believe that Vygotsky's ideas are of significance for management and leadership development and this is a view shared by those involve in training teachers.[40] We intend to cover two aspects of Vygotsky's contribution: first, the key idea of mediation in actions and secondly, the idea of a zone of proximal development.

Sociocultural learning is based on the idea that all human action takes place in a context: thus it is inevitably cultural but sociality is also very evident and this is best understood by use of what is referred to as Vygotsky's action triangle,[41] shown as Figure 14.5.

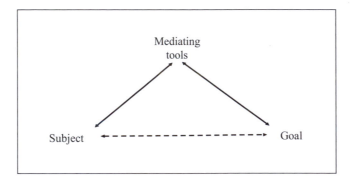

Figure 14.5 Vygotsky's action triangle

The triangle represents a single person, the Subject, participating in an action, for example, a manager conducting a meeting. Clearly, we are not focusing on the minutiae of action but the general action of conducting a meeting. In any action, there is a goal, not necessarily stated but always present. Consider someone who wants to not have a goal? However, one of the key contributions of Vygotsky was to show the importance of mediating tools in completing actions. By this he meant the obvious physical tools needed

---

40   Check the General Teaching Council's website on Vygotsky at http://www.gtce.org.uk/research/romtopics/rom_teachingandlearning/vygotsky_dec03/.

41   See Vygotsky, L. S. (1978) *Mind in Society: The Development of Higher Psychological Processes*, edited by M. Cole, V. John-Steiner, S. Scribner, and E. Souberman, Cambridge, MA: Harvard University Press.

to complete action and here we could point to tables and chairs, pens and paper, notepads and projectors, and so on. Obviously, such human artefacts reflect a particular time and society and the meanings of a culture. In addition to such physical tools, Vygotsky also showed the importance of psychological tools such as 'systems for counting; mnemonic techniques; algebraic symbol systems; works of art; writing; schemes, diagrams, maps, and technical drawings; all sorts of conventional signs, and so on'.[42]

These tools mediate how managers and leaders think, how they feel and behave. They also have a significant role to play in advancing understanding which we will consider shortly. Language is the most important tool and is acquired from society through interaction with others. Thus in a meeting, new ideas can be introduced and discussed and this will possibly impact on the manager, mediating feelings and behaviour, affecting memory and even stimulating imagination. But there is another process occurring; apart from mediating action towards a goal, tools also affect the subject in a process Vygotsky referred to as 'reverse action'. Thus, the wearing of a style of clothing, obviously cultural, can also affect the subject in terms how a person may see themselves, for example, someone dressing appropriately for a particular role. Language is not just used to work on goals but also provides a way of self-understanding in a time and place, for example, 'I am the chairman of the meeting and people need to listen to what I say.' This has important implications for those helping managers and leaders to develop: language as a tool enables the achievement of goals and how they understand themselves but it can also constrain. Thus managers and leaders who see themselves as lacking confidence in a particular area of work can restrict what they do accordingly. The very process of thinking in this way becomes part of their identity. Developers can understand a great deal about managers and leaders by listening to their talk about themselves. Does such talk enable or constrain?

This brings into play the second idea from Vygotsky, the zone of proximal development or ZPD. Learning as a process resulting in a change in behaviour, in terms of Figure 14.5, occurs by the introduction of new tools, physical or psychological or usually, both through interaction with others and/or some aspect of context, for example, how to use new software. The tools have the potential to enable managers and leaders do things better but, as we suggest above, they can also cause disturbance and contradiction to existing ways of understanding and behaving. Such a process needs support, or what others have called 'scaffolding'.[43] Such support needs to understand the gap between what is known now and what can be known, given the capabilities and and desires of managers and leaders. ZPD is described as 'the distance between the actual development level as determined by independent problem solving and the level of potential development as determined through problem solving under adult guidance or in collaboration with more capable peers'.[44] A consideration of ZPD is a consideration of existing capacity and skills to find solutions to problems that a manager or leader is facing and this forms the basis for a move towards more advanced learning that is relative to existing capacity. This has to be nurtured and be in line with a manager's concerns and potential, where the latter sets the limit of movement at a particular point in time. Stretching a manager beyond the limit is likely to fail. We believe that good developers, coaches or mentors will recognise

---

42   From Vygotsky, L. S. (1982) *Collected Works*, Moscow: Pedagogica, p. 137.

43   See Hobsbaum, A., Peters, S. and Sylva, K. (1996) Scaffolding in reading recovery, *Oxford Review of Education*, 22(1): 17–35.

44   See Vygotsky (1978) op. cit. p. 86.

how they work with such factors, so we suggest that ZPD is a rather useful 'tool' for them to consider.[45]

SITUATED LEARNING

Closely allied to sociocultural ideas on learning is the work of Jean Lave and Etienne Wenger[46] who provide an explanation of learning through practice in work situations. This more or less brings us back to the importance of natural, informal and incidental learning. Lave and Wenger make a clear differentiation between more formal approaches to learning and participation in work practices. It is within practices that a person will become part of a 'community of practice' with 'novices' learning about practice by working with and assisting those with more experience. Gradually, such novices become more 'legitimate' by copying those more skilled than themselves; thus there is a link here to Bandura's Social Learning theory which we discussed earlier. However, much of the learning occurs through conversations and the telling of stories about practices. So it is not just watching and doing which enables participation but also the ability to listen and work with stories that explain how to do things in particular situations. Whatever the method of learning, practice has to make sense to members of the community, who provide the judgement on what is acceptable or not. Where managers and leaders might be faced with new or different situations, there can be a degree of improvisation which, if successful, becomes a story to be told to others and this can then become an acceptable way of dealing with a similar problem in the future. However, any change in practice will require acceptance by the community, usually understood tacitly as a variation in norms or responsibilities.

In many ways, situated learning theory brings us back to where we started; that managers and leaders mostly learning informally, implicitly and acquire their 'know-how' tacitly. It is also a reminder that more formal approaches to leadership and management development are what Stephen Fox nicely calls 'the tip of a learning iceberg'.[47] It is in the iceberg that managers and leaders learn what they can and cannot do and this is bound to affect the value of more formal approaches to learning. There is a lot of evidence to suggest that there is an endemic problem in leadership and management development concerning what is called the 'transfer of learning' from formal events like training courses and education programmes back into everyday work practice. Some of this is due to the way cultural and historical factors mediate actions, as we saw in the section on sociocultural learning. However, there are other contextual factors that will enable and constrain all managers and leaders, as well as everyone else, in what learning can be applied in practices. This is bound to include those peers who make up the management and leadership community where practice occurs but it will also include decisions about responsibility and the boundaries for work, and the attitudes of more senior staff.

---

45 Learn more about ZPD in Cheyne, J. A. and Tarulli, D. (1999) Dialogue, difference and voice in the zone of proximal development, *Theory and Psychology*, 9(1) 5–28.

46 See Lave, J. and Wenger, E. (1991) *Situated Learning: Legitimate Peripheral Participation*, Cambridge: Cambridge University Press.

47 See Fox, S. (1997) Situated learning theory versus traditional cognitive learning theory: why management education should not ignore management learning, *Systemic Practice and Action Research*, 10(6): 727–747.

In addition, there are always more formal rules and informal norms which to varying degrees allow or prevent particular kinds of practice.[48]

LEARNING TO LEARN

Whichever theory of learning is used, it is crucial that it set against the requirements for effectiveness that are provided in Figure 14.2. Those whose job it is to provide and facilitate leadership and management development need to ensure this, but so do leaders and managers themselves. In particular, they need to take more responsibility for their learning by explicitly recognising their skills for learning and the theories which underpin such skills. This is part of a supra-skill of learning to learn, defined by Mumford in 2001[49] as 'a process through which individual or groups understand the principle of effective learning, an acquire and continuously improve the disciplines and skills necessary to achieve learning'.

Conclusion

This chapter has sought to provide managers, leaders and developers with an overview of some the key theories and ideas which are being used in management and leadership development. Which are the most useful? A brief answer is 'all of them'. However, depending on your preference or prejudice, it is likely that either implicitly or explicitly, just one or two of them will be used.

While we must remember that informal learning is most common, it is also more difficult to influence from the outside. We will return to this below. However, all the theories offer some help in providing experiences for managers and leaders, both in the context of work or off-site.

Behaviourism is a good reminder of the importance of providing stimulus for learning and setting objectives or outcomes that can be used to set standards for performance. Reinforcement or feedback is required to ensure that changes in behaviour become embedded. However, cognitivism reminds us that managers and leaders are not 'empty boxes' – they do have brains, and how managers and leaders respond to stimulus, reinforcement and feedback will vary from person to person. Mental states, mindsets and thinking styles can all affect how managers and leaders prefer to deal with new ideas and skills presented.

The focus on individual variations and preferences comes through more strongly in experiential and social learning theories. Remember some of the limitations: it still remains likely that managers and leaders will gain value from understanding their learning preferences and how the cycle of learning needs to be completed. There is also a need to understand less preferred styles or orientations for learning and how this might affect the managing and solving of problems. Social learning theory in particular reveals the importance of a manager or leader's conviction that that they can complete particular

---

48   This kind of consideration starts to move towards seeing contextual influences as an activity system, a position derived from cultural historical activity theory. Go to http://www.edu.helsinki.fi/activity/pages/chatanddwr/activitysystem/ for more details.

49   See Mumford, A. (2001) *How to Produce Personal Development Plans*, Maidenhead: Peter Honey.

behaviours in certain situations, referred to as self-efficacy and the importance of the role of others as models of the source of mastering new behaviours. This latter point starts to open up the contextual elements in learning for managers and leaders.

Sociocultural learning, as informed by the work of Vygotsky, allows a widening of scope in learning, revealing the influence of culture in social tools such as physical artefacts but most importantly, language and other signs. With tools, managers and leaders are enabled to complete action and, through interaction with others, learn new tools. However, the process is seldom straightforward and older tools can restrain receptiveness to new ones, especially where particular ways of talking are considered essential to preserve a valued identity and subjective understanding. In addition, particular ways of behaving, talking and understanding become shared in local communities. Situated learning helps us consider the importance of everyday practice and what becomes accepted as the norm for behaviour as a manager and leader.

It is very easy to see how informal learning and everyday practice can soon become embedded in any organisation as an accepted way of doing things and trying new behaviours. In some contexts, there is support; in others, there is constraint or prevention or even hostility. We are now in the realms of what is usually called a learning culture or climate and, if research has shown one thing, cultures and climates in organisations are very difficult to change from the outside. However, there are significant possibilities for making a difference if managers and leaders themselves become interested in what enables and constrains learning in their organisations: this has to start with understanding themselves as learners and as models for others. Managers and leaders must learn to learn.

15 *Choosing and Using Exceptional Events for Informal Learning*

LLOYD DAVIES

Introduction

A major difference between pedagogic and informal learning concerns the matter of *choices*. In the formal, pedagogic situation, from the point of view of the learner, all learning at primary and secondary levels, and much at the tertiary level, entails very little choice over what is learned, how, where, or when, or even why it is learned. The informal learner, by contrast, is faced with innumerable choices; what experiences to invest time and energy in exploring, how to go about it, which external resources (if any) to call on, how to frame its lessons, when to give up and so on. So the prompts or cues which initiate informal learning seem worthy of consideration, not least because even seasoned professionals often attribute much, or even, most, of their expertise to what they have learned by doing as opposed to what they were taught.[1]

In the literature on learning, *experiential* learning is often used as a synonym for informal learning, but in the context of this chapter it is necessary to make a distinction between the two terms. From the first paragraph it can be seen that in informal learning the onus of *all* decisions is assumed by the individual – whether to pursue a subject, how to do so and so on. The same can be said for much experiential learning, but in many other learning situations *experiences* form an integral part of the pedagogic syllabus. Thus police cadets learn the theory of crowd control in the classroom, but then have to split

---

[1] The use of the word pedagogy in the context of management education has troubled earlier writers. Holman (2000) in Contemporary models of management education in the UK, *Management Learning*, 31(2): 197–217, for example, dismissed other terms and concluded 'pedagogical' is therefore used in a broad sense to refer to the process of learning, the outcomes of learning, and teaching methods. It is recognised that it is not an ideal label (p. 212). Pedagogy is therefore formal in the sense that the learner is beholden to another person for his or her construct of the process of learning. If I am interested in philosophy, or the technique of basket weaving, or the interpretation of the laws of rugby football, and pick up an appropriate book in order to learn about the subject, I am relying on the author's preconceptions as to how the subject should be presented, on his/her formal approach.

Informal learning, as introduced above, may very well lead on to formal learning. In informal learning, one of the data sources which someone might choose to consult to help elucidate an experience is 'formal knowledge', which is broadly defined as information which is in the public domain, or may be sought through research. Linda, following her difficult experience, might well have referred to managerial texts in order to clarify and develop her practice of delegation, and in so doing moved from informal to formal learning. Other learning outcomes, however, such as her observations of the warning signs of excessive pressure on a colleague, would probably remain as the product of informal learning.

into groups and experience the practice of linking arms and feeling the pressure exerted on them by their 'crowd' colleagues. Chemistry students carry out experiments to observe chemical reactions. Outdoor training centres put their participants through demanding physical experiences so that they can learn about themselves and their colleagues. In each of these three examples, the teacher or trainer responsible for the learning has thought out how the actual experience will, hopefully, contribute to the learning, and will probably be present to monitor it.

The literature generally treats informal and experiential learning together, without distinguishing between them Kolb[2] starts the analysis of the four-stage cycle with *concrete experience*, taking it as a given: 'the abstract/concrete dialectic is one of *prehension* … [in which knowledge of the concrete is gained] through reliance on the tangible, felt qualities of immediate experience, what I will call '*apprehension*'. Boud, Keogh and Walker,[3] in a less positivist model of experiential learning, also take the experience as given. Indeed, they introduce Stage 1 of their model as '*Returning* to Experience (my emphasis), making the point that 'one of the most useful activities that can initiate a period of reflection is recollecting what has taken place' (ibid.). Whilst one can agree entirely with this observation, it does not address the question of why the experience was chosen for reflection. Jarvis's[4] learning cycle moves nearer by addressing what we might call 'second order' choices, that is choices on whether to pursue an experience. Under the category of 'non-consideration':

> *For a variety of reasons people do not respond to a potential learning experience; maybe because they are too busy to think about it or because they are fearful of the outcome, or even because they are not in a position to understand the situation within which they find themselves … This is another response that occurs quite often in everyday life.*

(p. 36)

The implications here are that the experience has been recognised before being discarded, but he does not comment on the mechanisms of recognition – which elicit the first order choices.

Moon[5] identifies *noticing* as the first stage in learning, and within it notes 'constitutive factors' such as the learner's self-esteem or emotions associated with the material or situation. She adds that 'the last factor is that the learner will not learn what does not reach their attention. One of the roles of a teacher is to bring the material of learning to the attention of learners' (p. 141), so experiential learning is being brought back into the domain of pedagogy.

Still the question remains: what is it about an experience, or the potential learners, that makes one person recognise and use it whilst another person may not even recognise it, or if they do, learn quite different lessons from it? Let us look at one, rather extreme, experience to explore some of the factors influencing these first order choices.

---

2   Kolb, D. A. (1984) *Experiential Learning*. Englewood Cliffs, NJ: Prentice-Hall, p. 41.

3   Boud, D., Keogh, R. and Walker, D. (1985) Promoting reflection in learning: a model. In *Reflection: Turing Experience into Learning*, p. 27. London: Kogan Page.

4   Jarvis, P (1994) Learning practical knowledge, *JFHE*, 18(1): 35.

5   Moon, J. (1999) *Reflection in Learning and Professional Development*. London: Kogan Page, p. 141.

Failure to 'Think On'

'Thinking on' is the Yorkshire term for considering the future or planning ahead, and planning ahead is one of the central requirements of managers and leaders. The following account of a failure to plan ahead was told by Linda (not her real name, and the identity of her firm has been concealed).

Linda's experience of a potentially disastrous organisational mishap is typical of the problems which face many managers. She is a professional in a consultancy firm, running a small team which advises clients on a range of significant day-to-day issues. After establishing the team and working for two to three years to build up a useful client base, she was taking a week's leave, delegating – as usual – a senior colleague to 'run the shop'.

After four days, when I was actually at home, I got a message to say that my colleague had become very ill very unexpectedly. Fortunately the timing wasn't a major problem, but the situation we faced overall certainly was. There was no handover, and we couldn't phone clients to ask what were the outstanding issues.

There were several elements to the problem. I did not know how long my colleague would be away, nor was there any certainty about their condition on return – if indeed return was possible. This caused several problems with my colleague's clients, who naturally were concerned with their work issues. I had to keep their confidence, but I could not say what the problem was, nor the longer-term implications.

By moving work around, and by my taking on more senior work with clients, we were able to keep going – but it was touch and go.

I soon realised, however, that the short-term solution was at the expense of our longer-term viability. Taking on client delivery work meant that I was unable to pull in new clients, which we needed in the longer term. I reckon that at least half of my time as a director is being 'out there', attracting clients whose needs would then be satisfied by the team, but this half was seriously eroded, and the results in the second half of the business year showed it.

My MD was a great help. I was concerned about my senior colleague – would they come back, and could I trust them and put them in charge again? But he encouraged me to work on a worst-case scenario, in which my colleague either did not come back, or, even worse, did come back but wasn't up to the job, which meant that I had to get a replacement. Emotionally, this last bit was awful for me, but he pointed out that what was at stake was the viability of the team, the interests of the clients, and even the reputation of the firm, so I had to take some hard decisions. I had to recruit an experienced replacement, knowing that if my colleague returned with capability unimpaired there could be still further issues to deal with.

Alongside this I had to encourage and help the existing team to do more. I was doing a lot, lot more myself, trying to attract new clients, keeping existing clients confident in our ability to deliver, and doing more hands-on delivering myself. And I was conscious that my own health was at risk, so there were limits!

In the event, despite the dip in earnings, it has worked out quite well. My colleague is back and working satisfactorily, the team is bigger and stronger, and our client base has expanded. But it has taught me that planning for the 'under the bus' situation can be crucial for survival. I need a flexible and robust team; client perceptions are terribly important; and the lead time for getting new work is at least six months.

In one sense, there are no surprises here. Intellectually, Linda could have predicted almost all of this had she sat down and thought about it beforehand, but the fact was that, in common with many other managers, she had not.

However, the need for planning was not the only 'lesson' which Linda had learned from this experience. It had given her valuable insights into the capabilities and characters of a range of people – her boss, her immediate colleagues, her customers and – not least – herself. She had a much sharper focus on the principal elements of her own job, as leader, planner, organiser and especially as business winner. It had especially exposed her to the commercial nature of her business; what had previously seemed relatively easy to accomplish, so that it ranked equally with the other aspects of the job, now ascended in her priorities to pole position: without business coming in from clients, she was lost.

For Linda those six to nine months were what can euphemistically be called 'a rich learning experience'. As an informal learning experience it illustrates some of the cardinal elements of most such learning events; it started with a severe disruption of Linda's *expectations*; it evinced a number of sometimes acute *emotions*; and it demanded *opportunities* for periods of serious reflection, when Linda was considering how she had arrived at this potential disaster and what she should do in the future.

These three elements constitute part of what I have called *the infrastructure of reflection*.[6] An infrastructure is a 'structure of component parts', and in this sense, along with Linda's particular ways of making sense and learning from events, her *learning orientation*, these elements appear to come into play when we encounter one of life's events, inside or outside work, and intentionally or unintentionally expend some effort and time to learning from it. The greater part of this chapter will therefore be devoted to looking at some of the underpinnings of these elements, to exam their key characteristics, and to suggest ways in which individuals can harness them in order to derive the greatest benefit – the greatest learning – from their own experiences.

Although an exploration of Linda's own individual learning orientation is outside the scope of this chapter, it is worth noting some of her personal attributes which probably contribute to her ability to learn so much from this experience. She comes across as clear-minded, and ready to see things both as they are and as they could be. So the implications of losing a key member of staff, both in the short and longer terms, were readily apparent to her, as were the possible problems which could arise if her colleague returned to work with their former capability but then found a replacement in the team. Most managers would recognise the short-term problems, but not all would discern the longer-term knock-on effects. Another relevant part of her learning orientation was the determination and persistence both to stay with the problem to the point of solution and to devote time to reflecting on its significance for her future managerial behaviour.

Underlying all these features is Linda's openness to change. She appears willing to innovate, to experiment, to contemplate a range of possibilities before deciding on the

---

6   Davies, L. (2008) *Informal Learning: A New Model for Making Sense of Experience*. Aldershot: Gower.

best – as she sees it. A closed mind, by contrast, would probably seek reasons for retaining the status quo: the present problem could be an exceptional blip in normality; the cost of any solution involving change would be excessive; the longer-term implications would outweigh short-term benefits; and so on.

The many facets of learning orientation are probably the key to why different people learn different 'lessons', or perhaps no lessons at all, from a given experience. The circumstances described above which Linda faced represent a fairly extreme situation from which almost all managers could be expected to learn, but there are many less dramatic situations which do not demand such urgent attention but nevertheless have the seeds of precepts or principles which could inform future understanding or action. How we attend to these experiences is often dependent on our particular learning orientation.[7]

Expectations

Linda's expectations when she went on holiday, based on previous experience, were that her team would continue to function as normal. She had no reason to doubt the health of her colleagues, or to fear that they would not perform as usual. Reeve[8] points out that there are two kinds of expectancy, an *efficacy* expectation, dealing with the question 'can it be done?', and an *outcome* expectation – 'will it work?'. The performance of her team during her past absences encouraged Linda to make a positive response to both these questions.

Expectations occupy the first place in the 'infrastructure of reflection' for the somewhat paradoxical reason that it is their failure that usually initiates the sense-making, and thus the learning, that comes from experience. (Learning and sense-making are used interchangeably because for most adults informal learning is founded on the ability to make sense, to see the rationality, of the lessons that the experience offers. Only after quite persistent attempts to see the logic behind the lesson would most adults, and certainly, one would hope, most managers, consign the outcomes of the experience to the category of heuristics or even superstitions.) Our expectations of a familiar event, such as when Linda departed on holiday, are usually in default mode, that is we expect things will be as they have been in the past. So as we approach, say, a routine meeting or a normal journey, we expect they will follow predictable patterns. After the events, from the distance of a few hours or days, they are probably almost or totally forgotten.

When an expectation is confounded we become alert to the possibility of some learning. Louis and Sutton[9] identify three causes for engaging in sense-making (p. 60) all of which to varying extents prompted Linda to reflect on her problem. These are *novelty*, when something stands out from the ordinary; *discrepancy*, for example an unexpected failure, and *deliberative initiative*, usually in response to a request. So Linda's observation that clients were challenging her and her team's ability to deliver was a new and disturbing circumstance. The experience that in her absence her team was not functioning as

---

7   A fuller description of learning orientation, together with its necessary concomitant element of memory, is given in Davies (op. cit. footnote 5).

8   Reeve, J. (2005) *Understanding Motivation and Emotion.* Hoboken, NJ: John Wiley.

9   Louis M. R. and Sutton, R. I. (1991) Switching cognitive gears: from habits of mind to active thinking, *Human Relations,* 44: 55–75.

expected was certainly discrepant, contrary to the normal pattern, and her experience of recruiting a replacement, and then reintegrating her returning senior colleague, provided much food for thought.

The fact that her expectations were so rudely shattered would have prompted Linda to ask herself, and possibly others, some questions designed to help her sense-making. Given her previous experience of satisfactory delegation during her holidays and other absences, what was different this time? Obviously it was the collapse of her senior colleague, but how was it that she had not anticipated this? Had she left in a hurry, focusing only on work issues without looking at the conditions – morale, workload, abilities and of course, health – of her colleagues? Did she habitually behave in this way? Thinking about the senior colleague, was there anything in their background which could have prompted her to consider health aspects more carefully? Were there any work circumstances, such as abnormally taxing issues or particularly demanding clients, which she should have addressed? Were there any foreseeable pressures from elsewhere within the firm which could trigger problems – organisational as well as health? If the answers to any of these questions threatened the smooth working of her team, to what extent should she have advised her boss beforehand? And what contingency plans could she have made?

These are some of the questions which arguably should precede and accompany any act of delegation, especially one when the principal actor is moving out of the scene, and they certainly form part of the pre-absence planning which Linda adopts before taking holidays in the future.

Emotion

If discrepant expectations are the starting point of experiential learning, they are closely followed by emotions. Linda's words convey some of the emotions she felt: her body language as she talked, and her tone of voice, re-enforced the impression of an exceptionally stressful and problematic experience. Her initial feelings of dismay were quickly followed by the twin, and to some extent competing, emotions of concern for her colleague, whom she esteemed as a workmate, and the worry of getting the work done. Her boss, drawing on his managerial experience and being able to be objective in the present circumstances, provided valuable advice which could reduce the emotional load to some extent, but his insistence that she recruited an additional member of staff, who could accomplish her colleague's work, transferred the anxiety to the potential problems if and when the colleague returned with an expectation of picking up as before.

Clore[10] argued that 'a primary function of emotion is to provide information' which could be communicated to oneself and others, through expression and behaviour. The information provided for Linda, by paying attention to her range of emotions, was obviously that of prompting her to reflection and action. Several writers identify the prompting phase as the first in a sequence of sense-making activities. Weick[11] includes it as one of his Seven Properties of Sense-making 'focused on and by extracted cues'. He describes cues as 'simple familiar structures that are seeds from which people develop

---

10   Clore, G. C (1994) Why emotions are felt. In P. Eckman and R. J. Davidson (eds) *The Nature of Emotions*, pp. 103–122. New York: Oxford University Press.

11   Weick, K. E. (1995) *Sense-making in Organisations*, pp. 49–50. Thousand Oaks, CA: Sage.

a larger sense of what may be occurring'. He cites Starbuck and Miliken who call the prompting phase 'noticing', and distinguish it from 'sense-making':

> *Sense-making focuses on subtleties and interdependencies, whereas noticing picks up major events and gross trends. Noticing determines whether people even consider responding to environmental events. If events are noticed, people make sense of them; and if events are not noticed, they are not available for sense-making.*[12]

Whilst one could query whether only 'major' events and 'gross' trends are subject to noticing, the trained and experienced eye would surely pick up significant but less obvious features. It is clearly the case that for sense-making to occur there has to have been a prior phase of noticing or prompting, and the information from emotions fulfils this purpose.

Arguably, the greater the emotion, whether of dismay or surprise, the greater the need, up to a point, to pay attention to it and consider it. (The qualification is required because some events cause emotion so extreme in nature that cognition is not possible, at least initially. Close involvement in the 9/11 disaster, for example, would probably have inhibited rational sense-making for the first few hours.) Moreover, as Bower[13] points out, the inertial persistence of emotion, and its slow decay, ensure that this attention should be maintained. Linda was describing an event which happened a few years ago, and there is little doubt that she will remember it for the whole of her working life. Bower sums up:

> *emotion and memory are related by several different causal strands. The inertial persistence of emotional arousal, and its slow decay, leads to continued recycling or rehearsal of those encoded events viewed as causally belonging to emotional reaction.*

This in turn confirms the place of memory, along with learning orientation, as part of the infrastructure of reflection.

It is worthwhile reflecting on the function of emotions associated with an experience, to the 'recycling or rehearsal' of events, and the tendency to dig into them with a view to sense-making. Reflexive questions which Linda could have posed for herself would have been clustered around her dismay at hearing about her colleague's absence, and her fear that her remaining team, including herself, might not be able to accomplish their added workload. Specifically, she could have asked herself: why did my colleague suddenly fall ill – should I have noticed any tell-tale signs? Did I contribute to it? And thinking about her remedial actions: are we going to survive? if so, at what cost (in terms of both internal morale and health, and client expectations and confidence)?

Linda's boss's help would have been helpful in reducing the emotional weight which she felt, because he was able to move on to the practicalities of the situation by posing other questions and he was able to point out that her fears and concerns regarding possible re-entry problems if and when her colleague returned to an enlarged team, whilst understandable, were hypothetical, and in any case, once anticipated, could be prepared

---

12   Ibid., p. 52.

13   Bower, G. H. (1994) Some relations between emotion and memory. In P. Eckman and R. J. Davidson (eds) *The Nature of Emotions*, p. 303. New York: Oxford University Press.

for. In this way, he was acting as a mentor; being apart from the action, although fully understanding of it; he could advise by posing questions, challenging assumptions, exposing alternative viewpoints. He comes across as a skilled manager and leader in that Linda never implies that he instructed her, although as her line boss that would have been entirely possible, but rather teases out her own views on possible courses of action.

Before leaving emotions as one of the prompting elements for experiential learning, it is worth noting that emotions cover positive feelings as well as the negative ones described in Linda's experience. The progress of science, engineering and technology, for example, is littered with examples where researchers' expectations have been disrupted by phenomena which surprise them, raising emotions of curiosity and puzzlement, which urge the researcher to explore why this has happened. Fleming's discovery of penicillin is a classic of this type. At a more everyday level, curiosity leads people to investigation and learning. Thus if a colleague displays a facility for languages, or a skill in statistics, our surprise might prompt us to explore these abilities, and possibly to encourage their further use.

Returning to the case above, however, the emotional awfulness of the experience has prompted Linda to keep near the forefront of her mind the need to have contingency plans for the 'under the bus' situation. The 'inertial persistence of emotion arousal', to repeat Bower's words, works to ensure that this was an experience which would not be repeated. It prompted her to make time for, and devote energy to, the use of an *opportunity* to reflect on the past with an eye to the future.

Opportunity

The opportunity to reflect on Linda's experience as it unfolded was not optional but obligatory. She *had* to address the problem as soon as it presented itself for commercial reasons, and no doubt those of self-pride. However, many experiences, indeed arguably, most, do not have the impact of Linda's, and the question arises for a particular experience: is this worth reflecting upon with a view to deriving its lessons, and if so to what extent? Naturally, time is limited and there is an opportunity cost in considering one experience at the expense of others. The choices an individual makes are mainly influenced by the extent of expectation disruption and the accompanying emotions, and the individual's learning orientation. As noted above, a mentor can play a role, as can other involved colleagues, in prompting reflection and suggesting lines of thought.

Given that time is scarce, the question of *when* to reflect is worth a little examination. For many people, the movement and mobility associated with physical effort seems conducive to reflection. Thus driving or cycling away from a meeting (providing the traffic is not too stressful), jogging, working out in a gym, mowing the lawn, or simply being a passenger in a plane or train, provide opportunities for the consideration of whatever issues are taxing us. Other time-management strategies we have encountered include diarising time *after* meetings to provide space for reflection, revisiting one's notes not only to refresh one's memory but to spark further reflection, and consciously thinking about, that is reviewing, the events of the day before falling asleep in bed. One colleague said that he had learned that a period of reflection at about 3 a.m., far from being an unwelcome break in his sleep, was positively helpful in reviewing the previous day and preparing for the next!

Other strategies which afford opportunities for reflection can involve other people. A coffee break chat, a pint after work with a friendly colleague, and of course a formal team review session, all provide time to look back, to explore what went well, and why, and what could be improved. The input from colleagues is particularly helpful because the additional data they can provide, the different perspectives they bring and the increased range of questions they can raise all add to the richness of the data available.

Finally, on the question of opportunities for reflection, Csikszentmihalyi and Sawyer[14] exploring the subject of creativity, make the point that following a period of solid work during which no particular insights may have come, a period of incubation is often necessary. This gives the subconscious mind the opportunity to make connections between items of data which the conscious mind would not consider, leading to flashes of inspiration – eurekas – or simply to more helpful insights. Thus the periods spent cutting the lawn, jogging, lying in bed, or chatting over a drink and so on, can be viewed as periods of incubation.

The forgoing paragraphs, drawing principally on Linda's organisational problem, have described how expectations, emotions and opportunity, allied to her personal learning orientation and memory, serve to initiate processes of reflection. Perhaps they are so commonplace that they are often overlooked when we attend to the potentially more complex processes of reflection itself. The argument is that by paying some attention to them, by not taking them for granted but exposing them to the why?, what?, how? and so on, questions, some of the outcomes of reflection will be better informed and more relevant.

What Next? How can We Stimulate Reflection?

The greater part of this chapter has been structured around the account of Linda's initial failure to 'think on' and the analysis of her subsequent reflections – which led to her learning. We have identified the elements of *expectations* and *emotions* as being the prompts that alerted her to the seriousness of her situation – from which she was able to learn some very significant managerial lessons, and *opportunity* as the necessary time or space in which to consider both the short-term and longer-term implications of her problem. In this final section I suggest some generic approaches to these elements.

Before offering diagnostic questions relating to these elements, I set out below a few tips or suggestions of ways, of settings, in which to pose these questions.

WORK WITH A COLLEAGUE OR MENTOR

Many experiences are shared in the sense that an event or incident which seems important to you is also one in which one or more colleagues were involved or observed. The experience may have stimulated them to reflect upon it, in which case it is easy to gain their insights or explore their quandaries, and the probability is that your learning will be the richer for their input. Even if it was passing them by as a learning experience they would feel flattered to have their views canvassed. If on the other hand it was a

---

14   Csikszentmihalyi, M. and Sawyer, K. (1995) Creative insight: the social dimension of a solitary moment. In R. J. Sternberg and J. E. Davidson (eds), *The Nature of Insight*, pp. 329–363. Cambridge, MA: Bradford Books, MIT.

solo experience, you may be able to discuss it with a mentor (perhaps an official, formal mentor, or more likely an informal, generally older and hopefully wiser person whose views you trust, and whose observations are worth considering), that too can yield good results. Like a good colleague, a mentor can ask the unexpected but perceptive questions, and challenge your sense-making. As we observed earlier, Linda's boss was acting more as a mentor than exerting his line authority.

TAKE TIME TO ALLOW FOR INCUBATION

The evidence from a great deal of research, including that of Csikszentmihalyi and Sawyer when they interviewed many creative people, is that insights very often take time to surface. You may well have had an experience when the realisation suddenly dawns on you to clear up an issue or problem which occurred some while ago. This is not a recipe for procrastination; the first question to ask oneself is 'Does this matter need an immediate answer or solution?', and if the response is 'yes' then action is obviously needed immediately. Many matters are not of such urgency, and in these cases allowing time for incubation is usually very productive.

OBSERVE A COLLEAGUE OR FRIEND WHO IS GOOD AT LEARNING FROM EXPERIENCE

Someone you know may appear to be particularly shrewd or wise, and it is often useful to watch them and try to work out what it is about their behaviour that conveys this appearance. When making this sort of observation we are beginning to dig into their *learning orientation*, the other element of the infrastructure of reflection, so we may be looking at their personality, their ability, or at techniques they have learned for enhancing reflection. The point of doing so is, of course, to see what aspects of their behaviour leading to their shrewdness or wisdom can be transferred and adapted to ourselves, to develop our own learning orientation. We say 'observe' a colleague, but if you are able to discuss their behaviour this could be much more rewarding. You could find a quiet moment and open the subject by saying something like 'I was impressed by comments/conclusions/analysis you made on that situation, and I am wondering how you made sense of it in that way. I would appreciate some guidance, if you can spare the time.' They would probably be moved by your interest, and very willing to discuss their approach.

TEST SOME OF THE SUGGESTIONS IN THIS CHAPTER IN A NON-CRITICAL EXPERIENCE

It is generally worthwhile experimenting with new techniques in non-threatening situations to see how they work for you. So it would be matter of using some of the self-directed questions on the three elements we list below, and perhaps following up the broader suggestions given in the preceding three paragraphs.

Let us then return to the three elements, and look at some internal questions designed to help us make sense of experiences.

1. *Expectations*, which have been disturbed when an event has not gone as we would have predicted:

   - what were we expecting from this event?
   - were they based on earlier similar events?
   - why did we link this event with the earlier ones?
   - what was novel or discrepant about this event?
   - how did this event differ from its predecessors?
   - how could our expectations change in the light of this event (if at all)?

2. *Emotions*, which have been roused by the failure of expectations:

   - what emotions have been generated from this experience?
   - given that emotions convey information, what information flows from this emotion? (Examples: the frustration caused by an abnormally delayed car journey could be telling us to allow more time in future journeys. The discomfort at seeing a friend perform badly in a meeting could tell us that the friend was under exceptional stress, or that we don't know them very well, or even that they thought they were OK when everyone else thought just the opposite.)
   - don't overlook positive emotions: to what does our pleasure at this success owe its origins? (The answer could be good planning, our own ability, or sheer luck!)

3. *Opportunity*: thinking about the time and space needed to reflect on an experience:

   - what opportunities do I already take or make?
   - given that opportunities are closely related to time management, what time management techniques could be harnessed? (The time management literature would almost certainly offer some useful suggestions.)
   - how can regular events, such as routine meetings, have opportunities built into them?
   - how can other people's views (following the first suggestion above) be elicited?

These are a few suggestions. The best questions, those you are most likely to use, are the ones you have customised and made your own; but a word of warning – they not intended to operate within your own particular comfort zone! Almost all questions of this type should contain a degree of self-challenge. They will mostly lead to increased knowledge and understanding, either of yourself or the circumstances in which you operate, and gaining this knowledge may be uncomfortable insofar as it requires effort and/or reveals unexpected truths – but the good news is that you will be more capable as a result of it all.

Conclusion

This chapter has been about some of the tools that are useful when setting out to learn from experience. Just as chisels and planes can be used when making a very wide variety of objects, so the elements discussed above come into play when looking at a wide variety of experiences. And just as chisels and planes are not the only tools needed, learning from experience generally requires more than these elements. Some of the literature mentioned earlier could be of direct help in enlarging your range of management development activities.

16 *Evaluation*

LISA ANDERSON

Introduction

There are many different ways in which evaluation can be conceptualised, although there is a general consensus that it is one of the most problematic and challenging aspects of management development. Evaluation of management development is usually aimed at answering questions about a particular learning programme and the impact which it may have had. Definitions of evaluation often focus on the 'value' element of evaluation. The Institute of Value Management defines value thus:

> *The concept of value relies on the relationship between the satisfaction of many differing needs and the resources used in doing so. The fewer the resources used or the greater the satisfaction of needs, the greater the value.*[1]

In addition to this idea of assessing the value and worth of management development activities there is also the process of justifying investment and measuring the return on investment: 'Evaluation is concerned with establishing the success or otherwise of development activities, and with assessing whether the associated benefits justify the investment.'[2]

In short, management development practitioners are under increasing pressure to prove the impact of their work in order to justify their continuing presence and their budgets. In doing so, they need to be clear about exactly what they are trying to achieve and be able to offer some form of measurement of their performance. This is particularly difficult given the nature of much of the 'soft' skills development which management development encompasses.

In this chapter, we consider a wider view of evaluation which takes in this notion of assessing the value of an investment, mainly carried out in a retrospective manner, but also considers how the evaluation of management development may be seen as *evolutionary*, that is, a key activity in the transformation of managers and organisations. In other words, we emphasise the potential of evaluation to be a 'prospective' practice.[3]

---

1   The Institute of Value Management: http://www.ivm.org.uk/vm_whatis.htm.

2   Stewart, J. (1999) *Employee Development Practice*. London: Financial Times.

3   I have borrowed the terms 'retrospective' and 'prospective' from Alan Mumford who first used them to describe approaches to management learning: Mumford, A. (1989) *Management Development Strategies for Action*. London: IPM.

You will also find here a summary of the debate surrounding the purposes of evaluation which provides a good starting point for a review of organisational evaluation activities and the range of attitudes which may exist towards them. A number of established models and methods of evaluation are discussed, including the ubiquitous Kirkpatrick model and its derivatives, which have dominated the evaluation landscape for over 40 years. We offer a framework for thinking about evaluation at three levels and present descriptions and case studies of a number of approaches and methods.

We hope that reading this chapter gives you the opportunity to reflect critically on your evaluation philosophy and practice and we encourage you to question your 'espoused' theory and your 'theory in use'[4] of evaluation.

The Purposes of Evaluation

The first step any evaluator needs to take is to consciously decide on the purpose or purposes of their work. Mark Easterby-Smith[5] suggests four possibilities:

1. Proving.
2. Improving.
3. Learning.
4. Controlling.

PROVING

If your evaluation sets out to prove the impact and worth of training and development, usually using some kind of cost–benefit analysis, then it falls into this category. This notion of 'proving' is linked to assessing the value of a programme. It is often used by public bodies to assess the payback from investments in projects and may include an analysis of gross value added (GVA) which measures the contribution to the economy of a particular sector or industry.

A less formulaic approach to proving the value of training and development activities is the use of 'stakeholder evaluation'[6] which seeks the views of all those with an interest in the programme (e.g. learners, trainers, bosses, funders) in order to assess its value. Stakeholder evaluation can be likened to 360° appraisal, producing a rounded or balanced picture of, in this case, a learning programme rather than solely representing either the trainer's or learners' views.

IMPROVING

This approach is also known as formative evaluation and is focused on improving the learning programme. The type of information collected here is particularly useful to the

---

4   Phrases created by Argyris, C. and Schön, D. A. (1978) *Organizational Learning: A Theory of Action Perspective*, London: Addison-Wesley, to expose the difference between how managers describe their practice (to themselves and others) and how they actually behave.

5   See Easterby-Smith, M. (1994) *Evaluating Management Development, Training and Education*. Aldershot: Gower.

6   An approach defined by Professor John Burgoyne.

trainer as it deals with process rather than outcomes and is helpful in assessing which elements of the programme were particularly effective for learners. However, learners may often be impressed with elements of the programme which are particularly enjoyable rather than potentially impactful on their work performance, so this method of evaluation is not only partial but may have little to do with the learning experience and more to do with the 'fun' factor in learning programmes. If we were to use this approach as our sole means of evaluation, trainers might be tempted to become crowd pleasers rather than facilitators of learning.

LEARNING

When evaluation activities have learning as a central purpose then they become collaborative, involving learners, trainers and evaluators (of course, very often trainer and evaluator are the same person). In this approach, there is no dividing line between the measurement of process and outcomes because they are interlinked. There is no artificial divide between what the trainer does and how the learner reacts to it, followed by an 'objective' assessment of cause and effect. The 'learning' approach to evaluation recognises the fluid and unpredictable nature of many learning experiences and acknowledges the influence of learners on any programme, rather than suggesting that trainers have total control in manipulating processes and outcomes.

CONTROLLING

This approach to evaluation is most often seen in large-scale learning efforts aimed at producing consistent behaviours in a large group of people. It is characterised by standardised and closely measured learning outcomes and is typified by the way in which the UK government uses the National Curriculum to standardise learning outcomes and encourages parents to judge schools on the basis of their national curriculum test results. National Vocational Qualifications are used in a similar way and individual or collective attainments are used as measures of evaluation. Many organisations use their own competency frameworks as a way of both designing and evaluating learning programmes. For an example, go to http://group.tnt.com/career/Leadershipdevelopment/CompetencyManagement/index.asp.

In addition to the above purposes, we might add another – influence.[7] This is an acceptance that findings from evaluation can be used to persuade others. For example, the continuation of a programme might require convincing results especially if it requires additional funding.

Deciding on the Evaluation Approach

The notion that evaluation approaches are based on an overall philosophy of management development provides a good starting point for thinking about how evaluation should take place. It is worth taking some time to think about your own philosophy; you may

---

7   Influence as a purpose of evaluation is suggested by Alan Mumford and Jeff Gold (2004) *Management Development Strategies for Action*. London: CIPD.

then choose to carry out your evaluation in line with your principles of management development. You may wish or need to take some to time to articulate these ideas as they often remain tacit and as such, may be woven into your practice yet difficult to describe in concrete terms.

Evaluation is often seen as an 'add-on' to management development practice as if the imperative were for the evaluator to work in a detached and distanced way from a learning programme. Whilst this audit approach may occasionally be useful, it does not allow for the learning which comes from evaluation to be fed back into the programme in real time. Also, in most cases, the trainer/developer *is* the evaluator so any attempt to take on the role of auditor is essentially flawed.

Case Study

Prospective evaluation

'Everyone has a Customer' was a year-long management development programme run by an external consultant for a major retail distributor in the north of England. The programme formed part of a change management exercise in the company, emphasising key messages about quality products, excellent service and partnership whilst developing managerial behaviours that focused on meeting the needs of both internal and external customers.

The consultancy which delivered the programme ensured that evaluation was carried out in a prospective way so that information gained from evaluation activities was used both to give feedback to the board about the progress of the learning programme and to adapt it to learner and business needs as these changed.

Plenty of informal evaluation occurred as a natural part of an ongoing dialogue between facilitator and learners; this was captured by the facilitator and used and incorporated into future sessions. Formal feedback was simple in format but powerful in terms of the information it produced; rather than just asking for feedback on the learning event itself, participants were asked to provide examples of changes which had occurred as a result of their learning. A later 'Pulse Check' evaluation exercise asked managers to think about company-wide projects which could add most value to 'Everyone has a Customer', the changes they could make in their own departments and their own leadership behaviours. The Pulse Check also asked managers about the feedback they thought they would receive from their team members and colleagues on their new behaviours and to plan their next steps.

The consultancy ensured that the programme had an ongoing impact on individual managers, departments and the business but did this in a way which was intrinsically linked to learning and development rather than detachedly gathering data which might somehow 'prove' that the learning was of value.

Consider the conceptions of management development shown in Table 16.1: they cover ideas of how learning may occur, what the relationship between trainers/developers and learners should be, how the organisational frameworks for learning might support learning processes and where the investment focus for evaluation could lie.

The links between conceptions may seem axiomatic; for example, behavioural approaches to learning seem to link well with other ideas at the same level such as the systematic training cycle. However, this is not always the case. If we examine Reid and Barrington's[8] purposes of evaluation framework, we can deduce their philosophy (shown in Table 16.2).

Table 16.1   Conceptions of management development

How individuals learn	Relationship between trainer/developer/ evaluator and learner	Model of learning and development	Investment focus
Changing behaviour as the result of instruction	Trainer in control as purveyor of knowledge	Systematic: structured and planned with clear steps	Clear learning objectives and behavioural outcomes for individuals (bottom-up approach)
Experiential: cyclical and thoughtful	Consultant	Dynamic: ongoing reassessment of needs perhaps linked to a competency framework	Business focus; bottom line measures (top-down approach)
Socially: by imitating others and/or participating in communities of practice	Partner	Integrated into work and management practice	Holistic focus on individuals and the business

Table 16.2   Reid and Barrington's purposes of evaluation framework

Evaluation purpose	Implied philosophy
It enables the effectiveness of an investment in training to be appraised in general terms and provides data that can justify expenditure	Business focus: bottom line measures (top-down approach)
It provides feedback to the trainer about their performance and methods	Trainer in control as purveyor of knowledge
It enables improvements to be made either in an ongoing way or on the next programme	Systematic: structured and planned with clear steps
It is an intrinsic part of the learner's progression around the experiential learning cycle	Individual learning as experiential: cyclical and thoughtful
It indicates which objectives have been met and where further training needs remain	Based on the systematic training cycle: structured and planned with clear steps

---

8   Reid, A. M. and Barrington, H. (1999) *Training Interventions*. London: CIPD.

It would seem that Reid and Barrington's overall philosophy towards learning and development is reflected in their evaluation approach. The implicit messages behind this evaluation approach are that it should be closely linked to the needs of the business, it is based on the experiential learning cycle[9] and that evaluation provides information for learning needs analysis (as per the systematic training cycle model).

We suggest that the starting point for evaluation is for everyone involved to have a clear idea of the philosophical basis for management and leadership development activities and for their evaluation. In large organisations, it is possible that individuals hold divergent views which can be surfaced through dialogue. However, small organisations and even one-person consultancies should not assume that they are immune from this tendency to operate without a clear set of principles and concepts which serve as a guide for practice.

Kirkpatrick's Model

No review of the work on evaluation is complete without an examination of Donald Kirkpatrick's[10] 'Chain Reaction' model of evaluation (Figure 16.1). This is the approach which most trainers and developers attempt to employ. It is based on the principle that there are five distinct stages of learning and change which can be measured to gauge the impact of the learning programme:

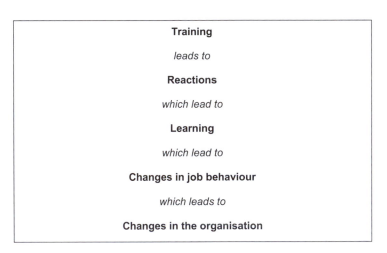

Training

leads to

Reactions

which lead to

Learning

which lead to

Changes in job behaviour

which leads to

Changes in the organisation

Figure 16.1 Kirkpatrick's chain reaction model

---

9   First developed by David Kolb in 1984.

10   This model shown here is based on Kirkpatrick, D. (1959) Techniques for evaluation programs, *Journal of the American Society of Training Directors (Training and Development Journal)*, 13(11): 3–9; (1059) Techniques for evaluation programs – part 2: learning, *Journal of the American Society of Training Directors (Training and Development Journal)*, 13(12): 12–26; (1960) Techniques for evaluation programs – part 3: behavior, *Journal of the American Society of Training Directors (Training and Development Journal)*, 14(1): 13–18; (1960) Techniques for evaluation programs – part 4: results, *Journal of the American Society of Training Directors (Training and Development Journal)*, 14(1): 28–32.

In this chain reaction model, evaluation starts with a formative look at the processes used on the programme, moving onto the measurement of reactions – how trainees felt about the programme and how they responded to various aspects of it. These reactions lead to learning, measured against learning outcomes set for the programme; in some cases, evaluators may also try to assess whether there are any unintended learning outcomes. This learning should result in individuals changing their behaviour in the workplace (in line with the learning outcomes) which will ultimately lead to changes in organisational performance.

If you were to ask a large group of trainers which approach to evaluation they used, many of them would say the Kirkpatrick or chain reaction model. In practice, the chain often breaks down when attempts are made to link learning outcomes achieved on the course to the effects on job behaviours and evaluation is then limited to an assessment of reactions through an end-of-course questionnaire and some testing of learning outcomes which can be built into the programme methodology. The reason this happens is that it is very difficult to measure learning transfer – when learners attempt to apply what they have learned in a training room in their normal work environment. One study shows that on average, 62 per cent of employees apply what they learn in training on the job immediately after the training event, 44 per cent are still applying it six months later and 34 per cent one year after training. It's quite worrying to think that 38 per cent of employees who attend training courses do not change their behaviour at all as a result of attending. Other studies suggest the transfer of learning over time seldom rises above 10 per cent!

The final step in the chain reaction evaluation process is the most problematic of all. This is particularly the case with management development because the way in which organisational impact can be measured is much less quantifiable than, for example, trying to assess the bottom-line effect of a compulsory accident-prevention programme in the workplace. The problem lies in trying to disentangle and then reconnect individual learning and organisational performance in a sterile 'cause and effect' way rather than acknowledging that a wide range of factors impact on how organisations perform and trying to understand which of these can be affected by management development initiatives. It is for these reasons that many organisations do not try to evaluate management development (MD) beyond the reactions stage and accept its contribution to organisation performance as an 'act of faith' – although we think they can do better.

Variations on the Kirkpatrick Theme

The idea that learning should be evaluated at a number of levels has been incorporated into a number of other models.[11] Rosemary Harrison[12] combines two models to produce her *CIRO* framework which suggests what the focus of evaluation should be. This model acknowledges the 'reactions' and 'outcomes' elements of the Kirkpatrick model and suggests that 'context' and 'inputs' should also be held up to scrutiny. It provides a more rounded view of where the focus of evaluation should lie but, as with other models considered so far, presents a picture of evaluation as a clear process with discrete steps

11   See, for example, Whitelaw (1972), Hamblin (1974).

12   Harrison, R. (2000) *Employee Development*. London: CIPD.

and measures. This seems to happen because the originators of such models base their work on the idea that management itself is a planned and ordered activity (as classical management theorists such as Fayol and Taylor would have us believe[13]) rather than understanding management as practice and devising management development learning and evaluation activities which reflect this view.

Modes of Learning

As you may have noticed, many of the models we have referred to so far derive from work which was carried out in the 1950s, in an era when it was quite acceptable for Kirkpatrick to make the observation that 'Most training men agree that it is important to evaluate training programmes'.[14] To illustrate how different approaches to evaluation are likely to be needed in a range of twenty-first-century management and leadership development situations, we draw a distinction here between two types of learning activity. The first we have called *abstract* learning approaches, covering learning programmes which generally take place off-the-job and have relatively fixed learning outcomes. These are the type of management development activities upon which many models of evaluation are based. The second category we have called *person-centred* learning. This includes techniques such as coaching, action learning and mentoring which are increasingly viewed as essential to effective management development

In making this distinction, we are emphasising the importance of basing evaluation measures on those philosophical choices described earlier in the chapter.

Abstract learning approaches include the many management and leadership development interventions that take the form of courses. These can be as short as half a day in duration or may involve attendance over a long period of time, particularly when they lead to a qualification. There will normally be a prescribed set of learning outcomes to be achieved by learners on the programme and one of the first stages of evaluation is to attempt to measure whether or not these learning outcomes have been achieved. In practice, however, this is sometimes the first *and* final stage.

Person-centred approaches to leadership development such as mentoring, coaching and action learning are much more clearly focused on personal development which is not fixed to any specific learning outcomes. Although it is possible to apply a chain reaction approach to person-centred learning, it is unlikely to produce helpful results. Rather than proving the value of the development initiative, evaluation in this case is much more likely to focus on learning and can be a collaborative activity between trainer (or coach/mentor) and learner. This does not mean that quantitative techniques cannot be used; in fact, when the evaluation focuses on one person, it is easier to produce figures to show how their learning has had an impact on the business.

---

13   Henri Fayol (1947) and Frederick Taylor (1949) presented their ideas of management as a rational, ordered and scientific activity. Although more recent studies have shown that the management task is complicated and characterised by disorder, earlier conceptions persist, perhaps because they offer a clear framework through which to understand management and upon which to base management development activities.

14   An excerpt from Kirkpatrick's classic 1959 paper.

Conceptualising Management as Practice

Anyone who has ever been a manager or been involved in or read an empirical study of managers will dispute the fact that management can be reduced to clear set of knowledge indicators, arranged in an orderly framework. This desire to crystallise the essence of the management task into a simple algorithm has been driven by concerns of government, academics and some managers themselves to professionalise management.

The MBA is seen as the pinnacle of achievement in the amassing and accreditation of management knowledge. However, there is plenty of evidence to suggest that MBA graduates are far from being the 'finished article' despite their accumulated knowledge. Mintzberg[15] is particularly scathing of MBA providers, students and the systems which surrounds them. He argues that management is neither a science nor a profession but a 'practice'. He criticises the MBA for its content and its approach to teaching and learning, resurrecting the old joke that the acronym actually stands for '*Management By Analysis*' to the exclusion of soft skills development and any discussion of the ethics of being a manager. He dismisses the claim that business simulations replicate the real-world environment as 'patent nonsense' and suggests that the case study method reduces management to decision making and analysis, ignoring the tacit dimension of managing. This leads to a second-handedness or third-handedness in learning which does nothing to prepare students for the realities of managing a business.

Clearly, there is a need to ensure that management development activities focus not only on what managers need to *know* but also on how they need to *be*. This idea of *being* a manager draws attention to the central activities of building relationships and promoting dialogue in the manager's role. In order to be effective, managers therefore need to have high levels of self-awareness and self-efficacy which can be enhanced by identity development work which is often a feature (although sometimes an unintended one) of management development.

So what does all this have to do with evaluation? It takes us back to the set of philosophical choices discussed earlier in this chapter and emphasises the need for developers and evaluators to be clear about the context in which the evaluation takes place. This notion of context goes further than Harrison's suggestion that evaluators pay attention to the organisational, analytic and diagnostic contexts. We suggest that there should be a recognition of how management *happens* within an organisation and the powerful role that management development and its evaluation can play in bringing about significant change in both arenas of knowledge and practice.

A Framework for Evaluation

Work carried out in the Northern Leadership Academy suggests that there are three possible levels of evaluation as shown in Figure 16.2.

---

15   Mintzberg, H. (2004) *Managers not MBA's*. Harlow: Pearson.

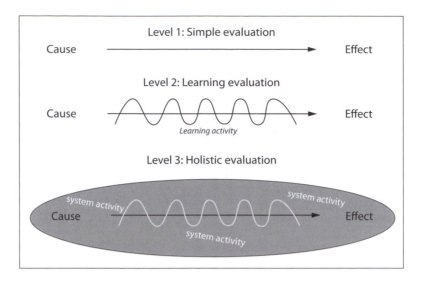

Figure 16.2 Levels of evaluation

Level 1: Simple Evaluation

Simple evaluation is typified by the chain reaction model; the evaluator identifies the prompts for change and then attempts to connect these to their effects. It is a simple and easily understandable way of collecting and analysing evaluation data. Evaluators are likely to be detached from the process (or adopt a quasi-detached position if they are involved in delivering the programme) and perhaps from the learners themselves, preferring to use 'hard' data to draw their conclusions. These data include information from end-of-course questionnaires to assess the learners' reactions, job performance information and ROI (return on investment) calculations.

A NOTE ON LEARNING TRANSFER

The Level 1 approaches described here are based on an assumption that learners will be able to apply any newly learned skills and knowledge in their workplace. However, this is not always the case; learners may lack the motivation to change their behaviour on their return to work and the environment in which they work may not support the intended changes. Bosses and colleagues are important in this respect; attempting to change one's practice whilst others remain sceptical or indifferent is difficult. It may well be that the learning event itself prompted new ideas and end-of-course evaluation would show that it had achieved its objectives. This is rather like claiming that the operation was a success but the patient died. Evaluation should seek to assess learning which persists; level 2 techniques (especially learning journals) attempt not only to measure how much learning has taken place but to ensure that this does not stop once the learning programme has ended.

Level 2: Learning Evaluation

At this level, the focus is still on cause and effect but there is a much heavier focus on the learning that happens in order to bring about those changes. Here, evaluators pay more attention to the process of learning than at Level 1 and this will probably involve including learners in the evaluation.

Level 3: Holistic Evaluation

At Level 3 there is an acknowledgement that cause, effect and learning are all important and interconnected but that any learning programme operates within a system and there is a need to understand how the system impacts on the learning event and vice versa. This involves asking some 'Why?' questions about the design and delivery of the programme and some 'How?' questions about the impact on colleagues and on the bottom line. Evaluating at this level provides information which can be used to inform organisational policy and strategy.

Evaluation Techniques

Having decided the purpose and level of evaluation, the next step is to decide on the techniques which are best suited to them. Choice of evaluation techniques depends on two main issues:

1. The level at which the evaluation is being carried out.
2. The time which has elapsed since the learning event took place (of course, some evaluation happens *during* the event itself).

Figure 16.3 gives examples of techniques and the appropriate level and timescale for their use.

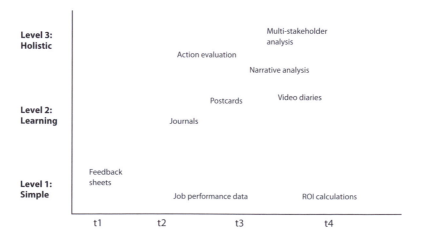

Figure 16.3 Examples of techniques

Level 1 Techniques

FEEDBACK SHEETS

End-of-course questionnaires or 'Happy Sheets'[16] are often what pass for evaluation on many programmes and although they attempt to assess both the effects of the learning event and the learners' reactions to it, they provide little more than a glimpse of how learners intend to apply their learning and are rarely followed up. Such questionnaires have become part of the ritual of training and development activities; trainers feel that they should issue one and learners feel short-changed if they do not complete one. There is a question about any purpose they really serve apart from making the trainer feel good (or bad) about themselves and for gaining feedback on things which can only be changed for the next group of learners (for example, the quality of the accommodation and the food). Evaluation should be concerned with assessing how learners learn and change rather than awarding marks for the trainer's performance. This type of evaluation could also encourage learners to place all of the responsibility for their learning on the trainer rather than acknowledging that this responsibility should be shared.

Return on Investment Calculations

This is the holy grail of evaluation for many people; the ultimate in the 'scientific' approach. Return on investment (ROI) is a technique derived from financial analysts which uses the formula shown in Figure 16.4.

On paper, this looks sensible and useable: in practice it is quite the opposite, particularly for leadership development activities. Calculating the costs of a programme are relatively easy, if somewhat time-consuming and disputable; the problem lies in defining gains made from a leadership development programme. For example, if the aims of a programme are to promote better communication and to encourage managers to become more entrepreneurial, it becomes difficult to make clear links between these objectives and business outcomes because of the effort and uncertainty involved in disentangling all of the variables involved as well as the likely time lag between learning and outcomes. If, however, you were to use one of the Level 2 or Level 3 techniques, you could still measure impact on the business without losing the thread of how learning, action and business performance are connected.

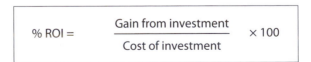

$$\% \ ROI = \frac{\text{Gain from investment}}{\text{Cost of investment}} \times 100$$

Figure 16.4 A simple ROI formula

16   Blanchard, P. N. and Thacker, J. W. (1999) *Effective Traning Systems, Strategies and Practice*, Englewood Cliffs, NJ: Prentice Hall, refer to end of course feedback sheets as 'love letters' or 'happy face data'.

Return on investment calculations are useful when they are used as part of a holistic evaluation that has a systemic aspect. The following case study shows how management and leadership development interventions often form part of a wider change programme, and as such should be evaluated in the context of the wider business and the environment in which it is operating. The Alliance and Leicester example illustrates how ROI calculations can take many forms including a calculation of cost savings, feedback from customers and employees and an analysis of actual performance against targets:

Case Study

Leadership and management development at the Alliance and Leicester

Alliance and Leicester Commercial Bank (now part of the Santander Group) is a subsidiary of Alliance and Leicester plc, one of the UK's major financial institutions. It provides competitively priced banking for all sizes of businesses; it is a market leader in cash management, handling more than £1 in every £5 of high street cash in the UK. Alliance and Leicester commercial bank employs around 1,500 staff.

During a strategic review in 2004, a new HR strategy was developed alongside the business strategy, ensuring that the people aspects of change were fully aligned to deliver business requirements. The HR strategy maximised an investment in technology by developing the organisational culture to deliver 'first touch' resolution of customer enquiries wherever possible.

The transformation programme has been a major theme across the commercial bank and has exceeded the bank's expectations against the agreed success criteria. A review has highlighted cost reductions of 30 per cent and achievement of ongoing service level targets. The culture of the operation is also changing, with an increased focus on customers, all positively reflected in the annual staff employee opinion survey.

A key driver was to change the approach of team managers, developing them as people managers to coach and develop their teams improving overall performance and effectiveness. A new organisation structure was designed as well as an assessment process which was outsourced to a specialist occupational psychologist. The HR team also developed a Leading Change programme with an external training consultancy to equip managers to support their teams whilst implementing major changes to jobs, team structures and technology. Training on 'experiencing change' was also provided to help staff with the changes they faced.

The Leading Change programme supported senior managers and team leaders in developing their leadership skills and giving a clear context on the message of change within the business. HR also led the communication strategy where senior managers briefed their teams so that everybody understood the strategy, the vision and the plans to deliver them.

The business achieved a 30 per cent cost reduction through implementing this strategy whilst customer service improved through quicker resolution of customer enquiries. 400 staff left the organisation through voluntary programmes with no business disruption and an improved working approach with unions is reported. A number of new team managers with key leadership skills were recruited alongside a number of new staff specifically into contact centres with relevant skills and experience.

Level 2 Techniques

Evaluation-led leadership development characterises evaluation as an activity which is integrated into the whole process rather than something which is tagged on at the end of a project. Evaluation is not a treatment which is applied to learners and the intervention but something which happens collaboratively and has beneficial outcomes for a range of stakeholders.

Level 2 evaluation techniques blend learning and evaluation by making evaluation part of the individual's learning process. Three example techniques described here:

1. journals;
2. postcards; and
3. narrative analysis.

JOURNALS

It is a widely accepted fact that reflection is one of the key components of effective learning. Nearly all of us reflect on what happens to us on a daily basis, perhaps mulling over the day's events on our journey home from work; thinking 'out loud' to our family and friends or coming up with bright ideas in the shower. Most of the time, these reflections are strikingly consistent but those bright ideas may never come to fruition. The reason for this is that the link between reflection and action is often tenuous. Learning journals are designed to help learners turn reflection into action. Leadership and management development programmes should help learners form insights into their own practice. Recording these thoughts and making decisions helps managers to think about how they might change their behaviour as a result and prompt them to take action.

Learning journals are also useful in that they can help to maintain the heightened consciousness of the learning process, which tends to decrease dramatically once learners return to work or end a programme. This occurs by ensuring learners keep a focus not only on what has been learned (in the past), how it might make a difference to practice (in the present) but also on the future opportunities for them to learn. This evidence of 'prospective' learning illustrates how learning programmes can have an impact on management practice in the long as well as the short term.

Case Study

Making sense of leadership in the voluntary and community sector

This programme, sponsored and co-organised by Greater Merseyside ChangeUp was designed to help leaders and managers in third sector organisations develop clear ideas about what it means to be in a management role in a voluntary, community or faith organisation; traditional models do not always translate well into this diverse and growing sector. A learning journal was incorporated into the programme to promote reflection and to help the programme team evaluate how learners were making sense of the programme and implementing their learning. This ongoing reflection enabled learners to bring 'real time' examples into the learning events and to be critical of theories and models which were presented.

A final session, held three months after the main programme had ended, contributed to the evaluation by asking participants to share excerpts from their learning journals, with a particular emphasis on how their practice had changed as a result of their learning.

The journal asked learners to focus on a number of key issues and provided a framework for reflection:

Section 1: Where am I now?

The first step in creating a journal is to think about where you are now. What kind of leader are you? What do you find easy about your role? What are the most challenging aspects? Which parts do you enjoy and which are the bits you dread?

What are the key leadership challenges which you currently face?

Section 2: Where do I want to get to?

What are your learning goals? Why are you willing to devote so much of your time to this programme? What do you want to get out of it? This may seem like a simple question to which the answer may be 'I want to be a better leader' but what does that mean for you?

Try to be specific in the goals that you set.

Section 3: How have I learned best in the past? How will this help me now?

Everyone learns in different ways. Some people are happy to listen and 'soak up' other people's knowledge whereas others can't sit still and listen for more than 20 minutes. Some learners can find inspiration in a book but others don't get past the first two pages. Some will tell you that there is no substitute for experience whereas others feel nervous at the thought of the 'error' in trial and error learning.

What kind of learning works best for you? How will you use this consciousness of your learning skills to help you now? Who do you need to help you?

Learners may also be asked to provide a 'highlight report' of the programme using their journal as the basis. In this way, information can be collected about three things:

1. *The process.* Learners' highlight reports provide evidence of which elements of the programme had the most impact upon them. These individual learner's stories show which topics have the most resonance for learners and which learning methods they responded to most positively. This is a useful way of measuring the impact of a programme on learners without setting up a scoring system for the trainers or the accommodation.
2. *Learning transfer.* By asking learners to record how they have changed their practice as a result of a programme, evaluators can gain insight into some excellent examples of learning transfer and make an assessment of which elements of the learning had little effect on learners' behaviour.
3. *The extent of 'learning to learn' skills.* Management and leadership development interventions should aim to give learners new skills and insights into their ability to learn in a range of circumstances. Evidence from journals can help to show if these metacompetences have been developed.

POSTCARDS

Postcards provide an excellent example of how evaluation should reinforce and extend the learning once the event has ended. Learners are asked to provide feedback on a learning event, often by reflecting on how their behaviour may have changed whilst helping them maintain a consciousness of their learning objectives and goals. Learners may be asked to reply to an e-postcard – an email or series of emails asking open-ended questions, requiring short answers – or you can use the old-fashioned way of supplying them with a series of real postcards with questions printed on them. The questions you ask will depend on the objectives of your programme, but here are some examples:

*   What was the most significant part of the learning programme for you? Why?
*   How have you changed your leadership practice as a result of something that happened to you on the programme?
*   When do you find time to reflect on your leadership practice?
*   What have you learned today?
*   What have you told your colleagues about the programme?
*   How will you use your learning from the programme to benefit others in your organisation?

Both journals and postcards involve leaders writing about their experiences; the written word is a powerful way of encouraging learners to give a considered view of how an experience may have helped them to improve their leadership practice. However, you may wish to use the spoken word to collect evaluation data and the next technique provides an example of how to do this.

NARRATIVE ANALYSIS

'Narrative' is a broad term covering stories, myths, fables, tragedy and painting.[17] When we use this phrase, we mean that we are interested in the stories that managers tell of their learning experiences. Giving learners the opportunity to tell a story out loud helps us capture the unique nature of individual experience and provides a richness that the written word does not always produce. As part of the learning experience, recounting events and feelings to someone else helps learners to make sense retrospectively of what has happened to them and often provides new insights in the telling of the story.

Storytelling can happen collectively as part of an evaluation 'event' which brings learners back together to reflect on how a programme has affected their leadership practice or narrative accounts can be collected from individuals. Evaluators may use a digital voice recorder to capture what is said rather than trying to write down snippets of information; you can even encourage individual learners to record their own accounts of learning and practice and send them to you for evaluation purposes.

Case Study

Analysing narrative accounts at Fujitsu Services

A pilot project at Fujitsu Services, supported by academics at the Universities of Liverpool and Lancaster, aims to evaluate the impact of management development interventions by analysing how managers talk about themselves and their work before and after experiencing a learning event. So far, the study has analysed interviews with a small number of managers who have attended the Fujitsu Management Academy's *High-performing Teams* event (an internally run programme). Managers were asked a series of open-ended questions before the event covering issues such as how they would describe themselves as a team leader and what they see as the elements of an effective team. Similar questions were asked shortly after the event and feedback on how individual managers might have changed their practice was also sought.

Transcripts of these interviews are then analysed using a software tool called Wmatrix* which is a tool for linguistic corpus analysis and comparison. This analysis provides information not just on the frequency of the words used but the context in which they are spoken. When the interviews with the Fujitsu Services managers were analysed using this method, it showed that after the learning event, they used certain words, much more frequently than before; for example, 'leadership' figured much more strongly than 'management' when participants were asked about new ideas. This could point to a change in attitude and practice which, when followed up, could then be used both to 'prove' the impact of a learning event and to pinpoint any unintended consequences of the learning programme.

* Rayson, P. (2008) Wmatrix: a web-based corpus processing environment, Computing Department, Lancaster University. http://ucrel.lancs.ac.uk/wmatrix/

---

17 For a comprehensive account of the nature and significance of organisational stories, see Gabriel, Y. (2000) *Storytelling in Organisations*. Oxford: Oxford University Press.

Level 3 Evaluation

Evaluation at this level takes account of the causes and effects of the changes brought about by the programme as well as the learning which prompts these changes and the impact, not only on individual learners but on a range of stakeholders within the system in which the programme is operating. This system might be confined to an organisation including its customers and suppliers or it may be much wider than one organisation especially if the programme is publicly funded. Two level 3 approaches have been described here: action evaluation places an emphasis on goal-setting by stakeholders whereas multi-stakeholder evaluation, referred to earlier, involves a retrospective analysis of the effects of a programme.

Both of these level 3 approaches require the evaluator to collect and analyse 'hard' (i.e. countable and quantifiable) and 'soft' (i.e. concerned with perception, attitudes and feelings) data. They allow us to achieve a well-rounded picture of how an event or programme has touched anyone with an interest in it. At first sight, they can appear daunting in terms of the amount of people to be consulted and the array of accounts and opinions to be listened to. However, they are scalable; you can choose to collect information from a sample of people who represent your stakeholder groups and you do not necessarily have to interview them all face-to-face.

Action Evaluation

Action evaluation (AE) was first developed as a technique aimed at conflict resolution within organisations.[18] Stakeholders of a learning event or programme are identified and are asked to set goals and to discuss the values and motivations associated with those goals. Actions based upon the achievement of these goals are then agreed. The goals become the focal point of the learning and the action taken and provide a touchstone for learners' reflection and feedback. Goals are continuously reassessed and redefined in the light of action taken and insights gained. The dynamic nature of goals means that evaluation is integrated into the programme and becomes the focal point of learning.

Conclusion

In this chapter, we have advocated an approach to evaluation which places it in a central rather than peripheral role to a learning event, experience or programme. This approach emphasises the need to keep learning objectives in clear focus and to start evaluating them both in terms of whether or not they are being reached and whether they are still appropriate and useful. There is not always a requirement for an *independent* evaluator: the ability to carry out this type of evaluation by management development providers themselves is one of the hallmarks of good practice. Acknowledging that elements of a programme need to change is not an admission of defeat but a recognition that the learning needs of the organisation and its groups and individuals are dynamic in nature.

---

18   For further information about action evaluation, go to http://www.aepro.org.

Evaluators need to be clear about their own conceptions of management knowledge and practice and how these may affect the learning and evaluation processes. Similarly, it is essential that the philosophical choices upon which management development is based are surfaced, discussed and acknowledged as the context for evaluation.

In summary, the successful evaluation of management development exists when a culture of feedback is created in a learning programme or intervention. This feedback can be obtained from a number of sources; the learners themselves, providers and facilitators and other stakeholders on whom the programme is likely to have or designed to have, an influence. The evaluation philosophy proposed here stresses the need for a high concern both for the learning experience itself and the likely impact of changed behaviours on the business.

Advanced Processes and Tools

17 *Neuro-linguistic Programming for Leaders and Managers*

PAUL TOSEY

Introduction

This chapter offers an introduction to neuro-linguistic programming (NLP) and its relevance for managers and leaders.

NLP is a practice that is used widely in management and leadership development. NLP training providers exist around the globe; the UK Association for NLP estimates that in the region of 30,000 participants have attended practitioner training courses in the UK over the past 25 years.[1] In 2008, more than 50 NLP training schools were operating in the UK alone.[2] As evidenced by literature from NLP associations, websites, magazines and conferences, it is used by professionals not only in business but also in education,[3] health,[4] law, the arts and more. It became a recognised mode of psychotherapy in the UK in the 1990s.[5] There are many popular publications that introduce NLP and its applications to business, such as Sue Knight's *NLP at Work*.[6] The UK's leading association for human resource professionals, the Chartered Institute for Personnel and Development, has a factsheet on its website about NLP and offers related training courses.[7]

Examples of practitioners' accounts of using NLP in business can be found in NLP magazines and websites. For example, *Rapport*, the magazine of the Association for NLP (ANLP), has reported on a communications skills training programme for the insurance company, Towergate,[8] and sales training in Coutts Retail.[9] In recent years NLP has been

1   Personal communication, Karen Moxom, ANLP Director, July 2008.

2   As listed at http://www.nlpconference.co.uk/training_schools.php, in September 2008.

3   See Churches, R. and Terry, R. (2007) *NLP for Teachers*. Carmarthen: Crown House.

4   See Henwood, S. and Lister, J. (2007) *NLP and Coaching for Healthcare Professionals*. Chichester: John Wiley and Sons.

5   See Wake, L. (2008) *Neuro-linguistic Pscyhotherapy: A Postmodern Perspective*. London: Routledge and The UK Council for Psychotherapy; http://www.psychotherapy.org.uk/index.html, accessed 16 September 2009.

6   See Knight, S. (2002) *NLP at Work: The Difference that Makes a Difference in Business*. London: Nicholas Brealey Publishing.

7   http://www.cipd.co.uk/subjects/maneco/general/nlp, accessed 16 September 2009.

8   See Coote, A. (2007) Walking in the shoes of the client: Towergate professional risks, *Rapport,* 10(Winter): 35–36.

9   Goodman, J. (2006) Team building, *Rapport,* 5(Autumn): 22–23.

marketed as a method of coaching, literature on which includes Grimley,[10] Linder-Pelz and Hall,[11] McDermott and Jago,[12] McLeod[13] and O'Connor and Lages.[14] As indicative data, nearly 400 of the practitioners listed on the ANLP website offer coaching as a service.[15] There is also much interest in NLP for leadership development;[16] in England, NLP has figured in the Fast Track development programme for teachers.[17]

Because NLP is about human communication in general, it can be applied to virtually any aspect of management and leadership, including self-management, presentation skills, managing meetings, setting targets, enhancing confidence, negotiation and so on. Sue Knight, who is well-known for her excellent work in applying NLP in business, gives this example:

> When Unipart managed a turnaround of its business against all market predictions, it did a number of things. One was to change the way that it ran meetings. Managers recognized that the emphasis in their meetings previously had been on problems, even though they were nominally called progress meetings. They acknowledged that they did not consider or imagine what they really wanted from their meetings or their projects prior to considering how to get there. So they began every meeting with a discussion of what they did really want – an outcome.[18]

This illustrates that NLP is outcome-focused; typically it suggests that people attend to what they do want, not to what they do not want. To build on this it encourages people to make their outcomes specific and 'well-formed', which has some similarity to the idea of making objectives SMART specific; measurable; achievable; realistic; timely. NLP refines this, however, by facilitating people to create an image or 'representation' of their outcome as it will be when it has been achieved. A similar principle is used in sports psychology to promote positive attitudes and effective performance. For example:

> Genie Laborde (1983: 14–18) describes coaching an engineer in a computer manufacturing company. The engineer, Jim, asks that she teach him to 'get out of his own way'. For a while he is only able to state what he wants to stop, such as feeling frustrated and upset. Laborde encourages him to identify what he wants instead. Eventually he identifies an outcome, saying that he wants to feel satisfied with his ability. By tapping into one of Jim's past experiences, Laborde finds that Jim has felt satisfied when he looks at the product of his work, then says to

10   Grimley, B. (2007) NLP coaching. In S. Palmer and A. Whybrow (eds), *Handbook of Coaching Psychology: A Guide for Practitioners*, pp. 193–210. London: Routledge.

11   Linder-Pelz, S. and Hall, L. M. (2007) The theoretical roots of NLP-based coaching. *The Coaching Psychologist*, 3(1): 12–17.

12   McDermott, I. and Jago, W. (2001) *Brief NLP Therapy*. London: Sage.

13   McLeod, A. (2003) *Performance Coaching: The Handbook for Managers, HR Professionals and Coaches*. Carmarthen: Crown House.

14   O'Connor, J. and Lages, A. (2004) *Coaching with NLP*. London: Element Books.

15   http://www.anlp.org/, accessed 16 September 2009. The ANLP is a membership organisation which practitioners join by choice, not a professional association, therefore its listings do not represent total numbers of practitioners.

16   For example, see Deering, A., Dilts, R. and Russell, J. (2002) *Alpha Leadership: Tools for Business Leaders who want More from Life*. Chichester: John Wiley and Sons.

17   See Hutchinson, G., Churches, R. and Vitae, D. (2007) *NCSL London Leadership Strategy, Consultant Leaders to Support Leadership Capacity in London's PRUs and EBD Schools*. Reading: Impact Report, CfBT Education Trust and the National College for School Leadership.

18   Knight (2002) op. cit. p. 80.

himself, 'that's a pretty good project'. The look of satisfaction on Jim's face as he recalls this experience provides behavioural evidence to support this. Laborde therefore helps Jim to identify the strategy he naturally uses to be satisfied with his ability. It involves Jim being able to see a representation of his work, then hear himself say 'that's a pretty good project', after which he feels the feeling of satisfaction.

This, of course, is just one small part of NLP, and more examples of applications follow below. What it illustrates is that NLP typically attends to the way people create their outer experience through their inner world. In the above examples, both the Unipart managers and Jim were, in effect, assisted to use their creative imagination to help them focus on their goals.

Its pragmatic emphasis can make NLP attractive within business settings. Yet it remains poorly understood, and prominent among the questions that managers, leaders and others raise are:

* What exactly is NLP?
* Is there research behind it?
* Does it have any theory?
* Is it safe to use?
* What can I use it for?

This chapter offers some comment on and, hopefully, some insights into, these questions. It reviews the origins of NLP, describes its working methods, and gives examples of how it can be applied. It then identifies key issues that are of concern to practitioners, users and researchers.

What is NLP?

NLP is an emergent, contested approach to communication and personal development, created in the 1970s, that has proved difficult to define.

The title 'NLP' reflects the principles that a person is a whole mind–body system, with consistent, patterned connections between neurological processes ('neuro'), language ('linguistic') and learned behavioural strategies ('programming'). It has been suggested that the founders, Bandler and Grinder, created this as a deliberately quasi-academic, tongue-in-cheek title.

In promotional literature NLP has been described as 'the art and science of human excellence in ... communicating'.[19] It can be understood as an innovative form of practical knowledge, comprising a wide range of frameworks, tools and techniques, which are presented in a copious popular literature and taught in training programmes.

A different type of definition is offered by NLP author Robert Dilts,[20] which is 'the study of the structure of subjective experience'. In highlighting the notion of 'study', this definition acknowledges that originally NLP was presented as a methodology, called

---

19   http://www.john-seymour-associates.co.uk/whatisnlp.htm accessed 19 September 2008.

20   Dilts, R., Grinder, J., Bandler, R. and DeLozier, J. (1980) *Neuro-linguistic Programming: Volume 1, The Study of the Structure of Subjective Experience*, p. 2. Capitola, CA: Meta Publications.

modelling,[21] the purpose of which was to investigate exemplary communication. I will describe the way NLP evolved shortly.

Early NLP publications espouse the autonomy of the individual and emphasise the potential for self-determination through overcoming learnt limitations.[22] Its motives were described, on the book jacket of *The Structure of Magic*,[23] as 'sharing the resources of all those who are involved in finding ways to help people have better, fuller and richer lives'. It embodies a discourse of self-improvement and, like the more recent field of positive psychology, emphasises well-being.

NLP attends to what works in practice, and values usefulness above theory. For example, the founders said – perhaps provocatively and a little disingenuously – 'We have *no* idea about the "real" nature of things, and we're not particularly interested in what's "true"'.[24]

NLP is also defined sometimes with reference to a number of working principles called 'presuppositions'. This is a collection of propositions and aphorisms espoused by, or derived from, the key figures who influenced NLP (Virginia Satir, Fritz Perls, Gregory Bateson and Milton Erickson, whose roles are described in the following section). For example:

- Mind and body are part of the same cybernetic system.
- The map is not the territory.
- There is no failure, only feedback.
- The meaning of your communication is the response that it gets.
- Every behaviour has a positive intention.
- People have all the resources they need to make changes.
- People make the best choices that present themselves to them.

For a more detailed discussion of the meaning of these principles see Robert Dilts' website (listed in the resources section) or Tosey and Mathison.[25]

It should be clear, therefore, that NLP does not boil down to a neatly packaged, logically consistent theory. Among other things, NLP was created in order to be used and has been developed through practice. The direction of this development has been emergent, not pre-planned, and was certainly not theory-led.

---

21   See Bandler, R. and Grinder, J. (1975a) *Patterns of the Hypnotic Techniques of Milton H.Erickson, M.D., vol. 1*, p. 6. Cupertino, CA: Meta Publications.

22   For example, Bandler, R. (1985) *Using your Brain for a Change*. Moab, UT: Real People Press.

23   Bandler, R. and Grinder, J. (1975b) *The Structure of Magic: a Book about Language and Therapy*. Palo Alto, CA: Science and Behavior Books.

24   Bandler, R. and Grinder, J. (1979) *Frogs into Princes*, p. 7. Moab, UT: Real People Press.

25   Tosey, P. and Mathison, J. (2009) *NLP: a Critical Appreciation for Managers and Developers*. Basingstoke: Palgrave Macmillan

Where Did NLP Come From?

NLP was developed in the 1970s by Richard Bandler, then a student, and John Grinder, an associate professor of linguistics, at the University of California, Santa Cruz. The founders went their separate ways several years ago.[26]

The story of the development of NLP appears to be one of a chance meeting of several creative minds. The gist of the story is that Robert Spitzer, publisher of Science and Behaviour Books, met the young Richard Bandler (then aged 17) in the early 1970s. Impressed by his skills, Spitzer invited Bandler to transcribe tapes of Fritz Perls, the founder of gestalt therapy, for a book that Spitzer wanted to publish.[27] Perls, who had died in 1970, was a key figure in the emergence of Esalen in California the 1960s as a centre of the growth movement. Spitzer also knew Virginia Satir, the renowned family therapist and wanted to produce a book about her work too,[28] so he asked Bandler to record her workshops on video. Bandler became so deeply interested in Perls and Satir that, apparently, he began to behave in similar ways, not just adopting their mannerisms but also demonstrating the same skills.

Bandler went on to attend Kresge College, at the University of California, Santa Cruz, in 1972. Kresge was a new, experimental college[29] that offered credits for students to run their own courses. Bandler began to offer experiential group sessions, and invited along John Grinder, an associate professor. Grinder, some eleven years older than Bandler, had a Ph.D. in linguistics[30] and a background in US intelligence work.[31]

Grinder joined with Bandler and others in various groups that experimented with personal development over the next two or three years. Some of those who became involved, such as Judith DeLozier, Steve Gilligan and David Gordon, remain key figures in NLP or related practices today.[32] Several of these people came to live in properties on land owned by Robert Spitzer.

Significantly, another person who later became resident there (in 1974) was Gregory Bateson, who had taken a part-time appointment at the University of California at Santa Cruz in 1972.[33] He had met Bandler and Grinder at Kresge and commented on the manuscript of their first book, *The Structure of Magic*.[34] Bateson was an English academic whose writing has influenced diverse fields including family therapy and communications studies. He was a prominent member of the Macy conferences, which began in 1946 and laid the foundations for the science of cybernetics.[35] In the 1950s, human communication became the main focus of his work, when he developed the 'double-bind' theory of

---

26   See McLendon, T. L. (1989) *The Wild Days: NLP 1972–1981*, p.117. Cupertino, CA: Meta Publications.

27   Perls, F. (1973) *The Gestalt Approach and Eyewitness to Therapy*. Palo Alto, CA: Science and Behavior Books.

28   Bandler, R., Grinder, J. and Satir, V. (1976) *Changing with Families: A Book about Further Education for being Human*. Palo Alto, CA: Science and Behavior Books.

29   See Grant, G. and Riesman, D. (1978) The Perpetual Dream: Reform and Experiment in the American College. Chicago, IL: The University of Chicago Press.

30   Grinder, J. T. (1971) On Deletion Phenomena, Ph.D., University of California, San Diego.

31   Dilts, R. and DeLozier, J. (2000) *Encyclopedia of Systemic NLP and NLP New Coding*, p. 460. Scotts Valley, CA: NLP University Press.

32   Ibid.

33   Lipset, D. (1980) *Gregory Bateson: The Legacy of a Scientist*, p.279. London: Prentice-Hall.

34   Bandler, R. and Grinder, J. (1975b) op. cit.

35   http://www.asc-cybernetics.org/foundations/history/MacySummary.htm, accessed 16 September 2009.

schizophrenia.[36] Bateson is probably the most important single intellectual influence on NLP, according to NLP literature such as *Turtles all the Way Down*,[37] Dilts and DeLozier's *Encyclopedia*,[38] and *Whispering in the Wind*.[39] Bateson also introduced Bandler and Grinder to Milton Erickson, one of the world's best known hypnotherapists. As a result, Erickson's distinctive use of language patterns became another key ingredient in the mix that became known as NLP.

This story of the origins of NLP emphasises that while there are clearly identifiable influences and antecedents, both practical and theoretical, NLP emerged through the creative interaction of people, and not through premeditated theoretical work. If we liken this to an alchemical process, we might say that Robert Spitzer provided the crucible in which Bandler, Grinder and others interacted, and from which NLP was formed.

The Meta-model

The Structure of Magic introduced the core language model of NLP, called the 'meta-model', which remains central to the field. If the appearance of the word 'magic' in the title prompts scepticism, we must remember that Bandler and Grinder were not claiming to be magicians. Their explicit project[40] was to show that the abilities of charismatic practitioners like Satir and Perls, whom many *perceived to be* magical, had structure and could be learnt by others. Their intent was actually to demystify practices, challenge the accounts of practice espoused by professionals, identify aspects that worked and enable these aspects to be learnt by others.

Based on Chomsky's ideas about language at the time, the meta-model categorises certain transformations, or ways in which the 'surface structure' of verbal communication can differ from the 'deep structure', which is effectively a fuller description of experience. These transformations, which are described in detail in *The Structure of Magic*,[41] arise through processes of deletion, distortion and generalisation, which sound undesirable but in fact help to make our communication more concise.

A good illustration of this, according to McDermott and Jago,[42] is Harry Beck's classic London Underground map (also known as the Tube map).[43] As a representation of London this *deletes* a huge amount of detail. For example it shows no streets or parks – the only geographical feature is the schematic representation of the River Thames. In terms of ease of use, for the purpose of travelling by Tube, you only have to compare Beck's map with a street map of London. On the latter it is difficult enough to identify stations, let alone track the lines.

36   Bateson, G., Jackons, D. D., Haley, J. and Weakland, J. *et al.* (1956) Toward a theory of schizophrenia, *Behavioral Science*, 1(4): 251–264.

37   DeLozier, J. and Grinder, J. (1987) *Turtles All the Way Down: Prerequisites to Personal Genius.* Bonny Doon, CA: Grindler, DeLozier and Associates.

38   Dilts, R. and DeLozier, J. (2000) op. cit.

39   Bostic St. Clair, C. and Grinder, J. (2001) *Whispering in the Wind.* Scotts Valley, CA: J and C Enterprises.

40   Bandler, R. and Grinder, J. (1975b) op. cit. p.6.

41   Ibid.

42   McDermott, I. and Jago, W. (2001) op. cit.

43   See the Transport for London website, http://www.tfl.gov.uk/, accessed 16 September 2009.

Second, Beck's map *distorts* in several ways. Thus the orientations of the Tube lines are stylised; they are either vertical, horizontal, or at 45° angles. Distances between stops are not to scale, so do not correspond to geographical distances. Nor are distances consistent on the map relative to each other (for example, from Piccadilly Circus to Oxford Circus is longer on the map than from, say, Baker Street to St John's Wood; in geographical distance the reverse is true).

The third feature is *generalisation*. An example is the way that all stations are shown as one of two symbols; either a small notch of the same size adjacent to the line, or a small circle if it is an interchange. Stations are treated as quite uniform, despite large differences in size, layout and facilities.

By virtue of its judicious use of deletion, distortion and generalisation, the Tube map is both functional and aesthetic. If it were more 'accurate', in terms of maintaining proportions and features we find in physical reality, it would probably be far less effective. Thus for travelling on the London Underground, Beck's map is excellent, while for finding one's way around the streets of London it is virtually useless.

The Tube map serves as a handy reminder of a central tenet of NLP, taken from Alfred Korzybski via Gregory Bateson,[44] which is the idea that 'the map is not the territory'. The same principle applies to verbal communication; it is like a map. Typically when someone else speaks, instead of seeking to understand more about the 'deep structure', the listener quickly, and largely subsconsciously, searches their own experience and constructs to make sense of the other person's words. In NLP this process is called a 'transderivational search',[45] which means that our brains make sense of other people's communication by searching across (trans) a variety of possible meanings and related contexts (derivations) until they find a reasonable fit. People don't always stop to check the validity of this sense-making.

To find out what another person is thinking or experiencing in more detail in any specific instance, we would need a way to elicit further information. The meta-model provides this, with forms of question that enable these more specific, and perhaps uniquely situational, meanings to be revealed. For example:

A coaching client complains about the need for 'better communication'. Using the meta-model, the coach can discover more by asking questions such as the following – remembering of course that the tone of voice used to ask these questions is also highly important:

- Who, specifically, is communicating with whom in an unsatisfactory way, and how specifically are they doing this?
- Better than what, specifically?
- What would happen if there wasn't 'better communication'?
- What stops person X communicating better with person Y?
- And so on …

The responses might reveal any of a wide range of issues; for example, the client could be feeling left out because they heard some important news second-hand; they could

---

44   Bateson, G. (2000) *Steps to an Ecology of Mind: Collected Essays in Anthropology, Psychiatry, Evolution and Epistemology*, revised edn. Chicago, IL: University of Chicago Press.

45   Bandler, R. and Grinder, J. (1979) op. cit. p.15.

be experiencing conflict with a colleague; or they could be advocating expenditure on training to improve the level of interpersonal skills in the company.

Bandler and Grinder also put forward the claim that matching the sensory predicates of another person's communication will influence the effectiveness of that interaction. For example:

> Sally's boss, Edith, uses visual terms in her everyday language (for example, 'things look bleak to me'; 'I need clarity on this'). Sally's own natural responses were either auditory ('I hear what you're saying') or kinaesthetic ('I grasp your meaning'). This meant that Sally was mismatching Edith's preferred sensory mode; Edith felt misunderstood and Sally was frustrated that her genuine attempts to empathise with Edith were unsuccessful. Sally then learnt to respond by matching Edith's visual terms ('I see what you mean'), and found that this helped to build rapport. Now she was in sympathy with Edith's way of processing information.

Thus NLP argues that forms or patterns in communication, such as the sensory mode of words in the above example, are often more significant than the content. Bandler and Grinder observed that effective communicators used these patterns skilfully, whether or not they were conscious of doing so. Less effective communicators tended to use their own preferred sensory mode regardless of that used by the other person.

NLP Applications in Business

While its origins lay in the study of psychotherapists, and its early books were addressed mainly to people in helping professions, the late 1970s saw something of a shift towards a more commercial market. NLP began to be offered as a public training in personal development and communication, with certificates denoting levels of expertise.

Business applications also began to appear at this time. The first published example was probably Grinder's adaptation of the NLP 'meta model', renamed for the business market as 'The precision model'.[46] The book refers to its contents as the 'technology of management' and carries a foreword by Dr Paul Hersey (of Hersey and Blanchard fame). Nowhere in this volume do the authors use the title 'Neuro-linguistic Programming'; the book jacket simply suggests that there is a need for management development theories to keep pace with breakthroughs in fields including neuropsychology. The categories of the core NLP language model, which were labelled with terms taken from academic linguistics, are re-named as 'blockbusters'. There is no reference to Bandler and Grinder's previous publications, or to the work from which the precision model was derived.

Internal Representations

NLP's insights into the structure and operations of people's internal imagery are also highly significant in its approach to people development. The role of internal representations in NLP was noted earlier, in the example of Genie Laborde working with Jim's outcome. Our

---

46   McMaster, M. and Grinder, J. (1980) *Precision: A New Approach to Communication*. Bonny Doon, CA: Precision Models

internal representations are a whole world of experience, yet some people can go through life blissfully unaware that this dimension exists. Those who discover this realm are often able to use it productively and creatively. For example:

> *Anne worked with a client, Felicity, who was extremely nervous about a forthcoming meeting. In particular Felicity was anxious about how to deal with a colleague, June, who had been something of a thorn in her side. Anne asked Felicity to notice how June looked 'in her mind's eye'. She replied that June was very large and close up, 'in her face'. In other words, Felicity's internal visual representation of June was a picture in which June was large – in fact larger than life-size, and larger than Felicity – and very close. Felicity said she felt hemmed in and panicky. Anne asked Felicity to explore what would happen if she were to move the image of June and change its size. As a result, Felicity discovered that she could make June smaller (in her mind's eye of course) and move her further away, far enough to give Felicity some breathing space and help her calm down. As it turned out, this was all Felicity needed to feel able to handle the meeting. She did not need to be coached in any other skills or strategies; the way she was representing June internally was the difference that made the difference.*

NLP has many ways of exploring the nuances of, and the dynamics of, internal representations. It is common to find, as in this example, that when a person can notice and start to experiment or play with these representations, the changes they were seeking begin to happen. This introduces another central plank of NLP, that it is first and foremost about enquiring into people's experience of the world, or the way they construct and create experience; it is not about trying to change the outer world. NLP is concerned with the meaning people make of events, which it sees as flexible and variable. Thus in the above example, it would have been contrary to NLP, and probably futile or worse, for Felicity to attempt to change June. The focus of the work was Felicity's construction of June as a scary prospect to handle.

State, Calibration and Rapport

NLP also works with bodily experience. In NLP, a person's physiological and neurological configuration is called their 'state'. If you are in a resourceful state then you are probably in a balanced posture, with freedom of movement, breathing regularly, feeling positive and generally sensing that you are capable. This would contrast with a state in which someone is anxious, breathing in a very shallow way, feeling physically frozen or rigid, and perhaps telling themselves that they are not good enough.

Generally NLP suggests that it is preferable to be in a positive state. It does not follow, however, that 'negative' emotions should be avoided, as some people appear to believe. More precisely, NLP suggests that one's state needs to be appropriate for the purpose (or outcome) at hand. A manager might want a very different state for a prominent business presentation compared with that for playing with their family on the beach, or compared with that for supermarket shopping.

Some NLP techniques, such as one known as the 'circle of excellence'.[47] are designed to improve one's 'state management' – the ability to change state intentionally. Thus:

The client accesses a number of highly positive experiences from their past, each time stepping into a vivid, imaginary circle in front of them. The combination of the positive experiences becomes linked or 'anchored' to the imagined circle. Then, whenever the person wants to access feelings of confidence and resourcefulness in future, they can imagine themselves stepping into that circle.

NLP emphasises that we have a degree of choice about our state. How much choice is possible is an issue for debate, as sometimes the degree to which control is possible or desirable seems to be exaggerated. The advantage of the NLP way of thinking about state is that instead of waiting until we get what we want before we feel good, we could choose to feel good first, which might in turn help us get what we want. In case that sounds odd or inauthentic, something like this has been shown by psychologist Richard Wiseman[48] to be a characteristic of people who experience good luck.

'Calibration' refers to observation of someone's state and their non-verbal behaviour. Sometimes, for example, we sense it is just not the right time to ask the boss for a day off, or we know as soon as we pick up the phone that the caller has good news. According to NLP these apparent intuitions are thought to result from sensory observation that is happening outside conscious awareness. A similar view is put forward by Malcolm Gladwell in his book *Blink*.[49]

In NLP it is deemed especially useful to be able to calibrate *changes* in another person's state, as this provides evidence of whether one is on track towards the relevant outcome. Earlier, the example of Genie Laborde coaching Jim mentioned her observation of non-verbal evidence that he was accessing feelings of satisfaction. Good sales people are excellent at calibrating whether a prospective buyer has any remaining objections. They will therefore deal with those objections rather than trying to bulldoze through the sale.

Skills of observation and calibration have played a part in NLP from the beginning. The first part of the *The Structure of Magic 2*.[50] is in one respect about the ability of effective psychotherapists to calibrate auditorily to whether a client's predicates are primarily visual, auditory or kinaesthetic. Most significantly, Bandler and Grinder learnt new possibilities of calibration from Milton Erickson, who exhibited an exceptional capacity for fine sensory discrimination.[51] Accordingly, NLP takes the view that people generally underuse the potential of their sensory apparatus, and NLP training is in part an endeavour to make fuller use of capacities people already possess.

Finally in this section, much emphasis is placed on the principle of rapport in NLP. This was discussed originally in NLP using the term 'trust' rather than 'rapport'.[52] In principle it should be easier to achieve a purpose with someone after rapport is established.

---

47   See Laborde, G. Z. (1988) *Fine Tune Your Brain: Next Steps to Influencing with Integrity*, p. 172. Palo Alto, CA: Syntony Publishing.

48   See Wiseman, R. (2004) *The Luck Factor: The Scientific Study of the Lucky Mind*. London: Arrow Books.

49   Gladwell, M. (2006) *Blink; The Power of Thinking Without Thinking*. Harmondsworth: Penguin.

50   Grinder, J. and Bandler, R. (1976) *The Structure of Magic 2: A Book about Communication and Change*, p. 14. Palo Alto, CA: Science and Behavior Books.

51   See for example Erickson's foreword to Grinder, J. and Bandler, R. (1976) op. cit. p. vii.

52   Grinder, J. and Bandler, R. (1976) op. cit. p. 14.

As a result, NLP is sometimes stereotyped as being about manipulating other people by mimicking their non-verbal behaviour in order to generate rapport artificially, and accused of encouraging inauthentic behaviour. Such instrumental use of non-verbal behaviour seems more likely to be counterproductive. We might also bear in mind that many social rituals – such as asking 'how are you', complimenting someone on their appearance, or showing sympathy for a misfortune – are regarded as natural and 'authentic' because they are socially and culturally familiar. Most of the time people create rapport in such ways without thinking, and people who are reckoned to be exquisite at these skills, for example Bill Clinton, are widely admired for this. If attending to this dimension of interaction consciously in order to improve one's social ability is seen as inauthentic, it could create a bind for someone who wants to improve in this area.

Modelling

As noted above, NLP began as a methodology called modelling,[53] which was the process used to identify the effective communication patterns used by Satir, Perls and Erickson. Bandler and Grinder both still emphasise modelling as the core process that generates NLP applications, for example through investigating exemplars of a chosen capability.[54]

Modelling is therefore more than a technique in NLP, it is a method for making human capabilities available for others to learn:

> The objective of the NLP modeling process is not to end up with the one 'right' or 'true' description of a particular person's thinking process, but rather to make an instrumental map that allows us to apply the strategies that we have modelled in some useful way.[55]

NLP can explore how human skills are constructed through sequences of representations. It can also identify the difference between the sequences used in excellent performance of that skill, and those used in less effective performance.

Modelling has been used to identify cognitive strategies that lie behind capabilities such as motivating oneself, negotiating and so on. A good practical guide is that by Gordon and Dawes.[56] For example, it has been suggested that people who are good at telephone communication will make an internal visual image of a successful outcome to their call before they pick up the phone – a simple strategy with which anyone can experiment to gauge its impact. Charles Faulkner, an internationally known NLP trainer and author, has modelled the intuitive judgements of leading traders, using the results of his modelling to become a successful trader himself. An interview with Faulkner about this work appears in

53   Grinder, J., DeLozier, J. and Bandler, R. (1977) *Patterns of the Hypnotic Techniques of Milton H. Erickson, M.D., vol II,* p. 4. Cupertino, CA: Meta Publications.

54   The nature of modelling is contested within NLP. Dilts emphasises a more conscious, analytical approach that employs conceptual frameworks, whilst Grinder (Bostic St. Clair and Grinder 2001, op. cit.) argues that modelling is essentially an unconscious assimilation of the exemplar's capability. In practice these two modes are often used in combination.

55   Dilts, R. B. (1998) *Modeling with NLP,* p. 30. Capitola, CA: Meta Publications.

56   Gordon, D. and Dawes, G. (2005) *Expanding Your World: Modelling the Structure of Experience.* Tucson, AZ: Desert Rain.

Robert Koppel's *The intuitive trader*.[57] Robert Dilts[58] even claims to have modelled a number of 'strategies of genius'. These include a creative process that can be used in business, based on Walt Disney's description of how he created stories, comprising three functions that Dilts termed 'dreamer', 'realist' and 'critic'.

Evaluating NLP

IS THERE RESEARCH BEHIND IT?

The specific nature of the studies that led to the NLP meta-model, including the form the data took and the analysis procedures used, is not set out in detail in published sources. It is therefore difficult to assess the research for this work. In an interesting development for the field, Bostic St. Clair and Grinder (2001)[59] have provided a more explicit retrospective account – albeit one that is hard to obtain – which describes how the meta-model emerged through both empirical work and the application of theory from linguistics.

Academic research into NLP is thin, with virtually no published investigation into how it is used in practice. Empirical research consists largely of laboratory-based studies from the 1980s and early 1990s,[60] most of which investigated two main features of NLP. These were the notion of the 'primary representational system', according to which individuals have a preferred sensory mode of internal imagery indicated by their linguistic predicates,[61] and a model concerned with eye movements.[62] Both models hypothesise correspondences between external behaviour and internal processing.

Heap[63] conducted a meta-analysis of such studies and argued that these particular claims of NLP cannot be accepted. He appears justified in criticising the way claims are made in unequivocal terms in NLP literature. However, Heap appears only to summarise the reported outcomes of these studies, making no attempt to appraise their validity, and others[64] have argued that some studies reviewed by Heap have problems affecting their reliability. Heap did conclude that 'the effectiveness of NLP therapy undertaken in authentic clinical contexts of trained practitioners has not yet been properly investigated'.[65]

While the existing body of empirical research certainly offers no support to NLP, it is also doubtful whether it can be regarded as conclusive. Contemporary research that seeks direct evidence for the efficacy or otherwise of NLP in clinical settings is being pursued today by the NLP Research and Recognition Project, based in the USA,

---

57   Koppel, R. (1996) *The Intuitive Trader: Developing Your Inner Trading Wisdom*. New York: John Wiley and Sons.

58   Dilts, R. B. (1994) *Strategies of Genius*. Capitola, CA: Meta Publications.

59   Bostic St. Clair, C. and Grinder, J. (2001) op. cit.

60   This body of work is catalogued on a site hosted by the University of Bielefeld, http://www.nlp.de/cgi-bin/research/nlp-rdb.cgi, accessed 16 September 2009.

61   Grinder, J. and Bandler, R. (1976) op. cit.

62   See Bandler, R. and Grinder, J. (1979) op. cit.

63   Heap, M. (1988) Neuro-linguistic programming – an interim verdict. In M. Heap, (ed.), *Hypnosis: Current Clinical, Experimental and Forensic Practices*, pp. 268–280. London: Croom Helm.

64   For example, Beck, C. E. and Beck, E. A. (1984) Test of the eye movement hypothesis of neuro-linguistic programming: a rebuttal of conclusions, *Perceptual and Motor Skills*, 58(1): 175–176.

65   Heap, M. (1988) Neuro-linguistic programming – an interim verdict. In M. Heap, (ed.), *Hypnosis: Current Clinical, Experimental and Forensic Practices*, p. 276. London: Croom Helm.

which was established in 2006, and by the European Association for Neuro-Linguistic Psychotherapy.

There is, on the other hand, considerable support for many models and ideas that NLP has borrowed, adapted or developed. Explicit linkage to psychology has been made by NLP authors such as Bolstad[66] and Linder-Pelz and Hall;[67] the field of cognitive linguistics, which is acknowledged for example by Andreas,[68] could also provide some badly needed updating of Chomsky's ideas, on which the meta-model was initially based. There is excitement too within NLP about contemporary findings in the field of neuroscience, for example through its discovery of mirror neurons,[69] which may provide support for NLP's view that one can sample another person's experience by adopting the same posture and movements.

The fact that it is in widespread use provides a case for conducting further research into NLP. It appears especially important to elucidate the experiences of users and clients, and there is also a need for evaluative case studies of NLP applications in business – as distinct from practitioner's anecdotal success stories. Outside the field of psychotherapy, the practitioner community has done little to date to sponsor or promote research. Trainers often espouse an evidence-based, sceptical approach, exhorting participants to test NLP's claims for themselves, but (in my experience) with insufficient awareness of likely constraints on such testing, such as the role of peer pressure, the propensity to believe in something for which one has paid substantial amounts of money, and the risks (whether perceived or actual) for participants of expressing dissent.

As a final thought on this issue, though, managers and leaders who worry about the lack of research evidence might also wish to reflect on whether they apply the same criterion as strictly to other business practices. If we take, for example, organisational change strategies, respected commentators Beer and Nohria, writing in the *Harvard Business Review*,[70] say 'the brutal fact is that about 70 per cent of all change initiatives fail'. There appears to be no strategy for organisational change that would meet the criterion of being 'evidence-based', yet businesses continue to spend large amounts on change programmes and the consultants who are hired to help implement them – rather more, I would speculate, than has ever been spent by businesses on NLP.

Does it Have Any Theory?

It seems sensible to regard NLP primarily as a practice that innovates by working across traditional academic disciplines. Although its founders originally identified NLP broadly with psychology,[71] NLP's contents and practices are eclectic and show diverse influences,

66   Bolstad, R. (2002) *Resolve: A New Model of Therapy*. Carmarthen: Crown House.

67   Linder-Pelz, S. and Hall, L. M. (2007) op. cit.

68   Andreas, S. (2006) *Six Blind Elephants: Understanding Ourselves and Each Other, vol. I, Fundamental Principles of Scope and Category*. Moab, UT: Real People Press.

69   Rizzolatti, G., Fogassi, L. and Gallese, V. (2006) Mirrors in the mind, *Scientific American*, November: 30–37.

70   Beer, M. and Nohria, N. (2000) Cracking the code of change, *Harvard Business Review*, May–June: 133–141.

71   Bandler, R. and Grinder, J. (1975a) op. cit. p.1.

including cybernetics,[72] cognitive psychology[73] and the work of the Palo Alto Mental Research Institute.[74]

The idea that all knowledge systems must have a unifying theoretical framework is not borne out by the history of ideas. Even so, no-one in the field of NLP has yet sat down and worked out how, if at all, these diverse strands might cohere theoretically. One author, Peter Young (Young 2004), has attempted a 'unified field' theory of NLP but I would argue that he has succeeded mainly in producing an alternative classification of NLP.

One of the resistances within NLP to academic theorising is founded on an understandable reluctance to impose a retrospective intellectual logic on a practice that today, drawing from theories of complexity, we might well describe as emergent. Such resistance may also reflect some of the influence of Fritz Perls, who scorned intellectualising. Yet this can also be seen as a resistance to critical evaluation, and carries the risk that the views of perceived authorities in the field become an unquestioned orthodoxy.

Attempts to theorise NLP are in one respect post hoc efforts to make sense of the trail it has left. Yet it is also important to acknowledge the intellectual traditions that prepared the ground for, and influenced, NLP. Conversely, a lack of dialogue about its conceptual basis is likely to hamper the further development of NLP as a field of practice. The potential to engage with this conceptual basis exists; as several authors have identified, NLP largely reflects the world view articulated in Gregory Bateson's ideas.

Is NLP Safe to Use?

There is little doubt that NLP has a reputation to live down in some quarters. I frequently hear the perception that NLP can be manipulative, a prospect noted in the early days of NLP.[75] What aspects of this issue are most relevant to leaders and managers?

I would certainly question any suggestion that there is anything in NLP that makes it inherently unsafe; it seems unlikely that NLP would have gained accreditation as psychotherapy if this were the case. Also, using NLP instrumentally for the practitioner's gain is clearly at odds not only with NLP's philosophy but also with its codes of ethics.[76]

Some concerns involve a significant misconception about NLP's insights into the nature of human communication. Through their study of Erickson,[77] the founders of NLP became convinced that 'all communication is hypnosis'.[78] This means that every one of us uses 'hypnotic' language patterns, often unwittingly, as part of our everyday

---

72   Ashby, W. (1965) *An Introduction to Cybernetics*. London: Methuen.

73   Miller, G. A., Galanter, E. and Pribram, K. (1960) *Plans and the Structure of Behaviour*. New York: Holt, Rhinehart and Winston.

74   Watzlawick, P., Beavin, J. H. and Jackson, D. D. (1967) *Pragmatics of Human Communication*. New York: W. W. Norton and Co.

75   Bandler, R. and Grinder, J. (1979) op. cit. p.7.

76   For example, the ANLP general code of ethics (http://www.anlp.org/index.asp?pageID=79, accessed 16 September 2009); the NLPtCA code of ethics for psychotherapists (http://www.nlptca.com/ethics.php, accessed 16 September 2009).

77   Bandler and Grinder (1975a) op. cit.; Grinder, DeLozier and Bandler (1977) op. cit.

78   Grinder, J. and Bandler, R. (1981) *Trance-formations: Neuro-Linguistic Programming and the Structure of Hypnosis*, p. 1. Moab, UT: Real People Press. The same quote points out that they would, at the same time, purposely state the counterview that 'nothing is hypnosis, hypnosis doesn't exist'.

communication. For example, Bateson wrote, long before NLP was created, that the unconscious does not recognise negatives in language, such as 'not'.[79] Thus saying 'do not touch that' can be regarded as a hypnotic command that conveys the opposite message (that is, 'do touch that'), which is why it is reckoned to be counterproductive to use the injunction 'don't' when trying to deter children from certain actions. This means that saying 'don't forget to deliver that report' is potentially quite different from 'remember to deliver that report on time'.

NLP has not invented these tools; they occur naturally in language. What NLP has done is to codify them, and make them available to the public at large. One could argue that NLP benefits people by making transparent some of the strategies of salespeople, just as much as it benefits sales professionals by applying its tools to the task of selling. For better or for worse, NLP challenges the idea that knowledge like this should only be in professional hands.

Clearly, an important issue is that of how ethics are addressed within a field in which it is possible for a layperson to acquire techniques and to practise after relatively brief training (for example, typically in the region of 20 days to become a certificated practitioner). Bodies such as the ANLP, which has a clear code of ethics for practitioners, and the Professional Guild of NLP, a membership body for NLP training organisations, are active in promoting ethical practice.

NLP began by extracting techniques and processes from holistic practices, such as those of Virginia Satir. Because of this, it maybe that NLP tends to be used best by people for whom it is complementary to, or an adjunct to, another mode of working. People trained in another mode can use NLP to enhance their existing skills and effectiveness. As probably happens with any mode of people development, potential purchasers and users of NLP seem more likely to assess the trustworthiness and effectiveness of individual practitioners than to accept or reject NLP wholesale as a method.

What is NLP Good for, and What is it Not so Good for?

As indicated, NLP can be applied in so many ways that it is difficult to define what it can and cannot do. If one treats NLP as a methodology, then what it is good for primarily is learning skills of virtually any kind from exemplars.

In addition:

- NLP practice is very client-centred. It is guided by the client's desired outcome, generally avoids labelling or diagnosing the client's problem, is non-intepretive, and has no list of pathologies. The strength of this is that it is focused on the client's needs and goals, similar to solution-focused approaches.[80] A potential weakness is that it could downplay the importance of a client's past history.
- NLP can be applied at multiple levels in business, so can be suitable for individual development, as in coaching; work with teams or groups, for example through

---

79   Bateson, G. (2000) op. cit. Bateson wrote this paper in 1967.

80   For example, Jackson, P. Z. and McKergow, M. (2007) *The Solutions Focus: Making Coaching and Change Simple*, 2nd edn. London: Nicholas Brealey.

assisting with meetings or with problem-solving; and training and management development programmes.

- In NLP, emotion is seldom in the foreground. While it is not purely cognitive, since it works with the whole body–mind, it probably would not be the method of choice for someone who likes attending to emotions first and foremost.
- NLP practitioners tend not to work directly with social or group dynamics, or with issues of power and politics (even though there is potential for its tools and frameworks to be applied in this way). That most NLP in practice seems to emphasise the development of the individual person, from a largely psychological perspective, may say more about the direction in which the field has developed than about its potential scope.
- Finally, much NLP can be used in self-help mode. Any manager or leader who picks up a book of NLP tools and techniques can put them into practice. At best this makes NLP accessible, democratic and empowering.

Conclusion

The practice of NLP, which is now more than 30 years old, offers an innovative, pragmatic approach to communication and personal development that appears to be widespread in business. This chapter has described some of its core content, including outcomes, language models, the idea of internal representations and the process of modelling.

The fact that NLP is in widespread use in business justifies the need to understand its principles and practices, and to investigate its claims. While it seems appropriate to retain a healthy scepticism about many of those claims, NLP deserves to be recognised and valued for its innovations, especially the way it can provide people with a means to achieve their goals and create their own solutions. The practice draws on many ideas and theories that are well established; attention in the field is turning increasingly to the need for dedicated NLP research, and to issues of ethics and professional accreditation.

Acknowledgements

I gratefully acknowledge the contribution to the material in this chapter of my colleague, Dr Jane Mathison; assistance from Karen Moxom of the Association for NLP; and support from the University of Surrey Scholarship Fund and the Higher Education Academy.

Glossary of Key Terms

Anchoring	The use of a behavioural stimulus (for example, a word, gesture, touch, and so on) to trigger a response (such as a particular physiological and emotional state, or a remembered experience).
Meta-model	A typology of patterns in the 'surface structure' of language that result from deletions, distortions and generalisations in the 'deep structure' (that is, experience), with corresponding

	questions. The first NLP framework, and still considered the core of the practice.
Modelling	A process by which a skill can be learnt from one or more people who are excellent exponents of that skill.
Predicate	A word (verb, adjective or adverb) that is assumed to indicate the sensory mode of corresponding internal processing. For example, in 'I see what you mean', 'see' is a predicate and corresponds to the visual representational system.
Presupposition	An axiom or underlying principle of NLP.
Rapport	A sense of trust between people. NLP suggests that a subtle, intentional mirroring of posture, gestures, breathing, and/or predicates (for example) can help to enhance rapport.
Representational system	The sensory mode of internal imagery and processing. For example, imagined pictures are in the visual representational system; sounds are in the auditory representational system.
State	A person's physiological and neurological configuration.

Web Links

The Association for NLP: http://www.anlp.org/
The European Association for Neuro-Linguistic Psychotherapy: http://www.eanlpt.org/
NLP Conference website: http://www.nlpconference.co.uk/
The NLP Research and Recognition Project: http://www.nlprandr.org/
The Professional Guild of NLP: http://www.professionalguildofnlp.com/
Robert Dilts' website: http://www.nlpu.com/
University of Surrey NLP research project: http://www.NLPresearch.org/

Recommended Books

Frogs into Princes (Bandler and Grinder, Moab, UT: Real People Press, 1979): a workshop transcription that conveys well the spirit of early NLP.

NLP at Work The Difference that Makes a Difference in Business (Knight, London: Nicholas Brealey Publishing, 2002): an accessible and practical introduction to NLP in business.

NLP for Teachers (Churches and Terry, Carmarthen: Crown House, 2007): whilst written for teachers, this provides an excellent practical introduction to NLP and has much that is directly relevant to HRD professionals and managers.

Steps to an Ecology of Mind: Collected Essays in Anthropology, Psychiatry, Evolution and Epistemology, revised edn (Bateson, Chicago, IL: University of Chicago Press, 2000): Bateson's work represents the philosophy behind NLP.

18 *Leading Reflection: Developing the Relationship between Leadership and Reflection*

RUSS VINCE AND MICHAEL REYNOLDS

Introduction

The other day, I (Russ) was invited to present my thoughts on organizational change to 60 senior managers at the headquarters of International Utilities plc.[1] Before I made my presentation, the chief executive took the opportunity to outline his own thoughts about the company going forward in a presentation called 'Possible Organizational Change'. He identified key issues and areas of growth, he pinpointed his view of the way forward, and he reaffirmed the corporate values underpinning managerial action. He finished his presentation by pointing to the title of his talk and he emphasized the word 'possible'. He explicitly invited all the managers present in the room to comment on this possible future, to communicate other ideas or issues that were important, and to be part of discussions on his thinking about taking the company forward. Thoughts and comments could be given directly to him, to any other member of the senior management team, or to individuals' line managers (who would then pass them up). We have two questions for the reader. How much feedback do you think the chief executive received? How much feedback do you think the chief executive wanted?

The answer to both of these questions is – not much. If we reflect on this leadership behaviour we can see that it represents a very common way of expressing who has responsibility to lead change, as well as a common way of attempting to include others in change. The approach to leadership implied in this example represents an *assumption* (a taken for granted idea about the way we do things here) that underpins behaviour; that makes this way of doing things seem like the way it should be done. The example we have provided represents a model of *individual* leadership, a form of leadership that is more about action than reflection, where organizational change is actually the responsibility of senior managers, despite the rhetoric that 'we are all part of making change happen'. This is not a criticism, because it is difficult to mobilize reflection in the organization to

---

1   This is not the actual name of the company, although it does describe what they do.

sustain more collective and critical approaches to leadership in practice. However, in this chapter we will explain why it is important to do so, and suggest how to go about it.

How could the chief executive at International Utilities have initiated a different way of mobilizing 'possible organizational change'? Our suggestion would be that, instead of listening to the chief executive and a senior academic, the time could have been better used to mobilize the ideas, preferences and suggestions of the 60 senior managers in the room in reflecting collectively on the possibilities for organizational change. We are suggesting this is because we think that leaders are responsible for *leading reflection*. We think that 'leading reflection' can make a difference to feelings of involvement and ownership of change; it can add value in an organization – whether this is financial, social or intellectual; it can generate invaluable knowledge; and it can support the emergence of contemporary ideas for effective leadership.

The main theme of this chapter is to help the reader understand the relationship between leadership and reflection, to explain why this is important, and to highlight some of the implications for action. Current thinking about leadership emphasizes its interactive nature – it is as much a collective process as a set of attributes located in a single individual, a process which responds to the particular context and to the ideas and expectations of the other people involved. From this perspective, a key function of anyone invested with the role of leader is to initiate and support attempts to think and act critically and creatively about the organization – hence 'leading reflection'. This theme of expressing an individual's role and responsibility through a collective process of reflection runs throughout the chapter. In the next section we will discuss key ideas and thinking about leadership and reflection.

Key Ideas and Theories

LEADERSHIP

In order to start to appreciate the relationship between leadership and reflection, it is useful to think about the ways in which our understanding of leadership has changed over time. The way we think about leadership has changed considerably in the past few years. (Leadership practice has been slow to catch up – but we get to this point later on in the chapter). Looking at the leadership literature we can identify three broad shifts in how leadership has been defined and understood. At first, leadership was seen as an individual responsibility and/or role. In any interactions with others, the expectations were that those others were required to accept the individual leader's *influence and stated goals*. The individual leader used their influence to shape agenda and actions, to ensure that what they wanted was implemented, and to take the blame for failure (although leaders have always been accomplished in avoiding this last one).

It did not take people too long to discover the problem with this very individually focused idea about leadership. It tends to create conflicts between competing versions of what could be done, it privileges the leader's version of reality, and it assumes dependency and willing ambivalence on the part of followers – thereby reducing the number of brains that could be mobilized in the service of making things happen. So the initial shift in understanding leadership has been from individual influence to *mutual influence*. It was no longer seen as the leader's task to shape what others were thinking and doing. Rather, it was realized that collaborative engagement in mutual goals and shared aspirations was more likely to support and sustain the successful implementation of decisions.

It did not take people too long to discover the problem with mutual influence. When people get together to make decisions they often have great ideas and aspirations. However, a gap inevitably develops between these ideas and aspirations and the reality of implementing them in the emotional and political turmoil of organizations. This is why so many change initiatives start off with great enthusiasm and fanfare, only to 'sink into the sand', never to be heard of or talked about again. The second shift in thinking about leadership therefore concerned the role of leaders in relation to *adaptive influence*. From this point of view, the specific role of the leader is to attend to the difference between espoused intentions and how these are lived in the complex realities of the organization. Leaders are responsible for addressing the organizational dynamics that underpin an organizational ability or inability to adapt, for example, the gap between what we said we were going to do and what actually happens. Such dynamics might include: the tendency of parts of the organization to form silos, one against the other; the organizational fallout created by competition between managers for power and resources; the general feeling amongst organizational members that they are undervalued; and the ambivalence many staff feel towards taking up roles that have unwanted responsibility and expectation. The leader can draw attention to these issues as part of the process of helping the organization to adapt to new threats and challenges, new markets or partnerships, new projects and aspirations.

It didn't take people too long to realize that all this engagement with the emotions and politics that lie beneath ideas, decisions and actions within organizations was exhausting, and that the gap between what was said and what was done was difficult to address (and after all, organizations pay consultants to fail to do that). This gave rise to the final shift in leadership thinking, one that emphasizes that leadership is not a significant individual skill; and that it is not expressed within a set of competencies. Rather, leadership is just one part of a number of processes that make up the *capacity within human community* to create value, to shape the future, to sustain change. This understanding of leadership sees it as an essential (but not exclusive) part of an ongoing process of learning and change.

One problem that this understanding of leadership seeks to address is that people in organizations have a tendency to desire and to avoid change at the same time. Change is something desired because we all know that change needs to happen – to support (for example) future profitability, competitiveness, job satisfaction or well-being. Change is avoided because in practical terms it often means more work for us, more hassle, more effort and all for no additional reward. Accepting the status quo means that we can get on and do what we are expected to do with the minimum of aggravation and fuss. However, this approach to leadership tries to identify those places within organizations where creativity, enthusiasm and innovation reside; and to resource and reward the initiatives that arise in teams, groups and projects, as the representation of the future business of the organization.

To summarize – there has been a noticeable shift in our thinking about leadership, from the individual, 'heroic' leader[2] to leadership as a process that is collective and distributed

---

2   The word 'heroic' could be substituted with many other descriptions of an individual's leadership approach. For example: confused, inspirational, narcissistic, bullying, competitive, irrational, authoritative, authoritarian, hateful, collaborative, etc.

between individuals. In organizations, the practice of leadership covers all of these ways of thinking about how leadership can be done. These different ways of understanding leadership connect to a broader set of insights about leadership, providing it with the richness and complexity that is inevitably part of human action and interaction within work environments. These insights are outlined at the end of this chapter in our section on Resources, readings and web links, in Table 18.1 ten things you should know about leadership.

REFLECTION

If you can accept that leadership is a collective activity, where collaborative energy and enthusiasm is mobilized within organizations to produce the maximum possible value, then you will begin to see why the interplay between leadership and reflection is important. In our example from International Utilities, we would contend that the day-to-day knowledge of the company contained within the minds of the 60 top managers provides a richer knowledge base for creating change than the combined minds of the senior management team. Transforming the way we think about what organizations know, as well as devising ways to access it and use it, is an essential part of organizational and individual change in the company. The ability to mobilize processes of collective reflection in the service of value creation is at the heart of modern ideas about the role of leadership in the organization. In this section of the chapter we will introduce you to some of our thinking about reflection in organizations, as well as explaining the importance of reflection in creating value, shaping the future and sustaining change.

The word reflection is a representation of human consciousness. It refers to 'the process or faculty by which the mind has knowledge of itself and its workings'.[3] Reflection is one of the key building blocks of human learning; it has become established at the core of management and organizational learning; and the relationship between reflection and action has inspired the two most well-known conceptual models in management learning and management education (Kolb's learning cycle and Schön's reflective practitioner – see the resources section at the end of this chapter). Through the writings of such authors the meaning of reflection has been refined to signify a process through which we engage with an event in order to make sense of it, providing a conscious and thoughtful connection between ideas and experience, past experience and future action. The appeal of these ideas in a professional context is that they link learning with action and experience within a management or leadership role. They offer the insight that it is possible to learn from the experience of work and to generate knowledge in ways that enable us to transform the practicalities, problems and challenges of organizations.

Schön's ideas on reflective practice[4] were (and perhaps remain) a significant challenge to our understanding of experience within work organizations. Schön was critical of the technical rationality which he saw as characterizing organizational problem solving. He wrote of the significance of interrogating the assumptions on which professional practice was based through reflecting on the ideas and norms that underpin judgements and

---

3   *The New Shorter Oxford English Dictionary* (1993) Oxford: Oxford University Press, p. 2521.

4   See Schön, D. A. (1983) *The Reflective Practitioner: How Professionals Think in Action.* London: Maurice Temple Smith; and Schön, D. A. (1987) *Educating the Reflective Practitioner.* San Francisco, CA: Jossey-Bass.

actions. In practical terms this involved both 'reflection-in-action' and 'reflection-on-action'. The former has been described as 'thinking on your feet'. It involves reviewing experiences, feelings and assumptions in order to create new ways of understanding and acting within a situation as it unfolds.

The reflective practitioner uses rather than excludes things that often seem irrelevant to rational processes of problem solving, for example the surprise, puzzlement, or confusion inherent within a situation. Reflection therefore implies critique of situations, and it is the 'wisdom of critique' that generates new understanding or action. Reflection-on-action is an inquiry process particularly connected to groups and teams. Organizational members have to develop ways of integrating inquiry into their everyday practices, in order to give rise to a better understanding of the processes that underpin doing tasks. (For example: making explicit use of the 'flip-chart knowledge' that organizations generate and then ignore.) Schön was well aware that organizational members often take refuge in practised and habitual ways of thinking and working; in established procedures and familiar approaches. His writing emphasizes efforts to see the unfamiliar within the everyday, to allow individuals to confront habits and attachments and to change those aspects of thought and practice that are taken for granted.

In recent years, thinking about reflection has shifted from a focus on the individual reflective practitioner towards the organization of reflection.[5] A more *organizational* view of reflection takes account of social and political processes at work in the organization. In particular, this approach argues for the transformation of implicit approaches to reflection in organizations, where the responsibility for reflection is often located with individuals, either to do it for themselves (when there's time), or to be responsible for the review of other individuals' performance, mostly in relation to people within subordinate roles. More emphasis would be placed on creating collective and organizationally focused processes for reflection. The question that organizations face therefore is not only how the collective knowledge generated through organizing can be captured and utilized through reflection, but also, what are the emotional and political processes in the organization that prevent or severely limit reflection?

There are three key ideas that have helped to underpin this shift.

1. Critical reflection.
2. Public reflection.
3. Productive reflection.

CRITICAL REFLECTION

- The task of critical reflection is to identify and question taken-for-granted beliefs and values, particularly those which have become unquestioned or 'majority' positions. It is a process of making evaluations, often moral ones, and not simply exercising judgements of a practical, technical nature.
- Critical reflection pays particular attention to the analysis of power, and it emphasizes the value of questioning and challenging existing structures and practices because individuals and organizations easily get stuck in defensive routines or bad habits.

---

5   See Reynolds, M. and Vince, R. (eds) (2004) *Organizing Reflection*. Aldershot: Gower.

- Leadership is always undertaken in the context of social and cultural processes. Critical reflection implies a focus on a collective, situated (contextually specific) process that assists inquiry into actual and current organizational projects. This enables managers to question critically those organizational practices and issues within their specific situation.

Critical reflection involves questioning assumptions that are implicit in the procedures, practices and structures which make up professional and organizational work. In addition to their physical and rational structures, organizations are built and maintained (emotionally, politically and relationally) from, for example, habits and attachments, established ways of working, rules and routines, political imperatives, techniques for compliance and demands for consensus. Critical reflection emphasizes the importance of engagement with emotional, moral, social and political as well as material considerations. The function of such reflection is to improve the possibility of unsettling established ways of working in support of change.

PUBLIC REFLECTION[6]

Public reflection is necessarily undertaken in the company of others, and as a result, creates different interpersonal dynamics of accountability, authority and action.

- As leaders we are often unaware of the consequences of our behaviour. Public reflection can bring these consequences to our attention in ways that might help to transform behaviour.
- Public reflection helps leaders to address the gap between what we say we will do and what we actually do in organizations. Public reflection is a necessary part of making this gap both visible and discussable, and in order to make change possible.
- As leaders we are often selective or biased in the information we obtain and/or communicate. Public reflection allows us to become aware of judgement errors that arise as a consequence of bias and to attempt to correct them.
- At times, leaders' prior solutions do not fit with new problems and issues. Public reflection provides an environment within which leaders can distinguish new knowledge and thinking from that which might be self-fulfilling and self-justificatory.

Public reflection encourages engagement with those others who are similarly caught up in the distinctive political processes that organizing creates, thereby seeking to make such processes both visible and subject to change. Reflection 'in public' makes the questioning of assumptions more likely because the act of giving voice to underlying assumptions can make them contestable. However, the extent to which organizational power relations allow assumptions to be contested varies considerably within different organizational contexts. Public reflection explicitly acknowledges the role of difference and dissent in improvement, and thereby seeks to offer an expanded view of authority relations. Authority is not a feature of individual behaviour or character, nor is it

---

6   These ideas are developed from a more academic perspective in Armstrong, S. and Fukami, C. (eds) (2009) *The Handbook of Management Learning, Education and Development*. London: Sage.

contained within the role that the individual occupies. Instead, it arises from the public testing, implementation and negotiation of individuals' authority; the negotiation of authority within groups; and the ways in which authority and legitimacy combine within specific organizational contexts. Making authority public suggests a willingness to test the boundaries of authority, making it easier (but not easy) to share and to distribute. Public reflection also mobilizes a wider accountability for those in positions of authority. Such willingness implies an understanding and practice of authority that is free from individual defensiveness and the regressive political consequences of this defensiveness in action.

PRODUCTIVE REFLECTION

Productive reflection emphasizes the dual goals of productivity and quality of working life. The continuous focus for collective reflection is the ability of an organization in combining productivity with well-being and work satisfaction.

- Productive reflection focuses on how competence is distributed inside companies and the processes of monitoring and intervention that are constructed to link competence to productivity, well-being and work satisfaction.
- Reflection is not confined to any one group in an organization (for example the HR department), but rather productive reflection seeks to make use of the distributed expertise within the organization, a form of expertise that is too often ignored or undervalued.
- Productive reflection has a developmental character with an intention to build agency among participants; to promote confidence that they can act together in meaningful ways; and that they can develop their own repertoire of approaches to meet future challenges. Reflection is seen as an open, unpredictable process, it is dynamic (it is likely to change over time) and it is unlikely that it can be turned into 'formal interventions to improve learning at work'.

The general aim of productive reflection is to maximize the learning potential of work by asking some key questions. For example: how does an organization make use of the existing knowledge produced through established ways of working when 'we don't have time to reflect'? How can expertise be distributed throughout an organization when organizational members have to compete for resources? What collective practices for reflection can be developed to promote collaboration between organizational members and confidence in the legitimacy of individual and collective voice? A more specific aim of productive reflection is to tie together collective processes of reflection on what and how productivity is achieved, with the search for ways of improving peoples' well-being and work satisfaction.

For many organizations, reflection is misunderstood, limited to individuals and often ignored. It is poorly developed because organizational members don't have time, don't know how, or don't see the point of it. It is poorly developed because reflection and the production of new knowledge and actions necessarily confront established ways of thinking and working, as well as authority relations, strategic decisions and approaches to leadership. Emotional, social and political relations are mobilized whenever organizational members meet. Making at least some of these relations overt is one way to reflect on and to create 'possible organizational change'. All of these approaches to reflection suggest that that it can be an essential part of the day-to-day life of leaders, not a disconnected, separate activity but integral, supported by structures and the culture of the workplace, affecting decisions and choices, policies and activities and the politics and emotion associated with them. In this way to be reflective is not a technique, learned and sometimes applied, but part of what it means to be a leader.

AN EXAMPLE

A practical example of the interaction between reflection and leadership can be found in a previous paper of ours,[7] where we discuss the case of a different international utilities company that wanted to reflect on organizational bids for contracts. The problem they faced was that the knowledge and expertise generated in bid teams was poorly linked to improvements in practice. Where bids had failed, reflection was ignored because organizational members did not want to dwell on their failure. Where bids had been a success, organizational members wanted to enjoy their success rather than reflect on it. This was not seen as a failure of the groups themselves to reflect, rather as a failure in the ability of the organization (and its leaders) to support reflection as an integral part of the process of bidding for contracts.

This raised the question of how the knowledge (about the procedures and dynamics of the bidding process) that was being lost could be recaptured. The company used an action-based approach that was integrated into each bid team. All bid Teams started to include an 'action researcher' (a role taken up by one of the existing members, who received training and support) whose job it was to record the process from beginning to end, to initiate discussions at each meeting on the group's processes and behaviour, and to pay attention to the emotions and politics that were having an impact on the team both from outside and from within. It was clear that this approach was not always easy or welcome within teams. Some team leaders thought that the action researchers were being critical of them; it took time for team members to understand that there was more happening in the team than the task at hand; and the action researchers often found it difficult to say what their inquiry had raised, as well as being believed when they did. However, despite these difficulties, the knowledge from both successful and unsuccessful bids was given public voice in the organization. The wider expression of this knowledge assisted in the practical task of evaluating the bidding process, as well as distributing this knowledge in the company.

Our example illustrates the case we have been making for leading reflection as an important part of a leader's role. It supports the way of seeing leadership as an interactive, negotiated process which is responsive to a particular situation. Also, it illustrates the characteristic of reflection as a collective, critical activity. The knowledge needed to resolve the situation was spread amongst the managers. The 'leader' in this example was not capable of improving the situation on his own. He was, however, in a position to initiate a process of reflection that was critical, public and proved to be productive. In other words, the leader takes the risk to initiate such a process, underlines its legitimacy by creating the space for it to happen, and judges the timing of the activity – in this case

---

7   Reynolds, M. and Vince, R. (2004) Critical management education and action-based learning: synergies and contradictions. *Academy of Management Learning and Education*, 3(4): 442–456.

the action research initiative – so that the focus remained on the problem which needed to be solved.

Guidelines on Practice and Implementation

We have discussed our background thinking, the ideas that make up leading reflection. The question we address now is: what does leading reflection mean in practice. There are two things we would like you to have in mind when using our recommendations about what to do. First, leadership and reflection are both continuous, organizing processes. This means that leadership and reflection are not mobilized only through individual skills, behaviours, competencies or actions. They both form part of the ongoing construction and reconstruction of 'the way we do things here'. A very controlling organizational culture seeks to minimize leadership and reflection; a very interactive organization seeks to maximize them. We have found that controlling organizational cultures tend to stifle creativity, awareness, enthusiasm and learning. We would argue for the development of more interactive organizational culture in organizations, built from a very broad and collective view of both leadership and reflection. We think that such an approach is good for both company productivity and for wellbeing. Second, all prescriptions (for example, 6 steps to success, the 9 essential components, 22 core competencies) are only as good as the effort you put into making them work in context. This often requires making changes to the original prescription. Prescriptions (including the one below) are only the starting point of development and they should be critiqued and changed as an integral part of going forward.

1. How to do leading reflection:

    –   Make the shift in the way you think about the organization, and what you do in the organization. This shift is from a focus on what individuals do, to a focus on the ways in which groups, teams and 'the organization' work. There are various bits of research to do and information that you need in order to go forward.
    –   Identify the taken-for-granted beliefs and values in the organization – those things that everyone knows about but are rarely talked about. Ask yourself: what is typical, what is characteristic, what are the ways in which we are being asked to do things here (whether implicitly or explicitly)?
    –   What are the key power relations in the organization? Remember, these may be in unexpected as well as the obvious places. For example, resistance can be a form of power as much as control.
    –   What are the bad habits in the organization? Sometimes, groups, teams, organizations get stuck in unhelpful ways of doing things, they support defensive routines and avoidance strategies, they mobilize limited ways of working. What are these in your group, team and/or organization?

Once you have this information, apply it within real and ongoing organizational projects in order to discover and to engage directly with the sticking points, emotional responses and political imperatives that underpin all action in organizations. The key task is to try to unsettle established ways of working in order to release, for example, creativity, conflict and dialogue in the service of learning, knowledge and action.

We can relate these points to our previously mentioned example. A 'taken-for-granted' in the bid teams, as well as within this organization, was that the action of making bids was more important than the need to capture knowledge and information about how to make bids. The process of making bids was therefore dependent on individuals' experience of previous bids, but did not include any broader reflection on the organizational knowledge that was being lost. This assumption was further reinforced by very individually focused power relations, where the onus was on the individual bid-team leader, not on the team. These power relations discouraged collective interest and ownership of the bidding process. Over time, the organization developed a bad habit in relation to bidding for contracts – that there was no process-level thinking and reflection about how and why bids were successful or not.

2. Make the shift towards reflecting openly, making decisions and raising issues 'in public'. Try to broaden the constituency within which decisions are made and actions undertaken. In other words, expand rather than reduce the accountability structures that exist in the organization or within the specific team or project you are involved in. The more that is negotiable in the organization (group or team) the more likely it is that you will collectively address the gap between what we said we would do and what we end up doing.

    –   The key to reflection and leadership 'in public' is taking the risk to make both simple and complicated organizational issues both visible and discussable. The fear here is often that this is overly time-consuming. However, it isn't, it is just a different focus in terms of how your time is used.
    –   Reflection and leadership 'in public' means that we have to learn to be more actively open to feedback. It is necessary to take active leadership on the process of generating feedback. This is because organizational politics and power relations often mean that people are as ambivalent about giving feedback as they are about getting feedback.
    –   Find ways to capture and to reflect on the knowledge (old and new) that is captured through increased interaction 'in public'. Much knowledge generated through reflection can be lost. Further reflective processes may be necessary in order to understand how this knowledge can be used.

Once you have taken these actions you should be able to understand that authority relations are more important than individual positions of authority. The key tasks are: (a) changing the implicit and explicit accountability structures within the group, team or organization and (b) changing the way in which authority is experienced and enacted within the group, team or organization.

We can relate these points to our example (above). When the bid teams started to include the reflective role (action researcher) they gradually became able to include discussions on the teams' own processes and internal relations, as well as the organizational politics coming from outside the team. Taking the risk to give voice to such information, to make it public, (eventually) increased team members' openness to feedback and allowed them to improve their ability as a team to engage with what worked well and what went wrong.

3. Make the effort to broaden notions of productivity, to include social well-being and responsibility as well profit. There should be a constant connection between the financial imperatives that are part of organizational life (profit, return, competitiveness, value) and the social issues that arise for people in work organizations (satisfaction, well-being, reward, being valued).

    – Ask questions about existing and potential processes and approaches in the group, team, organization that promote both productivity and work satisfaction. Are these in balance or is financial control seen as the key organizational issue? Mobilize reflective processes that will generate ideas about what can be done in the group, team and organization to promote satisfaction and well-being.
    – All organizational projects should be developmental in the sense that they include processes of reflection that enable learning and knowledge generation. This means making an effort to create the physical space for reflection, the time for reflective events, and the responsibility for feeding back the knowledge from these events (in public) within the group, team and organization.

The key task is to mobilize concern for satisfaction and well-being in balance with a concern for profit. This will involve identifying and utilizing expertise that is distributed around the group, team and organization, being inclusive, as well as seeking the connections and differences that exist between different parts of the group, team and organization. Greater balance between productivity and satisfaction will further underpin authority relations that are less controlling, more accepting of unpredictability and more open to change.

We can relate these points to our example (above). The more the bid teams gained experience at active reflection, the more they were able to identify their own competencies and incompetence in making bids. Underlying feelings of pressure to 'get the bid done and away' were balanced with feelings of making a contribution and working together. The evaluation of organizational processes where both success and failure can be potential outcomes was made easier in this more collective environment. In other words, the focus was on both winning bids and working together, rather than just on winning bids. This shift is a sign of the developmental effects of reflection, although not everyone in organizations wants to work in this way.

Potential Difficulties and Dilemmas

Of course, in practice, it's not that easy and there are two particular difficulties that you are likely to encounter.

1. The leadership contradiction: facilitation versus control. Leaders want feedback because we know that other people can have ideas and can contribute to improvements that add value to our own. Leaders don't want feedback because they fear it will undermine their ability to control a situation and their desired outcomes. This is not simply a

one-way problem that establishes leadership as the responsibility of an individual leader. This is a two-way problem of leadership in which individual understanding of how to lead is shaped and reinforced by the passivity and dependence of followers, as well as through an over-developed personal sense of position and responsibility.

2. The reflection problem: 'reflection isn't doing anything … it gets in the way of action'.

3. In many organizations, individual managers feel compelled to be seen to be doing something. This arises from the many and varied anxieties of everyday organizational life within organizational roles. For example: are we doing what we should be doing, if I'm seen not to be doing something then I might be given more to do, what is my role – if I keep on doing more will that help me to define it, if we stop doing then we might have to feel something about what we have been doing, and so on. Reflection is seen as something that *individuals* do, when and if they have the time. It is thinking back on or reviewing personal performance. There is a very poor appreciation that reflection can be an organizational process in addition to an individual process. This is further compounded by the idea that reflection is an interruption of action.

4. Problems with the idea of 'being critical'. Unfortunately, in everyday talk being critical is often seen as a negative activity, undermining someone else's position or their resolve. So that, in the same way that we noted about reflection, being critical is resisted because it is regarded as a formula for inaction. We take the view that *critical* reflection is by its nature likely to lead to action and change because it involves questioning underlying assumptions which have been lost sight of. Nevertheless being critical of current practices is not always well received, especially if it means being explicit about power relations and the interests invested in particular decisions, or raising questions which others were hoping would remain unasked. For a while at least reflecting critically and publicly may prove an isolating experience.

How Value can be Added

Our solution to these problems is to emphasize the importance of the relationship between leadership and reflection, and to connect this to a broader managerial responsibility, which we call leading reflection. Our final section therefore addresses why organizations might need to have leading reflection as one of the ways in which leadership is understood and implemented, as well as the value of this approach.

Let's just imagine that the chief executive of International Utilities, as a result of reading this chapter, wanted to test out his new-found awareness of leading reflection. What would he do? We think that he could do the following to start with.

He should reduce the number of senior manager meetings where there is an individual speaker, and where the most senior managers in the company tell the audience what they think/want. While it is good to listen to inspiring individuals with something to say (whether within or outside of the organization), this promotes an idea of leadership as expert-based and followership as passive. He should then provide leadership for the development of processes for reflection that engage and involve as many managers as possible. There's no one best way to do this; it will vary according to the existing power relations (the way we do things here), and as an unfamiliar process, it may need to be supported and sustained (until it becomes part of the way we do things here). For example, action learning has been used as a way of encouraging transformations of practice within organizations. However, action learning has also been used in ways that are divorced from the power relations in organizations, producing only localized impact. In terms of value added, such change will begin to extend organizational members' idea about what leadership means in practice, to include collective practices of leadership as well as individual leadership behaviour.

Having mobilized a shift from individual to collective leadership, part of the CE's role will be to give continuous support and legitimacy to collective and critical reflection. With increased reflection in the company, leaders, managers and staff throughout International Utilities can start to encourage *critique* of how things work. Particular encouragement can be given to reflection on the gap between what is said and done; to capturing and sharing existing knowledge in the company; and to revealing the assumptions that inform 'how we do things here'. In terms of value added, this will improve the social dynamics in the company and extend the legitimacy of difference and dialogue within and across hierarchical levels. Improved dialogue and the acceptance of conflict will help to encourage a shift away from double-edged responses to change (see problem 1 in the previous section of the chapter). This will allow increased opportunities to change bad habits and to unsettle established power relations.

Once underlying assumptions, knowledge, habits and power relations are more public, then leadership will be needed to create physical spaces within the organization where reflection can take place – public spaces within the organization that support interaction. There are two types of reflection that will take place within these spaces: first, continued reflection on processes and practices within work, and second, developing ways of supporting satisfaction within the workplace. (For example, International Utilities encourage workers' families to come into the HQ at lunchtime in order to make a deliberate break in work during the day. They have found that this has improved the way that individuals work.) In terms of value added, this will help to encourage something more than a focus on work. It will contribute to the energy within the company for the people who work within it. Attempts to combine productivity and satisfaction are about supporting organizational members' energy, as well as using this energy to create future stability, profitability and satisfaction.

Conclusion

In this chapter we are addressing two common organizational problems. First, organizations tend to be task-obsessed and therefore they undervalue reflection (we don't have time to stop and think). The imperative to get tasks done damages the ability to do them well, because such behaviour ignores reflecting on and capturing the valuable knowledge that is generated from action. Second, we think that a great deal of leadership behaviour in organizations is stuck in a very individual model, which keeps alive the rather outdated assumption that leaders tell people what to do and followers follow. This persistent assumption about leadership discourages collective engagement and thereby undermines the ability of organizations to learn from previous practice, to innovate and to change. We think that increased efforts within organizations to combine leadership and reflection will help to transform both of these problems.

We advocate expressing, enacting and exchanging leadership roles through collective and critical processes of reflection. We are looking to increase collaborative energy and enthusiasm in organizations in order to mobilize the maximum possible value, both financial and social. We discuss four different approaches to reflection: critical reflection, public reflection, productive reflection and organizing reflection, and offer examples of how they might relate to practice. In doing this we are seeking to create new practices, and there are two ways in which we think this can be achieved. First, through a shift of focus from what individuals do, towards a better understanding of the ways in which groups, teams and organizations work. This implies a change of emphasis from the individual as a source of knowledge to the organization as a system that can learn and change. Second, reflection is a political intervention within a system (which is perhaps why there is so much resistance to it). We think that critical, public, productive and organizing reflection will expand accountability structures, broaden the legitimacy to lead and make 'the way we do things here' more negotiable. The outcome of the development of the relationship between leadership and reflection will be leadership that can make the difference between performance and value-creating performance.

Resources, Readings and Web Links

BOOKS ABOUT LEADERSHIP AND REFLECTION

If you only want to read one book on leadership, then we would recommend:

Brad Jackson and Ken Parry (2008) *A Very Short, Fairly Interesting and Reasonably Cheap Book About Studying Leadership*, London: Sage. This book provides exactly what it says on the cover.

There are many other books available, and here's a brief list (of ones we like):

A. Dubrin (2006) *Leadership: Research Findings, Practice and Skills*, London: Houghton Mifflin.
K. Grint (2000) *The Arts of Leadership*, Oxford: Oxford University Press.
K. Grint (2005) *Leadership: Limits and Possibilities*, Basingstoke: Palgrave/Macmillan.
D. A. Kolb (1984) *Experiential Learning: Experience as the Source of Learning and Development*, Englewood Cliffs, NJ: Prentice-Hall.
P. Northouse (2006) *Leadership*, 4th edn. London: Sage.
J. Raelin (2004) *Creating Leaderful Organizations*, San-Francisco, CA: Berrett-Koehler.
D. A. Schön, (1983), *The Reflective Practitioner: How Professionals Think in Action*, London: Maurice Temple Smith.
A. Sinclair (2007) *Leadership for the Disillusioned*, Sydney: Allen & Unwin.
J. Storey (ed.) (2004) *Leadership in Organizations: Current Issues and Key Trends* London: Routledge.
G. Yukl (2005) *Leadership in Organization*, London: Prentice Hall.
We would suggest two books on the organization of reflection:
M. Reynolds and R. Vince (eds) (2004) *Organizing Reflection*, Aldershot: Gower.
D. Boud, P. Cressey and P. Docherty (eds) (2006) *Productive Reflection at Work*, London: Routledge.

Table 18.1 Ten things you should know about leadership

1. Leadership is context sensitive	The same set of leadership skills, behaviours and knowledge can work well in one situation and poorly within another. 'A change in the context changes leaders, leadership and leadership effectiveness.'* Context changes the meaning attached to leadership in an organization. Leadership is connected to social, political and ethical purposes and relations, it requires emotional not just rational endeavour, and it is characterized by irrationality as well as purpose.
2. Leadership is relational and collective	Leadership is rarely isolated or individually located. It is a collective activity, where collaborative energy and enthusiasm is mobilized within organizations to produce the maximum possible value. This speaks to the socially constructed nature of leadership. Our view on this phenomenon is that it is situated between individuals, rather than at the individual level. It resonates with the social construction of the self as well as political and cultural norms.
3. Leadership is distributed	There is a difference between leaders who act directly on a situation and leaders who discern how to encourage others to act. A challenge for leaders is to transform the processes that affect performance rather than directly affecting performance. This can be done directly and from a distance. Distributed leadership implies that the role of leaders is to stimulate organizing processes that support and encourage the leadership actions of others through the creation of ideas, promising practices, spaces and events within which diverse individual and collective voices can be heard.
4. Leadership is performance-sensitive; it is linked to value creation	The key product of leadership is added value. Value may be judged through improvements within one or more areas (e.g. profitability, competitiveness, social capital, knowledge generation, ethics, political credibility, or work satisfaction and well-being). Leadership can make the difference between performance and value-creating performance.
5. Leadership always has a political dimension	Leadership is an activity that both expresses and creates organizational power relations. It is a pivotal process in the construction and reconstruction of 'how we do things here'.
6. Leadership carries a tension between change and stability	There is a tension in the leadership role between the requirement to make change happen at the same time as being a guardian of corporate citizenship and status quo.

*   Osborn, R. N., Hunt, J. G. and Jauch, L. R. (2002) Toward a contextual theory of leadership, *Leadership Quarterly*, 13(6): 797–837.

Table 18.1 *Concluded*

7. Leadership and learning are inseparable	Leading is linked to learning within organizations and to organizational learning. For individuals, learning about leadership is action-based – it involves reflection and action on real and current work problems and issues over time. Therefore, the development of leaders occurs in the midst of action and through reflection, often in the company of other leaders who are similarly engaged. Leadership development can be understood as a lifelong journey rather than in terms of a specific set of skills, competencies or knowledge. Leadership is linked to the development of capability both for oneself and in others. To be in the role of leader is to be connected to the perpetual process of becoming a leader. Leadership is integral to organizational learning, and especially to the emotions and power relations that both promote and prevent an organization from learning.
8. Leadership is dynamic	Leadership is created and sustained in the interplay between promise and practice over time. Leadership encourages mobilization and capability development. It is important to consider leadership over time, to develop a longitudinal understanding of how we become leaders, as well as how this 'becoming' is linked to changes over time.
9. Leadership is transnational and/ or transcultural	Leadership is increasingly set within a global context and diverse groupings. It is enmeshed in cultural processes and the crossing of cultural boundaries.
10. These ideas about leadership were developed by the Leadership Forum at the School of Management, the University of Bath	The following individuals put their heads together to come up with this list: Ron Collard, Peter Hawkins, Andrew Pettigrew, Juani Swart and Russ Vince.The members of the Leadership Forum believe that all these ideas will be important in informing the future theory and practice of leadership.

USEFUL ONLINE RESOURCES

The Reflective Practitioner Donald Schon – http://www.infed.org/thinkers/et-schon.htm.

David Kolb, Experiential Learning – http://reviewing.co.uk/research/experiential.learning.htm#242.

The journal *Leadership* – http://lea.sagepub.com/archive/.

The journal *Reflective Practice* – http://www.tandf.co.uk/Journals/titles/14623943.asp.

National College for Schools Leadership (NCSL) has a variety of interesting resources available to all leaders (not just leaders in schools). For example, on systems leadership, http://www.ncsl.org.uk/publications/publications-systemleadership.cfm.

19 *Feedback and 360-degree Development*

PETER HOLT, SUZANNE POLLACK AND PHIL RADCLIFF

Introduction

The elusive nature of leadership is obvious in academic and practitioner circles, both of which reflect a wide variety of definitions, approaches and emphasis. Descriptors of leadership include emergent, transactional, transformational, inspirational, situational, action-centred, emotionally intelligent, primal, courageous, servant and principle-centred, to mention only a few that are included in book titles on the subject. The plethora of books and articles relating to leadership is a reflection of the importance of the topic and their contrasting approaches derive from the changing nature of the workplace – the context in which leadership takes place. Markets are now transnational and turbulent, telecommunications almost instantaneous, labour is portable, workplaces diverse and knowledge widely accessible and transferable. The future will see both big and small corporations, size being related to their purpose, but they will be international, extended and inclusive, fluid with constantly changing boundaries and continuously seeking to reinvent their products and processes. The consequence is that leadership is now more complex and performed in rapidly changing conditions. Moreover, given the added impetus of organisations' relentless drive for success, and increasingly the need for short-term, not just long-term success, more is demanded of leadership than ever before.

The Changing Nature of Leadership in a Local Context and the Implications for Leadership Development

Working within current organisations means operating in matrix structures, moving from one work group to another and building fleeting relationships that often don't last much longer than the current project. Leadership will often be displayed in these fluid circumstances but not necessarily by anyone with visible authority other than their ability to influence by personal persuasion and example. Commensurate with these trends is the pressure for organisations to develop leaders capable of functioning successfully in what appears to be a hostile environment. This poses a major challenge for the identification and development of desirable leadership skills and qualities. Thus leadership development is no longer a discrete area of activity but a holistic, collective and integrated process closely linked with myriad organisational practices and the wider context in which leaders operate.

Our Particular Perspective. Personal rather than Organisation Development and Specific Leadership not Generic Management Development: 360s need to be Fit for Purpose

An important response to the need for leadership development has been the rapid expansion in the use of 360 instruments seeking to provide the foundation for focused and rapid leadership development. 360s aim to provide leaders with relevant, multi-sourced and objective feedback that will result in changed behaviour and improved personal and organisational performance. Although they may be used for performance management purposes and wider organisational development[1] the essential focus of this chapter is the use of 360s for personal leadership development. This stems from the authors' collective responsibilities designing and running the public Leadership Programme based at Henley Management College[2] and from which we draw our experience and prime evidence. Thus we tend to approach the issue from a practitioner's perspective in which our prime concern is the development of an individual leader's impact. In essence we use our particular 360 because we believe, when integrated within a comprehensive development process, it leads to improved leadership performance.

A sound basis for judging current leadership effectiveness is to seek feedback from those who work closely with the leaders being assessed. 360 processes typically invite feedback from a participant's manager, or managers, their peers, direct reports and others including possibly customers and/or previous work colleagues. These feedback systems are now largely electronic and, with the exception of the individual manager's feedback, confidential. This encourages honest reporting and, although responses are always the subjective perception of the person providing feedback, the information provided is as objective to participants as they are ever likely to receive.

Well-designed and sensitively deployed 360s are unique development tools because they:

- Establish and reinforce the importance of organisations taking direct responsibility for developing leadership capacity.
- Send a strong message to the participants about the investment being made in their immediate learning and future career prospects.
- Provide a unique source of feedback for greater self-knowledge and leadership development.
- Contribute to the holistic, collective and interdependent perspectives of leadership and leadership development.

---

1   See the CIPD website for an excellent introduction to the generic use of 360s. This can be found at http://www.cipd. co.uk/subjects/perfmangmt/appfdbck/360fdbk.htm?IsSrchRes=1.

2   By the time of publication Henley Management College will have merged with Reading University Business School to become Henley Business School.

- Build stakeholder engagement with the individual's development agenda – this can be comfortably extended to other individuals and teams with which the participant is connected.
- Empower relationships and provide a foundation for future development conversations.
- Stimulate an expectation that behavioural change will take place and result in improved personal and organisational leadership performance.

However, development activities and supporting instruments have to be fit for purpose. The prime limitation of many 360s in our specific context is that they focus upon management, and not leadership, development. Whilst the two are closely related leadership tends to be longer-term, more a function of the person than the role, concerned with longer-term strategy rather than shorter-term delivery and concentrates upon vision and direction rather than detailed planning and control. Thus the emphasis of a 360 designed to support leadership development will differ from a more generic management 360. Additionally, 360s can be partial and one-dimensional by simply concentrating upon a range of visible behavioural competencies. In doing so they are neither holistic nor integrative, and tend to neglect the everyday challenges that leaders face and the wider organisational context in which leadership takes place.

The Wilber Model: An Integrative and Comprehensive Approach to Leadership Development

We have looked outside the leadership industry to find a model that will provide a framework to illustrate the complex holistic, interdependent and collective nature of leadership. This is provided by Ken Wilber's 'integral theory of consciousness'. After giving a basic interpretation of Wilber's model we will show how this demonstrates the value of 'Leadership 360 Plus', our particular 360, in developing leadership talent. Having done this we will then draw upon real life experiences to illustrate the progress individual leaders have made as they have responded to the results of their 360 by implementing personal change and improving their leadership capacity.

In his 'Iintegral theory of consciousness'[3] Ken Wilber seeks a model to incorporate the many approaches to consciousness. He identified 12 consciousness schools, each of which has 'much to offer'. And so it is for leadership. There are numerous approaches to leadership and a 360 based on any one of them is likely to reflect its own bias. However, we accept that most approaches will make a valuable contribution to the understanding and practice of leadership, but what is wanted as a foundation for a comprehensive 360 is 'a model sophisticated enough to incorporate the essentials of each of them'.

Wilber's four-quadrant model provides this foundation. It is based upon two axes: along the vertical he distinguishes between the individual and the collective perspective, whilst along the horizontal axis he distinguishes between the interior and exterior functions. This produces a figure (see Figure 19.1) in which the upper half refers to the individual and the lower half to the collective forums in which individuals exist. The

---

3   Wilber, K. (1997) An integral theory of consciousness, *Journal of Consciousness Studies*, February: 71–92. See also Wilber, K. (2001) *A Theory of Everything*. Boston, MA: Gateway.

right-hand side of the model refers to the exterior or objective aspects and the left-hand side to the interior or subjective forms.

The upper right, 'individual–exterior' quadrant, represents leadership behaviour displayed by the individual which, because it is external, can be defined, observed and objectively assessed. 360s which simply focus upon leadership competencies fit neatly into this quadrant. Similarly the lower right, 'collective–exterior' quadrant, represents organisation HR systems and processes (e.g. performance management, appraisal and management development processes) that impact upon leadership development. The organisation is the main 'collective' context within which leadership is deployed. The two right-hand quadrants are 'exterior' in the sense that their respective contents can be experienced objectively by our senses. In Wilber's words, they are all 'empirical phenomenon'.

In contrast the two left-hand quadrants differ from the right-hand side because they are 'internal' and comprise value-based belief patterns held internally by the individual or the teams and organisations within which they operate. In the upper left quadrant the 'individual–internal' reflects a person's values, beliefs and perceptions. The determination to succeed, humility and honesty are examples of personal values that fit neatly into this quadrant.

People do not exist in isolation – they live within their various communities, such as teams and organisations. These are represented by the bottom left 'interior–collective' quadrant. Communal identities are manifested in the form of organisation or group norms, ethics and values. Both of these left-hand quadrants are 'subjective' in the sense that they are internal to the person or the collective groups and organisation within which they are functioning and, unlike exterior factors, cannot readily be assessed objectively.

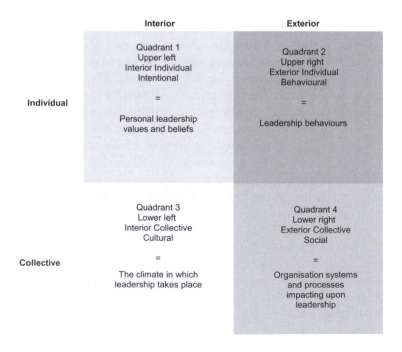

Figure 19.1 Applying Wilber's four-quadrant model to leadership

When applied to leadership Wilber's model reinforces the need for a holistic and integral perspective. For instance, simply focusing on behavioural competencies (top right) in isolation from where they originate and the context within which they operate is likely to have significant limitations. Behavioural competencies are value-driven (top left) and the top two quadrants both operate within a collective context. A holistic approach to leadership development will necessarily establish links between personal values and leadership behaviour and the situation in which leadership takes place and perhaps explains why leadership is not easily transferable. As one of our participants put it, 'Leadership is context-dependent, what works in one environment doesn't in another. Here we are quite collegiate – so certain things would not work.'

The instrument we use at Henley, Leadership 360 Plus, is a comprehensive model whose prime focus is leadership, not management, and, as will be seen, it maps neatly – but not precisely – onto the Wilber model.

Leadership 360 Plus: An Overview

'Leadership 360 Plus recognises that leadership is not vested in a particular person or small top team – so long as appropriate conditions exist then leadership exists at all organisation levels.[4] The instrument is based on the premise that there are three main dimensions to the practice of leadership:

Challenges:
The work that has to
be done

The need for balance

Capabilities:
The personal capacity
for leadership

Climate:
What is the mood like
around here?

Figure 19.2 Leadership 360 Plus

4   The model is a development of that found in Pedler, M., Burgoyne, J. and Boydell, T. (2004) *A Manager's Guide to Leadership*. London: Mc Graw Hill.

1. The first concerns the capacity for leadership reflected by individual leaders' capabilities and invariably manifested in observable behaviour.
2. The second relates to the specific challenges that leaders face on a relatively continuous basis.
3. The third concerns the particular context in which leadership takes place: we call this the leadership climate.

This model suggests that if we focus exclusively upon developing individual leadership capability, without taking account both of the challenges leaders face and the prevailing organisation climate, then we are only likely to obtain a partial solution. What is required is a holistic approach which analyses all three dimensions, explores their links and emphasises the need for balance.

LEADERSHIP CAPABILITIES

The ability to lead is based upon seven leadership capabilities (Figure 19.3) each with five key indicators. Sense of purpose is seen a 'core' whilst Self-leadership, Achievement focus and Open thinking are largely 'internal' to the individual leader. In contrast, Building relationships, Influencing and Developing performance are largely carried our in the 'external' environment.[5]

Each capability is defined within the instrument and feedback is collected from respondents scoring five associated indicators along a five-point scale. First they give the 'ideal' score for the particular leadership position (shown by a diamond) and second they score the leader's actual performance, as they perceive it (shown in the from of a bar chart). This is illustrated in Figure 19.4.

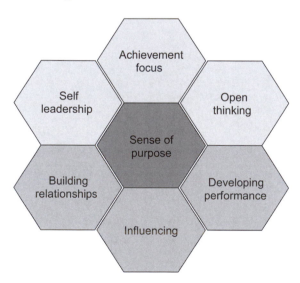

Figure 19.3 The seven characteristics of leadership capabilities

---

5   Particularly influential in our framework was the work of Daniel Goleman. See his *Emotional Intelligence* (1995, New York: Bantam), *The New Leaders* (2002, London: Little, Brown and Co.); and *Primal Leadership: Realizing the Power of Emotional Intelligence* (2002, Boston, MA: Harvard Business School Press) to mention just three of his books.

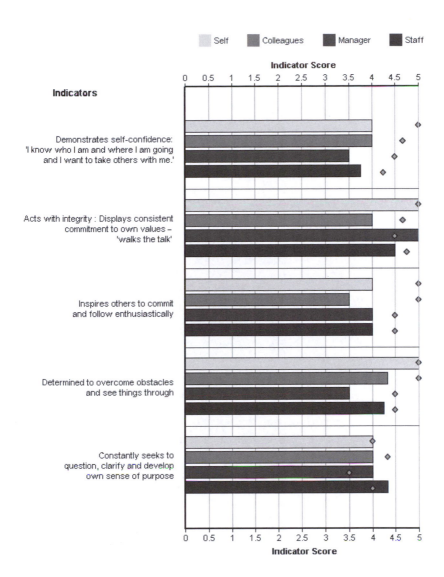

Figure 19.4 Detail for sense of purpose

From the above it can be seen that there are four reporting categories: Self (top bar), Colleagues (second bar), Manager (third bar) and Staff/subordinates (last bar). Each of the other six leadership capabilities is scored along the same lines.

Leadership Challenges

A similar procedure is used to provide feedback for the 11 leadership challenges, illustrated in Figure 19.5.

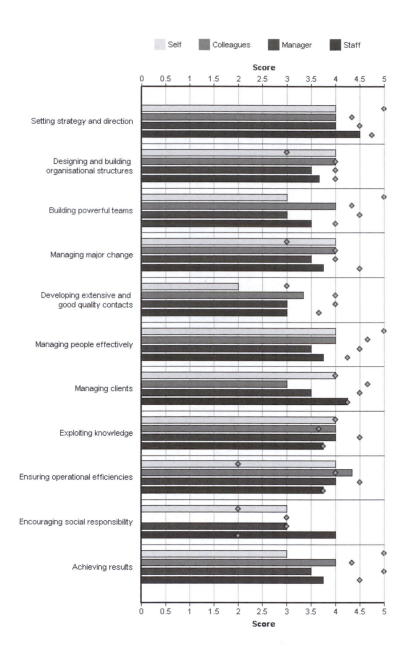

Figure 19.5 Example of detail for leadership challenges

What emerges from the above, but within the overall framework of Leadership 360 Plus, are four 'ideal' models of leadership each compiled by perhaps the most important constituents of leadership – those who practise it, witness it and experience it on a day-by-day basis. These ideals are reflected in the positioning of the diamonds. Similarly there are four assessments, including self-assessment, of the participant's leadership capability and level of performance when tackling leadership challenges. This provides the opportunity for each participant and their coach to investigate:

- The relevance of ideal types, their consistency and underlying logic.
- Comparisons between self-assessment and others' assessment for both their personal and ideal scores.
- The particular importance of staff scores – after all, it is they who are ostensibly being engaged as followers.
- Relative strengths and weaknesses: strengths are shown by the lengths of the bar extending close to, or beyond, the ideal score, weaknesses are shown by the gaps; it is particularly important to encourage participants to continue to develop and deploy strengths as well as address weaknesses.
- Trends: for instance identifying which group is tending to offer higher or lower scores – and why.
- Links between the two charts which indicate, for instance, which particular capabilities can best be combined to address a specific challenge.
- Developmental priorities – to include both building on personal strengths and limiting the impact of, or overcoming, perceived weaknesses.

LEADERSHIP CLIMATE

The climate in which leadership takes place is dealt with in the third section of the 360. This is not a reflection of, nor an assessment of, individual styles. After all, unless it is a small organisation, few leaders are solely responsible for establishing and maintaining a specific climate. In the context of leadership development, climate is important for the following reasons:

- It conditions leadership throughout the orgnisation and impacts upon the way individual leaders go about their job.
- It impacts significantly upon the morale of the workplace – and is therefore a crucial responsibility of leadership.
- It sets the context in which leadership development takes place.
- Leaders can do something about it – even if only talking to other leaders and persuading them that action is necessary to address issues of climate.

This focus on the climate within which each leader acts also impacts upon the realism and the ambition of the development plan established by the individual leader. It militates against ignoring the context within which the leader has to operate 'back in reality' and provides a test for the appropriateness of the course of action. It also challenges leaders to think about whether climate is a given or whether they should be rising to the challenge to change the climate in which they and their team have to operate.

We define seven dimensions of climate[6] to describe the context in which leadership takes place. They are listed in Table 19.1.

---

6   See Koys, D. and De Cotiis, T. (2001) Corporate culture and climate. In A. Furnham, *The Psychology of Behaviour at Work*, pp. 552–603. Hove: Psychological Press.

Each dimension is described in the 360 questionnaire at the extreme ends of a bipolar construct. Respondents are asked to score along the ten-point scale first for the ideal organisation and secondly for the organisation as currently experienced. The definition and format for 'autocratic' is shown in Table 19.2 as an example of this process.

Table 19.1 The seven dimensions of climate

Autocratic	Learning-oriented
Cohesive	Supportive
Fair	Trusting
Innovative	

Table 19.2 The definition and format of autocratic in the 360 questionnaire

Left-hand definition	Climate issue	Right-hand definition	Current climate	Preferred climate	Need for change
People have a high degree of freedom and personal responsibility to determine their own work targets and processes. Leaders adopts a hands-off approach.	Autocratic	People are closely supervised and have little individual responsibility. Leaders are not questioned – they initiate action and control what is going on.			

Thirdly, participants are then asked to indicate how important they think it is for change to take place (see the final column in Table 19.2). The data collected is illustrated in Figure 19.6.

Interpreting the 'Cohesive' scale in the Table 19.1 indicates that both the manager and colleagues show a significant gap between the ideal and actual scores and that change is important. Staff, however, have contrasting perceptions and part of the coaching and review process would be to investigate and possibly explain these differences. Interestingly the participants score their organisation beyond the ideal in five of the seven categories and feels that change would be 'useful' in each of them. So, from the participant's perspective, the climate is overly innovative and too trusting – matters that can be teased around in the coaching session.

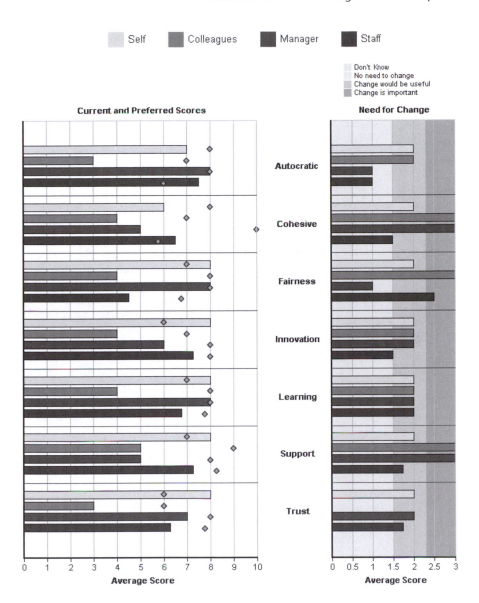

Figure 19.6 Example of detail for leadership climate

Free-form Comments

In addition to the above three quantitative sections, provision is also made to collect qualitative data as free-form comments under the headings:

- Stop doing;
- Start doing;
- Continue doing.

These comments give a valuable and additional personal insight into the important aspects of leadership performance that impact on work colleagues. They allow respondents to explain circumstances not covered by the questionnaire and to add a personal note. Not only do they include positive and negative feedback, in many cases they feedforward by giving helpful hints about possible areas for change. We find that these comments are often the most galvanising section of the 360.

The directness of the wording provides a clear indication as to where others see the priorities for behavioural change and are a catalyst for action. For instance, it is difficult for even the most hardened leader to ignore the observation: 'Get a better home–life balance. You have just had a new baby and you should bond more.'

However, the process of working through the three quantitative elements of capability, challenge and climate builds a framework for each individual's leadership reality. This incremental process is essential for informing the leader's decision about which behavioural changes will have the most beneficial impact and avoid the development agenda being simply a response to a collection of personal comments.

Action Planning

Finally an action planning process is built into Leadership 360 Plus profiles. At the end of each of the four sections is a short review process inviting participants to list their main learning points. The whole culminates in an action plan designed to encourage personal change, the implementation of learning and improved leadership performance.

Leadership 360 Plus in the Context of the Henley Leadership Programme

We firmly believe that positioning the 360 in a structured development process has a much more positive impact than its random deployment. Participants benefit because:

- It sets up expectations and whets the appetite. One participant, as we write, has just replied prior to his forthcoming programme: 'Provocative questions. I'm even more convinced that I'll get something out of the Leadership Programme.' This person is already on his development journey and we have not even met him. Interestingly, we have had similar responses from those providing feedback who are not even on the programme! One has just written, 'The survey was easy to use and, just from reading the questionnaire, some points came up that we have to think about on the trade desk.' So undertaking a 360 development journey may not be restricted to those attending the programme – it also has implications for those people providing feedback.
- Completing the 360 ensures that participants identify key stakeholders and think seriously about leadership issues and the context in which they are working. In short it helps them prepare for their leadership development journey and specifically, helps them prepare for the five days at Henley, which will focus and motivate the participants to take the next steps in honing their leadership style and skills.

- Along with the MBTI Step II ®[7] and FIRO-B ®[8] questionnaires it provides a battery of contrasting feedback to complement other aspects of the programme.
- The models from the programme are designed to help participants make sense of themselves and the world in which they lead. These models can be deployed immediately – and to good effect – to help them interpret and respond to their 360 feedback.
- There is a secure and supportive structure within which they can reflect about their leadership performance. They are not on their own. In addition to tutors and coaches there are also other participants going through a similar process with whom they can confer.
- The coaching process encourages them to make sense of all the data to which they are exposed and to think in terms of structured outputs: they know when they leave Henley that they will have had the opportunity to set themselves targets which they stand a good chance of achieving.

In short we believe that deploying a focused 360 specifically within a comprehensive development framework is likely to produce the most effective results and enhance the leadership performance of participants.

360 Case Studies

The following stories are real examples from our experience and illustrate the above points. Plainly we have taken steps to protect the confidentiality of those with whom we work. At the beginning of each case are a few words to indicate the reasons for including this particular story.

Case Study 1

The need for coaching support

The purpose of this story is to illustrate that, no matter how glowing the 360 profile may be, the need for professional coaching/feedback is essential. The interpretation of, and reaction to, 360 profiles will vary – and cannot easily be predicted by the coach no matter how closely they may have studied the profile.

Andrea is a senior manager in a large international organisation. Twelve people responded to his invitation for feedback and provided a positive report on his leadership capacity. The gaps in both the leadership capabilities and challenges sections were relatively small and, in general, the written comments were indicative of someone who was already an effective leader. For example one said: 'I think Andrea

---

7   MBTI ® MBTI is a trademark or a registered trademark of the Myers-Briggs Type Indicator Trust in the United States. OPP Ltd is licensed to use the trademark in Europe.

8   FIRO-B ® is a registered trademark of CPP Inc. OPP is licensed to use the trademark in Europe.

is a very good leader who needs to keep on working as he has been doing thus far, relying on his excellent personal and professional qualities.' A second wrote, 'In my view Andrea should continue doing what he does now – giving all who work for him a clear sense of support and appreciation. What I perhaps appreciate most is that he is always a very careful listener – doesn't jump to conclusions, encourages people to speak their mind, and only then takes a decision. I've also been impressed with Andrea's consistent practice of praising people publicly for their achievements.' A third reaffirmed the theme: 'Andrea has a very human way of managing. His way of being makes people feel guided and responsible at the same time. He has created an environment that motivates people and allows them to develop in different directions.' The overall impression was of a sensitive, empathic and skilled leader unafraid to take tough decisions when necessary. He was clearly valued by those providing feedback.

However, the coaching/feedback session showed someone who was uncomfortable with the 360 process. For him, 'It felt like the Stasi had been watching and reporting on me.' He was also ill at ease with himself seeking evidence from his profile to vindicate his inadequacies. So every performance gap, no matter how narrow, and every negative comment, no matter how constructive, reinforced this negative self-esteem. There seemed a mismatch between the person reported upon and the person being coached. In such situations it is particularly important that:

- The participant has realistic expectation of the coaching process and that a 'coaching contract' is understood by coach and coachee.
- The coach is experienced in handling tricky situations.

In this instance it was important for Andrea to accept the value of feedback in the development process and to recognise that negative comments were not malicious: it was a matter of challenging and reframing his perceptions to enable him to see his 360 feedback in a different light and to focus his energy on existing and future performance issues.

Case Study 2

Unearthing the unexpected

Superficially this looked like a typical 'time management' issue – but issues are almost never 'typical'. This coaching session dealt with a core problem whose symptoms appeared in the 360 and linked this to the prevailing leadership climate within the participant's organisation.

The common theme running through Ted's 360 was, in broad terms, work–life balance. His feedback reported that Ted was not only spending a lot of time on the job but also taking work home. During the coaching session this theme was taken up and, after a little while, Ted admitted that the reason for his troubles was caused by his dyslexia. He went to great lengths to keep this hidden from his work colleagues by avoiding situations that may expose him – and by assiduous preparation. For instance he would not spontaneously write on flip charts – they had to be prepared, emails were painstakingly answered and written work taken home to be checked each evening prior to circulation at work the next day. Touchingly Ted admitted that his young daughter used to help him with his work in the evening. But these demands were untenable in the long term – particularly as he was well thought of and being groomed for additional leadership responsibilities – which was bringing even greater pressure.

In the coaching session Ted decided that he wanted to address the fundamental issue 'how to deal with dyslexia'. We explored Ted's fear of becoming identified as dyslexic and linked this to the organisation climate. In the 360 this was reported as being generally supportive and learning oriented. Ted began to recognise and accept his paradox: he had a problem – but was not prepared to reveal this in spite of the supportive climate. Additionally, in preparation for the programme, he had read 'Why should anyone be led by you' in which the authors, Goffee and Jones,* make the point that inspirational leaders must be prepared to reveal selective weaknesses. Ted quickly reached the conclusion that he must be prepared to reveal his dyslexia. The remainder of the coaching session was spent exploring how to do so and assessing the likely consequences. In our experience it is not often that a single coaching session has such a marked impact. On the review day, held about three months after the core module, he told his story: first he took his manager into his confidence told him about the symptoms picked up by the 360 and the underlying cause. They prepared a joint strategy in which Ted would reveal his dilemma to his team and his manger would do his utmost to help Ted deal with the issue. The result was that he began to work more sensible hours, he ceased to take written work home with him and he was able to spend more time leading his people.

> *   Goffee, R. and Jones, G. (2000) Why should anyone be led by you?, *Harvard Business Review*, September–October: 63–70.

Case Study 3

Dealing with immediate emotional responses

Participants have wide-ranging responses when receiving their 360 feedback. This case illustrates the need for facilitators to be sensitive to participant's initial reactions, to encourage them to focus as much on positive as well as negative feedback and to allow time for balanced reflection.

After skim-reading his profile James was clearly perturbed. He remained behind at the end of the plenary session in which the 360 model was explained and participants received their profiles. His profile showed two different pictures: his peers saw him in a far worse light than did his manager and his team of direct reports. The distinction was marked. Although this was not the time for the scheduled coaching session the immediate concerns of a participant will not wait for formal coaching. It was time, first to allow him to express his initial feelings, second to reaffirm that what he was seeing was indeed the case – that his profile was as it was and there was no mistaking the facts portrayed and thirdly, it was necessary for James to have a balanced perspective before retiring for the night. The short-term fix was to allow him to ventilate his feeling – but then to encourage him to focus as much upon positive feedback, and there was positive feedback, as well as the negative. Simply listening to participants voice their anxiety will often result in them making some sense out of the mass of information they have received.

Allowing participants to digest their profiles overnight – in the knowledge that they have a coaching session the following day – encourages them to draw upon their learning from other parts of the programme. The 360 is not a one-off event, it is part of an integrated development process with a particular emphasis upon the importance of reflection. Receiving the profile one day and providing a coaching session the next day allows time for people to digest the information and establish considered priorities for their coaching session. The down side of this approach is that people like James often need the services of a coach fairly quickly.

But the 360 is only one source of information. At this stage participants will also have received feedback from the FIRO-B and MBTI questionnaires, will have come across various leadership models and case studies and had the opportunity to practice leadership through their involvement in various exercises. By reflecting upon this intense experience they will begin to establish what it is they wish to talk about with their coaches. Invariably it is closely linked with information emerging from their 360.

In James's case he knew he had a battle on his hands: the reason for him coming on the programme was because his chairman had selected him to become MD of his small company. The programme, and its integral 360, was part of James's preparation for taking on additional leadership responsibilities. James had not been the only candidate and it was this, he thought, that had put his colleagues' noses out of joint and which had been reflected in his 360. Colleagues anyway tend to report more negatively than other groups. Unlike the participants themselves, their managers and staff members, colleagues don't have a direct vested interest in the process. The line responsibility that managers have for participants means that they are very likely to become engaged in post-programme reviews – as are staff members – albeit from a different perspective. It may be that the formality of the relationship that people have with participants, and the anticipated aftermath from the programme, conditions their responses. Colleagues can be harsh, or perhaps more honest, without worrying too much about the consequences.

James colleagues were harsh – they had a perceived grievance to air. After his initial adverse reaction James took comfort from the positive feedback reported by his staff and, as the quality of leadership lies very much in the eye of the beholder, then this dimension is likely to be a good indicator of a leader's capability. During the coaching session James's identified his key 'stakeholders' and arrived at a strategy to build alliances with select colleagues – without whose support his job was going to be very difficult. He also reckoned it worth the risk to let people know – collectively – that the long-term future of the company could be undermined unless they were able to build a more cohesive and supportive climate. In short he quickly transferred his focus from denying to accepting his colleague's perspectives and planning a strategy to deal with their anticipated resistance.

Case Study 4

The need for a holistic approach

In this case there was particularly negative feedback from the participant's manager. The case illustrates the opportunistic nature of the 360, the value of a comprehensive and integrated approach and the length of time over which development programmes can continue to have an impact.

The single most striking aspect of Rosie's 360 was the critical feedback from her manager. During the coaching session she confirmed that the 360 was an accurate reflection of reality: her boss was extremely critical of her performance. Neither her colleagues nor her staff agreed and their feedback, she claimed, was fair and balanced. Indeed what was surprising about Rosie's 360 were the many positive written references about how she was handling a difficult boss. It was not surprising that the coaching session spent much time addressing the circumstances impacting upon Rosie. She was beginning to lose confidence and question her career prospects within the organisation.

When there are obvious differences between manager and participant then the 360 provides an ideal opportunity to at least discuss the situation. Given that in almost all circumstances the manager is also responsible for the more formal performance management of the participant then it is important to ensure that any significant differences in perception between the two are understood and tackled. Coaching provides the opportunity to prepare for these discussions and this is what happened in Rosie's case. The various options that Rosie had were considered, including the quite definite possibility that she would leave the organisation. She reached the conclusion that there was little possibility of changing the behaviour of her manager – what she could best do was to retain her self-belief and let him know her own thoughts about her department and his approach to her. To prepare for her meeting with Graham – her manager – she used the 'scripting tool' which encourages people to recognise their likely thoughts and feelings during a potentially threatening meeting – and that of her manager – and then to plan as precisely as possible how she was going to behave during a very short interaction with him. Like a good theatrical play this has to be well rehearsed before the first performance. From Rosie's perspective the meeting went well, as did her own career development, because it was not long before she took over her manager's job. Almost two years later she wrote to us saying: 'Since Henley, I have been promoted and taken on Graham's old job – he was my rather difficult line manager, who was perhaps a little threatened by me and I deeply struggled to work with. Thanks for your help which enabled me to do it – that week was as much about my realising I could perfectly well do a senior management job and should kick the habit of blocking off opportunities for myself, as any tool or technique I learnt. I remember it especially as it was one of the very few times I have spoken to someone who understood what it was like in my head, and I really appreciated it. I still use the "meeting scripting" tool you gave me from time to time'.

It was the 360 which provided the lever to unlock Rosie's predicament – but it was other aspects of the programme which provided her with the toolkit to rebuild her personal and professional confidence.

What Do Participants Do? A Summary of Development Actions

About three months beyond the core Leadership Programme is a follow-up day to review learning and re-energise the commitment to personal change. This day begins with a review of what has gone well. Some of the positive actions are listed:

- 'Previously I put a negative slant on things and used to emphasise risk. Now I am more optimistic and put a positive slant on things – look for the benfit as well as the risk.' This person scored themselves very harshly in the 360 process.
- 'The 360 helped me to understand my respondents and the leadership actions I needed to take to allow them to do their jobs better.'
- 'After the programme and the 360 I took a short break away from work to review my position. This allowed me to fundamentally challenge and change myself and ... to challenge the culture of the company.'
- 'Leadership is a journey. It is not something that is fixed. It is more a slow realisation of required change. As a result of the 360 and the programme I have started an organisation support network to help promote the leadership journey for myself and others.'
- The 360 involves 'learning about others. What is in my head is not always how people see me. Whether I like it or not they put what might be best termed a label on me and I have to live with that label – or I need to change.'
- It is interesting where people place their emphasis. 'I set "building powerful teams" as a high need where all others said this was a moderate need. I adjusted my leadership behaviour accordingly.'
- 'Overall the 360 was very useful. It gives a sound picture of how you are and the granularity of the areas is also useful. The main issue is how to translate this into action.'

- 'I used to count every nut and bolt that came on the site. The feedback told me that if I wanted to be an effective leader I had to change and rise above the detail that preoccupied me.'

People also refer to the occasional mixed message emerging from the 360 process and to its apparent inconsistencies, but this is an integral part of the complicated life that leaders live within the fluctuating fortunes of their organisations. Leadership is more about making sense of paradox and complexity than about coping with predictable routine.

Conclusion

There are costs involved in any 360 process: they are time-consuming exercises especially if they are to be carried out thoughtfully. This is particularly the case in small organisations where members of the top management team may find themselves giving feedback to each other and to other significant organisation leaders – often within a tight time frame. On the other hand, if the process does not demand time and thought, then it is reasonable to question the value of the outcomes of the process. 360s also set up expectations: at the personal level those who provide feedback will, entirely reasonably, expect beneficial personal changes to manifest themselves. If this does not happen then the future deployment of a 360 may be undermined. After all, if nothing changes, then why should people be expected to give up their time to provide feedback? In an organisation context this is even more the case: if previous 360 excercises deployed across the organisation have not resulted in anticipated benefits then why become involved in future 360 exercise? The danger here is of contagion into other areas. It is not just the 360 which is being called into question but the way the organisation does things across the board.

Nor does engaging in a 360 necessarily produce positive results. Its value may be compromised by the poor selection of feedback providers. By and large what participants receive in the way of feedback depends upon whom they select to provide it. If feedback providers feel aggrieved by generic organisation processes then they may use the 360 to ventilate their views rather than to aid personal leadership development. Additionally if they merely provide feedback which they feel a participant wants to hear then the exercise is also highly questionable.

However, most of the challenges to the 360 process can be addressed. The 360 instrument described in this chapter is part of a broader process of personal development whose prime focus is improved leadership performance, and the case studies illustrate our belief in the value of a holistic, comprehensive and integrated approach supported by experienced coaches. They also illustrate the contrasting development journeys being taken by different leaders facing very different challenges in different leadership climates. In spite of the uniqueness of individual journeys – or perhaps because of this uniqueness – it is very obvious how helpful the participants are towards each other. Empathy is an integral constituent of leadership and the opportunity for participants to listen and respond to each others' 360 stories is an important part of their learning.

To date we have been pleased with the progress that participants have shown in their leadership performance months after the completion of the 360 and the core programme module. However, the design of the 360 includes action planning guidelines to enable its use on a more prolonged self-development basis. We are also exploring its potential use to assess improved performance over longer periods. Apart from extending the developmental use of the 360 we further believe that this will aid participants and ourselves in tracking more longitudinal shifts in leadership behaviour. Additionally we are constantly collecting new data from the 360 and continuing our research in efforts to refine the process and help leaders meet their constantly shifting challenges.

20 *Building Quality into Executive Coaching*

DAVID E. GRAY

Executive coaching is now seen in many organisations, both private and public, as an essential professional development intervention. While in the recent past coaches may have been engaged by individual senior managers, it is increasingly the case that they are used throughout the management structure of organisations. As a result, many organisations have had to engage the services of teams or 'faculties' of coaches, either recruited individually, engaged en masse from coaching or management consultancy organisations, or developed internally. This raises a number of questions, not least of which are:

- Should an organisation use internal or external coaches?
- How should these coaches be recruited and selected?
- How should coaches and coachees be matched?
- How should the coaching faculty be managed?

This chapter will offer a tentative model for answering these questions, based partly on the author's personal experience of being recruited into a corporate coaching faculty, partly on recruiting a coaching faculty for a government-sponsored initiative and, in part, on recent research findings.

Why is Coaching Growing?

Coaching is on an upward trajectory.[1, 2, 3] One survey,[4] for example, found that nearly 80 per cent of respondents said that they now use coaching in their organisation. However, while the current trend seems to be one of continuous expansion, it is worth recalling that this is a relatively new phenomenon. Feldman and Lankau[5] suggest that executive

---

1   Eggers, J. H. and Clark, D. (2000) Executive coaching that wins, *Ivey Business Journal*, 65(1): 66–70.

2   Goldsmith, M., Lyons, L. and Freas, A. (eds) (2000) *Coaching for Leadership*. San Francisco, CA: Jossey-Bass/Pfeiffer.

3   Smither, J. W. and Reilly, S. P. (2001) Coaching in organizations: a social psychological perspective. In London, M. (ed.) *How People Evaluate Others in Organizations*. Mahwah, NJ: Erlbaum.

4   Jarvis, J. (2004) *Coaching and Buying Coaching Services*. London: CIPD.

5   Feldman, D. C. and Lankau, M. J. (2005) Executive coaching: a review and agenda for future research, *Journal of Management*, 31(6): 829–848.

coaching began to emerge as recently as the 1990s as an intervention aimed at changing the behaviour and performance of senior and middle managers. Today, coaching in general (that is, coaching is all its various guises, including 'life coaching') is growing exponentially, with probably about 10,000 coaches working in the USA, and maybe around 4,000 operating in the UK.[6] Palmer[7] suggests that between 25 and 40 per cent of US fortune 500 companies now use executive coaching. Coaching is also developing across Europe and there are active coaching communities in Australia and New Zealand.

Why is coaching so popular? From an organisational perspective, it offers a wide range of possibilities for the support, performance enhancement and personal development of managers and others. It is a truism, for example, to say 'it's lonely at the top', but many executives, as their star rises in an organisation, have fewer and fewer people to share their problems or concerns with. Just because someone becomes a CEO, for example, doesn't mean that their inner self-doubts and anxieties disappear – they may even grow! A coach, then, can be useful as a sounding board or as a confidante. They are also likely to have experience or knowledge of some of the business problems CEOs and other senior executives have to deal with.[8] Executive coaching typically involves, but is not confined to:

- Working with managers/leaders who have been targeted for promotion.
- Helping executives through organisational change processes.
- Increasing an executive's confidence, self-awareness, the recognition of 'blind spots' and developing their emotional intelligence.
- Improving an executive's leadership strategies and management skills.
- Helping a leader to coach their senior team through a major transition.
- Creating a collective vision for the organisation.

Increasingly the focus in many organisations is one of team coaching. Here the coach may work with an executive board or top management team, with the focus on how the group as a whole operates as a collective. The kinds of issues addressed typically include:

- Getting agreement and commitment to organisational strategy.
- Improving inter-group and intra-group communication.
- Resolving conflict.
- Managing communication, information and expectations upwards and downwards.

Many organisations see executive coaching as a direct performance-enhancing intervention which can be implemented not only at individual but also at team, section, department or organisational level. However, given the relatively high costs of coaching (certainly high relative to classroom-based professional development programmes), the introduction of a coaching programme has to be part of a strategic intervention, often high profile, and almost certainly sponsored or supported at senior level in the organisation.

---

6   Jarvis, J., Lane, D. and Fillery-Travis, A. (2006) *The Case for Coaching: Making Evidence-based Decisions on Coaching.* London: CIPD.

7   Palmer, B. (2003) Maximizing value from executive coaching, *Strategic HR Review,* 2(6): 26–29.

8   Schnell, E. R. (2005) A case study of executive coaching as a support mechanism during organizational growth and evolution, *Consulting Psychology Journal: Practice and Research,* 57(1): 41–56.

It is also likely that the design and implementation of a coaching programme will be undertaken or have the involvement at some level of the organisation's human resource professionals. Let us imagine, then, that a decision has been made to explore the options for implementing a large-scale coaching programme into an organisation. What are the next steps? The rest of this chapter offers a simple model.

An Overview of the Recruitment and Selection Process

As Figure 20.1 shows, the recruitment and selection model for recruiting the coaching faculty takes place in three stages: needs analysis, recruitment and selection, and matching. A training needs analysis is important because it is essential to determine 'what the training needs to achieve').[9] A simple 'let's get on and do it' approach does not work in today's dynamic world. Laying down some firm foundations for what is required allows the organisation to enter the recruitment process with more confidence. Within the recruitment and selection process, there are many alternative approaches available, but the use of assessment centres is one of the most successful because it makes use of many different predictors.[10] An assessment centre is at the heart of the suggested faculty recruitment model. Once applicants are shortlisted, the assessment centre is put into operation to identify high-calibre coaches whose skills and experience match the needs of the organisation. This is not the end of the recruitment process. Means have to be found for matching coaches with the beneficiaries of the coaching – the coachees. The rest of this chapter looks at each of these stages in more detail.

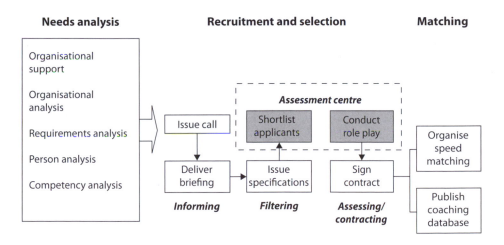

Figure 20.1 Coaching faculty recruitment and selection process

9   Arnold, J. (2005) *Work Psychology: Understanding Human Behaviour in the Workplace,* 4th edn. Harlow: Pearson Education Limited.

10   Goldstein, I. L. and Ford, J. K. (2002) *Training in Organizations: Needs Assessment, Development and Evaluation*, 4th edn. Belmont, CA: Wadsworth Thomson Learning.

Conducting a Coaching Needs Analysis

As with any training or development initiative, the essential first step is to ascertain whether a coaching programme is needed by the organisation. This means conducting a needs analysis, identifying the gap between the level of performance the organisation requires and what it currently gets. Given its intensive, one-to-one or small group format, coaching is one of the more expensive development interventions, so it is essential that its costs are justified. The needs analysis then may be conducted in an effort to assess the development needs of the organisation – coaching possibly emerging as just one potential solution. Alternatively, coaching may have been viewed as a worthy intervention from the start (for example, the CEO is impressed from reading about or having personal experience of coaching and wants it introduced). However, its scale, objectives and target beneficiaries can only be ascertained after a needs analysis has been performed. The coaching needs analysis comes in five stages: organisational support, organisational analysis, requirements analysis, person analysis and competencies analysis.

ORGANISATIONAL SUPPORT

Gaining organisational support and trust is a critical first step in any needs analysis process.[11] Stakeholders include all those who, for one reason or another, have an interest in the positive outcomes of the programme. Table 20.1 presents some of the likely stakeholders and the reasons why they might be important sources of information and 'buy-in' during the needs analysis process. Clearly, if we are talking about a large-scale, high-profile coaching initiative, then top-level management approval (and positive commitment) is essential. Getting the coaching programme discussed and approved at executive board level will be of enormous help in management buy-in throughout the organisation, as well as recruitment. It will help to sustain and protect the programme should any problems arise. Top-level commitment will also assist in eliciting the support of the next tier of senior and middle management, at least some of whom may be potential beneficiaries of the programme (see next section).

If the organisation is large enough to have its own human resources (HR) department or section, then it would be surprising if the people here were not involved at a strategic as well as operational level. Indeed, many coaching initiatives are promoted and managed by HR. It will normally be HR that plans, conducts and analyses the needs analysis data, the results of which will identify the beneficiaries within the organisation. But the focus on beneficiaries does not end here. Without the approval and support of coachees' line managers, it is unlikely that any coaching initiative could succeed. Line managers have the potential to smooth the way or to block the coaching programme because it is they who determine how much time coachees can be given to meet their coach (especially if this is off-site). Above all, they also have a key role in helping coachees to implement changes in knowledge, attitudes and behaviours into their everyday working lives. Line managers can also help to identify what these changes need to be.

---

11   Goldstein, I. L. and Ford, J. K. (2002) *Training in Organizations: Needs Assessment, Development and Evaluation*, 4th edn. Belmont, CA: Wadsworth Thomson Learning.

Table 20.1 Potential stakeholders for the coaching needs analysis

Stakeholder	Reasons for inclusion in needs analysis
The CEO, chairperson and executive board	Responsible for organisational strategy, including change management which the coaching might assist
Senior management	Responsible for planning and implementing change. Can help or (often subtly) block the coaching programme if their commitment is not achieved or maintained
The HR department, if the organisation is large enough to have one; if not, those responsible for the HR function	The HR function is best placed to understand the skills, knowledge and performance deficiencies in the organisation (often identified through appraisal processes)
Potential coachees	Their buy-in is essential. They must not see coaching as a threat or punishment for low performance
The line managers of potential coachees	May be key suppliers of support – must help to free up space for the coachee to meet their coach and try out new approaches and/or behaviours

In has to be borne in mind that there are also other important stakeholders who can play an influential role in making the coaching programme a success – or otherwise. These are:

- Opinion leaders. These are people who are influential in the organisation because of their status, knowledge or charisma. They might be useful allies, especially at an early stage, when the coaching initiative is being mooted or debated.
- Team leaders. These people are important, especially those who manage work areas where the coaching might need to take root.
- Blockers. These could be opinion leaders or those with power who, for whatever reason, dislike coaching or the coaching programme and have the ability to disrupt it. These people could exist at any level of the organisation.

ORGANISATIONAL ANALYSIS

Organisational analysis is concerned with systems-wide components of the organisation, including its goals, resources and any internal or external constraints present in the environment.[12] Of significance here are the strategic plans and direction of the organisation. The training development climate of the organisation is also important. For example, is training well integrated as part of the culture of the organisation? In terms of resource analysis, this could include an assessment of future human resource needs – what new skills or management competencies is the coaching required to develop, as the

---

12   Goldstein, I. L. and Ford, J. K. (2002) *Training in Organizations: Needs Assessment, Development and Evaluation*, 4th edn. Belmont, CA: Wadsworth Thomson Learning.

organisation adapts to its environment? At an organisational level the kinds of questions that can be asked here include:

- Does the organisation need a coaching intervention at this time? What kinds of strategic or operational issues need attention?
- What key behaviours, performance or attitudes require change? What is the view of the executive board on this matter, given the current strategic plans for the organisation? What is the view from middle management and those at the 'sharp end'?
- Has coaching been used in the organisation before; if so was the programme evaluated? What were the results? Were the stated aims of the coaching programme achieved? Are there currently people in the organisation who organised or were beneficiaries of the last coaching initiative who can be contacted and asked about it?
- What do the likely recipients know about coaching? Do they understand the difference between coaching, mentoring and consultancy? Do those conducting the needs analysis, understand the difference?
- What involvement will human resource professionals have with the programme? Who will have overall responsibility for championing, planning, implementing, leading and evaluating the coaching programme?
- What will the coaching programme cost and can the organisation afford it?
- Is coaching the right intervention or is an alternative development approach such as mentoring or consultancy more appropriate?

As Table 20.2 shows, coaching is usually a shorter-term relationship than mentoring and more focused on specific performance and outcomes.

Table 20.2 Summary of differences between coaching and mentoring

Coaching	Mentoring
A short-term relationship	Can be quite long-term
Structured with regular meetings	Informal, meeting 'as necessary'
Focus on specific issues and goals	Wide-ranging in focus
Focus on performance and development issues	Focus on career and personal development
Focus on the present	Focus on the future

Source: Gray (in print).[13]

In contrast to consultancy, coaching shies away from giving advice – the objective is to allow the coachee to find their own solutions (see Table 20.3). While both coaching and consultancy get the coachee/client to consider a range of potential options, consultancy (like mentoring) can focuses on giving advice. Coaches tend to avoid giving advice, expect in exceptional circumstances where the coachee is completely 'stuck' in a problem.

---

13   Gray, D. E. (in print) *Business Coaching for Managers and Organizations – Working with Coaches that Make the Difference.* Amherst, MA: HRD Press.

Table 20.3   Summary of differences between coaching and consultancy

Coaching	Consultancy
Gets client to consider a range of options	Also gets client to consider a range of options
Explores client's perspectives	Gives advice
Gets client to select options for action	Makes recommendations
Can be holistic in terms of work but also life and personal issues	Very business focused

Source: Gray (in print).

REQUIREMENTS ANALYSIS

A critical objective here is to identify the kinds of jobs or roles that are going to be subject to the needs analysis. Often job titles are unhelpful in specifying the nature of tasks being performed. An alternative would be to focus on specified activities such as all those managers whose function includes communication with external customers. Another step at this stage is determining who will be involved in the needs analysis process, with an attempt to co-opt as many key stakeholders as possible (including the kinds of people identified previously in Table 20.1).

PERSON ANALYSIS

According to Goldstein and Ford[14] person analysis asks two questions:

1. Who within the organisation needs development?
2. What kind of development do they need?

Coaching is expensive, so any coaching intervention needs to be carefully planned in terms of the balance between coaching and alternative, possibly cheaper, programmes such as mentoring (using internal mentors who are usually unpaid) or classroom-based workshops. A balance also has to be struck between the use of external and potentially cheaper internal coaches, and the number and levels of people to be coached. It is unlikely that a coaching programme will be aimed at all levels, so organisations have to take some tough decisions in terms of rationing coaching between competing claimants. So who should be coached? The following candidates are typical:

*   Executive coachees. These are obvious recipients of coaching, given the strategic decisions they will have to take. It is also 'lonely at the top', so, as stated earlier, executives often have few people to share their thoughts or fears with. Recipients, then, can range from the CEO and executive board members, through to other senior executives.

---

14   Goldstein, I. L. and Ford, J. K. (2002) *Training in Organizations: Needs Assessment, Development and Evaluation*, 4th edn. Belmont, CA: Wadsworth Thomson Learning.

- High-flying coachees. Obviously, these are candidates who have been assessed as having potential for positions of leadership or influence in the organisation. They may have been identified, for example, through a talent management process, as potential executive board members in the not-too-distant future.
- Key area coachees. These people are seen as important recipients of coaching because the tasks they perform are essential for the organisation. For example, they could be senior members of a marketing team who are involved in launching a vital new product, or the director and senior team implementing the organisation's new information technology system.
- Remedial coachees. Weaknesses or problems have been identified, possibly through annual appraisal or 360-degree feedback, that require attention. It is essential here that these recipients see the coaching being offered as a helping hand and not as a punishment. If coaching is only used as the focus of remedial issues, it will be seen as a punishment for 'bad behaviour' rather than as a positive development opportunity.

Having identified both stakeholders and beneficiaries, these people can be approached for information on their coaching needs and views on coaching.

At an individual level, the kinds of questions could, typically, include:

- Where are the potential coachees located?
- Are they ready for coaching and will they commit to it?
- How well does the performance appraisal system identify individual gaps in performance?
- How well does the current training system work to fill identified gaps?

With these kinds of questions in mind, the data gathering process could involve the use of an organisation-wide survey, one-to-one interviews with a purposively selected sample of beneficiaries or focus groups.

COMPETENCE ANALYSIS

Many conventional approaches to needs analysis refer to the next stage as 'Task and knowledge, skills and ability' analysis, KSA or similar terms. These models, however, tend to focus on manual or functional tasks. While coaching can enhance the performance of skills at any level, competency modelling is more appropriate, especially at management level for two reasons:

1. While some of the roles performed by managers include clearly identifiable tasks, managerial roles are often best described in more holistic terms.
2. Much of the knowledge managers use is tacit and often difficult for them to describe.

But, perhaps, an even more significant justification lies in the nature of coaching itself. While sponsoring organisations may set out the broad objectives of a coaching programme, coaches and coaches will usually then need to negotiate an agreement that is focused on performance-level objectives (competencies) right at the start of the coaching intervention. The questions here could include:

- What kinds of new skills or behaviours are required? These, of course, will be linked to the organisational changes identified above. Can 'families' of job roles be identified, providing a common focus for the coaching initiative?
- Are there any specific areas, projects or functions identified where there are gaps in performance?
- Is reorganisation changing the role that people perform and hence the competencies that the organisation requires?

Clearly, the needs analysis can be quite a major undertaking, but if completed thoroughly, it can provide the foundations on which the coaching programme can be built. Once the analysis is approved, and the organisation understands its requirements, the recruitment process can begin.

Recruitment and Selection

Following the needs analysis, the recruitment and selection process takes place in three stages: informing, filtering and assessing/contracting plus, in some cases, a number of sub-stages. These stages should be largely the same whether the organisation is recruiting a faculty of coaches who are external to the organisation, internal, or a mixture of the two – although the latter may make management and quality assurance processes slightly more complicated. However, there may be reasons for an organisation preferring external to the use of internal coaches (or vice versa) (see Table 20.4), and this preference may influence the design of the recruitment process. For example, it might be felt that experienced internal coaches are more valuable because they understand the culture of the organisation. Alternatively, external coaches are experienced in working and coaching in other organisations and may be able to bring in different perspectives.

Table 20.4 Pros and cons of using an internal versus an external coach

	Internal	External
Pros	Knows the internal culture and issues Usually permanently on hand Can help to promote a coaching culture in the organisation Has experience of the problems and obstacles in the organisation	Can bring an outsider's perspective Does not have vested interests or agendas inside the organisation Can provide external benchmarking criteria Coachees are more likely to be honest about their opinions Easier to maintain confidentiality Has access to external networks
Cons	Sometimes lack extensive training as a coach (e.g. short 'line manager as coach' programmes) Potential conflict between role as coach and role as line manager or HR member May be too much part of the organisational culture to be objective and innovative Confidentiality may be harder to keep May be too informal	Can be expensive May lack knowledge of the business Less 'known' by the organisation so higher risk of being inappropriate Organisation may worry about coaches gaining access to sensitive information

Let us now take a look at each of the recruitment and selection processes in turn.

INFORMING PROSPECTIVE COACHES

Issue a call for proposals

If an organisation is going to attract the best external coaches and the best coaching organisations, it needs to be crystal clear about what it is trying to achieve. What organisational agendas are being addressed? Why is a coaching programme needed? The needs analysis, of course, will hopefully have provided answers to these questions. It will help the recruitment process if a 'call' document is produced, setting out all the details of the proposed programme. This document will help, even if internal coaches are being recruited for the programme, because producing the document gets the organisation to clarify its own needs. The call document, then, could set out the following criteria:

- The background to the programme, including a brief history of the organisation, the key issues it faces, and the specific problems or challenges that now need addressing through coaching.
- The purpose of the coaching programme, including clear, measurable and specific objectives.
- The number of people requiring coaching, their positions in the organisation and their location (both nationally, and, if necessary, internationally).
- The kinds of skills, knowledge and experience the appointed coaches will need to demonstrate (and particularly if knowledge and experience of coaching in one kind of organisation/sector is essential).
- The number of hours of coaching proposed for each coachee.
- The duration of the programme including proposed start and finish dates.
- How progress will be evaluated and reported (for example, conference calls or written reports) and the stages at which this evaluation will take place.
- For programmes recruiting externally, either the highest price the organisation is willing to pay, or perhaps a band of indicative prices. Details of what costs are included and excluded – for example, transport costs.
- Cancellation arrangements.

There should be some encouragement for applicants to say how they might design and deliver the proposed programme, as this often produces some innovative ideas that the commissioning organisation had not thought of. Some of these ideas might be captured by incorporating them into the final contract for the work.

Deliver a briefing session

Rather than respond to lots of time-consuming individual questions from interested coaches and coaching organisations, a briefing session could be delivered consisting of:

- A 15–20 minute presentation (basically a reiteration of the call document).
- Responses to questions and comments about the programme.
- A summary of the session at the end and a call for written bids.

At the end of the formal element of the briefing session, there may be opportunities for networking and discussions with individual coaches on a one-to-one basis. Note, however, that it is essential here to divide the time fairly equally between them so as not to create an impression of favouritism.

FILTERING THE APPLICANTS

Issue specification of coaching experience and competencies

Obviously, the design of the form that coach applicants complete should be tied in with the kinds of knowledge, competencies and experience that are being sought in a good coach – as identified in the preceding needs analysis. Apart from the usual face data elements in the form (such as name, address, etc.) data should be sought on the coach's:

- Qualifications, including specific coaching qualifications. If coaching qualifications are held from the UK or European institutions, it would be appropriate to ask whether these programmes have been validated by the European Mentoring and Coaching Council (EMCC).
- Coaching experience, including the number of people they have coached, the sectors they have specialised in (if any), the types of organisation (large corporate, small and medium-sized enterprises, public sector, voluntary), and the levels of seniority coached (CEO, executive board, middle management etc.).
- The kinds of issues they have addressed in their coaching, such as leadership, strategy, work–life balance, stress, performance, motivation, etc.
- Coaching philosophy, style and models used.
- References, including people who have been coached by the applicant and who are willing to provide written recommendations. Similarly, case studies of successful coaching interventions could be asked for.

Shortlisting the applicants

Once the applications have been received, the organisation has to make systematic and rational choices between them. How can this be done objectively? One approach is to create a scoring system based on weighted criteria from the application form. For example, if the organisation thinks that having a first degree is only moderately important it could give this a weighting of 2, but if it considered a coaching qualification highly important, then this could have a weighting of, say, 5. The weighting system should be agreed and applied to each application by an assessment centre panel composed of:

- The director of coaching (probably a senior member of the HR department).
- An HR representative.
- A senior manager who is committed to the coaching programme (probably someone who has or is using a coach to beneficial effect).
- An independent consultant who is either a professional coach, or who is knowledgeable about coaching.

Although the scoring system gives the impression of being a 'scientific' approach, there should be plenty of opportunities for debate about the strengths and weaknesses of individual applications. Try to use the scoring system as a broad indication of a coach's strengths, rather than applying it rigidly. Also, the assessment centre panel could decide in advance approximately what level of score is deemed to be the benchmark for acceptance. Typically, much of the discussion will take place around those applications just above or just below the benchmark. By the end of the process the organisation will have arrived at a short list of applicants, ready for the next stage of the selection process.

ASSESSING AND CONTRACTING

Conduct role play

It would be all too easy (but also ineffective) to select between applicants on the basis of a 'traditional' interview. This would tell us remarkably little about how well (or otherwise) the coach can perform in practice. A possibly more reliable assessment process, would be to conduct an experiential role play, observed and scored by the assessment centre panel.

Let us see how this works. A member of the organisation plays the part of the coachee. This person should write out a short (possibly imaginary) description of their job role, and the kinds of issues, problems or developmental needs they currently face. This is given to the coach five minutes before they enter the room. Coaches are told that they will have 30 minutes to coach this person. Creating an imaginary scenario allows for greater creativity and flexibility. The members of the assessment centre panel act as observers and use a checklist (see Table 20.5) to score each candidate as well as adding further comments of their own. The nature of role play means that the interaction between coachee and coaching applicant is highly interactive and somewhat unpredictable. Observers should look out for:

- The ease (or otherwise) with which applicants respond to the coachee's questions and statements.
- Their general sense of confidence.
- Their body language with particular reference to defensive postures (such as arm folding), nervousness or hesitation.
- Their ability to ask open questions, provide supportive feedback and positive regard.
- Their ability to offer rapport, warmth, compassion and empathy and where necessary challenge.

Table 20.5   Checklist for evaluating the performance of the coach[15]

Competency	Strongly agree	Agree	Neither agree nor disagree	Disagree	Strongly disagree
Establishes rapport	O	O	O	O	O
Creates trust and respect	O	O	O	O	O
Demonstrates effective communication skills	O	O	O	O	O
Promotes self-awareness and self-knowledge	O	O	O	O	O
Uses active listening and questioning techniques	O	O	O	O	O
Assists goal-development and setting	O	O	O	O	O
Motivates	O	O	O	O	O
Encourages alternative perspectives	O	O	O	O	O
Assists in making sense of a situation	O	O	O	O	O
Identifies significant patterns of thinking and behaving	O	O	O	O	O
Provides an appropriate mix of challenge and support	O	O	O	O	O
Facilitates depth of understanding	O	O	O	O	O
Shows compassion	O	O	O	O	O
Acts ethically	O	O	O	O	O
Inspires curiosity	O	O	O	O	O
Acts as a role model	O	O	O	O	O
Values diversity and difference	O	O	O	O	O
Promotes action and reflection	O	O	O	O	O
Comments:					

As well as the positive criteria, the assessment centre panel might do well to look out for 'warning signals' about coaches to avoid. These signals might include coaches who:

* Talk too much, especially about themselves.
* Give advice and solutions (as in consultancy).
* Ask too many closed questions.
* Meet hostile responses with hostile questions.

Once all coaches have been observed, the task of the assessment centre panel is to compare scores and to go through the challenging process of making selection decisions. The experience of the author is that coaches at the high and low end of expert performance are identified quite easily by the panel. The debate usually revolves around those on the

---

15   Adapted from Jarvis (2004) op. cit.

borderline. Having an experienced coach on the panel can often help in identifying subtle strengths and weaknesses in a coach's performance. In the final analysis, the panel will need to agree on which coaches are going to be invited to join the faculty as members.

Sign the contract

It is important to distinguish between what organisations would regard as a contract, and what many coaches call contracts (which we will call here a coaching agreement). *Contracts* are negotiated between an organisation and individual coaches or a coaching consultancy for the supply of services. Contracts will typically include the overarching aims of the proposed coaching programme, timescales for the programme, payment scales, and how confidentiality and intellectual property rights of the organisation are to be protected. The contract might also contain details of how the programme is to be evaluated. Typically, contracts precede coaching agreements. Coaching *agreements* on the other hand, are generally made between the coach and an individual coachee and could include the coachee's goals, as well as what the coachee is committing to do, how records will be kept and issues of confidentiality. Of course, there needs to be some kind of synergy between agreements and the contract, otherwise the intentions of the sponsoring organisation may be undermined. For example, the contract might specify that the coaching programme deals with aspects of change management, so that the recipients of coaching are better able to cope with a major organisational restructuring. The organisation will want some reassurance from both coaches and coachees that this element features in the coaching agreements.

Matching Coachee with Coach

Once a cohort of coaches has been selected and contracts signed, the next step is to match them with those in the organisation who have been identified as eligible for coaching. This, however, is not necessarily a simple process. Some organisations make use of psychometric profiling of both coach and coachee, in order to identify attributes that in some way support or complement each other. However, there is no conclusive scientific evidence that this works or which psychometric tools are the most appropriate. In other organisations HR personnel, who may have quite detailed personal knowledge of the coachee, select a coach who they think is appropriate for them. This, however, relies heavily on the expertise and subjective opinions of the person responsible for this decision-making. Two alternative approaches are offered here, both of which empower the coachee themselves in making the choice.

This choice will be facilitated if diversity issues are planned for when appointing coaching faculty members, that is, the faculty should embrace an ethnic and gender mix. For many coachees, gender and ethnicity may not be factors in their choice of coach, but others, for example, may want a same-gender (or even cross-gender) coach when discussing, say, personal issues, or to act as a role model.

PUBLISHING A COACH PROFILE DATABASE

One way of matching coachees with a member of the coaching faculty is through the publication of a coach profile database, either as a booklet, or as a website. The use of the web allows for profiles to be updated quickly – for example, if a coach leaves the faculty or if a new coach is appointed. Each coach will have their own personal entry based, in part, upon the questions they answered as part of their application. The entry could also include a photograph. It is polite and prudent to ask all the coaches whether there are any details they would like to change or add to their entry before it is published.

Once the website (or booklet) is operational, coachees should be provided with simple instructions on what to do next. This might comprise asking them to:

- Browse the database for information.
- Select three potential coaches that they think they might be able to work with.
- Contact all three and ask to meet up with them or talk over the telephone.
- Talk to each coach, possibly looking for some of the competencies provided previously in Table 20.5.

Once a choice has been made, there should be clear instructions for what happens next – for example, notifying the HR department, or the section responsible for managing the programme, so that the pairing can be logged on file, progress can be monitored, invoices can be paid at the end of the programme, etc.

ORGANISING A SPEED MATCHING EVENT

The advantage of the coach profile database is that it allows for the coachee to view the biographical details of all the coaches. However, it is possible that not all coachees may feel they gain the right coach from using such an impersonal process. Also, while they get to talk face-to-face with a small number of coaches, the number is quite restricted. The advantage of 'speed matching' is that it allows the coachee to meet all the faculty of coaches and, subject to the amount of time devoted to the event, spend some time getting to know them. This will, of course, be helped if coachees have been encouraged to browse the faculty database to gain some advance knowledge of each coach profile.

The speed-matching event can be organised as follows:

- All the coaches and all the potential coachees are gathered in a room for the event.
- Each coach is seated at their own table.
- Each coach is then given three minutes to stand up and say something (to everyone in the room) about their experience, coaching approach, philosophy or anything else they think would be of interest.
- Once each coach has had their 'say' a whistle is blown to signal 'start'; everyone around each table then has an opportunity to ask the coach questions and listen to other peoples' questions (and the coachee's answers).
- After a set period of time (say, 15 minutes), the whistle is blown as a signal for everyone to change tables. The coachees have complete freedom to go to whichever table they want.

- The event continues for a pre-planned number of 15-minute time slots or until fatigue becomes obvious.

At this point, all the coachees complete a voting form containing every coach's name. They mark on this a '1' for their first choice, '2' for second and '3' for third and hand it in. The event organisers can decide in advance how to use the scoring system. Table 20.6 offers some possible approaches.

Using either the coach profile database or the speed-matching event, we emerge with matched pairs of coaches and coachees. However, as we saw in the needs analysis, there are many other potential stakeholders in the organisation who will want an involvement. Hence, the coaching programme needs a 'launch'.

Launching and Managing the Coaching Faculty

The coaching programme has to be launched in a blaze of publicity, but this is only half the story. The organisation also has to put in place long-term, robust management and quality assurance processes so that the programme is capable of sustainability.

THE LAUNCH EVENT

Given the relatively high costs of coaching and the significant number of stakeholders involved, it is essential that the coaching programme is given the level of publicity it deserves. Hence the need for a 'splash launch' event which should be designed to generate a sense of excitement and anticipation about the forthcoming coaching programme. Gaining a place on the programme as a coachee needs to be seen as a potentially career-enhancing move, and a sign of recognition.

Attendees at the launch should include:

- The CEO or MD (to provide the event with a sense of top level approval and sponsorship).
- The head of HR (who can talk about the logistics and organisation of the programme).

Table 20.6   Scoring system for speed matching event

Policy	Advantages	Disadvantages
Give all coachees their number 1 choice	All coachees are satisfied with their choice	Coach–coachee imbalance. Popular coaches get 'flooded' with coachees, others get few or none
Fill number 1 choices up to a maximum number of coachees per coach; then allocate number 2 choices up to another maximum, etc.	Each coach receives an equal number of coachees	Not all coachees satisfied with being allocated their number 2 (or even number 3) choice

- Previous recipients of coaching in the organisation (if any) who can informally discuss their experiences.
- All coachees and their line managers.
- The coaching faculty.

If name tags are provided, these should be colour-coded so the roles of those at the event can be clearly seen – especially previous recipients of coaching who can talk informally about how the process worked for them. Formal speeches should be short and kept to a minimum. The main activity during the event should be informal networking.

QUALITY ASSURANCE MECHANISMS

Monitoring mechanisms need to be put in place as part of quality assuring the programme. Underpinning these processes, organisations will have to use a variety of instruments for gathering useful data about the programme. Quality assurance aims to ensure that the products or services an organisation provides are 'fit for purpose'. This could include setting up an appropriate management structure, support mechanism (through a steering group – see below), and reporting mechanisms from both coaches and coachees (and their line managers).

Management structure

The kind of management structure will partly depend on where 'ownership' of the faculty lies within the commissioning organisation. If, as is often the case, the impetus for the introduction of coaching, and the recruitment of the faculty has been in the hands of the HR department, then management of the programme will probably lie here. A small team of HR professionals, one of whom can act as the director of coaching, can manage and administer the programme.

Steering group

The work of a steering group could be directed at:

- Establishing the aims of the programme, ensuring that these are in line with organisational objectives.
- Planning for measuring the programme's success and the timing of such evaluation.
- Tackling any problems that may arise including complaints from coaches, coachees or line managers.

Although overall control of the programme will still lie with its director, few people would want to manage a programme of this kind without the valuable input of other stakeholders. Hence, membership of the steering group will, typically comprise the director of coaching, two or three internal stakeholders such as senior managers from those departments or sections where the programme is focused, a number of coachees and representatives from the coaching faculty. The steering group should agree its own terms of reference which might state the overall purpose of the steering group's activities, its membership, and how often it will meet.

Reporting mechanisms

Quality assurance requires that there is a feedback loop of information about the impact of the coaching programme, using the coaches and coachees as well as other organisational stakeholders as suppliers of the data. This feedback could include telephone conference calls to coaches (on a monthly basis) or the use of a focus group to ensure that:

- Coaches and coachees are setting goals that fit organisational priorities. For example, the organisation does not want to be paying for 'personal therapy' sessions unless this kind of focus has been agreed in advance.
- Coachees are keeping to their appointments and engaging fully with the coaching programme. Many people are under time pressures at work, but these must not get in the way of the scheduled coaching.
- Coachees are completing any 'homework' (such as tasks that are designed to try out a new behaviour) agreed between them and the coach.

Feedback from coachees could be achieved through an email requesting this information or through a focus group. Feedback from line managers of the coachees is also vital, since such managers are in a prime position to recognise whether some of the skills, knowledge or attitudes gained by coachees are being put into practice in the workplace. Hence, line managers may request written action plans from staff who are beneficiaries of the coaching programme to ensure that coachees are making development gains.

Conclusion

This chapter has sought to highlight the growing importance of executive coaching, and to demonstrate a strategy for establishing the development needs of the organisation and individuals within it. A model for recruiting and selecting a top class coaching faculty has also been outlined. This, of course, may be a short-lived initiative unless the programme is successful and coaching becomes part of the cultural landscape of the organisation. Culture here is defined as the values of the organisation, its strategic goals, and the formal and informal systems that guide managers and employees in their everyday working life.[16] Strategic goals need to include the development of management skills necessary to achieve the desired organisational results. Coaching can become an important element in the development of these skills, although it must be realised that the achievement of a coaching culture is a lengthy and gradual process.[17]

This may be particularly so in small and medium-sized enterprises where management development cultures and processes are often less well established and funds for coaching in short supply. It would be optimistic to expect some of the full-scale strategies outlined in this chapter to fit into, say, an organisation of 20 employees. This does not mean that executive coaching cannot be built into small as well as large firms. The key here

---

16   Lindbom, D. (2007) A culture of coaching: the challenge of managing performance for long-term results, *Organization Development Journal*, 25(1): 101–106.

17   Clutterbuck, D. and Megginson, D. (2005) Creating a coaching culture, *Industrial and Commercial Training*, 38(5): 232–237.

is gaining the enthusiastic commitment of the CEO or senior managers to the coaching initiative – usually by being a beneficiary of coaching themselves. After this, a scaled-down approach to developing coaching could be implemented. The difference would be that small to medium-sized organisations are probably better advised to select a coaching consultancy that can help them with their needs analysis and matching processes. The assessment centre would focus on the identification of such consultancy organisations rather than the identification of individual coaches.

For coaching to really take root, it has to occur not only on a formal but also an informal level. A large proportion of individuals in the organisation should practise coaching behaviours as a means of relating to, supporting and influencing one another.[18] One approach to creating this permanent coaching culture is to enlist the services of 'coaching evangelists', people who are willing to act as ambassadors for the coaching programme.[19] It also helps if coaching is rewarded and recognised, for example, if people are rewarded for knowledge-sharing. Extensive training also has to be provided for coaches at all levels of the organisation, including the top team who should seek to become role models, seeking and using feedback.[20] As we can see, then, the introduction of coaching into an organisation via the recruitment of a coaching faculty is only the first (but important) step in creating a coaching culture in an organisation. The successful recruitment and integration of such large-scale coaching faculties may serve to drive the inexorable rise of executive coaching still further.

---

18 Hart, W. (2005) Getting culture: imbuing your organization with coaching behavior, *Leadership in Action,* 25(4): 7–10.

19 Tomlinson, D. (2008) Making coaching part of the culture, *Human Resources,* March: 20.

20 Clutterbuck and Megginson (2005) op. cit.

21 *Intuitive Intelligence*

EUGENE SADLER-SMITH AND ERELLA SHEFY

Introduction

In the 468 pages of the previous edition of the *Gower Handbook* published in 1994 there were, to the best of our knowledge, three references to intuition. The first of these was an exhortation to 'trust your intuition in decision-making' in a discussion of 'cultural pitfalls' in international alliances. The remaining two references were in the chapter on 'Developing women managers' and the potential value associated with the emergence of the 'female value' of intuition as a counterbalance to the prevalence of male values in organisations. Much has happened in the intervening 15 years in the study of intuition both in management and in the underpinning discipline of psychology. We will begin from the historical perspective in order to chart the emergence of intuition as an important aspect not only of management practice itself but, more latterly, of management development also.

BRIEF HISTORICAL PERSPECTIVE OF INTUITION IN MANAGEMENT

The roots of any explicit consideration of intuition in management can be traced back to the intellectualising not of a scholar, but of a practitioner – the AT&T executive Chester Barnard. In 1936 Barnard gave a lecture to the Engineering Faculty at Princeton University entitled 'The mind in everyday affairs', later to be included as the Appendix to his 1938 book *The Functions of the Executive*.[1] (It is salutary to reflect on the fact that at the time of writing this chapter Barnard's book was still available in print 70 years after its first publication.) In his lecture Barnard drew a distinction between what he termed the logical and non-logical mental processes that go on inside the brain of every manager. In using the term 'logical' he was referring to mental processes that are conscious, analysable by the thinker and expressible in words or symbols. In using the term 'non-logical' Barnard was referring to what would now be called intuition; in his terms mental processes that are non-conscious, un-analysable by the thinker and not expressible in words or symbols. For Barnard intuition was a rapid process that drew upon knowledge that was itself acquired non-consciously and based upon physiological conditions and factors in the physical and social environment.

From Barnard's suggestion that non-logical mental processes are a result of a combination of biological and social factors we may infer that his view of non-logical

---

1   Barnard, C. I. (1938) *The Functions of the Executive*. Cambridge, MA: Harvard University Press.

mental processes is that they are to some extent learned. This position accords well with the view of 'intuition-as-expertise' discussed later in this chapter. Not only was Barnard convinced of the value of intuition for executives because it enabled decision makers to handle a mass of experience or a complex of abstractions 'in a flash', but also of the insufficiency of logical processes alone for many of the day-to-day purposes of management. With uncanny foresight Barnard predicted that the increasing complexity of society and organisations allied to advances in technology, which he referred to as 'the elaboration of technique', will require greater reasoning for sure, but these conditions will also necessitate a better use of intuition in support of analytical reasoning. As we shall see, although he lacked the science to explain it, Barnard's conception of logical and non-logical comes close to modern conceptions of two contrasting modes of information processing (see next section).

From the publication of *The Functions of the Executive* we may fast-forward by a decade or so to the mid 1940s and the publication of one of the seminal works of management and organisation – Herbert A. Simon's *Administrative Behavior: A Study of Decision Making Processes in Administrative Organisation,* the Foreword to which was written by Barnard who 'exerted a major influence' on Simon's thinking. This is not the place to go into a detailed discussion of *Administrative Behavior* and the concepts of 'bounded rationality' and 'satisficing', suffice to say that in this work Simon sows the seeds of much subsequent research into the limits of rationality in decision-making processes. With his colleague William Chase, Simon conducted a now very famous series of small-scale experiments with chess masters which showed that the learned process of sophisticated pattern matching confers upon chess experts the ability for not only rapid recognition but also rapid, and accurate, execution of decisions – all the more significant since it is a finding that may be extrapolated to experts in many other domains.

From the perspective of our interest in intuition Simon made explicit reference to a pattern-matching view of intuitive judgement which he described as 'analyses frozen into habit', in a paper in *The Academy of Management Executive* in 1987.[2] Simon conceptualised intuition as a manifestation of expertise and a mental ability executed subconsciously and without deliberate and exhaustive analyses. Moreover, for Simon the ability to execute intuitive judgements was as indispensable to managers in complex, judgemental situations as analytical reasoning: 'The effective manager does not have the luxury of being able to choose between analytical and intuitive approaches to problems.'[3] Indeed there is a direct conceptual thread from Simon through to modern theories of recognition-primed decision making (RPD) which help to explain the deployment of intuition by experienced decision makers in complex, time-pressured situations, such as fire-fighting and neonatal care, as explicated by decision researcher Gary Klein in his books *Sources of Power* (1998) and *Intuition at Work* (2003).[4]

Also active in this field during the 1980s was Weston H. Agor, at the time Professor at University of Texas at El Paso, who wrote several influential publications on the subject and edited a widely-cited book called *Intuition in Organizations* and which included an

---

2   Simon, H. A. (1987) Making management decisions: the role of intuition and emotion. *Academy of Management Executive,* 12: 57–64; Simon, H. A. (1997) *Administrative Behavior,* 4th edn. New York: MacMillan.

3   Simon, H. A. (1987) Making management decisions: the role of intuition and emotion, *Academy of Management Executive,* 1(1): 57–64, p. 63.

4   Klein, G. (1998) *Sources of Power: How People make Decisions.* Cambridge, MA: The MIT Press; Klein, G. (2003) *Intuition at Work.* New York: Currency Doubleday.

article by Simon.[5] Agor was less concerned with the psychological processes associated with intuitive judgement and more with the practical use of intuition by mangers in organisations. Through his own field research Agor offered some invaluable insights into when and how managers used intuition. In a survey of 2000 executives in 1981–82 Agor found that, amongst other things, intuition varies with job level (senior managers are more intuitive than middle- or lower-level managers – a finding replicated on several subsequent occasions) and that females were more intuitive than males (a finding that is not consistent with more recent research).[6] In a follow-up survey in 1984 of the most intuitive 10 per cent of his original sample Agor found that managers were of the view that intuition should be used in situations in which:

1.   there is a high level of uncertainty and there is little previous precedent;
2.   variables are unpredictable, facts are limited and clearly don't point the way to go; and
3.   where several plausible alternative solutions exist and time is limited.

Agor's original findings were later extended by other researchers, including Jagdish Parikh in his large-scale international survey of over one thousand respondents published in 1994, and Lisa Burke and Monica Miller's qualitative study of a small sample of US senior managers published in 1999[7] (see below).

Alongside the earlier developments the 1970s and 80s saw considerable progress in the study of the biological bases of human information processing. Psychobiologists such as Roger Sperry, who was awarded the Nobel Prize for Physiology in 1981, investigated hemispheric functional specialisation in the brain of humans and animals. Sperry and his colleagues demonstrated that if communication between the two hemispheres of the brain is cut off (by severing the connecting bundle of nerve fibres – the corpus callosum – to treat severe epileptic seizures) patients are left, figuratively speaking, with two brains inside one skull between which information cannot be transferred. Further experiments revealed the nature of the specialisation of the two hemispheres: the left hemisphere is dominant in speech, language and arithmetic, whilst the right is dominant in facial recognition and spatial awareness. This work had a significant impact beyond psychobiology, for example Henry Mintzberg wrote a widely-cited article in the *Harvard Business Review* entitled 'Planning on the left [hemisphere], managing on the right', in which he argued that whether a person ought to be a planner or a manager may be determined by which hemisphere of their brain is 'better developed'. Interpretations of brain physiology have tended to be generalised into a fundamental, but as we shall see over-simplistic, assertion that analysis is 'in' the left hemisphere (of the brain) and intuition is 'in' the right. Simon referred to such extrapolations as 'romantic versions' of the split-brain doctrine, and notwithstanding the caveats and cautions from Simon

---

5   Agor, W. H. (ed.) (1989) *Intuition in Organizations: Leading and Managing Productively*. Newbury Park, CA: Sage Publications.

6   Hodgkinson, G. P. and Sadler-Smith, E. (2003) Complex or unitary? A critique and empirical reassessment of the Allinson–Hayes Cognitive Style Index, *Journal of Occupational and Organizational Psychology,* 76: 243–268; Sadler-Smith, E., Spicer D. and Tsang, F. (2000) The Cognitive Style Index: a replication and extension, *British Journal of Management,* 11: 175–181.

7   Burke, L. A. and Miller, M. K. (1999) Taking the mystery out of intuitive decision-making, *Academy of Management Executive,* 13: 91–99; Parikh, J. (1994) *Intuition: The New Frontier of Management*. London: Blackwell.

and others, such interpretations have spawned numerous 'brain training' programmes, often with the explicit aim of making participants more 'whole-brained' (http://www. hbdi.com).[8]

In the 1980s Bill Taggart, former Professor of Management at Florida International University, offered penetrating insights into different information processing modes (in spite of the fact that much of it was in tune with a 1980s zeitgeist of left brain/right brain differences). Taggart integrated the split-brain concept with a Jungian/Myers–Briggs Type Indicator (MBTI) typology (sensing–thinking and intuiting–feeling), classical Greek (Apollo–Dionysus duality) and Eastern philosophical traditions (the Taoist notion of Yang–Ying) to devise a simple and elegant metaphor for human dual information processing. The left hemisphere mode is concerned with processes that are active, logical, sequential, objective, causal, deductive and analytic, whilst the right hemisphere processes are receptive, non-logical, simultaneous, subjective, acausal, inductive and synthetic (and ultimately intuitive). Treated as metaphor this model shares a number of features not only with Barnard's logical and non-logical duality, but also with contemporary dual-process models of information processing. In terms of the practice of developing intuition Taggart was undoubtedly one of the prime innovators and made a major contribution by suggesting ways in which the intuitive mind (prefers to more holistic term 'the intuitive self') may be developed. Many of the resources he developed are still freely available on the web at the time of writing (http://www.the-intuitive-self.org).[9]

Beginning with Barnard's lecture in 1936 a common theme may be identified. It runs through Simon's work, whose major concern was the limits of rationality, to researchers and practitioners active in the 1980s such as Agor and Taggart (who focused specifically on intuition), through to advances in the past decade (discussed below) that have built upon these foundations. The historical context is important because it is a perspective from which we can identify this perennial theme of a duality of human thinking that is as relevant to management and management development today as it was in Barnard's time. At the present juncture, however, we are in the position of being able not only to define intuition in conceptual terms that have a solid foundation in the psychology of thinking, but are doubly fortunate in that recent years have witnessed a resurgence of interest amongst not only management researchers but management development practitioners searching for ways in which this sometimes ignored and undervalued but crucial aspect of managerial cognition may be both assessed and developed.

CONTEMPORARY PSYCHOLOGICAL INTERPRETATIONS OF INTUITION

How might this sometimes elusive concept that has stirred the interest over several decades in a variety of constituencies from the scientific and pragmatic to the mystical be defined and theorised? In a paper published in the journal *Academy of Management Review* in 2007 Dane and Pratt offered the following definition of intuition: 'intuitions

---

8   Herrmann, N. (1996) *The Whole Brain Business Book*, New York: McGraw-Hill; Mintzberg, H. (1976) Planning in the left-side and managing on the right, *Harvard Business Review*, July–August: 49–57.

9   Taggart W. and Robey D. (1981) Minds and managers: on the dual nature of human information processing and management, *Academy of Management Review*, 6: 187–195; Taggart, W. and Valenzi, E. (1990) Assessing rational and intuitive styles: a human information processing metaphor, *Journal of Management Studies*, 27(2): 149–172.

are affectively-charged judgements that arise through rapid, non-conscious and holistic associations'.[10] This definition encompasses six essential characteristics of intuition:

1. A judgement to be treated as a hypothesis and which can be tested by acting upon the judgement, rather than as any certain guarantee of an outcome (even though intuitions are often attended by strong feelings of certitude but which could be misplaced optimism);
2. Affect (feeling)-laden, in common parlance referred to as a 'gut feel' or a 'hunch'. Gut feelings can have a positive valence signalling attraction towards a course of action, or have a negative valence signalling avoidance. There are some who argue that the capability to experience intuition evolved in our ancestors as an aid to survival and therefore errs on the side of caution;
3. Holistic in two respects: first, thought and feeling (cognition and affect) come together in intuition, hence it may be thought of as a mind–body process; and secondly, intuitions arise in response to the perception and processing of an assemblage of cues which would be difficult to process analytically and within the time constraints that many real-world decisions have to be taken under;
4. Non-conscious to the extent that only the outcome (a gut feeling) is 'posted' into conscious awareness, whereas the reasoning processes leading to the gut feel are themselves not immediately available to introspection, although they may be accessed by skilled researchers using techniques such as applied cognitive task analysis or cognitive mapping;[11]
5. Rapid, involuntary and ubiquitous: intuitions, which are ubiquitous across many different languages and national cultures, arrive into conscious awareness unbidden and instantaneously, although in certain situations (for example when our attempts to solve a perplexing problem by analysis reach an impasse) intuition may operate with a slower pace giving rise to 'feelings of knowing' which materialise after an incubation period in a sudden insightful (eureka!) moment;
6. Potentially powerful if informed by expertise and feedback and used under the right conditions, but also potentially perilous if used in complex judgemental situations in the absence of the requisite expertise or developed in an environment in which good feedback has been lacking (for example, where a manager has been surrounded by colleagues who are not prepared to challenge her or his judgements, or who refuses to heed any critical feedback even when offered).[12]

It is not enough to define a construct, it is also essential that it is both adequately theorised, and measurable. From a theoretical standpoint the description of intuition offered above is commensurate with a body of theory in cognitive and social psychology known as dual-process theory. Although there is large variety of dual-process theories they all essentially posit the existence of 'two minds in one brain'. For our purposes we

10   Dane, E. and Pratt, M.G. (2007) Exploring intuition and its role in managerial decision-making, *Academy of Management Review*, 32(1): 33–54.

11   Clarke I. and Mackaness, W. (2001) Management 'intuition': an interpretative account of structure and content of decision schemas using cognitive maps, *Journal of Management Studies*, 38(2): 147–172; Militello, L. G. and Hutton R. J. B. (1998) Applied cognitive task analysis (ACTA): a practitioner's toolkit for understanding cognitive task demands, *Ergonomics*, 41(11): 1618–1641.

12   Sadler-Smith, E. (2008) *Inside Intuition*. Abingdon: Routledge

will adopt the conceptualisation offered by the social psychologist Seymour Epstein, who drew a distinction between a rational (in our terms 'analytical') system and an experiential ('intuitive') system. These two systems differ in a number of respects:

1. The analytical system's serial processing mode is affect-free, comparatively slow in operation, fast in formation, detail-focused, intentional, cognitively demanding, abstract and/or symbolic-based and open to conscious awareness;
2. The intuitive system's parallel processing mode of operation is affect-laden, comparatively fast in operation, slow in formation, holistic, involuntary, cognitively undemanding, imagistic and/or narrative-based and unavailable to conscious awareness. The intuitive system is considered by some to have evolved in *Homo sapiens* before the analytical system.[13]

The simple notion of gross hemispheric differences in brain functioning as an explanation of intuition and analysis has been largely dismissed, however new insights from cognitive neuroscience are pointing to more specific brain regions that may be implicated in intuitive processing. Without going into details (readers are referred to the excellent review by Liebermann in the 2007 *Annual Review of Psychology*[14]) it appears that an emerging neuroscience of intuition suggests that the brain regions involved in intuitive judgement and decision making may include the ventromedial prefrontal cortex (VMPC), the basal ganglia and the amygdala (the latter figures prominently in various discussions of 'emotional intelligence'). Whilst these discoveries are cutting-edge and can be seductive especially to those of a natural scientific bent, Herbert Simon cautioned psychologists working in management against getting carried away with brain biology by alerting us to the fact that 'The important questions for us are "what is intuition?" and "how is it accomplished?" not "in which cubic centimeter of the brain tissue does it take place?"'.[15]

The analytic and intuitive modes of processing are contextually appropriate – in this sense they are value-free in that neither is intrinsically better than the other. Although the deployment of intuition and analysis is situation-specific (for example in a particular context an individual may be highly intuitive and make major use of intuitive processes, whilst in another situation they might be analytical) individuals tend to exhibit fairly stable preferences for an intuitive or analytical mode of processing when averaged-out across tasks. Differences in managers' behaviour as a result of their exercising cognitive style preferences were considered by Simon to be a 'very plausible' hypothesis. If such differences exist they should be measurable, and indeed it is possible to assess an individual's preference for intuitive or analytical processing using valid and reliable self-report instruments that are relatively easy both to administer and score in occupational settings; these include: Epstein's Rational Experiential Inventory (REI); the Preference for

13   Epstein, S. (1994) Integration of the cognitive and the psychodynamic unconscious, *American Psychologist*, 49: 709–724; Epstein, S., Pacini, R., Denes-Raj, V. and Heier, H. (1996) Individual differences in intuitive–experiential and analytical–rational thinking styles, *Journal of Personality and Social Psychology*, 71: 390–405; Epstein, S. (2008) Intuition from the perspective of cognitive-experiential self-theory. In Plessner, H., Betsch, C. and Betsch, T. (eds) *Intuition in Judgment and Decision Making*, pp. 23–37. New York: Lawrence Erlbaum Associates.

14   Lieberman, M. D. (2007) Social cognitive neuroscience: a review of core processes, *Annual Review of Psychology*, 58: 259–289.

15   Simon, H. A. (1987) Making management decisions: the role of intuition and emotion, *Academy of Management Executive*, 12: 57–64.

Intuition or Deliberation (PID) scale recently developed by Betsch and her colleagues; and Allinson and Hayes' Cognitive Style Index (CSI).[16]

THE SIGNIFICANCE OF INTUITION FOR BUSINESS ORGANIZATIONS

So much for the historical antecedents, conceptualisation, theorisation and measurement of intuition; what about the practice of intuition in business organisations? When and how do managers use intuition? Under what conditions is intuition effective? These questions are essential precursors to any consideration of whether intuition is a skill worthy of development.

Since the ground-breaking work of Agor in the 1980s a number of researchers have followed in his footsteps and examined the situations in which managers deploy intuitive judgement. Parikh in 1994 surveyed 1300 senior managers from nine different countries with the aim of understanding how relevant they felt intuition to be across different functional areas of management. Intuition was judged to be most relevant (in descending order) in: corporate strategy and planning (80 per cent); human resource development (79 per cent); marketing (77 per cent); research and development (72 per cent); public relations (64 per cent); investment and diversification (60 per cent); and acquisitions, mergers and alliances (55 per cent). Intuition was judged to be least relevant in: operations and production management (28 per cent); finance (31 per cent); choosing technology and plant (35 per cent).

In the late 1990s Burke and Miller interviewed 60 experienced professionals holding significant positions in major US organisations with the aim of investigating the use of intuition in decision making. They discovered that intuition is most often used in personnel or people-related decisions, when decisions need to be made quickly or unexpectedly, when uncertainty pervades in novel situations, in situations lacking specific cues, and also in combination with analysis. The main perceived beneficial outcomes of intuition were that it expedites decision-making (for example, by avoiding 'analysis paralysis' and leading to quicker decisions), improves decision-making (for example, by providing a check-and-balance), and facilitates personal development (for example, by developing a 'full tool set'). They concluded that transcending traditional analytical approaches by appropriately integrating intuitive approaches into decision-making may represent a viable source of competitive advantage in the twenty-first century.[17]

As well as exploring managers' perceptions of intuition using largely qualitative methods, researchers have also conducted quantitative studies to look at the relationship between intuitive decision making and firm performance. For example, a study of non-profit organisations in the USA found that executive intuition was a significant and positive predictor of fiscal performance. A study of companies in the banking, computer and utility industries in the north-east USA found that intuitive processes are often used in organisational decision making and that they are positively associated with organisational

16   Allinson, C. W. and Hayes, J. (1996) The Cognitive Style Index: a measure of intuition-analysis for organizational research, *Journal of Management Studies,* 33: 119–135; Betsch, C. (2004) Preference for Intuition and Deliberation (PID): an inventory for assessing affect- and cognition-based decision-making. *Zeitschrift für Differentielle und Diagnostische Psychologie,* 25: 179–197; Epstein, S., Pacini, R., Denes-Raj, V. and Heier, H. (1996) Individual differences in intuitive–experiential and analytical–rational thinking styles, *Journal of Personality and Social Psychology,* 71: 390–405.

17   Burke, L. A. and Miller, M. K. (1999) Taking the mystery out of intuitive decision-making, *Academy of Management Executive,* 13: 91–99; Isenberg, D. J. (1984) How senior managers think, *Harvard Business Review,* November–December: 81–90; Parikh, J. (1994) *Intuition: The New Frontier of Management.* London: Blackwell.

performance in unstable environments but negatively related to performance in stable environments. This last finding adds further weight to the assertion that intuition is not appropriate across all tasks but rather is contextually appropriate, and most appropriate in the case of decisions that have to be taken under time pressure (for example to give 'first mover' advantage), with ill-defined goals, under dynamic and unstable conditions.[18]

Intuition is a key capability attributed to many successful entrepreneurs, giving them the knack of being able to identify business opportunities and assess their viability. The popular management literature, press and media are replete with examples of entrepreneurial individuals in businesses large and small attributing their success to business instinct, hunch, or gut feeling:[19] by the same token there are numerous books extolling the virtues of 'gut feeling': for example, *Straight from the gut; Head, heart and guts; Trust your gut;* or even simply *Guts*. Many of the anecdotes offered by entrepreneurs attest to the pre-eminence of expertise as the foundation of good intuitive judgement. Indeed, the rhetoric suggesting that certain individuals can consistently and successfully sense and exploit business opportunities over the longer-term is, on the face of it, convincing. We should never lose sight, however, of the fact that successful intuitions ('hits') tend to be highly visible and widely reported, whilst unsuccessful intuitions ('misses') tend to get under-reported if not 'buried'.

On the basis of the research conducted over the past two decades it is clear that intuition is used by managers, is deemed by them to be effective in certain situations, is related to firm performance under particular sets of conditions, and is important in innovation and entrepreneurship. On this basis intuition would seem to be a capability worthy of the serious attention of management and leadership development practitioners.

Intuition in management development is in its infancy, and a fundamental question is can intuition be developed? From the perspective of 'intuition-as-expertise' the answer to this question is yes: a fact attested to by the fact that experts in vastly different domains are able to perform with intuitive ease. Also, managers can develop a better knowledge and understanding of intuition's distinctive features and be able to distinguish it from related concepts and hence become better informed. Finally it is possible for managers to improve their self-awareness of their own intuitions in order to use intuition more effectively in their personal and professional lives. These three components – expertise (knowledge of a domain), understanding (knowledge of intuition), and self-awareness (knowledge of self) – comprise what we will term an 'intuitive intelligence' (see Figure 21.1).

DEVELOPING INTUITIVE EXPERTISE

Experts in any field ranging from management to musical performance have an extensive database of knowledge and skill held in long-term memory; the chunking of this information into patterns of meaningful units aids recognition, recall and processing.

---

18   Khatri, N. and Ng, H. A. (2000) The role of intuition in strategic decision-making. *Human Relations,* 1: 57–86; Ritchie, W. J., Kolodinsky, R. W. and Eastwood, K. (2007) Does executive intuition matter? An empirical analysis of its relationship with nonprofit organization financial performance, *Nonprofit and Voluntary Sector Quarterly,* 36: 140–155.

19   Becker, A. (2006) Kramer's latest platform, *Broadcasting and Cable,* August(28): 30; Champion D. and Carr, N. G. (2000) Starting up in high gear, *Harvard Business Review,* July–August: 93–100; Hyatt, J. (2002) The eureka moment: what sets legendary entrepreneurs apart isn't what they do – but how they do it, http://money.cnn.com/magazines/fsb/fsb_archive/2002/10/01. Accessed 25 February 2008.

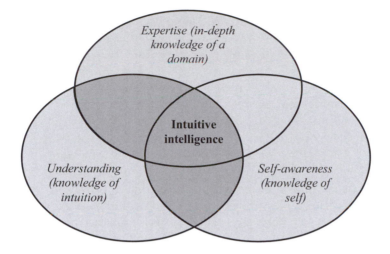

Figure 21.1 The components of an intuitive intelligence

These patterns make up mental representations or mental models of the world built up through formal learning, exposure to challenging real-world problems and feedback. The Skill Acquisition Model (SAM) developed by the Dreyfus brothers in the 1980s charts the route of progression from the novice who deploys rules and procedures in an un-nuanced way without taking the subtleties of the context into account, through to the expert with the ability to perceive and discriminate between a large number of contextual variables and exhibit a fluidity of performance which is as easy to execute as it is difficult to articulate.[20]

This ease of performance is born out of many years, consisting of thousands of hours, of learning and experience. Estimates vary, but expertise researchers often use the rule of thumb of 10 years or 10,000 hours of practising in a particular domain before expert levels of performance can be attained. Expertise researchers also make an important distinction between merely learning-by-doing (what some management developers might refer to as 'experiential learning') and the type of training required to become an expert. Expertise expert K. Anders Ericsson is firmly of the view that experts are more made than they are born, and that not all experience or practice makes perfect. Deliberate, focused and sustained efforts to do something that one cannot currently accomplish well or do at all extends one's performance, rather than routinely practising what can already be accomplished.[21]

Arie de Geus, the former head of planning at Royal Dutch/Shell, once observed that one of the most surprising things in management is that we experiment with reality (often justified as 'learning through mistakes' – as though this somehow made it excusable). As de Geus noted, one result of this approach can be that fear of failure and its consequences becomes the dominant emotion; not only that, there are real costs as well to capricious

---

20   Dreyfus, H. L. and Dreyfus, S. E. (1986) *Mind Over Machine: The Power of Human Intuition and Expertise in the Era of the Computer*. New York: Free Press.

21   Ericsson, K. A., Prietula, M. J. and Cokely, E. T. (2007) The making of an expert, *Harvard Business Review*, July–August: 114–121.

experimentation. Contrast this potentially dangerous form of 'play' with that of the golfer on the practice green or the tennis player on the practice court: they get as many chances as they want or need to perfect their swing or stroke, and it doesn't matter on the practice grounds if they get it wrong. In management, by experimenting with reality, the learner gets one or very few chances to get it right. From the perspective of the expertise-based view of intuition management learning and development can learn from sports practice grounds and the musical conservatories: safe environments are needed for managers to improve the skills they already have, to acquire new and relevant skills, and analyse their performance and the reasons for success and failure. It is important for managers that they are able to practice building their intuition without the fear that making mistakes may cost them, their employees, their customers or their businesses dear.

Needless to say there is a key role in the development of intuitive expertise for expert coaches both to impart skills and give feedback. Without the right kind of feedback it is possible for bad intuitions to go unchecked – a perilous state of affairs both for the individual and the organisation that they are a part of. The decision researcher Robin Hogarth distinguishes between different kinds of feedback environments and the different kinds of learning they engender. 'Kind' learning environments lead to the development of good intuitions, as in the example Hogarth describes of the professional tennis player: she has played tennis almost everyday since she was a child and has developed very good intuitions about where to hit the ball on the basis of accurate feedback from her coach and from experience in many matches, both practised and real, where the costs of and reasons behind bad intuitions are immediately apparent. 'Wicked' learning environments, on the other hand lead to the development of bad intuitions as a result of irrelevant and misleading feedback. In management, the acquisition of intuitions in kind learning environments with focused deliberate practice outside one's comfort zone in simulated and real settings with ongoing precise, relevant and candid feedback is likely to lead to intuitive judgements which will be valid but – since intuition does not come with any guarantee of success – nonetheless fallible.[22]

DEVELOPING UNDERSTANDING OF INTUITION

It is possible to confuse intuitions with other related phenomena, and the ability to discriminate intuitive judgment from other cognitive and affective processes has an important place in educating managers' intuitions and developing their knowledge and understanding of the concept as a basis for the development of self-awareness (see next section). There are three important distinctions.[23]

1. Intuition is not instinct: the latter term is best reserved for innate, automatic biological responses (for example, the homing instinct in some birds) whilst intuitions, as we have seen, are affectively charged judgements that arise through rapid, non-conscious and holistic associations in response to complex, judgemental situations – quite different from autonomous, instinctive responses.

---

22   Hogarth, R. M. (2001) *Educating Intuition*. Chicago, IL: University of Chicago Press.

23   Dane, E. and Pratt, M. G. (2007) Exploring intuition and its role in managerial decision-making, *Academy of Management Review*, 32(1): 33–54; Hogarth, R. M. (2001) *Educating Intuition*, Chicago, IL: University of Chicago Press; Sadler-Smith, E. (2008) *Inside Intuition*, Abingdon: Routledge; Sadler-Smith, E. and Shefy, E. (2004) The intuitive executive: understanding and applying 'gut feel' in decision-making, *The Academy of Management Executive*, 18(4): 76–92.

2. Intuition is not insight: when insight occurs a problem solver moves from the position of 'not knowing' to 'knowing' and being able to reason the solution (as in the various apocryphal tales of scientific discovery, such as Archimedes in his bath). An intuition of an impending solution may occur prior to the insightful moment – intuition may be an intimation that insight is about to happen. Some intuitions never emerge as insights, but remain as feelings of anxiety or promise, attraction or avoidance, which are verified or refuted only with the unfolding of events. Intuition allows us to sense coherences; insight allows us to see (and hence be able articulate) connections.

3. Intuitive judgements are not emotio*nal* judgements: the affect (feeling) which attends intuition (often referred to as a gut feel, but not literally in the gut necessarily) is of a different order than the feelings which attend emotions such as fear, love, hate or anger. The feelings associated with fear for example are typically intense bursts – they are emotional but do not persist. Gut feel on the other hand – typically feelings of anxiety, disquiet or potential – is less intense.

An important component of an intuitive intelligence is conceptual discrimination based on understanding: being able to distinguish between insight and intuition (and recognise the processes as they occur in one's own body), and between intuition and emotion, personal bias, prejudice or wishful thinking. Stories and anecdotes of other people's intuitions are also an important means of reflecting upon and benchmarking ones' own intuitions. The best-selling book *Blink: The Power of Thinking Without Thinking* by the *New Yorker* staff writer Malcolm Gladwell is a very readable account of intuition in action across all walks of life, from recognising art forgeries and speed dating to 'the delicate art of mind reading'.[24]

DEVELOPING INTUITIVE AWARENESS

Management development, like management itself, tends to be dominated by a rational, analytical paradigm, and without denying the value of rationality, one unfortunate consequence of this is that intuition tends to be ignored, overlooked or kept firmly in the closet. As a result managers, even though they inevitably experience intuition, often feel uncomfortable in admitting to its existence or in embracing it when it occurs. Intuitive self-awareness may be developed in a number of experientially based ways.

Acceptance of intuition: the systematic documentation in a journal, diary or logbook is a powerful protocol for documenting and exploring the strength, clarity and form of ones' intuitions, and ultimately for coming to accept the richness of ones' own personal intuitive experiences. Specific guidelines for journaling intuitions have been developed by Bill Taggart (see the Intuitive Self project website at http://www.the-intuitive-self.org) and the use of intuition journals has been evaluated and shown to be effective in a management education context.[25]

Creating the conditions: a number of management development researchers and practitioners have focused their efforts upon ways of 'quieting' the mind. The assumption behind this is that the voice of the intuitive mind (including subtle bodily sensations)

---

24   Gladwell, M. (2005) *Blink: The Power of Thinking Without Thinking*. London: Allen Lane/Penguin.

25   Sadler-Smith, E. and Shefy, E. (2007) Developing intuitive awareness in management education, *Academy of Management Learning and Education*, 6(2): 1–20.

may be drowned out by the constant verbalisations of the analytical mind. There are a variety of approaches to 'quieting' which range from simple physical and mental relaxation and switching-off to explicit meditative and contemplative techniques rooted in Eastern philosophies such as Buddhism. Techniques such as these are becoming increasingly common and more acceptable in the West and in business organisations. These approaches, along with a number of related techniques, have been evaluated in management education, for example in work with a group of practising managers on a part-time business school MBA programme.[26] Managers were trained in the use of various tools to create the conditions for an enhanced awareness of intuition and the impact of managers' use of these tools evaluated by an analysis of diarised accounts of the learning which occurred. Participants were accepting of methods which might be seen as unusual in the traditional business school environment; they reported positively on the programme and also documented effects in a number of areas including: their sense of perspective of issues, enhanced self-confidence, inter- and intrapersonal sensitivity, and a heightened awareness of their own thinking processes.

Balancing intuition and analysis: a fundamental precept of the dual mind idea used as the basis for this discussion of intuition is that the intuitive mind and the analytical mind each have an important role to perform in human reasoning, judgement and decision making. Consequently it is important that managers are aware of the strengths and the limitations of each mode of processing and are able to use each as a balance and check on the other.[27]

Specific guidelines on implementing intuitive awareness in leadership and management development are offered below.

Developing Mental (Cognitive) Awareness

Know the difference between instinct (a biological reflex action), insight (the explicit awareness of the solution to a problem) and intuition: for example, insight may be thought of as being in the head, instinct in the gut, and intuition in the heart. Acknowledge the distinction between the affect (feeling) which accompanies intuition and the feelings that come with emotions. Like intuitions, your fears, prejudices and biases may be felt – but they aren't intuitions. Hopes, cravings, desires and wishful thinking are also felt, but again they're not intuitions. Learn how to recognise when a genuine intuition is being experienced.

Developing Bodily (Somatic) Awareness

The body is the main sensor of both emotion and intuition. It's important to listen to your body in the context of daily events. For example, pay attention to your bodily response to stressful or challenging events. Emotions manifest in the body and can overwhelm our state of being. Connect with your body; listen to its signals and be an observer of its emotions

26   Sadler-Smith, E. and Shefy, E. (2007) Developing intuitive awareness in management education, *Academy of Management Learning and Education*, 6(2): 1–20.

27   Sadler-Smith, E. (2008) *Inside Intuition*. Abingdon: Routledge.

but without emotional involvement. Emotional intelligence and intuitive intelligence are closely linked. Greater attention to somatic phenomena – somatic awareness – is the starting point for the skill of distinguishing the affect that accompanies an intuition from that which comes with a more intense emotional experience (see below).

Developing Emotional (Affective) Awareness

Be aware of your automatic reactions to situations; anticipate the triggers that operate your emotional system. One way to cope with these powerful bodily responses is by creating a space between the triggering event and the thought that follows: observe your thoughts, as they pass fleetingly through your conscious awareness; learn to separate yourself from the content of the thoughts, treat them as though they were merely guests – temporary visitors – to your house. Overcoming the emotional waves that wash over you opens a new space for intuition to reveal itself.

Clearing a Space

Attention to your breathing is one of the most important ways to slow down your thinking; it clears a space between your thoughts, and opens up the window into the subconscious mind and its intuitions. Paying attention to your breath's rhythm and depth can create a clearing for intuition's quiet but persistent voice to be heard since its urge is to be expressed. The analytical mind's voices are powerrful and dramatic, constantly moving from one thing to the next (sometimes referred to as 'the monkey mind'). It can be the antithesis of intuition – the spokesperson of our educators' and society's norms and expectations. The voice of the intuitive mind is by comparison subtle; the challenge is to amplify the intuitive vibration, catch the moment, seize the hunch before the judging, analytical mind takes control.

Doing-Without-Doing

We cannot cause intuition to occur by an effort; on the other hand we can create the space within which it can flourish: a paradox of intuition is the harder you try the more likely you are to miss it. The Taoist notion of 'wei-wu-wei' expresses minimal effort activity accompanied by an instinctive and intuitive response to the present moment, to the state that is now. It involves condition of giving up control; for example, creativity can flourish in the when ideas are allowed to incubate. A number of scientists and artists have reported breakthrough ideas surfacing when they had given up control of their minds, for example in the apocryphal stories of Archimedes in the bath, Newton's 'nap at noon', and Kekule's fireside dream.

Being Mindful

Mindfulness involves cultivating a sense of awe and wonder, and savouring the things of the here and now. Mindfulness means being: (a) meta-aware: not just doing something but also being aware of what you are doing and how you are doing it; (b) undistracted: your mind isn't bogged down in the constant stream of stimuli that are vying for attention; (c) non-judgemental: you adopt the position of being a neutral observer of things that are going on around you. Being mindful can help to release your mind from its dependence upon habitual and norm-referenced patterns of thinking. It is a way of examining things in your environment that you might automatically take for granted. Cultivating mindfulness comes through slowing down the onrush of mental activity and focusing attention on the world of sensations. Mindfulness training can improve observational skills and enrich your direct perception of the current situation and can counteract the all too frequent hijacking of thoughts by emotions, fears, prejudices and biases.

Bypassing the Analytical Mind

Using 'mind bypass' tools can create a bridge between the conscious and the subconscious mind.[28] They are called mind bypass (MBP) because they help users overcome barriers erected by the analytical mind. By using MBP it is possible to attain a more direct and intuitive way of knowing. MBP tools take their inspiration and techniques from Eastern philosophies and artistic practices. They enhance a more 'holistic' self-awareness. The Eastern approach does not separate the body from the mind but sees conscious and subconscious as a holistic entity. Expressive arts, especially those involving movement and encompassing all the sensory modalities, use the body's own intuitive understanding of how we feel and what we think. These techniques can be deployed to bring separated parts (body and mind) together into a holistic relationship.

MBP tools developing intuitive awareness have been used in management learning and development in educational in corporate settings[29] and include: (1) Focusing: this is a technique developed by Eugene Gendlin at the University of Chicago starting in the 1960s.[30] Its aim is to train individuals in the ability to sense, recognise and articulate their bodily feelings – the 'felt sense'; (2) visual imagery: a number of practitioners[31] have argued that imagery is vital in accessing and articulating intuition. There are a variety of ways in which imagery can be used, for example a decision exercise based around an 'inner journey' and other forms of guided imagery exercises. Guided imagery relaxes the body, alters consciousness, turns attention inward and results in critical shifts in awareness towards the subtle signals of the intuitive mind;[32] (3) Metaphors:

---

28   Shefy, E. and Sadler-Smith, E. (2006) Applying holistic principles in management development, *Journal of Management Development*, 29(4): 368–385.

29   Sadler-Smith, E. and Shefy, E. (2007) Developing intuitive awareness in management education, *Academy of Management Learning and Education*, 6(2): 186–205.

30   Gendlin, E. T. (1969) Focusing. *Psychotherapy: Theory, Research and Practice*, 6(1): 4–15.

31   Vaughan, F. E. (1979) *Awakening Intuition*. Garden City, NY: Anchor Press/Doubleday.

32   Naparstek, B. (2003) Guided imagery and intuition. In A. A. Sheikh (ed.) *Healing Images: The Role of Imagination in Health*, pp. 437–447. Amityville, NY: Baywood Publishing.

are figures of speech in which a word that is usually used for one thing is applied to another (for example, describing intuition as the 'eye of the heart'). Since subconscious knowledge often contains pre-verbal content, metaphor can function as a mediator between the conscious analytical mind and the unconscious intuitive mind. Metaphors enable you to expand ordinary perspectives on the world and provide a medium for your affective, abstract, insightful and intuitive experiences.[33] Metaphor expands your realm of knowing and translates your felt senses into words. By using metaphor you can reach deeper layers of knowing that are impossible or difficult to access by other means. Once a metaphor arises, or is chosen, this can begin an intrapersonal or interpersonal dialogue and produce shifts in attitudes, beliefs and assumptions, and can be the lynchpin of the solution to a problem or a dilemma. Metaphorical ways of knowing can strengthen you to act from within in ways that would not be possible with a literal use of language.

Conclusion

In this chapter we have attempted to examine, initially from a historical perspective, the development of management thought on the subject of intuition: two seminal figures loom large in the early years of this endeavour – Chester I. Barnard (1886–1961) and Herbert A. Simon (1916–2001). In the 1960s and 70s intuition received a fresh impetus from 'split-brain' research, for example Henry Mintzberg, Bill Taggart and others utilised these ideas to bring the notion of intuition more into the mainstream of management in ways that managers could connect with. More recent research using the new generation of brain imaging techniques such as positron emission tomography (PET) and functional magnetic resonance imaging (fMRI) reveal a more complex neural geography than is suggested by the split-brain information-processing model – perhaps this heralds the inception of a neuroscience of intuition? In management research in the later decades of the twentieth century attention was focused upon identifying how and when managers use intuition, and the works of Isenberg, Agor, Parikh, and Burke and Miller are especially significant. More recently the application of dual-process theories to management intuition and the development of improved self-report assessment tools have been important steps forward.[34] The management development profession is also taking tentative steps towards designing and testing ways in which intuition can be embraced within educational and training settings.[35] These issues are summarised in Table 21.1.

---

33   Marshak, R. J. (1993) Managing the metaphors of change, *Organizational Dynamics*, 22(1): 44–57.

34   Hodgkinson, G. P., Langan-Fox, J. and Sadler-Smith, E. (2008) Intuition: a fundamental bridging construct in the behavioural sciences, *British Journal of Psychology*, 99: 1–27.

35   Burke, L. and Sadler-Smith, E. (2006) Instructor intuition in the educational context, *Academy of Management Learning and Education*, 5(2): 169–181; Sadler-Smith, E. and Burke, L. A. (2009) Fostering intuition in management education, *Journal of Management Education*, 33: 239–262.

Table 21.1 Summary of intuition in management and management development

Characteristics of intuition	A judgement; affect-laden; rapid; involuntary; holistic; non-conscious; potentially powerful and perilous
Chester Barnard's (1936) logical and non-logical mental processes	Logical mental processes: (1) conscious; (2) analysable by the thinker; (3) expressible in words or symbols Non-logical mental processes: (1) non-conscious; (2) un-analysable by the thinker; (3) not expressible in words or symbols
Herbert Simon (1987) on intuition	'Intuition and judgment – at least good judgment – are simply analyses frozen into habit and into the capacity for rapid response through recognition.'* 'The effective manager does not have the luxury of choosing between "analytic" and "intuitive" approaches to problems.'*
Dane and Pratt's (2007) definition	Intuitions are affectively charged judgements that arise through rapid, non-conscious and holistic associations
Epstein's (1994) Cognitive–Experiential Self theory	Rational (analytical) system: affect-free; comparatively slow in operation; fast in formation; detail-focused; intentional; cognitively demanding; abstract and/or symbolic-based; open to conscious awareness; evolutionarily recent Experiential (intuitive) system: affect-laden; comparatively fast in operation; slow in formation; holistic; involuntary; cognitively undemanding; imagistic and/or narrative-based; unavailable to conscious awareness; evolutionarily ancient
Selected Measurement Instruments	Cognitive Style Index (CSI) Preference for Intuition or Deliberation (PID) Rational Experiential Inventory (REI)
Isenberg's (1984) five managerial uses of intuition	Sense when a problem exists Perform well-learned behaviour patterns rapidly Synthesise isolated bits of data and experience into an integrated picture Check on the results of more rational analysis Bypass in-depth analysis and more rapidly come up with a plausible solution
Klein's (2003) conditions favouring intuition or analysis	Favouring intuition: time pressure; ill-defined goals; dynamic conditions; experienced participants Favouring analysis: conflict resolution; optimisation; justification; computational complexity
Techniques for developing intuition and intuitive awareness	Intuitive expertise: focused deliberate practice outside of one's comfort zone; simulated and real settings; precise, relevant and candid feedback Understanding of intuition: intuition is not instinct; intuition is not insight; intuitive feelings are not emotional feelings Intuitive self-awareness: acceptance of intuition; creating the conditions for intuition; balancing intuition and analysis

*   Simon, H. A. (1987) Making management decisions: the role of intuition and emotion, *Academy of Management Executive*, 1(1): 57–64, p. 63.

The learning approaches outlined in this chapter – developing intuitive expertise, understanding and self-awareness – represent initial attempts to build a repertoire of techniques for the integration of intuition into the management education curriculum and into management and leadership development programmes. As intuition becomes increasingly accepted in business it is to be hoped that the management and leadership development profession will move in this direction also, and not only build a range of innovative and creative approaches for the development of intuitive intelligence, but also evaluate rigorously their impact upon leadership, judgement and decision making in organisations.

Further Reading

Agor, W. H. (ed.) (1989) *Intuition in Organizations: Leading and Managing Productively*. Newbury Park, CA: Sage Publications.

Cappon, D. (1994) *Intuition and Management: Research and Application*, Westport, CT: Quorum Books.

Davis, S. H. and Davis, P. B. (2003) *The Intuitive Dimensions of Administrative Decision-making*, Lanham, MS: Scarecrow.

Davis-Floyd, R. and Arvidson, P. S. (eds) (1994) *Intuition: The Inside Story*, New York: Routledge.

Gladwell, M. (2005) *Blink: The Power of Thinking Without Thinking*, London: Allen Lane.

Goldberg, P. (1985) *The Intuitive Edge*, Los Angeles, CA: Tarcher.

Hogarth, R. M. (2001) *Educating Intuition*, Chicago, IL: The University of Chicago Press.

Klein, G. (2003) *Intuition at Work*, New York: Currency/Double Day.

Myers, D. G. (2002) *Intuition: Its Powers and Perils*, New Haven, CT: Yale University Press.

Parikh, J. (1994) *Intuition: The New Frontier of Management*, Oxford: Blackwell Business.

Robinson, L. A. (2006) *Trust your Gut: How the Power of Intuition can Grow your Business*, Chicago, IL: Kaplan Publishing.

Rowan, R. (1986) *The Intuitive Manager*, Boston, MA: Little Brown.

Sadler-Smith, E. (2008) *Inside Intuition*, Abingdon: Routledge.

Sadler-Smith, E. (2009) *The Intuitive Mind: Profiting from the Power of your Sixth Sense*, Chichester: John Wiley and Sons.

Vaughan, F. E. (1979) *Awakening Intuition*, New York: Doubleday.

Weintraub, S. (1998) *The Hidden Intelligence: Innovation through Intuition*, Woburn, MA: Butterworth Heinemann.

Wilson, T. D. (2002) *Strangers to Ourselves: Discovering the Adaptive Unconscious*, Cambridge, MA: Belknap Press.

22 *Critical Action Learning*

KIRAN TREHAN AND MIKE PEDLER

Introduction

Increased attention is focusing on the value of critical approaches to enhancing leadership and management development. This chapter examines how critical action learning perspectives can be harnessed to produce valuable learning and development through critically reflective practice. Critical action learning approaches not only explore underlying power and control issues, but actively engage in an examination of political and cultural processes affecting organizational life. These perspectives enable a move beyond instrumentalist approaches to embrace the complexity of leadership and management development.

The aims of this chapter are to explore what critical action learning is, to elucidate its core features, to highlight how it can be applied in leadership and management development and finally to illuminate some of the complexities and challenges of working with critical action learning in practice.

What is Critical Action Learning?

Critical action learning is a development of action learning;[1] an approach currently applied to a wide range of leadership and management development activities. Action learning is not a single practice and has been used to describe an eclectic variety of approaches, betraying either distinctive philosophical traditions[2] or merely the slippery use of the concept to describe almost any form of group activity. In essence it is based on the premise that learning is a process that can be developed when people are helped to reflect on their attitudes and actions taken when solving real organization problems.[3]

Pedler (1991)[4] further argues that:

> Action learning is an approach to the development of people in organisations which takes the task as the vehicle for learning. It is based on the premise that there is no learning without action and no sober and deliberate action without learning … The method … has three main

1   Revans, R. W. (1982) *The Origins and Growth of Action Learning* Bromley: Chartwell-Bratt.

2   Pedler, M. (1996) *Action Learning for Managers* London: Lemos and Crane.

3   McGill, I. and Beaty, L. (1995) *Action Learning*. London: Kogan Page.

4   Pedler, M. (1991) *Action Learning in Practice*, 2nd edn. Aldershot: Gower.

components – people who accept responsibility for taking action on a particular issue, problems, or the tasks that people set themselves and a set of six or so colleagues who support and challenge each other to make progress on problems.

Willmott[5] proposes critical action learning as a means to counter what he sees as an unquestioning, positivist tradition in management education. He suggests that management teaching in the Business Schools is largely a technical matter – a 'management by numbers' approach which promotes formulaic problem-solving rather than the ability to question, reflect and reach independent judgement.

In Revans' view action learning is founded in the 'wisdom of peers' and the sufficient variety of value systems to be found in the set:

Action Learning is to make useful progress on the treatment of problems/opportunities, where no solution can possibly exist already because different managers, all honest, experienced and wise, will advocate different courses of actions in accordance with their different value systems, their different past experiences and their different hopes for the future.[6]

Revans would agree with Kurt Lewin[7] that there is nothing so practical as a good theory, and Lewin might agree with Revans that it is necessary to get into action fairly quickly on the basis of your ideas. Any problem worthy of that name will not be simply resolved but deliberate ('sober and deliberate') action will generate new data and learning to guide the next steps. Taking a critical stance in the everyday sceptical and questioning sense of that word will certainly help to ensure that the actions chosen are sober and deliberate; a deeper examination of the situation via critical social theory will help to reveal the political and cultural dimensions in situations. Revans would welcome such an examination as long as the critical reflection and analysis did not displace the action and the learning; as he noted, action learners frequently emerge more aware of, and more skilled in, the 'micropolitics of organization'.

However, Willmott argues that 'conventional' action learning is unlikely to develop a critical perspective that can question the ends or purposes of managerial practices in organizational life. This requires supplementing the criticality of Schön's[8] reflective practice with an input of ideas from critical social theory' (CST). CST is a family term for idea systems that challenge current social norms. Marxism, feminism, post-structuralism, deep ecology and so on derive their analytical power by standing against the value positions and judgements that underlie current best practice. This is important in organizational life because so much management theory is normative, busy describing how things are rather than asking why.

In questioning her or his own practice, reflecting not only on but in action, Schön's 'reflective practitioner' practices a personal reflexivity, becoming aware of their own practice and the underlying ideas that lead to choosing this action over that. However, Willmott argues that this accepted view of critical thinking does not enable the action

---

5   Willmott, H. (1997) Critical management learning. In Burgoyne, M. and Reynolds, M. *Management Learning.* London: Sage.

6   Revans, R. W. (1998) *The ABC of Action Learning.* London: Lemos and Crane.

7   Lewin, K. (1951) *Field Theory in Social Sciences.* New York: Harper and Row.

8   Schön, D. (1983) *The Reflective Practitioner: How Professionals Think in Action.* New York: Basic Books.

learner stand outside the prevailing social or organizational situation in order to see how it could be different and changed for the better:

Critical thinking may be attributed to those who challenge received wisdom as they develop novel recipes for improving organizational performance. Total quality management (TQM) and business process re-engineering (BPR) may be described as 'critical' in the sense that they question the rationality and effectiveness of established production methods.[9]

In his ideal action learning recipe, Willmott adds a dollop of CST to standard critical thinking:

> *received wisdom, including that of experts, is subject to critical scrutiny, through a fusion of reflection and insights drawn from critical social theory ... CST is required, not just as a knowledge of some specific sets of ideas, but as a general source of political awareness and an understanding of the world as a 'psychopolitical field of action and change'.*[10]

From this perspective, the members of a conventional action learning set are unlikely to be able to critique the organizational and social world from an independent standpoint. Given the power of corporate cultures and the pressures to conform, what chance is there of managers, especially when drawn from the same concern, or from a range of similar concerns, being able to exert a critical view on their employing organizations?

Critical action learning is an important development in management and leadership development because it promotes a deepening of critical thinking on the daily realities of organizational life, and does this by emphasizing the value of collective as well as individual reflection. It attempts to supplement individual's experiences of action (learning from experience), with the reflection of existing organizational dynamics created in action (learning from organizing). The latter process, which Vince terms 'organizing insight', is an explicit recognition of the role that politics can play in facilitating, and constraining, the scope for learning.[11]

PERSPECTIVES ON CRITICAL ACTION LEARNING

Action learning, though broadly interpreted and open to contestation, is to do with collaborative enquiry, problem-solving and self-development. The potential for criticality in action learning derives from the tensions, contradictions, emotions and power dynamics that inevitably exist both within a group, in individual managers' lives and in their organizational contexts. Critical action learning emerges as a pedagogical approach when these dynamics are treated centrally as a site of learning about managing and organizing.

We acknowledge that many who already work with action learning see a critical perspective as intrinsic to the process. In a seminal paper that stimulated Willmott's later formulation, McLaughlin and Thorpe's argument was that:

---

9   Willmott (1997) p. 750, op. cit.

10   Willmott (1997) p. 753, op. cit.

11   See Vince, R. (2004) Action learning and organizational learning: power, politics and emotions in organizations, *Action Learning*, 1(1:) 63–78.

At the level of their own expertise, managers undertaking Action Learning programmes can come to know themselves and their organization much better. In particular, they can become aware of the primacy of politics, both macro and micro, and the influence of power on decision making and non-decision making, not to mention the 'mobilization of bias'.[12]

However, our choice to use the terminology critical action learning is deliberate for two reasons. First, as Vince has argued, critical action learning addresses the deficit in traditional action learning that offers little encouragement to or support in 'working with the emotional and power dynamics in learning processes'.[13] The second reason is to differentiate critical perspective from critique. Critical thinking as critique is central to action learning and is epitomised by Willmott:

Critical action learning explores how the comparatively abstract ideas of critical theory can be mobilized and applied in the process of understanding and changing interpersonal and institutional practices. By combining a pedagogy that focuses upon management as a lived experience with theory that debunks conventional wisdom, managers can be enabled to develop 'habits of critical thinking ... that prepare them for responsible citizenship and personally and socially rewarding lives and careers'.[14]

Critical action learning can be located via Lyotard's argument[15] regarding the purposes of knowledge on a continuum highlighted in Figure 22.1.

Pedler, Burgoyne and Brook[16] suggest that:

Action learning may be positioned on the line between P and E, and furthest from S. [Being] suspicious of canonical ideas (and the experts who trade in them) and distrustful of speculative knowledge untested in action. By contrast Operational Research falls between P and S, being concerned with the solution to practical concerns through the application of theory, and is perhaps the least concerned with human development. Critical Theory lies between P and E, being both concerned to build theory and emancipatory in intention, but is least concerned with practical action and reality testing.

Within this continuum, critical action learning would find a position somewhere between AL on the bottom line between P and E and critical theory (CT) on the right-hand diagonal in Figure 22.2.

---

12   McLaughlin, H. and Thorpe, R. (1993) Action learning – a paradigm in emergence: the problems facing a challenge in traditional management education and development, *British Journal of Management*, 4(1): 19–27.

13   Vince, R. (1996) p. 119, op. cit.

14   Willmott, H. (1997) Critical management learning, citing Porter *et al.*, 1989, p. 71. In J. Burgoyne and M. Reynolds (eds) *Management Learning: Integrating Perspectives in Theory and Practice*, pp. 161–176. London: Sage.

15   Pedler, M., Burgoyne, J. and Brook, C. (2005) What has action learning learned to become?, *Action Learning: Research and Practice*, 2(1): 49–68.

16   Ibid.

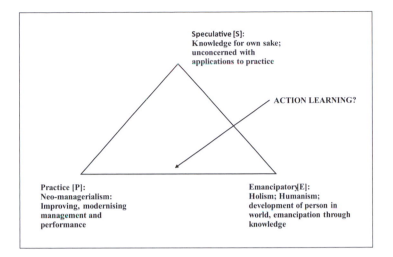

Figure 22.1 Lyotard's triangle

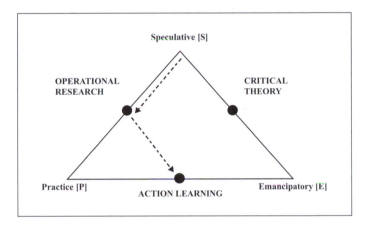

Figure 22.2 A trajectory of action learning

Core Features of Critical Action Learning

In the next section we illuminate the three key features of critical action learning. The central tenets we focus on are practical knowledge, collaboration and critical reflection and change.

RECOGNITION OF PRACTICAL KNOWLEDGE

Critical action learning synthesizes the practical stance of action learning[17] with the more sociological perspectives of critical theory. Critical action learning represents a shift from the traditional technicist approaches to learning; implicit within this tradition has been

---

17   Revans, R. W. (1982) *The Origins and Growth of Action Learning*. Bromley: Chartwell-Bratt.

the presumption that management knowledge and practice is objective and value free. Critical action learning challenges this position and argues for the need to deconstruct the discourse of policy and practice. As Edwards[18] illuminates '"practice" is already informed by overt or covert discursive understandings and exercises of power': and Schein,[19] writing on shared assumptions about nature, reality and knowledge, says:

> A fundamental part of every culture is a set of assumptions about what is real, how one determines or discovers what is real ... how members of a group determine what is relevant information, how they interpret information, how they determine when they have enough of it to decide whether or not to act, and what action to take.

This is central to critical action learning, which provides the 'means through which the individual find ways to learn about "oneself" by resolving a work focused project, and reflecting on that action, and on oneself in the company of others similarly engaged'.[20] Thus the potential for practical knowledge and criticality in action learning derives from action in situations of risk and confusion, to learning about power, politics and emotions in the process.

Critical action learning, as Mingers[21] highlights, allies to the recognition that individual experiences and learning always occur within institutional and social contexts, and that these both engender and constrain through relations of power and signification.

COLLABORATION AND ENGAGEMENT

A fundamental feature of critical action learning is collaboration. Vince[22] has advocated that critical action should be seen not as a group process for individual problem-solving, but as a collective process in a specific context for inquiring into actual organizational projects and practices. Within critical action learning, learning sets and the learning community are central in developing collaborative relationship, and offer rich opportunities to develop skills appropriate for working in partnerships, networks and across organizational boundaries. The distinctiveness of critical collaboration is that it provides a vehicle for self-government, shared decision making and problem solving which encourages people to own and be responsible for their actions.[23]

This approach favours self-empowered individuals and group learning, tackling the challenges that confront them in real time through questioning and reflection. Revans[24] argues that 'action learning sets are a small group of comrades in adversity, striving to learn with and from each other, confess their failures and expand on their victories'

---

18   Edwards, R. (1997) *Contested Terrain: The Transformation of the Workplace in the Twentieth Century*, p. 155. London: Heinemann.

19   Schein, E. (1992) *Organisational Culture and Leadership*, p. 97. San Francisco, CA: Jossey Bass.

20   Weinstein, K. (2002) Action learning: the classic approach. In Y. Boshyk (ed.) *Action Learning: Worldwide Experiences of Leadership and Organisational Development*, p. 6. Basingstoke: Palgrave.

21   Mingers J. (2000) What is it to be critical? Teaching a critical approach to management undergraduates, *Management Learning*, 31(2): 221.

22   Vince, R. (2004) Action learning and organizational learning: power, politics and emotions in organizations, *Action Learning*, 1(1): 63–78.

23   Trehan, K. and Rigg, C. (2007) Working with experiential learning: a critical perspective in practice. In *The Handbook of Experiential and Management Education*, pp. 400–416. New York: Oxford University Press.

24   Revans, R. (1980) *Action Learning: New Techniques for Management*, p. 8. London: Blond and Briggs.

(p. 16) and further highlights that 'the ultimate power of a successful [action learning group] lies not in the brilliance of its members, but in the cross-fertilization of its collective abilities'.

Vince[25] develops this further by highlighting 'Action learning sets are an environment within which the emotions, politics and social power relations that are integral to organizing can be viewed, discussed and potentially transformed.'

The dynamics of learning sets – their processes of organizing – often provoke emotions. Attending to and making sense of these is a rich source of experiential learning about organizational behaviour. The process of critical reflection provides language and concepts which help people acknowledge and make sense of feelings they may have long carried, but ignored, for example over tensions or contradictions they experience.[26]

Thus, critical collaboration supports the open and iterative nature of learning. Critical learning communities provide a space where comparatively abstract ideas can be mobilized and applied. Vince exemplifies the ways in which politics, emotions, learning and organizing interact in the context of open space and experimentation, by exploring the notion of 'organizing insights'. We would argue that organizing insights provides a synergy with critical action learning because, as Vince[27] says:

> When there is an examination of the politics that surround and inform organizing ... to comprehend these politics it is often necessary to question these political choices and decisions, both consciously and unconsciously.

This questioning of taken for granted assumptions is central to experimentation within collaborative learning communities.

Learning from peers is central in this process,[28] but what separates critical action learning from other approaches is the idea of engaging reflexively with peer dynamics, emotions and power relations. As Vince[29] highlights: 'it provides one way of thinking about the inseparability of emotions and politics, and acknowledges that this relationship is at the heart of what it means, both to learn and to organize'.

The social context is an often neglected perspective on learning. Some authors have argued that learning should always be understood as occurring within a social context,[30] and Vince[31] criticises Revans and Kolb's lack of analysis of the social and political context of action learning.[32] The implication for Vince is that learning communities are imbued

25   Vince, R. (2008) 'Learning-in-action' and learning inaction: advancing the theory and practice of critical action learning, *Journal of Action Learning Research and Practice,* 5(2): 5.

26   Rigg, C. and Trehan, K. (2004) Reflections on working with critical action learning, *Action Learning: Research and Practice,* 1(2): 149–165.

27   Vince, R. (2004) Action learning and organizational learning: power, politics and emotions in organizations, *Action Learning,* 1(1): 63–78.

28   Pedler, M. (1996) op. cit.

29   Vince, R. (2002a) Organizing reflection, *Management Learning,* 33(1): 63–78.

30   Reynolds, M. and Trehan, K. (2003) Learning from difference? *Management Learning,* 34(2): 163–180; Trehan, K. and Rigg, C. (2007) Working with experiential learning: a critical perspective in practice. In *The Handbook of Experiential and Management Education,* pp. 400–416. New York: Oxford University Press.

31   Vince, R. (1996) Experiential management education as the practice of change. In R. French and C. Grey (eds) *Rethinking Management Education,* pp. 111–127. London: Sage.

32   Revans, R. W. (1982) *The Origins and Growth of Action Learning.* Bromley: Chartwell-Bratt; Kolb, D. A. (1984) *Experiential Learning.* Englewood Cliffs, NJ: Prentice Hall.

with and surrounded by social power relations, which contribute to the construction of individual and group identity. As McGill and Beaty say, 'Action learning sets have a political dimension in that they replicate interpersonally and in the set, the sense of power and powerlessness that is found in any other group or organization.'[33]

CRITICAL REFLECTION AND CHANGE

The third core feature of critical action learning is critical reflection and change. The concept of reflection, particularly reflecting on experience, is central to the theories of learning which have come to inform action learning practice. Reflection is argued to improve the depth and relevance of individual learning,[34] to support emergence of self-insight and growth,[35] to develop the transferable ideal of the reflective practitioner, and to offer potential for organization learning and change,[36] for simply meaning introspection,[37] or for serving narrowly defined purposes of individual growth.

Critical reflection, however, goes beyond just problem solving and places an emphasis on understanding the whole person as mediated through experience, thus paying attention to:

> the process of how managers learn to manage has to be understood in the light of the individual's life, identity and biography as a whole. There is a clear continuity between the management of one's personal life and the formal work done in the organization.[38]

This form of critical self-reflection is qualitatively different from the concept of reflection in action learning. While reflection focuses on the immediate, presenting details of a task or problem, critical reflection involves an engagement with behaviour and activities geared towards rational task performance and those geared to emotional needs and anxieties. Vince[39] highlights the importance of moving away from reflective models that lead to reflection on experience being constructed or interpreted as managers 'thinking about their experience', emphasizing the rational nature of reflective processes rather than engaging with the emotional and political dimensions. However, others describe learning through critical reflection as creating new understandings by making conscious the social, political, professional, economic and ethical assumptions constraining or supporting one's action in a specific context.[40, 41] Similarly Brookfield[42]

33   McGill, I. and Beaty, L. (1995) *Action Learning*, p. 191. London: Kogan Page.

34   Moon, J. (2000) *Reflection in Learning and Professional Practice: Theory and Practice*. London: Kogan Page.

35   Miller, S. (2005) What it's like being the holder of space – a narrative on working with reflective practice in groups, *Reflective Practice*, 6(3): 367–377.

36   Vince, R. (2002b) The impact of emotion on organizational learning, *Human Resource Development*, 15(1): 73–86.

37   Hoyrup, S. (2004) Reflection as a core process in organisational learning, *Journal of Workplace Learning*, 16(8): 442–454.

38   Watson, T. and Harris, P. (1999) *The Emergent Manager*, p. 237. London: Sage.

39   Vince, R. (1996) op. cit.

40   Eccleston, K. (1996) The reflective practitioner: mantra or model for emancipation, *Reflective Practice*, 6(3): 146–161.

41   Mackintosh, C. (1998) Reflection: a flawed strategy for the nursing profession, *Nurse Education Today*, 18(7): 553–557.

42   Brookfield, S. (1988) Developing critically reflective practitioners: a rationale for training educators of adults. In S. Brookfield (ed.) *Training Educators of Adults: The Theory and Practice of Graduate Adult Education*, pp. 553–557. New York:

illuminates how, through the process of critical reflection, individuals come to interpret and create new knowledge and actions from their ordinary, and sometimes extraordinary, experiences. Thus critical reflection blends learning through experience with theoretical and technical learning to form new knowledge constructions, and new behaviours or insights.[43]

CRITICAL ACTION LEARNING IN PRACTICE

First illustration

So, what does a critical action learning look like in practices? In this section we illustrate two examples from practices; the first contextualizes a management development programme where a critical approach was applied in an education setting .and the second illuminates the application of critical action learning in an organizational context.

The example which follows is based on an approach called critical action learning adopted by Trehan and Rigg.[44]

First: the programme highlighted takes a critical learning approach where, supported by a small number of lectures, students spend two-thirds of their time working collectively in action learning sets (ALS) of six to nine people facilitated by a tutor.[45] The ALS fulfils a number of functions. It undertakes group tasks, which are predominantly real organization problems, and participants are encouraged through facilitation to reflect on how they work together and to work through process issues in some depth. Participants are also encouraged to exchange their experiences of working within the ALS, and of carrying out their individual course assignments. They are also involved in the assessment of their own and each other's work. In this sense students' dialogue and social support can be fundamental to the course.

Learning is through assignments that are almost entirely based on student-selected live organizational issues and based on their interpretation of tutor-written summaries. These are not organizational puzzles or problems with ready technical solutions, but are 'situations' in the sense that Schön[46] describes, characterized by uniqueness, uncertainty, instability and complexity and value conflict. Learning about leadership and developing the capacity to lead comes from the experience of working with these situations. A prime example is an overseas residential event in which the students' task is to undertake a comparative study of the market environment of a product or service in the overseas destination in contrast to their home context. Staff organize the destination, accommodation and travel arrangements, but task the participants to identify client organizations and arrange visits. Through this activity they not only learn about international market research in practice, rather than simply through lectures, but also learn about leadership experientially, about working outside their comfort zones and

Routledge.

43   Rigg, C. and Trehan, K. (2008) Critical reflection in the workplace: is it just too difficult?, *Journal of European Industrial Training*, 32(5): 374–384.

44   Trehan and Rigg (2007) op. cit.

45   See McGill and Beaty (1995) op. cit.

46   Schön (1983) op. cit.

about difference and cross-cultural comparisons in leadership development. They also learn from their involvement in leading and managing participative assessment.

This integration of critical reflection with action learning is a significant aspect of the programme, as the following extract from a participant highlights:

> *The action learning sets represented a move towards a critical approach to learning where the frustrations, power differentials, emotions, indifferences and conflicts which occur within groups can be focused upon and treated as tips for the exploration of management/leadership issues that are sensitive in our everyday experience. By focusing on our experiences as students in the action learning set context, a forum was provided for critical reflection on that experience, as a means of countering our conventional knowledge about the world. I had not considered leadership in these terms before.*

Comment: within each of these processes the task of learning about leadership and management development is focused on the group itself, its internal relationships, and relationships with other groups and the larger learning system of which the group is a part, which often generates strong emotions. During this process the programme draws from psychodynamic approaches to explore learning about the group dynamics, which includes a critical study of the leadership and management roles that participants take up and the roles that are imposed on them.

Throughout the programme many features aim to reinforce interdependence. The question of who owns the learning, diagnosis of issues or problems and the solutions to these are central to the students' learning. Facilitators take two basic, mutually supportive roles: those of task consultant – offering information, models or reading related to the task; and process consultant – making the participants aware of group processes. Facilitators take care in responding to participants' questions not to position students as dependent and passive. The course is structured around individual and group tasks framed in terms of learning outcomes. However, there is room for interpretation, which provides considerable leeway for participants to influence the content of the curriculum, but this is also a situation of uncertainty, through which students have to direct their own paths, individually and collectively.

Second: following on from working and learning about leadership and management development through critical action learning sets, the programme moves to the second step of developing participants' process skills.

Process skills are fundamental to leadership and organization development. Throughout the programme an equal emphasis is placed on process as on task content. In undertaking course tasks and investigating leadership situations, participants are supported by tutors in reflecting on how they work together as a group. This principle is also reflected in the course assessment in that many of the assignments require participants not only to demonstrate learning about content (for example, about leadership development, leadership behaviour or leadership performance models), but also to reflect on process issues they experienced in the course of undertaking the tasks, such as how they made decisions, what happened in their group, the strategic exchanges that occurred in the course of carrying out their research and how they felt throughout the activities.

Student evaluations of the group experience provide insight into their learning, with such comments as: 'It raised awareness of the complexities that exist within organizations';

'Most events in organizations are influenced by the way individuals interact in groups'. As one woman wrote:

> I would argue that my experience of being a member of these action learning sets has led me to experiencing a process of real personal 'change', which would not have occurred if, as students, we had been allowed to stay with the problem-oriented rationality of 'sharing' experience, rather than being made to 'work through' our experience within the group. It was in this forum that I was encouraged and supported in examining my values and attitudes, my behaviours in given situations and my understanding of the impact of group dynamics on what occurs within organizations. It is in this context that most change has occurred, both for me as a person and for me as a manager.

Comment: the action learning set is itself therefore a source of learning about leadership and management dynamics, in what Reynolds and Trehan[47] have termed 'classroom as real world'. The cohort each year is often a source of gender, cultural, class, religious, age and occupational diversity and each learning set consists of participants from a variety of roles and backgrounds, where issues mirror some of the patterns in organizations and society. Participants are encouraged to reflect upon, act on and learn from their feelings and experiences of these dynamics.

Thus, engaging with critical approaches to leadership and management development provides a mechanism for integrating the emotional, cultural and political context into the programme, which allows the participants to move beyond just thinking about leadership and management development as a rational process.

Third: the third step engages participants in critical reflection. On the programme participants write reflective papers, both individually on their learning, and collectively about their learning from the group process within their ALS. At the final stage they write a critical self-reflection paper, an autobiographical reflection on their leadership and management development practice. In this participants are encouraged to identify their core assumptions, to understand some of their patterns, and the contextual influences on them.

The following extract illuminates how engaging with critically reflective approaches can be a source of learning about, and transformation of, social relations within leadership dynamics:

> By being encouraged to look at issues about my power base and my influence over others within the context of the culture of my organization and my profession, I was moving towards a critically reflective position which began to question some of my underlying assumptions about leadership as a discipline, as well as about me as an individual. However, whilst considering issues in relation to both the personal power and position power I am able to wield, I began to reflect on how inequalities and power differences within society can be mirrored in organizations, obvious examples being in relation to equality of opportunity for staff; and the need for manager/leaders to address their personal role in perpetuating these inequalities.

Comment: this form of critical self-development is qualitatively different from the traditional concept of reflection in management development practice. While reflection

---

47   Reynolds, M. and Trehan, K. (2003) Learning from difference?, *Management Learning*, 34(2): 163–180.

focuses on the immediate, presenting details of a task or problem, critical reflection involves an analysis of power and control and an examination of the taken for granted within which the issues are situated. The potential for critical reflection derives from the tensions, contradictions, emotions and power dynamics that inevitably exist in managers' lives. Critical reflection as a pedagogical approach emerges on the programme because these dynamics are treated centrally as a site of learning about leading and leadership development.

In summary, the key advantages to this critical approach are that application of theory to practice and an iteration of practice to theory are advocated throughout the programme. They are tasked to relate concepts and models to live situations, and to make use of Lewin's adage that 'there is nothing so practical as a good theory'.[48] The approach to leadership and management development is informed by three key assumptions about learning: first, for participants to become aware of their theories-in-use; secondly, to think critically, so becoming as Carr and Kemmis write, emancipated 'from the often unseen constraints of assumption, habit, precedent, coercion and ideology';[49] thirdly, informed by Bateson's[50] theories of learning, tutors encourage participants to value their own experience and insights and to develop their own models; in other words, to create theory from practice:

I hope it will make me a better leader, but in a strange way that seems less important now. The main thing is that I have given myself permission to be a real live fallible person and I like myself much better for it.

Second Illustration – the Gladwell Story[51]

Action learning was employed as part of an attempt to introduce resident self-governance at neighbourhood level in Gladwell, a town of some 350,000 people on the edge of a major UK conurbation. With many disadvantaged people and alienated communities, the Council's recognition that it had failed its residents was the basis for its successive and mainly successful bids for European funding over several years. Such monies are intended to pump prime the redirection of mainstream spending by the agencies involved so that service delivery reflects local priorities and contributes to the social and economic regeneration of local communities.

We worked as consultants to the partnership board of local statutory agencies and voluntary sector and business organizations which led the initiative. A key part of this work was facilitating an action learning group of facilitators charged with empowering the residents in neighbourhoods towards self-governance via local neighbourhood committees to advise the partnership board on service delivery and improvement. This group met for a total of 15 days over a 13-month period and its collective experience forms the basis for this account.

---

48   Lewin (1951) op. cit.

49   Carr, W. and Kemmis, S. (1986) *Becoming Critical: Knowing through Action Research*, p. 192. Victoria: Deakin University.

50   Bateson, G. (1973) *Steps Towards an Ecology of the Mind*. London: Paladin.

51   The Gladwell Story – based on Attwood, M., Pedler, M., Pritchard, S. and Wilkinson, D. (2003) *Leading Change: A Guide to Whole Systems Working*, pp. 39–55. Bristol: Policy Press.

Giving the council back to the people

The idea of devolving more power to the community had been around for several politically fraught years. There were many criticisms of the local political system from both management and community quarters across the town. The community development effort began with public meetings in seven pilot neighbourhoods. From these meetings 'design teams' of local people were formed to engage representatives of 'the whole system' of diverse people, groups and interests in each neighbourhood. This process eventually led to two-day 'big events' to build a vision for the future neighbourhood. After this interim community forums were set up pending local elections to the neighbourhood committees. This process and these tasks were facilitated by a group of seconded council officers and agency staff.

THE FACILITATORS' ACTION LEARNING GROUP

By the time we arrived as consultants, the facilitators' group were already actively engaged on this demanding schedule of tasks. The background to this work on neighbourhood self-governance was not at all clear to most of the group, including ourselves, and much early effort went into trying to make sense of what was going on, partly because of the complexity of the system and partly because of the intriguing history of the group, some of whom knew each other, and some whom had been part of an internal bid for the consultancy contract eventually awarded to us.

In politically unstable conditions, the group members were attempting difficult tasks with demanding deadlines, and were often also feeling personally insecure. Most had short-term secondments to undertake this work and worried about their day jobs. Life in the group was difficult, exciting, depressing and joyful in turns; history remained with us, usually under the surface.

GROUP DEVELOPMENT

Meetings were pressurized, overloaded with information and several emerging conflicts. From the outset the imperative for urgent action created a steep learning curve for all concerned. People had many urgent questions:

- 'I'm interested in community work but I've never been out of the council, will I cope?'
- 'What will happen when we stand up in front of local people who are angry with us?'
- 'My manager didn't want to release me and told me I had to carry the extra workload – how do we get them involved?'
- 'Who should be in a design team'?
- 'How committed is the council to all this?'
- 'What's happening with the partnership board?'
- 'What logistical support do we get?'

The pace was such that these urgent preoccupations came and went very quickly. By the second meeting, a feverish concern with 'start-ups' had changed to an urgent focus on the next stages in the process – design teams and big events – which felt like ultimate goals at this point. By the third meeting we had spent four days together in a little over three weeks and by the fourth two members had already dropped out citing day job demands. But by now the group felt less fractured, more cohesive and committed. Outwardly, attention had again shifted from the stages in the process to different questions – 'Can we deliver?' and 'How much is in the pot anyway?' – and a concern not to over-promise to residents.

At this time we reflected on the rapid progression of the group from one urgent concern to the next, and to the personal development already evident as individuals tackled apparently formidable tasks, overcame them and moved on. We also noticed how we only remembered what and how much had been done when we managed to stop and reflect in this way.

Leadership, conflict and learning

This rapid development was reflected in a growing confidence both in particular individuals and the group as a collective. By now we had long passed the point where the big events were seen as an end point for the process and a much wider perspective had become evident. This maturing view emerged particularly in a clash with the council's chief executive, who, as promised to local politicians and the council's regional masters, was insistent on sticking to the original timetable of implementation in every case – despite the practical requirements for flexibility and local adaptations in individual neighbourhoods. A series of discussions culminated in a meeting with the entire council executive team. They listened carefully to the group and were impressed by the facilitators' experiences. Finally, the chief executive agreed it was necessary to be more flexible.

Some months later there was almost a repetition of this conflict over the timetable for neighbourhood elections, and with the same end result. The executive team wanted to stick to the promised May deadline, but the facilitators argued for a delay to September. At an uncomfortable meeting, the executives were experienced as prescriptive and the facilitators were left visibly angry. After various informal discussions, May was later dropped in favour of September.

This episode demonstrated the limits of formal leadership in complex, ambiguous situations where 'learning a way through' is the only workable course. By now the facilitators had acquired local knowledge that the executive team did not have, and were not only leading operationally but also had an important contribution to make to policy development. By understanding and accepting this, the executives eventually demonstrated flexible leadership and recognition of the importance of local knowledge beyond the limits of professional or expert knowledge.

Widening circles of inclusivity

The meetings and discussions with the executive team had the effect of setting neighbourhood events in a yet wider context. With timetables now agreed for elections to neighbourhood committee, the work of the group was redefined again. It suddenly became obvious that the need was now to engage with all the other 'patchworkers' (neighbourhood-based workers, including all the people from various council departments and partner organizations and agencies, who worked on the patch, including health, police and the numerous third sector or voluntary organizations. This was particularly because of the need to handover work in the pilot neighbourhoods to mainstream workers and officers.

This new task involved drawing in new people, briefing them and enrolling them into a different way of working. The facilitators' attention also began to shift to the other, non-pilot neighbourhoods in Gladwell. Patchworker events in each neighbourhood were complemented by a two-day 'Action with Communities' event, focusing on Gladwell as a whole, which brought together some 200 residents, council officers and staff from other agencies.

At this time, it also became apparent to the members of the facilitators' group that the hitherto single focus of community development had to be married to organization development work in the council and in the other member organizations of the partnership board. If neighbourhood governance was to be a reality, it had to be complemented with changes in the functioning of all organizations with a role at community level. The increasing ambition of this vision contrasted sharply with the will, time and resources available to bring it about. As we finished our contract the continuously shifting nature of things saw several key members leaving the facilitators group, and several new ones poised to join. Members of the executive team too were moving on. The chief executive had instituted regular meetings with the facilitator team which continued to meet, perhaps more in 'business mode' and perhaps with a tighter focus on the implementation of the process throughout the non-pilot neighbourhoods in Gladwell.

Comment

In the Gladwell case, it could be said that critical action learning happens naturally, as part of the territory of action and learning. Here the tensions, contradictions, emotions and power dynamics in the group and in the organizational and community contexts were all too clear. Confusion, fear, anger and excitement were often apparent, often openly discussed and often a core part of the learning about managing and organizing.

The experiences of the tensions and power struggles evident in the story – group members struggling with themselves and their sense of who they were, their skills and abilities; debating with each other about ways forward and collective direction; clashing with the executive team and so on – were a source of significant individual and collective learning. Other tensions were less discussed. Two members of the group were life partners and also part of the failed consultancy bid; there was a partially examined struggle between one of this couple (formerly an executive officer of the council who had lost this post via a reorganization of departments) and other members, sometimes including the facilitator. And there were myriad other tensions which appeared from time to time, concerning personal, departmental, intra- and inter-organizational relationships, some of which were discussed, some avoided and many unresolved.

The idea of critical action learning is primarily a product of practitioners whose purpose is the pursuit of a more critical management education. Of the few examples of critical action learning practice in print, most are, like our first example, found in academic settings which can more easily sanction space for reflection, for questioning and for the discussion of critical perspectives on managing, leading and organizing.

The Gladwell facilitators experienced intense pressures and as group facilitators we fought for reflective space and time. The tight, short-term focus of the group drove both action and the realization of learning as each task was anticipated (often in wonder and apprehension), planned for, tackled and accomplished. Each time an end was reached, the horizons opened wider to reveal a bigger picture. If this was a voyage of discovery, the facilitators' set only occasionally got their hands on any steering system, and were most of the time swept along on a tide of events.

So was the Gladwell experience an example of critical action learning? Certainly the facilitators group would understand that power and politics were an unavoidable aspect of managing, leading and organizing; certainly most would acknowledge the emotions and tensions inherent in the process of personal development and learning. Whether they were able to transfer these insights as reflective practitioners, and whether they could apply their learning, individually or collectively, to other situations of organizational learning and change, remain unanswered in this account.

Implications for Leadership and Management Development Practice

So far we have identified some of the ways in which the core facets of critical action learning can be developed in relation to leadership and management development practice. So what does this demand of the development practitioner? This is a question we turn to in this concluding section. We do not aim to offer a prescription, but present a set of ideas which include the importance of design in relation to content and process; the role of the facilitator; reflexivity; and engaging with experience.

A central aspect of critical action learning is the systematic examination of a commonly shared experience by participants as they work on individual or group projects This is the 'group dynamics' or process phase of learning in which the participants talk through issues related to the task and explore interpersonal relations within learning groups.

The Role of Facilitation

Process consultancy is where the facilitator helps the learning group to work on process issues and solve its own problems by helping participants become aware of group processes, of the likely consequences of patterns of behaviour and of techniques for accomplishing objectives. The facilitator is concerned with passing on the approach, methods and values of process consultancy so that the participant and the learning group can diagnose and remedy their problem.

The ownership of the learning, the diagnosis of issues or problems and the solutions to issues and problems are central to the facilitator's role. The degree of expertise required to complete the task effectively and the range of competencies residing in an action learning set will determine the nature and ownership of the issues and problems. In short, such issues are part of a negotiating process that involves all participants. In this way the learning strategy seeks to integrate the development-based activities with the participants' work and personal experiences and to instil in participants the desire and ability to take responsibility for their own learning.

The application of theory to practice and an iteration of practice to theory are also central in the design stages and could be developed as highlighted in Figure 22.3.

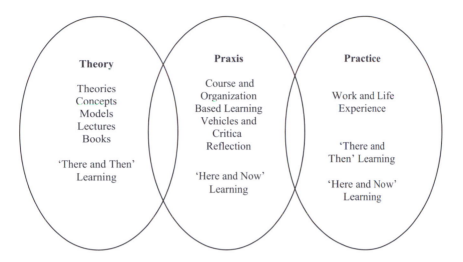

Figure 22.3 Critical action learning in practice

CRITICAL ACTION LEARNING IN PRACTICE

The establishment and facilitation of the action learning sets is therefore of great consequence, and presents important challenges for us as management developers, because first, the role and place of expertise and expert knowledge is open to scrutiny. All action learning accords a secondary place to the views and advice of experts and gives primacy to the knowledge and intuitions of the participants engaged with problems or opportunities that facilitate individual and organizational change. As Pedler[52] argues 'In action learning it is not so much the expertise itself that is questioned as the decision power that is taken and given to experts of all varieties.' A critical approach encourages reflection upon this experience of taking or giving power in active experimentation or in the evaluation of accepted knowledge and expertise.

Thus, in conclusion it is important to note that conventional management development approaches rarely embrace fully the tensions that inevitably arise from the ways in which the role of experts and the action learning groups are configured. By examining sites of tension, critical action learning 'can reveal the complex relationship between organizing and learning'.[53] The illumination of such conflicts is at the heart of critical action learning and can be vital in enhancing our understanding of how and why leadership and management development interventions work (or not). Critical action learning builds on earlier explorations in organization development, group dynamics and organizational learning, but also draws on more recent understandings from critical social theory, linguistics and social constructionism. The impact of these later ideas renders the social world of individuals, groups and organizations more problematic, more open to multiple interpretation, deconstruction and questioning.

Action learning is concerned with meaningful change in businesses, communities and individuals. This approach is increasingly seized upon as a means of overcoming the

---

52   Pedler, M. (2004) Editorial, *Action Learning: Research and Practice,* 1(2): 147–148.

53   Vince, R. (2001) Power and emotions in organizational learning, *Human Relations,* 54(10): 1325–1351.

gap between policy and practical implementation. Pedler[54] argues that this 'concern with finding ideas that will work in practice unites communities of interest amongst strategist, policy makers ... practitioners and professionals across a wide range of business'.

Conclusion

This chapter has highlighted the importance of critical action learning to leadership and management development. We have argued that there are compelling reasons for such a focus and approach. First, contemporary interest in the notion of evidence-based management development processes is indicative of resurgence in 'instrumental rationality' in organizational development. Yet there is growing scepticism over the extent to which 'scientist' assessments of training and development programmes can generate accurate and useful explanation in leadership and management development outcomes.

Critical action learning is informed by a commitment to practical knowledge and experience, which draws upon a range of intelligence rather than simply that of the expert. Learning in practical knowledge traditions emphasizes the importance of participation and deliberation. Participation is necessary since learning emerges from collaborative endeavours that generate new understandings. Deliberation draws attention to the fact that practitioner responses occur in a social context which needs to be taken account of and worked with. And when critical action learning does happen, people learn, not only about the task and about themselves and their own practice, but about 'the micro politics of organizations' – how you get things done around here.

---

54   Pedler (2004) op. cit., p. 5.

23 *Mentoring for Leaders and Managers*

BOB GARVEY

Introduction

This chapter is about mentoring managers and leaders. It starts by presenting some background to the mentoring phenomena and then goes on to discuss key ideas and theories relating to mentoring. Although mentoring is a very normal and ordinary human activity with a history of success over literally thousands of years, there can be some operational challenges: this chapter will discuss some of these and offer clear practical suggestions to address these. The chapter then goes on to outline guidelines for good practice, discuss the well-established benefits of mentoring and signpost some further reading and resources.

Background

Mentoring has a long and substantial history. It was first written about in Homer's epic poem, *The Odyssey*. King Odysseus, the king of Ithaca, is away fighting the Trojan wars and leaves his son, Telemachus, in the care of his trusted friend, Mentor. Under her Father Zeus' instructions, Athena, goddess of strategy and wisdom, replaces the earthly Mentor in disguise. The story tells of Telemachus' learning and development with a view to maintaining the kingdom in his father's absence and to taking his place as king. Since then mentoring has been associated with leadership development and in recent times has been employed in a range of contexts:

- Public and private sectors.
- Large and small businesses.
- Social and not-for-profit sectors.
- Schools, universities and colleges.

Key Ideas and Theories

Looking at some key ideas in mentoring, during the eighteenth century in Europe there was a flurry of writings. The first was a book, *Les aventures de Télémaque*, written by the

French Archbishop and tutor to Louis XIV's son, Fénelon (1651–1715). This describes the developmental journey of Telemachus supported by Mentor and introduces concepts of:

- Experiential learning and reflective questioning.
- Positive thinking, learning support, inspiration and wise counsel.
- Assertiveness, awareness and confidence.
- Charismatic leadership and role modelling.
- Trust in learning relationships.

Another writer, Caraccioli (1723–1803), develops these themes in a book, *True Mentor, or the Education of Young Men in Fashion*. Caraccioli develops Fénelon's themes and adds:

- Rapport building, empathy encouraging reflection.
- Goodness based on deep religious values.
- Understanding the cultural climate of the mentee.
- Acting from the principle of conscience and not self-interest.
- Encouraging varied reading and discussing literature.

Definition

Mentoring still retains some of the principles from the past, but mentoring activity has become formalised as part of an organisation's management development policies, succession planning, talent management and retention strategy. Mentoring is associated with change and it helps people to contribute to the organisational mission or strategy while supporting self-development and continuous improvement through meaningful and purposeful conversation. In essence, the ultimate aim of mentoring for the mentee is autonomy, empowerment and responsibility. It is not, as some say, about giving gratuitous advice. Perhaps the most straightforward definition is mentoring is 'off-line help by one person to another in making significant transitions in knowledge, work or thinking'.[1]

Mentoring can often reach the parts that other learning and development interventions can't reach! In mentoring, the relationship between mentor and mentee is all-important. There is a high degree of trust and mutual regard: the mentor helps the mentee become what they aspire to be and helps the mentee to realise their potential. In mentoring the learning is often two-way and the mentor learns and develops through being a mentor and doing mentoring. It is the quality of the relationship that has an impact on both the mentee's and the mentor's performance, often in quite dramatic and unexpected ways. This is discussed later in the chapter.

As illustrated in Case study 1, most people can remember being helped by someone who took an interest in their welfare, shared their own experience and knowledge with them, and enabled them to develop. Often they remember these relationships as playing a crucial part in their personal and professional development.

1   Megginson, D. and Clutterbuck, D. (1995) *Mentoring in Action*. London: Kogan Page.

> # Case Study 1[*]
>
> When I joined the organisation I was asked after a few weeks to find someone to be my mentor. I asked Peter since we worked in the same section and he was friendly and approachable. We set aside an hour a week so I could talk through issues that were concerning me. We ranged over many issues, personal as well as professional. Peter would make sure we finished the meeting with action points that I would try to follow up on, and that would often be where we started from the next week. But I could always ask him questions between our meetings as well. It was valuable to be able to turn to him over the kind of small matters that you would hesitate to bother some people with, especially your line manager. Peter helped me to get a picture of the whole organisation and my place in it. Thanks to him I settled in quickly and built up a sense of how my career might develop and what I needed to learn in order to make progress.
>
> [*]   Alred, G., Garvey, B. and Smith, R. (2006) *The Mentoring Pocket Book* (Management Pocket Book Series). Arlesford, Hants: Management Pocket Books Ltd.

Mentor vs Manager

Some are concerned as to the differences between a manager and a mentor. Mentoring and managing are not completely distinct, but a manager is concerned with the objectives of both team and organisation whereas a mentor is concerned with helping the mentee to learn within the context of a supportive relationship. A good manager may use mentoring as part of their line role and will recognise the value of an employee having a separate mentor to enhance their overall performance and their contribution to the team. A skilled manager may work with members of their team in the 'mentoring way', because they recognise that this enhances understanding, cooperation, performance and commitment.

If the mentor is somebody different from the manager this does not have to be a threat to the manager's authority. The benefits of mentoring to the manager and their team will emerge in the form of greater commitment, motivation and learning on the part of the mentee. In the end, it is important that there is as much openness and honesty as possible between the line manager, mentor and mentee while maintaining confidentiality within the mentoring relationship.

Mentoring vs Coaching

Some are concerned about the differences between mentoring and coaching.

Recent studies[2] suggest that mentoring and coaching have much in common and that in practice the differences are blurred and the similarities are more apparent. Willis's

---

2   Willis, P. (2005) *European Mentoring and Coaching Council. Competency Research Project: Phase 2.* Watford: EMCC.

research shows that the skills and process of both mentoring and coaching are virtually identical.

Coaching takes many different forms, for example, performance coaching, sports coaching and life coaching. Coaching tends to have a specific and tightly focused goal, or area of application.

Mentoring goes further in offering support and relevant advice to someone as a person, and whilst there is usually a focus, mentoring can touch on any aspect of a person's life. The mentor may offer coaching and training from time to time as appropriate, but may also encourage the mentee to seek help from specialists in these roles.

Broadly speaking, Megginson and Clutterbuck suggest that the differences are:[3]

Mentoring	Coaching
Implications beyond task	Task orientation
Capability and potential	Skill and performance
Best off-line or external	Online, offline or external
Agenda with learner	Agenda set with or by coach
Reflection by the learner	Reflections to the learner
Longer term	Shorter term
Feedback intuitive, implicit	Feedback explicit

However, it is important that the role is clearly understood at the outset and this is best done by both parties establishing ground rules and discussing mutual expectations. Sometimes, coaching activity can merge into mentoring and visa versa. This need not be a problem so long as both parties notice and acknowledge the shift by engaging in regular review of the ground rules.

Sponsorship or Development?

There are two main types of mentoring – developmental and sponsorship.

Developmental mentoring is aimed at supporting the mentee's learning and development as they experience change. This could be learning new skills, acquiring new knowledge, changing behaviours and attitudes, developing awareness of others and self.

---

3   Adapted from Megginson, D. and Clutterbuck, D. (2005) *Techniques for Coaching and Mentoring*. Oxford: Elsevier Butterworth-Heinemann.

This type of mentoring is the most widespread across all organisational sectors in the UK.

Sponsorship mentoring is about fast-tracking the mentee in their careers. This has been the dominant model in the US, whilst recently developmental mentoring has become more common across the Atlantic.

Key Areas of Practice with Examples

In 2004 a staff survey[4] in the NHS identified that 17 per cent of NHS staff experienced mentoring over the previous year. This amounts to approximately 240,000 people. This is significant because the NHS is perhaps the biggest employer in Europe. Within the private sector, for example, a major UK bank employing 70,000 people has a mentoring scheme for executives involving 800 senior managers as well as other schemes for graduates, front-line staff and other levels of management.

Mentoring is used for a variety of purposes:

- Developing managers and leaders.
- Supporting induction processes.
- Fast-tracking people into senior positions.
- Supporting change.
- Gaining long-term unemployed people employment.
- Reducing crime and reoffending.
- Improving school attendance, examination results and behaviour.
- Supporting anti-bullying policies in schools.
- Improving performance in whatever context it is employed.
- Improving skills.
- Transferring knowledge.
- Supporting diversity policies.

The following three case examples illustrate some applications of mentoring.

Case Study 2[*]

Mentoring for leadership

HBOS is a leading provider of financial services in the UK. The company currently employs approximately 70,000 people. Its executive mentoring programme contributes to growing and developing leadership capability at the most senior levels in the organisation. The aim is to broaden the mentees' business knowledge, grow their networks and prepare them for progression to even more senior roles.

---

4   The Healthcare Commission (2005) *NHS National Staff Survey 2004 – Summary of Key Findings*. London: Healthcare Commission.

The programme focuses on the top three layers of leaders in HBOS (levels 6, 7 and 8) and typically, the mentor will be directors and board members of various HBOS businesses at grade 8, and the mentees will be at grade 6 or 7.

The Learning and Development (L&D) consultant matches high-potential mentees with current executives from outside their division of the business.

Before the mentoring starts, the mentors attend a one-day skills workshop and the mentees attend a shorter workshop. Following the training, the mentee to schedules the first meeting with the mentor and they draw up an informal contract, agree the ground rules of the relationship, the length of the relationship (normally 12 months), confidentiality and draft an initial draft agenda of meetings. Typically, meetings are monthly and last up to two hours. They are usually face-to-face, although telephone sessions do happen, particularly once the relationship is established. The pair agrees to review the relationship at the end of the third meeting and, if either party feels it is not working, they may part. This rarely happens. Regular review within the relationship is encouraged. The L&D consultant may give support for the reviews but they do not police the scheme.

Discussions are normally around work-related issues, organisational issues, career development activities and behavioural issues. A common behavioural issue raised by mentees is their ability to influence their peers. Other topics commonly discussed are:

- behavioural aspects of time management;
- personal issues;
- conflict with others;
- team performance issues;
- business decision making.

The key success features in this scheme include:

- a strong element of voluntarism;
- ongoing support for mentors and mentees if they require it;
- light-touch management of the scheme.

The mentoring executives give the following reasons for wanting to be involved:

- 'I see it as my job.'
- 'What else can I do if don't help to bring someone else along?'
- 'I want to develop my own knowledge of the business.'
- 'I believe it is important for the future progress of the business.'
- 'I want to give something back to the organisation that has been good to me.'
- Strong participative influence on the shape of the scheme.
- Attention to mentor and mentee development.
- Further resources available, e.g. books, articles and videos.
- Responsive consultants to participants' needs.
- Informal evaluation.
- Regular review within the individual mentoring arrangement.

---

*   Adapted from Riddell, T. (2005) Mentoring for leadership in HBOS. In Megginson, D. Clutterbuck, D., Garvey, B., Stokes, P. and Garrett-Harris, R. (eds) (2005) *Mentoring in Action*, pp. 171–177. London: Kogan Page.

Case Study 3[*]

Mentoring women for leadership

The programme started with the Association of Business Women's (ABW) local chapter in Herning, a centre of commerce and innovation in the moors of Jutland, Denmark.

The purpose of the programme was to:

- create a learning arena for the mentees and clarify mentee's ambitions for top management;
- develop the leadership abilities of the mentees through personal development and insight;
- give the mentors more insight and skills for board membership;
- encourage networking among all the participants.

The scheme included:

- orientation, training and three networking days for all mentors and mentees;
- leadership development days for all mentees;
- a seminar on becoming/being a member of a board of directors.

Participants were found through a combination of advertising or direct marketing and direct contact. Men as well as women were mentors. The pilot group of mentors was mixed and included MDs, managers, headteachers and a chair. They were between 35 and 65 years old and the mentees were women between 28 and 45 from middle management positions.

The benefits for the mentor included:

- making yourself worthy of the trust and openness;
- developing self-insight;
- enhanced professionalism;
- personal learning;

The benefits for the mentees included:

- a male mentor can help put things into perspective for a woman working in a male-dominated company;
- opportunities for learning and networking;
- good insight into leadership;
- promotion to a new role.

Lessons learned – for mentor and mentee:

- mentoring should have a goal and purpose;
- confidentiality is vital;
- challenges have to be real not constructed;
- preparation and logging conversations is important;
- it takes time to create trust and openness;

- both will probably be nervous during the first phase of getting to know each other;
- mentor and mentee do not always agree.

Lessons learned about the programme:

Leadership development linked with a mentoring is a strong combination but it is very important to screen the mentees going into the programme so that they will benefit. It is important to involve the companies of the mentees to help facilitate the process and ensured that the companies also achieved visible and relevant benefits from mentoring. It is also necessary to screen the companies beforehand to ensure that they really support the programme. An important lesson is that mentoring accelerates change in the lives of the mentees and encourages networking which leads to strong relationships forming.

*   Adapted from Poulsen, K. (2005) Women and leadership: a development programme in Denmark. In Megginson, D., Clutterbuck, D., Garvey, B., Stokes, P. and Garrett-Harris, R. (eds) (2005) *Mentoring in Action*, pp. 156–162. London: Kogan Page.

Case Study 4*

The development of a lawyer

The mentor's account

The already established relationship really took off when I left the company in June 2000. When I departed it left a void for the company in terms of handling employment tribunals. I recommended that Eleanor should take on this responsibility. The company agreed but asked if I could continue to mentor her in this new role. Although she was a qualified lawyer, Eleanor needed help to become confident and competent in handling tribunals. She took over all the tribunal work with a relish. Initially I accompanied her and assisted by taking notes. Within a year she was performing the role excellently so I was able to withdraw from regularly accompanying her. At this point my role changed to one of 'sounding board'. I may have strayed into coaching and occasionally counselling during this process, but Eleanor and I continue to view my role as mentor. Eleanor gradually caught up and overtook my knowledge and she became a specialist in disability cases. My employment law experiences are more generalist. I kept up to date with the law by regularly sitting as a lay member in tribunals, by taking Employment Tribunals Service training and by researching for my lecturing role at university. Eleanor sometimes asks specialist questions and this prompts me to do research. This is always interesting and intellectually challenging and contributes to the now established two-way relationship. Although the relationship has always been about Eleanor's abilities, she does have a physical disability, arising out of a cerebral haemorrhage.

This impairs her mobility in one leg and one hand. It is not something that is relevant to the relationship, other than that it perhaps has brought out enormous courage and determination in Eleanor's personality. Eleanor left the company herself in March 2004 to work for Capital Law as a solicitor. She specializes in disability discrimination issues, provides training seminars and lectures on the subject and is now enjoying a broader unfair dismissal remit. My sounding board role continues.

Why do I do it?

1. I was brought up to do unto others as I would be done by and so the role of mentor is quite natural for me.
2. I have had the benefit of support from several mentors myself during my career and there is a 'giving back' element.
3. All of the professional institutions I have belonged to in my career have a strong focus on developing people, so mentoring is about professional development.
4. I take pleasure in seeing others benefit from my experience and ability to relate that experience to situations they find themselves in.

The mentee's account

Keith's role for me is like a driving instructor. Initially, there were dual controls, and I was only nominally driving. At that stage, Keith had to rev up my interest in driving, as I had grown disgruntled and apathetic about my career. He had to convince me that I could drive, as I and others had lost sight of my ability within my disability. He had to teach me the Highway Code, as he introduced me to employment law. He had to show me how to use the component elements of the car, as he showed me the tactics of employment tribunals – how silence is the most effective advocacy tool and so on. He taught me to navigate, as he counselled me to prepare for cases with thoroughness. But how did I end up in the car with him in the first place? I was quite a fierce 20-something then. No one could teach me anything! In retrospect, the reason I learned so willingly from Keith is that I could see he was a good driver. He interested me with his manias for wine, gardening and art. So I could quite understand how he was interested in me, because it was reciprocal! Certainly many miles have sped past. We already have nearly 10 years on the clock, as it were. We now drive different cars, but I am very conscious of how I need to communicate with Keith on the hands-free set from within my own vehicle on a regular basis. I am amazed when we talk that he has the same calm, methodical, mirror–signal–manoeuvre approach that he always had. It is important not to be fooled by this as it is this that underpins his roll with the punches, think on your feet, trust your instincts approach to litigation, when you need to move up a gear as you cross-examine a tricky witness. The result of this is that I now drive in Keith's style. If there is a single quality in my driving that is most clearly attributable to Keith, it is a degree of boldness. Keith taught me to have confidence in the car I drive and in my driving abilities. When I am on the skidpan of a tough tribunal case, it is definitely a Metcalf voice I hear inside my head, saying 'Shy bairns get nowt!' and I zoom ahead.

* Adapted from Metcalf, K. and Williams, E. (2005) Keith Metcalf mentors Eleanor Williams. In Megginson, D., Clutterbuck, D., Garvey, B., Stokes, P. and Garrett-Harris, R. (eds) (2005) *Mentoring in Action*, pp. 232–235. London: Kogan Page.

Issues from the Cases

Although the context of these cases is different, they share common features. First, in all cases there is an element of voluntarism in the mentoring relationship. How this features in each case is different but choice does seem to be an essential element for mentoring to be successful. In Case 2, both parties volunteer to participate but don't have choice as to who with! However, there is the safety valve of review and possible exit from the relationship. When it comes to putting people together for mentoring, as the cases illustrate, there are many ways to do it. Practice suggests that difference is a much better basis for successful mentoring than similarity.

Second, in all cases the mentoring has a purpose. This is not necessarily predetermined as a set of targets or goals but, in all cases, there is a broad focus on what the mentoring is about and what both parties want to achieve. In Case 4, the relationship has naturally developed over a long time and the nature of the role has shifted to a 'sounding board' relationship.

Third, in all cases, confidence seems to be a focus for the mentoring. This is not as a primary goal but it is often a consequence of good mentoring. With confidence comes improved performance and the development of leadership abilities.

Fourth, in Cases 2 and 3, the mentors and the mentees have some training and orientation towards mentoring. In Case 4, this doesn't seem to have happened but the mentoring, initially at least, was supported by the employer.

A further point is the mentoring role is not easy to define as in all cases the mentoring involved different roles and skills and these seem to be determined by the needs of the mentee.

In all cases, the quality of the relationship seems to be a very important issue. These can be characterised as involving trust and openness, rapport building, mutual interest and a sense of progressing learning and development and a key skill present in all cases is listening.

Potential Difficulties, Dilemmas and Weaknesses

Mentoring is a powerful human learning and development relationship, but because it is human it has the power to be both positive and negative. As humans, we are brilliant at relationships and we are dreadful at them at the same time!

As has been shown so far, mentoring takes many different forms, has different functions and it is influenced by its social setting and it is these variations that can lead to its success or failure. Additionally, genuine practical and structural difficulties contribute to the success or failure of mentoring and on occasions, mentoring is subject to social and cultural pressures.

According to Garvey,[5] there are three broad areas in which mentoring may go wrong:

---

5   Garvey, B. (2004) When mentoring goes wrong. In David Clutterbuck and Gill Lane (eds) *The Situational Mentor*, p. 162. Aldershot: Gower Press.

1. Practical or logistical issues.
2. Relationship issues.
3. Scheme and organisational-related issues.

PRACTICAL OR LOGISTICAL ISSUES

Time is one challenge in mentoring. This is because both mentor and mentee need to commit time to develop their relationship. Mentors need time to develop their mentoring skills and it takes time to learn and develop. Mentoring is not about quick fixes or plastering over the cracks!

Increasingly, people work in a time-pressured environment and this can sometimes challenge their commitment to mentoring. However, as shown in Case 2, mentors who see mentoring as a function of their job role do not experience the time pressures in the same way as those who see it as an extra.

The practicalities of time management are not that difficult. Most people have the knowledge and skills to manage time. They know, for example, the need to prioritise, to allocate time for activities, to work to deadlines and plan when to start an activity. If they do not know these things, they can learn them very quickly but this does not mean that they will apply this skill or knowledge. This suggests that time management is more about attitudes of mind and behaviours than about skills or knowledge. Individuals with time pressure problems can be difficult to deal because sometimes their environment or the cultural setting creates their problems. If this is the case, the changes in attitude or behaviour from the individual may need to take account of their social context. They need to understand the cultural pressures to behave in certain ways and learn to manage their behaviour within this context. In work-based mentoring relationships, mentors and mentees often report that a main topic of conversation is time. Here there is a real opportunity for the mentor to facilitate real changes in time-related attitudes and behaviours through dialogue, support and challenge.

RELATIONSHIP ISSUES

Many writers suggest that learning is fundamentally a social issue. We learn by and with and through other people. Mentoring is one aspect of this social learning. In learning relationships, Rogers[6] talks of the 'core conditions for learning', and these include empathy, genuineness, unconditional positive regard and an ability to communicate all these to others. All these 'conditions' need to be in place over time for learning to develop. Owing to the often intense and sometimes emotional nature of mentoring relationships these conditions take on particular significance. A mentoring relationship without these core conditions is inevitably under pressure.

Sometimes mentoring relationships may flounder because the pair fails to develop any sense of the dimensions, boundaries or assumptions held within the partnership. It is sometimes helpful to think about the mentoring relationship in terms of dimensions.

---

6   Rogers, C. R. (1969) *Freedom to Learn*. Columbus, OH: Charles E. Merrill Publishing Co.

```
Open------------------------------Closed
Public---------------------------- Private
Formal---------------------------- Informal
Active---------------------------- Passive
Stable---------------------------- Unstable
```

Figure 23.1 Relationship dimensions[7]

These dimensions are continuums and can be used to describe and discuss the relationship in order to establish ground rules or to evaluate progress or change in the relationship over time. For example, how open or closed would both parties like to be in terms of the content of the discussions? Or, who ought to know that they are in a mentoring relationship – should their relationship be public or private? How will they manage the relationship – formally or informally? Who is going to do what in the relationship or how active or passive will both parties be? How committed to the partnership are they and will they stick to their commitments?

Additionally, issues such as dependency and the ending of the relationship can have negative consequences for mentoring. There is always the potential for either greater dependency or a lack of trust evolving. The impending end is something that may affect the mentor relationship dramatically. It could bring the pair closer together and thus they become more dependent on each other. Or, trust may be put under strain as the potential ending draws nearer. Although some people may become concerned about dependency within mentoring and this is a natural concern, it is not necessarily a negative one. It is important for both parties to be able to 'let go' or change the nature of their partnership. However, sometimes dependency is an active and positive choice and sometimes it is beneficial. Eleanor from Case 4 said once, 'to look at dependency through the eyes of a disabled person is very different to an able-bodied person. Dependency is a good and positive choice for me and my mentor.' So, dependency can be both a temporary state and an active choice and it only becomes a problem if it is destructive, controlling or dominating.

Another relationship challenge is that a mentoring relationship may have run its course and neither party has noticed! This is when relationships may simply fizzle out. In a formal scheme vigilance is needed to reduce this risk through regular review and monitoring of the relationship within the relationship. The dimensions framework outlined above can be a good basis for a review.

Within mentoring another 'risk' is intimacy. This is often a natural consequence of a good learning relationship and may not be a problem. Intimacy is linked to the unique shared quality of the relationship which is special only to the two parties and this creates a strong and stable partnership. However, it could cause difficulties when the mentoring ends or the intimate relationship could move into an abusive or a sexual one. In both the UK and US work-settings, these are rare problems but they do occur more in the

---

7   Alred, G., Garvey, B. and Smith, R. (2006) *The Mentoring Pocket Book* (Management Pocket Book Series). Arlesford, Hants: Management Pocket Books Ltd.

US, where mentoring is focused on career sponsorship. In the UK, where mentoring is about learning and development, this is not big issue and statistically is about 1 in 500 relationships. This naturally leads on to the final potential difficulty in mentoring.

SCHEME AND ORGANISATIONAL RELATED ISSUES

In 1985, Kathy Kram[8] presented a four-stage framework for developing a mentoring scheme. This is adapted as follows:

- defining the purpose and scope of the scheme;
- diagnosis of factors that will encourage mentoring and those that will not;
- implementation plan;
- reviewing and evaluating.

If people don't know what or whom mentoring is for it becomes difficult to make a start, let alone sustain it, and this can lead to resentment and failure. Practice shows that developing a purpose and the scope of mentoring is best done collectively through dialogue with the interested parties and stakeholders.

Sometimes there are organisational factors that make it difficult to develop a mentoring scheme. These might include a lack of understanding among potential participants as to the importance of learning and development activities or lack of top management support for such a scheme.

There may also be practices and attitudes in the organisation that mentoring activity can associate with such as a management development programme, a talent management initiative or a staff retention strategy. In Case 2 for example, mentoring was linked to a newly developed competency framework called the Leadership Commitment.

It is also important to know where there is interest and where there might be resistance. Working with those who are for mentoring is a much better place to start than trying to persuade those who are against it!

Many organisations are tired of initiatives, and positioning mentoring as a new initiative is likely to cause problems. People being people might simply keep their heads down and wait for it to pass like a bus, only for the next one to come along five minutes later! Introducing mentoring slowly and organically is often the best way and gentle publicity for mentoring, support meetings and support materials help to keep it going and all contribute to successful outcomes and voluntary uptake.

As Case 2 points out, 'light touch' evaluation on an ongoing basis from the start of the scheme often leads to greater success than strict target-setting and retrospective evaluation. It is important to be mindful of what one of the great minds of the twentieth century, Albert Einstein, said in relation to evaluation: '*Not everything that counts can be counted and not everything that can be counted counts.*' This view is particularly important with a social process like mentoring. Research[9] shows that the single most important

---

8   Kram, K. (1985) Improving the mentoring process, *Training and Development Journal*, April: 40–42.

9   Neilson, T. and Eisenbach, R. (2003) Not all relationships are created equal: critical factors of high-quality mentoring relationships, *The International Journal of Mentoring and Coaching*, 1(1): available at http://www.emccouncil.org/index. phjp?id=55, accessed 3 August 2009.

factor in successful mentoring is the ability of both parties to give and receive feedback to each other about their relationship.

Moving on from scheme design, other potential problems with mentoring can be linked to power, status and hierarchy. An underpinning idea used to criticise mentoring can be drawn from earlier forms of mentoring, where mentoring is positioned as a parent–child relationship where 'father' knows best. Here the mentor may be the paternalistic, senior male who dominates those of lesser status. The ancient roots of mentoring do contain elements of paternalistic dominance, but mentoring is now part of a new language of learning and development. If within an organisational context mentoring is positioned as a hierarchical, power and control mechanism, there will be problems. Therefore, mentoring within the line is a problem. Mentoring is best developed outside of the line management arrangement, cross-functionally or in an interdisciplinary way to minimise these problems. Lessons from Case 2 illustrate this point.

Another real danger for mentoring is the tendency to adopt mentoring as a strategy for facilitating learning and change without consideration for the social setting or the cultural context. All too often mentoring is used to fix problems, fast track people to success or as a 'cure-all' for organisational ills. Organisations can talk development as much they like, but without real commitment it is just another initiative to squeeze a little more out of people!

Mentoring is influenced by organisational culture. In a strong task-focused culture people's issues may be disregarded. In such organisations mentors may believe in the mantra 'I did it the hard way and so should you!' Such people are not really mentors and may try to thwart developmental initiatives, or they may simply instruct the mentee in the ways of the organisation according to themselves and developmental progress then becomes blocked.

As already mentioned, mentoring is the kind of learning that changes lives, opens eyes, sets new horizons, values the person and is mutual and reciprocal. So while 'in at the deep end thinking' and advice-giving can create problems for mentoring, it can also create opportunities. The mentee may be able to play a part in the mentor's development and behavioural change in that they may influence the mentor's thinking just as much as the other way round. So we return to the issue of purpose and scope. It is important to consider who might be a good mentor and what they might contribute. Scheme organisers need to select their mentors and mentees by weighing-up many issues. There are few right answers here!

Conclusion

GUIDELINES ON PRACTICE AND IMPLEMENTATION

This section brings together the points made through this chapter and provides a quick guide to creating the conditions for success for mentoring in the workplace.

First, in scheme design, the Kram model (footnote 8) offers a good basis to work from as follows:

* defining the purpose and scope of the scheme
* diagnosis of factors that will encourage mentoring and those that will not

- implementation plan
- reviewing and evaluating.

Other factors that need to be considered are:

- *Voluntarism* – mentoring ought to be a voluntary activity but the degree of voluntarism will depend on the situation and the circumstances. In some cases, putting people together for a specific number of meetings before they review the relationship can be helpful. It can also assist the process if both parties agree on a 'no-fault divorce clause' or 'graceful exit clause' as a safe guard. In other cases, as in Case 4, total voluntarism is equally successful.
- *Matching* – matching for difference is often more effective than matching for similarity. Sometimes issue of age, gender and race may be considered but these will depend on the purpose of the scheme. Whatever choices are made it is important to have a transparent matching process.
- *Training* – both parties need some orientation towards mentoring. This could be skills training for both mentors and mentees and sometimes this can be done with both in the same programme.
- *Establishing reviewable ground rules* – clarifying the boundaries of the relationship at the start is important.
- *Whose agenda?* – mentoring is for the mentee, and research suggests that attempts to impose an agenda on the mentee can result in manipulation and social engineering. The benefits of mentoring for all stakeholders are derived from good practice and this means following the mentee's agenda.
- *Ongoing support* – mentors may need support and this could be as a mentor support group or one-to-one mentoring supervision – a mentor to the mentor. There is benefit in mentors from different sectors coming together to share practice and experiences, discuss mentoring process issues, debrief mentors, develop skills and to improve understanding.
- *Ongoing review* – once ground rules are established, they can become the basis for ongoing review and regular feedback within the relationship about the relationship.
- *Evaluation and monitoring* – there is little point in evaluating the scheme after, for example, two years to unearth problems that could have been resolved when they arose. Ongoing evaluation is important.

Adding Value

In a literature review Garvey and Garrett-Harris[10] looked at over 100 pieces of research into the benefits of mentoring and categorised them as follows:

- business performance and policy implementation;
- motivational benefits;
- knowledge and skills development;

---

10   Garvey, B. and Garrett-Harris, R. (2005) *The Benefits of Mentoring: A Literature Review, Report for East Mentors Forum, Mentoring and Coaching Research Unit*, Sheffield: Sheffield Hallam University.

- managing change and succession planning.

The majority of benefits cited in the literature relate to the mentee but they showed that businesses and the mentors also benefit in the following proportions:

Cited benefits for the mentee = 40 per cent

Cited benefits for the business = 33 per cent

Cited benefits for the mentor = 27 per cent

It is not really surprising that the most benefits cited are for the mentee. As already stated, mentoring is *for* the mentee. However, the closeness of the percentage number of citations for the business and the mentor suggest that mentoring activity is beneficial for all stakeholders.

Overall the percentages of citations for the specific categories of benefit break down as follows:

- motivational benefits – 33 per cent;
- business performance and policy implementation benefits – 30 per cent;
- knowledge and skills development benefits – 24 per cent;
- managing change and succession benefits – 13 per cent.

It is not surprising that the motivational benefits are in the majority, but the closeness of the citations in the business performance and policy implementation category is interesting and provides further evidence for decision makers that mentoring is good for the individual and the host organisation in terms of performance and the achievement of business policy imperatives.

Ranking the benefits for all three stakeholders results in the following:

- Mentee:

    - improved performance and productivity;
    - improved career and advancement opportunities;
    - improved knowledge and skills;
    - greater confidence and well-being.

- Mentor:

    - improved performance;
    - greater satisfaction, loyalty and self-awareness;
    - new knowledge and skills;
    - leadership development.

- Business:

    - staff retention and improved communication;

- improved morale, motivation and relationships (less conflict);
- improved learning and development within the business.

This was the largest literature review on the benefits of mentoring and it clearly shows that mentoring activity does add value to the business, the mentees and the mentors.

Resources, Reading and Web Links

The Mentoring Pocket Book by Geof Alred, Bob Garvey and Richard Smith (2006) published by Management Pocket Books is for mentors and mentees and contains a pocketful of tips and techniques to maximise the benefits of this highly effective human resource development process.

Mentoring in Action by David Megginson, David Clutterbuck, Bob Garvey, Paul Stokes and Ruth Garrett-Harris (2005) Kogan Page, London offers an extensive number of case studies for organisations and individuals interested in mentoring. There is an introductory section which offers guidance and best practice tips for mentoring.

Techniques for Coaching and Mentoring by David Megginson and David Clutterbuck (2005) Elsevier Butterworth-Heinemann, Oxford offers practical skills, processes and techniques for mentoring and coaching in practice.

Videos for Business

Mentoring for Business Excellence – a discussion and a case example of mentoring for business excellence in a small business context.

Mentoring Conversations – a live mentoring conversation illustrating a mentoring process and key skills. There is an introduction, discussion and a summary at the end.

Mentoring the Dream – a self-development film based on guided visualisation.

All videos are available from http://www.greenwood-partnership.com.

Weblinks

http://www.shu.ac.uk/research/ciod/coaching.html – the largest unit of its type in Europe: research, consultancy, training and MSc in Coaching and Mentoring.

http://www.emccouncil.org – the professional body representing mentors, mentees and organisations interested in mentoring.

http://www.clutterbuckassociates.com – training and consultancy provider.

http://www.mandbf.org.uk – mentoring mainly in the educational and social sectors.

http://www.mentoringforchange.co.uk – subscribe to a very interesting newsletter.

http://www.mentfor.co.uk – a mentoring network organisation based in the south-east and supported by the East of England Development Agency.

24 E-learning for Managers and Leaders

JIM STEWART

Introduction

This chapter examines what is now referred to as e-learning. I include the word 'now' here because e-learning has emerged as an accepted and dominant term from a range of other possible terms and acronyms associated with a set of approaches to learning and development which share very similar and common characteristics. As with other terms and concepts associated with leadership and management development, e-learning is not as straightforward as it might at first seem. It is perhaps obviously and clearly associated with learning and that might appear to be straightforward. However, the what, how and why of such learning are critical questions with argument and debate about the correct or best answers. The 'e' of e-learning may also appear straightforward. It is generally taken to be an abbreviation of 'electronic' and so may appear to simply mean electronic forms of delivering learning, but again there is dispute about what constitutes electronic when referring to e-learning. So this chapter will include an examination of various views and perspectives of e-learning with no definitive answers being provided. However, I will attempt to make a kind of sense of the varying views so that some indication of effective practice can emerge. An additional key point to make by way of introduction is that the focus of leadership and management development adds another dimension to debates around e-learning as such. This is because of the vagaries of understanding leadership, perhaps particularly in the context of management, and how leadership can and might be developed. The specific challenge for e-learning is how to harness the use of technology for developing skills in what is essentially a social process commonly involving face-to-face interaction between two or more individuals. But, as we will see, this is not a new challenge for the kind of approaches to development of which e-learning is simply the latest manifestation.

The chapter commences with a description of the history and origins of e-learning. This is important to establish some basic principles developed in similar contexts which are of value in informing practice. It then examines these principles in some detail before moving on to determine some useful and usable definitions of e-learning. The next section describes some contexts and applications and this is followed by speculation on how and why those might develop in the future. The chapter closes with some advice and guidance on the potential role and contribution of e-learning to leadership and management development.

Background and Origins[1]

The origins of e-learning can be clearly linked to approaches designed to accommodate learning at a distance. Historically these approaches were referred to as correspondence courses since they were based on paper-based learning materials sent and received through the post as are letters, or 'correspondence'. Correspondence courses were traditionally and are still generally those which lead to a qualification and are aimed at individuals wishing to change or advance their career. The term is not used today as much as in the past but when it is the meaning continues to have the association with qualification courses taken and generally but not exclusively paid for by individuals. Another feature already implied is that of learning at a distance and this feature is the key one of the related term 'distance learning'. This term can have a variety of meanings but is generally accepted to describe learning which has the following features:

- The learner is not immediately or continuously in the presence of or supervised by a trainer or tutor.
- The learner does though benefit from the services of a training or tutoring organisation.
- Such services may include support from a distance provided by a trainer or tutor.
- Such services always include learning materials provided by the training or tutoring organisation.
- Such materials can be a variety of forms and media and courses usually utilise a mix of these forms and media.

It is clear from these features that the concept of distance learning refers to a separation of learners in time and space from those who support them The points above deliberately use the terms 'training/trainer' and 'tutoring/tutor'. This is to denote the possibility of distance learning being used by employers for their employees and by educational institutions for their students. Distance learning has a history of being used for both purposes and in both contexts for leadership and management development practice. Correspondence courses have the longest history of distance learning for purposes of education and qualification provision, but the term has traditionally been applied to courses supplied by commercial organisations rather than educational institutions. Perhaps one of the most famous and certainly one of the first examples of the latter is the UK Open University which was established in 1968 and accepted its first students in 1970. It is interesting to note that the Open University Business School (OUBS) is the largest educator of managers and leaders in Europe through its management qualifications at various levels, up to and including its MBA. While not directly attributable to the creation of this institution, the name introduces yet a different term, that of 'open learning'. This approach is argued to offer and provide flexibility and autonomy to learners so that they can determine:

- What is learned.
- How it is learned.

---

[1]   This section is based on Stewart, J. and Winter, R. (1994) Open and distance learning. In Truelove, S. (ed.) *Handbook of Training and Development*, 2nd edn, pp. 197–230. Oxford: Blackwell Publishing.

- When it is learned.
- Where it is learned.
- At what pace learning occurs.

The ways in which the Open University and other similar institutions operate, and indeed how many if not all commercial and employer-based open learning programmes also operate, make it clear that flexibility and learner autonomy both have limits. The Open University, for example, has a finite number of courses and so limits the 'what'; their academics and course designers decide how to produce and present learning materials and so impose strict limits on the 'how' and finally as a university working to an academic year limits are also imposed on the 'when' and the 'pace' of learning. The OUBS is also a large provider of in-company programmes of leadership and management development through its qualifications for single or consortia of employers and these programmes are likely to have constraints of what, how, when and pace additional to those imposed by the OUBS itself. The characteristics of 'open' are therefore statements of ideal rather than actual conditions of learning. Even so, they also suggest a conceptual difference between distance learning and open learning. This difference rests first on the aim and ideal of learner autonomy as a central feature of open learning and the existence of distance as a central feature of distance learning. It is possible to imagine an open learning programme with no separation in time or place between learners and those who support them. Two examples of such programmes of particular relevance to leadership and management development are first what are referred as 'open space' events and second 'T' groups popular in the 1960s and 1970s for developing managers. Both of these types of programmes are based on open agendas of content and process. It is also possible to imagine a distance learning programme with no learner autonomy to determine the what, how, when, where or pace of learning. An example of this might indeed be an OUBS MBA programme. So the two concepts are separate and different. Despite this conceptual difference, common usage often links open and distance learning together as a single approach to learning or alternatively views distance learning as a form of open learning.

Some General Principles[2]

Both open and distance learning programmes can come in a variety of different forms and media. The first and traditional form was paper-based texts. These texts are different in presentation from traditional books. For example, it is considered effective practice in paper-based distance learning materials to make maximum use of white space, and related to this, to use larger font sizes than normally found in books. Research into such materials has over the years produced a number of other guidelines which include the following:

- *Presentation* – white space and font size is only one aspect of this. Others include high-quality paper, use of colour, print quality reproduction and attractive and high-quality packaging/binding and cover materials.

---

2   Ibid.

- *Layout* – this refers to the presentation of the content. Guidelines recommend breaking up text through use of boxed content such as summaries, activities and illustrative examples. Use of lots of and consistent headings and subheadings is also encouraged. A final recommendation is to break up the text with diagrams, graphics and photographs.
- *Ease of use* – a main purpose of the points so far is to make the materials more attractive, less daunting, and easy to use. There are additional suggestions related to this last point. A starting point is to organise the content into a logical structure and to then break it up into manageable chunks which are presented as a series of discrete units. Opinion varies on what is a manageable chunk, but a useful guideline is no more than 15 minutes of reading followed by an activity of some sort with the whole unit being capable of completion in no more than one hour. There are three more items under this heading. The first is use of clear objectives so that learners know what they are working towards. The second is use of a clear and consistent 'signposting' system; that is, use of different symbols to guide learners as to what they should be doing at any given point; for example different symbols for reading, responding to questions, an activity and taking a break. The third item is provision of a study guide and a key part of the content of that is explaining the signposting system.
- *Interactiveness* – this is probably the most significant and distinguishing feature of open and distance learning materials. It covers many items including learner activities and exercises, provision and use of self-assessment questions and model answers to enable self-monitoring of learning and progress and provision of trainer/tutor support for assessment of assignments and/or provision of guidance and advice on the content. Use of language and writing style is also included under this heading. The advice is to aim for language use consistent with a daily newspaper rather an academic tome and to adopt a conversational style to engage the learner.

You might recognise some of these features from this book and others you have read as textbooks on management and/or development. This is simply because features that have been found to support learning in paper-based texts used in open and distance learning programmes are now routinely used in textbooks and other forms of educational publishing for the same reason; that is, to support and facilitate learning. What is of more interest here is that the same features have been and are applied in different forms and media utilised in open and distance learning. The UK Open University led the way in many respects in use of alternatives to paper-based text through the use of television, radio, video and audio tapes among others. Use of different forms and media also lead to new names and acronyms such as technology-based training or learning (TBT/L) and, in higher education, resource-based learning (RBL) which encompassed paper as well as technology-based materials. Whatever the form and media used, the same principles have been applied.

The last two decades of the twentieth century saw more modern technologies such as personal computers being utilised (although the Open University has used computers for assessment and other activities from the start). This led to further names and acronyms such as computer-based training (CBT) and computer-assisted learning (CAL). In fact, such media had a longer history than recognised at the time, since what was referred to as programmed learning was used with specially developed machines from about the 1950s. Other technological advances led to interactive video (IV) and later digital video interactive (DVI), compact disc video (CD-V) and compact disc read-only memory (CD-ROM). All of these later developments relied on digital technology and in some cases and to a certain extent computer hardware. One point of commonality to do with all of these media, from paper to computer programs, is that their development was not – initially at least – for educational or learning purposes. To an extent the main purpose was either information storage and processing or entertainment. Opportunities for utilisation in support of learning were recognised after the media became established in other arenas and for other purposes. That is an important point which we return to later in the chapter. We will now move on to looking more closely at e-learning and the relevance of the discussion so far for understanding the potentialities and limitations of that approach in leadership and management development. It is worth reiterating that the principles which support and facilitate learning applied to paper have also been found to apply to other forms and media.

Definitions and Meanings

A useful starting point in examining the meaning and definitions of e-learning is to restate that it is connected to and is part of a long history of approaches developed as alternatives to face-to-face instruction, whether that face-to-face instruction occurs in a college classroom or an employer's training centre or, perhaps of more relevance to leadership and management development, an outdoor development centre. Given that, in this case it shares with all other media and technology the same features, characteristics and practice of open and distance learning. It is often an attempt to deliver learning at a distance and often an attempt to provide more autonomy over what, how, when, where and pace of learning to learners themselves. It is also, in common with other developments in open and distance learning media and technology, justified on both learning and cost-saving benefits. Those claimed benefits are often questionable, as they have been with earlier media and technology (see section on debates and controversies). What is less questionable is that e-learning as a form and medium of open and distance learning is subject to the same principles of effectiveness as earlier media and technology. In other words, the guidance suggested by research listed above on what supports effective learning through open and distance-learning approaches also applies to e-learning. So presentation, layout, interactiveness and ease of use, while having a different context for application, will be just as important in e-learning as they are in paper-based text. In fact, the principles are always applied differently in different media and technology since each different form has its own requirements, possibilities and limitations. Despite this, what helps and what hinders learning remains largely constant.

An initial point of debate in defining e-learning rests on what technologies to include and which to exclude. For example, one commentator defines e-learning as any learning activity supported by information and communication technologies (ICT).[3] This is similar to a definition from the Chartered Institute of Personnel and Development (CIPD) that asserts e-learning to be any that is delivered, enabled or mediated by electronic technology.[4] Both of these definitions have a focus on particular technology and seem to

3   Sambrook, S. (2003) E-learning in small organisations, *Education and Training*, 45(8/9): 506–516.

4   Sloman, M. and Rolph, J. (2003) *The E-Learning Curve*. London: CIPD.

be in agreement, although 'electronic' may be narrower in scope than ICT. However, in a later publication the CIPD elaborate their definition to emphasise what they describe as 'connectivity' on the basis of which they exclude any stand alone technology such as CD-ROMs.[5] Other authors have discussed and debated the same point and some at least have rejected the CIPD definition to include stand-alone technology in their definitions of e-learning. There is clearly disagreement here on what exactly constitutes e-learning.

In the same 2004 publication the CIPD provoke a different debate by introducing a further elaboration of their definition by adding the words '*that is for the explicit purpose of training in organisations*'. This narrows the definition even more and would, if accepted and applied, exclude any and all learning that meets the technological part of the definition but which occurs in non-work contexts, such as students learning in universities. It might also question any use of e-learning for leadership and management development since many might argue that goes beyond 'training'. It would in addition exclude many if not all of the OUBS students, and those on the many other distance learning and e-supported MBA programmes delivered by other providers, since they are clearly not being trained *in* the organisation. This element of the definition is clearly therefore too restrictive and so will be rejected here. That still leaves the problem of deciding what is included and what is excluded in terms of technology. Practice has moved on since both definitions were offered and it is a fast-moving and developing field. In addition, the 2003 CIPD report by Sloman and Rolph claims that the term e-learning was first used in 1999, so it is still very young in its life cycle. For these reasons it is reasonable not to expect or need a precise and settled definition. A debate about the inclusion of CD-ROMs will not take us very far. One point of relevance though to note is that Web 2.0 technology (see section on current ad future developments) utilises and emphasises the potential of connectivity even more that previous technology and so there may be a case for giving greater weight to that factor in deciding on a definition. What seems to be the case is that use of ICT for purposes of education, training and development seems to be a useful defining feature of e-learning, so any use of ICT to support leadership and management development will constitute e-learning.

A further area of debate in understanding the meaning of e-learning is the role of what is referred to as *stuff* and *stir*. The use of these words was introduced by Rossett[6] to distinguish between the content of learning and the process of learning. This is a well-established distinction in management learning and refers to *what* is to be or is learned (the stuff) and the *how* or way it is learned (the stir). Stuff and stir though are words applied specifically in e-learning for this distinction. The argument is that *stir* is more important and significant in both defining e-learning and in making it effective. Examples of stir are the collaborative learning tools such as virtual classrooms and online discussion boards. There is a clear link here with the notion of 'connectivity' and so perhaps an explanation for the CIPD excluding CD-ROMs in their definition. Learning content (stuff) delivered by ICT but without supporting collaborative processes (stir) is in this view not considered to be e-leaning. This argument may in part be based on not utilising the full functionality and associated benefits of ICT, but it is a partial argument. As we saw in the previous section, support for open and distance learning can be in a variety of forms and does not rely necessarily on collaborative processes. Since ICT can

---

5   CIPD (2004) *Inclusive Learning for All*. London: CIPD.

6   See Sloman and Rolph (2003) op. cit.

and does provide those other forms of support it seems somewhat esoteric to exclude those programmes that do not provide online collaboration from the meaning of e-learning. A possible reason for doing so might be to support a case that e-learning is a genuine fundamental departure from what has gone before. However, any familiarity with ICT programmes without collaborative *stir* will lead to the conclusion that they are simply open and distance learning programmes which utilise new and different technology. In addition, open and distance learning programmes, including those that are primarily paper-based, have for many years sought to include collaborative processes using whatever technology was available at the time. The UK Open University is perhaps a good but by no means the only example of this with their personal tutor telephone system, study groups and summer schools. So, it seems reasonable to conclude that e-learning is simply and primarily a continuation of established approaches to management and leadership development which utilises the latest technology to deliver learning content while at the same time supporting learners and facilitating learning. That is what all development practice, including all forms of open and distance learning, seeks to achieve. E-learning simply utilises particular forms of technology to achieve those aims.

Contexts and Applications

The rise in popularity and use of e-learning, just as with all innovations, is not easy to explain in practice. There do seem to be a number of factors though that has been significant. According to a CIPD survey published in 2004,[7] one of these is undoubtedly the role of vendors. Both technology companies and those already selling technology-based education and training products identified the potential for utilising ICT in developing new products. The technology companies developed products to support the *stir* of e-learning. These are generally referred to as learning platforms, which are basically computer programs that enable and support a variety of applications to support learning through ICT. These support systems usually rely on enabling connectivity to varying extents, but that is never an exclusive support feature. A major market for these products has been and remains educational institutions such as colleges and universities, although large employers have also adopted commercially available systems. The established education companies developed the *stuff* of e-learning and so brought products to market that required ICT hardware and software. Early examples of these were mainly in the form of CD-ROMs but they also quickly became more sophisticated and relied on the availability of learning platforms. Technology companies developing the learning platforms also developed *stuff* to accompany their system products, but to a lesser extent. The education market of colleges and universities is less significant for learning content than are large employers. Respondents to the CIPD survey were clear that those companies selling products related to e-learning were a major factor in driving adoption and increases in use. It is perhaps worth noting that the role of vendors in influencing and shaping approaches to management and leadership development is not restricted to e-learning. A similar argument could be made in relation to outdoor development, for example, and indeed to the myriad theories of effective leadership that have emerged and gained currency over the years. Most of those also led to new approaches to developing

---

7   CIPD (2004) *E-Learning Survey Results*. London: CIPD.

managers and leaders so that they could learn to behave in accordance with the associated theory. I will leave readers to fill in their own examples of this point.

An additional factor has been public policy. A number of writers identify a focus by national governments and their agencies on for example lifelong learning (LLL) as part of the explanation.[8] A similar focus on work-based learning (WBL) by governments as part of their policy initiatives is also argued to be relevant. The focus in recent years by the UK government on the importance of leadership and the creation of a number of leadership academies for a range of public sector services is an additional and specific factor of relevance here. Use of and growth in e-learning has been in part the outcome of public policy support and funding and other government led initiatives for its promotion. The notions of LLL and WBL are not of direct relevance here but Sambrook[9] provides a useful model of the latter which helps to explain government interest. The model simply distinguishes between *learning in work,* which denotes learning through and on the job, *learning at work,* which denotes learning which occurs at the place of work but away from the job, for example in a training or learning centre, and *learning outside work* which denotes learning relevant to work but occurring perhaps at home or at a college. The UK government, for example, has been keen to promote the latter two in order to improve skills and economic performance and e-learning is seen as relevant to both those contexts. Similar arguments apply to LLL and enabling and promoting it through e-learning has been part of the UK government's strategy on vocational education and training, including that directed at improving leadership and managerial capability.

This brief examination of some of the reasons for the growth in use of e-learning suggests a number of different contexts of practice. One is society and communities. E-learning is seen by governments as a way of increasing the amount of learning as well as spreading the range of people involved. A second context is formal education. The rise in use of e-learning in this context is also associated with government policy in the UK at least since they provide the majority of funds for education. Such funds have been directed in part at promoting e-learning at all levels of education from compulsory schooling to first and higher degree-level education at universities. The emphasis has been more on the flexibility and autonomy of open learning rather than creating distance learning in these contexts, but most programmes associated with government policy and funding have elements of both. The final major context of practice is that of work organisations. This has occurred mostly in large employers with a greater emphasis on distance rather than open learning, although again most programmes have elements of both.

All of these contexts are relevant to leadership and management development. It has long been recognised that in and at work is a significant locus of learning to lead and to manage. Experiences outside of work but not necessarily part of formal development programmes are also recognised and considered to be significant. Whether for performing community, social or organisational managerial and leadership roles, e-learning is now established as a potentially effective support to and for learning through and at work, and through outside experiences. While e-learning may have been developed and improved more in other contexts, such as life skills and academic as well as vocational qualifications,

---

8   Sambrook, S., Geertshuis, S. and Cheseldine, D. (2001) Developing a quality assurance system for computer-based learning materials – problems and issues, *Assessment and Evaluation in Higher Education,* 26(5): 417–426; Sambrook (2003) op. cit.

9   Sambrook (2003) op. cit.

its potential for supporting leadership and management development is increasingly acknowledged in public policy.

In relation to the work and employment context, e-learning has not seen the continued growth anticipated in earlier years. The most recent survey in the UK[10] shows less than half (47 per cent) of respondents using more e-learning than previously and a quarter (26 per cent) saying they don't use or no longer use e-learning. An additional interesting finding of the survey is that while over half of those surveyed use e-learning, the figures for the public sector are 82 per cent and only 42 per cent for the private sector. There is clearly a much higher rate of usage in the former compared with the latter. The survey has no data on the question but it might be that this greater use in the public sector is related to the policies of national government, in that they are likely to have more influence on development practice in the public sector. Indeed some of the respondents in that sector will be government organisations at national, regional and local levels. In relation to leadership and management development the figures are likely to reflect the emphasis just described on leadership development in the public sector. However, they may also reflect a different view of what constitutes leadership and so how it can and might be developed in the two sectors. This is not the chapter to address the question of whether leadership is leadership wherever it is exercised, or indeed the same question applied to management. The different contexts of the public and private sectors are however one factor in the perennial debate as to whether leaders and managers face different requirements in the two sectors.

The application and use of e-learning raises a number of issues of significance for leadership and management development practice. The first is the role of the development professional. There is an established debate on this issue and e-learning is only one element. However, there is an argument that there has been a shift in emphasis in recent years from *training* to *learning* and that the role of the development professional has and is changing accordingly. The CIPD has done a lot of work on this and their website has a number of free publications on their research. It may be that the recent introduction and rise in use of e-learning has some connection with the changing role of the development professional. Less emphasis on direct and face-to-face instruction, or training delivery, is certainly a feature of the claims on the changing role. Use of e-learning, as with other forms of open and distance learning, certainly demands less direct training delivery. Another claimed feature of the changing role reflects increasing responsibility for initiating and managing learning being passed to individual employees in work organisations. This is probably especially true of managers and leaders, who in any case are likely to want to exercise more individual control over their development. Such control and personal responsibility, as with open learning more generally with its focus on learner autonomy, is enabled and supported to an extent (but see next section) by e-learning. A requirement for changed attitudes towards both training and learning on the part of both development professionals and leaders and managers in relation to development is highlighted as critical to the success of e-learning by the majority (over 90 per cent) of respondents in the 2008 CIPD survey.[11] This finding supports the general arguments on the role of the development professional and the role of individual leaders and managers in managing their own learning. Similar findings on a changed role and

---

10   CIPD (2008) *Annual Learning and Development Survey*. London: CIPD.

11   CIPD (2008) op. cit.

changed relationships between learners and those who support them have been revealed in research into use of e-learning in higher education.[12] It seems to be the case, therefore, that application and use of e-learning has significant implications for leadership and management development practice and the role of development professionals.

A second issue questions the nature and extent of this argued shift in role for development professionals. A clear lesson of experience of e-learning to date is that is not a panacea and cannot be applied to all learning needs and that even where it is relevant and useful it needs to be utilised as part of an overall design and set of methods. The 'mixing' of e-learning with other methods is now generally referred to as *blended learning*. The effectiveness of blended learning as opposed to using e-learning as a single approach is supported by nearly all respondents (95 per cent) to the CIPD survey. It is also supported by research in both employment and education contexts as being more effective than using e-learning alone. The particular mix of methods can and does vary according to the particular learning being sought, but as a rough rule of thumb it is argued that e-learning is effective in relation to learning knowledge-related content but needs to be combined with other methods when developing skills. This is also argued to be particularly the case in relation to social and interpersonal skills. These are of course the skills focused on most in leadership and management development, so it seems sensible to conclude from this that blended learning approaches rather than e-learning in isolation are of more relevance to leadership and management development

There is nothing new in these arguments: similar points have been made in relation to all forms of media used in open and distance learning. They do suggest that there is still a place and role for direct, face-to-face delivery in the role of development professionals, perhaps especially so when the focus is leadership and management development.

A third and final issue raised by the application of e-learning is another element of the argued new role for development professionals. We do not have to accept the arguments on connectivity in defining e-learning to recognise that online collaboration is a feature of many e-learning programmes. This suggests a new context and set of tools for development professionals in supporting and facilitating learning. Encouraging discussion and interaction among learners, designing and applying activities and exercises, facilitating participation and answering questions are all part of the normal and established role of the development professional in direct and face-to-face delivery. The same kinds of contributions are also required in supporting online interaction, but this shift in context is argued to be so significant that it constitutes a different role and new and different skills.[13] This role and the associated skills go beyond those that arise simply from using new and different technology. A new term has come into common usage to accompany the new role and that is *e-learning moderator*. The role of e-moderator is said to be very different to face-to-face roles: there is both extensive research and extensive comment on how the role needs to be performed and the knowledge and skills required to perform it effectively. One particular example of where and how this might apply to leadership and management development is in relation to action learning. The extent of involvement and the role of a facilitator in action learning sets is an established debate.

12   See for example Smith, P. J., Murphy, K. L. and Mahoney, S. E. (2003) Towards identifying factors underlying readiness for online learning: an exploratory study, *Distance Education*, 24(1): 57–67.

13   Salmon, G. (2004) *E-moderating*, 2nd edn. London: RoutledgeFalmer.

How those arguments might apply in relation to virtual action learning sets who meet and interact solely online utilising an e-learning platform is a new and emerging debate.

We can conclude this section by saying that e-learning can be and is being applied across all of the major areas and arenas of development practice, including leadership and management development. E-learning has not been applied in any of these arenas to the extent once predicted, although it is now well established. It also seems to be clear that effective use of e-learning requires in most if not all cases well-designed combinations of blended learning, and that its use has some implications for the role of development professionals. These last two points are the subject of some debate and e-learning still retains some controversies. We will identify what those are and examine some of them in the next section before speculating on the future of e-learning in the penultimate section of this chapter. The final section will offer some guidance on use of e-learning specifically for leadership and management development.

Debates and Controversies

We have already seen that defining e-learning is a matter of some debate and controversy. This is related in part to the differing views on the extent to which e-learning represents a radical new departure in development practice or is simply a continuation of established approaches under the wider approach of open and distance learning. The view here is clearly in support of the latter. This view receives some support from the work of academic research into e-learning.[14] Work by some researchers on the use of e-learning by employees shows first that attitudes towards and confidence in learning per se, then specific learning materials in particular and finally e-learning as an approach influence responses to and effectiveness of e-learning. In other words, e-learning is not seen as a radical or significant departure from previous learning experiences by learners themselves. A second finding of this research is that a range of factors common to most approaches to and methods of learning influence learners' responses to and the effectiveness of e-learning. The most significant of these factors was found to be 'user-friendly'. That factor might be applied to any form of learning experience but it is certainly one that has been applied for many years in open and distance learning. A final outcome of this work was use of the notion of *getting in, getting on, getting out.* Applied to e-learning this refers to ease of entry to the materials, engaging with the materials and exiting the materials. Again, this notion could be applied to most if not all forms and approaches to development practice, but clearly it does apply to all open and distance learning materials. There is no reason to believe that these points do not apply to those learners experiencing leadership and management development, so it seems safe to say that they should be applied in use of e-learning used to develop leadership and management ability.

Another focus of debate and controversy is the extent to which practice is led by the 'e' or by the 'learning' of e-learning. We saw earlier that many professionals believe growth in use of e-learning was in part driven by vendors which suggests technology rather than learning principles led development of e-learning. A recent focus of this debate has been on what are referred to as *learning objects*. These are the 'stuff' of e-learning and have been subject to international attempts to set technical standards by intergovernment agencies.

---

14   See for example, Sambrook *et al.* (2001) and Sambrook (2003) op. cit.

Friesen,[15] an educationalist, makes a strong argument based on three objections against the process adopted to set these standards. The objections are first, difficulty in specifying a learning object from a purely technical perspective, second, a challenge to the assumption that learning objects and related technical standards can be pedagogically neutral, and third, the undue (according to Friesen) influence of the US military–industrial complex in the intergovernmental agencies and standard setting process. Friesen's basic argument is that the case of standards for learning objects is illustrative of the development of e-learning being led by technology and technical specialists rather than by educational, development and learning specialists. No doubt technology specialists will take a different view, but Friesen does show that there is debate and controversy over the emphasis on and significance of e and of learning. This is an important point and consideration for leadership and management development because such practice has a penchant for the latest fad or fashion and so is often led by whatever that is at a particular point in time rather than the learning needs and preferences of those being developed. In this sense, the 'e' of e-learning is simply an example and perhaps a metaphor for a wider problem in leadership and management development. Even so, it is also a real problem that needs to be recognised and dealt with.

The academic research referred to earlier highlights two further areas of debate and controversy. The first of these is the costs and benefits of e-learning. Sambrook[16] argues that the full costs are almost impossible to establish and so therefore is any worthwhile cost–benefit analysis. Evaluation of development activity is of course always difficult, and perhaps particularly so in relation to leadership and management development (see Chapter 16 this volume). According to Sambrook it is particularly true of e-learning, so evaluating the use of e-learning in leadership and management development has a double problem. Despite this, there is a well-established view that e-learning brings both cost savings and learning benefits, although there is little evidence other than reported claims to support such a conclusion. Similar arguments on cost savings and learning benefits have been made in the past for new technologies in open and distance learning, but again with very little evidence to support them.[17] It seems that this is another continuing thread connecting e-learning to previous approaches to development practice.

A second debate arises out of academic research centres on the issue of trust. Many e-learning platforms have a monitoring functionality which enables the activity, engagement and progress of individual users (learners) to be checked by those with administrative access to the system, normally e-moderators. The extent to which such functionality is utilised signals the level of trust, or otherwise, placed by the provider or facilitator of e-learning in individuals using the programs. I can say from personal and direct experience that e-learning programs are sold with the monitoring functionality as a major selling point. The issue of trust is also related to the notion of learner autonomy in open learning, since any degree of monitoring suggests a very low level of learner autonomy. It also raises ethical questions for development professionals, not least in connection to their relationship with clients and learners engaging in leadership and management development. A specific example of this kind of issue is the notion of

---

15   Friesen, N. (2004) Three objections to learning objects and e-learning standards. In McGreal, R. (ed.) *Online Education Using Learning Objects*, pp. 59–70. London: Routledge.

16   Sambrook (2003) op. cit.

17   Stewart and Winter (1994) op. cit.

'lurkers'.[18] This term is applied to those members of online communities – a discussion group or virtual action learning set for example – who engage much less than others, perhaps not at all, but gain benefit from accessing the work of those who do engage. The first question that arises is whether to have a system that enables lurkers to be identified. The second question is what to do about it, if anything, and there are probably questions between, before and after those two. It might be said that similar or even the same issues arise in 'normal' delivery. However, the first question of whether to have the capability of identification does not arise in 'normal' circumstances as in those it cannot be avoided. It can be avoided in e-learning, so the question has to be faced and answered.

This discussion of trust raises two final and related controversial issues. The first is the potential for control and standardisation presented by e-learning. A claimed benefit is to guarantee that all learners receive and so experience the same learning. That claim is questionable on the simple grounds that individuals are unique and so experience the same phenomena differently and uniquely. The more important point is the desirability of attempting to achieve standardisation. Related to this is the role of the development professional and the extent to which it is desirable that this includes monitoring, control and standardisation; another ethical issue. Answers to these questions may vary from context to context; for example, a lecturer in a university may take a different view to a management development professional in a commercial work organisation. However, it is a question that arises when considering use of e-learning and one which is particularly relevant to leadership and management development. The OUBS lecturer may be content that all participants receive the same material in the same form and are subject to the same assessment requirements as this can be easily justified on the grounds of an academic qualification such as a MBA being awarded. But do leadership and management development professionals wish to standardise management and leadership learning? Is that the best way to develop leaders and managers?

The topics of debate and controversy highlighted here are by no means exhaustive and there are others within research and practice of e-learning. Most will continue into the future. New topics may emerge as e-learning and in particular the use of new technologies continues to develop. We will now turn our attention to speculating on those developments.

Current and Future Developments

We have seen that a wide range of development contexts other than leadership and management development have adopted e-learning. The spread of contexts is likely to continue in the future, in part influenced by new technological possibilities (see below). E-learning is already used in all levels of education and in all types of work organisations as well as at societal levels. Three contexts that could encompass its use to greater degrees in the future are first within communities, second among voluntary and social groups and third by individuals for their own personal development. Some use in these contexts no doubt already happens. What we are suggesting here is that these contexts will be arenas of future growth in use. This will lead to more and more leaders and managers in those contexts both embracing e-learning and being subject to its use in their formal

---

18   Salmon (2004) op. cit.

development programmes. It might also lead to more opportunities to take leaders and managers out of their familiar worlds and utilise new and unfamiliar contexts for learning and development. An example of this might be mixed online communities drawn from different contexts and sectors working on a common project sponsored by a local voluntary group. The spread of members of such an online community need not be limited to contexts and sectors but might also be geographic and international in composition. In this scenario individual leaders and managers seeking new experiences and opportunities to develop will not have to rely on their employers or others organising a formal programme; they will initiate it themselves.

The growth just referred to will be facilitated by technology. Two current developments are likely to be significant. The first is the emergence of social networking enabled by Web 2.0 technology within the Internet.[19] A key feature of this is the ability of individuals and groups to build and control their own networks. Some sites which utilise Web 2.0, such as Second Life, are already being used by universities and others for educational and development purposes. However, the same technology enables communities and voluntary and social groups to utilise the same systems for their own purposes, which are likely to include learning and development at some point. What is likely to facilitate more individual and personal use is technology that enables what is referred to as *m-learning* – for mobile-learning. As Sambrook[20] identifies, m-learning is likely to grow in the future and the argument here is that this will lead to greater use of e-learning by individuals for their own personal learning and development. An earlier section argued that individual leaders and managers are and have to take more responsibility for their own development. Web 2.0 and mobile technologies will both enable, facilitate and support this happening to a greater extent than is presently common or possible.

These speculations are based on current knowledge of current technologies. What is not a speculation is that by the time the speculations are read technologies and applications of existing technologies not currently known will have emerged and may lead to different developments. However, as with existing e-learning, the developments are unlikely to represent radical or new departures in the essence of development practice or the ways in which people learn. They will however present new opportunities for and ways of supporting learning.

GUIDANCE ON PRACTICE

There is no simple set of rules that can be offered or applied in ensuring the best use of e-learning. One reason for this is the variety of ways in which it can be used and the different methods that might be combined with e-learning to produce an effective blended learning programme. What follows therefore are some general principles which will have more or less relevance and application depending on particular circumstances.

- Utilise wherever possible tailored and specifically designed learning objects and e-learning 'stuff'. There are many learning objects and commercially available e-learning stuff for leadership and management development. However, in lots of cases they are so generic and generalised that they are unlikely to be as effective as tailored

---

19   See CIPD (2008) *Web 2.0 and HR*. London: CIPD for discussion of this point.

20   Sambrook (2003) op. cit.

content. Bear in mind of course that tailored content will be very expensive, or at least relatively so. However, within learning platforms there are usually programmes and systems for creating content which are easily mastered to enable development professionals to produce good-quality materials. There are also similar programmes and systems available without buying a full learning platform.

- Apply the principles of effective open and distance learning to either produce e-learning content or as criteria in making buying decisions. The principles outlined in this chapter are not hard and fast rules that apply in all places and all times. They are though based on research and experience over many years and reflect application of sound lessons on how to enable, facilitate and support learners and learning outside of formal face-to-face contact. Current technology allows use of a wide variety of media in a single development programme; for example, streamed video, music and speech, interactive film, podcasts and other downloads as well as written material. Variety for its own sake is not good, but for clear and useful purposes it increases learning effectiveness.

- Support learners through effective design and operation of e-learning 'stir'. Applying the principles of effective 'stuff' is not really getting the most out of e-learning. Current and future technology has one big advantage over previous technology, and that is the potential for synchronous and asynchronous connectivity between learners and development professionals. We know from long experience and research that leaders and managers learn through and with other leaders and managers and e-learning can facilitate that happening. Stir though does need to be thought through and fit with stuff and so shouldn't be an afterthought or add on. It also though has the potential to be the stuff as well as the stir, but in that case stir should be the basis of the programme design from the start.

- Utilise e-learning as part of a blended learning approach to leadership and management development. Experience over the last 10 years or so has shown that e-learning alone is less effective than when combined with other methods. These other methods can be and often are more traditional face-to-face events. They can also include more or less formalised mentoring and coaching programmes, for example. Whatever the particular combination of methods designed, the place, role and contribution of e-learning elements needs to be clear with specified aims and objectives. As with leadership and management development more widely, the more tailored to individual needs the better and more effective the use of e-learning and a whole blended learning programme is likely to be. Use of e-learning can enable a greater degree of variety and flexibility and so can also enable and support a greater degree of individualisation as well as the arguable benefit of greater standardisation.

Conclusion

This chapter has explored the origins and development of e-learning as well as the meaning of the term. A clear conclusion to be reached is that e-learning is not a universal panacea for all leadership and management development needs and that it cannot provide a solution to all related problems. That said, e-learning does have relevance to a wide range of contexts of development practice. Gaining benefit from its application in those contexts is more likely to be achieved by adopting well-researched principles of effective learning and in particular those which have been established in open and distance learning. There is a danger though that technology and the work of technical specialists will have greater influence than development professionals and other learning specialists. The role, contribution and influence of these two groups are only one of many debates and controversies within research and practice of e-learning. Debates and controversies are likely to continue and are likely to be added to as new possibilities emerge through new technologies and applications. These are also likely to open up different contexts and methods of leadership and management development to e-learning systems and programmes. In summary, we might say that e-learning has brought some benefits to development practice and has the potential to bring more, but realising and achieving that potential is by no means automatic or guaranteed.

Useful Resources

BOOKS

The E-Learning Revolution (2002) Martyn Sloman, London: CIPD.
E-tivities (2002) Gilly Salmon, London: RoutledgeFalmer.
E-moderating, 2nd edn (2004) Gilly Salmon, London: RoutledgeFalmer.

WEBSITES

http://www.e-learningcentre.co.uk/ E-learning content and research, some free.
http://www.direct.gov.uk/en/EducationAndLearning/AdultLearning/LearningOutside TheClassroom/DG_4016860 An official government website with free if partial advice but also useful links.
http://www.wwwords.co.uk/elea/ An online journal on e-learning. Requires a subscription.
http://www.elearningage.co.uk/HOME.ASPX Includes guides to resources and suppliers but is also a useful and free online magazine.
http://www.elearning.ac.uk/ Mainly focused on use of e-learning in higher education but content is of wider relevance and value, especially research reports.
http://www.elearningnetwork.org/ A voluntary network of individuals interested and involved in e-learning. Various categories of membership including one free level which gives access to some useful information/advice/guidance.
http://www.c4lpt.co.uk/index.html Mainly commercial site operated by a consultant but with some very useful resources which are very good value, including a useful introductory guide to e-learning.

25 Leadership and Management Development in the Voluntary and Community Sectors

ALISON TRIMBLE AND BECKY MALBY

Introduction

In our view there are two types of leaders in the voluntary and community sector (VCS). Those employed in voluntary organisations, whose *raison d'être* is a commitment to the sector, and who are required to be organisational leaders as well as sector leaders; and those who have 'become' community leaders, as a result of wanting to do something about their own experience as for instance a migrant, a carer for someone with specific needs; someone learning to live with a lifelong condition. These are two very different starting places.

Development for the VCS seems to us to be focused on making the VCS a 'proper' sector to work with – on the premise that its not well organised, and that makes it difficult for the public sector and private sector to work with it. This leads to the solution of developing more business-like leaders in the VCS. Leadership and management development therefore focuses on programmes that mimic what is provided for the public sector, rather than taking the specific motivations and requirement of people in the voluntary and community sectors.

Perhaps the biggest learning curve for those providing development is that there is a great sense of hunger amongst VCS leaders for learning which is both skills-based, for example, communication and negotiation skills, as well as process-based, for example, developing meaning-making capacity which would facilitate better understanding of the systemic issues of social change.

Who are Community Leaders?

The term 'community leader' has a broad range of meaning and association, all of which are valid in their different contexts, but may be very diverse and even contradictory. For example, community leaders are democratically elected members of local government and have a formal mandate to represent their community's interests and views. Community leaders are also those who consciously stand outside of elected democratic structures and specifically represent their community to elected leaders or even act in opposition to elected community leaders.

The ambiguity of the term community leader is a point of debate nationally but has recently had particular local resonance in Newcastle, where the debate has been public and focused around issues of decision-making and accountability.

For us community leaders are those who exercise leadership outside of public and private sector organisations. They may be elected political leaders; employees of a VCS organisation; volunteers; tenant or community-based representatives or they may be individuals living and working on the margins of mainstream social frameworks and taking up a leadership role in whatever community they find themselves within.

We use the shorthand 'voluntary and community sector' (VCS) here to cover the spectrum of community leaders, recognising that it is a catch-all phrase and that the complexity of understanding, articulating and supporting community leader identity is an important issue to be explored in advancing an integrated leadership agenda across all sectors.

The Policy Context

Until recently the imbalance of investment in VCS training has received little policy attention, but the partnership emphasis of recent change agendas for health and social care, and the wider social regeneration objectives of the current government, have brought this imbalance more sharply into focus. There are now numerous initiatives and government departments designed to redress the deficit such as the Neighbourhood Renewal Unit, the Home Office, initiatives such as ChangeUp[1] and Futurebuilders,[2] establishing of Social Enterprise units at DTI and DoH and, since November 2006, the setting up of 'The Office of the Third Sector' in the Cabinet Office. These amongst others have produced a commitment of resources and policy drives to support the VCS to become a viable third sector partner in the delivery of mainstream services, and to encourage statutory partners to work differently in their approach to commissioning from the multiplicity of potential VCS providers.

What Leadership Development do Community Leaders Need?

To find out we undertook a short inquiry comprising:

- Two diagnostic café events, held in Sheffield and Newcastle, attracting over 70 people to explore the questions of community leadership. These events were co-hosted by the Centre for Innovation in Health Management at the University of Leeds, and local groups or organisations who reflect some of the diversity of community leadership

---

1   ChangeUp http://www.changeup.org.uk/hubs/workforce.asp.

2   Learning and Skills Council (2007) *Future Skills, Yorkshire and Humber Voluntary Sector. Workforce Development Action Plan 2007–2009*. Coventry: Learning and Skills Council.

systems. A number of people working within the public and private sectors were also invited to the events in order to ensure that ideas and experience from the whole system of community leadership were reflected in the discussions.

- A broad range of telephone and face-to-face conversations with community leaders and their partners, allowing some of the subtleties and painful personal difficulties of community leadership to be included.
- Desk-based research into national policy frameworks and existing local/regional research on community leadership.

There is clearly a broad range of national and regional policies, research, reviews and findings on the question of third sector and community leadership. The aim of this brief inquiry was not to scope the range in itself but to identify key findings for developing leadership support to third sector leaders.

The inquiry process set out to consider the following:

- What is the experience of community leaders in accessing personal and leadership development training?
- What are the themes and issues of community leaders?
- What are the development needs of community leaders?
- What ideas do community leaders have for meeting their personal and leadership development needs?
- What can the process of engaging with community leaders for this task teach us as a public sector consortium about engaging with the voluntary and community sector?

Assumptions Underpinning the Inquiry

There seem to be two sorts of questions about community leaders:

1. Is there a deficit of capacity within the VCS; have community leaders not had the same kind of access to personal and leadership development support as people from other sectors? Or,
2. Is 'capacity building' an interpretation influenced by the power dynamic which crackles between players within the whole system of communities in our society? In other words, are community leaders lacking in their capacity to exercise leadership, or is their capacity assumed to be 'lacking' because their leadership practices don't necessarily match up to the dominant practices of Western-oriented public and private sector leadership?

The view that emerged from our inquiry was that both are true: there is a deficit of experience in the VCS in terms of quality and access to leadership training, but there is also an underlying power dynamic at play.

COMMUNITY LEADERS EXPERIENCE OF TRAINING – AN OVERVIEW

We found that whilst there is clearly a plethora of training opportunities for VCS leaders, there are many questions about the quality of training and relevance to the specific and yet very diverse needs of the sector.

The experience of many participants suggested that lack of awareness or responsiveness by training providers to these specific and diverse needs were key factors in poor take-up of training or became issues for people during the training, itself leading to drop out or dissatisfaction.

Practical issues such as cost, organisational capacity – for example, to release one person onto training programmes – had an impact on the take up of training for some groups, whilst the need for senior-level strategic leadership interventions was a critical issue for others who were operating at a more strategic level within local partnerships.

Some training initiatives are specifically named as 'Leadership' training, but much of this has an undertone of capacity-building and enabling VCS leaders to take up a more effective role in statutory-led decision making or commissioning systems, rather than looking at what is distinctive about VCS leadership experience or exploring genuine (as opposed to tokenistic) co-creation of partnership agendas.

The association of leadership training to capacity building was frequently alluded to and points to significant underpinning assumptions about notions of leadership amongst VCS leaders and their partners, in training provider agencies or statutory sectors.

The Experience of Community Leaders in Accessing Personal and Leadership Development Training in Detail

Many of the community leaders involved in this process knew of, or had taken part in, personal development and other training programmes set up for the VCS. These were often provided by voluntary sector networks such as NCVO; Neighbourhood Renewal Partnerships such as local area partnership (LAP) training events or the neighbourhood renewal unit (NRU)'s national training organisation Renewal Academy; regional training providers such as the Academy for Community Leadership (ACL) who have secured public sector funding such as single regeneration budget (SRB) or regional development funds to offer a range of training programmes; or local authority/PCT training programmes.

It was felt that there was a plethora of VCS training and frequent inducements for community leaders to attend these courses. One person commented that she could easily spend her days 'going on training to have my capacity built'. However, whilst there is clearly quantity of training for community leaders (an outcome of recent policy objectives such as the Home Office Third Sector strategy and capacity building initiatives such as the ChangeUp and Futurebuilders programmes) there are nevertheless some questions about the *quality* and *type* of training available and a wide range of reasons why people don't access or benefit from current provision.

These reasons include the following:

1) TRAINING WAS NOT APPROPRIATE OR RESPONSIVE ENOUGH TO PARTICIPANTS' PERSONAL NEEDS AS LEADERS FROM DEPRIVED OR MARGINALISED COMMUNITIES

The VCS is made up of a diverse range of organisations and individuals, with large professional organisations at one end of the spectrum, and individual activists and community advocates on the other. Whilst many of the people employed by VCS organisations will have the same level of personal needs as the average citizen, a distinguishing feature of the VCS leadership spectrum is that service providers and service users are often the same people and, unlike the public sector where clear lines are drawn between service users and service providers, this factor needs to be acknowledged and addressed in training for community leaders.

Community leaders are often people who find themselves in a leadership role because they are trying to resolve difficulties related to their own lives, or to that of their families and communities. It is the struggle to resolve these difficulties that has pushed them into the leadership frame, and not necessarily their own leadership ambitions. The personal context of community leaders, particularly those from deprived or marginalised communities, is therefore a significant factor in whether and how they can access training programmes.

Factors which can affect the ability of leaders from deprived or marginalised communities to access training include: cost, childcare or other care responsibilities, the debilitating impact of day-to-day survival in deprived communities, self-confidence and mental health, and not least the 24/7 nature of being a leader in their own community. The 24/7 life of community leaders keeps home and work in the same physical and emotional space, and can create conflicts which often lead to isolation within their own community. The psychological shift from being community member to community leader can be a demanding one, especially on the bad days when community leaders need support for their own difficulties.

Many people talked about how difficult it was to go on training programmes because the structure of the programme didn't take these practical factors into account, nor was there sensitive enough understanding of the complexities of life for many community leaders. The need for a highly supportive, flexible learning environment was stressed, along with an understanding of the personal cost and struggle which many vulnerable people experience when they take up a leadership role.

Zenab is an Ethiopian community leader whose experience of taking up leadership in her community is described below and who expressed her anxiety about participating in training programmes where the complexity of her situation wasn't understood. On a previous leadership training programme Zenab had so many unprocessed questions about her role as a community leader that she left the programme, and despite the significant leadership role she plays in her community, she continues to be anxious about it and to underplay the critical impact she has.

The trauma of torture and death in response to challenging government are real for Zenab and the personal and psychological risks which she incurs when she takes up the challenge of critical social leadership are immense. Her children are growing up in a culture with different values and expectations and at the same time have a sense of being denied the same opportunities as their friends who are not refugees. Her children's expression of challenge to her family and cultural norms are also confusing for Zenab.

Zenab's story

Zenab is an Ethiopian community leader. In Ethiopia, Zenab grew up in a cultural system which was very different from the cultural context of the UK. She was expected to conform to the rule of the regime and also to conform to internal community systems which, although patriarchal, also took care of the needs and rights of all community members. Opposition to the regime or the community patriarchy was not allowed.

In Zenab's situation she and her family challenged the prevailing rule of government and expressed opposition to government actions. They were imprisoned, tortured and eventually found asylum in the UK. Zenab's struggle is how to translate her experience of conformity and challenge into a Western culture with its expectation of democratic challenge and rule of law, notions of personal responsibility and rights and the different social norms which underpin interpersonal relationships.

Add to this the wider social and policy context of being an asylum seeker in the UK today and working out how to act as a leader becomes a minefield. Zenab's experience is that she is grateful for the asylum she has received in UK and yet is also aware of UK society's expectation of her unquestioning gratitude. Refugees often feel they have to follow the rules in the UK, but what should they do when those rules are discriminating and continue to oppress her family and community?

A key leadership question for Zenab is how should she be, how should she behave, what kind of risks can she afford to take, how can she manage herself and the anxiety created by the fundamental changes happening in her life, and how can she balance the personal and social demands of taking up her leadership role in this context?

Zenab's situation is not an isolated one, and in many respects her story mirrors that of many refugees and asylum seekers in the UK today. The question as to Zenab's response to the question 'Would you be interested in a leadership development programme?' was 'How would you cope with my needs as a community leader?' The question for the Northern Leadership Academy (NLA) is how best to work with community leaders such as Zenab to release the huge potential of her leadership insight and experience, and to better facilitate her contribution to the creation of meaningful change in our society.

2) PROGRAMMES DIDN'T OFFER APPROPRIATE INTERVENTIONS TO MEET THE LEARNING NEEDS OF COMMUNITY LEADERS

Much of the training available to community leaders was felt to be very content focused, e.g. information input about new policies or strategies such as the Every Child Matters agenda, rather than focused on experiential learning or strategic skills development which would support capacity to engage with these agendas, for example, knowledge-gathering, sense-making, communication skills, political intelligence, influencing and negotiating skills and strategic thinking.

There was a strong view that training programmes were mostly targeted at technical skills (often low level) such as budgeting skills, chairing meetings, or at project management skills (at senior level) such as establishing performance management systems, or successful finance and fundraising skills, which arguably reflect public sector system needs more than the organic needs of VCS groups.

It also emerged that many people choose to attend the practical, technical skills-based programmes because they are usually cheaper than experiential or leadership development programmes.

One group who participated in the café events were incensed by the experience of one person who had taken part in a two-day event on community participation, which had been run as theoretical training programme on models of community participation. Whilst there was acknowledgement that input on theoretical models and new thinking was useful, the debate centred on whether experiential learning was a more appropriate way to explore issues such as community engagement, and there was a feeling that too many training programmes on these kinds of issues were overly theoretical and not adequately complemented by a reflective, experiential process.

During the individual and group interviews the researcher modelled some reflective double-loop working, and invited participants to comment on whether they had experienced this kind of process before, and whether it was something they would find useful if offered in leadership development programmes. The overwhelming response was positive. One person suggested that what was needed was a more reflective emotional intelligence-based process which would be a welcome addition to the training market for community leaders.

A key question which emerged from discussions about the learning needs of community leaders was whether there was anything distinctive about community leadership, and if so how did that impact on leadership development support. This also provoked vociferous debate, and a struggle to disentangle notions of leadership which were common to all leaders, and notions of leadership which were unique to community leaders. Some of the distinctive features were about styles of working, forms of accountability and legitimacy, the nature of the blurred relationship between service user and service provider and the informal, often entrepreneurial modus operandi of community leaders.

The need to explore community leadership as a process which has much in common with, and could borrow from, wider notions of leadership was acknowledged. At the same time, an exploration and articulation of the distinctive manifestations of leadership in a community context was also felt to be an important theme for future programmes.

A critical issue which also emerged from this discussion was the 'professionalisation' agenda, which is often made explicit by training providers and without apology, underpins many community leader training programmes. This was felt to be a highly inappropriate response to the learning needs of community leaders, and symptomatic of a more subtle power agenda at play.

3) THE PROFESSIONALISATION AGENDA OF MANY TRAINING PROGRAMMES

Some training initiatives are specifically named as 'leadership development', but much of this has an undertone of capacity-building and enabling VCS leaders to take up a more effective role in statutory-led decision making, or commissioning systems, rather than looking at what is distinctive about VCS leadership experience or exploring genuine (as opposed to tokenistic) co-creation of partnership agendas.

The association of leadership training with capacity building was frequently alluded to in the scoping process, and points to significant underpinning assumptions about notions of leadership amongst VCS leaders and their partners in training provider agencies or statutory sectors.

It was felt that technical skills-based programmes are often advocated by statutory partners in the guise of offering capacity-building support to VCS activity indeed the focus of most NRU and Home Office community leadership training is on skills-based capacity building, rather than personal development. The seminal Egan review[3] on developing skills for sustainable communities prepared for the Office of the Deputy Prime Minister (ODPM) in 2004 is one such example. The recent Department of Health 'health trainer' initiatives are another example. In this case the impetus to identify local people who can support improving health agendas in their own communities is a positive one, but instead of working with the distinctiveness of local knowledge, and finding ways of using it collaboratively with health professiona, local people are trained as health workers who can work professionally and understand better the parameters of professional working. This makes it easier for health professionals to work with local people, but does it really capitalise on the distinctive resource of local people to shape interventions in their community using the subtleties of their local knowledge and connections? The evidence of previous pilots to access this local resource, for example, the Community Mothers Schemes, suggests that this kind of training actually diminishes the distinctive role of local people, and simply assimilates local people into the professional class.

The question of intent here is important. Is the aim of capacity-building training about the assimilation of VCS groups into a statutory-led system, or is it about developing a more radical leadership agenda for change? This is an issue for further exploration on the prototype programmes, and should be borne in mind when designing the content of programmes and designing the facilitation emphasis, for example, ensuring that the focus is less on problem solving and more creating meaning.

4) POOR-QUALITY TRAINING

There was a view that many VCS training programmes were low cost, and therefore accessible to people from organisations and communities with limited budgets, but a key frustration was that low cost often meant low quality. The consequence was that this person rarely signed up for VCS training programmes. There was a view that the output demands and target-driven nature of many local authority and Neighbourhood Renewal-based training, has led to a scattergun approach, which targets as many people as possible with a small amount of training and has subsequently sacrificed quality for quantity.

---

3   Office of the Deputy Prime Minister (2004) *Egan Review: Skills for Sustainable Communities*. London: Office of the Deputy Prime Minister.

Comments about quality made reference to poor training environments, mediocre trainers who often had limited understanding or sophistication in terms of the VCS context, and training methods which were often unimaginative and based on traditional 'chalk and talk' approaches. One person commented on the stereotypical 'second cousin' image of the voluntary sector, which was expected to deliver at the soft end of services rather than deliver core mainstream services, and made the corresponding connection to the second cousin nature of VCS training.

In contrast to the opportunities for high-quality training and support available to leaders from the public sector, training for community leaders often seems less ambitious in terms of the quality and scope of what is offered.

Public and private sector leadership development has a long tradition and a strong base of experienced training organisations, with a range of qualitative frameworks to deliver interventions. There is a much less mature framework for delivering personal and leadership development within the VCS.

A critical additional factor for community leaders from deprived or marginalised communities is that many are also struggling to manage difficult personal and social needs. This needs to be worked with sensitively and flexibly by facilitators who have experience of working in this field, and can use their contextual knowledge to underpin the learning process.

There is a need to develop VCS training provider capacity in northern regions, an issue which the Greater Merseyside ChangeUp Consortium acknowledged in its report *Heartfelt: Aspects of Leadership*.[4]

The consortium consciously set out to test the National ChangeUp observation that 'training providers do not always understand the culture and context of the voluntary and community sector or the skills that people working and volunteering for frontline organisations need'.[5]

The consortium found that their local experience chimed with this national view, and recommended that:

> Commissioners/funders satisfy themselves that providers who propose to develop and deliver activity to benefit leadership in the Third Sector either have the capacity to do so using the recent expertise of third sector practitioners, or that the 'experts' to be used possess the necessary skills to translate practice and principles from the private and or public sectors to a third sector context.

There is clearly a gap for training leadership development facilitators who can work in the VCS community. These might be trainers from other sectors who need to learn more about the context of VCS, or they may be experienced VCS practitioners who are moving into a leadership development and training role, but who need further opportunities to develop facilitation and consulting skills.

---

4   ChangeUp Merseyside (2006) *Heartfelt: Aspects of Leadership*, p. 30. Liverpool: Sefton Council for Voluntary Service.

5   The Home Office (2004) *ChangeUp: Capacity Building and Infrastructure Framework for the Voluntary and Community Sector*, p. 27. London: The Home Office.

5) THE NEED FOR PRACTICAL TRAINING WHICH IS RELATED TO WORK CONTEXT

The articulation of practical training needs is a recurring theme in reviews of the development needs of community leaders, for example, the Egan Report, and was certainly a theme emerging from this scoping exercise. This is partly because there is a need to address the practical skills deficit across the sector, for exampoe, the Leitch review which was commissioned to identify the optimal skills mix needed by 2020 in order to maximise economic growth, productivity and social justice in the UK has produced an interim report which declares that 'the government targets for skills improvements by 2020 will not be met by existing measures'.[6]

There is clearly an important wider strategic agenda for developing practical skills at cross-training initiatives in the VCS. However, the emphasis on practical training may also be in part an expression of the working context and personal commitment of community leaders who frequently see themselves as activists; as 'doers' – doing this work to make real and practical changes to people's lives.

This may be a consequence of many years of community leaders trying to differentiate themselves from public and private sector leaders who are often stereotyped as pen pushers or bureaucrats, and who are often negatively perceived as trying to prevent community leaders from delivering the changes they want, because they don't fit neatly into statutory frameworks.

Additionally, community leaders are often (though not always) people who find themselves in a leadership role because their desire for practical change has pushed them into the leadership frame, and not necessarily because they have leadership ambitions or employment/training needs. Many of the community leaders involved in this enquiry process were hesitant about acknowledging their leadership role, or were adamant that they were not leaders but practitioners who made things happen.

The notion of practitioner leadership is therefore a key issue to be explored within any leadership intervention for community leaders. An analysis of training needs often becomes a red herring for training providers, because the urgent practical imperative for 'doing' things often masks the more fundamental need for reflecting on 'how' one does things, and the importance of developing reflective learning skills in order to intervene more effectively in practical work.

The need for practical work-based learning is, however, a clear issue for community leaders and the challenge will be to ensure that any interventions meet this need within a critical reflection and review frame, rather than simply be seduced by consumer demand for practical skills-based learning.

6) PRACTICAL OBSTACLES

There were a number of practical issues which affected the take up of training for VCS leader. These include:

Cost: For some individuals, particularly those operating outside of organisations or on benefits, meeting the cost of programme fees and additional costs such as travel, materials,

---

6   Learning and Skills Council (2007) *Future Skills, Yorkshire and Humber Voluntary Sector. Workforce Development Action Plan 2007–2009*. Coventry: Learning and Skills Council.

childcare, and so on. was a barrier to participation. Cost was also a factor for many VCS organisations, even large ones, as budget choices tend to be tight and stark, for example, the choice between having a training budget or a project delivery budget. Some organisations clearly have training budgets, particularly those who operate across sectors and at a strategic level, for example, registered social landlords (RSLs), large care providers and whilst some are committed to funding personal development opportunities many more are focused on skills-based development and budgets are often eschewed towards these programmes.

Time: many smaller VCS organisations find releasing staff for long periods of time difficult because the size of the organisation means there is limited capacity or budgets to provide cover. This experience is borne out by the findings of a Yorkshire and Humber study who cite 'Organisational capacity (backfill) issues are a major barrier to training uptake by managers.'[7]

The experience of individuals was similar in that people who offered their time to community activity voluntarily often had to take time off work to fulfil their voluntary role and taking further time off for training was an additional pressure. One person who led a summer camp for young people every year spoke of how she had to use two weeks of her annual leave to do this. She drew a parallel with TA volunteers who are given additional leave by employers to train to serve their country, and wondered about extending this kind of government incentive to encourage community leaders to train to serve their communities.

Training didn't take account of the strategic integrated context in which community leaders are required to work. Many of the senior community leaders pointed to the fact that as leaders they were required to work not just with their local communities, but also with strategic partners, in other sectors and organisations. Their role was often a brokering one, but they were also required to contribute to both local strategic agendas and to nationally driven changes to the third sector role in service delivery.

Few people had participated in, or knew of, leadership programmes which were targeted at the senior and strategic end of the community leadership role. In '*Future Skills*' report this was identified as a key issue:

> There is a prevailing problem of access to generic level 4 and 5 leadership and management training for paid managers e.g. Chief Officers, especially strategic and business planning. The barriers are predominantly time, cost and distance as opposed to a lack of appropriate learning provision. However, there is an issue that some provision, which would otherwise be relevant, can lack a voluntary sector focus, or does not take sufficient account of the operating environment for voluntary organisations. A recurrent complaint was lack of support for the senior manager from trustees. A 'lonely at the top' culture seems to be prevalent in the sector, with a significant number of CEOs having no appraisal or supervision from their board.[8]

It was also felt that there were few opportunities for leaders across the sectors to think together about the leadership implications of, for example, current commissioning policy and partnership agendas, beyond making it up as they went through the process.

---

7   Learning and Skills Council (2007) *Future Skills, Yorkshire and Humber Voluntary Sector. Workforce Development Action Plan 2007–2009*. Coventry: Learning and Skills Council.

8   Learning and Skills Council (2007) *Future Skills, Yorkshire and Humber Voluntary Sector. Workforce Development Action Plan 2007–2009*. Coventry: Learning and Skills Council.

This was recognised as being a Herculean task, given the embedded lines of power and role which have been traditionally drawn between the sectors, the backdrop of repeated radical change and reorganisation in statutory sectors (particularly in the NHS), and the struggle of all parties to realise the government's vision for change in service delivery at a local level.

The need for reflective learning opportunities and development of advanced communication skills for leaders across the sectors is also borne out by the findings of countless government reviews into partnership working and third sector commissioning strategies.

One of the key findings of these reviews is that while there is a need to build the capacity of the third sector in order to fulfil its role as a mainstream provider of services, there is also a need to support the capacity of statutory partners and commissioners to work more creatively with the multiplicity of providers which this will produce.

The conclusion of the Report of the Third Sector Commissioning Task force is that 'a partnership approach, based on mutual trust and understanding between organisations concerned with commissioning and delivering services that people want and value will be achieved by improved communication and changed behaviour'.[9]

However, the opportunities for developing advanced communication skills and supporting behaviour change across the sectors are rare. Most of the leadership training in the region is sector specific, and whilst it is clearly important to support the specific needs of people working in different sectors, there is also a pressing need to bring different parts of the system together to explore the leadership implications and required skills of this integrated agenda.

The Office of the Third Sector report has declared that government's role is not to set up social enterprises but to 'create the conditions that enable social enterprises to thrive'.[10] For example, the Office of the Third Sector is currently working with the North East Regional Centre of Excellence to tackle barriers which prevent social enterprises from delivering public services. A pilot has been proposed to develop template social clauses in commissioning contracts and to use the development of these templates as a vehicle for learning about new practice in commissioning strategies.

This kind of critical policy initiative would be an important one to locate in a reflective cross-sector leadership programme, which brought together commissioners and leaders from the multiplicity of social enterprises and organisations that will be required to engage with this new funding regime. Exploring and testing the practical aspects and issues of developing a social clause is important, but it is also important to explore what the underlying emotional, organisational and political aspects inherent to this agenda are (e.g. hidden assumptions about the different sectors and working cultures, managing self in radical change and transition periods, understanding the impact of one's own behaviour on the outcomes of change, surfacing the power dynamics implicit in new – and old – commissioning structures.)

The role of charitable funders was also referred to in this context. Most VCS organisations rely on funds from charitable trusts, and/or grants administered through statutory funding bodies. Very few achieve sustainability through service level agreements

9   Third Sector Commissioning Task Force (2006) *No Excuses. Embrace Partnership Now. Step Towards Change*. London: Department of Health.

10   Office of the Third Sector (Cabinet Office) (2006) *Social Enterprise Action Plan: Scaling New Heights*, p. 3.

(SLAs) or commissioning contracts, and managing the diversity of grant funding requirements is a significant part of VCS activity. The power dynamics of supplicant and donor are a major factor in this interplay between funders and VCS groups, often leading to inappropriate use of resources and frustration on all sides.

For example, many community leaders feel they have to dance to the tune of funders even when they know that they are being asked to deliver impossible outputs or services, inappropriate to local need, yet the weight of authority and priority setting is rarely held in the hands of community leaders. Bringing the funders into an objective reflective learning process would support better communication and understanding of the different agendas, and support all parties to exercise their leadership roles in these situations more effectively.

Another issue which has strategic implications for leaders across the social policy agenda is social cohesion, including integration and the role of leaders from new communities and black and minority ethnic (BME) communities in the UK.

Many of the refugee participants in the Sheffield café event were regarded as pivotal players both in their previous home country and within their current UK communities, but very few felt that they were able to contribute to the strategic thinking or service planning processes within their communities. This is an issue for individual community leaders as much as it is an issue for the VCS organisations who often broker the interface between refugee groups and the statutory sector. There was a strong feeling that developing the capacity to engage more effectively with strategic agendas was fundamental to a refugee community's integration into UK society, and that current working practice often marginalised refugee groups from planning and decision making. There was additional disillusionment about even the much proclaimed consultation process for refugee communities, which was seen as tokenistic, often meaningless, divisive and held firmly in the hands of governments and statutory agencies.

There was a very strong sense of the leadership expertise within refugee communities being a wasted resource, not just in relation to work with refugee communities, but also in relation to refugee contributions to mainstream agendas. A key question arising from the scoping exercise was how the leadership experience and expertise of refugee and asylum seekers might be used more effectively across UK social policy agendas.

7) THE VALUE OF THE NETWORKING ROLE OF TRAINING PROGRAMMES

Training programmes, whilst useful in themselves, also served a critical role in supporting the development of a coherent, networked VCS by bringing people together from across the sectors to explore common issues.

Whilst this was often seen as an unintended consequence of community leader training programmes, it is nevertheless a key aspect in the development of the sector, and could usefully be planned into the objectives of any NLA training interventions.

Several people referred to the fragmentation of the voluntary sector in this context, for example, between refugee communities, between refugee and BME communities, between BME communities and wider VCS groups. The need for supporting 'sector' development, as much as supporting individual groups within the sector, was therefore emphasised as a critical task if VCS groups were to take appropriate advantage of the opportunities for a distinctive third sector role in mainstream services. The role of a coherent and inclusive regional third sector which could connect to national sector agendas whilst balancing the focus of local agendas was seen as a real need and one which any new training programme should consciously address.

What Community Leaders Want

The inquiry revealed a great hunger and enthusiasm for supporting VCS leaders, both within the sector, and also amongst other sectors who want to work in partnership with the VCS. This local energy, together with the commitment and policy drive of government, are evidence of a strong market opportunity for the development of a range of innovative and effective leadership interventions for VCS leaders.

Summary of findings

- Training was not appropriate or responsive enough to participants' *personal needs* as leaders from deprived or marginalised communities.
- Programmes didn't offer appropriate interventions to meet the learning needs of community leaders.
- Professionalisation agenda of many training programmes.
- Training was often low cost and low quality.
- There is a need for practical training which is related to the work context.
- Practical issues were often obstacles for individuals and organisations.
- Training didn't take account of the strategic, integrated context in which community leaders are required to work.
- Training programmes had the additional value of peer networking for sector development.

Themes and Issues for Community Leaders

- *Notions of leadership*: is there anything distinctive about community leadership, how can this be articulated and consciously developed? What can be borrowed or adapted from other forms of leadership and contemporary thinking about leadership to enhance VCS leadership?
- *Sector development*: what are the issues which underpin development of the sector and what organisational and sector-based infrastructure building needs to take place?
- *VCS role in mainstream policy development and service delivery*: how can the third sector develop a viable role within current policy and delivery opportunities without losing the distinctiveness of its third sector identity? In particular how can the specific experience of leaders from deprived or marginalised communities, including refugee and asylum seeker communities, be better understood, developed and accessed to the benefit of mainstream agendas?
- *Policy planning and decision-making*: how can VCS groups engage in policy planning and decision making, for example, about the needs of deprived and marginalised communities, in a way which goes beyond consultation or participation in the current structures and facilitates a more systemic appraisal of the decision making process?

- *Leading partnerships together*: how can VCS leaders come together with leaders from other sectors to explore the implications of integrated 'partnership leadership'? A distributed model of leadership has particular appeal in this context but what would it look like in a diverse cross-sector context which is mutually owned by all the stakeholders? Exploring these issues via practical initiatives such as new commissioning strategies for social enterprises would be a creative and topical way of doing this.
- *Power*: what are the power dynamics underpinning the relationship between VCS leaders and leaders from other sectors? Is there a hidden professionalisation agenda? Similarly, what are the power dynamics within the diversity of the VCS itself, for example, between asylum seeker and BME communities, between community activists and voluntary sector organisations?
- *Personal needs and context of community leaders*: how can the significant personal needs of many community leaders are addressed in leadership programmes?
- *Practical work-based learning*: how can leadership development programmes balance the need for technical and practical workplace support, with a reflective whole systems approach to learning and personal development?
- *Young people*: how can the energy and ideas of young people be more effectively combined with the experience and maturity of adults? How can we support leadership development in our young leaders, both to learn more about notions of leadership, and to support them in their preparation for adult leadership roles?

Conclusion

The leadership development experience of community leaders suggests that the following issues need to be taken into account in the provision of any leadership and management development programmes for the VCS:

- Support for personal circumstances and the complexities of being a leader in deprived or socially excluded communities. This might mean the provision of programmes specifically geared to the needs of leaders from within these communities, and/or it might mean consciously taking account of these needs in general programmes.
- Support for the specific and more strategic level of need experienced by leaders and managers of VCS organisations.
- Emphasis on high quality both in terms of environment and facilitation.
- Practical issues: training opportunities needs to be accessible for participants with limited personal or organisational resources, for example, in terms of cost and time.
- More opportunities for experiential, personal development training and less focus on theoretical, content-based and technical training.
- An emphasis on confidence building, sustaining self and managing relationships is needed across the sector, that is, for both local leaders/activists and for leaders of community organisations and more senior leaders.
- Practically based: focusing on real (not theoretical) work and community issues, and which are as much about creating meaning as problem solving.
- Training programmes must be cognisant of and appropriate to the wider power dynamics within communities, and between different sectors and government.

The question of professionalisation of community leaders and the wider systemic implications of the mainstreaming agenda are key themes here.

- Networking objectives: programmes need to contribute to strengthening the sector objectives as well as strengthening individuals. Opportunities for peer learning and information exchange were important in this respect.
- There is a need for trainers and facilitators who have experience and expertise in working with the voluntary sector, and also the subtleties and complexities of leaders from marginalised or deprived communities. There is potential for developing new career paths and employment opportunities for VCS leaders within the leadership development sector.
- Incorporating key strategic themes and issues into the programme, for example, commissioning agenda, social enterprise developments, and using these as opportunities for exploring the practical and personal implications as much as an opportunity for information input. This could be facilitated by inviting contributions from people in other sectors into the programme, and/or by offering a programme which consciously sets out to bring together a mixed group of leaders to explore the implications of leading these initiatives together.

26 *Leadership and Management Development for the Environment*

ALAN MURRAY

Introduction

A few years ago this topic would have been an unlikely inclusion in a handbook on leadership and development. Leadership and development were seen to be so closely aligned to growth and expansion that issues of environmental care were considered to be a distraction. No more! In February 2007 the Intergovernmental Panel on Climate Change pronounced for the first time that the connection between global warming and industrial activity was 'unequivocal'. A cursory glance at their website (http://www.ipcc.ch) and their fourth report should be sufficient to persuade the most sceptical that things are not going well for the environment and that things will have to change. The report was seen to be so influential that the US finally accepted the findings and despite the intense lobbying of the petroleum industry, President Bush endorsed this 'inconvenient truth'. In the UK, the government formed the Committee on Climate Change (http://www.theccc.org.uk) and their first report was more challenging than anyone anticipated – calling for a reduction in CO_2 emissions of 80 per cent by 2050.

This creates a huge challenge for business and industry throughout the world, and calls for levels of leadership rarely seen outside the field of combat, because hugely difficult choices will have to be confronted and decided upon; choices which may lead to economic disruption in certain sectors and general uncertainty in financial markets, and if anyone was unsure of the consequences of such uncertainty before 2008, they will be acutely sensitive to its significance now. Governments, including the UK government which both sponsored and accepted the recommendations of the report, are dithering about how to make policy on these matters; at the same time as endorsing this report, another UK government department was relaxing airport traffic restrictions at a number of UK Airports.

This means that business needs to take the lead in forging policies to meet these challenges, because business is the only institution that can adapt quickly enough, with enough innovation and investment to make the necessary changes required. Leadership in this phase will bring great reward for those successful innovators, and markets will recognise their leadership with increased value. A new era of responsible business is heralded to restore confidence in the corporate world and demonstrate that enlightened self-interest encompasses issues of social and environmental sustainability. If that is not reason enough to embrace the challenge, there are sound business reasons for becoming engaged in this area.

In this chapter I will review the core theories and ideas that inform notions of sustainable development, and how sustainable development is subtly different from what often passes for corporate (social) responsibility. I will illustrate these differences with examples showing how leading corporations have responded to the challenges presented. I will look at some of the best practice examples, and plot a way for potential leaders to map this tortuous terrain.

Background to Sustainable Development

It is now over 21 years since the Brundtland Commission deliberated on, amongst other things, 'environmental strategies for achieving sustainable development by the year 2000 and beyond'.[1] Having sat for almost three years the Commission finally agreed on a definition of sustainable development which has set a challenge to industry that, to this day, few companies have confronted let alone embraced.

The Commission concluded by remarking:

> *Humanity has the ability to make development sustainable – to ensure that it meets the needs of the present generation without compromising the ability of future generations to meet their own needs. The concept of sustainable development does imply limits – not absolute limits, but limitations imposed by the present state of technology and social organization on environmental resources and by the ability of the biosphere to absorb the effect of human activities.[2]*

This definition of sustainable development – 'meet[ing] the needs of the present generation without compromising the ability of future generations to meet their own needs' – carries with it a number of implications and equally, a number of challenges to the business world. The implications of the phrase meeting the needs of the present generation suggest fair distributions across the present population of the world in terms of quality of life, measured, perhaps, by comparative standards of living or benefits from sharing the resources of the planet. They also suggest that what resources are utilised are done so in as efficient a manner as possible. The same notions pertain when applied to the needs of successive generations.

The Commission had warned:

> *Sustainable development is not a fixed state of harmony, but rather a process of change in which the exploitation of resources, the direction of investment, the orientation of technological development, and institutional change are made consistent with future as well as present needs … painful choices have to be made. Thus in the final analysis, sustainable development must rest on political will.*

---

1   WCED (1987) *Our Common Future*. Oxford: Oxford University Press.

2   Ibid., p. 8.

The contributors to the report may well reflect with some disappointment on the lack of progress made since its publication. Rather than witnessing the political will required, perhaps the real irony is that as the report was being compiled the inexorable move towards a free-market global economy was beginning to take hold in the developed world. Moreover, multinational companies were moving in to developing economies to take advantage of the low cost bases offered. Their efforts were supported by Western governments who, for the next two decades, would enjoy an almost unprecedented period of continual economic growth combined with low inflation.

It is also likely that they would be even more alarmed had they been able to foresee the escalation of the threat to the environment posed by the effect of continued industrial growth on global warming. Of course, in 1987 such connections were considered my many as mere conjecture. The Intergovernmental Panel on Climate Change (IPCC) was established in 1988, and although its first report was used to inform the first Green Summit in Rio de Janeiro in 1992, it was not until much later that the connection was established beyond doubt. Even the findings of the second report, key input for the negotiations of the Kyoto Protocol, failed to persuade many leaders, especially those in the USA, of the scientific reality of climate change. It was only after publication of the third report in 2001 that the sceptics were confronted by such weight of evidence that their resistance began to buckle. In the USA, however, President Bush under the relentless lobbying of the petroleum industry refused to concede. It was not until the fourth report was published in 2007 and the 'unequivocal' connection was made, that all but the most intransigent gave way, including the US administration.

The challenge to business is to organise itself in a way that makes itself sustainable in the way envisioned by Brundtland. Consider preparing a presentation for your board where the two main proposals relate to (a) reducing growth forecasts, and (b) redistributing profits, and you begin to see the magnitude of this challenge! This might appear flippant, but these are the issues that call for true leadership, and some of the examples of those who have shown such commitment are highlighted below.

However, before looking at these case studies, I want to spend a moment looking at how the quest for sustainable development differs from what can happily pass as corporate responsibility (or corporate social responsibility, corporate citizenship, or whatever).

Corporate Responsibility

In contrast to sustainable development, the origins of corporate responsibility can be traced back as far as the corporate form, certainly to the time of the Industrial Revolution, when factory owners, initially probably in their own self-interest, provided services for workers, and latterly as acts of philanthropy built legacies which still remain. In the UK, the villages of New Earswick, near York, developed by Rowntree, and Bourneville, near Birmingham, by Cadbury, stand as two of the most obvious examples of this approach. This was mirrored in the USA by the likes of Carnegie and John D. Rockefeller. Indeed, Rockefeller is still regarded by many as the pioneer of a form of 'targeted philanthropy', designed to have maximum effect on medicine, science or education.

Ideas about the responsibilities of corporations to undertake non-commercial activity have since waxed and waned as sociopolitical developments have shaped the landscape of business activity. As the power of corporations grew so society voiced concern and corporations adapted. The Wall Street Crash damaged the reputation of corporations, and Roosevelt's New Deal was, in part, designed to limit their powers. After the Second World War many European countries moved over to state control of key industries, and in the UK the welfare state was established, with the notion that government was best placed to decide the needs of the people it governed, and that the benefits of commercial activity should be distributed more widely than purely to the shareholders.

In the 1970s and 80s a number of political changes took place which saw the emergence of powerful non-governmental organisations (NGOs) in response to corporate environmental disasters, such as Love Canal, Bhopal, Chernobyl and the Exxon Valdiz. Western political thought was moving to the right, championed by Regan and Thatcher, and there seemed little that individuals could do to counter the free-market arguments which were taking hold throughout the developed world. Paradoxically, this re-statement of capitalism provided the backdrop to the resurgence in ideas of corporate responsibility.

Until 2000 the only sectors that seriously engaged with environmental disclosures were those in 'sensitive' industries, and the larger corporations (often one in the same). However, since the turn of the twenty-first century all corporations have become aware of the concept of corporate responsibility (CR) and have engaged to some extent or another with CR programmes. All FTSE 100 companies now have a CR department, and most produce some form of CR report.

However, even a peripheral glance at their programmes demonstrates the wide divergence in the understanding of what CR means to different companies. In many ways this is not surprising. There is no history of CR as a discipline as such. There is no professional body, no recognised conceptual framework or other body of knowledge which might act as some technical resource, and indeed, those who find themselves in the field have arrived there from other backgrounds, often with an uncertain remit and little guidance. I recall in a series of interviews undertaken in the late 1990s before CR departments had become commonplace, there was a practice of pursuing policies because others were doing the same, rather than fundamentally understanding the purpose behind the initiatives.

For many, honestly believing that they have signed up to a full CR remit, the programmes are designed purely for the company's benefit. There are many articles, reports and books which extol the business benefits of CR. The business case is almost beyond dispute for these authors. In their tracts you will find trite references to 'win–win' situations, and all the other comforting platitudes to remove any doubts about adopting whichever strategy is being advocated. That is not to dismiss out of hand all the CR initiatives that companies undertake, far from it! But considering the benefits requires a critical evaluation and an understanding not only of the issues, but the rationale behind the adoption of CR policies.

The Questions

HOW DO I GET STARTED?

Embedding corporate responsibility across the organisation may not happen overnight, and may be met by some scepticism across the organisation! This should not be surprising

– many hark to the mantra attributed to Milton Friedman[3] that 'it is the social responsibility of business to make profits'! However, Friedman was astute enough to accept that under certain circumstances it was acceptable for certain companies to follow a social agenda. Concepts such as the value of reputation were not so clearly understood in 1970, when the comment was made, and the spectre of shares in a major UK bank dropping by 99 per cent of their value, bears testament to need for trust to return.[4]

For many commentators, the stance of responsibility taken by the company equates to the measure of trust shown in the company by external parties. It is quite clear that during the autumn and winter of 2008 trust was completely lost in the banking sector as each government bail out was followed by disclosures of yet further undisclosed debts. As this chapter was being written so analysts were speculating on where the next scandal would arise and which bank would follow the fate of RBS.

It is also interesting to dwell on the fact that it was in the same period that banks and financial institutions were espousing CR as 'core values' that they must equally have been embarking on a whole raft of questionable activities. This gives rise to the first issue:

1. EXAMINE YOUR CORE BUSINESS ACTIVITIES AND DETERMINE WHO ARE MOST AFFECTED BY YOUR OPERATIONS

This aspect can, perhaps, be best illustrated by examining the CR approaches of two contrasting companies. If we stick with the RBS as our example we find that they have, 'as a top priority for 2008' a programme to 'cut financial crime', a second priority of 'customer service', and so on.[5] To this reader, these CR priorities sound very much like sensible business policies that have little to do with anything outside conventional business practice. Surely the business of banking is lending and investing? Should not also, therefore, policies of responsibility concentrate on these issues? Amid reports that as part of the discredited lending policies of RBS one loan of £2.5bn to a Russian émigré living in the US had to be written off,[6] RBS talk about staff volunteering and Community investment.

This can be contrasted with a wholly different approach taken by Fuji Xerox who open their 2008 Sustainability report with a statement of their vision of 'A Sustainable Society and Beyond', by taking a holistic view of the life-cycle of their products.[7] In seeking to understand their 'ecological footprint', that is, the effect their operations have on the planet's resources and biosphere, they do not just examine the life-cycle in relation to their own activities, but look at how their products are used after they have been sold and factor in 'energy in use' and disposal/recycling costs to gain an impression of the realistic impact over time of their products and their operations, and also to raise awareness through the supply chain and customer base of the issues surrounding sustainable development.

---

3   See Friedman, M. (1970) A Friedman doctrine: the social responsibility of business is to increase its profits, *The New York Times Magazine*, 13 September: 32–33, 122, 124, 126.

4   Shares in the Royal Bank of Scotland fell from 413.5p on 26 February 2008 to 10.5p on January 19 2009, a fall of 97.46 per cent.

5   http://www.rbs.com/corporate03.asp?id=CORPORATE_RESPONSIBILITY/2008_PRIORITIES.

6   http://www.independent.co.uk/news/business/news/the-oligarch-who-cost-royal-bank-of-scotland-1631bn-1451512.html.

7   http://www.fujixerox.co.jp/eng/sr/2008/.

2. STAKEHOLDER ENGAGEMENT

In an interesting review essay on social and environmental accounting Jan Bebbington,[8] looks at the *Oxford English Dictionary* definition of 'to engage', and finds that it involves 'urging, exhorting, persuading and inducing people to see a particular point of view and, in doing so, to win them over as adherents to that point of view'.

Indeed, the notion of winning over through argument betrays the manangerialist credentials of stakeholder engagement, a side which is rarely acknowledged, as the term is so often used to portray what is, in effect, the reverse position, i.e. that the company might be persuaded by the stakeholder's view. This might be viewed as something of an academic point, except for the fact that any form of dialogue with interested or aggrieved parties must surely take account of their concerns. In the terms of adopting a CR strategy, companies must be open to the challenges presented by stakeholders, and consider how best to deal with their unease.

The situation that arose for Drax Plc in 2006 amply demonstrates what can go wrong when the 'management' of certain stakeholder groups is mishandled. Early in 2006 Drax power station, the largest coal-fired power station in the UK, which produces 7 per cent of the UK's electricity needs and 23 million tonnes of CO_2,[9] switched from using a proportion of biomass back to coal as energy prices increased. The result on the one hand was an increase in profits, but on the other, it brought a week of protest, with coal trains stopped, a protest camp set up outside to stop deliveries, and the daily presence of police at the power station gates.[10] It drew attention to its own ongoing activities, made itself the focus for environmental action and incurred the wrath of environmental NGOs who continue to monitor its activity closely.[11]

The decision to meet with parties who have grievances or are concerned about aspects of a company's activities is not one to be taken lightly, and without thinking through the consequences fully. If the decision is taken to ignore a groundswell of public opinion and retreat behind police lines, then so be it. However, if a company is serious about its wider responsibilities, it must surely understand the sociopolitical climate and, in the case of a coal-fired power station, the prevailing scientific evidence on climate change. On their website, in a section on the environment, Drax simply remark:

As the largest, cleanest and most efficient of the UK's coal-fired power stations we take our environmental responsibilities very seriously. At Drax, environmental protection and, where possible, enhancement is at the heart of our decision-making process and underpins our overall approach.[12]

---

8   Bebbington, K. J. (1997) Engagement, education, and sustainability: a review essay on environmental accounting, *Accounting, Auditing and Accountability Journal,* 10(3): 365–381.

9   *The Guardian*, 9 March 2007.

10   *The Guardian*, 13 September 2006.

11   See, for example, http://www.corporatewatch.org.uk/?lid=2711.

12   http://www.draxpower.com/corporate_responsibility/environment/, January 2009).

3. WHOM DO YOU WANT TO INFLUENCE?

There should be a clear notion of who the intended audience should be, developing from the theme of 'understanding your stakeholders'. An examination of many CR reports and websites often begs the question 'who is this stuff for?' In common with the question in accounting, 'who are the *users* of accounts?', a clear notion of audience makes developing strategies of CR more focused and relevant. For example, research into the reaction of financial markets to social and environmental information suggests that market participants take little notice when making investment decisions.[13] This means that if you are aiming to influence market participants, reporting CR initiatives by traditional means is probably not the best way.

Indeed, understanding how markets are assimilating this sort of information is particularly complex. For many traders and fund managers, who see trading in financial markets as an essentially *amoral* activity, issues of sustainability and responsibility are viewed as issues of financial risk. Many will recall one of the issues that blighted Shell in 1990s when they made the decision to sink the redundant oil platform in the deep waters of the Atlantic, 250 miles off north-west Scotland. Following protests that spread across Europe, and a fall in the share price between April and August, the plan was abandoned. However, although Greenpeace admitted that its data was wrong, and despite the share price recovering, the damage to Shell's reputation had been done and Brent Spar is still mentioned in the context of financial risk, and as a metaphor for issues that can derail a company's progress.

On the other hand, what is the point in producing reports that might only be read by NGOs and others who may either on the periphery of the company's activities or disaffected in some way or other?

The potential audience will also depend on the nature of the business. A company with a strong retail sector, possibly with an online sales facility, like Boots or WH Smiths may expect its customers to check out CR policies while logged on for other purposes. Conversely, companies with little connection to such a wide customer base, perhaps like Amec or Bunzl, will deliver to a different constituency, and concentrate on a different approach, as can be seen on their websites.[14] BP for their part aim their report at 'our shareholders, employees, governments and joint venture partners, academics, non-governmental organizations and other parties or individuals with a working interest in BP'.[15]

4. WHAT ARE MY GOALS?

This relates to what you seek to achieve within a chosen timescale, and what your vision for the company might be. For example, do you envision your company in terms of long-term sustainability, or are your aims more modest and company centred?

---

13   See Gray, R. H. (2006) Social, environmental and sustainability reporting and organisational value creation? Whose value? Whose creation?, *Accounting, Auditing and Accountability Journal*, 19(6): 793–819 and Murray, A., Sinclair, D., Power, D. and Gray, R. H. (2006) Do financial markets care about social and environmental disclosure? Further evidence and exploration from the UK, *Accounting, Auditing and Accountability Journal*, 19(2): 228–255.

14   http://www.bunzl.com/bunzl/responsibility/; http://amec.com/about_us/sustainable_development.htm.

15   See BP (2008) *Sustainability Report*, p. 1. London: BP plc. Also available at http://www.bp.com/sustainability.

Achieving sustainability, in the Brundtland terms of environmental stewardship and social justice across generations, presents such major challenges that most companies have failed to get close to this goal. Indeed the goal of reducing consumption and distributing income beyond shareholder entitlement, for most is one step too far. Indeed to embark on such a course might have a challenge in law!

It also may explain why many companies redefine the term to something that is deliverable. For example, in their 2007 *Sustainability report*, BP define sustainability thus:

> *At BP we define sustainability as the capacity to endure as a group: by reviewing assets: creating and delivering better products and services that need the evolving needs of society: attracting successive generations of employees: contributing to a sustainable environment and retaining the trust and support of our customers, shareholders and the communities in which we operate.*[16]

Here, the notion of sustainability as 'meeting the needs of the current generation without compromising the ability future generations to meet their own needs' has been replaced with an idea that sustainability refers to the 'endurance of the group', and the 'needs of the current generation', to 'developing better products and services'. In essence a definition which presents acute challenges has been replaced with one which has deliverable aims, likely to enhance profit and please capital markets.

There is an alternative. Interface is one of the largest companies in the area of carpets and floor-coverings. The history of Interface goes back to 1973 when Ray Anderson led a joint venture between a group of American investors and Carpets International Plc, a UK-based manufacturer of carpet tiles. It began with only 15 employees, but within 5 years had a turnover of US$11m. It went public in 1983, changed its name in 1987 and through the acquisition of more than 50 companies it became one of the world's largest producers of carpets and carpet tiles in four continents and with sales to 110 countries.

In 1994, Anderson read a copy of Paul Hawken's book,[17] *The Ecology of Commerce* and was mesmerised by Hawken's analysis of the environmental crisis that was approaching. Hawken's analysis of the connection between the 'carrying capacity' of the planet, the potential for 'overshoot', where the planet is called upon to produce more than it is able, leading to collapse and species extinction, acted like 'a spear in the chest' to Anderson, who then embarked on an ambitious quest to turn his company from a 'voracious plunderer' to a responsible leader in the quest for sustainable development. His epiphany is explained in his own book, *Mid-course Correction*.[18]

Anderson developed his vision by constructing a programme of change in a seven-stage process, a system that any company could follow to some degree. It is based on an internal examination of core activities with the aims of:

1. eliminating waste in every area of business;
2. eliminating toxic substances from products, vehicles and facilities to bring about 'benign emissions';

---

16   Ibid., p. 1.

17   See Hawken, P. (1993) *The Ecology of Commerce: A Declaration of Sustainability*. New York: HarperCollins.

18   Anderson, R. C. (1998) *Mid-course Correction: Toward a Sustainable Enterprise. The Interface Model*. Atlanta, GA: Peregrinzilla Press.

3. adopting the latest technology in renewable energy generation to bring economic as well as environmental benefits;
4. examining the life-cycle of products to allow the redesigning of processes to use bio-based materials;
5. re-evaluating the way people and products are transported in all aspects of the business cycle, thereby reducing waste and emissions;
6. communicating values to stakeholders to obtain support for these actions, and
7. creating a new business model with a culture that places sustainability at the centre of the decision-making process.[19]

Anderson demonstrates that even running a company that depended on the petrochemical industry and facing the most intractable challenges, he was able to work through the problems and find solutions.

How Do I Persuade the Board and Colleagues?

The reluctance shown by some to adopting the CR agenda is often linked to the feeling that there might be a lack of enthusiasm on the part of the board or other key colleagues. It is easier if there is board support form the outset, of course, but in a changing economic environment the case for strategic change can be pushed home if couched in terms that all can identify with.

THE BUSINESS CASE

The business case for change is, itself, compelling. In February 2007, Achim Steiner, executive director of UNEP, at the launch of the most authoritative scientific report on climate change by the intergovernmental Panel on Climate Change to date, made the following statement:

The 2nd of February 2007 will one day hopefully be remembered as the day the question mark was removed from the debate on whether human activities are driving climate change. The new Intergovernmental Panel on Climate Change report says there is 90 per cent certainty that the burning of fossil fuels and other human activities are driving climate change.

The word unequivocal is the key message of this report ... those who have doubts about the role of humans in driving the climate can no longer ignore the evidence.

The IPCC report says the rise in global temperatures could be as high as 6.4°C by 2100. The report also predicts sea level rises and increases in hurricanes. It is the work of 1200 climate experts from 40 countries.[20]

This was the report that finally persuaded the US administration that they could no longer resist the science: reluctantly they accepted the role of industry in global warming.

---

19   For full details, see: http://www.interfacesustainability.com.

20   See the IPCC website for all the scientific research which went into the report at http://www.ipcc.ch/.

In the UK, it prompted the government to establish its own Committee on Climate Change in March 2008. It published its first report on 1 December 2008, and its recommendations were more startling than anticipated by many, though they mirrored the warning calls that have emanated from the likes of the Tyndall Centre[21] for some time:

> *The Committee's recommendations on the first of these issues – the target for 2050 – have already been presented in a letter to the Secretary to State delivered on 7th October 2008. We recommended that the UK should commit to reducing its GHG emissions by at least 80 per cent below 1990 levels by 2050.*[22]

These findings represent a sea change in the way government views climate change. A reduction in emissions of the magnitude of 80 per cent means all sectors will need to think carefully about the way they do business or face the consequences, the most probable of which is regulation.

There is an accepted business case for acting in advance of regulation, for remaining in control and shaping the agenda. Lobbying costs are reduced and there is normally a 'first-mover' advantage. Regulation brings with it uncertainly. Uncertainty creates nervousness in financial markets and in the face of uncertainty markets discount prices. This uncertainty can be removed by signalling to the market that perceived issues of financial risk are being handled promptly and with skill.

REPUTATION

Another driver for strategic change is in terms of reputation, where the benefits of being seen to be leading the way in innovation and re-engineering work processes and products in the face of an evolving business environment may far outweigh the perceived costs. As noted, markets react to such signals in a positive way, and analysts on the 'buy' side rarely miss this analysis.

It is thus likely that colleagues, and the board, may see the rationale for strategic change.

Measuring the Impact of CR Initiatives

Another way of deciding which approach to take in defining CR strategies is to examine what impact the strategies are supposed to achieve; what outcomes the company wants. Equally the causal links in a chain of activities need to be explored.

In their recent book on corporate responsibility, Blowfield and Murray[23] devote a chapter to discussing the impact of CR initiatives. They invite the reader to consider the subtle difference between the notions of outcomes and outputs:

---

21   The Tyndall Centre is a research hub based at the University of East Anglia which publishes research on climate change on a regular basis. See http://www.tyndall.ac.uk.

22   Committee on Climate Change (2008) Building a Low Carbon Economy: the UK's Contribution to Tackling Climate Change. London: TSO.

23   Blowfield, M. and Murray, A. (2008) *Corporate Responsibility: A Critical Introduction*. Oxford: Oxford University Press.

In its most general sense, 'impact' refers to the outcomes associated with particular actions. Although this is too simple a definition, it draws attention, first, to the importance of outcomes (cf. outputs) and, second, to the significance of causality. As examples in this chapter reveal, discussion of impact often confuses 'outputs' for 'outcomes'. But although the two words overlap in some contexts, the former is narrower in meaning, referring to the specific actions that are needed to achieve a larger result, whereas the latter is the larger result itself. (For example, degrees are an output of university that have the outcome of creating a better educated population.) Thus, in the corporate responsibility context, a corporate responsibility report is an output, not an outcome, if our aim is to enable business to manage its relationship with society better.[24]

They explore in some depth the means through which impact might be assessed but, more relevant to these discussions, by reviewing the works of others they have devised a simple five-dimensional framework which can be used by those who want to gauge the impact their approach might effect.

The Big Picture

If it is the aim of the company to become truly sustainable, then the company is pitching at a level which will impact on the higher levels of concern. It will look at 'the big picture'. It will, while seeking to achieve stable and sustainable economic growth, be prepared to:

1. address the pressing issues of climate change;
2. examine and reverse the adverse effects of globalisation;
3. deal with violations of human rights;
4. work for justice and equity; and
5. stamp out corruption and poor governance.

This is to embrace the stronger tenets of sustainable development, to consider the social and environmental aspects of corporate activity, mindful of such issues as the Millennium Development Goals and, in essence, the principles behind the UN Global Compact. Although many companies are signatories to the Global Compact few can be seen to be demonstrably engaged in this agenda. However, there are some notable examples, such as Interface, Fuji Xerox and others, to add weight to the notion that is just takes leadership and courage.

Instrumental Benefits

The question here relates to whether or not the business case can have demonstrable effects. Indeed one might expect that, if companies undertake various CR initiatives, there should be some way of demonstrating the financial implications. It should come as no surprise that this has been the focus of considerable research over a long period.

---

24   Ibid., p. 309.

Margolis and Walsh,[25] for example review 95 studies that sought to provide evidence of a link between social and financial performance yet failed, in common with others, to find any definitive correlation. Indeed, this whole area of study was summed up by two researchers[26] as 'twenty-five years of incomparable research', referring to the difficulty in assessing the correct measure to use to capture what 'social performance' really is. Unfortunately, the consensus of research opinion is that the connection between doing well and doing good is not strong, and little has changed in the last decade to alter these findings.

Business Attitudes, Awareness and Practices

In the way that the 1990s were seen as the decade of corporate governance,[27] so the first decade of the twenty-first century may be seen as the decade of corporate responsibility. From a standing start, every company in the FTSE 100 now has a dedicated CR department. In their most recent report on trends in global sustainability reporting, KPMG report that 'corporate responsibility reporting has gone mainstream – nearly 80 percent of the largest 250 companies worldwide issued reports, up from about 50 percent in 2005'.[28] Despite some scepticism, and some misunderstandings, as I have illustrated above, there has been real progress and the understanding of supply chain implications, and life-cycle analysis. The willingness of multinational companies (MNCs) to consider working with NGOs and involvement of organisations like Business in the Community in the UK promoting partnership activity between companies and NGOs bodes well for the future.

Non-business Stakeholders

Another way to examine the impact of CR is to think about how it impinges on wider society. We might consider, for example, the number of framework agreements between international trade unions and MNCs that have been negotiated. Indeed union recognition is one of the criteria for membership of the FTSE 4Good.

The Impact of Corporate Responsibility on Itself

The final observation in terms of impact refers to the effect that research in to, and the implementation of, CR initiatives has had on the evolution of the concept itself. If we consider, for example, the Global Reporting Initiative, we note that it is now in its third iteration, the criteria for reporting has widened considerably, and guidance is now included for small and medium-sized enterprises (SMEs). The Global Compact continues

---

25   Margolis, J. D. and Walsh, J. P. (2001) *People and Profits: The Search for a Link Between a Company's Social and Financial Performance*. Mahwah, NJ: Lawrence Erlbaum.

26   Griffin, J. J. and Mahon, J. F. (1997) The corporate social performance and corporate financial performance debate: twenty five years of incomparable research, *Business and Society*, 36(1): 5–31.

27   Charkham, J. (2005) *Keeping Better Company*. Oxford: Oxford University Press.

28   KPMG (2008) *KPMG International Survey of Corporate Responsibility Reporting 2008*. Amsterdam: KPMG International.

to expand its reach and now includes an initiative to embed principles of responsible education across the curricula of business schools across the globe.[29]

Conclusion

Taking a responsible attitude in developing a firm's corporate overall strategy is often viewed in terms of the bottom line cost to the company. It is nearly always one of the first questions raised as new initiatives are trailed. It is interesting that other 'expenditures' are not viewed in the same light. The decision on the level of dividend payment, for example, is seen as an important signal to the market,[30] where the effect on the bottom line is not always the top priority in making the decision. The fact that responsibility initiatives are not seen as market-sensitive is one of the main reasons they are often viewed as peripheral to the core activity of the business. What I have attempted to do in making the case for adopting responsible strategies is to suggest that the landscape of business is changing. Nationalisation of major banks which is, to a greater or lesser extent, occurring around the world as the complex interlinking of financial contracts unravels is likely to bring about a change in attitudes within financial markets. Also, as new scientific research into climate change presses home the need for more rapid acknowledgement from governments that industrial practices have to change, so markets will become sensitive to the way companies respond, and these issues may yet become more relevant to markets.

To show leadership in managing this period of change, executives need to understand the issues and be able to make a case, based on the collective need by business to alter course, to embed responsible practice within their organisations. Sustainable development, in many ways, is an issue for society rather than for business. It is for governments to protect their citizens against corporate excess, and if this is viewed in terms of climate change, then fierce regulation may be the only way to achieve some of the aims to cut emissions we have referred to above.

If Adam Smith's view of capitalism is, as many suggest, based on notions of enlightened self-interest, the same motivation may drive the need for a change in the way we see business. In terms of self-interest, most thinking people would want for their children and grandchildren what they want for themselves – a pleasant place to live, with enough resources left to allow successive generations to thrive. That seems a perfectly reasonable aspiration! However, this will only be possible if leaders of today have the vision to change the way we do business; to examine their core activities and work out new ways of meeting the challenges that not only face us today, but will become crucial as we approach the midpoint of the twenty-first century.

---

29   See http://unprme.org.

30   There is a considerable literature on this issue. See, for a full summary, Stern, J. M. and Chew, D. H. (2003) *The Revolution in Corporate Finance*. New York: Blackwell.

27 *Leading and Managing in Global Contexts*

KIM TURNBULL JAMES AND JAMES COLLINS

Introduction

In this chapter we explore the idea of global leadership and the development of global leaders. Global leadership has been discussed extensively during the last 30 years: it is a contentious notion. There is no consensus as to what global leadership is – is it leadership exercised in a variety of locations over the course of a career? Is it leadership in an organization operating on a global scale? Is it leadership that rises to global challenges? We first explore the literature relating to global leadership and its development and find that this literature embraces a competence approach. We consider what is rarely discussed in this literature in relation to ethical and responsible leadership and how leaders need to face up to globalization responsibilities. We consider new thinking on leadership and question whether the global leadership literature and these new developments can be brought together. We then turn to practice – what do companies faced with the need to respond practically actually provide for their leaders? – and offer five case studies of corporate practice in global leadership development. We conclude that companies aim to contextualize their leadership development and that the leadership development literature needs to address potential disconnects between literature addressing global leadership, corporate social responsibility (CSR), ethical and responsible leadership and contextualized leadership development.

What Does it Mean to be 'Global'

Global leadership has received considerable attention in the academic and practitioner literatures, and we begin with a brief examination of the literature as a starting point for explaining how the global leader can be conceptualized and how that in turn informs global leadership development.

In their frequently cited article, Bartlett and Ghoshal[1] pose the question 'What is a global leader?' They explore this by first seeking to understand what might be understood by the 'global organization', and like many authors, differentiate between domestic,

---

1   See Bartlett, C. A. and Ghoshal, S. (1992) What is a global manager?, *Harvard Business Review,* 70: 124–132.

international, multinational and transnational businesses.[2] For these authors it is the latter that is the truly global organization.

An executive in an international organization can be likened to the expatriate manger; their focus is on a single overseas subsidiary. On the other hand, the transnationally competent manager needs to take a global perspective. This requires highly specialized groups of managers with different sets of competencies to those utilized by their international peers. They need to maintain a balance between international scope and local responsiveness. So, if organizations are to develop into truly global entities they need to develop transnational strategies, and that this requires a parallel shift in managers' skills and competencies. A slightly different perspective is taken by McCall and Hollenbeck[3] who recognize that executives are required to work across borders at different levels; the borders of business, of product, of function and of country. All executive jobs are therefore more or less global depending on how many borders are crossed and the complexity of these borders.

In this regard there is no one type of global executive; global business leaders look and think beyond their local environment in every aspect of their operation, but in many ways this also can be represented by the notion 'think globally act locally'.

The need for an organization's human resource strategy to match their business strategy is important[4] and the notion of a 'war for talent' described in the wider contexts of HR[5] can be found in the global leadership context.[6] This particularly concerns a continuing shortage of skilled executives who have experience of operating in a global world constrains the creation of truly transnational organizations. Adler, for example, says 'a new breed of multiculturally competent managers will be needed to lead business to promised vision'.[7] In a similar vein, citing Gardener's remarks about the exceptional qualities of global leaders: '[leadership] that goes beyond the nation-state and seeks to address all human beings [is] the most important, but rarest and most elusive, variety of leadership',[8] Adler, Brody and Osland[9] remark that 'today the "rare" is becoming a necessity'. These commentaries clearly place the subject of the development of global leaders at the heart of any conversations or discussions that concern management learning and education.

---

2   See for example, Adler, N. J. and Bartholomew, S. (1992) Managing globally competent people, *Academy of Management Executive*, 6(3): 52–65; and McCall, M. W. and Hollenbeck, G. P. (2002) *The Lessons of International Experience: Developing Global Executives*, Boston, MA: Harvard Business School.

3   McCall and Hollenbeck (2002) op. cit.

4   Adler and Bartholomew (1992) op. cit.

5   See McKinsey Quarterly (1998) The war for talent. *The McKinsey Quarterly*, 3: 44–57.

6   See for example Rhinesmith, S. H. (1995) Open the door to a global mindset. *Training and Development*, May: 35–43; and Adler, N. J. (2002) *International Dimensions of Organizational Behaviour*. Cincinnati, OH: South-Western.

7   Adler, N. J. (2002) *International Dimensions of Organizational Behaviour*, p. 297. Cincinnati, OH: South-Western.

8   See Gardner, H. (1995) *Leading Minds: An Anatomy of Leadership*. New York: Basic Books.

9   The quote is from Adler, N., Brody, L. W. and Osland, J. S. (2001) Advances in global leadership: the women's global leadership forum. In W. H. Mobley and M. W. McCall (eds) *Advances in Global Leadership*, pp. 351–383. Los Angeles, CA: JAI Press.

What Does it Take to be a Global Leader?

A focus on the competencies, capabilities and skills of leaders has dominated much of what has been written about leadership in the twentieth century, and this theme continues to be an area that attracts a large volume of research. The central tenet is that the right competencies distinguish effective managers from those whose performance is ineffective or inferior.

Given that this is the focus in much of the mainstream leadership literature it is perhaps no great surprise that in the global leadership context managerial abilities and competencies have been, and remain, a central focus. From an examination of the published literature we find that a large volume of writing discusses the capabilities, competences, skills or qualities that make a leader effective in a 'truly global' context. In essence, the assumption in the models that these authors present is that it is the right competencies that enable executives, at a strategic level, to be effective global leaders, and that this is crucial to the success of global organizations.

Like many articles reporting research on competencies in the mainstream leadership literature, authors writing about global leadership present models describing a list of attributes; these are sometimes centred around core competencies. For example, Adler and Bartholomew list seven competencies required of competent transnational business leaders. In their model Moran and Riesenberger[10] report 12 core competencies that are crucial to managers' ability to implement an effective global business strategy, and Brake's model reports 15 global personal leadership competencies – around three core themes which he labels the 'the global leadership triad'.[11] Kets de Vries and Florent-Treacy[12] describe 12 essential dimensions of global leadership that are crucial for exemplary global leaders. In an approach which describes universal leadership qualities, Rosen *et al.* include four core constructs which they label 'global leadership literacies'.[13] In a model that explores the requirements of future global leaders Goldsmith, Greenberg, Robertson and Hu-Chan[14] introduce five crucial factors.

Whether these authors depict four, five, six or more constructs in their model most describe a common set of competencies or skills. As illustrative examples of the competence approach we set out the dimensions described by Kets de Vries and Florent-Treacy and the five factors described by Goldsmith *et al.*

Kets de Vries and Florent-Treacy argue that effective global leaders are engaged in two simultaneous functions. First, a 'charismatic' role, which involves envisioning, empowering and energizing activities and actions with the aim to inspire and motivate followers. Secondly, what they describe as an 'architectural' role, which is a concern for the implementation of processes that improve organizational design, and which controls

---

10   Moran, R. and Riesenberger, J. (1994) *The Global Challenge: Building the New Worldwide Enterprise*. New York: McGraw-Hill.

11   Brake, T (1997) *The Global Leader. Critical Factors for Creating the World-class Organization*. Chicago, IL: Irwin.

12   Kets de Vries, M. F. R. and Florent-Treacy, E. (1999) *The New Global Leaders: Percy Barnevik, Richard Branson, and David Simon, and the Making of the International Corporation*. San Francisco, CA: Jossey-Bass.

13   Rosen, R. H., Digh, P., Singer, M. and Phillips, C. (2000) *Global Literacies: Lessons on Business Leadership and National Cultures*. New York: Simon and Schuster.

14   Goldsmith, M., Greenberg, C. L., Robertson, A. and Hu-Chan, M. (2003) *Global Leadership: The Next Generation*. Upper Saddle River, NJ: Prentice Hall.

and rewards employee behaviour appropriately. They describe twelve essential dimensions of global leadership which are crucial for exemplary global leaders:

1. envisioning;
2. empowering;
3. energizing;
4. designing and controlling;
5. rewarding and giving feedback;
6. team-building;
7. outside orientation;
8. tenacity;
9. emotional intelligence;
10. life balance;
11. resilience to stress;
12. global mindset.

Goldsmith *et al.* suggest that in order to address the global challenges of the future leaders require five crucial factors. These are:

1. thinking globally;
2. appreciating cultural diversity;
3. developing technological savvy;
4. building partnerships and alliances;
5. sharing leadership.

Is there Anything Different about the 'Global' Leader?

A large number of authors have described how global specific competencies are central to an organization's competitive advantage and organizational performance.[15] However, an important question here is that concerning the difference, if any, between the capabilities and competencies required of the global leader compared to good or effective leaders who not have the 'global' label.[16] In other words, does operating in the global environment require that leaders employ a unique set of leadership skills? Are the skills that are required for global leaders any different to those needed in domestic or local businesses? We believe that the debate concerning the universal nature of leadership is relevant here: can a 'one size fits all' model of leadership be appropriate to the global context? Many definitions of leadership and leadership theories do not reflect global relevance. These essentially domestic models, mostly US-based, might not be transferable to the world at large and it may even be dangerous to apply these ethnocentric models to the global environment.[17]

---

15   See for example Caligiuri, P. M. and DiSanto, V. (2001) Global competence: what is it, and can it be developed through global assignments?, *Human Resource Planning Journal*, 24: 27–38.

16   For example, Lobel, S. A. (1990) Global leadership competencies: managing to a different drumbeat, *Human Resource Management*, 29: 39–47.

17   Bartlett and Ghoshal (1989) op. cit. and Adler, N. J. (2001) Future issues in global leadership development. In M. E. Mendenhall, T. M. Kühlmann and G. K. Stahl (eds) *Developing Global Business Leaders*, pp. 257–259. London:

This is a topic that has attracted considerable debate and central to the work of Project GLOBE.[18] This large global project found that many leadership characteristics or behaviours are universal and generalizable to leadership across the world. In this regard the authors describe the following – charismatic leadership, visionary, inspirational, decisive, performance oriented, integrity, enthusiastic, encouraging, motivational and dynamic. Overall these characteristics are described as a value-based leader syndrome. The authors report three further leadership dimensions that are culturally contextual; they may be perceived favourably or unfavourably in different cultures. These dimensions concern a leader's power orientation (autocratic leadership), their humane orientation and a bureaucratic–collective approach.

In most cases the notion of global leadership described in the academic and practitioner literature is not dissimilar to the implicit view of an effective leader[19] and many leadership characteristics of the global leader can be mapped on the transformational/charismatic/visionary model.[20] In this regard we have sympathy for Miller's comment that the term global leadership used so widely and arbitrarily as to make it of no practical use to academics or practitioners.[21]

Furthermore, putting a dominant focus on competencies reinforces a view that there is some sort of ideal profile of a global leader, and that effective global leaders are required to develop this ideal profile. Perhaps the logic is that by defining the competencies required of global leadership, management education programmes can be directed toward the development of these specific competencies. This places undue importance on the deficiencies model of management learning. Such a simplistic approach reignites some of the criticisms surrounding leadership theories that focus on traits, behaviour and competencies. A central criticism of these approaches is that they fail to properly consider context. Although the notion of cultural appreciation and the ability to adapt across cultures might at first sight appear to address, or at least partly address, the contextual issue, global leadership is exercised in a complex environment and under a multitude of conditions and thus the problem of tackling leadership under different contextual conditions cannot be explained by a set of skill or competencies. As Mintzberg states: 'learning a set of competencies does not per se make a manager competent'.[22]

Quorum Books.

18   See House, R., Javidan, M., Hanges, P., Dorfman, P. and Gupta, V. (2004) *Culture, Leadership, and Organizations: The GLOBE Study of 62 Societies*. Thousand Oaks, CA: Sage.

19   See for example, Lord, R. G., Foti, R. J. and Phillips, J. S. (1982) A theory of leadership categorization. In J. G. Hunt, U. Sekaran and C. A. Schriesheim (eds) *Leadership: Beyond Establishment Views*, pp. 104–121, Carbondale, IL: Illinois University Press; and Schyns, B. and Meindl, J. R. (2005) *Implicit Leadership Theories: Essays and Explorations*, Charlotte, NC: Information Age Publishing.

20   See the work of Bass and colleagues. For example Bass, B. M. (1985) *Leadership and Performance Beyond Expectation*, New York: Free Press; and Bass, B. M. and Riggio, R. E. (2005) *Transformational Leadership*, Mahwah, NJ: Lawrence Erlbaum Associates.

21   Miller, E. L. (2001) Future issues in global leadership development. In M. E. Mendenhall, T. M. Kühlmann and G. K. Stahl (eds) *Developing Global Business Leaders*, pp. 260–264. London: Quorum Books.

22   The quote is from Mintzberg, H. (2004) *Managers not MBAs*, p. 140. London: Prentice Hall.

Dominant Approaches to Developing Global Leaders

As we have described above, there is strong competition for organizations to attract global talent. Researchers writing before 2000 report that many organizations do not have effective global leadership development plans in place.[23] However, a more recent view is that in response to a perceived lack of competent global leaders more companies have developed their own global leadership development strategies or programmes.[24]

Although the nature of global leadership corresponds to much of the literature on effective leadership in general, the development of managers, leaders and executives in the global context has been separately reported: the principal focus is the concern for acquiring the cultural awareness necessary for the leadership role. Although acknowledging that global leadership development programmes should include classroom-type formal training and simulations, it is the experience of foreign cultures that is crucial. Many authors suggest that a central part of development is the use of overseas assignments or other forms of social interaction in a local environment, including those outside the immediate business context.[25]

The idea is that through exposure to alternative perspectives this form of development enables individuals to challenge existing assumptions and cultural bias. The developmental advantage of overseas working is that in addition to technical and functional overseas assignments, which can be considered as operational appointments, this form of development permits personal development, particularly for high-potential individuals and for executives about to enter senior management positions.[26] Gregersen, Morrison and Black offer a succinct summary of the strategies that are important to the development of the required global leadership competencies.[27]

• Classroom and action learning projects.
• Forming teams of individuals with diverse backgrounds.
• Immersion in the country's way of life through foreign travel.
• Broaden the outlook of potential global leaders through overseas assignments.

Support for the approach to development through overseas assignments and other forms of cross-cultural social interaction can perhaps be captured by the view expressed by John Pepper, the former CEO of Proctor and Gamble, who stated: 'Of all the career changes that I have had, the international assignment was the most important and developmental. It changed me as a person.'[28]

---

23   See Bartlett, C. A. and Ghoshal, S. (1989) *Managing Across Borders: The Transnational Solution*, Boston, MA: Harvard Business School Press; also Gregersen, H. B. Morrison, A. J. and Black, J. (1998) Developing leaders for the global frontier, *Sloan Management Review*, 40: 21–32.

24   Mendenhall, M. E. (2006) The elusive, yet critical challenge of developing global leaders, *European Management Journal*, 24(6): 422–429.

25   See Gregersen *et al.* (1998) op. cit.; Caligiuri and DiSanto (2001) op. cit. and Mendenhall (2006) op. cit.

26   Caligiuri and Di Santo (2001) op. cit.

27   Gregersen, Morrison and Black (1998) op. cit.

28   The quote is from Bingham, C. B., Felin, T. and Black, J. S. (2000) An interview with John Pepper: what it takes to be a global leader, *Human Resource Management*, 39: 287–292.

The literature on development through cross-cultural training or overseas assignments is not without contrasting views. For example, Dowling and Schuler[29] report that senior managers in organizations do not believe that there is a need for cross-cultural education or training, as such training is ineffective. May[30] suggests that although an overseas posting might serve to develop the skills to work with one culture, in other words acting locally, he questions whether there is the transferability necessary for global awareness. The argument put forward by Adler and Bartholomew is that the kind of expatriate management which is reflected by overseas assignments of headquarters or home personnel is an historic approach which is no longer relevant. A more pertinent system reflecting transnational human resource management and development is found where:

> transpatriates from all parts of the world are sent to all other parts of the world to develop their worldwide perspective and cross-cultural skills, as well as developing the organization's cadre of globally sophisticated managers ... transnational firms need to create transnational cultures that are inclusive of all their members, not wait for the world to converge on a reality that looks like any particular firm's national culture, even one that looks 'just like us'.[31]

This perspective reflects the notion that the geographical representation of the leadership of a truly global organization should be a proper reflection of the spread of its global assets. Sulieman[32] offers further support for how the concept of transnational HR is suitable for the future with a hypothetical example in which the organization with 20 per cent of its assets in India and 20 per cent in China should have a similar representation in its top teams and in the boardroom. He suggests that if such a team exists, this is a global leadership team. Although this is perhaps currently no more than a hypothetical premise what is clear is that many global organizations have, or are attempting to, reduced their reliance on expatriate managers at middle management level, by developing their local talent. However, at the executive level this is not happening, more than 15 years after Adler and Bartholomew's paper. For Sulieman the process of localization is an antecedent to global leadership and although widely implemented, the globalization of leadership requires a change in the paradigm in the way that senior executives are selected and this remains a significant challenge.

The Challenges of Globalization

Although our examination of the global leadership literature provides an organized description of what has been written about global leadership, we are struck by an absence in this literature of much discussion about the challenges of globalization, and how these are perhaps crucial to leadership in a global context. Two principal concerns come to mind.

---

29   See Dowling, P. J. and Schuler, R. S. (1990) *International Dimensions of Human Resource Management*. Boston, MA: Kent.

30   See May, S. (1997) Think globally – act locally! Competences for global management, *Career Development International*, 2: 308–309.

31   This quote is from Adler and Bartholomew (1992) op. cit., pp. 60–63.

32   Sulieman, B. (2005) The global leadership marathon, *Employment Relations Today*, 32: 11–17.

Reverse Globalization

First, the changing nature of the global organization – the traditional notion of a global organization which is owned and operated by Western interests requires reassessment.

The nature of the transnational organization is not necessarily represented by historic Western and Asian conglomerates whose sphere of influence stretches across the globe (witness for example organizations such as Shell, British Petroleum and Coca Cola). New transnational organizations include companies whose ownership and headquarters may be in countries such as Russia, China and India, with subsidiaries in Britain, France or the US (for example, the Severstal, Mittal and Tata steel giants and their diverse interests).

Responsible and Ethical Leadership and Corporate Social Responsibility

We consider a second, and considerable, challenge for global leadership is that posed by concerns that are broadly captured by discussions about corporate social responsibility (CSR).

Common global concerns reflect environmental degradation, poverty and illness, political conflict and corporate practices. Political and business meetings, for example, Davos and G8 summits, and UN discussions – and initiatives such as UN Compact – which address issues such as trade and the environment, dominate the news. In recent years world summits, such as the Group of Eight (G8), have attracted large anti-globalization rallies. It would appear that, at least in the eyes of many members of the general public, the concept of business globalization is associated with these common global concerns. This underlines that the globe, as both a geopolitical and business environment, is faced by many threats and challenges and although businesses may not be set up in order to directly meet these challenges, their sustainability is influenced by such threats, and as organizations they impact the world's social, economic and physical environments.

In the context of the challenges faced by business, many news stories (and academic journal articles) about corporate practice commence by introducing the topic of business ethics and corporate social responsibility. Typically, stories about financial misdeeds describe the downfall of organizations such as Enron, WorldCom and Parmalat, and the ethical and moral practices of the leaders of these organizations. The notion of acting in ways that move beyond self-interest applies equally to egocentric individual behaviour and the business-centric actions of corporate organizations.

What needs to be recognized is that organizations, and their leaders, have an impact that goes beyond their organizational boundaries and that the governance of such organizations is far from simple. Although at one level the issues of the social and environmental challenges of globalization, and of ethical and responsible governance, may be a concern that needs to be addressed by nations and states, this is clearly an issue that is of importance to business and hence to global leadership and the way that corporations develop their global leaders.

Organizations have a greater ability to take a transnational approach to social responsibility than does government. Adler writes:

Given their global influence, which by definition transcends national borders, global leaders have a responsibility for the well-being of society that far exceeds that of their domestic counterparts of yesteryear … Since no government body can regulate companies that span the globe, the social-responsibility function must be internalized by the company and its leaders in ways that have never been needed or seen before.[33]

In the face of environmental challenges Shrivastava describes examples of environmentally leading organizations that have an awareness of issues that concern social and ecological welfare.[34] He calls for an ecocentric approach to leadership which encompass 'a concern for global social, economic, and environmental problems … and the globally inequitable distribution of resources and wealth. These global issues create special responsibility to address problems of developing countries.'

In the context of business school education rather than leadership development specifically, Ghoshal comments:

By propagating ideologically inspired amoral theories, business schools have actively freed their students from any sense of moral responsibility … As long as all the other courses continue as they are, a single, stand-alone course on corporate social responsibility will not change the situation in any way.[35]

Moral, ethical and authentic leadership are developing areas in the field of leadership despite the focus of the global leadership literature being principally on the skills and competencies said to be crucial to global leadership. This ignores the matter of how global leaders learn to face the social and environmental challenges of today's global environment. These issues are addressed more extensively in the literature on responsible,[36] moral,[37] ethical,[38] authentic[39] and values-based leadership.[40] The challenge for global leadership development that takes account of global leader responsibilities is to bring these concepts into frameworks that are more focused on company strategy and results.

Leadership: Beyond Competence

The global leadership literature reflects a concern for competencies associated with a leader's personality traits – their behaviour, skills, expertise and cognitive mindset. Whilst

---

33   The quote is from Adler (2001) p. 259, op. cit.

34   Shrivastava, P. (1994) Ecocentric leadership in the 21st century, *Leadership Quarterly*, 5(3/4): 223–226.

35   Ghoshal, S. (2005) Bad management theories are destroying good management practices, *Academy of Management Learning and Education*, 4: 75–91.

36   See for example, Maak, T. and Pless, N. M. (2006) *Responsible Leadership*. London: Routledge.

37   See Pellicer, L. O. (2003) *Caring Enough to Lead: How Reflective Thought Leads to Moral Leadership*. Thousand Oaks, CA: Corwin Press.

38   See Ciulla, J. (2006) Ethics: the heart of leadership. In T. Maak and N. M. Pless (eds) *Responsible Leadership*, pp. 17–31. London: Routledge.

39   See for example, George, B. (2003) *Authentic Leadership: Rediscovering the Secrets to Creating Lasting Value*. San Francisco, CA: Jossey-Bass.

40   For example, Grojean, M. W., Resick, C. J., Dickson, M. W. and Smith, D. B. (2004) Leaders, values, and organizational climate – examining leadership strategies for establishing an organizational climate regarding ethics, *Journal of Business Ethics*, 55: 223–241.

this fits with much mainstream leadership research in which, for example, transformational leadership features strongly, new additions to the leadership literature have emerged. These new constructions of leadership could have relevance for the global context. Goldsmith *et al*. suggest that sharing leadership is one competence for global leaders but beyond team leadership this is an emerging concept now attracting attention.[41]

The idea that leadership can be exercised by a group of people collaborating together – often but not invariably associated with the term shared leadership – and by individuals at many levels in an organization – often but not invariably associated with the phrase distributed leadership – is central to post-traditional leadership models.[42] Post-heroic leadership[43] suggests rethinking our perspective on leadership away from the endeavour of single identifiable individual leaders and focusing on the teams and the invisible actions of many in organization achievements. Co-leadership or collective leadership[44] is often used in relation to co-responsibility, for example a strategic team in which all members bear shared responsibility for the organization. In shared and distributed leadership, patterns of behaviour must change: such leadership requires the emergence of collaborative interaction and the possibility of being influenced by peers and of acquiring lateral influence, compared with traditional top-down leadership.

At the same time as discussions about shared and distributed leadership are flourishing, the notion of strategic leadership is emerging. However, strategic leadership is not a simple reinvention of top-down leadership, and indeed strategic and distributed leadership appear to be related concepts. For example, Sosik, Jung, Berson, Dionne and Jaussi[45] argue that outstanding strategic leadership creates a culture of shared leadership, in which the organization as a whole shares and participates in the leadership tasks of the organization, and this contributes to an organization's ability to learn and transform for continuous change. It also suggests that context is very important – if leadership is about a plethora of networks and relationships, and about ways of meeting organization challenges we may need to know more about the differences in the meaning of leadership in different organization contexts. Whether we add to the leader competence and capability lexicon or revise the relevance of thinking of leadership as a characteristic of an individual, this move to understanding leadership as embedded in a system and not just as a transferable skill enabling an organization 'under new leadership' to turn things around or drive through change, could have profound impact on leadership learning events.

Leadership as a contextualized activity has been a growing interest and may have a number of sub themes. The idea is that leadership is not the same activity *wherever* it is exercised. In other words, from this perspective it is questionable whether there can be

---

41   Goldsmith, M., Greenberg, C. L., Robertson, A. and Hu-Chan, M. (2003) *Global Leadership: The Next Generation*. Upper Saddle River, NJ: Prentice Hall.

42   See for example, Pearce, C. L. and Conger, J. (2003) *Shared Leadership: Reframing the Hows and Whys of Leadership*, Thousand Oaks, CA: Sage; also Raelin, J. A. (2003) *Creating Leaderful Organizations: How to Bring Out Leadership in Everyone*, San Francisco, CA: Berrett-Koehler; also Senge, P. and Kaeufer, K. (2001) Communities of leaders or no leadership at all, in S. Chowdhury (ed.) *Management 21 C*, pp. 186–204, New York: Prentice Hall; Pearce, C. L. and Sims, H. (2000) Shared leadership: toward a multi-level theory of leadership, in M. Beyerlein, D. Johnson and S. Beyerlein (eds) *Advances in the Interdisciplinary Studies of Work Teams*, vol. 7, pp. 115–139, New York: JAI Press.

43   See Fletcher, J. K. (2004) The paradox of postheroic leadership: an essay on gender, power, and transformational change, *Leadership Quarterly*, 15: 647–661.

44   Denis, J. L., Lamothe, L. and Langley, A. (2001) The dynamics of collective leadership and strategic change in pluralistic organizations, *Academy of Management Journal*, 44(4): 809–837.

45   Sosik, J. J., Jung, D. I., Berson, Y., Dionne, S. D. and Jaussi, K. S. (2005) Making all the right connections: the strategic leadership of top executives in high-tech organizations, *Organizational Dynamics*, 34(1): 47–61.

one set of competences that can be transferred effectively from one context to another. Instead leadership tasks need to be constructed bottom-up from an understanding and interpretation about the strategic demands and cultural issues the leader faces in the specific role they take up in the organization. This is not a generic notion of good leadership style (although interpersonal skills are required) but the leader's ability to relate to the various groups and people involved in such a way that they can work together in the system to create the change or improvements needed.

This leads to another emergent theme: the relational dimension of leadership. Leadership has often been discussed in relation to followers but this notion of the follower is often about the leader's ability to influence a person in a positive way, such as to increase motivation or create a relationship where the follower feels empowered to produce their own ideas. The onus is on the leader to create a climate where the follower can blossom: this is often reflected in leadership competence frameworks. However, a different view of the relational aspects of leadership is emerging in which leadership is seen to be operating within a political system. This view recognizes that leadership has to be exercised across many different organization boundaries and works to influence groups with very different perspectives and agendas. In this way leadership can be seen to operate within a network of mutually influencing and influenced relationships. Maintaining these and being able to live with the complexity they foster while undertaking the leadership tasks of the individual's role is hard and emotionally taxing.

Turnbull James and Ladkin[46] argue that these new additions to leadership thinking have implications for leadership development practice. Development based on competences is underpinned by a 'deficit model' in which leaders need to acquire missing or underdeveloped behaviours, attitudes and traits. This can be contrasted with the need to develop individuals' capacity for collaboration, sharing and dealing with the complexity of organization networks, systems change and working across boundaries. The focus is on the leader working within a particular context, rather than the attainment of generic capabilities, and is underpinned by a view of leadership primarily as an intervention into a system dynamic rather than as a function of style or interpersonal skill. This suggests that development activities put context in the foreground and involve learning about organizations systems, working with different interest groups and understanding how these impact on the individual and how individuals can use their understanding of the organization to shape appropriate interventions. For the global leader this would be learning in and for the context in which leadership is practised rather than about the cultural context to which one's leadership will be applied.

Global Leadership Development: Case Studies

In the following section we report the findings from five case studies which focus on what organizations are doing to develop their global leadership cadre. The cases represent organizations involved in different kinds of business all of which operate in a global environment. The cases provide some detail of the global challenges faced by the

---

46   See Turnbull James, K. and Ladkin, D. (2008) Meeting the challenge of leading in the 21st century: beyond the 'deficit model' of leadership development. In K. Turnbull James and J. Collins (eds) *Leadership Learning: Knowledge into Action, pp. 13–34.* London: Palgrave.

organizations and the approach they take to global leadership development. In order to explore the assumptions and origins of their development practice we examine the focus of their development programmes rather than explore IHRM practices around overseas assignments in detail.

Case Study 1

Driven by meaningful corporate values

The organization is a public company with a European headquarters which primarily operates as a manufacturer and as a multimedia technology, communications, and services organization in the communications industry. The company employs over 100,000 people in regions across the globe (source: company website, May 2008). An interview with the Director of Group Leadership Development and Learning provided the data that contributes to the case study.

Global challenges

One of the main challenges for this organization is adaptation and change in a world of continued fast-moving technological change: maintaining a leading position and developing a strategy for the future against unknown future global developments is of course not unique to this company; but for organizations such as this, at the forefront of technological change, there are added pressures.

Who or what is a global leader?

In the past (that is, over 15 years ago) corporate experts and leaders from HQ were sent to regions in which new business development was taking place. The emphasis now is on developing global talent – a global leader could be a national from Europe, North or South America, or Asia or countries who need to be able to work anywhere in the world (not solely their own country or continent). This is a challenge for global leadership development.

Within the organization potential leaders are mostly identified through methods such as personal assessment in a personal development plan (PDP, 360) and talent mapping and career coaching dialogues. Great importance is placed on developing the best talent for key positions. This is crucial because 'we will not get anywhere with our transformation if we do not manage and have the best leadership in the industry'.

Global leadership development programmes.

In the past, the organization focused on 'leadership profiles': team leader, business leader, strategic leader. However, given the challenges of transformational change the company now take a more integrated approach to leadership development. Development is viewed as 'a journey, during which there are some key changes which requires a special attention to ensure that it will be smooth and successful'. This new approach gives special attention to the key transition moments between four key changes and 'there are consolidation periods, during which leaders are evolving and growing in a specific role, environment, and so on'. There is special attention at the key transition moments to ensure the rest of the journey is smooth and successful. The leadership model on which this is all based was developed in 2007 by a taskforce of senior HR managers through extensive dialogue within the organization (all tiers of management and the executive board) and with external interests such as key customers, business partners and the academic community. In comparison to other organizations, this organization considers itself to be advanced in working with a 'global mindset'. An important issue has always been that of cultural sharing – this term suggests something more than an awareness of local culture; rather there is a mutual understanding of each other's culture. Great importance is placed on corporate values and how these are disseminated throughout the organization.

Although recognizing that there is a need to identify and develop a number of capabilities important to leadership, it is corporate values and culture that are central to the leadership development programme. These are supported by an understanding of how the individuals lead themselves, their team, their business. Although the importance of capabilities remains, a reassessment of focus is underscored by this organization moving from placing great importance on their 'catalogue' containing in excess of 100 capabilities, to a more manageable 20 capability indicators; Although 'the new model includes elements of the old the challenge was to hold on to the good bits and let go of the not so good to ensure that the new model was not anchored down or restricted by prior thinking. This provided an opportunity for to engage in real transformational change of the programme.'

Post the 2007 leadership model launch, the portfolio was streamlined and the organization works with internationally renowned business school providers and other global partners as co-creators and facilitators within their 'leadership community'. The learning design is based on a 70/20/10 approach – 10 per cent formal training, 20 per cent self-awareness and 70 per cent action learning. The focus is on classroom and formal delivery at lower managerial levels based on 'an assumption that when you are more junior, you probably need to learn more, through traditional type of training'. For senior executives innovative experiential learning is employed: 'the more senior you become the less traditional training you want to go through; first you don't have the time, second you get bored, and thirdly you don't get the benefits of networking in the more traditional classroom environment'.

Case Study 2

Privately owned working in global markets

The organization is a US privately owned company which primarily operates in the agriculture sector. The company employs over 150,000 people in regions across the globe (source: company website, May 2008). An interview with the head of global leadership development provided the data that contributes to the case study.

Global challenges

The organization operates in global markets and all regions of the globe, thus world trading conditions and local circumstances can be difficult and fast-moving.

Within this context the organization has developed a corporate strategy for 2015 and beyond which identifies strengths and opportunities. These have had an influence on the organization's leadership development plans

What/who is a global leader?

Developing talent is at the heart of the organization's ethos and a leader can be 'anyone in the company anywhere'. In essence global leaders are the senior managers who are required to work with colleagues or customers across regions.

Global leadership development programmes

The full set of leadership development programmes is based on six individual leadership programmes that represent the lower levels of leadership responsibility to the highest executives (approximately 30 people). At the lowest level managers receive training in the 'fundamentals of management' and at the top level 'transformational leadership'.

The overall programme was developed in 1999 by a senior headquarters executive team who took themselves to a secluded environment to address the leadership development issue. The structure of the programmes was designed by the organization's leadership academy. Although, up to middle management levels, programmes are delivered locally, they are applied consistently across the regions; 'we have learning and development sectors each of those regions who are in charge of facilitating and coordinating those programmes ... regardless of if you are sitting in Latin America or Asia Pacific, you'll have the same modules. There will be some differences in terms of the use different examples, but it really is consistent.'

The model is principally a competency framework with four quadrants: leadership behaviours, knowledge, execution and learning capacity. Incorporated into the model are three crucial themes: a concern for integrity, conviction, and courage; it is used in recruiting, it's expected that anyone who is hired really has those three core heart qualities.

In programmes for senior regional leaders (for example, 'Future Focus Leadership') participants come together from across the globe; here they can introduce their own regional or global challenges such as concerns around sustainability and social responsibility – however, such issues are only introduced at the instigation of cohort participants.

The programmes are modular with each module having a particular focus – e.g. self reflection, awareness and emotional intelligence, customer engagement. Development is not confined to the classroom and can include visits to developing markets and to customers; 'for example, our Europe and Pacific group are going to Japan in the next few months to take a look at a Japanese customer and really work with that customer to understand their business. Participants will learn skills that will help them to engage with the customer better. For example, having learned something about emotional intelligence they may explore how EI affects customer relationships.'

As part of development senior managers engage in the development of their junior colleagues: 'they're developing others and coaching others it is something we stress in all of our leadership programmes, we have individuals from Future Focus Leadership and High Performance Leadership, who volunteer to come and help facilitate with programmes in the academy: they'll also volunteer to be mentors and coaches'.

Case Study 3

Focus on top regional roles: autonomy, common world wide identity, multicultural teams

The organization is a public company with a European headquarters which primarily operates in offshore exploration and engineering sector. The company employs over 40,000 people in regions across the globe (source: company website, May 2008). An interview with the head of organization development provided the data that contributes to the case study.

Global challenges

A principal challenge is to provide a common organizational identity across the globe in a corporate structure organized to have regional autonomy; regional targets and profit and loss accounting. The issue is reflected in the expectation (the demand by customers) that a common standard of services is provided across all regions. The organization contracts with the world's largest corporations working in regions where local demands may be inconsistent with global messages and therefore 'from a client's perspective, one of the things that they want is that the experience that they have of us in Singapore is the same that they get in South America'. The need for a global identity built on consistency and regional autonomy is a dichotomy and the organization wishes to invert the current practice of 70 per cent local variation and 30 per cent global consistency, but maintain a structure of autonomous regions. This is a challenge for the organization as whole and 'our leadership population who experience a tension in their role, because they have their local lords and masters to whom they report ... but at the same time, particularly at the senior level, being asked to operate as global thinkers and global leaders; to take a much more global perspective'.

There is a high reliance on overseas expatriate assignments. This creates multicultural teams working in local conditions and cultures different from home. Different expectations and practice (e.g. prescribed systems compared to experiential learning of a local workforce) is a challenge 'is an issue that we need to address head on; it is the whole challenge working cross-culturally'.

In additional to the technical challenges of working in harsh environments there are social and political challenges to working in some parts of the globe. For this organization it raises the questions they ask as to whether they should operate in these regions at all.

What/who is a global leader?

Leadership development is offered at many levels but global leadership development principally concerns for 'the top 100 people who have significant regional roles, as well as those people who are being seen as high potential and therefore coming from the layer underneath'. Leaders in the organization principally come from traditional sources (the developed world). There has been a big rise in the use of extended expatriate assignments 'from almost nil 3 years ago to 120 current projects'.

To create a cadre of potential global leaders there is a need to move from expatriate to *'looking to identify local people who can step up to these roles, once expatriates move on'*. This requires a move away from a culture that expatriates will *'teach the local managers because we know best'*. The current approach is to Westernize local talent – bringing them in from the regions changing from local cultural behaviour to western leadership culture (consistent with the organization) and returning them later. This is because 'our experience of the local people is unless they have been Westernized to a considerable extent, it is very difficult for them to step up and accept responsibility, to demonstrate initiative and express a meaningful opinion. So where we have got young high flyers in the business population we export them to European centres for a period of time to give them that different perspective.'

Global leadership development programmes

A challenge for HQ is to develop a consistent leadership programme within a corporate structure of regional autonomy. For example, the head of organization development is not empowered to apply a company-wide programme because region directors control local development needs and opportunities; this introduces a tension in the development strategy which is unresolved. A previous attempt to integrate leadership development 'into a centralized system had been a disaster'.

The global leadership development programme which was developed in 2005 is based on the Kouzes–Posner Leadership Practices model as the organization considers it important to have a robust model. However, there is an admission that other models could have served equally well. The head of organization development views the original model to be somewhat 'Americanized' and with the support of a 'leading international business school' who deliver the programme are tailoring aspects of the model to make it relevant to their particular context.

Middle and junior high-potential professionals are identified through formal talent review processes and receive development on programmes that include international 'outward bound' type training 'outside of the formal learning environment'. This provides an opportunity to reflect and learn about themselves and about working in different and challenging environments.

Case Study 4

Long-term expatriate assignments, regional autonomy and common identity

The organization is a public company with a European headquarters which primarily operates in the construction and services sectors. The company employs in excess of 18,000 people in regions across the globe (source: company website, May 2008). An interview with the director HR development provided the data that contributes to the case study.

Global challenges

Although this organization describes itself as 'global' it is structured so that that regional parts operate independently and have autonomy; 'perhaps should not call ourselves a global organization, we are more multinational in that we are not absolutely joined up and global across the whole group'. Within this structure the challenge is how to convey a common global corporate identity; how can this be maintained in an autonomous regions structure.

Although regional structures are a challenge, through the use of technology virtual teams facilitate global connections which permits the 'utilization of the talent from around the group to design/deliver whatever we agree in the contract. We are not really saying that leadership needs to be globally orientated.' The paradox of working in one's own profit centre while aiming to develop a greater use of global virtual teams is that this has the potential to produce 'silo rather than "boundaryless" behaviour'.

A further challenge for the organization is a recognition that 'people in other companies are continuously challenging our business model, and inventing new ones, different ways of doing things … So part of our development push is to get employees to accept that the future will be more ambiguous.'

What/who is a global leader?

In this organization career success is not perceived solely in terms of leadership of one of their businesses. Experienced professionals can decide to remain technical gurus, a project manager, or move to a position to run a business; the challenge is to ensure, through a system of equality of rewards and recognition, that individuals can select career paths and the talent within the organization can be retained. This contrasts with perceptions that success equates to a leadership position and means that 'we have not set out to design programmes for global leaders. What we set out to do is to paint a picture that the future will be different and engage with managers and leaders on the difference.'

The organization does not send experts around the world on multiple assignments during a career – leaders currently tend to be from the developed world on long-term expatriate assignments (rather than short-term trips). The organization recognizes the need to develop local talent to become leaders and potential global leaders; such high-potential talent (in the emerging economies) is identified locally and may be sent to HQ and to established projects, where corporate (Western) culture prevails, to learn the company's corporate way. Regional businesses are therefore 'exporters of local talent; through development these individuals are given a different perspective – they are almost indoctrinated and then sent back after a period of two, or three years'.

Global leadership development programmes

Traditional development methods such as personal development plan (PDP) discussion around capabilities, and understanding one's self are offered in early career. At senior executive level – the top 100 executives – the organization runs leadership masterclasses and has developed their Development Dialogue programme. This requires that leaders reflect on how they consider their future (and provides some tools to do so) and that they engage in a one-to-one dialogue with an individual on the board. This approach is a challenge for board members and the potential senior executive and both can find the experience difficult. The head of development views this approach as a move away from a programme in which competences are central. As an approach the 'Development Dialogue is different and certainly we are never going to create a competence matrix, although I can't say that I have banned the word in my organization.'

So, rather than developing the necessary competences for global leadership you can regard ours as a programme that helps to develop global leaders, but we are doing things in our context which hopefully will give us the leadership capability for the future context.

Case Study 5

A need for local managers to join the international cadre

The organization is a public company with a European headquarters which primarily operates in the automotive and construction engineering sectors. The company employs over 5,000 people in regions across the globe (source: company website, May 2008). An interview with the director of group leadership, learning and development provided the data that contributes to the case study.

Global challenges

One of the key challenges is managing the consequences of being a global organization. In this regard 'globalization means managing, on the one side company new opportunity and growth, and on the other side cutting back some traditional business areas. The big challenge, from a leadership perspective, is to handle that and to handle it properly.' The organization has become increasingly global and this has necessitated greater strategic responsiveness, particularly the speed you have to react to changes around you and to manage change in your own organization - this is closely linked to globalization, as you always need to react quickly'.

An increased global presence requires that attention is paid to managing cultural diversity, particularly real and perceived difference between organizational culture and local national culture. Within this context managing the war for local talent, for example developing leaders from Brazil, China and India is a leadership development challenge which recently become a greater priority.

What/who is a global leader?

In the past global or executive leadership has been dominated by individuals from headquarters (UK) or those from developed (Western) countries. However, it is recognized that leaders (and potential global leaders) need to be recruited and developed from the emerging nations (where the organization owns and operates manufacturing plants). The organization recognizes that 'we need to do much more, and there is a big workload to develop our leadership potential in the growing areas like India, China and Brazil. That is a big challenge for us from the leadership development.'

Development programmes in long-established regions of manufacture (e.g. Western-located plants) have been in place for many years. However, the organization has many divisions and regions and 'in some regions nothing happened, but in some divisions a lot more; so currently we are focusing on aligning the activities'. A common programme has therefore now been established.

High-potential candidates are identified in traditional ways through personal development reviews. To develop future global leaders from emerging economies there is a need, in early career, to bring people from different regions to work in different and difficult markets; this helps them develop new perspectives. In addition specific development activities have been established in order that local leaders are developed at home.

Global leadership development programmes

The common model at all levels of seniority (from executive to first level manager) 'stretches laterally, geographically, but also vertically within the structures of the organization. This is a different approach to the idea of there are five or six models of leadership depending on where you sit in your position in the hierarchy, and different regional needs.'

A team of executive directors was involved in developing the approach. The model includes four quadrants representing capability, personal attributes, knowledge and experience. Added to this some variation is introduced according to context; for example to 'differentiate between managing change required by a plant manager, to that required at regional or global director level'. Incorporated into the model is the organization's respect of values. These values are reflected in a set of mutual promises about expectations and standards of behaviour; 'six promises to the employee and the six promises from the employee'.

At the time of implementation a major concern was the transferability of the programme into different cultural contexts 'and the first time that we actually brought it to Asia, I was personally quite nervous. We tried to prepare everything and asked how can we make sure that it is culturally sensitive? I was surprised that we could actually transfer it very easily.'

Ideas of social responsibility are incorporated into the programme. For example, as part of the programme mangers engage in a business project and are required to choose and carry out a social project.

Case Study Discussion

Each of these organizations operates in highly globalized fields and face different challenges. Although this is not at all surprising, it underlines that in terms of global leadership and global leadership development context is a crucial issue.

IN WHAT WAY ARE THESE GLOBAL ORGANIZATIONS?

Although each of the case study organizations operate in regions across the globe, it is perhaps only three that are 'global' in terms of the way this is notion is described in the academic literature.[47] These three organizations appear to have transnational strategies rather than operating at a local level in many regions across the globe. Indeed, reflecting

---

47   Bartlett and Ghoshal (1992) op. cit. and McCall and Hollenbeck (2002) op. cit.

on this issue and talking about the structure of his organization, one of the participants described the organization as 'multinational rather than global'.

For the two organizations which operate autonomously in different regions there appears to be a tension between operating at a multinational level – Bartlett and Ghoshal's notion of an organization that is represented in regions – and operating as a 'global' enterprise.[48] Although their corporate identity and modus operandi are required to transcend national or regional boundaries, fiscal and executive arrangements remain local, and the reality is that local demands can supersede the need for global uniformity. The notion of 'think globally act locally' is therefore a challenge for these organizations.

GLOBAL LEADERS

Although the organizations recognize that global leaders can emerge from any part of the organization, only one confidently expressed the view that their current leadership cadre included individuals from across the globe who might have responsibility for activity for operations in any of the regions where business operations currently take place. In one of the organizations senior regional leadership tends to be in the hands of individuals from these regions, but in three of the cases there is a strategy of senior executives coming from headquarters or developed (Western) parts of the organization.

In this respect, only the first two of these organizations could be viewed as approaching Sulieman's notion that global leadership should represent the global assets of the organization.[49] But it is still a far cry from this – in one case it is at regional level that leadership can be viewed as representing organizational structure, and for another it is more a concern that global leaders are the best talent available and they can come from anywhere. In many respects the latter might not only be a more realistic counterview to the notion of global leadership as representative of diversity, but is perhaps a more worthy approach. The idea that high potential from any region can lead in any part of the world is a message consistent with the quote attributed to Napoleon: 'Every soldier carries in his knapsack the baton of a Field-Marshal.'

OVERSEAS ASSIGNMENTS

For some of the organizations there is still a reliance on traditional overseas assignments. However, they recognize that the development of local talent is a strategic HR priority[50] and development programmes for high-potential talent, which includes developing local talent, are in place. Rather than short term overseas assignments – hopping from one to another – for one of the organizations working overseas is a long-term career position. Certainly Adler and Bartholomew's view a decade and a half ago that expatriate leadership development through overseas assignments of headquarters personnel is an historic and irrelevant approach is not supported.[51] In fact, for three of the organizations, high-potential local talent is brought in from the regions to headquarters so that these individuals can learn the company approach to business and what are essentially Western

---

48   Bartlett and Ghoshal (1992) op. cit.

49   Sulieman (2005) op. cit.

50   Adler (2002) op. cit.

51   Adler and Bartholomew (1992) op. cit.

views of management and leadership, before being returned to their own regions. Perhaps this will lead to a point when these candidates have become experienced enough to work in positions across the globe, but this is not yet the case, and by the time they are in such a position there is an argument that they will then be steeped in Western approaches to leadership.

CROSS-CULTURAL WORKING

Cross-cultural working is a challenge for some organizations. First, they need to develop local talent, but in their organizations the need is for the local talent to fit into the company rather than expatriate managers to simply have to accommodate to local cultures. Thus cross-cultural working applies to the local managers working for a global organization. Secondly, expatriate managers experience a tension between sensitivity in working with people from different cultures and the different approaches at a local level, with the need to adopt approaches which cross the entire company – from corporate values to corporate practices and ways of working. This is accentuated by the demands of corporate customers who expect the same response wherever they happen to touch or deal with the company. Finally local managers with local customs need to fit with a global approach, but act locally according to domestic demands and customs; this tension is a real challenge as corporates seek uniformity of service.

COMPETENCY FRAMEWORKS

In four of the cases competence frameworks still have an important place in the development programmes. However, they are complemented by additional issues which are central to development programmes. Here concerns such as organizational values and valuing local culture are a reflection of how the organization would like to be perceived by employees and the wider world. This suggests a recognition that a list of competency attributes or behaviour is not enough.[52] For example, one of the organizations reduced its 'competency catalogue' from over 100 attributes to a core of 20. Furthermore, another of the organizations does not include a competency framework for its most senior managers, and explicitly stated that they considered the approach inappropriate to the development needs of these individuals.

CORPORATE SOCIAL RESPONSIBILITY

Although concerns such as values and integrity are important, CSR is not in a prominent position in the programmes. However, the challenge of working in areas where conditions are difficult is recognized by one organization whose comment about working in regions of questionable social, environmental and political integrity – 'should we work there at all' – does indicate that these issues are part of strategic decision making.

Although in at least two organizations a social project is included in development programmes the explicit connection between CSR and global leadership development does appear to be generally absent – at least three interviewees said more could be done. For example, in one organization it was up to the participants of the programme designed

---

52   Mintzberg (2004) op. cit.

for regional leaders to decide whether issues such as CSR should be included in their particular development programme; in other words there was space for participant-generated concerns. However, this is not the same as bringing globalization issues to participants to generate discussion about their role as leaders in global challenges and finding ways of working with dilemmas between corporate interests and global concerns. Whilst engaging in CSR projects such as building schools in developing countries is undoubtedly educational and mind-opening, it is not the same as bringing issues of direct business relevance and strategic decision-making into play during development activity.

NEW IDEAS ABOUT LEADERSHIP AND LEADERSHIP DEVELOPMENT IN CONTEXT

There is evidence in these cases that organizations do in practice go beyond the competence frameworks that are significant in the literature. The notions of corporate values and development dialogues are examples of this. The companies each develop a leadership development strategy which is tailored to their needs – even where existing models of leadership are adopted they are carefully adapted to fit the context.

There is not yet much evidence of different concepts of leadership underpinning leadership development – no one talked of shared or collaborative leadership, for example. Perhaps these notions sit better within development activity which is based on consulting to teams or in executive coaching. The challenge for most global learning and development executives is to formulate approaches which can be adopted by their own staff and understood by managers wherever they are located. Programmes offered centrally are by their nature focused on individual attendance.

Conclusion

It is clear that for leadership development practitioners there is a need to create strategies that are specifically tailored to their context. This context includes an understanding of the nature of the global challenges facing the business combined with identifying who the global leaders are in the business. Global leadership development can be focused on people who go out from the company main base to various regions in the world, can be from focused on nationalities from across the globe playing on the world stage, might be the very top executives, long-term ex-pats or combinations of these. A new challenge is to bring people from developing countries into the international cadre.

The challenges often centre on the practical difficulties of 'think global, act local': allowing operations to have a regional flavour to meet local customer needs has to be balanced with global customers expectations of corporate consistency and who can touch the company anywhere in the world. For other organizations the issue is their technical and professional excellence operationalized with local sensitivity, and they may think of themselves more as more multinational than global.

From a theoretical perspective we noted the growing complexity of the leadership literature, with the emergence of new concepts reflecting the need for leadership that is ethical and responsible on the one hand and collaborative and widely distributed to meet the perceived adaptive challenges of the early twenty-first century. This is not always reflected in the literature on global leadership and one challenge for academics is to make sense of these burgeoning ideas in a way that can inform practice.

Finally we note the lack of explicit connection between leadership development and corporate responsibility: whilst many companies give generously to charitable projects and may offer development opportunities for executives to spend time on these projects, the leadership issues of global responsibilities, ethical choices under pressure and the development of decision-making processes that incorporate the CR commitments companies make, are not central to the leadership literature or to companies leadership development strategies, which lean towards achieving business goals. One company, acknowledging that at present CR and leadership development were not strongly connected unless participants themselves raised these issues as part of their action learning, coaching or classroom discussions, recognized that this was something that would be needed in their global leadership development practice in future. This is an important direction for global leadership development.

28 Conversations and Learning: Narrative and Development in Practice

JOHN LAWLER AND JACKIE FORD

Introduction

The aim of this chapter is to reconsider professional development and to propose an approach which can be used alongside or indeed instead of more traditional development approaches in a range of contexts. It is based on dialogue between professionals, their peers and other significant people with whom they interact.

There is much written about development in the work context, ranging from the broad strategic approaches of human resource development, through generic functions such as management development and leadership development, down to the micro level of development in the identification of specific competences required in individual jobs or professions. Our aim here is provide details of an approach, initially used in leadership development, then in management development more broadly, which can be applied in a range of contexts. We have used the broad terms of 'professional development', 'professionals' and 'professional staff' to encompass the wide range of jobs and their contexts within which this approach can be used. We realise that the term 'professional' itself might be seen as being problematic in that it is open to different and possibly contradictory interpretations, but our focus here is development, rather than a review of the literature which considers definitions of professional work. Thus we see this approach being appropriate in a broad range of professional contexts where there are certain identifiable core skills, expertise and knowledge which are deemed essential for the particular range of tasks within the profession but where these alone do not constitute the overall requirements of the job. The additional element is that of *interaction* with the user of the services, however they are described: client, student, customer, patient, and so on, and with other colleagues within and beyond the employing organisation. Thus we see this approach as being an important addition to approaches to development in a range of professions: not only within the more traditional professions including legal and medical, education and health care but also within professions in their broader sense, including engineering, IT, architecture, design, and so on.

The approach detailed here takes a narrative perspective. This focuses on relationships and interrelationships, on intersubjectivity as a means of creating and exploring meaning within work and thus within development. What we mean by intersubjectivity is the sharing of our individual subjective impressions, feelings and views. In this respect this approach provides an addition to rather than a substitution for an individual focus of development. It implies a collective and interactive process and examines a wider range of potentialities and meanings than is usually accommodated in individually focused methods. The chapter acknowledges the contribution of such individually based approaches, considers literature which promotes the use of dialogue in development and explores an interactive, narrative perspective which draws heavily on themes developed in social constructionism and existentialist thinking. The chapter is structured as follows: we aim first to outline a shift in thinking in relation to professional development in organizations and then to consider the potential contribution of two related lines of enquiry, existentialist thinking and social constructionism, to this area. We then discuss how these approaches can provide new insights into professional development and into professional relationships at work. The chapter concludes with a demonstration of how this approach can be translated into a practical development process.

Professional Development: Current and Developing Approaches

At a basic level, the development of professional staff has as its primary concerns questions, such as 'What is the potential of staff in relation to what is required of them, and how can such potential be developed?' In addition, professional standards are consciously transmitted and reinforced through this process. Currently there appear to be expectations within organisations of greater self-determination in relation to professional development, in that models and approaches within the literature suggest a shift from responsibility for training resting with training departments. Megginson[1] proposed that cutbacks in staffing levels within human resource development departments, together with recognition of the value of on the job rather than off-site training and development, have moved the focus of responsibility to line managers. However, this transfer occurs at a time of flattening hierarchies and wider spans of managerial responsibility which prevent line managers taking on responsibility for development. There has therefore been an 'inexorable' shift[2] in responsibility for professional development onto individuals themselves.

Nonetheless, this is not the whole story and some individuals have been more actively supported by a range of others including mentors, line managers, peers, staff, learning sets colleagues and so on – what we have termed 'significant others' in our work. Within the context of professional development, there is an implicit assumption that professional workers are bright and motivated and would not have reached the status of professional worker without some potential and the capacity to realise part of that at least. Increasingly in development the focus has been on this second aspect – what are professionals required to do in their professional roles, and what are they likely to be required to do in the future? This is exemplified particularly in competency-based approaches where the particular skills, attributes, and so on necessary to effective

---

1   Megginson, D. (2004) Planned and emergent learning, consequences for development. In C. Grey and E. Antonacopoulou (eds) *Essential Readings in Management Learning*, pp. 91–106. London: Sage.

2   Megginson, D. (2004) op. cit., p. 93.

execution of the duties of the post are detailed and the individual's current performance and development needs are considered alongside.

The identification of skills, competences and standards is generally the result of the close scrutiny of much professional work and the identification through job analysis of sets of generalised abilities which in combination are seen to be the major contributors to professional standards of work. Once identified as being necessary, the next task is to focus on how best to develop or inculcate these skills in existing and future professionals. Approaches to the identification of these qualities is justified by a functionalist rationale, namely, enabling the employing organisation to operate more effectively and/or efficiently. Such approaches take what we term an objectivist view, that is, they objectify and externalise particular qualities in a way which separates them from, or transcends, the individuals who might possess them. Such an approach assumes the pre-existence of these qualities or at least their potential, and also assumes a common understanding of what those qualities are.[3] Approaches used as part of job analysis similarly objectify job tasks through identifying and externalising them from the context of the job, detailing specific components which, when put together with other tasks, make up the job as a whole. Thus, in relation to management Cunliffe[4] notes: 'objectivist forms of inquiry view management as a set of formalized activities, competencies, functions, roles'. In similar vein, when such approaches are adopted in other areas of development, the result is a generalised and standardised account of the necessary qualities of professional practice. Whilst such results are useful in some respects, there are concerns that in the context of development in the professional arena, they do not take into account the complexities of professional work beyond the strictly technical or the context in which it is conducted. They constitute a technical rather than a relational view of professional work and present a means by which professional skills and values are transmitted acontextually down the generations with the inevitably individual professional seen in a largely passive, or at least unquestioning role of recipient of such skills and values. Richardson[5] highlights this in relation to the development of teachers. She argues that development:

Derives from the short-term transmission model; pays no attention to what is already going on in a particular classroom, school, or school district; offers little opportunity for participants to become involved in the conversation; and provides no follow-up. We have been engaged in this form of staff development for years, knowing full well that this approach is not particularly successful.

Richardson argues for a collaborative, collegiate style of development focusing on an inquiry approach and dialogue. In this way, the specific context in which the individual is working, including other participants in the context, can be taken more into account. She argues that there are several reasons why this is not incorporated into development programmes, which include the possibility that the open-ended nature of such an approach might be perceived as being beyond the desired control of employing organisations and

---

3   Ramsey, C. (2005) Narrative: from learning in reflection to learning in performance, *Management Learning*, 36(2): 219–235.

4   Cunliffe, A. (2002) Social poetics as management inquiry, *Journal of Management Inquiry*, 11(2): 128–146, p. 131.

5   Richardson, V. (2003) The dilemmas of professional development, *Phi Delta Kappan: The Journal for Education*, 84(5): 401–406, p. 1.

also that, particularly in the US, a culture of individualism operates against such a collegial approach. Others agree that professional development is largely instrumental, serving the needs of employing organisations and the professions themselves, and is unremittingly individualistic in its focus.[6, 7, 8] Little attention is given to the dynamics of relationships or other contextual matters and universal or generalised aspects of professional work are emphasised.

In addition to the generalised skills and qualities which predominate in development, Ramsey[9] notes the dominance of objectivist models of learning, such as Kolb's learning cycle, which she argues are adopted uncritically and again provide oversimplified and inadequate models of learning for development. She argues that a more detailed, reflexive and engaged process is required for more effective development. Much professional work is informed by tacit knowledge, contextual meanings and habitual practice, which are not open for immediate reflection. Developing subjective approaches opens up the possibility for reflection, for questioning assumptions and for surfacing different meanings and so creating, through the acts of dialogue, new meanings and understandings. Allowing a subjective perspective or intersubjective exchange opens up wider possibilities for development. In many respects this might be seen as anathema to objectivist views as it presents the opposite of the universal or immediately generalisable experience, which competence approaches, for example, dictate.

Relational Dialogue

There is an increasing literature which considers relational exchanges between people at work and the possibilities of exploring and developing shared understandings through dialogue and narrative. In this chapter, we use dialogue to refer to the unrestricted, open interaction a person has with other individuals which enables that person to develop their own individual narrative or set of narratives – their own story. Writers such as Shotter and Katz[10] and Cunliffe[11] refer to 'social poetics' in dialogue. By poetics, they indicate that words alone are limited in what they can convey but that words in inter-personal dialogue can convey feeling as well as intellectual components. Poetics signifies a creative process, not a ritual process of question provoking answer; it focuses on the use of imagination rather than the literal signification associated with the exchange of words.[12] Cunliffe particularly considers language following the 'postmodern turn', arguing that it is no longer sufficient to consider it as representational in describing some external objective reality. This she describes as monological, that is, singly authored. She sees language

6   Boud, D. (2006) Creating space for reflection at work. In D. Boud, P. Cressey and P. Docherty (eds) *Productive Reflection at Work: Learning for Changing Organisations*, pp. 158–169. London: Routledge.

7   Fook, J. (2006) Beyond reflective practice: reworking the 'critical' in critical reflection. Keynote speech for the conference Professional Lifelong Learning: Beyond Reflective Practice. 3 July, 2006. http://www.leeds.ac.uk/medicine/meu/lifelong06/papers/P_JanisFook.pdf, accessed 28 January 2008.

8   Ramsey, C. (2005) Narrative: from learning in reflection to learning in performance, *Management Learning*, 36(2): 219–235.

9   Ramsey, C. (2005) op. cit.

10   Shotter, J. and Katz, A. M. (1998) 'Living moments' in dialogical exchanges. Dialog og Refleksjon: a Festschrift for Tom Andersen on the Occasion of his 60th Birthday. V. Hansen. Tromso: University of Tromso, Norway.

11   Cunliffe, A. (2002) op. cit.

12   Cunliffe, A. (2002) op. cit.

now as being used more creatively, dialogically, where language constructs reality and helps in the formation of social experience. Dialogical exchanges present the opportunity of moving away from universal understandings to examine the unique elements which unfold in personal exchanges. Shotter and Katz's view is that the activity of explaining things does more than explain them. They argue:

> *words do nothing on their own. They do not stand for things, nor represent ideas. They have a meaning only in those situations in which living human beings make some use of them in relating themselves to other human beings.*[13]

Words in dialogue are not representing some thing second hand. They are actions: they do something – people can be moved by them – the talker and the listener and both together: hence the 'poetic' aspect of dialogue. This can lead to an understanding that is both ordinary and extraordinary in that it considers both commonplace aspects of life and the unfamiliar which is the direct product of the dialogue.

This 'going beyond' involves the incorporation of feeling and individual understanding. In many practices we measure ourselves and others against an external set of standards or values, as happens, for example, in competence-driven development. In such cases Shotter and Katz argue, 'one feels that one must act in one's practices according to a set of pre-established standards and one must talk and write about things in accord with procedures for proving one's statements are true'.[14] However, conversations are not just about informing, as might be the case for an individual seeking traditional feedback, but are themselves formative – forming relationships, most importantly but formative in other ways also – forming impressions, plans, even forming aspects of the self. If we are 'struck by' something someone says – or something we say – that can be a change in our being, not just a new bit of something we know. Shotter and Katz refer to Bachelard's work on poems and their influence, namely that the words and their reverberations bring about a 'change of being' – we read or hear a poem and the images from it become our own, they do not constitute a representation of an entity already in existence. Dialogue then is not bringing forward something which was previously hidden in someone's head, but occurs in a conversational space between people, and it is in that space and the developing relational talk that meaning can be created. This enables people to go beyond prescribed roles to take a part in constructing a shared view of their activities; to go beyond what exists currently to examine what might be created collectively.

> *It is only by being able continuously to create new links and connections between events within that 'play', in practice, that those involved in a dialogue with each other can reveal both themselves and their 'worlds' to each other … It is in such living moments between people, in practice, that utterly new possibilities are created, and people 'live out' solutions to their problems they cannot hope to 'find' solely in theory, in intellectual reflection on them.*[15]

---

13   Shotter, J. and Katz, A. M. (1998) op cit, p. 2.

14   Shotter, J. and Katz, A. M. (1998) op cit, p. 2.

15   Katz, A. M. and Shotter, J. (1996) Hearing the patient's 'voice': towards a social poetics in diagnostic interviews, *Social Science and Medicine*, 43(6): 919–931, p. 920.

This process then encourages development but on a broader scale that traditionally considered. We are not focusing on skill or competence-development here. Rather this process allows the development of 'knowing of a third kind', that is, not developing knowledge by adding to facts – knowing *that* – or skills – knowing *how* – but 'knowing from within'.[16]

The above approaches indicate that a development focus on skills and knowledge acquisition alone is by no means irrelevant, rather it provides a partial picture. Objectivist accounts of professional standards and practices have their value, but objectivist research concerning social relations has particular limitations. Certain professional skills or knowledge might be regarded as technical rather than social, but social interactions form a significant basis for much professional work both in delivering services directly to those who use and need them, and in engaging with others in the organisation and provision of such services, hence its importance here. A prime example of this is exemplified in the doctor–patient relationship where 'the doctor is the medicine'.[17]

Cooper[18] argues that the disengaged, objective, disinterested research stance leads to 'standard accounts' of the world or aspects of it, the generalised or universal as referred to above. This is useful in dealing with constants such as inert matter, chemical reactions and physical forces and may be useful in some aspects of social interactions. However, this is not fully adequate in reflecting the nuances of the social world. We have several 'standard accounts' of development in development models, professional characteristics, standards and competences. How accurately do these reflect the lived experience of professional life in all its settings? 'What the standard accounts ignore is the degree to which the world is a human one, whose structure, articulation and very existence are functions of human agency'.[19] What is largely missing from standard accounts is the subjective voice, especially that of those who may not be the immediate focus for development activity but who form a crucial part in organisational relations. Writers such as those above draw on a range of thinking to inform their analysis. Our approach has much in common with these perspectives but draws specifically on social constructionism and existentialist thinking. The next section introduces and compares those lines of thought, before going on to explore how they can both be used to inform a narrative approach to development.

Existentialism and Constructionism

Existentialist and constructionist thinking have some commonality in that they are both influenced, to varying degrees, by phenomenology (though we recognise that themes in each area go beyond this approach, as we have argued elsewhere.[20] We do not intend here to provide a detailed examination of the origins of these lines of thinking but to

16   Shotter, J. (2005) Inside the moment of managing: Wittgenstein and the everyday dynamics our expressive–responsive activities, *Organization Studies*, 26(1): 113–135, p. 122.

17   Hearn, J. Lawler, J. and Dowswell, G. (2003) Qualitative evaluations, combined methods and key challenges: general lessons from the qualitative evaluation of community intervention in stroke rehabilitation, *Evaluation*, 9(1): 26–50.

18   Cooper, D. (1999) *Existentialism: A Reconstruction*, 2nd edn. Oxford: Blackwell.

19   Cooper, D. (1999) op. cit., p. 58.

20   Ford, J. and Lawler, J. (2007) Blending existentialist and constructionist approaches in leadership studies: an exploratory account, *Leadership and Organization Development Journal*, 28(5): 409–425.

consider the potential contribution of these perspectives. This we hope will add to the existing and predominant objectivist orthodox approaches to development thinking. One commonality of existentialism and social constructionism is the value they place on the individual, subjective, relational experience (though subjectivity is interpreted differently in each, as we will note in due course). Having said this, it would erroneous to regard existentialism as a subjective philosophy,[21] as this would privilege subjective experience over active experience – over 'being in the world'. Existentialism appears to be less fashionable in the attention it receives than was the case in the twentieth century, for a variety of possible reasons. However, there are themes within existentialism which still merit attention as is evident in recent, critical writings.[22, 23, 24] Our intention here is to consider such themes, in combination with constructionism, with a particular focus on interrelationships and intersubjective dynamics in the context of professional development.

Existentialism: Essence and Existence

'Existence precedes essence' is the aphorism said to characterise existentialist thinking. An assumption underpinning much organisational thinking and research is that the 'essence' of something precedes its existence. It is important here to distinguish between things which exist in themselves, as *things*: such as a chair or a stone; and things which exist as conscious *beings*, with the capacity to choose, reflect, and so on. Sartre develops the notion of consciousness and 'being' as having different abstractions or conceptualisations – 'being in itself' (*en soi*), 'being for itself' (*pour soi*) and 'being for others' (*pour-autrui*). According to Murdoch[25] 'being in itself' implies an unreflective awareness. 'Being for itself' involves reflection and a heightened consciousness of ourselves in the world. 'Being for others' is the least individual mode of being as we operate with allowance for the expectations of others. In existential thinking though we exist primarily: unlike things, we have no underlying 'essence'.

Research grounded in physical science is often focused on identifying the underlying essence of a thing and to bringing it to light. This approach to identifying essential aspects of something has an influence on how research is conducted in other areas, such as human personality, behaviour and interaction. An existentialist approach to relationships challenges this: in fact it takes a diametrically opposite view in that, if an essence of effective relationships exists at all, it comes into being through the relationship itself rather than being seen as pre-existing in some way. Thus the professional brings their core knowledge and skills to the relationship but how that relationship develops is not predetermined by this, there remains a significant element of flexibility and unpredictability. Indeed the professional his/herself might change in some respects as a result of practice – their 'being' may be altered. To identify an individual's essence would

21   Cooper, D. (1999) op. cit.

22   Levy, N. (2001) *Being Up To Date: Foucault, Sartre and Postmodernity*. New York: Peter Lang.

23   Lawler, J. (2005) The essence of leadership? Existentialism and leadership, *Leadership*, 1(2): 215–231.

24   Martinot, S. (2006) *Forms in the Abyss: A Philosophical Bridge between Sartre and Derrida*. Philadelphia, PA: Temple University Press.

25   Murdoch, I. (1999) *Sartre: Romantic Rationalist*. London: Vintage Books, p. 118.

be to limit further development: this essence would restrict development so that the person's being could not alter beyond what it was.[26, 27]

Taking this perspective of identifying essential aspects of particular professions or professional activity is to miss the uniqueness both of each individual and of each individual relationship. This in itself is of prime importance in professional activity. Kierkegaard argues strongly for the uniqueness of each individual:

> (Kierkegaard) held that the most difficult task facing each person is that of becoming an individual. Objective discussion inevitably misses the truth about the individual. To be an individual is to recognise one's own uniqueness, to face the necessity of decision and ultimately to take the 'leap of faith'.[28]

The unique nature of interpersonal relationships in the context of professional work is relatively unacknowledged. 'Clients' take a leap of faith in trusting themselves to the abilities, competences and sensitivities of others in the process. Professionals trust their own abilities (and are trusted by the community more broadly) to apply their knowledge to this new set of circumstances presented by a new unique client. The other aspect of the above quotation which is relevant to note is the individual task of 'becoming'. We argue here that professional development similarly is an uncertain process of becoming which is severely restricted by focusing exclusively on skills and competences. Using competencies alone as a guide to development restricts our reflection on the interpersonal aspects of our work activity. We may reflect on the technical aspects of our work but less on our own situation and the choices which perpetually face us.

Our unreflective selves represent an implicit awareness of ourselves when we are not actively engaged in thinking reflectively. In this mode of being we are more conscious of the world around us and its immediate challenges and demands than we are of our own reflective selves. We may quickly shift to a more reflective consciousness where we consider our own position, perceptions and judgements, perhaps to question their validity or to justify an opinion we are forming. Part of our aims in developing a narrative development process is to change conscious thinking: to bring to consciousness certain elements of ourselves and our professional lives which might not previously have been brought to consciousness.

Todres and Wheeler[29] take an existentialist approach to relationships (in their case within the context of nursing) which highlights the importance of subjective experience and the need to incorporate a reflective, existentialist perspective. We argue similarly that the subjective experience of human relationships needs to be explored and articulated more effectively, the better to understand and develop them. Existentialist thinking argues that 'we live before we know'. An external objective perspective restricts the range of understandings and interpretations of those involved which give particular meaning to experience. Life is lived as a continuous stream of events. Individual events are indeed

---

26   Sartre, J.-P. (1958) *Being and Nothingness*, translated by H. Barnes. London: Methuen.

27   Sartre, J.-P. (2000) *Being and Nothingness*, translated by H. Barnes. London: Penguin Classics.

28   Woodhouse, M. B. (2002) *A Preface to Philosophy*, p. 136. Belmont, CA: Wadsworth/Thomson.

29   Todres, L. and Wheeler, S. (2001) The complementarity of phenomenology, hermeneutics and existentialism as a philosophical perspective for nursing research, *International Journal of Nursing Studies*, 38: 1–8.

important, but overall our lives only make sense when we see events as a whole, in relation to each other: in other words, as a narrative or set of narratives.

Social Constructionist Perspectives

Consideration of the existentialist perspective enables us to explore meanings and choices in relation to work relationships and development. Using this perspective alongside a constructionist approach further enhances our scope to explore some of the influences on the relationships and interrelationships.

There are many strands of inquiry within social constructionist perspectives, ranging from both multi- and interdisciplinary fields of anthropology, cultural studies, history, literary studies and sociology, and it has been identified that no single classification can capture the range of perspectives and theorising within this area of thought.[30, 31] Indeed the same comment is made in relation to existentialist thinking and writing.[32]

Despite the impossibility (and undesirability) of capturing one clear approach to social constructionism, there are nevertheless a number of what could be construed of as underlying assumptions to such approaches. Burr,[33] (drawing on Gergen's writings) proposes four key assumptions that inform social constructionist approaches. The first of these is the adoption of a critical stance in relation to our taken for granted understandings of ourselves and our world, rather than a more objective, fixed and positivist of traditional perspectives. Secondly, there is the importance of recognising the historical and social influences and how they impact on our understanding of our lives. As Burr[34] has argued:

> The particular forms of knowledge that abound in any culture are therefore artefacts of it, and we should not assume that our ways of understanding are necessarily any better (in terms of being near the truth) than other ways.

The third assumption underpinning social constructionist approaches is that our knowledge of the world is the product of ongoing and unique co-constructions through daily interactions between individuals. Finally, she argues that the knowledge imparted through these interactions alters over time so as to create infinite available social constructions.

Adopting a social constructionist perspective encourages an analysis of the ongoing and relational acts between people. In relation to professional development, this reinforces the importance of examining the social and local context in which these professionals are located, and the recognition that individuals co-create their realities and senses of their professional identities. Adopting a social constructionist perspective encourages an analysis of the ongoing and relational acts between people. This adds a subjective

---

30   Burr, V. (1995) *An Introduction to Social Constructionism*. London: Routledge.

31   Gergen, K. (1985) The social constructionist movement in modern psychology, *American Psychologist,* 40: 266–275.

32   Friedman, M. (ed.) (1999) *The Worlds of Existentialism: A Critical Reader*. New York: Humanity Books.

33   Burr, V. (1995) op. cit.

34   Burr, V. (1995) op. cit., p. 4.

counterpoint to the dominant objectivist development discourse: a focus on relations rather than just on skills and knowledge.

In this way, constructionist perspectives challenge traditional accounts of individuals having a core and single sense of who they are. This multiple, polyphonic approach enables recognition of the significance of relational and dialogical understandings. Adopting a social constructionist perspective encourages analysis of ongoing, relational and intersubjective acts between people 'adding a subjective counterpoint to dominant objectivist perspectives'.[35] Professional development approaches based on individual perspectives alone, omit consideration of interactive experiences whereby individuals absorb numerous understandings of themselves through discourses enacted within personal interactions with self and others. Social, local and contextually aware interpretations encourage greater recognition of the construction of meaning in relation to professional development within the specific community that is using the term – at organisational, departmental, team or individual levels.

Viewing professional development as socially constructed enables a consideration of ways in which certain aspects of it are produced and reproduced between the individuals as well as consideration of the hegemonic professional development discourses that dominate organisational life. Such approaches encourage greater attention to features such as the local circumstances, practices, processes, situations, ideas, and so on, that may be creating repressive climates or preventing new and creative practices of development.

Using Both Approaches

Our intention here is not to reconcile existentialist and constructionist thinking but to point out the potential of using them alongside one another – what Klugman[36] refers to as a 'bipolar approach'. Rather than see these approaches as representing different poles, we see the contributions each can make as being different but equally valuable.

Both approaches value the subjective experience but their views of subjectivity vary, as they stem from different views of the self. Thus we are not proposing one interpretation of subjectivity but accepting the value of different subjectivities through which individuals make sense of the world. Klugman[37] provides a useful summary of the different ways in which the self is viewed in each of our chosen approaches:

For constructivism, the self is a construction with local characteristics, rather than an entity with universal features; a function rather than a being. For existentialism, the self is in and of itself a substance, a being, a fundamental given … So on the one hand it is argued that the self is a socially constructed set of contextual functions, attributions and beliefs, while on the other it is held that the self is ultimately a free and given being, an entity in its own right.

---

35   Ford, J. and Harding, N. (2007) Move over management: we are all leaders now?, *Management Learning,*38(5): 475–493.

36   Klugman, D. (1997) Existentialism and constructivism: a bi-polar model of subjectivity, *Clinical Social Work,* 25(3): 297–313.

37   Klugman, D. (1997) op. cit., p. 298.

According to existentialist thinking, the self is a developing 'being' - an entity which is constantly 'becoming' through actions and interactions in the world. This contrasts with the constructionist perspective which views the self as a social construction, or set of constructions which we occupy as we react to and interact with the varied challenges of everyday life.[38] The individual, from the existentialist perspective, is an aware and conscious being, which can experience the moment and which is free to exercise choice over, or to will, whom to become. Thus, the individual being 'participates in the construction of reality'.[39] The individual, in the constructionist view, can reflect on the 'selves' which develop through 'being', manifesting and using individual awareness. For Klugman the constructionist's 'reality does not exist in any ultimate, empirical way, but it is rather a construction of the person who is viewing or experiencing reality at any given moment'.[40] Existentialism thus offers the concept of consciousness of the present and of future intention to act, alongside a constructionist view which emphasises reflection and awareness of past and present influences. Klugman stresses the value of this combination in the context of a psychotherapeutic relationship, particularly that 'experience of personal identity may be fruitfully conceived as a progressive, ongoing dance between existential and constructivist modes'.[41] We believe this 'dance' is equally appropriate in the context of development.

Multiple models of subjectivity which allow (us) to modulate between one conception and another may broaden our ability to make meaning of ... subjective experience and the sense of self and identity that is so closely linked to that experience.[42]

From this, *intersubjectivity* provides the means of understanding the subjective experience of others. As we noted earlier, by intersubjectivity we mean the sharing of our individual subjective impressions, feelings and views. This provides us with a detailed understanding of each others' perspectives and enables us jointly to construct an understanding of the context and our own positions within that.

We suggest that a combination of existential and constructionist thinking allows particular insights into development. It permits a subjective view which in turn encourages a far greater appreciation of the complexities of work and development. In particular it highlights the constructions made both by the individual professional and those with whom they operate. It also highlights conscious choices and intentions and in particular allows the consideration of each individual participant not solely as operators but within their particular social and work contexts. Our intention though is not to critique the current thinking on professional development but to develop a means of introducing these perspectives into the development process. We noted earlier the role of language and dialogue in developing reflective and reflexive creative thinking. Our suggested process is using dialogue to examine work and development in an existentialist and constructivist framework.

---

38   Holstein, J. A. and Gubrium, J. F. (2000) *The Self we Live by: Narrative Identity in a Postmodern World*. New York: Oxford University Press.

39   Yablon, I. (1980) *Existential Psychotherapy*, p. 24, New York: Basic Books; Klugman, D. (1997) op. cit., p. 303.

40   Klugman, D. (1997) op. cit., p. 304.

41   Klugman, D. (1997) op. cit., p. 298.

42   Klugman, D. (1997) op. cit., p. 298.

This next section is intended to outline how a dialogical approach might be used in development. There is a problem for those with a desire to improve practice, of becoming overly critical of traditional methods of development without offering any suggestions about how criticisms of such approaches can be incorporated into practice. Our approach is the encouragement of more critical, reflexive and dialogical relationships that take cognisance of the emotional investment of individuals and their significant others and which encourage a questioning of how individuals make sense of their experiences as they construct their realities.[43, 44, 45, 46] The process detailed here is an attempt to avoid a means of development that offers formulaic and oversimplified notions of what constitutes effective professional work and development. Instead, the process focuses on the meanings we make, with others, on our way through organisational life. To do this, individuals need to be given the opportunity to speak freely, to reveal and examine their own preferred interpretations. These dialogues can thus provide rich sources from which to explore local understandings and local relationships, and how these can be developed in order to promote more inclusive and collegiate work relationships. This whole process is based on a developmental, rather than judgemental model, so that participants in development can increase their knowledge and understanding of how they are perceived by others within their organisations and share their own interpretations and meanings which develop in the organisational context.

A Narrative Approach to Development

The philosophy of the narrative approach that we explore below is that constructionist and existentialist dialogues provide alternative perspectives and different lenses to examine development. Whilst accepting their differences, they each encourage recognition of the centrality of relationships and interrelationship both to our understandings as well as in relation to human well-being.[47] As Ochberg[48] has argued:

Lives, like stories, are the way we fashion ourselves: encountering and temporarily surmounting the projected demons that would diminish us. This is what a narrative perspective allows us to notice: not only about the way we talk, but also about the way we live.

43   Elliot, C. and Reynolds, M. (2002) Manager–educator relations from a critical perspective, *Journal of Management Education*, 26(5): 512–526.

44   Ford, J. and Harding, N. (2007) op. cit.

45   Gray, D. E. (2007) Facilitating management learning: developing critical reflection through reflective tools, *Management Learning*, 38(5): 495–517.

46   Rumens, N. (2005) Extended review: emotion in work organizations, *Management Learning*, 36(1): 117–128.

47   Gergen, M. and Gergen, K. (2003) *Social Construction: A Reader*. London: Sage.

48   Ochberg, R. L. (1994) Life stories and storied lives. In A. Lieblich and R. Josselson (eds) *Exploring Identity and Gender: The Narrative Study of Lives*, p. 143. Thousand Oaks, CA: Sage.

Intersubjective dialogues present the opportunity for reflexivity in development as argued for by a range of writers[49, 50, 51, 52] and provide us with a means of developing our own narrative. To reiterate, it is in this way we distinguish dialogue and narrative: the former is the unrestricted interaction with another individual which enables us, supported by other dialogues, to develop our own individual narrative or narratives. This approach to development gives due emphasis to the importance of dialogue and structured conversations for professionals. There is a need for critical reflection on the roles that these professionals perform, their very 'narratives of the self'[53] that they co-construct with their colleagues and significant others, both in relation to their past achievements and failures as well as present ones and future plans. Encouraging the use of dialogue and narrative to explore professional work and development thus provides the opportunity to go beyond the 'standard accounts' of the profession and to examine the experience of professional relationships. The individuals concerned then have the chance to discuss what their roles mean to them rather than working to preordained definitions. Dialogue presents the opportunity to explore locally constructed and locally interpreted meanings. 'Concepts and things will have the meanings they do only through membership of an immense network which, however many of its elements we care to articulate, will remain as a whole *unsurveyable*.'[54] So engaging in dialogue enables exploration of professional activity in the world not abstracted from its context.

Buber proposes dialogue as the key to creating intersubjective understanding and realising potential. He argues that there are three types of dialogue:

> Genuine dialogue ... where each of the participants really has in mind the other or others in their present and particular being and turns to them with the intention of establishing a living mutual relation between himself and them. There is technical dialogue, which is prompted solely by the need of objective understanding. And there is monologue disguised as dialogue in which two or more men, (sic) meeting in space, speak each within himself in strangely tortuous and circuitous ways and yet imagine they have escaped the torment of being thrown back on their own resources.[55]

Buber talks of seeing 'the other' in different ways. As an *observer* particular characteristics of the other are identified, enabling that person to be categorised in one or several ways. One can argue that this reflects the traditional approach to development where a number of skills or competences are identified and ascribed to an individual. As an *onlooker* the other is viewed in a more rounded, contextualised way. Buber argues that through acting as onlooker a new perspective emerges, when the other 'says something' to a person which cannot be grasped in an objective way. It is in this relationship where meaningful dialogue occurs, when someone becomes 'aware' of the possibilities.

49   Cunliffe, A. (2002) Reflexive dialogical practice in management learning, *Management Learning*, 33(1): 33–61.

50   Gray, D. E. (2007) op. cit.

51   Ramsey, C. (2005) op. cit.

52   Vince, R. and Reynolds, M. (2004) Critical management education and action-based learning: synergies and contradictions, *Academy of Management Learning and Education*, 3/4: 442–458.

53   Ford, J. (2007) Managers' working lives and the interplay of social and family discourse. British Academy of Management Conference, September.

54   Cooper, D. (1999) op. cit., p. 52, italics in original.

55   Buber, M. (2002) *Between Man and Man*, p. 22. London and New York: Routledge. Originally published 1947.

The approaches have in common an emphasis on potential: individual potential and the potential of relationships. As such, they take a different view of potential rather than the more static approach of categorising people according to competences or skills, even ones which are yet to develop. This then forms the basis of the narrative process of development. As we have said previously, by narrative we mean that we develop a narrative or number of narratives or storied accounts of ourselves, our careers, our development as a result of the dialogue(s) we conduct with others. The dialogue gives us more than the opportunity to gather new information but through our interaction to develop our being – to *become*. This approach encourages much deeper exploration of professional and other potential. A key dynamic in this process is consideration of the centrality of a reflective and reflexive process. This goes beyond the reflective practitioner approach advocated by Schön and others[56, 57] and invites individuals to make connections and test understanding through seeking patterns, logic and order in our experiences. Our belief is that the active pursuit of reflexive and dialogical space encourages individuals to increase their awareness of how they constitute, maintain and thereby retain some control over their realities and sense of who they are and how they account for their experiences and professional development. We aim to encourage professionals to adopt a critical self-reflexive approach, drawing predominantly on Cunliffe's[58] two themes of problematising the nature of language and questions of reflexivity, as cited above, but also influenced by a number of writers within the field of critical reflexivity.[59, 60, 61, 62, 63] We therefore encourage professionals to adopt both a *reflective* approach (using expert knowledge and practical theory) and a *reflexive* approach (recognising the assumptions made and how these impact on our constructions of reality). In doing this, we recognise the notion of reflexivity as intersubjective reflection,[64] as being an important feature in our approach to development, wherein the individual explores the mutual meanings emerging in working relationships. Gray[65] similarly argues the importance of reflection and reflexivity as a tool both in learning and in developing a consciousness for action – for change – in organisations. The process we advocate goes beyond reflection and towards the pursuit of a 'radical self-reflected consciousness'[66] in which the self-in-relation-to-others becomes both the aim and object of focus. This process is explored in more detail below.

---

56   Schön, D. A. (1983) *The Reflective Practitioner: How Professionals Think in Action*. New York: Basic Books.

57   Ghaye, T. and Lillyman, S. (1996) *Learning Journals and Critical Incidents: Reflective Practice for Healthcare Professionals*. London: Mark Allen.

58   Cunliffe, A. (2002) Social poetics as management inquiry, *Journal of Management Inquiry*, 11(2): 128–146.

59   Hardy, C. Phillips, N. and Clegg, S. (2001) Reflexivity in organisation and management theory: a study of the production of the research subject, *Human Relations*, 54(5): 531–560.

60   Perriton, L. (2000) A reflection of what exactly? A provocation regarding the use of critical reflection in critical management education. Paper presented at the second Connecting Learning and Critique Conference, Lancaster University, July.

61   Reynolds, M. (1997) Towards a critical management pedagogy. In J. Burgoyne and M. Reynolds (eds) *Management Learning: Integrating Perspectives in Theory and Practice*, pp. 312–328. London: Sage.

62   Reynolds, M. (1999) Critical reflection and management education: rehabilitating less hierarchical approaches, *Journal of Management Education*, 23(5): 537–553.

63   Watson, T. (1994) *In Search of Management*. London: Routledge.

64   Finlay, C. (2002) Negotiating the swamp: the opportunity and challenge of reflexivity in research practice, *Qualitative Research*, 2(2): 209–230.

65   Gray, D. E. (2007) op. cit.

66   Sartre cited in Finlay, C. (2002) op. cit., p. 216.

A Practical Process for Development

This section details the practicalities of using this approach. This process involves highly individualised discussions and a personal review that complement other development processes. Our process emphasises dialogue between professionals and peers and it is through this dialogue that we form narratives about ourselves. The practical application of this approach requires a framework to initiate dialogue between the individual and a number of 'significant others'. The individual is then asked to reflect on these dialogues, summarise their main interpretations and identify the implications for their own practice and development. To do this, we advocate an approach which starts with events that assist individuals to focus on the meaning of their work and role; to co-construct its practice in organisations; to have due regard to the significance of the interrelations; and to be sensitive to individuals' values. In doing this, we attempt to avoid a rigid definition either of their own role or of development. Instead, we pay attention to the constructed (and co-constructed) meanings and experiences by which we make our way as individuals through organisational life. To that end, individuals needs to be given the opportunity to speak freely, thus revealing preferred constructions. These dialogues can thus provide rich sources from which to explore the local understanding of professional practice. Such methods of inquiry or analysis enable people to place themselves at the interface between persons, stories and organisations, and to place themselves within a particular emotional and organisational context. Dialogue is used to elicit richer and unique insights into how professional practice and development are co-constructed between the individual and their peers, staff and direct manager.

Taking development as a social process implies that meaning is made through the individual's network of relations. So significant others in these relationships need to be identified, to explore individual meaning. These other significant people who will contribute to this narrative, are those chosen by the individual his/herself. Language is the means we use to communicate and to construct meaning, so we need to encourage our peers, staff and those to whom we report to tell us stories, to converse with us about our development in meaningful ways.

Our process for development is divided broadly into four main phases: preparatory; writing reflection notes; providing a narrative summary; discussions in a development workshop.

Stage One: The Preparatory Phase

In the preparatory phase participants initially decide who they would like to include in the process and then they conduct individual, preparatory discussions with these people. Ideally this would include two or three peers, two or three members of their staff and their current boss. A range of people is recommended, each of whom know the participant reasonably well and are likely to engage in constructive dialogue. The main aim of this discussion is to generate a conversation that explores perceptions about the individual as a professional at the centre of this development. The aim is that through each discussion, participants gain a greater appreciation of themselves and their personal development within their organisational contexts.

So as to look beyond the immediate circumstances faced in the organisation, we encourage the discussion to be explored in three elements: the *past*, the *present* and the *future*. We do not suggest that a rigid set of questions is followed in the form of a questionnaire, but that questions are used as prompts for the development of a genuine dialogue and the eliciting of storied accounts. By way of illustration, we have used the prompts in Table 28.1 as part of a developing leaders programme:

This aim of this framework is to provide an initial structure to the conversation. It is not intended to constrain dialogue to these questions alone, but to provide an opening for further discussion and exploration. Participants are encouraged to probe further during the course of the discussion to elicit specific behaviours and/or examples as appropriate. Thus it is envisaged that a dialogue will develop organically as it were, rather than the mechanistic administration of a structured set of questions.

Table 28.1   A framework for the discussion

The past	How long has the individual worked with this person and in what context(s)? How would the other person describe the mutual work relationship? How have the work relationship and the relevant work roles developed? Other questions may be considered which help develop the dialogue and encourage participants to consider the factors which have influenced work and work relationships and those aspects of the individual (knowledge, behaviour, skills, interests, and so on) which are valued by others.
The present	How the current context is affecting how the individual is perceived in their professional role? How the current context influences what participants need to do and how I do it? What particular opportunities the current context might present?
The future	Where might the individual's particular professional qualities best be applied? (For example: in terms of service delivery; relations with staff and colleagues; and impact on the organisation more broadly.) Where can they focus their development for greatest benefit?

Stage Two: Reflective Notes

The second stage involves participants writing reflective notes from each of their conversations (after each meeting, rather than waiting until they are all complete). In this way each participant has a set of notes where the issues which emerged from each discussion can be considered separately. On completion of the structured conversations, and consideration of the reflection notes, participants are then able to prepare a summary document as the third stage in the process.

Stage Three: The Narrative Summary

The purpose of the narrative summary is to capture aspects of the developing narrative: it is not intended as providing a fixed or static point of assessment. The summary is based on questions such as those below, for discussion and further exploration at the fourth stage, the development workshop.

Key questions might include:

- What are the significant moments and/or main themes from these dialogues?
- What are the (say) four key messages/issues for the individual's development?
- In what ways has an understanding of the perception of others changed?
- What are the priority issues for the individual to take from this to explore further during the development workshop?

Stage Four: Development Workshop

The development workshop typically takes the format of a one-day programme of activities designed to introduce the participants to reflexive and dialogical approaches to development. This provides a framework for them to consider further the feedback they have received and to discuss this in small groups of three of four. The results of these discussions are first, that participants clearly identify the key issues raised by the feedback; and secondly, that they consider incorporating their own response to these issues into their own personal development plans. Typically, participants prepare a short presentation and work in small groups, making their presentations to each other and discussing the implications of their reflections for their further development.

Feedback from some of the leadership development workshops that we have facilitated indicates that participants find the storied nature of the workshop sessions of considerable benefit in generating new insights into shared and intersubjective understandings of their role as leaders and participants in the leadership process. This has led to participants generating a range of creative plans for their personal development but, as importantly, has established an enhanced dialogue with a range of colleagues. In this way development, and in this example leadership development, can be viewed as continuous and integrated activity, not sectioned off into a formalised process, separated from the everyday work environment.

Conclusion

We feel it is particularly valuable for us to become aware of the various discourses and subject positions that constitute our subjectivity. Using the two different perspectives discussed in this chapter promotes such an awareness. We recognise that in terms of the hierarchies of power and status, some people are bestowed greater formal degrees of influence than others and it is these individuals with greater power and status who may, consciously or otherwise, impress their meaning and 'sense-making' of situations on others. Furthermore, these perspectives needs to take account of the values held by individuals and needs to recognise that there is no value-neutrality. So, a development programme should make explicit the values that it is attempting to reproduce and reinforce within its process. Using this narrative approach, professional development is thus viewed as an 'intersubjective' phenomenon, that is, it is a process which participants themselves define together. The process enables new insights into individual learning and development and, as importantly, promotes the development of new professional relationships as a result.

29 Public Sector Leadership and Management Development

JEAN HARTLEY

Introduction

There is an interesting paradox about leadership and management development (LMD) in the public sector. It is a large sector of the economy and society and also contributes in myriad ways to a nation's competitiveness and well-being – yet it is also a neglected sector in terms of leadership and management development, both in terms of expenditure and also in terms of attention from academics. This chapter will explore the opportunities for conceptual development and practices in this field. This is of interest not only to those practitioners who work inside the public sector, but also for those who provide contracted services for the public sector or whose organizations work in partnership with public sector bodies. There are also wider implications for LMD across all sectors.

The Public Sector as Big Business

Hartley and Skelcher[1] note that, globally, public services have emerged from a period of considerable criticism and devaluing. This period of challenge to public services and the role of government generally was generated by the rise of neoliberal ideologies in the 1980s and 1990s. These ideologies promoted 'free' market solutions at the expense of state provision and so this period witnessed substantial privatization and disinvestments in public services. Now, in the early years of the twenty-first century, a new settlement between state and society has emerged. This more refined version of neoliberalism recognizes the role of government and public services in creating stable social and economic conditions, but in a new coalition with business and civil society actors. In addition, the 'credit crunch' in Western societies has shown very vividly the limitations of an unfettered market approach. It is the public sector which has stepped in to try to sort out market turmoil through nationalizing banks and other institutions, through regulatory activities and through fiscal adjustments. Some commentators are

---

1   Hartley, J. and Skelcher, C. (2008) The agenda for public service improvement. In Hartley, J., Donaldson, C., Skelcher, C. and Wallace, M. (eds) *Managing to Improve Public Services*, pp. 1–21. Cambridge: Cambridge University Press.

now suggesting that the new settlement between state and market will be reinforced as a result of the financial crisis of 2008.[2]

Public services are important in a number of ways. First, they matter because of their scale. Public services consume a major part of gross domestic product (GDP). Jackson,[3] using OECD data, notes that the ratio of government spending to GDP across the Organization for Economic Cooperation and Development (OECD) countries in 2000 was 37 per cent, just over a third of GDP. In recent years there has been a substantial increase in UK public expenditure, particularly for health and school education services, reaching 43.4 per cent in April 2008.[4]

Public services are therefore big business when it comes to expenditure. They are also substantial in terms of employment, organization size, investment and the production of goods and services. For example, over 5.8 million employees, or 20.2 per cent of total employment in the UK, worked in some part of the public sector in 2006. Of these, 2.9 million worked in local government.[5] The National Health Service is also a substantial employer, with over 1 million employees across the UK. While the civil service was 'downsized' in the early 1980s, there still remain 558,000 direct employees.[6] The criminal justice system, the armed services and other parts of the public service also employ substantial numbers.

This analysis of employment is based on direct employees. However, it is also necessary to include the workforce providing public services in contracted-out services, such as some street-cleaning and prisons; in privatized services such as water, electricity and railways and in hybrid organizations which are a mixture of public and private services, such as universities and some museums and art galleries. Ferlie et al.[7] and Benington,[8] amongst others, have pointed to the increasing interrelationships between the public, private and voluntary sectors in the design and provision of public services. Public sector and public services are no longer co-terminous.

Public services are critical to the competitiveness of a nation. The welfare state is an important part of the public services; but so too is the role they play in building the conditions and infrastructure for an entrepreneurial and prosperous private sector, and for the integrity of the nation state. At a local level, public sector organizations (such as the health service and the local authority) may be the largest employers and have a significant impact on the local economy and on regeneration.[9] On a larger, national scale, governments provide 'positive freedom goods' such as education, health, pensions and unemployment benefits which enable a country to develop economically.[10] Governments

---

2   Marquand, D. (2008) Situation vacant: a theorist is sought to succeed Mr Keynes, *The Guardian*, 11 October.

3   Jackson, P. (2003) The size and scope of the public sector: an international comparison. In Bovaird, T. and Löffler, E. (eds) *Public Management and Governance*, pp. 25–39. London: Routledge.

4   Office of National Statistics (2008) http://www.statistics.gov.uk/cci/nugget.asp?id=206.

5   National Statistics (2006) www.statistics.gov.uk/pdfdir/pse1206.pdf, accessed February 2007.

6   Ibid.

7   Ferlie, E., Hartley, J. and Martin, S. (2003) Changing public service organizations: current perspectives and future prospects, *British Journal of Management*, 14: S1–S14.

8   Benington, J. (2000) The modernization and improvement of government and public services, *Public Money and Management*, 20(2): 3–8.

9   Geddes, M. (2001) What about the workers? Best value, employment and work in local public services, *Policy and Politics*, 29: 497–508.

10   Jackson op. cit.

also provide other infrastructure to support manufacturing and commercial development such as roads and transport, business development, labour market training, trading regulations and inspections and so forth. It is not surprising that global institutions such as the World Bank and the United Nations Development Programme see 'good governance' as central to effective economic and social progress in developing countries.[11] Marquand[12] also notes the crucial role of the public sphere in producing collective rules by which a society agrees to be governed (including the rules that govern markets, trading and aspects of international relations).

But the Dearth of Literature on Public Services LMD (Until Recently)

Despite the size and role of the public sector, it has been underrepresented – or even misrepresented – in the leadership literature until recently. Look in any major book or review of leadership and it is unlikely that 'public' will be in the index or that the public context of some leadership is theorized.[13]

Of course, much of the early work on leadership was undertaken with the armed services (army, air force and navy) in both the UK and USA, but this was not theorized in terms of the public sector context of the military. Another example is the emphasis on 'great leaders' such as Winston Churchill, Margaret Thatcher or Nelson Mandela, all of whom exercised a particular form of public leadership known as political leadership. Yet the political, policy and public context of their work is rarely acknowledged or the institutional channels for their relationship with their followers analysed. A third example comes from the work of Burns[14] who coined the terms 'transformational' and 'transactional' leadership in relation to politicians, but whose work was stripped of its context (and often origins) as it was relocated to the sphere of (private sector) business. These examples show that public leadership is present throughout the leadership literature but has not been theorized as such and there has been relatively little interest in how the institutional context has an impact on the constraints and opportunities of leadership – with implications for LMD.

For their part, public sector academics have been slow to theorize leadership (as opposed to administration or management) although this is now changing,[15] with an explosion of interest in leadership in the public sector and a huge hike in the provision of leadership development over the last decade. However, until recently, in the field of

---

11   United Nations Development Programme (UNDP) (2002) *Deepening Democracy in a Fragmented World*. New York: Oxford University Press.

12   Marquand, D. (2004) *Decline of the Public*. Oxford: Polity.

13   See, for example Avolio, B. (1999) *Full Leadership Development*, Thousand Oaks, CA: Sage; Yukl, G. (2006) *Leadership in Organizations*, 6th edn, Upper Saddle River NJ: Pearson Prentice Hall; Parry, K. and Bryman, A. (2006) Leadership in organizations, in Clegg, S. Hardy, C., Lawrence, T. and Nord, W. (eds) *The Sage Handbook of Organization Studies*, London: Sage.

14   Burns, J. M. (1978) *Transformational Leadership*. New York: Harper and Row.

15   Terry, L. (1998) Administrative leadership, neo-managerialism and the public management movement, *Public Administration Review*, 58(3): 194–200; Van Wart, M. (2003) Public sector leadership theory: an assessment, *Public Administration Review*, 63(2): 214–228; Denis, J.-L., Langley, A. and Rouleau, L. (2005) *Oxford Handbook of Public Management*, Hartley, J. and Allison, M. (2000) The role of leadership in modernization and improvement of public services, *Public Money and Management*, April: 35–40.

public administration, the traditional political science view that politicians (national and local) make policy and managers (civil servants and local government officers) execute policy left little room for leadership. For politicians, leadership and leadership development were not countenanced because they saw themselves as mandated by their political party, their election manifesto and the electorate so that leadership and particularly leadership development were irrelevant (that is now changing as the chapter will explore). At the same time, public managers, working within the organizational form of large bureaucracies, acted either as clerks (impassive officials implementing political will) or martyrs (holding private views about the wisdom or necessity of action but continuing to implement political decisions without comment).[16] Thus, leadership was not much discussed in relation either to politicians or to managers.

More recently, there has been a greater interest in 'entrepreneurial government' which includes a role for leadership. Initially, this came about initially under the rubric of 'new public management'[17] which articulated a role for managerial leadership, though interestingly it continued to fail to articulate a role of leadership by politicians. The emphasis in managerial (but not political) leadership was based on the importing of private sector management practices and ideologies into the public sector.[18] The worldwide interest in public sector reform[19] was accompanied by a language more receptive to the idea of leadership.

The interest in leadership was given a further boost by the recognition of an approach to public policy and public management which went beyond 'new public management' and focused on the more recent paradigm shift to 'networked governance'.[20] In a networked governance approach, it is widely recognized that public sector renewal has resulted in a weakening of the hierarchically organized state in favour of more differentiated partnership arrangements that cut across the boundaries of public, private and third sectors as well as across different levels of government. This means that political leadership, managerial leadership and civic leadership may all have a place (or a voice) in how democracy is conducted and public services created and produced (or co-produced). There are, of course, some countervailing tendencies. The new dynamic image of public leadership and the apparently enlarged opportunities for managerial discretion seem to be counterbalanced by a strengthening of central interventions and control, and explicit and rigorous standards and performance regimes. Managing the tensions and paradoxes of these governance regimes has become the order of the day for politicians and public managers, strengthening the need for leadership.[21]

16   Moore, M. H. (1995) *Creating Public Value*. Cambridge, MA: Harvard University Press.

17   Hood, C. (1991) A public management for all seasons. *Public Administration*, 69(1): 3–19.

18   Ibid.

19   Pollitt, C. and Bouckaert, G. (2004) *Public Management Reform: A Comparative Analysis*. Oxford: Oxford University Press.

20   Benington, J. (2000) op.cit; Stoker, G. (2006) Public value management: A new narrative for networked governance? *American Review of Public Administration*, 36(1): 41–57.

21   Pedersen, D. and Hartley, J. (2008) The changing context of public leadership and management: implications for roles and dynamics, *International Journal of Public Sector Management*, 21(4): 327–339.

The Leadership Development Signals in the Public Sector

Leadership was signalled as central and critical to the reform of public services in the UK with the policy document from the Cabinet Office's Performance and Innovation Unit entitled 'Strengthening leadership in the public sector'[22] symbolizing a surge of interest in leadership at the beginning of the millenium. The document noted, amongst other things, that the public sector was not attracting or keeping the best leaders and that there was an increasing need for leadership across organizational boundaries (to reflect the concern of central government to be more 'joined up' and to support partnership working at local and regional levels). Other policy papers, such as white papers and discussion documents highlighted leadership in titles and in text. There was no escape from the prevalence of leadership in public service reform under the Labour Government from 1997 onwards.

The PIU report also noted the need for more intense development of leaders and potential leaders, including those capable of operating in a partnership or joined-up government world. Leadership development became much more prominent in the field. In England and Wales, new leadership development institutions were either set up for the first time, such as the National College of School Leadership or the National Health Service Leadership Centre (later incorporated into the NHS Institute for Innovation and Improvement); or were substantially revamped to reflect a clearer leadership focus, such as the National School of Government and Centrex, the national police leadership college (later becoming the National Policing Improvement Agency). For the first time, there were 11 major national leadership colleges or virtual colleges covering all major parts of the public sector, and linking up with each other to 'share good practice'. These are shown in Table 29.1. In Scotland and Northern Ireland, there are counterpart leadership development bodies, though not on the same scale, and Wales aims to create some degree of integration across the public sector with Public Sector Management Wales (PSMW) while also participating in many of the English leadership development bodies (in part because England and Wales tend to come under similar legislation and legal frameworks).

These leadership development bodies vary in how much they are involved in operational training (e.g. managing critical fire and rescue incidents at the Fire Service College; developing clear knowledge of parliamentary procedures in the National School of Government) but all have substantial sections of their staff and budgets devoted to leadership development (out of the estimated £130 million or so spent on learning and development across the public sector). Several of these bodies developed their own models of leadership, such as the Aspire leadership model in the Fire Service (for aspiring chief officers) or the Leadership Qualities Framework of the NHS.

There are varied views about whether 'management' and 'leadership' are different or not. For example, Kotter[23] argues that organizations need both leadership and management but that they are different: leadership is concerned with setting a direction for change, developing a vision for the future, while management consists of implementing those goals through planning, budgeting, staffing and so on. Kotter comments that most organizations are over-managed and under-led. However, there is an alternative view which is also strongly held. Mintzberg[24] described leadership as a key managerial role

---

22   Performance and Innovation Unit (2000) *Leadership in Delivering Better Public Services*. London: Cabinet Office.

23   Kotter, J. (1990) *What Leaders Really Do*. Boston, MA: Harvard Business School Press.

24   Mintzberg, H. (1973) *The Nature of Managerial Work*. New York: Harper and Row.

Table 29.1   Members of Public Service Leadership: National leadership bodies in England (2009)

Leadership development institution	Area of public sector
Defence Leadership and Management Centre, Defence Academy	Armed forces
Fire Service College	Fire and rescue service
Improvement and Development Agency for Local Government	Local government
Leadership Centre for Local Government	Local government
Leadership Foundation for Higher Education	Universities
Learning and Skills Improvement Service	Further education
National College for School Leadership	Primary and secondary education
National Health Service (NHS) Institute for Innovation and Improvement	Health
National Policing Improvement Agency	Police
National School of Government	Civil service

and Yukl[25] argues that defining leadership and management as distinct roles, processes or relationships may obscure more than it reveals: 'Most scholars seem to agree that success as a manager or an administrator in modern organizations necessarily involves leading'.[26] Glatter[27] argues that there is a danger for public leadership development if the focus is solely on leadership without the technical skills required for management.

In addition, in relation to the public sector it is clear that managers are not the only kinds of leaders in any case. The existence of formally elected leaders or politicians is important to recognize, as is the existence of community or civic leaders, who may hold formal leadership roles in society or who may assume informal leadership roles (e.g. in social movements and local activism). So managers are potentially leaders but they are not the only ones. Behn[28] argues that it is essential that public managers exercise leadership if they are to work on implementing policies (which are necessarily incomplete) and with communities as well as organizations, which themselves exert leadership.

The Distinctive Context of the Public Sector

A 'convergence' view of the public and private sectors makes the implementation of management ideas and practices as straightforward (or as problematic) as the use of management ideas and practices in the private sector, and universalizes the provision

---

25   Yukl op. cit.

26   Yukl op. cit., pp. 6–7.

27   Glatter, R. (2008) *Of Leadership, Management and Wisdom. A Brief Synthesis of Selected Reports and Documents on Leadership Development. Report.* Nottingham: National College for School Leadership.

28   Behn, R. (1998) What right do public managers have to lead?, *Public Administration Review,* 58(3): 209–224.

of leadership development. But this convergence view is increasingly out of kilter with the prevailing approach in the UK, many European countries and around the world. The management of public services is recognized as distinct because it must operate in a complex political environment, with due regard to questions of legitimacy, accountability and social outcomes. We now explore these issues in more detail, exploring the implications for leadership development. As the boundaries between the public, private and not-for-profit organizations become increasingly permeable,[29] there will be new kinds of interchange and adaptations between leadership in the various sectors.

Leadership Development for Understanding and Shaping Context

It is generally agreed that a key prerequisite of effective leadership is the need to understand the context in which it is being exercised. Theorists have looked at this from a number of perspectives, exploring both the influence of contextual factors on leadership and the influence of leadership in shaping context. However, there is much less work than might be expected on this crucial set of interactions between leadership and context. Porter and McLaughlin[30] review the theoretical and empirical knowledge about the organizational context and leadership (across all types of organization) and conclude that while leadership context is much discussed in fact there is little research. Grint[31] classifies theories about leadership according to the degree to which they pay attention to, or ignore, context, as an aspect of leadership.

An important element of context for public service organizations is that they do not choose their 'markets', but are required, usually by legislation, to provide services to anyone meeting the eligibility criteria (e.g. anyone living in a particular defined administrative area, or anyone with particular needs). This contrasts with the market-led approach of private sector organizations, which can choose, seek or create their own markets and are free to exit from that market at any time.

Public organizations also operate in arenas of 'market failure' or where the market is thought to be unlikely to operate effectively in the short or longer-term. Climate change, terrorism and the ageing of the population are examples of such complex and cross-cutting challenges, where government is often expected to play a lead role. Of course, there may be a role for private organizations in addressing part of the challenge, often in partnership with public organizations. The leadership challenge for both political and managerial leadership may then be to orchestrate the response across a range of stakeholders.

The role, or sometimes duty, of public service organizations to address broad social and economic questions means that:

> there are more stakeholders with a greater variety of interests, and the stakeholders are more present. The boundaries between organizations and the external environment are more permeable

---

29   Ferlie et al, op. cit..

30   Porter, L. and McLaughlin, G. (2006) Leadership and the organizational context: like the weather?, *Leadership Quarterly,* 17(6): 559–576.

31   Grint, K. (2000) *The Arts of Leadership.* Oxford: Oxford University Press.

... Public management is at least as much about managing the external environment as about managing the internal organization.[32]

The need to pay considerable attention to the external environment has substantial implications for leadership development. It means that formal programmes often need to pay considerable attention to policy analysis and policy evidence, not only in relation to the specific area of service provision but also in relation to the evidence available about changes in the economy and society more generally. A key skill, therefore, for a public sector leader is to be able to 'read the context' in which leadership actions and decisions have to take place and to be able to sense and interpret trends and changes in the political, economic, social and environmental context of governance and service provision. Many public sector leaders gain considerable skill in interpreting the environment in relation to their own specific service area (sometimes called a silo), but many appear to be less skilled at understanding and interpreting the wider environment within which their own service is located. Is there sufficient provision for developing the skills of strategic scanning, planning and action across the public sector? The existence of the separate leadership development bodies would seem to make this more difficult. While some of the colleges welcome and engage with managers from across the public sector and outside (e.g. the National School of Government runs some leadership courses with participants from central government and local government, and sometimes with the private sector), the main work of the colleges is with leaders from their own service. There is scope for more cross-sector leadership development which would have substantial advantages in terms of helping to understand and interpret the external environment.[33] Currently, the main location where analysis of the external environment with leadership development across sectors is in university degree and diploma courses.

In terms of informal or emergent leadership development, which can come through job experience, on-the-job mentoring, secondments and so forth, the emphasis on leadership development across the whole of the public service has been limited over the last 20 years or so, but is starting to be recognized as an important avenue to wider understanding of the external environment, although there is still some distance to travel. This is evident in two ways.

First, there is a greater emphasis on having wider leadership experience as part of career progression to the higher echelons of public leadership. For example, the Cabinet Secretary, Gus O'Donnell, has been quoted on a number of occasions as saying that to be a senior leader 'you have to get out to get on', meaning gain experience of management and leadership outside the civil service. Increasingly, senior leaders are likely to have had leadership experience in more than one sector, for example, the voluntary sector, local as well as central government, the private sector and so forth. This is now seen as career-enhancing rather than career-limiting, as it was in the past.

Second, there is a greater interest in and valuing of knowledge which is learnt in the field, not just from books and policy papers. There is a recognition that tacit knowledge (hard to articulate or explain to others) as well as explicit knowledge is important in

---

32   Feldman, M. (2005) Management and public management, *Academy of Management Journal*, 48(6): 958–960, quotation on p. 959.

33   Benington J and Hartley J (2009) *Whole Systems Go! Improving Leadership across the Whole Public Service System*. Ascot: National School of Government.

leadership. Leadership includes the 'practical wisdom' or judgement which comes from looking at actions and decisions in context not solely from theory. So, the social exclusion policy staff who visit a run-down housing estate in east London, or the health service manager who visits a prison learn from such experiences to take wider account of the environment and how it might affect their own service. It is not clear how far the leadership development bodies take such forms of peripatetic learning seriously beyond the occasional 'organizational raid'. Yet research suggests that this can be a powerful form of learning about leadership.[34]

Leadership Development for Complex Problems

There is increasing recognition that many of the issues which societies and governments are having to address are 'wicked' as opposed to 'tame' problems. Wicked problems are not exclusive to the public sector, but there are a substantial number which the public expect governments and public services to try to address.

Tame problems are ones which have been encountered before, for which known solutions already exist and which can be addressed by a particular unit, profession or service. Tame problems may be complicated but they are resolvable through existing practices and organizational arrangements. Wicked, or cross-cutting, problems have no definitive formulation (different people may formulate the problem differently), are incomplete and have changing requirements. Solving a wicked problem may throw up other problems because the problems are interrelated. Often, large groups of people have to contribute to solving the problem, through changing their behaviours. An example of a tame (though complicated) problem is surgery. An example of a wicked problem is tackling the health issues of childhood obesity. Grint[35] introduces a third type of problem – a critical problem where immediate and urgent action is needed (e.g. dealing with major road traffic injuries in the accident and emergency department; or stabilizing and then controlling a major fire). These are different types of problems, which are likely to require different types of leadership (see Table 29.2).

If these are different types of leadership, then they may require different types of leadership development. For example, the leadership development bodies are well-equipped to address the technical or tame problems, as they have the knowledge, the expertise and the accumulated history, culture and wisdom to address these (there may be room for improvement, but the overall parameters of the problems are broadly known).

The work of Heifetz[36] has become particularly relevant in the UK for thinking about the leadership of complex and difficult problems, where either the outcomes or the means are not clear or are not agreed upon. Adaptive problems require a type of leadership 'which rejects the pressure from followers to provide magical solutions to complex problems, and instead works with stakeholders to take responsibility for grappling with

34   Hartley, J. and Rashman, L. (2007) How is knowledge transferred between organizations involved in change? In Wallace, M., Fertig, M. and Schneller, E. (eds) *Managing Change in the Public Services*, pp. 173–192. Oxford: Blackwell.

35   Grint, K. (2005) Problems, problems, problems: the social construction of 'leadership', *Human Relations*, 58: 1467–1494.

36   Heifetz, R. (1994) *Leadership Without Easy Answers* Cambridge, MA: Belknapp Press.

Table 29.2 Tame, wicked and critical problems

Type or problem	Form of authority
Tame problems: Complicated but resolvable Likely to have occurred before Limited degree of uncertainty	*Manager*: Manager's role to provide the appropriate processes to solve the problem
Wicked problems: Complex and often intractable Novel with no apparent solution Often generates more problems No right or wrong answer just better or worse alternatives High level of uncertainty	*Leader*: Leader's role is to ask the right questions rather than provide the right answers (as answers may not be self-evident) and to require collaborative process
Critical problems: A crisis situation Urgent response needed with little time for decision-making and action Uncertainty managed through clear decisions	*Commander*: Commander's role to provide a decisive answer to the problem

these problems and for the changes in one's own thinking and behaviour required'.[37] It is the type of leadership which asks questions rather than immediately proposes solutions, because one of the tasks is to get people to recognize that they may be contributing to the problem and that therefore addressing the problem requires changing thinking and behaviour (including one's own) in order to grapple with the difficult issues.

The concept of adaptive challenges – or wicked problems – is widely talked about in public policy circles but leadership development approaches have only recently taken on board the ideas about adaptive leadership as a way to tackle these. For example, if the issues are complex and cross-cutting then it makes sense to develop leaders in programmes and situations where leaders from different services learn and develop alongside each other. Yet although partnership working is increasingly embedded in public service working, this has not affected leadership development to a similar extent. Much of the leadership development still takes place in the service silos and colleges rather than between those leaders who need to work together to explore and address the problem. In addition, wicked issues, requiring adaptive leadership, often requires working with and in communities, voluntary and community sector groups, informal and formal civic leaders and so on. This is complex territory to navigate, and helping leaders to develop the emotional and political skills as well as rational skills to address these issues is important.

Leadership development for critical incidents is now fairly well-established. It has become better resourced, in the wake of the 9/11 terrorist bombings in the USA, and there is regular cross-service simulation training and critical incident events for the 'blue light' services (police, fire and rescue and ambulance) along with the emergency planning service of the local authority. They are able to use sophisticated virtual simulations, as well as complex and varied physical 'rigs' to practise not only the operational techniques on the ground, but also the strategic challenges of 'gold command' leadership concerned with communicating to and creating meaning for local communities, the media, the nation and central government.

---

37   Benington, J. and Turbitt, I. (2007) Adaptive leadership and the policing of Drumcree demonstrations in Northern Ireland, *Leadership*, 3(4): 371–395.

Leadership Development to Deal with Diverse Interests and the Contested Public Domain

The private sector is used to thinking about its markets in terms of 'customers' but this is insufficiently complex for public service organizations. While the concept of customer, familiar in new public management, has been important in improving the quality of services to the public, it is not enough because there is a range of stakeholders who hold views about, and have legitimate interests in, the work of public service organizations. The recipients of services may not only be customers (e.g. users of services), some are likely to be taxpayers. They are also citizens, in a democratic society, able to exercise their rights to vote and debate and try to influence the priorities of the local and central governments that they have elected. Public organizations may have to provide not only services but also remind people of duties as unwilling 'customers', because they can use state authority to require citizens to submit to obligations, such as criminal prosecutions, planning regulations or environmental health, using the law or state authority to achieve outcomes for the public good.

Public services are under the formal control of politicians (either directly in the case of national or local government, or more indirectly in the case of health organizations and some other public services). Politicians themselves are elected representatives of wider constituencies and stakeholders, with a democratic mandate to represent the whole, which includes future generations as well as the current voters. The fact that services are funded primarily through the public purse means that there is the potential for a high level of debate, accountability and scrutiny – not to mention contested values and priorities – which may all affect the management of public organizations. Hoggett[38] notes that goals in the public domain are inevitably ambiguous and contested because of the different values, interests and priorities which exist amongst 'the public'.

Leadership development is still a fairly new idea for political leaders and there are relatively few formal courses to help them develop their leadership skills. Many report learning through sometimes bitter experience and in the past, a number of national politicians have reported going straight from being backbenchers to a minister with only a red box thrust into their hands. Leading edge practice started with some local authorities, which have analysed, articulated and developed the leadership skills of local politicians in the mid 1990s. In the year 2000, the nationally funded Leadership Academy was established by the Improvement and Development Agency and has now provided leadership development for local politicians in England and Wales through three two-day modules for elected members on personal, political and community leadership. Scotland has set up a similar scheme. Over 1500 elected members have now taken this programme in England and Wales. While this is a relatively small offering in the context of the 22,000 local politicians, the Leadership Academy has been crucial in raising both the profile and the acceptability of leadership development for politicians. There is also a developing appetite for leadership development at the UK level amongst Westminster politicians and increasingly provision is made both for individual ministers (of all ranks) through the ministerial team at the National School of Government.

---

38 Hoggett, P. (2006) Conflict, ambivalence and the contested purpose of public organizations, *Human Relations*, 59(2): 175–194.

It is too soon to evaluate provision or impact across both local and national politicians, but analysis of the skills of the first 201 local politicians who completed the Leadership Academy suggested that leadership development are at least partly learnt (nurture rather than nature). The study,[39] based on work using the Warwick Political Leadership Questionnaire for politicians, found that more senior local politicians self-reported a higher level of skill on four key dimensions of leadership. These were:

1. Personal effectiveness: self-awareness, ability to work with and understand other people, and to handle difficult relationships
2. Strategic direction: the ability to be strategic and take an overview
3. Political intelligence: the ability to understand and work effectively with the political currents and dynamics, both within and across political parties
4. Organizational mobilization: the ability to mobilize others in and across organizations to bring about substantial organizational and cultural change in the local authority.

There are three possible interpretations of these findings. The first might be that senior politicians are more lenient in their ratings of themselves compared with those local politicians not in major leadership positions. However, the Warwick Political Leadership Questionnaire has ten dimensions of skill and this effect was not found in the other six dimensions. The second possibility is that that 'born leaders', or at least those with particular leadership skills, have come to take up more senior leadership positions on the council. However, the results in relation to demographic variables, leadership roles and the organizational characteristics of the local authority shows that the capabilities (skills) of strategic direction and political intelligence are improved by length of service and length of time in a senior position. This suggests that some skills at least are acquired and is an important finding for the policy and practice of leadership development for politicians.

Managers in the public sector are not legitimated to act as politicians: they do not have the authority of the ballot box, but they may often need to act with political awareness – that is, with sensitivity to the diverse interests which are served by particular actions and decisions. Organizational leadership theory and research, and therefore leadership development, has tended to focus on leadership *in* the organization rather than leadership *of* the organization (i.e. both inside and outside) and this is a limitation. Increasingly leadership activities and meaning-making take place not only inside the organization but in the networks of stakeholders and other organizations that organizational leaders have to, or choose to, interact with.[40] This is an issue for leadership across all sectors (private, public and voluntary) but it is particularly salient because of the contested nature of values and goals of public service organizations. Leadership outside as well as inside the organization requires the effective use of political skills. This is because a leader needs to be able to understand and work with a range of stakeholders, who may have diverse interests, values and goals and who may sometimes collaborate but at other times compete. This is likely to happen inside the organization as well as outside its

39   Leach, S., Hartley, J., Lowndes, V., Wilson, D. and Downe, J. (2005) *Local Political Leadership in the UK*. York: Joseph Rowntree Foundation.

40   Hartley, J. and Fletcher, C. (2008) Leadership with political awareness: leadership across diverse interests inside and outside the organization. In James, K. and Collins, J. (eds) *Leadership Perspectives: Knowledge into Action*, pp. 157–170. London: Palgrave.

formal boundaries. There is a need to anticipate and shape challenges arising from diverse interests, not just respond to them.

So there is a pressing need for managers to be able to work not only with the formal institutions and representatives of the state, but also across and with a diverse range of organizations. Many managers have to work with stakeholders who advocate or lobby on behalf of consumer, pressure and political groups. Other managers may have to understand and work in a complex and dynamic environment of legislation, regulation and policy advice. A globalizing world creates a range of uncertainties about world governance, national stability or local priorities which managers need to understand and take account of, and which may have unexpected or substantial repercussions which have to be addressed. The impact of politics (both formal and informal) may vary according to the sector the organization is in, the degree to which it has a high and visible public profile, the sensitivity of some of its activities and its accountability and governance structures. Work we conducted at Warwick, in conjunction with the Chartered Management Institute, created and tested a model of the skills of political awareness for managers.[41] This has particular (though not exclusive) salience for public sector managers in positions of leadership. The framework has five dimensions.

PERSONAL SKILLS

An essential foundation for being able to be effective in managing with political awareness is to have self-awareness of one's own motives and behaviours, and the ability to exercise self-control. It is also about being open to the views of others so that it is possible to listen and reflect on the views of others. It is also about having a proactive disposition, initiating rather than waiting for things to happen.

To some extent, these are skills which are valuable in any effective manager and are not solely about political awareness. Yet understanding motives, interests and influence is central to leading with political awareness, and the personal skills are the bedrock on which other skills are built.

INTERPERSONAL SKILLS

Political awareness seems to require strong interpersonal skills. These concern having the interpersonal capacity to influence the thinking and behaviour of others, and getting buy-in from people over whom the person has no direct authority, and making people feel valued. These are 'tough' as well as 'soft' skills because the ability to negotiate, to stand up to pressures from other people and to handle conflict in ways to achieve constructive outcomes are important.

Again, these skills may be viewed as core management and certainly core leadership skills, but they also constitute foundational skills for political awareness. There are some elements which go beyond direct leadership skills such as cultivating relationships which have potential rather than immediate value, and on knowing when to rely on position and authority and when to rely on less direct methods of exerting influence.

---

41   Hartley, J., Fletcher, C., Wilton, P., Woodman, P. and Ungemach, C. (2007) *Leading with Political Awareness*. London: Chartered Management Institute.

READING PEOPLE AND SITUATIONS

This dimension has a strong analytical aspect to it, and is based on thinking and intuition about the dynamics which can or might occur when stakeholders and agendas come together. There is a recognition of different interests and agendas of a variety of people and their organizations, and an interest in discerning what may be the underlying as opposed to the espoused agendas which people bring to situations. It includes thinking through the likely standpoints of varying interest groups in advance of dealing with them, and using a wider knowledge of institutions, political processes and social systems to understand what is or might happen. It also includes recognizing where you may be seen as a threat to others and their interests (rightly or wrongly, because this is about the ability to view situations from other people's perspective).

This dimension concerns the power, influence and interests of different groups and is primarily concerned with analytical rather than influencing skills (influence is particularly salient in the following dimension of building alignment and alliances).

BUILDING ALIGNMENT AND ALLIANCES

This dimension is a crucial skill of action, which requires the previous elements of skill in order to be effective. Building alignment out of different interests, goals and motives requires a detailed understanding and appreciation of the context, the players and the objectives of each stakeholder, as far as these can be ascertained. Building alignment and alliances is about recognizing difference and plurality of interest but being able to forge these into collaborative actions even where there are substantial differences in outlook or emphasis. This dimension goes beyond much of the literature on partnerships where finding consensus and commonality is the key skill. It recognizes but works with difference and with conflicts of interest in order to forge new opportunities. It builds on the proactivity of the first dimension (personal skill) in actively seeking out alliances and partnerships rather than relying on those which are already in existence or which are expected to contribute. It includes being able to bring out into the open and deal with differences between stakeholders, not conceal them or hope that if they are ignored they will somehow go away. Tough negotiation skills (from interpersonal skills) may underpin the capacity to build a realistic and useful consensus without ending up with the lowest common denominator.

STRATEGIC DIRECTION AND SCANNING

This dimension brings in the important question of purpose – what these political awareness skills are being used for. This includes two major elements. The first is a sense of strategic thinking and action in relation to organizational purpose, so that the understanding of power, interests and influence is set within a strategic aim. This includes thinking long term and having a road map of where the manager wants to go so that they are not diverted by short-term pressures. The second element is about not just a focused sense of strategy but also a skill in strategic scanning – about thinking about longer-term issues which may have the potential to have an impact on the organization. This is about not just looking at what is on the horizon but what may be over the horizon. It requires analytical capacity to think through scenarios of possible futures, to think about small changes which may herald bigger shifts in society and the economy, and being able to find ways to analyse and manage (as far as possible) the uncertainty which lies outside the organization. This last includes being about to keep options open rather than reaching for a decision prematurely.

This research suggests that an effective leader in a complex set of interrelationships across organizations will require skills in each of these dimensions in order to show astuteness, 'nous' or political awareness. While personal and interpersonal skills are the foundation of building trust and understanding the needs and interests of other people and organizations, there is also a need for the skills of building alliances across those differences and being able to sense or interpret wider changes in the external environment which may have an impact on plans and objectives.

Thus, the five dimensions of the framework outlined above are those which the research suggests are needed by individuals to achieve outcomes in complex and dynamic settings inside and outside the organization where diverse interests are in play.

Across the public sector, a number of organizations have shown interest in using this framework as a diagnostic tool as part of leadership development. We are now working with two government departments (Home Office and the Department for Work and Pensions) along with the NHS nationally (Institute for Innovation and Improvement) in order to create tools to help individual managers and their organizations to identify, improve and hone their political awareness skills so that they are able to work with and across stakeholders with diverse interests. A number of organizations, such as the Fire and Rescue Service, and the Health Service, have developed leadership development models which include the need to acquire and enhance political awareness skills to be used for organizational purposes – a constructive view of politics in and across organizations. This is an area which may well grow in the future.

Leadership Development for Outcomes

The salience of the external environment is also related to purpose – while private sector organizations have principal aims of profit and market domination and development, public organizations primarily aim to produce not profit or market positioning but public value.[42] Public value means what is added to the public sphere and this may be social or economic, or it may be political, environmental or even more broadly about the quality of life. The unit of analysis of benefit may not therefore necessarily be the single organization and its outputs but also extends to consideration of outcomes across an 'institutional field'. For example, schools may not be just concerned with examination results but with developing broadly educated and informed citizens capable of contributing to society. (Private sector organizations may also contribute to public value, for example, through innovation, philanthropy or service delivery, but it is rarely a primary objective.) In addition, a public value perspective requires examining the impact of public services on customers and users but also the impact on them as citizens.

The implications for leadership development are important. It means that leadership development needs to focus on the purpose(s) of leadership rather than just on the

---

42   Moore, M. H. (1995) *Creating Public Value*. Cambridge, MA: Harvard University Press; Benington, J. and Moore, M. (in press) *Public Value: Theory and Practice*. Basingstoke: Palgrave.

processes or the personal characteristics which underlie leadership behaviours. All the time, leadership development has to be cognisant of 'leadership for what' – what are the outcomes to be achieved through leadership actions. This means a wider view of organizational performance than imposed (or self-imposed) inputs or activity targets, but rather thinking about the values and purposes to which the talents of public sector managers and leaders are being put. These are larger questions than many leaders have been encouraged to think about in the recent period of performance targetry. It takes us back to leadership development implications of understanding the wider environment or context, working with others collaboratively where appropriate (sharing learning, sharing leadership and sharing good or promising practices may all potentially enhance the public sphere). The language of public value is filtering into leadership development programmes and experiences but there is still some way to go.

Conclusion

From this brief consideration of public leadership development we may conclude that there are some differences in context that either only exist in public organizations or that exist to a greater degree in public organizations. This suggests that generic leadership and management theory may not be universally applied, but rather that there are some issues which require consideration of context and circumstance.[43] Pettigrew[44] supports this when he states: 'The process of public transformation cannot be explained just by appeals to managerial action and associated drives for efficiency and effectiveness. Context does matter.'

In this chapter, I have concentrated not on giving an overview of all the concepts, activities and outcomes from the public sector – as this is about 20 per cent of UK employment it would be too large a task. Instead, I have concentrated on those aspects of public sector leadership development which either only occur in the public sphere or else occur to a greater degree. Context matters in leadership development. There are also ideas and practices here which will be of wider interest across the private and voluntary sectors.

43   Christensen, T., Laegreid, P., Roness, P. and Røvik, K. (2007) *Organization Theory for the Public Sector*. London: Routledge.

44   Pettigrew, A. (2005) The character and significance of management research on the public services, *Academy of Management Journal*, 48: 973–977, quotation on p. 976.

30 *Developing Leaders as Futures Thinkers*

PERO MIĆIĆ

The figures within this chapter refer to colour throughout. Please ask for your copy of a coloured presentation about the Eltville Model by e-mail to CS@FutureManagementGroup. com.

Introduction

The global flux of the 2000s surely raises two fundamental questions for leadership development. First, how can leaders use knowledge about futures as a source of orientation, inspiration and innovation? Secondly, how can they see and understand more of the future in a meaningful and rational way?

Futurists have produced an enormous quantity of forecasts and scenarios about the future. The problem is that most leaders and managers have difficulty in making profitable use of this knowledge in order to make better assumptions, be less surprised, develop vision and perceive and seize opportunities before their competitors.

One of the major reasons for the difficulties people have with managing the future is the fact that futures experts and their clients often speak different languages. Even futures experts do not understand each other. This leads to significant confusions about the goals, the roles and the methods for future management. It is the complex nature of the many types of futures and as a consequence the variety of mental models that causes the confusions and the problems.

In this chapter, we present the idea of five futures glasses and the Eltville model[1] as a simplified model to help leaders learn to think and communicate about the future. The Eltville model has been developed and used in almost a thousand interactions with top management teams. It is a profound and practical model used to resolve futures confusions and to see more and understand more of the future.

A case study of the company MyBeauty (name changed) explains how the model can be applied in practice and how it can contribute to remarkable success in business.

---

1   Mićić, P. (2006) *Das ZukunftsRadar* (The Future Radar). Offenbach: GABAL Verlag GmbH.

From Futures Research to Future Management

Before we were able to talk specifically of future management in the narrowest sense of the word, futures research had first to become established as a discipline to be taken seriously. We started using the term future management in the mid 1990s when professionally managed companies increasingly systematically concerned themselves with an analysis of the future beyond strategic planning.

Futures research is the interdisciplinary discovery and analysis of possible, plausible, probable and creatable long-term futures.[2] It aims to help to:

- understand the (present) world;
- improve the well-being of the human race;
- increase awareness for the long-term future;
- make better decisions;
- understand thinking about the future.[3]

The word 'research' is much discussed, and many people dispute the fact that futures research is a science as the word implies. Futures research is not scientific if you support the positivistic science paradigm that only things that can be measured, counted, weighed and generally confirmed or refuted can be researched. But the future does not exist in a strict ontological sense. After all, no one can measure history either. If the quality of being scientific means that the methods used meet the demands of validity, reliability, replicability and generalization, then futures management *can* indeed be scientific.

Future Management as a Bridge

Managers and entrepreneurs often consider futures research and the related trend research as imprecise, non-committal and unreliable. There is often a huge gap between their need for knowledge and the knowledge offered by futures researchers and trend researchers. Future management (Figure 30.1), which we define as follows, closes this gap:

> Future management is the bridge between futures research on the one side and strategic management on the other side. It describes the totality of all systems, processes and methods for early perception and analysis of future developments and their inclusion in strategy.

Future management is entrepreneurial and corporate futures research. Compared to futures research, future management is a more practical concept and fundamental to human nature because it turns futures research, which is primarily focused on anticipation,

---

2   Mićić, P. (2007) Phenomenology of future management in top management teams. Unpublished Ph.D. thesis, Leeds Metropolitan University.

3   See Bell, W. (1997) The purposes of futures studies, *The Futurist*, November–December(1): 42–45.

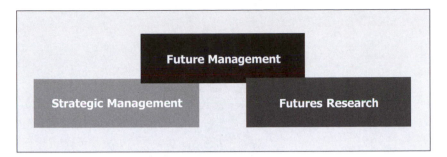

Figure 30.1 Future management as a bridge

into a holistic concept with interfaces to strategic and operative management. It closes the gap between futures research, which is often abstract and theoretical, and the practical requirements of companies, by systematically recognizing the future of markets and developing practically implementable strategies out of these findings. Future management builds on the findings of general futures research and creates the connection to (business) decisions and actions in everyday life.

Future Confusions

Good future management is one of the most important success factors in private and in corporate life. Regardless of whether you are the chairman of a corporation or your own life enterprise, it is easier to build and maintain your success the better you are able to perceive and use future changes and the opportunities they conceal at an early stage. Future management is the missing link between futures research and business, and it is likely to be the only function leaders cannot and must not delegate.

Leaders and managers often lament and complain about their attempts to work with futures experts and with futures tools. In our work with several hundred management teams, we often heard the following statements:

- We have looked at earlier forecasts and are very disappointed by the forecast quality of the future expert.
- We can't cope with all of these forecasts, scenarios and visions – we have no clear picture.
- We know the results of futures research, but haven't been able to translate this knowledge into our language, our concepts and practicable strategies.
- We have worked with scenarios, but it didn't meet our needs.
- We have listened to the futures researchers, but what they had to say didn't have enough new, helpful and reliable information for us specialists.

Numerous projects and plans in future management practice fail due to the sort of futures confusions in Figure 30.2. There are three kinds of futures confusions: the objectives confusion about what future management is for, the role confusion about

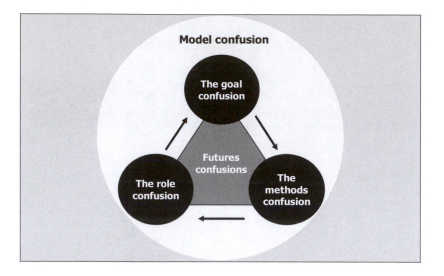

Figure 30.2 The futures confusions

what the futurist is aiming at and the methods confusion about which methods shall be applied for which task in future management.[4] Table 30.1 summarizes these:

Table 30.1   The futures confusions

Objectives confusion	*Forecast versus creation* The more strongly humans are able to form their own future, the less predictable the future becomes. Forecast and creating the future are opposing, mutually exclusive objectives. Since people can create their future to a large extent, the future cannot be predictable.
	Forecast versus warning Scenarios of extreme and surprising futures are misunderstood as forecasts. They should, however, serve exactly the opposite purpose, namely to prevent these futures.
	Vision versus plan The description of a long-term future to be aimed for is understood as planning and rejected. Planning in the narrowest sense can nowadays only be done for a very short period. Vision is not planning.
	Pragmatism versus science fiction Many people understand the future as being only what is new, utopian and never imagined before. However, the future is usually already here. Most of its ingredients can already be seen today.

---

4   See Micic, P. (2007) *Die fünf Zukunftsbrillen* (The Five Futures Glasses). Offenbach: GABAL Verlag GmbH.

Table 30.1 *Concluded*

Role confusion	*Prophet or future manager?* The client usually sees the futures expert as a prophet or forecaster. The futures expert sees himself more as a future manager in most cases. *Prophet or inspirer?* Trend researchers' trend creations are understood as forecasts. In reality, however, they provide inspiring ideas and thoughts rather than predicting the future. *Universal expert or innovator?* Futures experts are often assumed or expected to know the future better than the specialists. Their competence has its basis in their interdisciplinarity and methodological knowledge.
Methods confusion	*Tool catalogue without a construction drawing* The suitability of the methods and tools for various approaches to the future is hardly mentioned in the catalogues of methods. Hence, some methods are overused and misused for purposes which they were not aimed for. *Limitations of classic scenarios* The classic scenario method does not cover many of the requirements for practice. As scenarios are considered to be state of the art, the result is often disappointed expectations.

Many of these futures confusions result from the different views on the future. People tend towards the subconscious assumption that everyone understands the way they think and talk about the future and that others thin in the same way too. They assume that everyone is wearing the same futures glasses and thus form the premise for frustration, misunderstanding and failure.

What is Required in Practice

The dilemmas, irrationalities and future confusions can be positively reformulated into requirements for practice in Table 30.2. The five futures glasses and the Eltville Model are intended to meet these requirements as far as possible.

Table 30.2 Requirements for practice

A holistic approach Above all, the method needs to be holistic in the sense that it integrates all necessary process steps and all results types in one model and links them with each other.
Futures differentiation The method must clearly differentiate between the various perspectives of the future (possible, probable, feared, surprising, planned, etc.).
Active–passive clarity It must be clear in the process whether one is regarding oneself or the environment, mixing the active and passive views is systemically not practicable.

Table 30.2 *Concluded*

Orientation The method must provide an orientational picture of a probable future, even if the future cannot be (exactly) predicted.
Variety of surprises The method needs to consider a large number of potential surprises, not just a few scenarios.
Opportunity-focus The method needs to guarantee a strong element of creative formulation of future opportunities and options and thus support competitive differentiation.
Vision The method needs to provide a comprehensive picture of the future desired by the actor or the team.
Strategy and planning The method needs to have clear connections to the operative business.
Permanence The method needs to be suitable for supporting a permanent radar process in daily business.
Efficiency The method needs to be efficient in the sense that the above-mentioned requirements can be met with an appropriate amount of time and money.
Independent application The method needs to be suitable for independent use by an averagely qualified team, at least in its basic functions.

The Complex Nature of Types of Futures

The future. If all we mean by that is the time in front of us, then the definition of the future seems simple and any further inquiry superfluous. However, if we look at it more closely, then it quickly becomes clear that this initial unambiguous and exhaustive understanding of the future is often unsatisfactory and hardly does justice to the complexity of the future. Futures researchers try to categorize the future, using terms such as possible, probable and preferred. Yet this structure also remains unsatisfactory. As the future is a very complex thought object, it is dangerous to look at it with too radical a simplification. Complexity can only be understood and handled with complexity.

If we look through the relevant literature, we notice that hardly any futures thinker has ever attempted a comprehensive categorization of the future. The map presented here can be seen as such an attempt.

Figure 30.3 shows the types of futures from our viewpoint. The initial complex categorization enables appropriate simplification by bringing structure and a system into the term and the nature of the future. Let's therefore accept the temporary confusion initially in order to then develop a simple and practicable model. It is only possible to comprehend and understand why it is important and necessary to get to know and use the five futures glasses when you see how many different terms and definitions there are for the future.

The types of futures suggested here need to be regarded under the following assumptions:

1. The futures are defined from the perspective of an individual actor, meaning a person, a team or an organization. The content of every type of future is therefore subject to the subjectivity and incomplete knowledge of each individual.
2. The definitions of the types of futures are dependent on the time at which they are

considered. The contents of the categories change over time. A certain future, such as the contact with extraterrestrial life, can develop from the imaginable future to the possible future and plausible future to the probable future, before it falls out of the futures and into the present or the certain owing to factual evidence.

3. The types of futures depend on the sequence in which they are looked at. If you begin with the planned future, you can come to a different categorization if well argued.

4. Table 30.3 describes systematically the different types of futures documented in the literature as well as those used in our workshops and interactions with top management teams. The types of futures were identified by using the criteria number, knowability, probability, desirability and controllability which were developed by critical analysis of the literature. The same applies to the classes and the descriptions. The types of futures in bold print are used as generic. The other terms in standard print are viewed as synonymous with the generic terms to a great extent.

A Simplified Model: the Five Futures Glasses®

Due to the complex character of the future shown in the types of futures, even the experts produce a Babylonian confusion of language concerning the most important concepts and terms on the future. There is no conclusive language for the phenomenon of the future: much of the benefit of futures research and future management therefore remains hidden. We need a model that enables us to express exactly, or at least more exactly than usual, what we see and feel and what we think of with regard to the future. We need a map for futures terminology. A layman can only describe the taste of wine with a few words such as dry, mellow, sweet. The expert has a vocabulary of a thousand words.

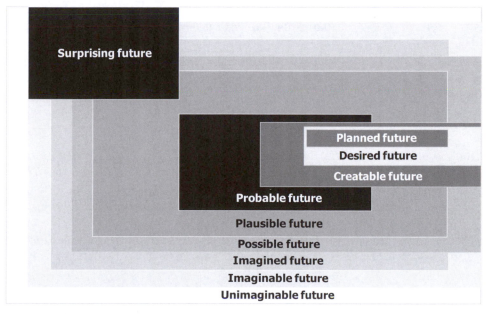

Figure 30.3 Types of futures

He has models and terms for the various occasions on which wine can be enjoyed and experienced and differentiates very clearly between the different impressions of the same wine in different situations. How much clearer and richer his perception of the world of wine must be!

The types of futures create a good understanding of the complexity of the seemingly simple and unambiguous term 'future'. This also gives us a reason to apply a portion of modesty and humility when wanting to manage the future. However, in order to be able to master the complexity shown in the map of the futures, we need a simplified model that helps us to understand the future without being oversimplified. The following table summarizes the types of futures into the considerably simpler model of the five futures glasses. This model has been developed in a comprehensive phenomenological analysis of workshops with top management teams.[5]

Table 30.3   Types of futures and futures glasses

Types of future	Five futures glasses
Probable and improbable futures (Plausible futures)	*Blue futures glasses* Assumption analysis: knowing about the probable development of the environment
Surprising futures	*Red futures glasses* Surprise analysis: knowing the possible surprises
Creatable futures	*Green futures glasses* Opportunity development: knowing the possible courses of action for the future
Desired futures	*Yellow futures glasses* Vision development: determining the long-term orientation
Planned futures	*Violet futures glasses* Strategy development: determining the action necessary for the future
Imaginable futures Imagined futures Possible futures	Futures which cannot be clearly assigned to one pair of futures glasses since they apply to all of them

The colours are assigned to the futures glasses to make them easier memorable. Blue reminds us of clinical, reserved and logical analysis. We think of green as the colour of creativity, opportunities and options. We understand yellow as the colour for a decision in a certain direction, in the sense of a vision. Red is for surprise and (usually) for threats. Violet finally is considered as the colour of planning and action.

The categories 'imaginable futures', 'imagined futures', and 'possible futures' are so basic and relevant for every perspective that they cannot be clearly assigned to any pair of

---

5   Mićić, P. (2007) Phenomenology of future management in top management teams. Unpublished Ph.D. thesis, Leeds Metropolitan University.

futures glasses. They can be included in all five perspectives and provide the mental raw material for different ways of looking at the future.

For a better understanding of the five futures glasses, let us look at five statements about the year 2020 that could appear in your daily newspaper today:

1. In a research report to the government by the Federal Statistics Office, a demographer writes that 30 per cent of the population will be older than sixty in 2020.
2. A WHO virologist writes that there could be a pandemic by 2020, as a result of which several million people could die within a short period.
3. A young engineer writes that virtual meetings will replace half of all business trips in 2020.
4. The Works Council writes that it will have enforced the 30-hour week for all employees in its company in 2020.
5. A multi-billionaire says in an interview that he will have donated most of his wealth by 2020.

What is the difference between all of these future statements about the year 2020? Is it their intentions? Is it the methods the statements are based on? Is it the verifiability of the statements? Is it the level of predictability of the subject area? It is a little bit of everything.

The difference quickly becomes clear very if we offer each of these future thinkers a bet. If we propose that they bet 10 euros of their own personal taxed money that their statement will come true. If they are right, they stand to make a substantial profit, as the rate is 1:10. How will they react?

Will the demographer accept the bet? They are possibly more likely to agree than the others. Demography is, after all, one of the few areas in which the future can be estimated with at least some degree of certainty. The rate of 1:10 would probably convince them. The demographer has formulated a clear assumption on the future: they are looking into the probable future with the blue glasses.

What will we hear from the WHO expert if we offer them the bet? It is possible that they will insult us, show us the door. All they wanted to do was to warn people and to achieve a change in their attitudes towards hygiene, prevention and emergency planning. They will reject our offer for moral reasons alone and perhaps even add that they wouldn't bet on the very thing they are trying to prevent: they are looking through the red glasses for the surprising future. This doesn't have to be negative as in this example; it can also be positive.

How will the engineer react if we ask them to bet 10 euros that 50 per cent of all business travel really will be virtual in 2020? We can assume that they would qualify their statement. They didn't really mean it as a concrete forecast, they spoke about the possibility. It is simply an option, an opportunity we could already use today, if only we could get used to it: the engineer is looking through the green glasses and sees opportunities in the sense of possible courses of action and options.

What will the Works Council do? They will probably say that is their vision. Money and material things are not everything. In the 1970s, the union used the advertising slogan 'Dad belongs to me on Saturdays'. Now it's time for the next step, despite globalization. There is value in spending more time with the kids and the family. It is, of course, not certain that this vision can be realized. Therefore, they won't bet on it. The Works Council is looking through the yellow glasses, for the desired future, for the vision.

The multi-billionaire certainly won't be impressed by the 10 euros, but a game is a game after all. Will he accept the bet? Almost certainly, because he has planned it and decided to do it. He has already announced it and no one can prevent him from doing exactly that. He is looking at the future through the violet glasses of planning and action.

There is evidence of various perspectives on the future in the history of mankind. People have consciously occupied themselves with the future since antiquity, and then more extensively since the Renaissance. People have always adopted all five perspectives on the future and therefore worn all five futures glasses, but those concerned with the long-term future of markets and the world on a professional basis have had a focus.

The Characteristics of the Five Futures Glasses

Table 30.4 provides a comprehensive overview of the characters of the five futures glasses:

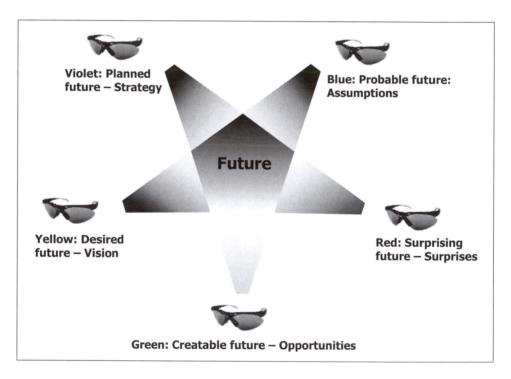

Figure 30.4 The five futures glasses

Table 30.4 Overview of the five futures glasses

Futures glasses	The blue futures glasses	The red futures glasses	The green futures glasses	The yellow futures glasses	The violet futures glasses
Primary objective	To know the probable future developments in the environment	To know the possible surprises the future holds	To know the possible options for action	To determine the desired future and direction	To determine the necessary action to achieve the desired future
Secondary objective	To improve assumptions To make better decisions To reduce risks	To prepare for surprises To be less surprised to reduce peak level of stress To secure existence	To expand the potential for success To increase the number and quality of ideas for the vision and the strategy	To follow a clear direction To seize potential for success To initiate and coordinate action	To link the futures strategy to operational strategy To coordinate action
Example	In 2020, one third of the population will be 60 or older.	A pandemic with an unknown virus could kill millions of people. 11 September 2001, 9 November 1989 (fall of the Berlin Wall)	We can increase our efficiency by using videoconferencing	We will be the first provider of a conversational user interface for simple communication between man and computer	We will establish a cooperation with a software research institute to develop the conversational user interface
Objects of thought concerned	Assumption questions Future factors (trends technologies, issues) Signals Future projections Future scenarios Assumptions about the future	Surprise questions Surprises (event-based) Surprises (process-based)	Opportunity questions Future opportunities Vision candidates	Visions questions Mission (mission elements) Vision (Vision elements) Strategic guidelines	Strategy questions Objectives Projects Processes Systems Development opportunities Contingency strategies
Perspectives	Macro perspective Outward orientation	Macro perspective Outward orientation	Micro perspective Inward orientation	Micro perspective Inward orientation	Micro perspective Inward orientation
Attitude	Detached Passive Observing	Detached Passive Observing	Involved Active Intervening	Involved Active Intervening	Involved Active Intervening
Mindset	Realistic Critical Analytical Experience based Conservative	Calculatedly pessimistic Analytic Creative Imaginative Progressive	Optimistic Creative Intuitive Imaginative Progressive Transformative	Optimistic and realistic at the same time Intuitive and analytic at the same time Progressive	Realistic Pragmatic Analytic Experience-based Progressive
Destructive factors	Wanting to creatively develop the future Wishful thinking Being too optimistic Being too pessimistic Including one's own action	Probability thinking Underestimating the benefits Suppression and avoidance	Critical thinking Experience-based thinking	Being too ambitious Not being ambitious enough	Being too ambitious Not being ambitious enough Under or overestimating the importance of finance and resources
Typical methods	Projections and scenarios Delphi Roadmapping	Assumptions reversal Scenario methods Wild card analysis Wargaming	Impact analysis Creativity techniques	Decision techniques Conception techniques (e.g. morphologies)	Planning Project management Roadmapping

From the Five Futures Glasses to the Eltville Model

Each pair of futures glasses implies a process of analysis for the external development or a process of development for internal action.

1. Assumption analysis (assumption view/blue futures glasses)
2. Surprise analysis (surprise view/red futures glasses)
3. Opportunity development (opportunity view/green futures glasses)
4. Vision development (vision view/yellow futures glasses)
5. Strategy development (strategy view/violet futures glasses).

The Process Model

Two further process steps need to be added. First, any view of the future requires a certain degree of knowledge about future factors, that is, trends, technologies and issues of the future. Gathering this knowledge is not attached to a particular view. It is a scanning and monitoring process that provides information for all futures glasses and usually in a neutral manner. Following Ansoff[6] and his idea of a 'strategic radar', this process phase is referred to as 'future radar' and precedes all other steps. Secondly, future management needs to become an ongoing process. It is therefore necessary to develop and agree upon rules and procedures on when, how and under which circumstances activities in the future management of the organization should be carried out. This phase is referred to as 'institutionalization', and comes at the end of the process.

With these two additional process steps, the process part of the Eltville model is complete and can consequently be linked to the results part of the Eltville model.

The Results Model

Each pair of futures glasses is clearly linked to certain objects of thought that together form the results part of the Eltville model. The process of future radar leads to future factors, that is, trends, technologies and issues as drivers of change. In addition, available projections and scenarios are collected. Wearing the blue glasses leads to assumptions, which appear in the form of expectations, non-expectations and eventualities, depending on the degree of probability. The green glasses lead to opportunities to create futures. The yellow glasses result in a clear mission and an attractive, ambitious but achievable vision as well as in strategic guidelines. The red glasses take into account surprising events and developments of the future in order to relativize the assumptions and make the strategy more robust. Finally, the violet glasses describe the way to achieving the vision in concrete terms of goals, projects, processes and systems. Developing opportunities are not yet suitable for action and need to be researched further. Eventual strategies are prepared in case surprising events and developments with strong impact on the organization take place.

---

6   See Ansoff, I. (1975) Managing Strategic surprise by response to weak signals, *California Management Review*, 18(2): 21–33.

Table 30.5   The two parts of the Eltville model

The process part	The results part
Description of a general process in seven steps. Five of the seven steps are characterized and described by the five futures glasses. The introductory step, FutureRadar, and the closing step, institutionalization, round off the process model.	Description of interconnected core concepts (objects of thought). The core concepts form a 'mental letter case' for all important future management terms. With their clear relations, the core concepts form a semantic network.

The Eltville model is an integrated model for future management. It is a descriptive model of the notions or objects of thought that managers use in practice. However, with its clear definitions of the character and the interrelations of the objects, its purpose is also to be prescriptive, that is, to serve as a template for systematically thinking about the future.

The Eltville model is simple enough to provide a complete framework for thinking and acting in practice as a kind of mental letter case. On the other hand, it is complex enough to fully portray the processes and results of future management while remaining neutral towards individual methods, techniques and tools.

The following section presents a case study about a European company which has been using the Eltville model for seven years.

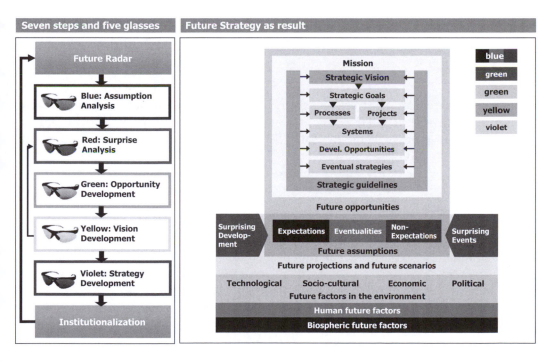

Figure 30.5   The process and the results parts of the Eltville model

Case Study

MyBeauty

One of Europe's largest producers of cosmetics has been practising future management and using the evolving versions of the Eltville model for seven years. We will call the company MyBeauty to keep its identity secret. 'We are successful because we are systematically managing our future', the CEO likes to say. MyBeauty was in a situation of stagnancy. The products, the clients and the way to do business have not changed over years. On the official surface, everything was in order and running well. The predecessor of the new CEO had been running the company for almost 20 years without any major effort as well as without real progress. After he took over, the new CEO soon had the feeling that substantial changes of customer preferences and behaviour are ahead and that MyBeauty needed to react and act according to a changing environment. However, it was not at all obvious what the new future strategy should be like.

A futures team of 12 people which consisted of the first and second leadership level as well as the CEO of one of the core suppliers and two procurement officers of two major retailers was put together. We were hired as external process experts, facilitators and researchers. We are describing the process in the way it was used for the third time in 2005 since in 2001 the model had not evolved to its current state. The seven project steps were executed and the objects of thought shown in Figure 30.3 were elaborated as results of the project.

Future Radar

The aim of Future Radar was to collect existing knowledge about the future of the cosmetics market and its environmental factors. The necessary mindset is attentive, open-minded and critically neutral. We scanned what experts and futurists have published and we did a set of telephone interviews with them.

After defining the central future questions (see detailed questions in later steps), the major future factors were selected. We ended up with one set with high relevance and one set with arguable relevance, but potential for innovative ideas. Extensive research on information and signals was done and the results were prepared in appealing slides and posters.

The result of Future Radar was summarized in some 60 slides about future factors, that is, trends, technologies and issues as drivers of future change in the cosmetics industry. These slides were used to cover the walls of the conference room.

Assumption Analysis (Blue Futures Glasses)

Assumption analysis, the working step taken in the first workshop, serves to identify, question, complete and substantiate the future assumptions on probable developments in the environment. Every decision and every strategy is based on future assumptions. Therefore, the essential factors need to be established and recognized in the core assumptions. This provides a realistic picture of the probable future without predicting the future. Since future assumptions are about the external environment, which cannot be significantly influenced, the required mindset is detached, analytic and critical.

The central assumption questions were as follows (generalized for purposes of secrecy):

1. How will the needs, expectations and preferences of consumers change?
2. How will the relevant technologies and methods change?
3. How will the competitive landscape change?
4. How will the regulatory environment change?

The possible answers to each question were identified in the form of projections of potential developments in the environment. The projections were elaborated by members of staff and by us as well as taken from publications of experts and futurists and from their answers in the interviews.

For each projection, we developed argumentations as a basis for the evaluation of the expectational probabilities. The projections were evaluated by surfacing the expectational probabilities that each internal member of the futures team attributes to each projection. Thus, the projections became individual assumptions which in a process of systematic argumentation became collective assumptions of the futures team. The individual assumptions with the biggest deviations were discussed most intensively. Finally, the assumptions were classified in expectations (will happen), non-expectations (will not happen) and eventualities (might happen).

As a result, a future panorama with 11 assumption questions and 47 projections was elaborated. We refrained from classical scenario development because for the purpose of checking assumptions we needed to work with expectational probabilities. But in scenarios the probabilities of each projection in the scenario need to be multiplied which almost inevitably leads to scenarios with a total probability of less than 1 per cent.

Surprise Analysis (Red Futures Glasses)

Assumption analysis aims at surfacing and improving the assumptions about what the management team of MyBeauty believes what the probable future will be. Surprise analysis, however, aims at expanding the imagination of the management team of MyBeauty concerning possible surprises. Without this, many possible but low-probability future developments, like a huge boom in cosmetic surgery, would not have been taken into account. Surprises are very likely. Surprise analysis was to immunize the organization against surprising developments and to transform potential surprises into opportunities.

In order to prepare for possible surprises which could put an end to MyBeauty's existence, we did research and carried out another workshop with the futures team. As with each process step, a set of specific questions was posed. These surprise questions were (generalized for purposes of secrecy):

1. How could the technologies and methods in cosmetics change suddenly and dramatically?
2. How could consumer behaviour change rapidly?

We developed several scenarios of unexpected and rather surprising developments in the environment. In the first project, we used three-dimensional scenarios; in the later project we produced scenarios with six dimensions (variables). In addition to theses rather systematic scenarios, we developed a set of eleven simple, that is, one-dimensional scenarios or stories, about surprising events in the world of cosmetics. Evaluating the MyBeauty's vulnerability by checking each element of their strategy against the scenarios revealed the threats and risks which were consequently covered through a set of eventual strategies.

Surprise analysis for MyBeauty resulted in a surprise panorama, that is, a systematic overview of possible and relevant surprises with the respective eventual strategies.

Opportunity Development (Green Futures Glasses)

The more opportunities an organization or an individual perceives, the higher is their potential success. Opportunities are consequences of the assumed developments. Even threats are expressed in opportunities since a threat, recognized early, means an opportunity to avert the threat. Furthermore, opportunities are the 'raw material', i.e. the possible elements of the future strategy.

In order to perceive as much of the doable and creatable future as possible, a creative, progressive and imaginative mindset is recommended. The two days of the second workshop started with the definition of central opportunity questions (shortened and generalized for purposes of secrecy):

1. How can we increase and secure our success in present businesses concerning product and solutions, marketing and sales, people and culture, systems and processes, partners and suppliers or finance and resources?
2. What are our opportunities in new business segments?

The opportunities, that is, the answers to the opportunity questions, were developed through analysis of future assumptions concerning necessary and favourable action as well as through analysis of future factors concerning resulting and conceivable opportunities. The opportunities were evaluated according to their potential to strengthen or improve the competitive position of MyBeauty.

The research and the two workshop days of opportunity development led to a total of 615 opportunities as answers to the nine opportunity questions. The opportunities were presented in the form of an opportunity panorama, a comprehensive table.

Vision Development (Yellow Futures Glasses)

MyBeauty started this project because the new CEO felt that without a major change in the organization's direction of development, they would soon experience a substantial crisis. The vision of MyBeauty was meant to be a concrete picture of a fascinating, jointly desired and feasible future of the organization. The strategic vision provides a demanding but realistic future perspective and activates people for higher performance. The vision is the foundation for all strategic and operative decisions. The vision focuses the attention and activities of the management team and all employees, thus leading to more efficiency and effectiveness. Together with the vision, the mission and the strategic guidelines are set. The necessary mindset for the yellow view is visionary, but realistic, nevertheless.

The vision questions were virtually the same as the opportunity questions, only we did not ask for options, but for the best choice. In order to arrive at a really special and unique strategic vision, we did not develop just one vision, but eight alternative vision candidates. This opened the entire scope of possible ways into the future. One of the vision candidates was 'MyBeaty continued', another was 'MyBeauty worldwide group'; further vision candidates were more specific and attractive. The vision candidates were evaluated according to a set of four criteria, among which were the degree of compatibility with the assumptions about the future development of the market and the appropriateness of the involved risks, which were identifiable through the results of the surprise analysis. This process resulted in a list of ranked vision candidates. After intensive discussion, the first and the third vision candidate were put together to form the core of the new strategic vision for MyBeauty. This core was then completed with additional vision elements and strategic guidelines. The mission was implicitly changed from producing cosmetics to helping customers to grow their business in a specific area.

This work resulted in a comprehensive and well-structured strategic vision, which can be visualized in pictures or drawings of needed.

Strategy Development (Violet Future Glasses)

The strategic vision was broken down into clear and well-defined stage goals, which are achievable within one to three years. Crucial tasks and responsibilities were assigned to members of the futures team: thus a link to the traditional strategic planning and management was created. The violet view is to plan for the preferred future with a realistic and pragmatic mindset, that is, to show what needs to be done to achieve the strategic vision.

Strategy development meant to define strategy questions, to elaborate goal candidates, to rate and rank them according to their suitability to achieve the vision, to describe the best goals and to elaborate them in the form of projects with goal managers and project managers. Finally, the strategy was checked against possible surprise and consequently improved at some points. This resulted in a robust future strategy with measurable goals, projects, processes, systems and eventual strategies efficiently leading to making the strategic vision come true.

Institutionalization

After the first project, a future management system had been introduced to make future management a regular process which nevertheless does not cause significant additional expenses. MyBeauty had pursued a certain kind of future management before, but not as professionally and effectively as needed.

With a systemic and pragmatic mindset, the futures team developed a radar system, which consists of a network of people who worked as sensors and linked themselves to experts from outside the organization. Furthermore, a communication process and schedule was defined. Finally, MyBeauty introduced a software system to manage the results of their future strategy and to manage the interrelations between the objects of thought like assumptions, opportunities, surprise, vision elements, goals and projects.

Success

Before the project described here, MyBeauty had been experiencing growth rates of 2 per cent at most and even negative growth rates before the new CEO took over. Through systematic future management, the CEO says, MyBeauty doubled the sales and multiplied the returns within five years.

How You can Use the Eltville Model

The five futures glasses is a model simple enough to provide a complete framework for thinking and acting in practice. On the other hand, it is complex enough to fully portray the processes and results of future management while remaining neutral towards individual methods, techniques and tools.

The following applications relate to your personal life enterprise as well as the future management in your company or your organization.

ORGANIZE YOUR THOUGHTS AND RESOLVE FUTURES CONFUSIONS

The five futures glasses help to resolve and/or avoid the futures confusions. The five futures glasses support you through clear, interrelated definitions of the thought processes and the core concepts of future management unambiguously connected to them. You are now in a position to clearly differentiate the various futures and handle them in an experienced way.

COMMUNICATE WITH A BETTER OVERVIEW AND MORE PRECISION

The improved orderliness in your mind will enable you to talk and write about the future in a much more precise way. Experience and enjoy the confidence with which you use the processes, terms and concepts of future management. The holistic approach of the five futures glasses also provides you with a good overview of what you know and what you don't know.

HELP OTHERS TO COMMUNICATE BETTER

Use the clarity of your thoughts and communication and your confidence to support other people's discussions. Knowledge of the five futures glasses makes you into a highly suitable facilitator in your organization. Resolve misunderstandings and conflicts with just a few words and examples.

GAIN MORE INSIGHT FROM NEWSPAPERS, BOOKS, LECTURES AND FILMS

You learned how statements about the future can be literally 'coloured'. Now that you know the five futures glasses, their characteristics and principles, you can much better understand, evaluate and use texts, statistics, novels and films about the future.

USE THE FUTURES GLASSES AS A TEMPLATE FOR DESIGNING FUTURES PROJECTS

Whether you want to compile a study, give a talk, hold a seminar, carry out a workshop or organize and plan a complete strategy project for your company – the five futures glasses provide you with a tried and tested template for designing futures projects.

STRUCTURE YOUR FUTURES STRATEGY

The five futures glasses provide you with the structure for your future strategy and additionally interconnects the core concepts of future management in a semantic network. You save a lot of explanation due to the precise definitions and their interconnections. This model is a basis to put forward arguments to your employees, colleagues, supervisory boards, partners and other interested parties.

ORGANIZE YOUR TOOLBOX

The five futures glasses are deliberately neither method-specific nor tool-specific. You can use several different methods to work on the process steps and the core concepts. In this way, the futures glasses are an ideal structure for your toolbox. Each single pair of futures glasses becomes a 'compartment' in your toolbox.

SEE MORE OF THE FUTURE THAN YOUR COMPETITORS

Use your ability to look clearly at the future and communicate about it as a strategic advantage in the competition for foresight. We have experienced hundreds of times that even the most professional management teams can be totally helpless with regard to a clear structure and methodology for looking at the future. Since the turn of the millennium, a competition for foresight has developed between companies, organizations and even countries. Anyone who is better at handling the future than others will recognize the threats and, above all, opportunities which lie in it earlier and is therefore better able to use them to his advantage.

Conclusion

In this chapter I have presented a new model for future managment thinking. The five futures views as well as the object model are not a development that needs to be painstakingly learned. They are more of a discovery of what is already present in human beings. The perspectives that are illustrated by the five futures glasses are familiar and peculiar to each person in a very natural way, except that the terms are defined a little differently in each mind. The core concepts are sorted in a different way and both are connected in an individual way.

Until now, there has been no consistent model in practice or in science which completely integrates the more or less natural thought processes and core concepts for the future in a simple way, describes them with clear definitions and relations and makes them applicable in practice. The five futures glasses and the Eltville model are the result of an attempt to form such a model.

Index

If you have found this book useful you may be interested in other titles from Gower

Requisite Organization:
A Total System for Effective Managerial Organization and Managerial Leadership for the 21st Century
Elliott Jaques
Hardback: 978-0-566-07940-5

The CEO: Chief Engagement Officer:
Turning Hierarchy Upside Down to Drive Performance
John Smythe
Paperback: 978-0-566-08561-1
E-book: 978-0-7546-8180-9

Change Leadership:
Developing a Change-Adept Organization
Martin Orridge
Hardback: 978-0-566-08935-0
E-book: 978-0-566-09243-5

59 Checklists for Project and Programme Managers
Rudy Kor and Gert Wijnen
Paperback: 978-0-566-08775-2
E-book: 978-0-7546-8191-5

GOWER

Accelerating Business and IT Change: Transforming Project Delivery
Alan Fowler and Dennis Lock
Hardback: 978-0-566-08604-5
CD-ROM: 978-0-566-08742-4

Communicating Strategy
Phil Jones
Hardback: 978-0-566-08810-0
E-book: 978-0-7546-8288-2

The Essentials of Project Management
Dennis Lock
Paperback: 978-0-566-08805-6

**Transformation Management:
Towards the Integral Enterprise**
Ronnie Lessem and Alexander Schieffer
Hardback: 978-0-566-08896-4
E-book: 978-1-4094-0342-5

Visit **www.gowerpublishing.com** and

- search the entire catalogue of Gower books in print
- order titles online at 10% discount
- take advantage of special offers
- sign up for our monthly e-mail update service
- download free sample chapters from all recent titles
- download or order our catalogue